THE SHAKEN AND THE STIRRED

THE YEAR'S WORK
Edward P. Comentale and Aaron Jaffe, editors

THE SHAKEN AND THE STIRRED

The Year's Work in Cocktail Culture

EDITED BY
**STEPHEN SCHNEIDER
AND
CRAIG N. OWENS**

INDIANA UNIVERSITY PRESS

This book is a publication of

Indiana University Press
Office of Scholarly Publishing
Herman B Wells Library 350
1320 East 10th Street
Bloomington, Indiana 47405 USA

iupress.org

© 2020 by Indiana University Press

All rights reserved
No part of this book may be reproduced or utilized in any form or by any means, electronic or mechanical, including photocopying and recording, or by any information storage and retrieval system, without permission in writing from the publisher. The paper used in this publication meets the minimum requirements of the American National Standard for Information Sciences—Permanence of Paper for Printed Library Materials, ANSI Z39.48-1992.

Manufactured in the United States of America

Cataloging information is available from the Library of Congress.

ISBN 978-0-253-04973-5 (hardback)
ISBN 978-0-253-04974-2 (paperback)
ISBN 978-0-253-04975-9 (ebook)

1 2 3 4 5   24 23 22 21 20

CONTENTS

Introduction: The Shaken and the Stirred
(Stephen Schneider and Craig N. Owens)   *1*

PART 1: *Muddled Mythologies*

1. "The greatest of all the contributions of the American way of life to the salvation of humanity": On the Prehistory of the American Cocktail (Jonathan Elmer)   *25*
2. The Boulevardier: Craft, Industrialism, and the Nostalgic Origin in Cocktail Culture (Antonio Ceraso)   *37*
3. A Continued Stream of Fire: Professor Jerry Thomas Invents the "Blue Blazer" (Christoph Irmscher)   *58*
4. The Sazerac Mixing Ritual: Storytelling, Parody, and New Orleans (Joseph Turner)   *75*
5. My First Time (Albert W. A. Schmid)   *93*

PART 2: *Spirits of the Age*

6. "They made me feel civilized": The Martini as Modernist Culture (Michael Coyle)   *103*
7. At Home with Postwar Cocktail Culture and the Cocktail Dress (Lori Hall-Araujo)   *121*
8. Middlebrow Cosmopolitanism and the Canadian Cocktail (Lisa Sumner)   *145*
9. Absolut Psychosis (Craig N. Owens)   *169*
10. Joy Perrine and the Bourbon Cocktail's Renaissance (Susan Reigler)   *195*

PART 3: *Mixed Messages*

11. Inventing Margarita: Femininity, Fantasy, and Consumption (Marie Sarita Gaytán)   *203*

12. Polynesian Paralysis: Tiki Culture and the Aesthetics of American Empire (Andrew Pilsch)   *224*
13. The Irish Car Bomb (and One Other Disreputable "Cocktail") (Stephen Watt)   *244*
14. Bar Trek (William Biferie)   *261*
15. The Taming of the Shrub (Dan Callaway)   *282*

PART 4: *In a Glass, Darkly*

16. The Lingering Louche: Absinthe, the Green Demon of Alternative Modernity (Aaron Jaffe)   *289*
17. Rye Take on the Past—The Old-Fashioned Cocktail: A Glass of Crooning Sophistication (Judith Roof)   *305*
18. The Manhattan (Edward P. Comentale)   *321*
19. Cocktails That Aren't Cocktails for Gentlemen Who Aren't Men: Recovering the Metaphorical Body of the Fictional Drinker (Michael Jay Lewis)   *345*
20. The Cold Gray Dawn of the Morning After: Hangover Cures and the Inevitability of Excess (Stephen Schneider)   *370*

Afterword: Confessions of a Cocktail Nerd (Sonja Kassebaum)   *384*

Contributors   *395*

Index   *399*

THE SHAKEN AND THE STIRRED

INTRODUCTION

The Shaken and the Stirred

STEPHEN SCHNEIDER AND CRAIG N. OWENS

IN AN ESSAY ENTITLED "IN Search of the Auden Martini" (2009), Rosie Schaap embarks on a mission to discover what kind of martini it was that poet and martini devotee W. H. Auden actually drank.[1] But more importantly, Schaap sets out to disprove John Lancaster's contention in *The Debt to Pleasure* that Auden made martinis not with a properly English gin but rather with vodka. And as the essay progresses, what is at stake is nothing less than saving Auden himself from the accusation of pedestrian taste. As Schaap puts it,

> Maybe what I'm trying to say is: I don't *want* to believe it. I don't want to lump Auden in with the cocktail consumers I've seen belly up to bars at innumerable happy hours, lean their elbows on the polished wood or marble or zinc, and, with an air of sophisticated authority, order an extra-dry vodka Martini with extra olives.[2]

After all, these drinkers require not pity, nor scorn, but rather an intervention: "I want to pry away their drinks," Schaap continues, "and replace them with real martinis—made with gin and considerably more than a rumor of vermouth, and garnished, if garnished they must be, with clean, curly twists of lemon peel."[3] (But, as Michael Coyle's essay in this volume shows, opinions on the question of the garnish differ even among the most orthodox of *martinistas*.)

For Schaap, drinking a vodka martini is akin to reading "Ayn Rand, when one's time could be spent with Milton or Wordsworth—that is, with something beautiful and humanizing and good."[4] And in an essay on a poet such as Auden, the analogy is no doubt fitting. Yet Schaap—despite not wanting to believe that Auden made his martinis with vodka—can't dispel the possibility. She notes that Auden's brother "is ambiguous with respect to his brother Wystan's

Martinis," sometimes describing them as "vodka Martinis" and sometimes as "plain Martinis"—though "plain" likewise proves ambiguous.[5] In the end, Schaap chooses to believe an anecdotal story about a New York writer and editor who swore off gin after one too many of Auden's martinis: "Anecdotal, sure, but it suggests that Auden could go both ways with the Martini, sometimes deploying gin, sometimes vodka."[6]

We shouldn't be surprised that Schaap, herself an authority on the cocktail, wants to prove that Auden's martinis were every bit the equal to his poetry. As both Paul Fussell and Eric Felten remind us, we often imagine that what we drink says something about who we are. And contemporary cocktail culture is a culture that demands not just a refined sense of taste, but also a sense of cocktail craft and cocktail history. In other words, Schaap's own status as a bon vivant depends as much on her knowing for a fact what kind of martini Auden drank as it depends on her knowing that the vodka martini is to cocktails what *Atlas Shrugged* is to literature.

Any martini enthusiast would likely agree with Schaap on this last point, but they would also note that her own recipe for a martini—and especially her disdain for the inclusion of a garnish—would make much the same point even if the consideration of Auden's drinks were missing. After all, every serious martini drinker has a theory of how a proper martini is to be mixed, and that theory in turn tells you whether that martini drinker is to be taken seriously: for, cocktail culture is as much about reading the craft and form of the cocktail itself as it is about anything else. But as Schaap's essay makes clear, cocktail culture is a loquacious culture—one that has turned the witty banter associated with the cocktail party into a discourse on the cocktail itself. The cocktail that emerges is not so much a drink as a provocation: an occasion to think not just about what we'd like to drink, but also about the broader cultural symbolic systems that render those preferences meaningful.

COCKTAIL CULTURE

It seems only proper to open a volume on cocktail culture with a discussion of the martini, perhaps the drink most closely associated with cocktail culture. After all, the martini is nothing if not iconic: a crystal-clear drink, served in an elegant and geometrically exact glass, with only an olive to trouble its otherwise placid depths. Of course, if Schaap and other martini enthusiasts are to be believed, not even an olive should interrupt the visual perfection of the martini (therein, too, lies the injunction against shaking your martinis, lest shards of ice end up in your drink). The martini has an entelechy, an aspiration toward formal perfection that has been the stuff of discussion and debate for as long as the martini has had its modern form.

We might suggest, then, that the martini most perfectly represents cocktail culture because it is a drink that demands theorizing. It isn't enough to mix a martini, one has to mix it right; and to mix it right, one must account for one's choices and preferences. Gin or vodka? How much vermouth? Olive, lemon twist, or unadorned? It isn't enough to answer these questions. One must also answer why—or why not—and the myriad other questions of meaning and value that inevitably arise.

Perhaps the most detailed answer to these questions—and arguably the earliest study of contemporary cocktail culture—can be found in Lowell Edmunds's *Martini, Straight Up* (1998).[7] Edmunds offers a thorough examination of the martini's history and cultural resonance in an effort to answer the question "What does the Martini communicate?" His answer takes the form of seven simple messages and four ambiguities:

1. The messages of the Martini
    - The Martini is American—it is not European, Asian, or African
    - The Martini is urban and urbane—it is not rural or rustic
    - The Martini is a high-status, not a low-status, drink
    - The Martini is a man's, not a woman's, drink
    - The Martini is optimistic, not pessimistic
    - The Martini is the drink of adults, not of children
    - The Martini belongs to the past, not the present[8]
2. The ambiguities of the Martini
    - The Martini is civilized—the Martini is uncivilized
    - The Martini unites—the Martini separates
    - The Martini is classic—the Martini is individual
    - The Martini is sensitive—the Martini is tough[9]

Edmunds's approach is "to focus on the Martini as an image—or, in semiotic terms, a sign or a sign-vehicle—without going any more deeply into social contexts than a sketch of the sign requires."[10] The messages and ambiguities that Edmunds identifies seem to bear out Roland Barthes's contention that the ideal drink "would be rich in metonymies of all kinds."[11] And perhaps that's why, despite Edmunds's ostensible eschewing of social context, he concludes that "the net result for the Martini is politically incorrect, to say the least."[12]

However, Edmunds also makes clear that "the Martini provides 360 degrees of opportunity for anyone who wishes to look into or through this drink."[13] Understood as a sign, the martini might be associated with any number of competing social visions, from "the fabulous Martini of the swingers," from the movie of the same name, to the "sinister Martini of noir style."[14] Add to that the shaken vodka martinis of James Bond, the questionable martinis mixed by FDR, or the "civilized"[15] martinis of Hemingway's *A Farewell to Arms*, and you have a drink for seemingly any occasion. But each of these drinks establishes the martini not just as a sign, but also, as Edmunds suggests, a vehicle for thinking more broadly about drinking; about drinks culture; and about the location, traditions, mythologies, ideologies, and histories of that culture.

A slight shift in perspective allows us to see cocktail culture not just as the drinking culture that has historically surrounded mixed drinks, but also as culture as it might be viewed through the lens of the cocktail. And while the martini throws into sharp relief the masculinity and misogyny that often attend hard drinking, it also highlights the many other forms the martini ritual might take. Similarly, the old-fashioneds and martinis that litter the world of *Mad Men* point to the excesses of a masculine Madison Avenue, while the cosmopolitans of *Sex and the City* offer us instead a symbol for the frivolity of a New York that is centered instead on Fifth Avenue. And, indeed, we need not search far to find plenty of other instances where the cocktail functions as a metonym for larger cultural trends and questions.

Albert W. A. Schmid draws our attention, for example, to the way the mixing of an old-fashioned serves as a means of seduction in the movie *Crazy, Stupid, Love*.[16] The old-fashioned appears in a similar scene in the film *How Do You Know*, though this time the mixology is left to a bumbling Paul Rudd rather than the handsome, self-assured Ryan Gosling.[17] But in both movies, it isn't the drinking of the old-fashioned that establishes a character's masculinity, but rather the mixing of the drink for a female character. Potency, typically coded masculine, isn't simply a matter of consumption, but also one of craft and skill.

Perhaps it goes without saying then that cocktail culture is built upon the fact that cocktails generally, much like martinis in particular, seem to demand a certain degree of theorizing. Cocktails invite us to muse on their origins, their names, their ingredients, and their proportions. Cocktail writers have noted this fact for as long as they've been writing on cocktails. Harry Craddock, for example, reflects in *The Savoy Cocktail Book* on the origins of the Alaska cocktail (two parts gin, one part Yellow Chartreuse, one dash orange bitters) when he notes that "so far as can be ascertained this delectable potion is NOT the staple diet of the Esquimaux. It was probably first thought of in South Carolina hence its name."[18] Craddock's humor points our attention not just to the manner in which cocktails invite us to obsess over drink names and origins, but also to the manner in which they often resist such inquiries. Craddock's witty dismissal of the drink's name also suggests that as much as a cocktail seems to demand this sort of intellectual consideration, there also comes a time to simply drink it and be happy.[19]

Maybe, then, as the essays in this volume attest, we need to add a few ambiguities to Edmunds's four: The cocktail is serious—the cocktail is frivolous. The cocktail demands investigation—the cocktail resists investigation. The cocktail has a history—the cocktail is timeless. The cocktail is just a drink—the cocktail is rich in metonymies of all kinds.

COCKTAIL REVIVAL

General theories of the cocktail notwithstanding, the term *cocktail culture* has another, far more specific set of referents on the cusp of the third decade of the twenty-first century. Far from alluding to the cocktail's presence as some sort of cultural cipher, cocktail culture today references that far more specific set of events, trends, and forces that has come to be known as the "cocktail revival." Beginning in the mid-1980s with Dale DeGroff's resurrection of the Rainbow Room's cocktail menu, and with the publication of books such as DeGroff's *The Craft of the Cocktail* and Gary Regan's *The Joy of Mixology*, the cocktail revival has come to describe the renewed attention given to craft cocktails in the contemporary American drinks scene.[20] Many high-end restaurants have restored or revamped their cocktail offerings, and even more casual haunts have added respectable craft cocktails to their menus. Cocktail bars have likewise popped up in most major cities, and even in some smaller locations. While famous institutions such as New York's Death & Co and Milk and Honey, or Philadelphia's Franklin Mortgage and Investment Company, or Chicago's Aviary have become established trendsetters, one can also get an exemplary cocktail at the 715 Club in Denver or The Bourgeois Pig in Lawrence, Kansas.

Much as books like *The Savoy Cocktail Book* attended the drinking culture of the Prohibition era, a host of new books, websites, magazines, and articles have grown out of the cocktail revival. Slate.com devotes regular columns to cocktails and cocktail culture, and even published a sixty-four-drink competition called Martini Madness (M. F. K. Fisher's Gibson won).[21] Meanwhile, magazines and websites such as *Imbibe*, *Punch*, *Chilled*, Liquor.com, and Difford's Guide provide a never-ending list of trends, recipes, bars, and personalities for the bon vivant. Meanwhile, Mud Puddle Books has brought back into print those older volumes of cocktail lore, including Jerry Thomas's *How to Mix Drinks* (1862), Hugo Ensslin's *Recipes for Mixed Drinks* (1917), Frank Meier's *The Artistry of Mixing Drinks* (1936), Charles H. Baker's *South American*

Gentleman's Companion (1951), and David Embury's *Fine Art of Mixing Drinks* (1948). Alongside other classics, such as Craddock's *Savoy Cocktail Book* and Stanley Clisby Arthur's *Famous New Orleans Drinks and How to Mix 'Em* (1938), these volumes provide the foundation—and indeed the raw ingredients—for today's cocktail revival.

David Wondrich's *Punch!* (2010) and *Imbibe! From Absinthe Cocktail to Whiskey Smash, A Salute in Stories and Drinks to "Professor" Jerry Thomas, Pioneer of the American Bar* (2015), alongside Ted Haigh's *Vintage Spirits and Forgotten Cocktails: From the Alamagoozlum to the Zombie: 100 Rediscovered Recipes and the Stories Behind Them* (2009) and Jeff "Beachbum" Berry's *Sippin' Safari* (2007), offer the cocktail aficionado careful histories of both drinks and drinking cultures from the saloons of the nineteenth century to the tiki bars of the 1940s and 1950s. Philip Greene's *To Have and Have Another* (2012) examines the cocktails of Ernest Hemingway,[22] while Olivia Laing's *The Trip to Echo Spring: On Writers and Drinking* (2013) offers a broader cultural examination of the relationship between literature and alcohol.[23] Each of these volumes also represents years of painstaking research, with these authors consulting literature, newspapers, archives, and living authorities in an attempt to catalog the broader history of the cocktail.

More recent volumes have also taken the craft of the cocktail to new levels of specificity. Kazuo Uyeda's *Cocktail Techniques* (2010) makes available the fundamentals of Japanese bartending, including techniques for the "hard shake" now popular in many cocktail bars and for crafting ice spheres.[24] Kevin Liu's *Craft Cocktails at Home* (2013) and Adam Rogers's *Proof* (2014)[25] reflect on the science behind the creation and mixing of alcohols, while Amy Stewart's *The Drunken Botanist* (2013) examines the plants from which we derive much of what we drink.[26] Tony Conigliaro's *The Cocktail Lab* (2012), Dave Arnold's *Liquid Intelligence* (2014), and Tristan Stephenson's *The Curious Bartender* (2014) draw on molecular gastronomy in an effort to marry food science and cocktail culture in the act of mixology.[27] Even the Jell-O shot gets a gourmet makeover in Michelle Palm's *Jelly Shot Test Kitchen* (2011).[28]

Naturally, there are also celebrity volumes issued by top bartenders and by other outposts of the contemporary cocktail revival. DeGroff and Regan, two leading figures in current cocktail culture, have both issued multiple volumes on the craft of the cocktail. Meanwhile, New York bars such as PDT, Death & Co, and The Dead Rabbit all offer volumes containing their most famous drinks. New Orleans gets a similar treatment in *In the Land of Cocktails* (2007) by Ti Adelaide Martin and Lally Brennan of Commander's Palace and Café Adelaide fame, and Kerri McCaffety and Andrei Codrescu's *Obituary Cocktail:*

The Great Saloons of New Orleans (2011).²⁹ Finally, journalistic efforts such as Jason Wilson's *Boozehound* (2010) and Max Watman's *Chasing the White Dog* (2011) provide entertaining accounts of what it means to really get enthusiastic about one's drinking.³⁰

Alongside these books, one also finds an active blogging community (many cocktail authors also maintain blogs, or have converted blogs and other internet ventures into books) and conference scene. The latter is often centered around events like Portland Cocktail Week, the Manhattan Cocktail Classic, or Louisville's Kentucky Bourbon Affair, which seem like a combination of trade show, food festival, and celebrity event all shaken—or stirred—into one. But perhaps the most famous conference is the annual Tales of the Cocktail, which attracts around twenty thousand to New Orleans each July. Alongside tastings and parties, Tales of the Cocktail organizes educational seminars devoted to the histories, techniques, and current issues associated with cocktail culture.

In short, we might say of the cocktail revival what Theodor Adorno and Max Horkheimer said more broadly of the culture industry: "Something is provided for all so that none may escape."³¹ Even as the cocktail revival looks in many ways like Edmunds's seven messages and four ambiguities writ large, it also speaks to the current enthusiasm for niche marketing, craft production, and gourmet reinventions of classic foods and drinks. The nineteenth-century cocktail is now presented as the craft cocktail—an artisanal masterpiece involving handmade syrups, hard-to-find spirits, and a liberal dose of muddling, stirring, shaking, and straining. As Antonio Ceraso makes clear in his essay for this volume, the craft cocktail speaks as much to our contemporary moment as does the boulevardier to modernist Paris. The cocktail revival isn't simply a recovery of nineteenth-century mixology, but rather a reconception of that mixology to meet the needs of twenty-first-century ideas about taste, craft, and refinement.

It goes without saying, then, that the cocktail revival is most certainly not about recovering nineteenth-century cocktail *culture*, a culture centered on hotels and saloons and more than occasionally viewed with skepticism. Instead, the cocktail revival extends the foodie-driven logic that has led to gourmet food trucks, farmers markets and locavore restaurants, and upmarket re-inventions of such homey dishes as grilled cheese and shrimp and grits. And insofar as this cocktail culture presents itself as a response to the premixed, mass-produced, sugary cocktail culture of the 1970s and 1980s, it is a culture premised on refined taste and sensibilities. Where a nineteenth-century old-fashioned might be mixed to make both cheap whiskey and medicinal bitters more palatable, the contemporary old-fashioned likely combines small-batch or single-barrel whiskey with housemade bitters. Add a hefty price tag, and you have a drink that reflects the conspicuous consumption that has come to surround middle-class restaurant culture in the last twenty years.

We might suggest, then, that the cocktail revival is defined by postmodern pastiche: a historicism that speaks less to the past and more to the present, and as much to contemporary consumer society as to the craft of mixology. This historicism to some extent helps explain the discursive nature of the cocktail revival, with its emphasis not just on crafting sublime cocktails but also on the stories, theories, and cultures surrounding them. The cocktail revival seems, then, as invested in producing a historically situated, erudite, and refined cocktail culture as it is in producing a better standard of drink. For the contemporary bon vivant, the metonymies of the cocktail prove to be just as compelling as the cocktail itself.

COCKTAIL LOGIC

One particular component, then, of cocktail culture is the logic of the supplement. As used by Jacques Derrida, in laying out an idea central to deconstruction, the supplement is the mark that conveys meaning, attests to the impossibility of conveying meaning perfectly, and adds to the meaning to be conveyed, all at once.[32] Thus, the supplement—a phoneme, a word, or any sign—is both too little and too much: it is a mark of a failure, and at the same time it is the excessive, necessary, and insufficient corrective to that failure. Cocktail culture is replete with supplementarity, which manifests itself in different forms but always according to the same dynamic of lack, excess, and failure. The essays in this book continually examine that dynamic—most frequently implicitly, but occasionally explicitly as well.

The cocktail itself is built first and foremost on supplements: liqueurs, vermouth, sugar, limes, bitters, all of which transform liquor into something more meaningful. But even as these ingredients inaugurate this transformation, they are themselves relegated to the role of adjuncts. The martini, for example, is a "gin cocktail"; but it isn't a cocktail at all without the addition of French vermouth. Likewise, the daiquiri might more accurately be described as a sugar-and-lime drink than as a rum drink. And yet it is the addition of rum that separates the daiquiri from other sours, suggesting that rum is also a supplement—albeit the supplement that makes the "daiquiri" possible.

This semiotic supplementarity also defines cocktail culture, where all manner of cultural artifacts and practices attend the production and consumption of mixed drinks. For example, the hangover cure, probably the most obviously supplemental of the collations discussed in this volume, offers a stiff drink as the remedy for too many stiff drinks—the excess to end all excesses, as Schneider's essay in this volume argues. Likewise, as Andrew Pilsch's essay will show, tiki culture emerges as the representation of a fantasy ideal of a seemingly utopian Polynesia and yet continuously puts its colonizing, exoticizing impulses under erasure, articulating at the same time to the emerging military-industrial complex of the postwar decades. The accessories that accompany cocktail drinking—from cocktail dresses to barware—both reinforce the polysemy of the cocktail and, in surrounding its creation and consumption, attest to its emptiness and insufficiency as a sign on its own. And vodka, always disappearing both into the drinks of which it is an essential ingredient and behind the thematics of the advertisements that hawk it, is always both there and not there: too much and too little at the same time. Whether a given essay in this volume focuses on filmic, televisual, or literary representations of cocktails; on the advertisements and rituals that surround them; or on their history, folklore, and mythology, they all attest, to a greater or lesser degree, to the contradictory problematic at the heart of cocktail culture: it is both about drinking and *not* about drinking, about limits and excess, about refinement and abandon. The cocktail both fortifies and weakens, hastening both resolution and dissolution, its speech always slurred and its vision always doubled.

Indeed, it is at times difficult to determine whether cocktail culture is the supplement that defines the allure of the mixed drink, or if cocktails serve as the punctuating artifacts for cultures that surround them. Perhaps this simultaneously overdetermined and underdetermined logic of the cocktail accounts for its longstanding fascination. While certain cocktails have come into and gone out of fashion, cocktails, as a class of drink, have always been in style and have always accrued semiotic and cultural addenda of all kinds. Wine culture and beer culture, by contrast, strike us as quite limited in their semiotic possibilities, even accounting for the explosion of micro- and craft-brewed beers and the perennial popularity of wine. Indeed, perhaps no other category of commodity speaks so loquaciously and so multidiscursively as the cocktail. As the chapters that follow show, there is almost no aspect of culture on which the cocktail is silent: gender, sex, sexuality, class, race, geography, politics, economics, psychology, and technoscience all find themselves speaking through, and spoken by, cocktail culture.

Taken together, then, the essays in this volume offer an archaeology, to borrow Michel Foucault's term, of the particular cultural formations and the moments they investigate. The essays see the cocktail both as the distillation of cultural desires, anxieties, and beliefs, and as an entryway into the examination of those cultural phenomena that extend beyond the cocktail itself. Thus, they offer insights not just into cocktail culture narrowly defined, but also into culture at large. In short, the cocktail serves as both object and method.

LINE 'EM UP

The essays in this volume evolve much like a night of drinking might. Between the *aperitif* and the hangover, the essays grow increasingly voluble, increasingly attenuated in their connection to a particular drink or a particular drinking tradition, just as the conversation at a bar or during a party becomes increasingly decentered—untethered, even. While the part titles we have offered suggest some salient distinctions and some cogent similarities, even those distinctions are apt to blur.

The first part, "Muddled Mythologies," comprises investigations into origins and origin stories. Jonathan Elmer's "'The greatest of all the contributions of the American way of life to the salvation of humanity': On the Prehistory of the American Cocktail" serves as a kind of aperitif, whetting the palate for the essays to follow. In this first essay, Elmer recounts his own search—framed by a posh afternoon drinks party—for an originary cocktail upon which cocktail culture itself might rest. While acknowledging colonial precursors to the cocktail, and an active drinking culture surrounding mixed drinks even in the American revolutionary period, Elmer also discovers that these drinks nonetheless never quite conform to the definitions offered of "the cocktail." Indeed, even these definitions seem never to quite accurately get to the original, ur-cocktail, replete as they are with conflicting histories and theories of what it is that makes a cocktail a cocktail. And yet, Elmer concludes that perhaps what makes the cocktail an American institution is not a singular origin, but (to paraphrase) the mess that lies seething beneath the idea of the cocktail itself. The essay thus serves as both a prologue and a forewarning about what is to come as the volume unfolds—the sometimes speculative, always qualified arguments about origin, history, and meaning that serious drinking engenders.

Taking its cue from Elmer's opening piece, Antonio Ceraso's essay "The Boulevardier: Craft, Industrialism, and the Nostalgic Origin" takes a moment of erudite conversation over drinks as the occasion to investigate the origins of the title cocktail among expatriate American culture in 1920s and 1930s Paris. In doing so, however, Ceraso is less concerned to provide a definitive narrative of the cocktail's invention than to understand the way that twenty-first-century cocktail culture's fascination with the origin and revival of such cocktails as the boulevardier seems to enable a kind of critical consumption—a kind of consumption enacting a cultural aesthetic that both allows for highly classed consumption of vintage cocktails and works against the mass-market-driven aesthetic of late-industrial capitalism. Approaching his investigation from an explicitly Marxist and post-Marxist theoretical point of view, Ceraso is careful not to endorse vintage cocktail culture's promise of liberation from industrial capitalism; rather, his essay shows that, dialectically, the very anxieties induced by industrial commodity production enable vintage cocktail culture's animating nostalgia in the first place.

Christoph Irmscher's "A Continued Stream of Fire: Professor Jerry Thomas Invents the 'Blue Blazer'" remains grounded—or seated—in licensed premises even as it carries on the search for origins and originals. While mixed drinks had been around for a long time before the appearance of Thomas's volume in the mid-nineteenth century, *The Bartender's Guide* represents a turning point—in Irmscher's view, a democratization of mixology that has made contemporary cocktail culture possible. But, just as importantly, it gave us the cocktail's first advocate in the person of Thomas himself. As his own spectacular career attests—a career defined by the fire-throwing ritual involved in the mixing of the Blue Blazer—cocktail culture thus emerged not only out of popular interest in the mixing of drinks, but also out of the celebrity that culture bestowed on such bartenders as Thomas.

Joseph Turner provides the last of our four mythologies, turning our attention to the Big Easy, perhaps America's most mythologized city—particularly where alcohol consumption is concerned—in his essay "The Sazerac Mixing Ritual: Storytelling, Parody, and New Orleans." For Turner, the Sazerac is defined less by ingredients and more by the particular mixing ritual involved in its creation. While the reliance on ritual also proves to be a constitutive element in other New Orleans cocktails—and, as Turner reminds us, a constitutive element of New Orleans culture more broadly—it also reminds us that the authenticity we often look for in cocktails may be defined more by the mixing and drinking rituals we share than by the accuracy of any recipe or the authenticity of any story. Indeed, these rituals allow for the proliferation of recipes and origin stories, and they have provided the means for drinks such as the Sazerac to take on new meanings and resonate in new ways.

While four of the five essays in this book's first part concern themselves with cocktail culture's origins, the essays in the second part, "Spirits of the Age," stagger slightly beyond the ambit of drinks and drinking to consider the historical and cultural contexts that adhere to particular spirits and cocktails. To be sure, the question of origins continues to arise in several of these essays, but more central to their concerns are the cultural contexts, including marketing, and historical developments that influence these potables' interpretation as individual beverages and as symptoms and markers of the cultures in which they emerged and gained popularity.

In considering the martini as a representation of modernist culture, Michael Coyle links historical developments in the way the martini has been conceived over the years with reflections on the martini's symbolic value. Drawing us back to Lowell Edmunds, Coyle suggests that the messages and ambiguities that surround the martini result from that drink's function as a modern and modernist sign. This function accounts for not only the martini's status as the ideal cocktail, but also that drink's ability to balance ideas about purity and the mixing of cultures. And it is this balancing act—one in which the martini combines "disparate elements to form convivial new wholes"—that makes the martini a civilized and modern, if conservative, drink.

Lori Hall-Araujo's "At Home with Postwar Cocktail Culture and the Cocktail Dress" continues the examination of modernity, this time by considering midcentury developments in couture and middle-class homelife that marked the emergence of the cocktail party as the occasion for negotiating gender roles in the domestic sphere. Reading film, advertising, and home décor through developments in women's cocktail dresses, Hall-Araujo sees cocktail culture, and specifically the domestic space of the cocktail party, as a site for ideological negotiation, not only among those in attendance at such parties, fictional and real alike, but also over larger questions of gender and class identity. The cocktail dress emerges as an object apposite to such negotiations because, in selecting and wearing one, the middle-class woman performed her relationship to gender expectations, to middle-class respectability, and, given the international origins of these dresses and their designers, to the production and proliferation of globally inflected tastes. Neither long nor short, professional wear nor evening wear, formal nor informal, the cocktail dress, under Hall-Araujo's analysis, becomes a dynamic object, indexing and analyzing at the same time the liminal flux of the cocktail hour, the cocktail party, and the newly designed midcentury domestic spaces created to contain them.

Lisa Sumner expands on the international orientation of Hall-Araujo's analysis in "Middlebrow Cosmopolitanism and the Canadian Cocktail." Focusing its attention primarily on Seagram's marketing efforts around the 1967 Montreal World's Fair, Sumner's essay grounds the fantasy of intercultural understanding examined in the cultural milieu of late-midcentury pan-American conceptions of hospitality, nationality, and worldliness. For Sumner, the cocktail consumption practices promoted by Canadian distillers and advertisers—in particular, Seagram's—and the ideals of worldly savoir faire promoted by the

World's Fair itself, are decidedly classed: for they reify neoliberal middle-class narratives of upward mobility, equality, and identity, even as they seek to elide international cultural difference, reducing foreignness to a few polite phrases and stereotypical accoutrements.

In "Absolut Psychosis," Owens situates the rise in popularity of vodka among American drinkers in the 1980s and 1990s as symptomatic of larger shifts in conceptions of corporate masculinity. Like Sumner's, his essay attempts to understand the relationship between spirits advertising on the one hand and the cultural preoccupations they point toward on the other. Pairing an analysis of print ads for Smirnoff and Absolut vodkas with a reading of Brett Easton Ellis's 1991 novel *American Psycho* and its 2000 film version, Owens argues that we witness a progressive emptying out of identity figured as neo-Cartesian subjectivity and a concomitant aesthetic and ethical investment in surfaces: the hard (male) body, haute couture, mass-market branding, and corporate masculinity of the 1980s. For Owens, vodka, repeatedly represented as pure absence, becomes a particularly crystalline lens through which to read this emergent fascination with surfaces, which, with its emphasis on image, its paranoiac anxieties, and its resistance to stable symbolic discourse, engenders a kind of cultural psychosis.

The third part, "Mixed Messages," includes essays that focus explicitly on international and intercultural exchange, a theme already suggested in essays from the previous part. Marie Sarita Gaytán's "Inventing Margarita: Femininity, Fantasy, and Consumption" considers the multiply inflected, often overdetermined origin stories of the margarita cocktail, linking it to a late-midcentury American fascination with Mexican culture. But, as Gaytán points out, the Mexico evinced by the margarita—wily, seductive, feminine, and exotic—is constructed upon a particularly American fantasy of consumption, cultural domination, and masculinity. Her essay draws on the history of tequila advertising, origin stories, and cultural mythologies to show that the margarita, as much as it may seem to index an alluring idea of Mexico, always points more saliently toward the ideologies and assumptions inherent in the American culture for which it was created and to which it is marketed.

Andrew Pilsch's essay "Polynesian Paralysis: Tiki Culture and the Aesthetics of American Empire" recapitulates the theme of cultural appropriation and colonial fantasy as it examines the dialectic, and often surreal, relationship between midcentury American culture and the faux-Polynesian aesthetic of tiki. Pilsch argues that the rise of tiki culture and its infiltration into middle-American, middle-class tastes—not just in food and drink, but in décor and home appliances—index the confluence of the post–World War II era of easy airline travel, military-industrial entanglements, and a fantasy-ideal of American influence in southeast Asia and the south Pacific. His essay follows developments in commercial bar and restaurant technologies, the rise in middle-class standards of living, and the conversion of military transport industries to the service of civilian transportation to show that subtending tiki's artificial ideal of Polynesian exoticism and otherness is the rise of the United States as a global military superpower and an American neo-colonialism. This latter development, in Pilsch's essay, accounts for the perverse re-encoding of native Polynesian cultures, whereby popular south Pacific tourist destinations began to recast themselves in terms of the commercial American tiki aesthetic.

In his essay on "Irish" cocktails such as the Irish Car Bomb and the black and tan, Stephen Watt asks us to attend to how the naming of cocktails both invokes and obscures cultural history in ways that prove more ethically complex and challenging than a drinker's easy assumptions might first suggest. Far from turning our attention to Irish history, and the often-violent relationship between England and Ireland throughout the twentieth century, the Irish Car Bomb and the black and tan threaten to trivialize our engagement with what it has meant to be Irish since 1916. As Watt contends, "perhaps the maintenance of a keen memory of historical events, international ones no less, is too much to expect of American or other drinkers." But he also demands that we understand our drinking from within the collective memories that our drinks evoke—even if doing so demands that we no longer order those very same drinks.

William Biferie extends this transcultural analytical impulse, focusing his attention on the way the Star Trek television and film franchise uses cocktail culture to create opportunities for intergalactic intercultural rapprochement in twenty-fourth-century deep-space human and alien encounters. "Bar Trek" draws on Homi K. Bhabha's notion of "third space": formal and informal interstices where dominant and subaltern cultural codes and ideologies find themselves in flux, enabling the mutual rethinking and reorganizing of those ideologies in relation to one another. Biferie's essay thus demonstrates that alcohol not only remains, in the imagination of Star Trek's creators, an agent of the carnivalesque but also allows for the preservation of conservative notions of binary gender and the norms by which those notions are governed in present-day US culture. Once again, cocktails emerge as the lynchpin for the preservation of American cultural fantasies threaded through highly artificial conceptions of the foreign—or alien—other. And yet, Star Trek suggests a future where "the best parts of human culture—friendship, laughter, and curiosity—remain intact" within a drinking culture that offers not just the preservation of older, masculine notions of consumption, but also the possibility of something more.

By the fourth part of this volume, "In a Glass, Darkly," the essays have taken a decidedly tangential line of thought. In them, cocktails and cocktail culture serve to spark reflections and conjectures that stray—or stumble—at times quite far from the drinks themselves. In "The Lingering Louche," the most booze-grounded of the final set of essays, Aaron Jaffe offers a consideration of absinthe's occupation of the "intermediate zone between the just-now (what's assuredly modern) and the not-now (the just-before, the not yet modern)." His examination of the decadence surrounding absinthe offers a counternarrative to the cool and clean history that Coyle associates with the martini. Absinthe's is a history defined by disruption and excess, by negative mystique and the threat of ruin. Jaffe locates this history as the lingering opacity that continues to haunt cocktail culture and its drinking rituals.

Judith Roof's essay "Rye Take on the Past—The Old-Fashioned Cocktail: A Glass of Crooning Sophistication" analyzes the disorienting chronology of influence and influences at play in Ethel Merman's development as an actress in American musicals and films, particularly in her work with Cole Porter. Roof's essay takes as its frame Merman's sung deconstruction of the old-fashioned in Porter's 1940 musical *Panama Hattie*, in a song titled "Make It Another Old Fashioned, Please." Roof argues that the cocktail itself, and the very notion of the origin, as evinced by its labored and multiple origin myths and by Merman's increasingly self-referential performances throughout her career, always has been its own origin already. The comforting narrative coherence promised by the old-fashioned cocktail and the celebrity biography alike, according to Roof, is always threatened by a Janus-faced temporal duality in which the present moment—in narrative or in history—continually emerges as the fraught and never-quite-present fulcrum between an idealized past and the idealized future that will continue to constitute, and deconstitute, chronology and causality.

Like Roof, Edward P. Comentale suggests, at least as far as the manhattan is concerned, that narrative coherence may be little more than an empty promise. Locating the manhattan as an aspirational cocktail, Comentale investigates how quickly the same drink becomes ruinous. The manhattan emerges as a gauche and overwrought counterpoint to the martini, a drink that evokes masculine success via its excessive and overbearing nature. Not surprisingly, then, the manhattan surfaces in the writings of authors like Theodore Dreiser as an augur of dissipation—of collapse and ruin—as assuredly as it is a marker of success and aspiration. Comentale asks whether the manhattan might offer an antidote to aspirations of cocktail culture in general and how we might drink manhattans with such concerns in mind.

Michael Lewis's essay, "Cocktails That Aren't Cocktails for Gentlemen Who Aren't Men: Recovering the Metaphorical Body of the Fictional Drinker," examines tonics and the secondary figures in literature and film who serve them up. Like Roof and Comentale, whose essays come as tonics against the jejune coherence of narratives of all kinds, Lewis focuses his attention on the relationship between the cocktail, in this case the pick-me-up, and narrative as such. His essay argues that narrative is itself a tonic, a means of organizing readerly experience and setting to rights the disorder of the fictional world. This reorganizing force operates both within the narrative, to restore order to memory and events that threaten to succumb to disorder, and in the reader's experience of the diegesis, promising wholeness and coherence by the narrative's denouement.

Just as the book begins with a partygoer's early optimism, evinced by Elmer's essay, so too must it end with a regretful retrospective. Schneider's essay "The Cold, Gray Dawn of the Morning After: Hangover Cures and the Inevitability of Excess" reflects on the numerous recipes offered over the past century as cures for the hangover, the inevitable aftermath of a night of heavy drinking. Balancing the often-oversold claims of revival and well-being that these tonics offer with Kingsley Amis's coldly rational reflections on the hangover, Schneider argues that the hangover cure functions not so much as an antidote to excess as a testament to the logic of excess already inherent in cocktail culture itself. Despite its representation as the cure, the end of excess's torment, because of the highly alcoholic nature of most pick-me-ups, the hangover cure, in fact, doubles down on the logic of excess. Under Schneider's analysis, it always points back toward the very overindulgence that makes it necessary in the first place by administering yet further indulgence. For Schneider, this excess is at the core of cocktail culture, its only kept promise.

Taken together, these essays offer a partial and provisional map of cocktail culture's vast and diverse geography. But they do not, by any means, exhaust their territory. Rather, this volume offers ways of reading cocktails and cocktail culture, and of reading culture through cocktails, that will enable continued questioning and analysis of elements of cocktail culture beyond those offered here. By asking what ways of reading, interpreting, and knowing are made possible by the cocktail and what kinds of subjectivity, identity, and self-representation the cocktail enables, these essays offer cocktail enthusiasts and cultural critics alike ways of situating drinks and drinks culture within larger contexts. On the one hand, this book serves as a complement to the many resources available—recipe books, guides, and reviews—meant to refine the consumer's tastes and habits. On the other, it offers an alternative to the discourse of consumption that unproblematically offers contemporary cocktail culture as an enlightened, or at least more sophisticated, way of being in the world by subjecting that culture to rigorous examination and analysis.

But not even the heartiest drinker or most attentive reader can get through the rigors of constant booze and chatter without an occasional pick-me-up. These tonics come in the form of three brief interludes, essays by professional mixologists, authors, and distillers active in the creation of the drinks discussed throughout this book. Albert W. A. Schmid, award-winning chef and author of books on the old-fashioned and the manhattan, offers us the provocatively titled reminiscence "My First Time," in which he recalls the first time he worked as a bartender, and reflects on those aspects of bartending that do not always find their way into cocktail books, articles, and reviews. Food and beverage writer Susan Reigler profiles an innovative and celebrated Louisville (by way of St. Croix) mixologist in "Joy Perrine and the Bourbon Cocktail's Renaissance," situating Perrine's rise to prominence within the context of Kentucky's bourbon culture. In "The Taming of the Shrub"—with apologies to Shakespeare—Dan Callaway provides a glimpse into the process of inventing new cocktails and refining old practices, processes that involve not just experimenting with ingredients but collaborating with kitchen staff. Sonja Kassebaum will have the last word in "Afterword: Confessions of a Cocktail Nerd," although she will by no means have been the first to geek out on drinks and drinking in this collection. Kassebaum describes her own adventures through the cocktail revival, adventures that saw her transformation from cocktail enthusiast to distiller and co-owner, with her husband, of Chicago's North Shore Distillery. Taken together, these four brief essays help ground the book in the practices and practicalities of the spirits industry.

Finally, a word about this collection's title. The reader familiar with anthropology will no doubt recognize the book's not very subtle reference to Claude Levi-Strauss's seminal volume *The Raw and the Cooked*, a structural analysis of almost two hundred Amerindian myths, deploying a series of binary oppositions as organizing axes for the author's investigations.[33] The binarity of his method presages the martini's oppositional messages and ambiguities described by Edmunds, above, and a similar either/or (and, at times, both/and) logic arises in a number of the essays to follow: authentic or contrived, domestic or foreign, original or imitation, representation or reality. Our title, though, does more than just indicate some homologies in method—not very strong ones, in any case. More than that, it suggests that for as long as cocktail culture has been a loquacious culture—certainly since before James Bond's punctilious and unorthodox preferences became famous—it has been a culture of debate, dialogue, analysis, and argumentation, traditions that these essays unabashedly carry on.

A number of individuals beyond those named in the table of contents have had a hand in affording us the privilege of continuing those debates and analyses in the present volume. Its genesis was the April 2014 Cocktail Culture Conference in Louisville, Kentucky, co-hosted by the University of Louisville's Department of English and the Center for the Humanities at Drake University (Des Moines, Iowa). Many individuals and businesses had a hand in making that conference possible: Tracy Heightchew (then of the University of Louisville's Commonwealth Center for Humanities and Society); Sean Thibodeaux, Aaron Price, and the staff at St. Charles Exchange; The Brown Hotel; and sponsors Heaven Hill Distilleries, Angel's Envy Bourbon, and North Shore Distillery. At Indiana University Press, Gary Dunham and Janice Frisch have been invaluable in guiding this project from its early stages through publication. Contributors to this collection, including This Year's Work series editors Edward P. Comentale and Aaron Jaffe, have invariably shown generosity of spirit and wisdom as the project has taken shape. For lending us their expertise and energy, we are deeply grateful to them. Finally, without the support and patience of our colleagues, friends, and families, who have allowed us the space and time to bring this collection together, *The Shaken and the Stirred* would not have seen the light of day.

Louisville and Des Moines
February, 2020

NOTES

1. Rosie Schaap, "In Search of the Auden Martini: How to Make a Cocktail Beautiful, Humanizing, and Good," Poetry Foundation, September 9, 2009, https://www.poetryfoundation.org/articles/69354/in-search-of-the-auden-Martini.
2. Schaap, "In Search of the Auden Martini," n.p.
3. Schaap, "In Search of the Auden Martini," n.p.
4. Schaap, "In Search of the Auden Martini," n.p.
5. Schaap, "In Search of the Auden Martini," n.p.
6. Schaap, "In Search of the Auden Martini," n.p.
7. Lowell Edmunds, *Martini, Straight Up*, rev. ed. (Baltimore: Johns Hopkins University Press, 1998).
8. Edmunds, *Martini, Straight Up*, xxiv.
9. Edmunds, *Martini, Straight Up*, vii–viii.

10. Edmunds, *Martini, Straight Up*, xxvi.
11. Roland Barthes, *Barthes: Roland Barthes by Roland Barthes*, trans. Richard Howard (New York: Hill and Wang, 2010), 96.
12. Edmunds, *Martini, Straight Up*, xxv.
13. Edmunds, *Martini, Straight Up*, xxvi.
14. Edmunds, *Martini, Straight Up*, xxvi.
15. Ernest Hemingway, *A Farewell to Arms* (New York: Scribner's, 1929), 245.
16. Albert W. A. Schmid, *The Old Fashioned: An Essential Guide to the Original Whiskey Cocktail* (Lexington: University Press of Kentucky, 2013), xv–xvi.
17. James L. Brooks, dir. and writer, *How Do You Know* (Los Angeles: Columbia Pictures, 2010).
18. Harry Craddock, *The Savoy Cocktail Book* (London: Constable and Co., 1930; Mineola, NY: Dover, 2018), 18. Citations refer to the Dover edition.
19. For those interested in how a gin-and-Chartreuse drink came to be called the Alaska, we can likely consider the drink's golden color and its early-twentieth-century birthdate as clues that the drink was named after the Alaska gold rush. In *The Fine Art of Mixing Drinks* (Garden City, NY: Country Life Press, 1948), David Embury gives some indirect support for this theory, when he provides a slight variation named the Nome. Nome, Alaska, was one of the central sites for the Alaska gold rush and still claims to be home to the world's largest gold pan (213).
20. See Dale DeGroff, *The Craft of the Cocktail* (New York: Clarkson Potter, 2002), and Gary Regan, *The Joy of Mixology: The Consummate Guide to the Bartender's Craft* (New York: Clarkson Potter, 2003).
21. Troy Patterson, "Martini Madness," Slate.com, April 10, 2013, http://www.slate.com/articles/life/drink/features/2013/martini_madness_tournament/final_four_and_championship/m_f_k_fisher_s_gibson_and_bertrand_russell_s_famous_martini_question_from.html.
22. See Philip Greene, *To Have and Have Another: A Hemingway Cocktail Companion* (New York: Perigee, 2012).
23. See Olivia Laing, *The Trip to Echo Spring: On Writers and Drinking* (New York: Picador, 2013).
24. See Kazuo Uyeda, *Cocktail Techniques* (New York: Mud Puddle Books, 2010).
25. See Kevin Liu, *Craft Cocktails at Home: Offbeat Techniques, Contemporary Crowd-Pleasers, and Classics Hacked with Science* (self-pub., Kevin Liu, 2013), and Adam Rogers, *Proof: The Science of Booze* (New York: Houghton Mifflin Harcourt, 2014).
26. See Amy Stewart, *The Drunken Botanist: The Plants That Create the World's Great Drinks* (Chapel Hill, NC: Algonquin, 2013).
27. See Tony Conigliaro, *The Cocktail Lab: Unraveling the Mysteries of Flavor and Aroma in Drinks, with Recipes* (New York: Ten Speed Press, 2013); Dave

Arnold, *Liquid Intelligence: The Art and Science of the Perfect Cocktail* (New York: Norton, 2014); and Tristan Stephenson, *The Curious Bartender, Volume I: The Artistry and Alchemy of Creating the Perfect Cocktail* (London: Ryland Peters and Small, 2013).

28. See Michelle Palm, *Jelly Shot Test Kitchen: Jell-ing Classic Cocktails—One Drink at a Time* (Philadelphia: Running Press, 2011).

29. See Ti Adelaide Martin and Lally Brennan, *In the Land of Cocktails: Recipes and Adventures from the Cocktail Chicks* (New York: William Morrow Cookbooks, 2007), and Kerri McCaffety and Andrei Codrescu, *Obituary Cocktail: The Great Saloons of New Orleans* (Gretna, LA: Pelican Publishing, 2011).

30. See Jason Wilson, *Boozehound: On the Trail of the Rare, the Obscure, and the Overrated in Spirits* (New York: Ten Speed Press, 2010), and Max Watman, *Chasing the White Dog: An Amateur Outlaw's Adventures in Moonshine* (New York: Simon & Schuster, 2011).

31. Max Horkheimer and Theodor W. Adorno, *Dialectic of Enlightenment*, trans. John Cumming (New York: Continuum, 1998), 123.

32. See Jacques Derrida, *Dissemination*, trans. Barbara Johnson (Chicago: University of Chicago Press, 1981), esp. 156–171.

33. See Claude Levi-Strauss, *The Raw and the Cooked*, vol. 1, *Mythologiques*, trans. John and Doreen Weightman (New York: Harper and Row, 1969).

BIBLIOGRAPHY

Arnold, Dave. *Liquid Intelligence: The Art and Science of the Perfect Cocktail*. New York: Norton, 2014.

Barthes, Roland. *Barthes: Roland Barthes by Roland Barthes*. Translated by Richard Howard. New York: Hill and Wang, 2010.

Brooks, James L., dir. and writer. *How Do You Know*. Los Angeles: Columbia Pictures, 2010.

Conigliaro, Tony. *The Cocktail Lab: Unraveling the Mysteries of Flavor and Aroma in Drinks, with Recipes*. New York: Ten Speed Press, 2013.

Craddock, Harry. *The Savoy Cocktail Book*. London: Constable and Co., 1930. Reprint, Mineola, NY: Dover, 2018.

DeGroff, Dale. *The Craft of the Cocktail*. New York: Clarkson Potter, 2002.

Derrida, Jacques. *Dissemination*. Translated by Barbara Johnson. Chicago: University of Chicago Press, 1981.

Edmunds, Lowell. *Martini, Straight Up*. Rev. ed. Baltimore: Johns Hopkins University Press, 1998.

Embury, David A. *The Fine Art of Mixing Drinks*. Garden City, NY: Country Life Press, 1948.

Greene, Philip. *To Have and Have Another: A Hemingway Cocktail Companion*. New York: Perigee, 2012.

Hemingway, Ernest. *A Farewell to Arms*. New York: Scribner's, 1929.
Holland, Barbara. *The Joy of Drinking*. New York: Bloomsbury USA, 2007.
Horkheimer, Max, and Theodor W. Adorno. *Dialectic of Enlightenment*. Translated by John Cumming. New York: Continuum, 1998.
Levi-Strauss, Claude. *The Raw and the Cooked*. Vol. 1, *Mythologiques*. Translated by John and Doreen Weightman. New York: Harper and Row, 1969.
Laing, Olivia. *The Trip to Echo Spring: On Writers and Drinking*. New York: Picador, 2013.
Liu, Kevin. *Craft Cocktails at Home: Offbeat Techniques, Contemporary Crowd-Pleasers, and Classics Hacked with Science*. Self-published, 2013.
Martin, Ti Adelaide, and Lally Brennan. *In the Land of Cocktails: Recipes and Adventures from the Cocktail Chicks*. New York: William Morrow Cookbooks, 2007.
McCaffety, Kerri, and Andrei Codrescu. *Obituary Cocktail: The Great Saloons of New Orleans*. Gretna, LA: Pelican Publishing, 2011.
Palm, Michelle. *Jelly Shot Test Kitchen: Jell-ing Classic Cocktails—One Drink at a Time*. Philadelphia: Running Press, 2011.
Patterson, Troy. "Martini Madness." Slate.com. April 10, 2013. http://www.slate.com/articles/life/drink/features/2013/Martini_madness_tournament/final_four_and_championship/m_f_k_fisher_s_gibson_and_bertrand_russell_s_famous_martini_question_from.html.
Regan, Gary. *The Joy of Mixology: The Consummate Guide to the Bartender's Craft*. New York: Clarkson Potter, 2003.
Rogers, Adams. *Proof: The Science of Booze*. New York: Houghton Mifflin Harcourt, 2014.
Schaap, Rosie. "In Search of the Auden Martini: How to Make a Cocktail Beautiful, Humanizing, and Good." Poetry Foundation. September 9, 2009. https://www.poetryfoundation.org/articles/69354/in-search-of-the-auden-martini.
Schmid, Albert W. A. *The Old Fashioned: An Essential Guide to the Original Whiskey Cocktail*. Lexington: University Press of Kentucky, 2013.
Stephenson, Tristan. *The Curious Bartender, Volume I: The Artistry and Alchemy of Creating the Perfect Cocktail*. London: Ryland Peters and Small, 2013.
Stewart, Amy. *The Drunken Botanist: The Plants That Create the World's Great Drinks*. Chapel Hill, NC: Algonquin, 2013.
Uyeda, Kazuo. *Cocktail Techniques*. New York: Mud Puddle Books, 2010.
Watman, Max. *Chasing the White Dog: An Amateur Outlaw's Adventures in Moonshine*. New York: Simon & Schuster, 2011.
Wilson, Jason. *Boozehound: On the Trail of the Rare, the Obscure, and the Overrated in Spirits*. New York: Ten Speed Press, 2010.

PART 1

Muddled Mythologies

ONE

"THE GREATEST OF ALL THE CONTRIBUTIONS OF THE AMERICAN WAY OF LIFE TO THE SALVATION OF HUMANITY"

On the Prehistory of the American Cocktail

JONATHAN ELMER

THERE IS A PARADOX AT the heart of the question of the American cocktail. Everyone seems to agree that the cocktail is American, but nobody really knows what that means. H. L. Mencken observes that the "*cocktail*, to multitudes of foreigners, seems to be the greatest of all the contributions of the American way of life to the salvation of humanity, but there remains a good deal of uncertainty about the etymology of its name and even some doubt that the thing itself is of American origin."[1] Mencken is writing in the immediate aftermath of World War II—the "American way of life" and "the salvation of humanity" were phrases often uttered in that moment with no trace of irony. But Mencken, I think, never removed his tongue from his cheek in anything he wrote. "Multitudes of foreigners" seem agreed that "the cocktail" is American. People *need* it to be so, evidently: as if American exceptionalism—Redeemer Nation bringing about the "salvation of humanity!"—was a status bestowed by others rather than fomented by American self-regard.

David Wondrich, our best contemporary authority on the history of mixed drinks, understands well that self-regard, and he offers a slightly different paean to the cocktail's Americanness:

> Anyone who has spent any time pondering the origins of the Cocktail ... will agree that it's a quintessentially American contraption. How could it be anything but? It's quick, direct, and vigorous. It's flashy and a little bit vulgar. It induces an unreflective overconfidence. It's democratic, forcing the finest liquors to rub elbows with ingredients of far more humble stamp. It's profligate with natural resources (think of all the electricity generated to make ice that gets used for ten seconds and discarded).

"In short," Wondrich concludes, "it rocks."[2]

Some time ago, I was given the task of writing about the "early American cocktail." (This essay is the result.) It was my time to ponder the origins of the cocktail, and I was not exactly in a state of "unreflective overconfidence." I knew the cocktail was American—as Mencken and Wondrich make clear, *everybody knows that*—but I was actually much more familiar with drinking in general in early America than I was with how and when the cocktail emerged from the mists of time. What I knew was this: *people drank a lot*—in early America, and elsewhere. Or perhaps I should say they *used alcohol*. Not merely something to imbibe in the seventeenth and eighteenth centuries, alcohol was the go-to liquid for all manner of everyday tasks. Until at least the mid-nineteenth century, most women bathed babies in spirits rather than water. Women applied wines stewed with thyme, sage, winter savory, sweet marjoram, and rosemary to their faces to maintain fairness, and rubbed their bodies with mead mixed with rose juice and petals. Women cleaned hats and boots with beer, silver and mirrors with gin, and metal with rum.[3]

I also knew some of Benjamin Franklin's writings on booze, and the value of abstaining from it. As early as the 1720s, Franklin is publishing pieces with titles like "On Drunkenness," "A Meditation on a Quart Mugg," and "The Drinker's Dictionary," this last an alphabetically arranged compilation of phrases for being wasted. I offer here my own reduction of Franklin's "dictionary":

> He's Biggy, Burdock'd, Been at Barbados, and has a Head Full of Bees.
> He's Cherubimical, Crocus, Wamble Crop'd, and Half Way to Concord.
> Sir Richard has Taken off his Considering Cap.
> He's Dipped his Bill and is Wet both Eyes—he's in his Element.
> Fox'd, Fuddled, and Fetter'd, His Flag is Out and he Fears no Man.
> He's Glaiz'd, Globular, Been with Sir John Goa, and Got the Glanders.
> Hardy, Hiddey, He's Got on his little Hat.
> Jagg'd and Jambled, he's seen the French King.
> He sees two Moons, has Rais'd his Monuments, Eat the Cocoa Nut, and is altogether Nimptopsical.
> He scalt his Head Pan and Been Among the Philistines and In his Prosperity.
> He's been too Free with Richard, like a Rat in Trouble. He's half seas over, in the Sudds, As Stiff as a Ring-bolt, Stew'd, Stubb'd, Soak'd.
> Top'd, Wet, and got the Indian Vapours.[4]

Being "too Free with Richard" was behavior observed only by the abstemious Franklin, who was called the "Water-American" by his beery colleagues in the printing house: "My Companion at the Press, drank every day a Pint before Breakfast, a Pint at Breakfast with his Bread and Cheese; a Pint between Breakfast and Dinner, and another when had done his Day's-Work."[5] He goes on: "I drank only Water; the other Workmen, near 50 in Number, were great Guzzlers of Beer. On occasion I carried up & down Stairs a large Form of Types in each hand, when others carried but one in both hands. They wondered to see from this & several Instances that the Water-American as they call'd me was *stronger* than themselves who drunk *strong* Beer."[6] These passages are vintage Franklin: preening and wily and satirical all at once. He looks down on drinking and drinkers, but he also takes delight in the slang of it. Franklin might be called the first theorist of American drinking. He sets the stage for the uniquely American conjunction of exuberance and censoriousness that marks the country's relation to its alcoholic ways.

But I had been tasked with writing about the early American *cocktail*, not boozing in general, and the responsibility of understanding origins weighed heavily on me. It was perhaps for this reason that, when I made the acquaintance of a major collector of early Americana, I blurted out: "I have to write an essay on early American cocktails! I bet you have some awesome punch bowls!" He raised his eyebrows at my enviable commission. He did indeed have some awesome punch bowls. Thus did I wangle an invitation to a late-summer gathering at my acquaintance's country retreat, the other guests being other collectors and experts in early American material culture.

Of course, the punch bowls were a bit of a red herring. Punch may have been the "Monarch of mixed drinks," as Wondrich calls it, but punches are not cocktails.[7] My collector friend told me he would not be making punch or mixing drinks but that I was welcome to do so if I liked. I boned up on punches, shrubs, toddies, and flips. I learned that the American Revolution began outside a bar, which probably should not have surprised me. An engraving by Amos Doolittle shows the "Battle of Lexington" with Buckman's Tavern in the background.[8] The story goes that the militiamen who met the British had been knocking back flips in the dead of night. Of all the named drinks from this colonial era, the flip is the most attractive to me: a mélange of ale, rum, sugar or molasses, a beaten egg, and a scrape of nutmeg. But the proper preparation of a flip involves plunging a red-hot poker into the mix, to create a smooth, frothy, slightly burnt finish, and I thought brandishing a hot poker amidst the priceless objets d'art was probably ill-advised.

What did I think I would learn at this event? Hard to say, exactly. Expertise certainly—given all the authorities there, I might learn some hard facts useful to my writing. But more generally, I was drawn to the aura of authenticity itself, as if being in the company of these amazing artifacts would rub off on me, and I'd be able to bottle some of that in my essay. And I did learn about authenticity, though not what I had expected to learn. My host had written a few days before that his concession to my assignment was the procuring of some fine thirty-year-old Madeira. This was hardly a cocktail, of course, but I had no objections: if it was good enough for George Washington, who reportedly drank several glasses of Madeira every evening, it was good enough for me. As promised in the invitation, we "dined *al fresco* in the potting shed." We dined—and we drank. By the time we sat down to a delicious meal, we had been through some bubbly and a Côte de Beaune. The Madeira made a round. I had prepared some notes to share with the other guests—including Franklin's funny "dictionary"—but we were well into it now, and the notes would have to wait.

One difficulty with nailing down the early American origin of the cocktail is that name and thing don't always coincide—in fact, they rarely do. This "lexical flexibility" bedevils all discussion of cocktails.[9] As Wondrich points out, the word *cocktail* is used to denote all manner of drinks today—he has a special horror of the "Chocolate Martini"—that have no right to the name, and the same was true early on: "For a while there in the very early part of the [nineteenth] century that name appears here and there attached to drinks that in later years any self-respecting saloon denizen would have looked at with slantindicular gaze had it been proffered to him as a Cocktail—things such as 'rum and honey,' which may be a fine drink but ain't no Cocktail."[10] To study this subject, one must become lexicographer and linguist, in addition to historian. Mencken offers seven possible etymologies for "cocktail." Two of these trace to the French: that it derives from *coquetier*, an eggcup, which non-French speakers in New Orleans pronounced "cocktay"—this traces the drink to Henri Peychaud, famous for Peychaud's Bitters; or that it derived from *coquetel*, the name of a mixed drink from Bordeaux. On the English side, the possible origins are more grotesque. Surely the idea that "cocktail" derives from "cock-ale"—a concoction involving a bird beaten to a pulp suspended in the cask so that its fowl essence pervades the whole—is just a sick joke. Then there's the idea that it comes from *cock-tailed*, meaning "having the tail cocked so that the stump sticks up like a cock's-tail."[11] Some historians aver that this effect was achieved by the application of raw ginger to a horse's rear end.

Mencken's researches have been superseded by those of Wondrich, who confirms evidence for this last narrative. "Feaguing" was the practice of putting "a clove of ginger up the poor tired [horse's] 'fundament' before showing it," explains Wondrich. "We may take the name cock-tail to be what linguists call an 'exocentric noun-verb compound,' like *breakwater, scarecrow,* and *pickpocket*. A cocktail is something that cocks up your tail . . . that something being a glass of ginger beer or ginger extract mixed with ale. In America, the tails took a little extra cocking."[12] This sketchy business with the ginger draws Wondrich into still deeper linguistic waters: "The issue has been confused by its use of the old rhetorical trick of hypallage or transferred epithet: In reality, it's the drink that's ginger, and *cock-tail* is the vulgar appellation."[13] But Wondrich's citations indicate something different: "Cock-tail—is ginger," writes John Badcock in *Sportsman's Dictionary* (1825), and the same author's *Boxiana; or, Sketches of Ancient and Modern Pugilism* (1828) describes fight fans in a country pub drinking "gin and [that is, or] beer, or both combined with a scratch or two of cock-tail in it."[14] Wondrich asserts that this "scratch or two of cock-tail" "has to be something like ginger extract," but how do you *scratch* an extract?[15] Leaving aside such quibbles, this much is clear: The word *cock-tail* seems to be first associated with a drink not in America, but in England. It refers to a drink with ginger in it, which by association with the practice of feaguing suggests a perking or picking up of spirits (or tails).

On this side of the pond, the crucial perking agent was not ginger but bitters. An 1806 article in *Hudson (New York) Balance and Columbian Repository* explains to a puzzled reader that "Cocktail . . . is a stimulating liquor, composed of spirits of any kind, sugar, water, and bitters—it is vulgarly called the bittered sling, and is supposed to be an excellent electioneering potion, inasmuch as it renders the heart stout and bold, at the same time that it fuddles the head. It is said also, to be of great use to a democratic candidate: because, a person having swallowed a glass of it, is ready to swallow anything else."[16]

Back in the potting shed, I too was ready to swallow pretty much anything. The thirty-year-old Madeira was drained, and our host had brought out some items for perusal—including some fuddling cups, a kind of colonial dribble glass in the shape of three vessels interlocking handles like friends linking arms. The trick is to know how to drink from the correct cup without dribbling from the others: a test for the drink-befuddled. A curator of early Americana was challenged and passed with flying colors, despite the fact that he had been enjoying the Madeira just as much as I had. The conversation had taken a more surreal turn. One guest muttered bitterly about the loss of standards at *Antiques & Fine Art*, the main journal for collectors. Our host described his search for a period greenhouse, which sent him to some godforsaken town in the Netherlands that specializes in such rarities. One guest tried to sell our host a seventeenth-century house that had been disassembled, proposing that it be reassembled on his grounds. Earlier, as we had stood next to Benjamin

Franklin's sundial—a gift to Franklin from an English admirer—our host had described how the wood with which his 1710 house was clad had been salvaged from the timbers of an eighteenth-century shipwreck. Now, in response to the offer of another house on his property, he mused, "I'd have to find another shipwreck."

Authenticity is a beautiful dream. My lunch companions knew full well that it was strictly inaccessible, but they luxuriated in the dream no less fervently for that. I was tapping into a dead-serious species of play, a hide-and-seek with origins, a dream-authenticity. And this play helped me understand the resurgence of interest in historic cocktails today. Perhaps the best place to observe it is in the reappearance of the speakeasy. I once visited the Bathtub Gin bar in Manhattan: I arrived in a kind of vestibule, like those used by car rental agencies. There was one person there, doing nothing. I said, "Too early?" A nod. Twenty minutes later, I returned, to be ushered through a nondescript door into a large saloon with brass fixtures and delicious cocktails. Cocktails are tied up with the pleasure of such passages through the looking glass, such inhabitations of a dreamworld where fantasies are authentic and the authentic is a fantasy. My lunch companions seemed able to live the dream, as it were (having loads of money helps): that is, the intense persnicketiness about historical accuracy was finally more in the service of enjoying the present than of (merely) understanding the past. Cocktail history enthusiasts share a similar commitment to historical recreation in the service of pleasure in the present: as with Civil War reenactors, it's the *experience* of history that is sought. Watching my lunchmate handle the fuddling cups like a pro, I briefly considered opening a speakeasy called The Potting Shed.

What Mencken calls the "Gothic Age of American drinking," Wondrich calls the "Archaic Age." It's the period from the Revolution to the antebellum years, the era in which the cocktail, as word and thing joined, came into being (initially, probably, as a "spiced sling").[17] Evidence allows us to narrow its place of emergence: "Whatever the precise circumstances of its birth, it's clear that the Cocktail enjoyed its first fame in the rough triangle between Boston, Albany, and New York, and in the absence of any evidence to the contrary we must consider that its homeland."[18] James Fenimore Cooper agrees. In 1821, Cooper published the first American historical novel, *The Spy: A Tale of the Neutral Ground*. Set in Westchester County in 1780, the novel presents the Revolution not as a heroic battle of freedom against tyranny but rather as a kind of jockeying between pretenders and spies, fake loyalists and spurious patriots, all on the disputed "neutral ground" of Westchester. It's all very vague and unsettled; Washington himself appears mostly incognito. Taken as a whole, it's a weirdly compromised origin story. But in this game changer of a novel, Cooper inserts another origin story involving an Irish woman named Elizabeth Flanagan who follows the troops:

> Her faults were, a trifling love of liquor, excessive filthiness, and a total disregard of all the decencies of language; her virtues, an unbounded love for her adopted country, perfect honesty when dealing on certain known principles with the soldiery, and great good-nature. Added to these, Betty had the merit of being the inventor of that beverage which is so well known, at the present hour, to all the Patriots who make a winter's march between the commercial and political capitals of this great state, and which is distinguished by the name of "cock-tail." Elizabeth Flanagan was peculiarly well qualified, by education and circumstances, to perfect this improvement in liquors, having been literally brought up on its principal ingredient, and having acquired from her Virginian customers the use of mint, from its flavour in a julep to its height of renown in the article in question.[19]

I have no idea what this "beverage" is supposed to be. It's not a julep, since it is distinguished from one. Perhaps the liquor is whiskey, because one assumes the immigrant Flanagan hails from Ireland, where her "education and circumstances" might have led her to be "literally brought up" on that national beverage. In any case, Cooper's little story suggests two important things: first, the cock-tail is tied to the Revolution, to the founding of the United States (even today, writes Cooper—in 1821—the "Patriots" availing themselves of cock-tails "make a winter's march" between New York and Albany); second, the cock-tail comes from elsewhere—in this case, Ireland.

The relation between drink and the American political experiment is intimate, as Franklin and Cooper attest. Consider here another founding Benjamin. In *An Inquiry into the Effects of Spirituous Liquors on the Human Body: To Which Is Added a Moral and Physical Thermometer* (1790), Benjamin Rush details the threats to self-governance posed by different kinds of drink (see fig. 1.1).

Rush's way with lists is more a product of Enlightenment confidence than is Franklin's whimsical treatment, but the two Benjamins share a pleasure in nomenclature. As the drinks get more inflammatory in Rush's "Thermometer," from Small Beer to Pepper in Rum, so too does the gravity of the attendant vices, diseases, and punishments. It is easy to see how "Peevishness" might well be a consequence of a "morning after" involving "Puking and Tremors of the hands," but as we move to more dire conditions, some puzzles emerge. It may initially seem odd that "hatred of just government" represents a more severe

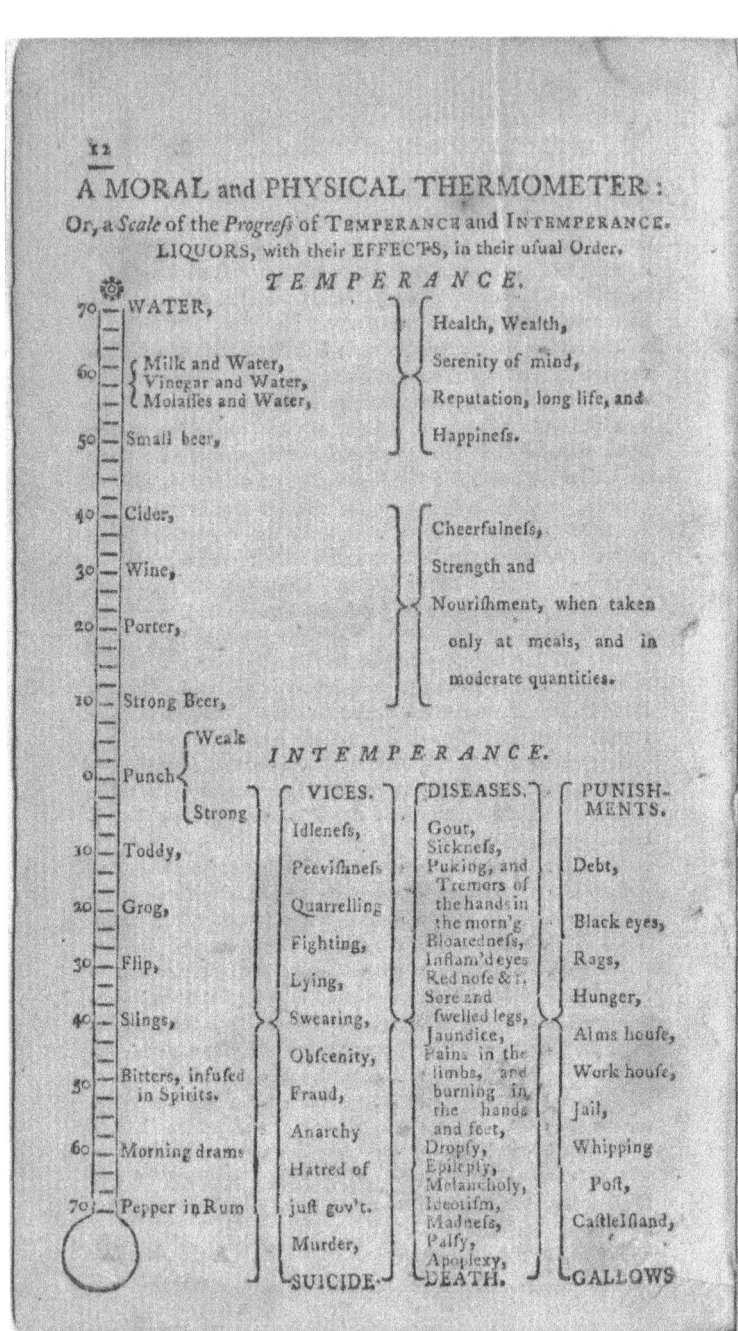

Figure 1.1. Rush's "Moral and Physical Thermometer."

vice than "anarchy," but in a new republic committed to the establishment of precisely such "just government," its rejection represents the ultimate political sin—one exacerbated by too much fiery rum. Rush's approach was moral and medical, all in one. Indeed, it was Rush who first proposed alcoholism as a disease.[20] From "Water-American" Franklin's pert Puritanism to Rush's scientific symptomatology, the way was paved for the Temperance movements of the nineteenth century and Prohibition in the early twentieth.

Turning back to the drinking side of the American alcoholic bipolar condition, we can make a final point about the cocktail and Americanness. Let's say that what is distinctive and original about America, paradoxically, is its secondariness: that is, rather than focusing on the creation of anything absolutely new and ex nihilo, we need to look, when considering the "contribution of the American way of life to the salvation of humanity," at a different and opposed vector—what Cooper calls "improvement." This is Wondrich's take as well: "If the Cocktail is American, it's American in the same way as the hot dog (that is, the Frankfurter), the hamburger (the hamburger steak), and the ice-cream cone (with its rolled gaufrette). As a nation, we have a knack for taking underperforming elements of other people's cultures, streamlining them, supercharging them, and letting 'em rip—from nobody to superstar, with a trail of sparks and a hell of a noise along the way."[21] This improving "facility with mixing drinks," asserts Wondrich, "was the first legitimate American culinary art, and—along with the minstrel show, but that's another book—the first uniquely American cultural product to catch the world's imagination."[22] Actually, the American Declaration of Independence was the first "uniquely American cultural product to catch the world's imagination," as David Armitage has shown.[23] That the cocktail emerges during the Revolution, according to Cooper, makes, then, a kind of ideological sense. In *Notions of the Americans* (1828), Cooper writes that "Americans had no revolution, strictly speaking; they have only preceded the rest of Christendom in their reforms, because circumstances permitted it."[24] Neither the cocktail nor American independence claims absolute originality: like Flanagan offering an "improvement of liquors," her taking of "underperforming elements" and making something better and new out of them, the American project itself is less a revolution than an opportune seizure of the "circumstances" allowing for an improvement.

The "Gothic Age of American drinking" thus puts in place the world within which the meaning and ideology of the American cocktail make sense. Even if we settle, for now, on the bittered sling as the earliest instance of a drink that satisfies our sense of what makes a cocktail, and was called such by its nineteenth-century inventors, the fact is that word and thing are never stable in this history. And what's more, as Cooper and Wondrich agree, and as I learned in the potting shed, authenticity is what we need it to be, and it is less about origins than about improvements.

So let me venture an ideological (and antihistoricist) conclusion. *There is no such thing as the original American cocktail.* Rather the word and the concept name the dialectic of excess and discipline, ebullience and opprobrium. This dialectic was what powered the ideal of "improvement," the word Cooper used. Politically, the United States was a mess seething beneath one idea—the nation. Alcoholically, the United States was also a mess. The wild invention of an entrepreneurial, shaggy, and individualistic country needed a single name under which to categorize all the "improvements" being offered—and that name eventually became *cocktail*: "In the Gothic Age of American drinking as of American word-making," writes Mencken, "a great many fantastic drinks were invented, and some of them were given equally fantastic names, *e.g., horse's neck, stone-fence (or stone-wall), brandy-crusta, brandy-champerelle, blue-blazer, locomotive, bishop* and *stinkibus*.... Bartlett ... adds many more, *e.g.* the *bald-face*, the *black-jack*, the *bust-head*, the *ching-ching*, the *deadbeat*, the *deacon*, the *floater*, the *fiscal agent*, the *knickerbocker*, the *moral suasion*, the *pine-top*, the *phlegm-cutter*, the *ropee*, the *shambro*, the *silver-top*, the *snap-neck*, the *split-ticket*, the *stagger-juice*, and the *vox populi*."[25] Many are the voices proffering improvements! And very nearly infinite are the possibilities. Mencken "employed a mathematician to figure out how many could be fashioned of the *materia bibulica* ordinarily available in a first-rate bar. He reported that the number was 17,864,392,788. We tried 273 at random, and found them all good, though some, of course, were better than others."[26] Vox populi, indeed.

Indiana University

NOTES

1. H. L. Mencken, *The American Language, Supplement One* (New York: Knopf, 1956), 256.
2. David Wondrich, *Imbibe! From Absinthe Cocktail to Whiskey Smash, A Salute in Stories and Drinks to "Professor" Jerry Thomas, Pioneer of the American Bar*, rev. ed. (New York: Perigee, 2015), 209.
3. Sarah Hand Meacham, *Every Home a Distillery: Alcohol, Gender, and Technology in the Colonial Chesapeake* (Baltimore: Johns Hopkins University Press, 2009), ch. 1, passim.

4. Benjamin Franklin, "The Drinker's Dictionary," in *Franklin, Writings*, ed. J. A. Leo LeMay (New York: Library of America, 1987), 266–71, passim.

5. Benjamin Franklin, "The Autobiography of Benjamin Franklin," in *Franklin, Writings*, 1348.

6. Franklin, "Autobiography," 1348.

7. Wondrich notes that the 1887 revision of Jerry Thomas's foundational mixographic guide, *How to Mix Drinks, or the Bon Vivant's Companion* (New York: Dick & Fitzgerald, 1862), marks the "displacement of Punch as the Monarch of mixed drinks by moving punches to the back of the book and putting Cocktails at their rightful place at the front" (226). Wondrich has also written an entire volume on punch, with a characteristically ornate title: *Punch: The Delights (and Dangers) of the Flowing Bowl. An Anecdotal History of the Original Monarch of Mixed Drinks, with More than Forty Historic Recipes, Fully Annotated, and a Complete Course in the Lost Art of Compounding Punch* (New York: Perigee, 2010).

8. Corin Hirsch, *Forgotten Drinks of Colonial New England: From Flips and Rattle-Skulls to Switchel and Spruce Beer* (Charleston, SC: American Palate, 2014), 16–18.

9. Wondrich, *Imbibe!*, 210.

10. Wondrich, *Imbibe!*, 218.

11. Mencken, *American Language*, 257.

12. Wondrich, *Imbibe!*, 215.

13. Wondrich, *Imbibe!*, 215n.

14. Wondrich, *Imbibe!*, 215n. Brackets Wondrich's.

15. Wondrich, *Imbibe!*, 215n.

16. Wondrich, *Imbibe!*, 216.

17. Wondrich, *Imbibe!*, 224.

18. Wondrich, *Imbibe!*, 221.

19. James Fenimore Cooper, *The Spy: A Tale of the Neutral Ground*, ed. Wayne Franklin (New York: Penguin, 1997), 189.

20. Matthew Warner Osborn, *Rum Maniacs: Alcoholic Insanity in the Early American Republic* (Chicago: University of Chicago Press, 2014).

21. Wondrich, *Imbibe!*, 209.

22. Wondrich, *Imbibe!*, 11.

23. David Armitage, *The Declaration of Independence: A Global History* (Cambridge, MA: Harvard University Press, 2008).

24. James Fenimore Cooper, *Notions of the Americans, Picked Up by a Traveling Bachelor, in Two Volumes* (Philadelphia: Carey, Lea, and Blanchard, 1838 [1828]), II, 339.

25. Mencken, *American Language*, 260–61.

26. Mencken, *American Language*, 260.

BIBLIOGRAPHY

Armitage, David. *The Declaration of Independence: A Global History*. Cambridge, MA: Harvard University Press, 2008.

Cooper, James Fenimore. *Notions of the Americans, Picked Up by a Traveling Bachelor, in Two Volumes*. Philadelphia: Carey, Lea, and Blanchard, 1838 [1828].

Cooper, James Fenimore. *The Spy: A Tale of the Neutral Ground*. Edited by Wayne Franklin. New York: Penguin, 1997.

Franklin, Benjamin. "The Autobiography of Benjamin Franklin." In *Franklin, Writings*, edited by J. A Leo LeMay. New York: Library of America, 1987.

Hirsch, Corin. *Forgotten Drinks of Colonial New England: From Flips and Rattle-Skulls to Switchel and Spruce Beer*. Charleston, SC: American Palate, 2014.

Mencken, H. L. *The American Language, Supplement One*. New York: Knopf, 1956.

Meacham, Sarah Hand. *Every Home a Distillery: Alcohol, Gender, and Technology in the Colonial Chesapeake*. Baltimore: Johns Hopkins University Press, 2009.

Osborn, Matthew Warner. *Rum Maniacs: Alcoholic Insanity in the Early American Republic*. Chicago: University of Chicago Press, 2014.

Wondrich, David. *Imbibe! From Absinthe Cocktail to Whiskey Smash, A Salute in Stories and Drinks to "Professor" Jerry Thomas, Pioneer of the American Bar*. Rev. ed. New York: Perigee, 2015.

Wondrich, David. *Punch: The Delights (and Dangers) of the Flowing Bowl. An Anecdotal History of the Original Monarch of Mixed Drinks, with More than Forty Historic Recipes, Fully Annotated, and a Complete Course in the Lost Art of Compounding Punch*. New York: Perigee, 2010.

TWO

THE BOULEVARDIER

Craft, Industrialism, and the
Nostalgic Origin in Cocktail Culture

ANTONIO CERASO

RECENTLY, MY SPOUSE AND I were meeting friends for dinner at a small restaurant in Chicago. We arrived early, and decided to order a predinner cocktail. Since it was early in the evening and early in the summer, and since the restaurant was Italian, we asked the waitperson for "two Americanos"—an *aperitivo* cocktail of Campari, sweet vermouth, and club soda. She seemed perplexed by this order *before* dinner, and soon headed off not in the direction of the bar, but toward the restaurant's hulking espresso machine, where she began fussing with the various levers. Sensing a misunderstanding (she thought we were ordering caffè Americanos), we gestured to the bartender, who—it turned out—was also the restaurant's owner, and explained the mix-up. He immediately went back to the bar, carefully measured and mixed our drinks, and brought them out to us himself. But he also wanted to talk about cocktails. "Did you know the Americano had another name?" he asked excitedly. We conversed about the Milano e Torino, also excitedly. The talk soon turned to cocktail history: we debated the Americano's origins, talked of Americans in northern Italy, and discussed the Americano's relationship to two other classic cocktails with similar ingredient patterns—the negroni and the cocktail at the center of this essay, the boulevardier.[1] What began as a simple order, a basic exchange, had become a conversation, a social and symbolic encounter that surpassed its exchange functions.

Americano
1 oz Campari
1 oz Italian vermouth
Soda water
Half orange slice to garnish
Build ingredients over ice in a collins glass. Garnish with half an orange slice.

I begin with this admittedly privileged scene because it highlights a number of elements that are central to my discussion of the boulevardier cocktail, and of cocktail and craft cultures more generally. The first is a kind of historical compulsion in cocktail rhetoric. In contemporary writing on and discussion of cocktails, we often find a turn toward their origins, mythologized or otherwise. We narrate when and by whom a particular cocktail was invented, debate questions of provenance, speculate about alternate histories. To be immersed in cocktail culture today means to have a sense of cocktail history, and with it, a historical sensibility about what might be called cocktail-centric historical eras. Indeed, this sensibility often functions more as a general relation with a historical moment; cocktail consumption easily couples with and complements ways of dressing and of furnishing one's home, the architecture of cocktail bars, typographic styles for menus—a whole historical repertoire or stylization that becomes, for some, a life performance. I will call this relationship the "nostalgic origin" in cocktail culture, though it will become clear that I don't consider it to be a matter of pure nostalgia. Rather, the obsessive turn toward historical narratives about cocktails and their seemingly linked historical enactments (the Jazz Age party, the mid-century modern furniture style) performs social and symbolic functions at our own particular moment—functions that exceed mere nostalgia, or even branding through nostalgia. A resurgent cocktail culture (and craft culture more generally), I argue, deploys these narratives as a means of inventing new forms of social, symbolic, and economic exchange.

But cocktail culture, like other craft cultures, enacts these new modes of exchange during a period in which work, consumption, and the forms of power that organize them seem to be in transition. The conversation with the bartender/owner of the little Italian restaurant also depicts a conceptual scene: *the encounter between the mixologist and the cocktail aficionado.* As a specific emerging mode of a producer-consumer dyad, this pairing provides us with conceptual personae for thinking through transformations and experimentation in the realms of work and consumption, as well as pointing us to emerging values in craft cultures more generally. I will, however, note here a figure who has dropped out of this pairing, a figure who perhaps reflects both the conceptual difficulty and the evaluative difficulty of emerging craft production and consumption: the waitperson who misunderstood the order. The waitperson—in being mistaken—is displaced from the social and symbolic exchanges centered on cocktail *knowledge*. The displacement of this particular kind of worker by the mixologist/aficionado pairing stands in for both a changing economic landscape and its rhetorical enactments. Among such enactments, of course, is this essay itself—and perhaps this book as a whole. As we excitedly discuss the points of intersection between the historical, the rhetorical, and, well, the liquid, we should also keep this fundamental displacement in mind. Where a particular historical compartment in cocktail culture is one theme of this essay, the narrative displacement of a particular form of work is another.

ALWAYS HISHTORISHIZE

The boulevardier cocktail is first mentioned in Harry McElhone's classic cocktail recipe book, *Barflies and Cocktails: 300 Recipes*—a text produced in 1927 by the staff of Harry's Bar (or Harry's New York Bar), one of the more famous watering holes for Prohibition-era Americans in Paris.[2] However, rather than appearing as one of the featured recipes in the text proper, the boulevardier recipe appears in a supplementary text written by American journalist and editor Arthur Moss. This supplement, titled "Cocktails Around Town," is a winking set of in-jokes and anecdotes about well-known personalities in the then-vibrant Paris expatriate community, paired with at times bizarre cocktail recipes that the listed person purportedly had invented. If the main text recipes are cocktail standards endorsed by McElhone, Moss's supplement provides the humorous custom-ordered cocktails. Among the thirty-five entries (alphabetized by the inventor's last name, with the exception of the boulevardier) are the following:

> As a jazzband impresario, its [sic] only natural for Billy Arnold to take to the "Black Bottom Cooler" which he makes with 1/3 champagne, 1/3 coca-cola, and 1/3 stout, all well-iced.... J. W. Janicki, remembering certain things about the Sovietland, is all for the "Bolo": 1/2 sloe gin, 1/2 Gordon gin.... And you'll probably need someone to tow you away after H. Verstappen's "Ambulance Cocktail": 1/5 Swedish punch, 2/5 gin, 2/5 lemon juice, 2 dashes Angostura.[3]

Tucked in with these often-unsavory listings, the boulevardier cocktail makes its first modest print appearance. Moss notes, with a reference to classic typing filler text, "Now is the time for all good Barflies to come to the aid of the party, since Erskinne [sic] Gwynne crashed in with his Boulevardier Cocktail; 1/3 Campari, 1/3 Italian vermouth, 1/3 Bourbon whisky [sic]."[4] The reference, which nobody in the expatriate community would have missed, points out the prominent Parisian-American Erskine Gwynne, and, more specifically, Gwynne's then brand-new society and literary magazine, the *Boulevardier*.

The drink's origin narrative, then, locates it historically within a fully romanticized cultural hotbed of the expatriate and particularly American literary community in 1920s Paris, a minor but not unexpected variation on the "Prohibition-era" fascination that drives many cocktail narratives today. Its lead character—Edward Erskine Gwynne Jr.—only ramps up the cluster of cultural associations, operating virtually as a prototype for an American expat gadabout. Raised in a formerly wealthy, if often run-on-hard-times family, Gwynne grew up among Long Island, New York City, and Paris. His father, Edward Erskine Gwynne Sr., came from the prominent Cincinnati Gwynne family (Cincinnati's Gwynne Building, completed in 1914, is on the National Register of Historic Places). Gwynne Sr.'s aunt, Alice Claypoole Gwynne, married Cornelius Vanderbilt II in 1867 (she is Gloria Vanderbilt's grandmother, and journalist Anderson Cooper's great-grandmother). The younger Erskine Gwynne's status as a Vanderbilt, often cited in descriptions of the boulevardier cocktail, is thereby assured, though Gwynne's actual ties with the Vanderbilt side of his family were likely far looser in practice, just as his actual relationship to his Vanderbilt relatives is often misstated in cocktail narratives.[5] Further connections with society fame were closer to home. Gwynne's sister, Alice Gwynne, achieved some fame of her own under her assumed name Kiki Preston. A virtual moving scandal sheet, Gwynne/Preston was notorious among Paris expatriates for her drug use; she was also a key figure in the Happy Valley set, a group of British and American expats who founded an upper-crust commune in Kenya and devoted themselves to drug and sexual experimentation. For his part, Gwynne was no stranger to expat antics, being known at one point as the "Playboy of Paris."[6] The image of him crashing into a party with a cocktail was likely familiar enough to Moss's readers that they didn't need further explanation.

These familial connections and personal traits certainly lend an amusing society (and, ultimately, modernist) veneer to the boulevardier cocktail's supposed inventor, but the cocktail's story also remains focused on the *Boulevardier* magazine itself. Most accounts identify the basics: that the *Boulevardier* was envisioned as a Paris expat version of the *New Yorker*, mixing society gossip, satire, event reviews, and cartoons with some minor attempts at serious literary work and light—often parodic—journalistic fare; that Gwynne founded the magazine in 1927; and that it folded in early 1932. The magazine's place in the prolific scene of 1920s expatriate journalism, however, is perhaps most adeptly explored by Ronald Weber in his book *News of Paris: American Journalists in the City of Light Between the Wars*. For Weber, the *Boulevardier* was far more a tongue-in-cheek satire and society sheet than a literary magazine, whatever its initial aspirations may have been. A latecomer among Anglo-American periodicals in Paris, the *Boulevardier*, like its rival the *Paris Comet* (also founded in 1927), captured the tail end of a prosperous period for expatriate elites. It's no surprise that both magazines failed once the Depression really started to make itself felt, even among Gwynne's crowd. Weber notes wryly that Gwynne—long after the magazine had folded—continued writing on "the posh world he traveled in" right up until the "German forces swept into Poland."[7] It is an appropriate judgment on what was largely a frivolous enterprise, but this quality of the *Boulevardier* magazine may be part of what recommends it as a site of cocktail nostalgia.

A history of American news and literary journalists in 1920s Paris draws our attention back to the author of the "Cocktails Around Town" supplement itself, Arthur Moss. At the time that *Barflies and Cocktails* was published, Moss was already well known for his initial Paris literary magazine foray, the *Gargoyle*,[8] as well as for his "Around the Town" column in the Paris edition of the *New York Herald* and his "Over the River" column in the *Paris Times*; both columns were collections of expat gossip and literary news that Moss had been publishing for several years.[9] Moss's more relevant position for his one-line callout of Erskine Gwynne, however, was his job as the editor of the *Boulevardier* magazine. If Gwynne was something of a popular figurehead of the magazine, Moss seemed to be the day-to-day editor who made the *Boulevardier* run. As Weber notes, "With *The Boulevardier*'s fourth issue in June 1927, Arthur Moss appeared on the masthead as the magazine's editor, though judging by the writing style of editorial statements and the 'Boulevard Brainwork' column he was at the helm from the start."[10] Moss's close involvement with Gwynne and the magazine helps contextualize his mention of both in the supplement to *Barflies and Cocktails*: when Moss listed the inventor of the boulevardier cocktail, he was essentially advertising—with a wink, perhaps—his new business venture with his partner Erskine Gwynne. Indeed, if the winking cocktail-dubbing entry in his "Cocktails Around Town" served as surreptitious publicity for the new magazine, *Barflies and Cocktails* ends with a more public announcement: a full-page ad for the *Boulevardier* magazine closes the little volume (see fig. 2.1).

The story of the boulevardier's origins would be mild and interesting enough: American expatriates with a pseudoliterary bent living (and drinking) it up in Prohibition-era Paris. But the story now seems to come packaged, in some cases literally, with the drink itself. Rarely does a mention of the boulevardier cocktail go by without reference to Gwynne and Moss's little magazine, or some conveyance of an imagined general atmosphere of between-the-wars Paris. A *T: New York Times Style Magazine* piece on the cocktail presents the cocktail's inventor as "a wealthy young American lad who flitted off to Paris to start a literary magazine in 1927, something along the lines of The Dial, The Transatlantic Review and other English language pamphlets that reaped a

Figure 2.1. Full-page ad for the *Boulevardier* magazine.

bountiful harvest by giving an early forum to writers like Hemingway, Joyce, Dos Passos, Sinclair Lewis, Noël Coward, Thomas Wolfe and others."[11] Cocktail historian Ted Haigh also provides the origin narrative, though his focus is on how American liquors (bourbon) came to be mixed with unheard-of (in the United States) European ingredients (Campari) as a result of Prohibition: "One amply palatable drink of that milieu, The Boulevardier, appeared in... *Barflies and Cocktails*. It was the signature drink of Erskine Gwynne, expatriate writer, socialite and nephew of railroad tycoon Alfred Vanderbilt. Gwynne edited a monthly magazine, a sort of Parisian *New Yorker*, named *The Boulevardier*."[12] A *New York Times* feature noting the cocktail's popularity provides the following: "According to most accounts, the cocktail was created in the late 1920s by Erskine Gwynne, an expatriate writer, socialite and Vanderbilt family relation who founded a Paris literary magazine called the Boulevardier."[13] And Gary Regan recounts the story in *The Negroni*, attributing Moss's entry to McElhone himself, and nodding to Gwynne, Kiki Preston, and Hemingway in the bargain.[14] This list of origin narratives could be extended; even a short video by cocktail expert Dale DeGroff on how to make a boulevardier cocktail includes a quick mention of Erskine Gwynne and his magazine.[15] When the High West Distillery decided to produce a premixed version of the boulevardier, the company included the cocktail's origin story on the bottle itself; the label announces that "Erskine Gwynne, the creator of the Boulevardier Cocktail, moved to Paris and began The Boulevardier, a monthly magazine patterned after The New Yorker, catering to the upper-class expatriate." Reviews of the new product repeat the story.[16]

It is, of course, possible to chalk up the obsessive rendition of the boulevardier's origin with the odd romance of Gwynne himself, or with the clear provenance of the drink's beginnings. But the focus on a cocktail's origins functions as a subgenre within cocktail writing itself. While the boulevardier's origin narrative may be exemplary in its specificity, its appearance nearly whenever the cocktail is mentioned is hardly isolated. Origin narratives appear alongside drink recipes across cocktail writing. Take, for instance, the entry for the aviation cocktail appearing on the Gin Foundry website. The entry includes where the cocktail first appeared in print (in the 1916 edition of Hugo R. Ensslin's *Recipes for Mixed Drinks*), how variations on the cocktail agree with or depart from its origin (it began to be made without crème de violette, "most likely due to a scarcity of the liqueur"), and historical reasoning for or arguments about its proper ingredients and proportions (because the German Ensslin's book included numerous drinks featuring the "Alps produced liqueur Crème de Violet," those who argue that an aviation can be made without it are presumably incorrect).[17] Becoming immersed in cocktail culture, becoming a consumer of classic cocktails, involves a rhetorical encounter with these historical narratives.

Aviation
2/3 gin
1/3 lemon juice

2 dashes maraschino
2 dashes crème de violette
Shake well in a mixing glass with cracked ice, strain, and serve.

This recipe gives proportions rather than measures; 2 oz of gin and 1 oz of lemon juice work well.

From Hugo R. Ensslin, *Recipes for Mixed Drinks* (1916).

The search for an origin narrative in cocktail rhetoric is not limited, however, to so-called classic cocktails, such as the boulevardier and the aviation, or even those cocktails whose beginnings present persistent mysteries, such as the old-fashioned. Rather, the tendency appears even for cocktails of fairly recent vintage. Most cocktail writers agree, for instance, that the American trilogy cocktail was developed at the New York City bar Little Branch in 2007. But the story of the drink (rye whiskey, Laird's applejack bottled in bond, sugar, orange bitters) draws on a deeper history, recalling the colonial American period when rye whiskey caused rebellions, and "George Washington's records mention 'cyder spirits.'"[18] By drawing on the early American pairing of rye whiskey and apple brandy, the recently invented cocktail dresses itself in a nostalgic colonial-era origin: once the Prohibition and pre-Prohibition eras have been exhausted for atmosphere, the American Revolutionary era would seem as good a place to land as any for cocktail aficionados.

American Trilogy
1 cube brown sugar
2 dashes orange bitters
1 oz rye whiskey
1 oz bonded applejack
Orange peel, to garnish

Add sugar cube to an old-fashioned glass, dash with bitters, and muddle thoroughly. Add ice, rye whiskey, and bonded applejack, and stir until combined and cold. Garnish with orange peel.

From Richard Boccato and Michael McIlroy,
Little Branch cocktail bar, New York (2007).

Cocktail culture, through its writing at the very least, has a strong historicist tendency—a desire to place that which is ingested within not so much a context as a stylized historical scene. There are, no doubt, particular argumentative functions that explain why such generic features take hold in cocktail writing. A form of authorship is granted to drink inventors through such narratives—even early cocktail books followed this ethic of attribution. In arguments about "proper" ingredients, furthermore, an appeal to the origin is a powerful rhetorical tool. In discussions about why a drink contains this or that ingredient, or whether the drink should be made one way or another, tracking down its provenance can help adjudicate disagreements. But these functions—really, discussions about *making* cocktails—fail to explain the detail, the stylized historical atmosphere that we imbibe with our drinks. What does the *Boulevardier* magazine have to do with Campari or vermouth or how the boulevardier cocktail should be served? What arguments are adjudicated for the modern mixologist by tales of Erskine Gwynne's Paris escapades? In the next section, I suggest a broader function for these narratives: that they allow the cocktail aficionado—after the waning of industrialism—to reclaim a sort of craft knowledge of consumption, or what Bernard Stiegler calls *savoir vivre*.

AGAINST THE INDUSTRIALIZED CONSUMER

If the resurgence of craft cocktails in bars and restaurants and specialized cocktail establishments since the late 1990s tells us something about labor, it is this: the mixologist is not a worker. I mean this, of course, in a very specialized sense. The mixologist, even down to the invention and scientification of the title, is not an *industrial worker*—or, at the very least, is not imagined to be. Indeed, the mixologist may serve as a sort of conceptual prototype for this negative relation to industrial work. Across a resurgent sense of labor as craft (from mixology to foody-ism to craft beer to various DIY and "maker" movements), whatever the positive concept of such work may be, it remains marked by its negative concept as *not-industrial*. Before we turn to the question of an industrialized consumer, then, it is worthwhile to revisit the older question of the relation between the industrial worker and the craft maker.

The classic analysis of the worker of industrialism would, of course, take us back to Marx's insights on the disarticulation of knowledge and labor. For Marx, the industrial labor process, which *makes* the industrial worker, is marked above all by the extrusion of a knowledge of making from the craft producer and its reinstallation in a process or a machine. The result is the interchangeability of any given producer and, with it, the flattening of any concrete worker to units of (deindividualized, abstract) labor power. This reading of Marx, which comes to be known as the deskilling of the craft maker—the transformation of the craft maker into an industrial worker—is most closely associated with Harry Braverman, who argues in *Labor and Monopoly Capital: The Degradation of Work in the Twentieth Century* that "deskilling" is the essential quality of all forms of labor under capitalism, including specialized and "mental" labor as well as service work. For Braverman, the primary turn is what he calls the "separation of conception and execution," or the "dissociation of the labor process from the skills of the workers."[19] This dissociation constitutes the main historical departure of industrial work from the tradition of craft making, which Braverman describes as follows:

> From the earliest times to the Industrial Revolution, the craft or skilled trade was the basic unit, the elementary cell of the labor process. In each craft, the worker was presumed to be the master of a body of traditional knowledge, and methods and procedures were left to his or her discretion. In each such worker reposed the accumulated knowledge of materials and processes by which production was accomplished in the craft.[20]

The industrialization process, Braverman argues, strips away the traditional knowledges of making, along with any discretion in the production process. With the onset of Taylorist principles of scientific management, moreover, it is not simply knowledge but also a bodily sensibility of production that is extracted and abstracted, as specific ways of making are extracted from living bodies, and new workers are shaped according to abstract processes.

The specter of deskilling haunts contemporary craft practices and discourses, functioning as their negative concept. From the standpoint of production, craft becomes an act of reskilling, or reclaiming "a body of traditional knowledge" of materials and processes. It's not surprising, in this sense, that a historical tendency toward postindustrialism in wealthy nations should produce a resurgent craft *ethos*: the two are intimately connected as forms of making, ideologically if not in practice. The production side of this ethos seeks to recreate the knowledge of making, to reconnect conception and execution, or reassociate a labor process with the skills of the worker, in Braverman's terms.

On the surface, this would seem an odd enough task for series of recipes, the apparent *knowledge* of craft cocktails. In the case of the boulevardier, the clear statement of proportions ("1/3 Campari, 1/3 Italian vermouth, 1/3 Bourbon whisky") appears easier to handle than your proverbial McDonald's fryer. A few minutes on the cocktail forums, however, would fast disabuse you of this notion. One must gauge the intensity of the various spirits, know the rye content of the bourbon, adjust the proportions, understand the effects of the different ratios. And so we learn that McElhone's (or rather, Moss's) classic one-to-one-to-one formula is probably inappropriate, at once too sweet and too bitter; that the Campari overwhelms the bourbon (perhaps Aperol would be better?); that perhaps you would need one and a half ounces of bourbon, perhaps three-quarters of an ounce of Campari; or that maybe you should chuck it all and use a strong rye, bottled in bond, and name it anew: the 1794 cocktail. One must be able to invent. Notably, it is not only the mixologist who escapes industrial deskilling, given a resurgent craft ethos. The workers in craft beer breweries take on a cultural air of the craft producer (a "creative"), even if the craft producer is functionally the same as a worker in a big, industrial brewery. You may mostly operate the forklift or move between the tanks in the brewhouse, but you can name the hops in this batch and switch up the process from time to time to create a one-off, and that's what makes you *not an industrial worker*. Cocktail culture—as a species of craft culture—retains this relationship with industrialism; reskilling (as a reclamation of traditional knowledges, materials, and procedures) structures its forms of work for production.

Boulevardier
1 1/2 oz bourbon
1 oz Campari
1 oz Italian vermouth
Orange peel, to garnish

Combine ingredients over ice in a mixing glass. Stir until glass begins to frost, maybe a minute or two. Strain into a cocktail glass and garnish with orange peel.
From Ted Haigh, *Vintage Spirits and Forgotten Cocktails* (2009).

But what of the consumption side?

Bernard Stiegler's paired concepts of *savoir faire* and *savoir vivre* shed light on the way a craft ethos addresses both making and consuming. Throughout his works, Stiegler is (like Braverman) intensely focused on the way knowledges, practices, and even capacities (or potentialities) are externalized and made discrete—or what he calls (after Derrida) their grammatization. For Stiegler, *savoir faire* is a knowledge of making, or doing; its externalization and discretization looks very much like classical deskilling in Braverman's reading of Marx. Indeed, Stiegler echoes this reading, noting that "with the industrial revolution, the process of grammatization . . . discretizes the gestures of producers with the aim of making possible their *automatic reproduction*."[21] Marx's analysis, then, sees the "loss of savoir-faire," or the externalization of the knowledge of making, as the basis of a proletariat—a class of workers for whom skill (as knowledge of making) and labor (as action of making) have been disassociated. Stiegler argues that this analysis is correct as far as it goes but that it does not recognize a larger trajectory of grammatization. This trajectory, on the one hand, makes Plato the first great thinker of the proletariat, given his concern in the *Phaedrus* with the central role of the externalization and discretization of memory through writing.[22] On the other hand, the trajectory continues into the age of consumer society—a development that Marx could not have anticipated. Where Marx (and Braverman) may have (given Stiegler's reading) correctly analyzed the externalization of savoir faire, they do not grasp the externalization of savoir vivre, or the loss of a knowledge of living. This process, for Stiegler, constitutes a "proletarianization of the consumer."[23]

Stiegler argues that, for its economic subjects, the loss of knowledge of living is as devastating as the loss of a knowledge of making. The destruction of savoir vivre, which doubles as a loss of a knowledge of consumption, is characterized by its externalization into systems and processes of mass markets. Both processes "short-circuit" a collective and creative coevolution of humans and their tools—what Stiegler calls, after Gilbert Simondon, transindividuation. The loss of savoir vivre is somewhat more difficult to conceptualize than deskilling in the classical sense, since the loss of savoir vivre seems to include an externalization of desires and affects, and not simply a loss of "knowledge" akin to what at one time might have been called taste. It is the grammatization neither of speech nor of gesture, but rather of something like pleasure. In the extraction of savoir vivre, a multiplicity of human desires is externalized into calculable systems, and the systems reinstall those desires as *more automatic* and deindividualized drives linked with industrial production. One might blanch at a seeming consumer elitism in this view (you don't really want what you want—we've lost a memory of our own pleasures), but pairing this view with the extraction of savoir faire provides a cultural flip side to the craft challenge of reclaiming a knowledge of making.

Stiegler begins his analysis by comparing commerce and the market, where *commerce* functions as a sort of enlightened exchange relation, always "an exchange of *savoir-faire* and *savoir-vivre*" while "the *consumerist* market presupposes the liquidation of both *savoir-faire* and *savoir-vivre*."[24] If contemporary cocktail culture is constituted in part by its resistance to deskilling *as making*, it is also constituted by a resistance to the loss of savoir vivre, or the industrialization of consumption. The mixologist is not a worker, but neither is the cocktail aficionado a consumer, at least in the sense of the industrialized consumer of the late twentieth century. The meeting of the mixologist and the cocktail aficionado is not the same as the ordinary exchange relationship on the market. It is a "commerce," in Stiegler's exalted term; the word in French can also "refer to conversation and more generally to all forms of fruitful social relations."[25] The transformation can be applied to the craft relation in general; it's why stopping by a local craft brewery for a growler is different from grabbing a twelve-pack of Bud Light at the supermarket. It may also indicate why "craft" functions as so powerful an identity draw. It is not merely that craft provides a level of distinction akin to the old taste, but that it produces the appearance of a radically transformed—individuated—market relationship. Craft's draw may be located in this relational force prior to its identity functions.

In any case, the reclamation of savoir vivre in response to its externalization in consumer society serves to explain the genre function of the origin narrative in cocktail culture—first in terms of its iteration, and second in terms of content. If we return to our original scene—the restaurant owner and the cocktail aficionados commercing, as it were, over Americanos—we might detect the consumption side of the knowledge of making that drives craft production. The telling of these narratives cements an appearance of knowledge in the space of consumption; our collective understanding of how to *live well through consumption* was reinforced through the telling, through the narratives, which is to say, rhetorically. It's not surprising, in this regard, that cocktail culture is so deeply linked with other forms of "enlightened consumption," from foodie-ism to an obsession with sartorial representation.

The reclamation of a lost knowledge of consumption might also explain why such narratives so often seem nostalgic. One must go back to 1920s Paris—or 1940s Los Angeles, or the early 1960s lounge culture, or even the days of the Whiskey Rebellion—to recapture the savoir vivre expropriated by the consumer culture that developed over the second half of the twentieth century. If cocktail culture's focus on craft production rebuilds savoir faire, its nostalgic narratives are perhaps not nostalgic at all. Rather, they seek to situate a commerce prior to its degradation into a market; they both imagine and perform exchange relationships outside those of the (degraded) market (the flip side is, of course, a rampant craft futurism: molecular gastronomy and the like). If those people dressed in their Jazz Age clothing seem gripped by an odd nostalgia in the darkened speakeasy-styled bar, it certainly may be because the world they're performing never actually existed. But they may not be *replaying* anything at all. Rather, what appears as nostalgic in cocktail narratives (and in cocktail culture) may be in fact aspirational and inventive. The obsession with the origin narrative and its frequent performance may serve as unspoken strategies for rebuilding savoir vivre, for re-inventing a commerce outside the market.

COCKTAILS AND ECONOMIES OLD AND NEW

It would be tempting to stop here, with both cocktail culture and our assembled craft culture in general inventing our new worlds, standing up to the industrial expropriation of knowledges—commercing, so to speak, collectively. Of course, this is how craft cultures have thought of themselves since the Arts and Crafts movement. That's clear enough, and not a particularly interesting observation at this point. That our desires for commerce, in Stiegler's sense, can be replaced as consumer drives and repackaged as the essence of the competitive market should be obvious to anyone who's watched half an episode of *Top Chef*, or the endless similar craft "competitions." In the world of craft cocktails, such appropriation or co-opting—the re-industrialization of craft, again and again—might be seen in the remarkable proliferation of craft cocktail bars, or in the way the transnational liquor companies have recognized the market upside of craft across their various product lines. The craft ethos itself is always available to industrial repackaging.

It is time, however, to return to the waitperson, standing over by the espresso maker, left out of the conversation/commerce that defined the mixologist/aficionado pairing. Her absence from the conversation points up a difficulty that goes beyond mere recuperation into an industrial model. Her absence suggests that we take seriously the mixologist/aficionado pairing as a real reflection of emerging work and power relationships. The problem of the new craft cultures is not only that they are vulnerable to "co-optation," or to endlessly being recuperated into the bad old norms of industrial production. Rather, emerging craft cultures have to be approached as sites of emerging power relationships in themselves: not in their failure to distance themselves from the old forms of production and consumption, but in their success in doing so. If the new craft cultures oppose themselves to industrialism, they do so on this basis: where industrialism normalizes, the new craft differentiates. The resurgence of savoir faire and savoir vivre might thus be understood through an analysis of normalization and differentiation as forms of power.

The kinds of externalization examined by Marx, Braverman, and Stiegler can be seen as historically limited, a function of a particular period or moment. What's notable about all these accounts—and this includes Stiegler, though he goes furthest in suggesting that the industrial production/consumption dyad is breaking down—is that once knowledges are externalized, they are then standardized (in machines, in processes, etc.). One end of grammatization—and this seems to be the opponent of craft cultures in general—is both an automaticity and a *normalization* of production/consumption. For Stiegler, the more positive side of grammatization is its ability to serve as the basis for commerce, for those externalized knowledges to be, in essence, shared. That is, if the externalization of knowledge is a *pharmakon*, both poison and remedy, its poisonous trait is its capacity to *deindividuate* through normalization, as industrialism does to both the worker and the consumer. The remedy that externalization provides, on the other hand, is the capacity of cognitive and affective worlds to be shared, and, through that sharing, to generate novel (that is, different, nonnormalized) sociotechnical forms—"long chains of transindividuation." It is for this reason that Stiegler opposes to industrialism (or what he calls an "economy of carelessness") not "craft," but rather an "economy of contribution." What becomes clear, in any case, are the values attributed to either side of externalization: Where externalization normalizes, it is destructive. Where it proliferates differences (through the sharing of cognition and affects), it is both productive and laudable.

It is easy enough to map these values onto emerging craft cultures. To the extent that craft resists normalization and proliferates differences, it takes part in a positive "sharing" economy. Cocktail culture is exemplary in this regard: it thrives on variation and invention. Even the classic cocktails (like the boulevardier) call for constant rejiggering, so to speak. Cocktail culture spurns the mass production of Jack and Cokes and cosmopolitans (one high-end Chicago cocktail establishment even puts "No Cosmos" on a sign!), and even the plain old gin and tonic comes in for endless reinvention (surely you make your own tonic water!). This narrative of an emergent craft culture overcoming the normalizing mass culture of industrialism with happy innovations is, of course, familiar: it is the story that contemporary capitalism tells itself. I will suggest another mapping here; it is not a mapping that contests this story, but rather one that locates it within multiple systems of power.

In his series of lectures on the genealogy of neoliberal economic philosophy, Michel Foucault ends a chapter with a predictive statement: "What appears on the horizon of this kind of analysis [specifically, an economic analysis of criminality]," Foucault says,

> is not at all the ideal or project of an exhaustive disciplinary society in which the legal network hemming in individuals is taken over and extended internally by, let's say, normative mechanisms. Nor is it a society in which mechanisms of general normalization and the exclusion of those who cannot be normalized is needed. On the horizon of this analysis we see instead the image, idea, or theme-program of a society in which there is an optimization of systems of difference, in which the field is left open to fluctuating processes, in which minority individuals and practices are tolerated, in which action is brought to bear on the rules of the game rather than on the players, and finally in which there is an environmental type of intervention instead of the internal subjugation of individuals.[26]

What's notable about this passage, appearing in *The Birth of Biopolitics*, is that it maps out very clearly the three forms of power Foucault is famous for analyzing (sovereign power, disciplinary power, and biopower), linking the first two with normalization and linking the last—contemporary biopower, neoliberal analysis—with "an optimization of systems of difference." Where sovereign

Table 2.1. Foucault's Forms of Power Mapped against
Craft and Industrial Production

Form of Power	Craft/Industrialism	Power works by ...
Sovereign power	Guild craft	Normalizing and excluding
Disciplinary power	Industrial	Normalizing and including
Biopower	Entrepreneurial craft	Optimizing differences

power (usually associated with monarchy) was marked by "general normalization and exclusion," and disciplinary power (usually associated with modernity and industrialism) was marked by "normative mechanisms" that impinged on and extended themselves through individuals, biopower actually functions *through* a proliferation of differences, by generating differences (say, innovation) in a controlled environment. This organization of the mechanisms of power might be mapped against craft/industrial periodizations as shown in table 2.1.[27]

Viewed in this manner, the poisonous side of externalization as imagined by Stiegler (and Marx and Braverman) bears a distinct relationship to the forms of internalization associated with industrialism. That is, grammatization retains a negative value to the extent that the worker/consumer submits to the normative mechanisms of the workplace/market. What comes after industrialism, this kind of grinding normativity, is the proliferation of difference associated with craft cultures: not just Budweiser and Coors, but dozens, hundreds of beer choices; not just Jack and Cokes and cosmos, but American trilogies, aviations, boulevardiers. The emergence of craft contra industrialism is this movement away from normative mechanisms. But this is also the image of a form of power that Foucault sees emerging in mid-twentieth-century economics. Where craft pits itself against industrialism, it can be said to be shifting between these two forms of social power. Craft opposes normalization (of the worker and consumer) after normalization has already waned. Craft promotes the proliferation of differences just as social power shifts from enforcing sameness to requiring the proliferation of differences (on the market, of subjectivities, etc.).

The externalization of savoir faire and savoir vivre was in some sense necessary for the normative work in both industrial and disciplinary economies. Put another way, standardizing production and consumption by extracting and normalizing the knowledge of making and living was both an economic function and an effect of its particular regime of power. But that would suggest that their reclamation is similarly implicated. That we relearn a savoir faire and a savoir vivre—that we become, figuratively, mixologists and aficionados—may itself be an effect of our own economic form and its attendant regime of power: biopower, for the entrepreneurial economies of constant innovation.

The entrepreneurial, yes. Table 2.1 introduces a notable distinction between "guild craft" and "entrepreneurial craft." We might find one more lesson in the cocktail narrative, then, if this analysis holds. The mixologist is not a worker, to be sure, and the cocktail aficionado is not a consumer in the degraded sense. But the mixologist does increasingly appear to function as the hero of the innovative economy: the entrepreneur. The cocktail aficionado is similarly entrepreneurial, both in the quest for authentic (as opposed to automatic) satisfaction and in the seamlessness of the aficionado's own inventive drink-making. And how very familiar and admirable a figure our Erskine Gwynne would appear in the world of the tech start-up! The content of the *Boulevardier*'s narrative, a winking Erskine Gwynne out to make his way through sheer pluck and risk in Paris, is telling in this regard. It is quite possible, in fact, that the boulevardier is not a classic Prohibition-era cocktail at all—that it was simply a throwaway joke like the other joke cocktails in Art Moss's appendix, a little jibe at the Cincinnati American (bourbon) in Europe (Campari, vermouth). It's quite possible, that is, that the boulevardier did not become an actual cocktail until our present cocktail revival found reason to reinvent it, complete with an apparent narrative. It may be nostalgic in a pure sense. But like so many of these narratives, it captures a scene of savoir vivre by focusing our attention on the capitalist entrepreneur and innovator. The cocktail narrative (and many craft narratives besides)—for all the other work they do—is a narrative of the entrepreneur. It is perhaps for this reason that the worker—our missing waitperson, relegated to the shadows—disappears from view, not excluded from the cocktail narrative, exactly, but rather both placed and displaced within it.

—⚜—

Cocktail culture today of course exists in many forms and encompasses a wide set of activities. Here, I've restricted this variety to a very particular symbolic meeting: the meeting of the mixologist and the cocktail aficionado. This site of exchange is particularly intense—precisely because, ultimately, one person can play both economic parts, as in the aficionado at home, trying to work out a drink for herself from the supplements of *Barflies and Cocktails*. But that meeting is also the site of imagined worlds, *new economies* that will be the location of social struggle. In one world, knowledge of making and knowledge of living/consumption free themselves from the automaticity of our former ways of producing and consuming, reclaiming something like commerce, inventing forms of exchange that allow for care. In the other, a relentless innovationism simply extends carelessness through new channels, all entrepreneurs for themselves—a form of exchange that we know only too well, and that may just be getting worse. The meeting of the mixologist and the aficionado is ultimately both of these at once, as are the other craft relations we currently lionize: the craft brewer and the beer aficionado, the chef and the foodie, the artisanal paper maker and the paperhead. Craft is proliferation of these meetings, of these exchanges, of these imagined worlds. In working out how these new exchanges will operate we will, of course, turn to rhetorical resources and to narratives. So now is the time for all good Barflies to come to the aid of the party.

DePaul University

NOTES

1. Much of our discussion was no doubt drawn from Gary Regan's book on the negroni, *The Negroni: Drinking to La Dolce Vita, with Recipes & Lore* (Berkeley, CA: Ten Speed Press, 2015), a book that also mentions the boulevardier.

2. Harry McElhone, *Barflies and Cocktails: 300 Recipes*, intro. by David Wondrich (New York: Mud Puddle Books, 2008), first published in 1927.

3. Arthur Moss, quoted in McElhone, 80–83.

4. Moss, quoted in McElhone, 80.

5. Erskine Gwynne Jr.'s grandfather was David Eli Gwynne, brother to Alice Claypoole Gwynne. Ted Haigh, in his *Imbibe Magazine* feature on the boulevardier cocktail, mistakenly identifies Erskine Gwynne Jr. as "nephew of railroad tycoon Alfred Vanderbilt." See Ted Haigh, "History Lesson: The Boulevardier," *Imbibe Magazine*, December 4, 2009, https://imbibemagazine.com/the-history-of-the-boulevardier-cocktail/. "Alfred Gwynne Vanderbilt I was actually Erskine Gwynne's first cousin once removed (first cousin to Gwynne's father), though Haigh probably means Cornelius Vanderbilt II, Gwynne's great-uncle through marriage. Haigh's erroneous description is picked up by other cocktail sites that list Gwynne as a "Vanderbilt nephew."

6. Ronald Weber, *News of Paris: American Journalists in the City of Light Between the Wars* (Chicago: Ivan R. Dee, 2006), 203.

7. Weber, *News of Paris*, 215–16.

8. Malcolm Cowley, writing from Paris, mentions Moss familiarly in a 1922 letter to Kenneth Burke: "We have been doing the Dôme as usual. The crowd: Art Moss, Percy Winner, several nice boys, several Jewish girls, Ivan Opffer." Paul Jay, ed., *The Selected Correspondence of Kenneth Burke and Malcolm Cowley,*

1915–1981 (New York: Viking Press, 1988), 123. Presumably, the three knew each other from their Greenwich Village days in the late 1910s, when Moss had edited the literary magazine the *Quill*, and collected a compilation of poems published in the magazine as *A Greenwich Village Anthology of Verse* (1919). Cowley had published in the literary magazine the *Gargoyle*. See also Jack Selzer, *Kenneth Burke in Greenwich Village: Conversing with the Moderns, 1915–1931* (Madison: University of Wisconsin Press, 1996).

9. Weber, *News of Paris*, 141–43.

10. Weber, *News of Paris*, 206–7.

11. Toby Cecchini, "Case Study: The Boulevardier," *T: New York Times Style Magazine*, February 2, 2012, https://tmagazine.blogs.nytimes.com/2012/02/02/case-study-the-boulevardier/.

12. Haigh, "History Lesson," n.p.

13. Robert Simonson, "The Boulevardier Is Back on the Menu," *New York Times*, January 28, 2014, http://www.nytimes.com/2014/01/29/dining/the-boulevardier-is-back-on-the-menu.html.

14. Regan, *The Negroni*, 40.

15. Dale DeGroff, "How to Make a Boulevardier Cocktail," web video, February 20, 2016, http://bartenderhq.com/how-to-make-a-boulevardier-cocktail-by-dale-degroff-via-liquor-com/.

16. Nathan Borchelt, "The Barreled Boulevardier Cocktail Review," *Paste Magazine*, December 5, 2013, http://www.pastemagazine.com/articles/2013/12/the-barreled-boulevardier-cocktail-review.html.

17. "Aviation," Gin Foundry, September 20, 2013, https://www.ginfoundry.com/cocktail/aviation-cocktail/.

18. Lesley Jacobs Solmonson, "Cocktail of the Week: Eveleigh's American Trilogy," *LA Weekly*, January 10, 2014, https://www.laweekly.com/cocktail-of-the-week-eveleighs-american-trilogy/.

19. Harry Braverman, *Labor and Monopoly Capital: The Degradation of Work in the Twentieth Century*, 25th anniv. ed. (New York: Monthly Review Press, 1998), 78–79. Italics in the original. It should be noted that what has come to be called the "deskilling" thesis is, like everything else associated with Marx, a subject of controversy. For an alternative reading that disputes Braverman, see Paul Adler, "Marx, Machines, and Skill," *Technology and Culture* 31, no. 4 (October 1990): 780–812, https://doi.org/10.2307/3105907. Adler argues that deskilling was seen even by Marx as a temporary stage in a larger process that could include the "upgrading" of skills, while Braverman sees it as an intensifying and inescapable trait of capitalist production.

20. Braverman, *Labor and Monopoly Capital*, 75.

21. Bernard Stiegler, *For a New Critique of Political Economy*, trans. Daniel Ross (New York: Polity, 2010), 32–33.

22. Stiegler, *For a New Critique*, 29–30.
23. Stiegler, *For a New Critique*, 28.
24. Stiegler, *For a New Critique*, 16 (italics in the original).
25. Stiegler, *For a New Critique*, 16.
26. Foucault, Michel, *The Birth of Biopolitics: Lectures at the Collège de France 1978–1979*, trans. Graham Burchell (New York: Palgrave, 2008), 259–60.
27. This table is based roughly on similar tables produced by Jeffrey T. Nealon in *Foucault Beyond Foucault: Power and Its Intensifications Since 1984* (specifically, pp. 45 and 59). In one significant difference, Nealon identifies biopower's primary practice with "norms." Nealon further specifies, however, that norms in Foucault's sense are a set of forces that "introduce a heightened productivity into the disciplinary apparatus" (49). The passage from *The Birth of Biopolitics* perhaps renders the same operation as an "optimization of systems of differences," with the accent on *optimization*.

BIBLIOGRAPHY

Adler, Paul. "Marx, Machines, and Skill." *Technology and Culture* 31, no. 4 (1990): 780–812. https://doi.org/10.2307/3105907.

"Aviation." Gin Foundry. September 20, 2013. https://www.ginfoundry.com/cocktail/aviation-cocktail/.

"The Barrelled Boulevardier." High West Distillery. http://www.highwest.com/products/the-barreled-boulevardier/.php.

Borchelt, Nathan. "The Barrelled Boulevardier Cocktail Review." *Paste Magazine*. December 5, 2013. http://www.pastemagazine.com/articles/2013/12/the-barreled-boulevardier-cocktail-review.html.

Braverman, Harry. *Labor and Monopoly Capital: The Degradation of Work in the Twentieth Century*. 25th anniv. ed. New York: Monthly Review Press, 1998.

Cecchini, Toby. "Case Study: The Boulevardier." *T: New York Times Style Magazine*. February 2, 2012. http://tmagazine.blogs.nytimes.com/2012/02/02/case-study-the-boulevardier/.

DeGroff, Dale. "How to Make a Boulevardier Cocktail." Web Video. February 20, 2016. http://bartenderhq.com/how-to-make-a-boulevardier-cocktail-by-dale-degroff-via-liquor-com/.

Foucault, Michel. *The Birth of Biopolitics: Lectures at the Collège de France 1978–1979*. Translated by Graham Burchell. New York: Palgrave, 2008.

Haigh, Ted. "History Lesson: The Boulevardier." *Imbibe Magazine*. December 4, 2009. https://imbibemagazine.com/the-history-of-the-boulevardier-cocktail/.

Jay, Paul, ed. *The Selected Correspondence of Kenneth Burke and Malcolm Cowley, 1915–1981*. New York: Viking, 1988.

McElhone, Harry. *Barflies and Cocktails: 300 Recipes*. Introduction by David Wondrich. New York: Mud Puddle Books, 2008. First published 1927.

Nealon, Jeffrey T. *Foucault Beyond Foucault: Power and Its Intensifications Since 1984*. Stanford, CA: Stanford University Press, 2007.

Regan, Gary. *The Negroni: Drinking to La Dolce Vita, with Recipes & Lore*. Berkeley, CA: Ten Speed Press, 2015.

Selzer, Jack. *Kenneth Burke in Greenwich Village: Conversing with the Moderns, 1915–1931*. Madison: University of Wisconsin Press, 1996.

Simonson, Robert. "The Boulevardier Is Back on the Menu." *New York Times*. January 28, 2014. http://www.nytimes.com/2014/01/29/dining/the-boulevardier-is-back-on-the-menu.html.

Solmonson, Lesley Jacobs. "Cocktail of the Week: Eveleigh's American Trilogy." *LA Weekly*. January 10, 2014. https://www.laweekly.com/restaurants/cocktail-of-the-week-eveleighs-american-trilogy-4310331.

Stiegler, Bernard. *For a New Critique of Political Economy*. Translated by Daniel Ross. New York: Polity Press, 2010.

Weber, Ronald. *News of Paris: American Journalists in the City of Light Between the Wars*. Chicago: Ivan R. Dee, 2006.

THREE

A CONTINUED STREAM OF FIRE

Professor Jerry Thomas Invents the "Blue Blazer"

CHRISTOPH IRMSCHER

MR. JEREMIAH "JERRY" THOMAS IN his natural habitat—behind the bar of the Metropolitan Hotel in New York City or at the Occidental Hotel in San Francisco—must have been quite a sight. As you watched his diamond-studded fingers pour amber liquids into frosted tumblers or cut blocks of ice into pieces, whatever temperance vows you might have sworn, to yourself, to your family, to your friends, were quickly forgotten.[1] But there was nothing more memorable than witnessing "the Professor," as he was also called, prepare his signature drink, the Blue Blazer (see fig. 3.1).

The recipe was not complicated, and it is the same today. All you need are a few ounces of Scotch whisky, sugar (syrup will do, too), some boiling water, a lemon peel, two large silver-plated mugs with handles, and a small tumbler. Leave the syrup and the lemon peel in the tumbler, pour one ounce of boiling water into one of the mugs, add three ounces of scotch, set the liquid on fire, and mix the ingredients by pouring them, four or five times, from one mug to the other while gradually increasing the distance between the two. Finally, pour all that flaming liquid into one mug, transfer it into the tumbler, and extinguish the flames by using the bottom of one of the mugs. Stir and enjoy. Note: Don't try this at home, or at least not until you have cleared sufficient space around yourself and locked Fluffy in the other room. While it is actually not all that easy to set diluted whisky on fire, pouring the liquid back and forth creates a kind of bellows, furnishing the air that feeds the fire. And once you've got that fire going, collateral damage is a distinct possibility. So, on second thought, don't even think of trying this at home.[2]

Figure 3.1. Jerry Thomas and his "Blue Blazer." From Jerry Thomas, *The Bar-tender's Guide*. First edition. The Lilly Library, Indiana University Bloomington.

What I have provided above is a somewhat modernized version of Mr. Thomas's recipe. His original description was more impressionistic. He included it in his *Complete Cyclopaedia of Plain and Fancy Drinks*, the substantial first section of what was likely the first collection of cocktail recipes ever published, a book originally called *The Bar-tenders' [sic] Guide*. At $1.50 a copy—the equivalent of $28 today—the *Guide* cost a pretty penny. The publisher Dick & Fitzgerald, known for popular books on subjects ranging from minstrel songs to ballroom dancing to the writing of love letters, had registered copyright for the book on June 23, 1859. When the *Guide* finally came out three years later, its cover featured a gold-stamped image of a satisfied looking, comfortably whiskered and goateed gentleman raising a glass in one hand and holding a cheroot in the other, with the title artfully wrapped halfway around the vignette (fig. 3.2).

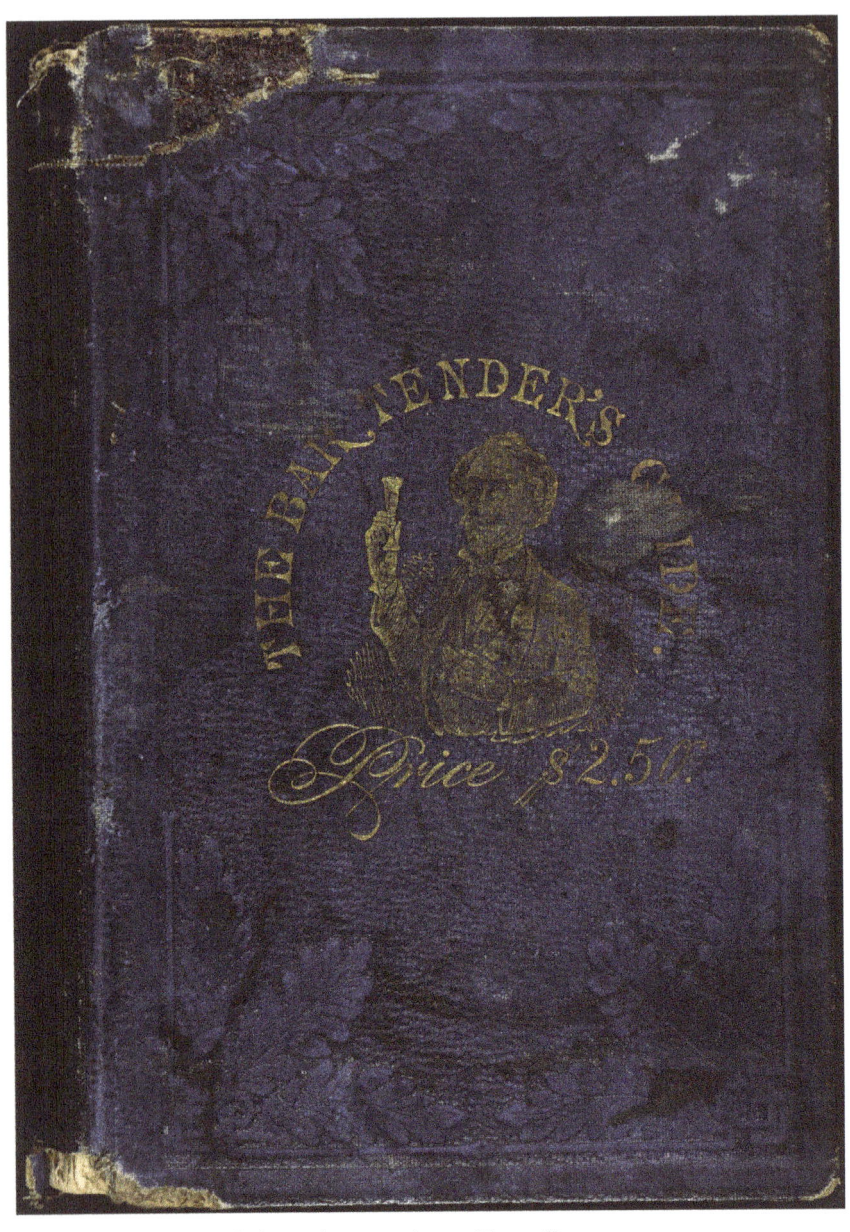

Figure 3.2. *The Bartender's Guide*. First edition. The well-worn copy in The Lilly Library, Indiana University Bloomington.

As the book became popular, the title underwent subtle changes, and the cost of the clothbound copy went up, too—first to $2.00 and then to $2.50 (about $61 today), a level that only well-heeled topers could have afforded, especially in times of war (for the sake of comparison, a bookbinder in New York City would have made $1.42 a day in 1862).³ The cover switched from brown or green to blue, then back to green; the apostrophe in the title migrated to a more proper place, and the hyphen disappeared, turning *The Bar-tenders' Guide* into *The Bartender's Guide*, while Jerry Thomas's contribution was rechristened *How to Mix Drinks, or the Bon-Vivant's Companion*.⁴ The bibliographical puzzle of the different states of the first edition is further complicated by the fact that in 1866 Dick & Fitzgerald began advertising yet another edition, which I have not seen anywhere: *Jerry Thomas' Bar Tender's Guide; or How to Mix All Kinds of Fancy Drinks*, described catchily as "an entirely new edition; new plates; new drinks." That book was available either in cloth or as a paperback, for 75 cents or 50 cents, respectively (about $18 or $12 in today's money).⁵

The first edition of Jerry Thomas's compendium had another small book attached to it, one that I imagine would have been a kind of embarrassment to him. *A Manual for the Manufacture of Cordials, Liquors, Fancy Syrups, &c. &c.* was a handbook for rectifiers, including descriptions of the machinery needed. The author of the dubious manual was one Christian Schultz, whose claim to authority in these matters derived from his previous job as a professor of chemistry in Berne, Switzerland, and from sundry visits he had paid to the "best distilleries in Paris and Bordeaux."⁶ Let us hope, then, that France was not where Professor Schultz learned how to produce Bordeaux in sufficient quantities to satisfy greedy American customers: take four gallons of the original beverage, mix it with six gallons of cheap, plain wine, and solve the resulting visual problem by coloring the potion with a "tincture of alderberries [sic]."⁷ Fortunately, the official second edition of the *Guide* dispensed with most of the shady Professor Schultz's recommendations, reducing the number of recipes from 463 to 95. Although it's impossible to prove, one would like to think that Jerry had a hand in that decision.⁸

—※—

The Bartender's Guide, with its impossibly long full title, a symphony of words and different fonts crowded on the title page, was thus addressed to several audiences—those who made drinks and those who faked them; those who enjoyed them; those who did all of the above; and, perhaps, also those who just liked to read about such things. A guide and companion to many, *Bartender's Guide* spoke multiple languages. In his description of the Blue Blazer, for example, Jerry cheerfully mixed several discourses. Overall, his recipe spent less time on details ("1 wine-glass of Scotch, / Do. [ditto] boiling water") than on technique and impact: "If well done this will have the appearance of a continued stream of liquid fire."[9]). Minutiae are for those who, like T. S. Eliot's Prufrock, measure out their lives with coffee spoons. Jerry was a master of the grand gesture. Comparing him to the average poison-slinger behind the counter of a grubby bar, according to Herbert Asbury, was like comparing Michelangelo to the cartoonist Bud Fisher or, to use a contemporary analogy, Renée Fleming to Taylor Swift.[10]

It had taken Dick & Fitzgerald three years to get the *Guide* out, and it's not clear at what point Thomas joined the enterprise and how extensively he revised an already existing manuscript. That said, there is a uniformity of tone throughout the book that suggests it wasn't just the result of a hack job. Another likely reason for the delay, suggested by Andrew Smith, was that originally there didn't seem to be any need for such a publication at all. Imbibing mixed drinks was an upper-class activity, limited to upscale bars, and bartenders working there tended to have their own recipes, which they kept to themselves. The advent of the Civil War changed all that. Alcohol sales soared, and bars became the places where one went to numb the soul.[11] And there, if you were lucky, you would run into Jerry Thomas, looking just the way he did in the woodcut attached to the description of the Blue Blazer (see fig. 3.1), in all his mustachioed, grim-faced, bow-tied splendor, his back arched slightly backward, his eyebrows lowered in fierce concentration as he was making his signature drink, conjuring his shimmering arc of fire while holding nothing but two mugs in his hands. And Jerry would remind you that imbibing was not about seeking oblivion. Against the shadow barrels of whiskey in the background, Professor Thomas was the unconventional master of alcoholic revels, the expert who knew how to transform matter into spirits.

—ᴡ—

Mixing drinks is not really an art, not in any strict sense. The products of the bartender's work are ephemeral, created only to be consumed. For Jerry Thomas, however, even if the product was evanescent, the process by which it came about was not. Which is why—to his own mind, at least—he was an artist of sorts or, rather, a scientist and an artist in one convenient package, with more than a touch of the writer added: "The 'blue blazer' does not have a very euphonious or classic name," he informed his readers, "but it tastes better to the palate than it sounds to the ear." If our ears mislead us, we cannot trust our eyes either: "A beholder gazing for the first time upon an experienced artist, compounding this beverage, would naturally come to the conclusion that it was a nectar for Pluto rather than Bacchus."[12] Confronted with Jerry's pyrotechnics, wouldn't the uninitiated observer think that this was a drink from hell? In his poem "Bacchus," written in 1846, Ralph Waldo Emerson had briefly imagined such a beverage, grown "From a nocturnal root / Which feels the acrid juice / Of Styx and Erebus," but he had then recommended that we follow his example and become intoxicated with the Spirit rather than with spirits.[13] That was, emphatically, not Jerry's solution. To him, the drink, any drink served in his bar, was real. But such a concern with substance over form didn't make the mixer of the drink less of an artist, an "experienced artist," as he clarified. Amateurs beware: "The novice in mixing this beverage should be careful not to scald himself." Mixology was a new science, but it required expertise like any other discipline: "To become proficient in throwing the liquid from one mug to the other, it will be necessary to practise for some time with cold water."[14]

Mixing was a mind game, a bid for total control over the drinker's thoughts and, eventually, body. The Blue Blazer was "nothing but sweetened hot water and burned whisky [sic], flavored with a big dose of imagination," an unknown bartender in Cincinnati explained a few years after Jerry's untimely death. "The sight of the burning whisky as it slips through the air from one mug to the other makes an impression upon the mind that retracts upon the palate, so that while the fluid is slipping down the drinker's throat he has an indistinct idea that he is swallowing fire, and at the same time a very substantial assurance that such fire is good."[15] Once a man has four or five Blue Blazers inside his vest, observed the *Milwaukee Daily-Journal*, be ready for some "startling and dramatic effects."[16]

—⚜—

How and when Jerry became such a proficient drink-preparer remains shrouded in mystery. Born in 1830 in Sackets Harbor, not far from the Canadian border, he led a colorful life, which included a trip to Cuba as a sailor, when he was seventeen or eighteen years old, and a stint working in a saloon in San Francisco; he also tended bar on the ground floor of Barnum's American Museum in New York, at the City Hotel in New Haven, at the Planter's House hotel in St. Louis, and finally, in 1858, at the Metropolitan Hotel. Which is not to say that he never tried his hand at anything else: at one point, he was touring towns up and down the Sacramento River, a member of what he claimed was the first band of minstrels in California. But mixing drinks was in Jerry's genes; the barroom was his stage. His younger brother George had felt the call, too, and it was with him that Thomas opened his own barroom on Broadway, the first of a variety of independent enterprises that usually ended in bankruptcy.

In 1863, he ended up in San Francisco again, where he penned a second book, now lost, called *Portrait Gallery of Distinguished Bar-Keepers*, perhaps a sly allusion to photographer Mathew Brady's *Gallery of Illustrious Americans*. Along the way, he invented drinks that he named as if they were poems he had written.

After his return to New York at the end of the Civil War, Jerry was back at his old game. Over the next decade and a half, now married and a father of two, he ran a series of establishments, sometimes in partnership with his brother, that became known both for the drinks that they offered and the art that hung on the walls, among them works by cartoonist Thomas Nast, who, if he did not invent the image of "Uncle Sam," helped popularize it. At least one of Jerry's enterprises included billiard tables and—perhaps not the wisest addition to a place where powerful drinks were served—a shooting range. But Thomas's ingenuity could not compensate for what must have been a fundamental lack of financial savvy. In March 1882, Jerry sold his last saloon, located on Sixth Avenue and Tenth Street, across from the Jefferson Market police court.

The bar culture that Jerry's pioneering book had made possible would soon be hijacked by the great merchant princes of the Gilded Age, who, inside their ritzy hotels, erected veritable temples to the cocktails Jerry had conjured, places where wealthy patrons could lounge comfortably as they sipped. The new Palmer House in Chicago, for example, completed in 1875, sported a sixty-foot bar—no shooting range to be seen.[17] However, for Jerry Thomas from Sackets Harbor there had never been anything particularly idle about the making of drinks or anything particularly luxurious about the drinking of them. He was still working, though in a job hardly adequate to his talents, when death caught up with him on December 14, 1885. He had just finished his shift at the bar of the Hotel Brighton on Broadway and Forty-Second Street, a gambling place not known—or, as Jerry the eternal optimist would have said, *not yet* known—for the quality of its drinks, when his heart gave out. He was fifty-five years old.[18]

In *The Bartender's Guide*, however, Mixmaster Thomas lives on. His only surviving book is more than the first comprehensive collection of American cocktails ever published. It is, rather, a brief for the necessity of the profession Jerry so flamboyantly embodied. Jerry did not take his task lightly: the hidden themes of Jerry's *Guide* are practice, patience, and perfection. But Jerry wanted to illuminate and educate, not prescribe. "The precise portions of spirit and water, or even of the acidity and sweetness, can have no general rule, as scarcely two persons make punch alike," he said.[19] Hence there was no point in being too precise in his instructions: "what quantity might suit one person would be to another quite distasteful."[20] Being a bartender requires creativity and imagination. But most of all, one has to learn to wait. While the Blue Blazer is quick—a flash in the cup, so to speak—other drinks necessitate hours or weeks of preparation and patience as they mature: "let it stand six weeks in a warm cellar"[21]; "put all in a cask, and leave it for six weeks"[22]; "let it remain for three days."[23] If fire is one of the bartender's main tools, ice is the other one: "Refrigerate with all the icy power of the Arctic," Jerry Thomas exulted in the recipe for Regent's Punch, a concoction for a party of twenty, made up of no fewer than three bottles of champagne; two bottles of Madeira and soda water; one bottle each of Hockheimer wine, curaçao, and cognac; and a half bottle of Jamaica rum. To which, Jerry recommended, add four pounds of raisins, oranges, lemons, rock candy, and, instead of water, green tea, "to taste."[24]

The deeply dialogic nature of Jerry's instructions amounts to more than just the typical cookbook rhetoric. *The Bartender's Guide*, despite its price, is a profoundly democratic book, and the desire to share knowledge that informs Jerry's writing has its equivalent in the sharing of drinks. A large section of his book is devoted to that most collective of drinks, the punch. A well-mixed punch is the potion of democrats, fit for a country where everybody is royalty: "This is a composition worthy of a king," writes Jerry about the Royal Punch, especially when the materials are "admirably blended" and the "inebriating effects of the spirits" are "deadened by the tea, whilst the jelly softens the mixture, and destroys the acrimony of the acid and sugar."[25] Nineteenth-century drinks were usually based on rich liquors like brandy, rum, and sweet gin, which were imported from Europe. Though ingredients may have come from abroad, the drinks themselves were the result of American ingenuity. When making a perfect mixture out of different ingredients, the bartender symbolically mixes the nations the way America as a country, on a larger scale, blends them, too. For in order to make the perfect "Claret and Champagne Cup, à la Brunow" you need Caribbean liqueur, French brandy, and German seltzer: "Stir this together, and sweeten with capillaire or pounded sugar, until it ferments."[26] Mixed drinks are the American antidote to those beverages that too closely reflect the taste of one nation only, as in the combination of "Rhine Wine and Seltzer-Water," a German drink, which "is not very likely to be called for at an American bar."[27] This is not to say that Jerry is averse to foreign concoctions, as long as they have been sufficiently Americanized, such as "Satina's Pousse Café," a kind of multitiered liqueur, offered in a celebrated Spanish café in New Orleans, or the French equivalent of that beverage, sold in Monsieur Faivre's establishment in New York City.[28]

Figure 3.3. Professor Jerry Thomas preparing a "Blue Blazer"; "Our Bartenders," Under the Gaslight (1878–79). From Jerry Thomas, *The Bon Vivant's Companion, or How to Mix Drinks*, ed. Herbert Asbury (New York: Knopf, 1929).

Enjoying mixed drinks the way Jerry Thomas describes it might seem like an experience for gentlemen only, and in the best-known illustration of Thomas preparing his Blue Blazer he is indeed surrounded exclusively by males even more impressively bewhiskered than he (fig. 3.3). Note the difference between the charismatic performer and his passive, awestruck audience. The bartender is the only one moving here—a reminder that the bar is a place of leisure only for those who go there to drink, not for those who make the drinks.

But, as Jerry points out, women drink, too, and when that happens, a well-prepared beverage will serve as a great equalizer. In Jerry's provocative view, women are less likely to practice moderation, especially when the taste of the alcohol is masked, as in "punch jelly." Give them access to such a drink and they will end up incapacitated for distinctly feminine pursuits: "The strength of the punch is so artfully concealed by its admixture with the gelatine, that many persons, particularly of the softer sex, have been tempted to partake so plentifully of it as to render them somewhat unfit for waltzing or quadrilling after supper."[29] Drink levels gender differences.

And in his recipe for mulled wine, uncharacteristically written in verse, Jerry explicitly addressed women, not as consumers but as the makers of drinks: "First, my dear madam, you must take / Nine eggs, which carefully you'll break." Breaking, dropping, beating, pouring, stirring, heating, the female drink-mixer creates a product no man can resist: "he's a fool, / who lets such precious liquor cool."[30]

While the Blue Blazer, with its emphasis on courage, speed, and danger, appears to cater only to male imbibers, this is not true of other recipes in Jerry Thomas's book. In fact, the sheer excess involved in decorating many of the drinks ultimately challenges conventional gender expectations, as we watch the bartender's hand daintily arrange orange and pineapple slices on his creations or add sprigs of mint or verbena to them.[31] Women adore the mint julep, which Jerry, perhaps for that reason, learned to make just right: "Put into a tumbler about a dozen sprigs of tender shoots of mint, upon them put a spoonful of white sugar, and equal proportions of peach and common brandy, so as to fill it up one-third, or perhaps a little less." Take rasped or pounded ice and fill up the tumbler. The final touch: "Epicures rub the lips of the tumbler with a piece of fresh pineapple" and leave the outside encrusted with veritable stalactites of ice. "As the ice melts, you drink." After all this preparation, how could anyone say no? A well-prepared, beautifully arranged mint julep will win over even the most indifferent among the ladies: "I once overheard two ladies talking in the next room to me, and one of them said, 'Well, if I have a weakness for any one thing, it is for a mint julep!'" Adds Jerry: "A very amiable weakness, and proving her good sense and good taste."[32] In its attention to the multiple connections between taste, presentation, and décor, *The Bartender's Guide*, then, is not so different from the traditional cookbooks written for female readers.

Showy, dangerous, theatrical, to be performed only by those who know what they're doing, the Blue Blazer was a far cry from drinks more commonly imbibed today, such as the olive-crowned martini sipped at dusk during cocktail hour, stirred, not shaken, *pace* James Bond, so that its molecules may "lie sensuously, one on top of one other," as one of the drink's devotees, Somerset Maugham, demanded.[33] But in its raw splendor, Jerry Thomas's signature drink stands at the beginning of the history of a type of drink that has been considered archetypally American. Joseph Lanza has called the cocktail America's "calico contribution to modern civilization" and "a portable melting pot."[34] Mixology might, then, be understood as a symbolic way of celebrating the mix that is America. Its gaudy performative element would be in line, then, with other displays of American excessiveness, like Barnum's bizarre American Museum, with its mermaids, fat babies, bearded ladies, and Abyssinian minstrels. That Jerry should, at one point, have shared a building with that establishment is a rich irony indeed, given that Barnum, in his theater hall, loved to stage temperance plays, at the end of which patrons could sign pledge cards. But as Barnum knew only too well, the lure of what's bad for you is too strong to be resisted—hence the loving care he invested in a voyeuristic display of wax figures called "The Drunken Family."[35] Shades of Jerry Thomas, 2016: the *New Yorker*, reviewing a new bar called "The John Lamb" in the basement of the Sago Hotel on the Lower East Side, described a drink called "Bad Judgment" (Jameson, cornflower syrup, egg white).[36]

Back in 1862, Jerry Thomas's publisher was clearly worried that temperance fanatics might sink his book. Therefore, *The Bartender's Guide* begins with an apology in the form of a preface, written either by the publisher or by Jerry Thomas himself. A reference to an experience the writer of the preface had in London does point us in the direction of Jerry's authorship, since we know that he had indeed gone there in 1860: "We very well remember seeing one day in London, in the rear of the Bank of England, a small drinking saloon that had been set up by a peripatetic American, at the door of which was placed a board covered with the unique titles of the American mixed drinks supposed to be prepared within that limited establishment."[37] The restaurant critic William Grimes takes this anecdote at face value and suggests that if we find this establishment we will have also found the first American bar on British soil.[38] I do suspect that this "small drinking saloon," hilariously located in the building of the Bank of England, was a figment of the writer's imagination. The "American" drinks he mentions—the "Alabama fog-cutter," the "Connecticut eye-opener," the "thunderbolt-cocktail," and "lightning-smash"—do not appear in Jerry Thomas's book, and for good reason. The way I see it, his anecdote accomplishes two things: it establishes social drinking as one of the first really successful American cultural export items, while it also parodies the expectations of Europeans that everything American is necessarily vulgar—of course their drinks cut, smash, ignite, and explode. When Benjamin Franklin was in London, he was known for his healthy habits, which included swimming and imbibing copious amounts of water—hence his nickname, the "Water-American."[39] But the days of the Water-American are over. Move over, Ben Franklin. Make room, Bank of England. Enter Jerry Thomas.

The preface of *The Bartender's Guide* thus views the mixing of drinks within an explicitly nationalist or patriotic framework. Americans are, claims the author, more likely to enjoy drinks socially than the citizens of other nations. Temperance advocates, worried about the lonely alcoholic drinking his wife and children out of a house and home and all their savings, need not fret. The objective of *The Bartender's Guide* is, says the author reassuringly, not to introduce the delights of drinking to readers who otherwise might never have touched such concoctions or to cheer on the lonely addict who's about to go on a bender. Instead, he claims unconvincingly, this is a book for those who already know, *color che sanno*, a book for fastidious connoisseurs.[40] The language Jerry uses mirrors such fastidiousness to almost comical excess: "We do not propose to persuade any man to drink, for instance, a punch, or a julep, or a cocktail, who has never happened to make the acquaintance of those refreshing articles under circumstances calculated to induce more intimate relations; but we *do* propose to instruct those whose 'intimate relations' in question render them somewhat fastidious, in the daintiest fashions thereunto pertaining."[41] Of course, the author protests entirely too much. But there's a serious message buried under all that verbiage. Taking on the temperance alarmists who lament that booze wrecks families and homes, the author suggests that mixing and drinking, when exercised rightly and in the appropriate social context, are matters of choice and that both activities require taste and dedication. The phrase "intimate relations," used twice (amusingly, the second time the phrase appears the author seems to be quoting himself), adds yet another dimension to the practice: mixing drinks and drinking mixed drinks bring people closer together. The *spiritus rector* presiding over the loving union between a man or a woman and a drink is none other than Professor Jerry Thomas himself, who has scoured the world in search of his recipes, "of all that is recondite in this branch of the spirit art." There is no excuse anymore for downing any of the barbarous compounds that travelers will encounter abroad, made by "bar-keeping Goths and Vandals" who know as little about the "amenities of *bon vivant* existence," the author adds with more than a touch of casual racism, as "a Hottentot can know of the *bouquet* of champagne."[42]

If the preface had indeed flown out of Jerry's own pen, and this seems likely, what fun must he have had celebrating himself in such glowing terms. This "Jupiter Olympus" of the cocktail—a phrase from the preface—wielded the pen almost as confidently as he handled the tumbler. Jerry ended his preface by quoting from Shakespeare's *As You Like It*: "Good wine needs no bush."[43] But if there's any lesson to be learned from *The Bartender's Guide*, it's actually the reverse. Good drinks need their advocates. Illuminated by the blue blaze casually created by his bejeweled hands, a beaming Jerry Thomas, both Lucifer and Jupiter, winks at us across the distance of more than a century, whispering to our guilty consciences that it's okay and that making drinks together, drinking drinks together, is, at heart, an act of love.

Indiana University

NOTES

1. In 1863, Edward Peron Hingston, a British theatrical manager and friend of humorist Artemus Ward, found Jerry Thomas behind the bar of the Occidental in San Francisco, "all ablaze with diamonds." See Hingston, *The Genial Showman: Being Reminiscences of the Life of Artemus Ward and Pictures of a Showman's Career in the Western World* (London: John Camden Hotten, 1871), 245.

2. William Grimes, *Straight Up or On the Rocks: The Story of the American Cocktail* (New York: North Point, 2001), 65–66. For more detailed instructions, see David Wondrich, "Dangerous Knowledge: The Blue Blazer," *Esquire*, November 16, 2007, https://www.esquire.com/food-drink/a3525/blueblazer1107/.

3. *History of Wages in the United States from Colonial Times to 1928. Revision of Bulletin No. 499 with Supplement, 1929–1933* (Washington, DC: Government Printing Office, 1934), 336.

4. Jerry Thomas, *The Bartender's Guide: How to Mix Drinks, or the Bon-Vivant's Companion, Containing Clear and Reliable Descriptions for Mixing All the Beverages Used in the United States, together with the Most Popular British, French, German, Italian, Russian, and Spanish Recipes, Embracing Punches, Juleps, Cobblers, Etc., Etc. Etc., in Endless Variety. By Jerry Thomas, Formerly Principal Bar-tender at the Metropolitan Hotel, New York, and the Planter's House, St. Louis, to Which Is Appended A Manual for the Manufacture of Cordials, Liquors, Fancy Syrups, &c. &c., after the Most Approved Method Now Used in the Distillation of Liquors and Beverages, Designed for the Special Use of Manufacturers and Dealers in Wines and Spirits, Grocers, Tavern-Keepers, and Private Families, the Same Being Adapted to the Trade of the United States and Canadas. Illustrated with Descriptive Engravings. The Whole Containing over 600 Valuable Recipes. By Christian Schultz, Professor of Chemistry, Apothecary, and Manufacturer of Wines, Liquors, Cordials &c. &c., from Berne, Switzerland* (New York: Dick & Fitzgerald, 1862). All other quotations from this edition are drawn from an inexpensive facsimile reprint produced by Ross Bolton in 2015. Original first-state first editions are rare and fetch prices upward of $3,000 when offered for sale. For some of the bibliographical details, I am indebted to an exhaustive description of a first-state first edition by the British bookseller Peter Harrington, http://www.peterharrington.co.uk/the-bar-tenders-guide-a-complete-cyclopaedia-of-plain-and-fancy-drinks.html.

5. See the catalog attached to Arthur Martine, *Martine's Handbook of Etiquette and True Politeness* (New York: Dick & Fitzgerald, 1866), [182]. WorldCat has no listings for that edition.

6. Apart from authoring the *Manual*, Schultz seems to have left few other traces in life; *Trow's New York City Directory for 1862* lists Mr. Jeremiah P. Thomas and his saloon at 622 Broadway but has no entry for Christian Schultz.

7. Thomas, *The Bartender's Guide*, 204.

8. *The Bartender's Guide, or How to Mix All Kinds of Plain and Fancy Drinks* (New York: Dick & Fitzgerald, 1876) was the only revision to appear in Jerry's lifetime. Since the cheap edition advertised in 1866 is lost, it is hard to say if the 1876 *Guide* was indeed entirely fresh. By contrast, the 1887 version of the *Guide*, beginning with the introductory "Hints and Rules for Bartenders," is, in many ways, a new book. See https://euvs-vintage-cocktail-books.cld.bz/1887-The-bar-tender-s-guide.

9. Thomas, *The Bartender's Guide*, 77.

10. T. S. Eliot, "The Love Song of J. Alfred Prufrock," *The Complete Poems and Plays of T. S. Eliot* (London: Faber and Faber, 1969), 14; Herbert Asbury, "Introduction," *The Bon Vivant's Companion, or How to Mix Drinks by Professor Jerry Thomas*, ed. Herbert Asbury (New York: Knopf, 1929), xvi.

11. Andrew F. Smith, *Drinking History: Fifteen Turning Points in the Making of American Beverages* (New York: Columbia University Press, 2013), 125–26.

12. Thomas, *The Bartender's Guide*, 77.

13. Ralph Waldo Emerson, "Bacchus," in *Poems: A Variorum Edition*, vol. 9, *The Collected Works of Ralph Waldo Emerson*, ed. Albert J. von Frank (Cambridge, MA: Belknap, 2011), 232.

14. Thomas, 77. The term *mixology* was first used, humorously, in *Knickerbocker Magazine* in 1856; see David Wondrich, *Imbibe! From Absinthe Cocktail to Whiskey Smash, A Salute in Stories and Drinks to "Professor" Jerry Thomas, Pioneer of the American Bar*, rev. ed. (New York: Perigee, 2015 [2007]), 54.

15. "Some Winter Drinks," *The North American*, January 1, 1887. Eric Felten, not an admirer, calls the Blue Blazer "a triumph of showbiz, though not exactly a lip-smacker" (*How's Your Drink? Cocktails, Culture, and the Art of Drinking Well* [Chicago: Surrey, 2007], 128).

16. "Some Fancy Drinks," *Milwaukee Daily Journal*, March 20, 1885.

17. Justin Kaplan, *When the Astors Owned New York: Blue Bloods and Grand Hotels in a Gilded Age* (New York: Viking, 2006), 69.

18. For an unconventional, impeccably researched biography of Jerry Thomas, see Wondrich, *Imbibe!*

19. Thomas, *The Bartender's Guide*, 11.

20. Thomas, *The Bartender's Guide*, 53.

21. Thomas, *The Bartender's Guide*, 33.

22. Thomas, *The Bartender's Guide*, 64.

23. Thomas, *The Bartender's Guide*, 74.

24. Thomas, *The Bartender's Guide*, 23.

25. Thomas, *The Bartender's Guide*, 33.

26. Thomas, *The Bartender's Guide*, 67.

27. Thomas, *The Bartender's Guide*, 80.

28. Thomas, *The Bartender's Guide*, 65.
29. Thomas, *The Bartender's Guide*, 22.
30. Thomas, *The Bartender's Guide*, 54–55.
31. Thomas, *The Bartender's Guide*, 25, 44, 74.
32. Thomas, *The Bartender's Guide*, 44.
33. Robin Maugham, *Conversations with Willie: Recollections of W. Somerset Maugham* (New York: Simon & Schuster, 1978), 112.
34. Joseph Lanza, *The Cocktail: The Influence of Spirits on the American Psyche* (New York: St. Martin's Press, 1995), 13.
35. John W. Frick, *Theatre, Culture, and Temperance Reform in Nineteenth-Century America* (Cambridge: Cambridge University Press, 2003), 120.
36. Jiayang Fan, "Bar Tab," *The New Yorker*, December 19 and 26, 2016, 40.
37. Thomas, *The Bartender's Guide*, [3]–4.
38. William Grimes, "Letters: On the Trail of the Cocktail," *The Guardian*, November 21, 2000, https://www.theguardian.com/theguardian/2000/nov/22/guardianletters1.
39. Benjamin Franklin, "The Autobiography of Benjamin Franklin," in *Franklin, Writings*, ed. Leo Lemay (New York: Library of America, 1987), 47.
40. Dante Alighieri, *La Divina Commedia: Inferno*, ed. Emilio Pasquini and Antonio Enzo Quaglio (Milano: Garzanti, 1980), 41, line 131.
41. Thomas, *The Bartender's Guide*, [3].
42. Thomas, *The Bartender's Guide*, 4.
43. From Rosalind's final speech in Shakespeare's *As You Like It*, Act V, iv. The "bush" is a reference to the branch of ivy (the plant sacred to Dionysus or Bacchus) that vintners used to hang out when advertising their wares (*As You Like It*, ed. Agnes Latham, The Arden Shakespeare [London: Methuen, 1975], 131, note to lines 200–1).

BIBLIOGRAPHY

Asbury, Herbert. "Introduction." *The Bon Vivant's Companion, or How to Mix Drinks by Professor Jerry Thomas*. Edited by Herbert Asbury. New York: Knopf, 1929.

Eliot, T. S. "The Love Song of J. Alfred Prufrock," *The Complete Poems and Plays of T. S. Eliot*. London: Faber and Faber, 1969.

Emerson, Ralph Waldo. "Bacchus." In *Poems: A Variorum Edition*. Vol. 9, *The Collected Works of Ralph Waldo Emerson*. Edited by Albert J. von Frank. Cambridge, MA: Belknap, 2011.

Fan, Jiayang. "Bar Tab." *The New Yorker*. December 19 and 26, 2016. 40.

Franklin, Benjamin. "The Autobiography of Benjamin Franklin." In *Franklin, Writings*, edited by Leo Lemay. New York: Library of America, 1987.

Felten, Eric. *How's Your Drink? Cocktails, Culture, and the Art of Drinking Well.* Chicago: Surrey, 2007.
Frick, John W. *Theatre, Culture, and Temperance Reform in Nineteenth-Century America.* Cambridge: Cambridge University Press, 2003.
Dante Alighieri, *La Divina Commedia: Inferno.* Edited by Emilio Pasquini and Antonio Enzo Quaglio. Milano: Garzanti, 1980.
Grimes, William. "Letters: On the Trail of the Cocktail." *The Guardian.* November 21, 2000. https://www.theguardian.com/theguardian/2000/nov/22/guardianletters1.
Grimes, William. *Straight Up or On the Rocks: The Story of the American Cocktail.* New York: North Point, 2001.
Hingston, Edward Peron. *The Genial Showman: Being Reminiscences of the Life of Artemus Ward and Pictures of a Showman's Career in the Western World.* London: John Camden Hotten, 1871.
History of Wages in the United States from Colonial Times to 1928. Revision of Bulletin No. 499 with Supplement, 1929–1933. Washington, DC: Government Printing Office, 1934.
Kaplan, Justin. *When the Astors Owned New York: Blue Bloods and Grand Hotels in a Gilded Age.* New York: Viking, 2006.
Lanza, Joseph. *The Cocktail: The Influence of Spirits on the American Psyche.* New York: St. Martin's Press, 1995.
Martine, Arthur. *Martine's Handbook of Etiquette and True Politeness.* New York: Dick & Fitzgerald, 1866.
Maugham, Robin. *Conversations with Willie: Recollections of W. Somerset Maugham.* New York: Simon & Schuster, 1978.
Smith, Andrew F. *Drinking History: Fifteen Turning Points in the Making of American Beverages.* New York: Columbia University Press, 2013.
"Some Fancy Drinks." *Milwaukee Daily Journal.* March 20, 1885.
"Some Winter Drinks." *The North American.* January 1, 1887.
Thomas, Jerry. *The Bartender's Guide: How to Mix Drinks, or the Bon-Vivant's Companion, Containing Clear and Reliable Descriptions for Mixing All the Beverages Used in the United States, together with the Most Popular British, French, German, Italian, Russian, and Spanish Recipes, Embracing Punches, Juleps, Cobblers, Etc., Etc. Etc., in Endless Variety. By Jerry Thomas, Formerly Principal Bar-tender at the Metropolitan Hotel, New York, and the Planter's House, St. Louis, to Which Is Appended A Manual for the Manufacture of Cordials, Liquors, Fancy Syrups, &c. &c., after the Most Approved Method Now Used in the Distillation of Liquors and Beverages, Designed for the Special Use of Manufacturers and Dealers in Wines and Spirits, Grocers, Tavern-Keepers, and Private Families, the Same Being Adapted to the Trade of the United States and Canadas. Illustrated with Descriptive Engravings. The Whole Containing over 600 Valuable Recipes. By Christian Schultz,*

Professor of Chemistry, Apothecary, and Manufacturer of Wines, Liquors, Cordials &c. &c., from Berne, Switzerland. New York: Dick & Fitzgerald, 1862.

Shakespeare, William. *As You Like It*. Edited by Agnes Latham. The Arden Shakespeare. London: Methuen, 1975.

Wondrich, David. "Dangerous Knowledge: The Blue Blazer." *Esquire*. November 16, 2007. https://www.esquire.com/food-drink/a3525/blueblazer1107/.

Wondrich, David. *Imbibe! From Absinthe Cocktail to Whiskey Smash, A Salute in Stories and Drinks to "Professor" Jerry Thomas, Pioneer of the American Bar*. Rev. ed. New York: Perigee, 2015 [2007].

FOUR

THE SAZERAC MIXING RITUAL

Storytelling, Parody, and New Orleans

JOSEPH TURNER

"Handy's recipe also calls for a glass rinsed with absinthe, but that's just New Orleans being New Orleans."

David Wondrich[1]

FOR DAVID WONDRICH, THERE IS something quintessentially New Orleans about the presence of absinthe in a Sazerac. Absinthe makes the Sazerac more than just another bastardized old-fashioned, even if it started life that way. An old-world ingredient such as absinthe makes the Sazerac worthy of a city like New Orleans, a city that has always straddled the old world of Europe and the new world of the United States. In a rare act of governmental effectiveness, the Louisiana House of Representatives even named the Sazerac the official cocktail of New Orleans in 2008.[2] But even if New Orleans loves the Sazerac, the cocktail itself doesn't exactly make sense. As Wondrich seems to say, *of course* New Orleans would put absinthe in an otherwise civilized cocktail—and *only* New Orleans would think of it. David Embury likewise picks up on what makes the Sazerac quintessentially New Orleans, describing the Sazerac as an excessively mixed cocktail of discordant flavors, which, in the end, is not terribly pleasing to drink[3]:

> The Sazerac is a sharp, pungent, thoroughly dry cocktail. To most people, however, the combination of absinthe and whisky [sic] is not particularly pleasing. Whisky lovers do not like the sharp, biting taste that the absinthe imparts. Absinthe lovers prefer their absinthe straight, dripped, frapped, or mixed with gin rather than whisky. Nevertheless ... various hotels, clubs, and other bars [in New Orleans] have created simplified Sazerac-type

cocktails—drinks with pretty much the same flavor as the Sazerac but which can be made with much less fuss and loss of time.[4]

The Sazerac, as Wondrich and Embury suggest, is improbable. In an effort to curb the discordant notes Embury identifies in the Sazerac, other cocktails, such as the Crescent City cocktail and the Cocktail la Louisiane, eventually turned to Bénédictine to avoid incorporating absinthe. If the addition of absinthe is New Orleans being New Orleans, then the mixing ritual is, too—it's a drink of improbable flavors that is, as Embury makes clear, a pain to mix. It is not the absinthe alone that makes the Sazerac the official drink of New Orleans. It is also the labor-intensive mixing practice that produces it.

So how do we account for the popularity of the drink, a drink that is both difficult to make and, to some, unpleasant? The Sazerac is, like the city of New Orleans, showy, exotic, and ritualistic. That combination is precisely what makes the Sazerac the ideal drink for a group of Louisiana politicians to elevate to the status of official cocktail of New Orleans. Mixing a Sazerac recalls the ritualistic nature of the Catholic Mass and voodoo practices, with French brandy (in the original recipe) being augmented with absinthe, a spirit evoking witchcraft as much as voodoo does. The Sazerac cocktail is the result of a practice that many, like Embury, consider excessive. Moreover, the Sazerac is not only a *product* of the Sazerac mixing ritual. The drink also *is* that ritual. As I argue below, part of the Sazerac mythos is locating *this* Sazerac in a particular origin story (imagined, authentic, or anywhere in between). Muddling a sugar cube in one glass as ice chills a second glass—a process that takes several minutes—opens time for the rehearsal of an origin story. Moreover, the ritual and rehearsal of origins are part of the spectacle of New Orleans. We expect New Orleans to be excessive, performative, and loud. Perhaps most importantly, we expect a drink that tastes good, and the relative truth-value in tracing the drink's origin is dependent on a drink that is made well. The performative mixing ritual is self-authorizing: make a good drink, and I'll believe whatever version of history you provide. Playfully riffing on "authenticity," the Sazerac is both old world and new, a classic remade through excess, parody, and ritual. The Sazerac, that is, deserves to be the cocktail of New Orleans.

CARNIVAL

We expect ritual from New Orleans. It is a city steeped in Catholic, Creole, and voodoo pasts, and a city that emerges from the ways in which those pasts intermingle. New Orleans is a city in which French culture, already creolized in many ways, met an expanding port city in the nineteenth-century United States. New Orleans is the second-oldest Catholic archdiocese in the United States (so named in 1793). One can still take tours of the city's many Catholic shrines, alone or via guided tour.[5] Historically, the city passed hands between Catholic countries, first as a French settlement, then run by the Spanish, before finally incorporating into the vast United States. These roots in a Catholic past color New Orleans differently than Protestantism does New England—Boston might tolerate the excess of a Saint Patrick's Day celebration, but a carnival parade there seems out of place. *Mardi Gras*, French for "Fat Tuesday," is a Catholic celebration preceding (or, for some, authorizing) the austerity of Lent— a kind of excessive spectacle that paves the way for contrition. In Catholic culture, Fat Tuesday is also called Shrove Tuesday—"shrove" from *shrive*, to confess—and is one last day of indulgence before Ash Wednesday. It is a kind of storm before the calm. As Byron puts it, writing about carnival celebrations in Venice in 1817:

> 'Tis known, at least it should be, that throughout
> All countries of the Catholic persuasion,
> Some weeks before Shrove Tuesday comes about,
> The people take their fill of recreation,
> And buy repentance, ere they grow devout,
> However high their rank, or low their station,
> With fiddling, feasting, dancing, drinking, masking,
> And other things which may be had for asking.[6]

In the liturgical calendar, *carnival* (perhaps from the Latin *carne vale*, "farewell to meat") is yet another term for the festival period that precedes Lent.[7] Mardi Gras may be an extension of Roman Saturnalia, a festival that, like Mardi Gras, is similarly focused on ritual, public display, and parody. In all likelihood, Mardi Gras was an older, pagan fertility festival co-opted by early Christians who sought to make the Gospel more palatable to nonbelievers. New Orleans's carnival festivities are cut from the same cloth as Byron's Italian carnival: excess, then contrition; serious partying before serious penitence. It is, in some ways, a festival season that mimics a night of hard drinking and the morning after. With the arrival of Lent, the Christian nature of absolution, however, cuts off the oldest advice about curing a hangover (i.e., drinking more booze). Or as Kingsley Amis puts it, the "hair ... of the dog that bit you."[8]

Mardi Gras is also about the ritual of masking, a ritual likewise imported from Catholic Europe. At its essence, masking is the ability to be someone or something else, if only for a day. It affords the opportunity for the poor to be rich, for women to dress as men, and for the infusion of all manner of exoticism into the everyday. As Byron describes it,

> And there are dresses splendid, but fantastical,
> Masks of all times and nations, Turks and Jews,
> And harlequins and clowns, with feats gymnastical,
> Greeks, Romans, Yankee-doodles, and Hindoos,
> All kinds of dress...
> All people, as their fancies hit, may choose.[9]

As Byron suggests, there are strong elements of creativity and fantasy in carnival celebrations. People are drawn to the exotic, to racial difference, and to spectacular displays of clowns and gymnasts. Lyle Saxon, the famous twentieth-century New Orleans journalist, recalls his first Mardi Gras in his 1928 *Fabulous New Orleans*. Harkening back to his childhood in the early twentieth century, the role of masking occupies a large part of his memory. Saxon recalls an African American family servant, Robert, dressed as a devil:

> His grinning face seemed unbelievably comic to me, and try as I would, I could not believe that the mask hid the black face of Robert. He seemed so completely a devil. And I felt much the same way toward the other maskers; I could not believe that these simpering masks concealed the everyday faces of men and women such as I knew constituted the workaday world. Soon I gave it up and accepted the madness as something altogether delightful.[10]

Carnival, and particularly masking, is about finding delight in the strange and the exotic. As Saxon makes clear, masking is a welcome, temporary "madness." In its roots as an old-world European Catholic festival, carnival in New Orleans of the nineteenth and early twentieth centuries meant that African Americans and women could be served in bars.[11] Masks allowed celebrants to flout conventions: to openly mock laws, religious beliefs, and social propriety. The circumscribed nature of the festivities, however, sets clear limits—Robert may pretend to be a devil, but he must cast the devil down during Lent.[12] Byron's Venetians choose to dress as any nationality or of any time period, as "their fancies hit," only to return to normalcy on Ash Wednesday (and the beginning of Lent). There is a ritual element to these festivities, where flouting social customs re-inscribes just how important those customs and mores are. Parody reinforces the centrality of the customs being mocked. Like medieval schoolmasters moving aside to let schoolboys pretend to be in charge, carnival gave people license to vent their energy in the spirit of civic cohesion. It fostered, as Mikhail Bahktin argues, a "two-world condition," or an unofficial (but very real) world of carnival in opposition to the official world of ecclesiastical and civic duty.[13] This two-world condition allowed people to inhabit fully the spirit of excess characteristic of carnival as seriously as they would inhabit the spirit of contrition that followed. Even in old-world cities such as Venice or the new-world New Orleans, already socially and racially diverse in the nineteenth century, Catholic carnival festivities encouraged the performance of difference within ritualized practices of fantasy and role reversal.

NEW ORLEANS DRINKS—CRUSTA, GIN FIZZ, AND THE SAZERAC

It is perhaps unsurprising that a city so linked to ritual, and to the subversion of ritual, is often credited with the invention of the cocktail. Making any cocktail is ritualistic to some extent. However, those cocktails most associated with New Orleans—the Crusta, the Ramos gin fizz, and the Sazerac—are all noteworthy for their particular rituals. The Sazerac is the quintessential New Orleans cocktail not only because it is weird, as Wondrich suggests, but also because it, like the Crusta and the Ramos gin fizz, ritualizes the spirit of parody and creativity so central to carnival culture. The citizens of New York can claim to have produced many cocktails; that is perhaps unsurprising: even in the mid-nineteenth century, when many cocktails were first mixed, New York was home to some five hundred thousand souls. The productivity of those thirsty New Yorkers was (and is) rivaled, however, by what is perhaps the American city most associated with the bon vivant lifestyle: New Orleans. With roughly a fifth of New York's population in 1850 (and less than 5 percent in 2010), New Orleans nevertheless claims a place in the history of the cocktail with the iconic Sazerac, the Ramos gin fizz, the Crusta, and such modern innovations as the Obituary (a gin martini with absinthe). Although the city of New Orleans cannot claim to be New York's equal in terms of quantity, it can claim a place in the history of cocktails and cocktail culture in terms of innovation (and, as a happy by-product, drop New York City down a healthy peg or two). New Orleans is serious about the bon vivant lifestyle. But New Orleans's signature cocktails demonstrate that its citizens have repeatedly remade classic cocktails, co-opting them (the old-fashioned, the fizz, the martini) and, through spectacular, ritualized creation rites (and some degree of parody), given birth to new versions.

Consider the preparation of the brandy Crusta, which Wondrich calls "the absolute pinnacle of the nineteenth-century bartender's art."[14] The Crusta is a cocktail on steroids—and it was, of course, invented in New Orleans, at the New Orleans City Exchange somewhere around 1840. Nowadays, the drink is a combination of cognac, Grand Marnier, lemon juice, simple syrup, maraschino, and bitters. Not so very different from a brandy old-fashioned. But the preparation and presentation are excessive—New Orleans being New Orleans. Jerry Thomas, in his 1862 *The Bar-tender's Guide: How to Mix Drinks, or the Bon-Vivant's Companion*, devotes an inordinate amount of attention to the Crusta. Thomas's usual pattern can be seen in the Brandy Cocktail: after listing ingredients, he writes simply, "Squeeze lemon peel; fill one-third full of ice, and stir with a spoon."[15] But the Crusta directions include both a picture of the drink and an evaluation:

> Crusta is made the same as a fancy cocktail, with a little lemon juice and a small lump of ice added. First, mix the ingredients in a small tumbler, then take a fancy red wine-glass, rub a sliced lemon around the rim of the same, and dip it in pulverized white sugar, so that the sugar will adhere to the edge of the glass. Pare half a lemon the same as you would an apple (all in one piece) so that the paring will fit in the wine-glass . . . and strain the crusta from the tumbler into it. Then smile.[16]

As Wondrich describes the elaborate mixing and garnishing ritual, "Excellence has never been easy."[17] And in New Orleans, cocktail excellence is always showy and labor-intensive. The result is something to be in awe of, a spectacle to behold and to be smiled over. Smiling is necessary, as Thomas suggests, not only because the drink is beautiful, but also because the mixing ritual renders the cocktail virtually undrinkable. Because the cocktail offers no conspicuous point of access, Elizabeth Williams and Chris McMillian advise the would-be drinker to "drink from the citrus band."[18] Even that advice seems likely to produce messy results. This excess is what makes the Crusta, like the gin fizz or the Sazerac, quintessentially New Orleans.

The Ramos gin fizz, another great New Orleans cocktail to emerge from this period, is similarly reliant on spectacle and ritual. Henry C. Ramos, in the Imperial Cabinet Saloon and later in the Stag Saloon, mixed up his famous cocktails—which take about three minutes each. The Ramos gin fizz is a mixture of gin, lemon juice, orange flower water, sugar (or simple syrup), egg white, cream, and seltzer. (It's an update of the then-popular silver fizz.) In the heyday of the Stag Saloon, there were as many as thirty-five men lined up behind Ramos's bar, shaking the famous Ramos gin fizz in unison. Cream and citrus, of course, curdles the milk, but the addition of egg white and vigorous shaking emulsifies the drink into something frothy and refreshing. Saxon recalls:

> Across the street from the St. Charles was the old Ramos bar, where twelve barkeepers stood in a line, shaking the silver containers which held the famous gin-fizz. . . . In the Ramos saloon there were many women, beautifully

dressed.... Later I learned that on Mardi Gras all police regulations regarding bar-rooms were put aside, and on that one day it was permissible for women to go into these places.[19]

We can never be sure if time has embellished the number of bartenders from twelve to thirty-five, or if Saxon miscounted. As with the Sazerac, the Ramos gin fizz relies on spectacle, exotic ingredients—egg *and* flower water—and ritual.

What the drinks of New Orleans make clear is the role of ritual in the mixing of drinks. Putting things into a shaker and shaking (or stirring) is the heart of this ritual. Chris McMillian, perhaps the most famous New Orleans bartender, provides the ultimate example of New Orleans mixology: that is, he places an extravagant and perhaps excessive focus on ritual. On YouTube, one can watch McMillian mix a variety of cocktails, each of which he embellishes with New Orleans ritual. Take, for example, the mint julep, a Kentucky Derby–time favorite. McMillian is not satisfied with simply mixing a mint julep. Instead, he tells the story of the mint julep, linking it to Milton's *Comus* and, via etymology, to ancient Persia. At his most spectacular (and engaging), McMillian recites Kentucky colonel Joshua Soule Smith's "The Mint Julep" as he mixes his mint julep[20]: "Then comes the zenith of man's pleasure. Then comes the julep—the mint julep," he says as he lightly muddles mint. This type of over-the-top ritualistic performance and storytelling, situated as it is in a particular history of the cocktail, is the marker of New Orleans mixology.

That same ritualistic preparation characterizes McMillian's take on the Sazerac. Also on YouTube, you can watch McMillian's Sazerac ritual: the camera is positioned so that the viewer feels belly up to the bar, as McMillian begins by giving a history of the Sazerac.[21] McMillian relates the story of Antoine Amedie Peychaud, an apothecary from the French colony of Santo Domingo (now Haiti), who fled to New Orleans circa 1795 following the slave revolt.[22] In this version of events, Peychaud served his signature bitters in a series of stomach-calming drinks. One booze–bitters combination that stuck was cognac and bitters, which Peychaud served in small egg cups, or *coquetiers*, in the 1830s. English-speaking Americans, whose Anglo-Saxon ancestors had been mangling French pronunciation since at least 1066, hammered the liquid smoothness of *coquetier* into the harder, more guttural *cocktail*.[23] McMillian then goes on to explain why Americans shouldn't be scared of "bitters" before mixing a Sazerac. It's a great story, and if some nineteenth-century New Orleans native had waxed poetically about the Sazerac, you can bet that McMillian would have quoted him.

The Sazerac mixing ritual as performed by McMillian is something to behold. You must use *two* old-fashioned glasses (*not* a mixing glass). Pack the first with ice and set it aside; let the glass chill thoroughly. In the second glass, add a small bit of water and a sugar cube. Muddle well until the sugar dissolves, usually in the neighborhood of two minutes. Then, add Peychaud's bitters (although some recipes call for Angostura as well, at a 3:2 or 2:1 ratio). Add rye whiskey, or cognac if you're going for historical authenticity, and stir.[24] If you choose to add Angostura bitters, they can help to marry the flavors in a Sazerac, similar to if you added a slice of lemon peel. However, as Jeffrey Morganthaler cautions, "Do not use orange bitters in a Sazerac. I've seen this done and I can't possibly understand the rationale."[25] As we watch McMillian make the drink and tell his story, it seems unimportant that his version of history is almost undeniably false. As Eric Felten puts it, the etymology of *cocktail* from *coquetier* is "spurious, to be sure."[26] The term *cocktail* had been in use since at least 1806.

Historical authenticity is subordinated to, and even reliant on, a drink that is both spectacular and well made. Once the first glass is chilled, toss out the ice. (This step seems entirely in the spirit of spectacle: the Sazerac recipe is born before the widespread availability of commercial refrigeration. The first ice manufacturing company in New Orleans was founded in 1868.)[27] Then, take a few dashes of absinthe (or absinthe substitute, such as Herbsaint) and swirl it around in the glass. Avoid any puddling in the glass; toss any excess absinthe. Then, strain the rye–bitters–sugar mixture into the chilled glass. Add a twist of lemon and serve. The Sazerac mixing ritual ensures that the drink is served at full strength. Mixing a drink in a chilled glass rather than an ice-packed mixing glass (as is the case with the manhattan or the old-fashioned) avoids a drink that, through contact with ice and through the addition of friction, could be one-quarter water. This mixing practice is also true of the venerable sling, which was likely served at room temperature. Such a mixing practice—preserving the full-strength drink—perhaps offers more proof of the Sazerac's origin in the time period before widespread refrigeration. The Sazerac, in being defined by this ritual, links it to the very oldest cocktail mixing practices.

Even if McMillian's version of events is engaging, the more historically verifiable account of the Sazerac's genesis finds its origin at New Orleans's Merchants Exchange Coffee House in 1850. The Merchants Exchange Coffee House, which operated as a bar, is central to this history of the Sazerac. Sewell T. Taylor, who ran the bar for some years before turning to a career as a liquor importer, owned that business. One of his wares was the cognac *Sazerac de Forge et Fils* (originally of Limogenes, France, but which was recently revived by the Sazerac Company).[28] Aaron Bird took over the Merchants Exchange, but renamed it the Sazerac House, after its signature cocktail. This version of events also incorporates Antoine Peychaud, whose bitters are more floral and fruity than Angostura. Cognac was used until the late 1870s, when rye whiskey replaced it. There is some disagreement about why this change took place. Stanley Clisby Arthur claims that "American rye whiskey was substituted for the cognac to please the tastes of Americans who preferred 'red likker' to any pale-faced brandy."[29] That may be so, although I am suspicious of the implied jingoism. Wondrich, avoiding cultural bias, turns to science. He claims that rye becomes the de facto Sazerac base at precisely the same time as the *Phylloxera vastatrix*, or wine louse, a microscopic aphid, ravaged wine grapes of western Europe. Then an abundant whiskey, rye was added to replace the diminishing cognac—likely by Thomas Handy, who owned the Sazerac House for some twenty years. Handy was a Maryland native, and throughout the 1700s and 1800s, rye whiskey was produced all along the Susquehanna River in Maryland and Pennsylvania. (Early recipes call for Old Overholt, originally a Pennsylvania rye, now made by Jim Beam.) Handy would have been all too familiar with rye whiskey. In spring, distillers would send rye whiskey via riverboats along the Ohio River to the Mississippi, eventually snaking into New Orleans.[30] By the time *The World's Drinks and How to Mix Them* was published in 1908, the drink included whiskey (read: rye) and absinthe. The truth, then, is probably somewhere in the middle—that American rye became the de facto choice for mixing the Sazerac because it was more plentiful. It is also quite possible that Arthur is also onto a truth as well: that American tastes indeed shifted to rye, but less as a rejection of cognac than for the same reasons of plentitude.

How the absinthe was first added has remained a mystery. Wondrich chalks it up to New Orleans mystique, saying that "Handy's recipe also calls for a glass rinsed with absinthe, but that's just New Orleans being New Orleans."[31] New Orleans is home to the Old Absinthe House, which claims to have been serving their signature Absinthe House Frappé since 1874.[32] That drink was commemorated in the 1904 Broadway musical *It Happened in Nordland*, in a song titled "Absinthe Frappé." The song goes like this:

> The deed is done so waste no woe o'er yestereen.
> Nor swear to shun a year or so the festive scene.
> Remorse will pass, despair will fade with speed away
> Before a glass of rightly-made absinthe frappé![33]

The Absinthe Frappé ritual sweetens the strong, bitter taste of absinthe with the addition of sugar and cold water, a process that releases the liquor's signature cloudy color (or what's called *la louche*).[34] In the nineteenth century, absinthe was often 120 proof or higher. At this proof, the bitterness and alcohol can be unpleasant. Shake and serve the Absinthe Frappé. Like all cocktails, the Absinthe Frappé was a hangover cure. The logic of that cure was not any kind of Lenten absolution. On the contrary, it was designed as a palliative that, like Peychaud's bitters and the Sazerac itself, enabled further carousing. A kind of machine for forgetting "remorse" and preparing oneself anew for the "festive scene" so central to the spirit of New Orleans. Absinthe was a popular liquor in New Orleans, and one can locate advertisements for it in Louisiana as early as 1837.[35] Those advertisements point to the Sazerac as we know it, with its absinthe, post-dating Peychaud's apothecary.

PARODY

McMillian's videos offer perhaps the best of what New Orleans ritualistic mixology can be—charming, affable, and educative. The performance of ritual, however, can easily slide into the excessive and, as a result, invite parody. That is a lesson that fine-dining critic Alan Richman learned in the HBO series *Treme*. In *Treme*, the Sazerac cocktail became a literalized metaphor of the city's fighting spirit—a city that was a key strategic site in the Revolutionary War and in the War of 1812, and a city that had to fight to reestablish itself after the devastation of Hurricane Katrina. In 2006, Richman wrote a scornful review of the city and its food, saying that New Orleans "was always a three-day stubble of a city."[36] He excoriates the "scuzzy bars" of New Orleans, a city he considers to be a "destination for tourists seeking the worst possible experience." In conflating New Orleans with the excesses of Bourbon Street, Richman seems to miss the point: anyone who has walked Bourbon Street *knows* that it isn't *real* New Orleans. The New Orleans of Bourbon Street is one known for bad, overly sweet drinks (the Hurricane, daiquiris served from machines, or any other sugary monstrosity served by the Tropical Isle chain restaurant). Bourbon Street is a parody of itself, fully enmeshed in the orders of simulation that separate it from the "real" city surrounding it.

Much of *Treme* (David Simon's first major project after *The Wire*) focuses on restaurant culture in New Orleans. A major character of the show, chef Janette Desautel, defends her city against Richman's depredations. While a fictional Richman (played by the critic himself) dines in VIP fashion, Desautel approaches Richman's table with a cocktail in hand, her white chef's outfit contrasted with Richman's stylish suit. The chef interrupts Richman's conversation with "This is how the Creole fairy folk back home cure their three-day stubble," throwing the cocktail—a Sazerac, of course—in Richman's face. "Sazerac?"

Richman exclaims, "You've got to be kidding! Nobody throws a Sazerac!" In a follow-up *GQ* article, the real Richman offered modest contrition, saying that the Sazerac is "a whiskey cocktail and a good choice of weaponry, since it symbolizes the city." The vacillation between reality and fiction is a dizzying mixture of simulation and simulacra, as Richman moves between real man writing for *GQ* and fictionalized self in *Treme*, before returning to "real" self in *GQ*. That is, a man whose opinion of a city is based on the simulacra of Bourbon Street and whose faulty opinion is assaulted within the fiction of the show.

It seems obvious, then, why Sazerac is the drink used to fight back against Richman's criticisms. As a cocktail with deep roots in the city's past, the Sazerac is the ideal weapon to metaphorically battle against Richman's assumptions about New Orleans. The Sazerac is not the cocktail of Bourbon Street barcrawling. It is a cocktail with deep roots in the city, born in the 1850s, when New Orleans straddled the old and new worlds. Born at a time when French was still taught in New Orleans primary schools.[37] If New Orleans pulls strands of identity from all over—new American and old European, poor and gentrified, white and black—that multiplicity is why *Treme* turns to the Sazerac. Like *The Wire* before it, *Treme* is a show acutely aware of how poverty, race, and institutional neglect shape the worldviews and lived experiences of the inhabitants of a city. *Treme* takes on the problems of social stratification in the pre- and post-Katrina city, and especially in such rapidly gentrifying neighborhoods as the eponymous Treme. It is also deeply interested in questions of authenticity: what's "real" New Orleans and what's for the tourists.[38] The Sazerac, like New Orleans, is similarly plural: it is European in name, American in ingredients, humble in origins, and iconically (perhaps authentically) New Orleans. It is like a "Creole fairy folk" legend, with a deep history that has morphed into mythology. The importance of the Sazerac in New Orleans culture and mythology reflects the spectacle, ritual, and festivity of the city's old-world roots. Catholic in its ritual, excessive in procedure, relying on subtle hints of exotic ingredients, the Sazerac owes much to the traditions of Catholic carnival Europe imported into the new world.

But carnival, as Bahktin has argued, isn't about simply ridiculing social structures and hierarchies. It isn't about dressing up as a devil, or a Hindu, for just the pleasure of doing so. The degradation implicit in lampooning social mores is ultimately generative. As he puts it, "Degradation digs a bodily grave for new birth; it has not only a destructive, negative aspect, but also a regenerating one . . . it is always conceiving."[39] The addition of absinthe to an otherwise civilized drink such as the old-fashioned offers such a generative parody, turning the flavor profile of a traditional cocktail into something radically different.

So different that Embury describes the drink as offensive to anyone who loves either whiskey or absinthe. The generative nature of the parody, however, risks overtaking the original (and thus destroying it). Absinthe can easily turn into the fat, loud guy in the room, crowding out everyone else. The strong and sharp anise flavor is why early recipes call for rinsing the glass in absinthe and throwing out the excess. The incorporation of absinthe is like a carnivalesque parody, adding an unexpected, exotic flavor to reinvigorate the original.

The Sazerac not only offers a parody of the old-fashioned, but also grows from the cultural logic of the mask, of fantasy and projection. Masked carnival-goers knew implicitly that a mask, covering part of the face, was about the management and creation of desire. That a mask could turn the familiar into something exotic. The ritual of mask-wearing, like carnival itself, allowed for a space in which otherwise good (or bad) Catholics could pretend to be someone new. It also allowed them to pretend to be *with* someone new. Making a Sazerac with only hints of absinthe creates subtlety, a hint of exoticism in an otherwise familiar drink. A drink that is strikingly different and familiar—a kind of uncanny old-fashioned. Amy Stewart, in *The Drunken Botanist*, says that the Sazerac "is the perfect gateway drink for anyone unaccustomed to licorice-flavored cocktails."[40] It is and it is not. A traditional Sazerac will have only hints of licorice, enough to be provocative without becoming overpowering. A mask of the exotic placed atop an old-fashioned. But the licorice is *definitely* there, if only in hints.

CODA: ON THE "FUSS" OF THE SAZERAC

As Embury says, the Sazerac is a fussy drink. When I make Sazeracs at home, my fussiness lies in using local ingredients. In some ways, my take on the Sazerac both is and is not as authentic as McMillian's or Wondrich's. I'm combining the old and the new in the spirit and tradition of New Orleans, making a very old drink with new ingredients, navigating the Sazerac mixing ritual. I sit in Louisville, Kentucky, the city that drinkers know better as the bourbon capital of the world. But my Sazerac isn't about bourbon. It's about brandy. This particular brandy was made by Copper & Kings, a craft distillery along the Ohio River in downtown Louisville. Copper & Kings is making a name for itself with a variety of brandies, absinthe, and other spirits, in a state otherwise synonymous with bourbon. The company relies on a series of new technologies to reinvigorate old-world brandy. For example, Copper & Kings uses bourbon barrels to age their brandy, they rely on "sonic aging" processes and "non-chill filtering," and they insist on being a "craft" distiller. Copper & Kings's approach evokes the ritualistic, artisan-based economy embodied by the Sazerac.[41] They make, in other words, a very old spirit with new-world exactitude and science. And the result is a fine product.

The Sazerac was born in a time when Americans were forging new drinks from old-world ingredients—French cognac and French or Swiss absinthe alongside local bitters. Then, Handy went with rye, a local specialty from his native mid-Atlantic. Sazerac purists might scoff at using brandy in a Sazerac today, but it strikes me that the cocktail's history is grounded in tradition and innovation, in old and new. The Sazerac has always been about sourcing local ingredients to remake the old-fashioned. Brandy, of course, is cognac without the AOC designation (Appellation d'Origine Contrôlée, which stipulates the liquor's composition and geographical origin).[42] So, today I'm paradoxically retreating from the "fuss" about the Sazerac's history by embracing it. I'm time-traveling to when the Sazerac was made with cognac, except I'm using Copper & Kings brandy.[43] I'm breaking rules but, in an odd way, cherishing the drink's New Orleans French roots. Louisville was originally settled by French immigrants (and called *La Belle*), before taking the name Louisville in honor of the French king Louis XIV. Those early French settlers used the Ohio River to send goods south, fostering trade relationships with New Orleans. In that way, making a Sazerac with local brandy, a spirit with deep French roots, in a city that owes its origin to French immigrants, seems a fitting way to honor the ways in which the nineteenth-century Sazerac embraced the old and new worlds.

My Sazerac honors the French roots of the drink (and of New Orleans and Louisville). I'm also using Copper & Kings absinthe. As a result, the drink is thoroughly American while nodding to the drink's rich French history. I also happen to prefer a Sazerac that is a bit louder and dryer than other versions: more absinthe-heavy, using the anise notes less as a mask and more as the life of the party. A drier Sazerac is, perhaps, more in line with the drink's past as well. As Robert Simonson recalls, he instantly fell in love with the Sazerac while in New Orleans, before learning "that bartenders have been erring on the sweet side regarding their Sazeracs, adding too much simple syrup."[44] As Simonson wonders, "Had I been enjoying bastardized Sazeracs? Did I know a true Sazerac when I saw it?"

A brandy Sazerac with a bit more absinthe, three dashes of Peychaud's bitters, going easy on the sugar, produces a drier, less sweet, and (perhaps) more authentic Sazerac. The brandy Sazerac is rich, smooth, and less sharp than the rye Sazerac. This version of the drink is both less and more pure than the Sazeracs served at many Louisville bars (which generally use Rittenhouse rye). Most rye is now made in Indiana.[45] If Handy turned from French cognac to rye because it was local to his mid-Atlantic roots, then perhaps using a local brandy is more in the spirit of the drink than using rye produced in Indiana. Whether you prefer your Sazerac with brandy or with rye, you can still claim to be authentic: that's part of the drink's ritual. Just stake out a claim. As Simonson puts it, what's most important about the drink is that you enjoy it. "Just make sure it's properly chilled, and don't feed me any fucking Bourbon," he says. I take Simonson's point to be about the Sazerac mixing ritual: when making your Sazerac, choose your liquor (rye or cognac) and your origin story. Put on whichever mask you prefer, and enjoy.

University of Louisville

NOTES

1. David Wondrich, "New Orleans Cocktail of the Week: The Sazerac, Quintessential Cocktail of New Orleans," *Day of the Dead Celebration*, August 18, 2014, http://dayofdeadnola.blogspot.com/2014/08/new-orleans-cocktail-of-week-sazerac.html?m=1.

2. "New Orleans Declares Sazerac Its Cocktail of Choice," National Public Radio, June 26, 2008, http://www.npr.org/templates/story/story.php?storyId=91912549.

3. This author does not share Embury's criticisms of the Sazerac.

4. David Embury, quoted in Simon Difford, "Sazerac Cocktail," *Difford's Guide for Discerning Drinkers*, https://www.diffordsguide.com/encyclopedia/504/cocktails/sazerac-cocktail.

5. "Catholic Shrines of New Orleans," Blessed Francis Xavier Seelos, C.Ss.R., http://www.seelos.org/NOLA_Shrines_8.5x11_sm.pdf.

6. Lord George Gordon Byron, "Beppo," in *Lord Byron: The Major Works*, ed. Jerome J. McGann (Oxford: Oxford University Press, 2000), 316, lines 1–8.

7. *Oxford English Dictionary*, s.v. "carnival," n1, http://www.oed.com/view/Entry/28104?redirectedFrom=carnival#eid. The *OED* offers this explanation: "The history of the word is illustrated by the parallel medieval Latin name *carnem laxare*..., corresponding to Italian *carne lasciare 'leaving or forsaking flesh', whence, apparently by contraction, the modern *carnasciale = carnevale*" (* indicates a word or form not actually found, but of which the existence is inferred).

8. Kingsley Amis, *Everyday Drinking* (New York: Bloomsbury, 2008), 83.

9. Byron, "Beppo," 317, lines 17–22.

10. Lyle Saxon, *Fabulous New Orleans* (Gretna, LA: Pelican, 1988), 21–22.

11. Saxon, *Fabulous New Orleans*, 52.

12. Mikhail Bahktin, *Rabelais and His World*, trans. Helene Iswolsky (Bloomington: Indiana University Press, 2009), 9.

13. Bahktin, *Rabelais*, 6.

14. David Wondrich, "Brandy Crusta," *Esquire*, November 6, 2007, http://www.esquire.com/food-drink/drinks/recipes/a3823/brandy-crusta-drink-recipe/.

15. Jerry Thomas, *The Bar-Tender's Guide: How to Mix Drinks, or the Bon-Vivant's Companion* (New York: Mud Puddle Books, 2008), 50.

16. Thomas, *The Bar-Tender's Guide*, 52.

17. Wondrich, "Brandy Crusta."

18. Elizabeth M. Williams and Chris McMillian, *Lift Your Spirits: A Celebratory History of the Cocktail Culture in New Orleans* (Baton Rouge: Louisiana State University Press, 2016), 30.

19. Saxon, *Fabulous New Orleans*, 52.

20. Chris McMillian, "New Orleans' Best Cocktails: The Mint Julep," YouTube, 7:55, December 19, 2007, https://www.youtube.com/watch?v=gJV-O1e1oz8&t=272s.

21. Chris McMillian, "New Orleans' Best Cocktails: The Sazerac," YouTube, 5:22, July 12, 2007, https://www.youtube.com/watch?v=sfhaxHYb46E.

22. See, for example, Stanley Clisby Arthur, *Famous New Orleans Drinks & How to Mix 'Em* (Gretna, LA: Pelican, 1937 and 1977), 10–11.

23. See, however, Jonathan Elmer's essay earlier in this volume for alternatives to this etymology.

24. For the original version of the drink, see David Wondrich, *Imbibe!* (New York: Perigee, 2007), 200–2. Wondrich also advises against using both Peychaud's and Angostura bitters, but he does suggest a cognac/rye mixture.

25. Jeffrey Morgenthaler, "The Dos and Donts [*sic*] of Sazeracs," March 28, 2008, http://www.jeffreymorgenthaler.com/2008/the-dos-and-donts-of-sazeracs/.

26. Eric Felten, *How's Your Drink? Cocktails, Culture, and the Art of Drinking Well* (Evanston, IL: Agate Surrey, 2007), 16.

27. Williams and McMillian, *Lift Your Spirits*, 44.

28. "Sazerac Cognac Returns with Sazerac de Forge & Fils 'Finest Original,'" *Alcademics*, September 24, 2019, https://alcademics.typepad.com/new_booze/2019/09/sazerac-cognac-returns-with-sazerac-de-forge-fils-finest-original.html.

29. Arthur, *Famous New Orleans Drinks*, 18.

30. Sarah Rense, "How to Make a Sazerac," *Esquire*, March 8, 2019, http://www.esquire.com/food-drink/drinks/recipes/a3876/sazerac-drink-recipe.

31. Rense, "How to Make a Sazerac," para 4.

32. "Old Absinthe House: History," *Rue Bourbon*, https://www.ruebourbon.com/history/.

33. "Absinthe Frappé—Absinthe in Music From 1904," The Wormwood Society, http://wormwoodsociety.org/index.php/history-articles/absinthe-frappe-absinthe-in-music-1904.

34. Amy Stewart, *The Drunken Botanist: The Plants That Create the World's Great Drinks* (Chapel Hill, NC: Algonquin, 2013), 201.

35. Doris Lanier, *Absinthe: The Cocaine of the Nineteenth Century* (Jefferson, NC: McFarland, 2004), 124.

36. Alan Richman, "Yes, We're Open," *GQ*, November 3, 2006, https://www.gq.com/story/katrina-new-orleans-food.

37. Jay Gitlin, *The Bourgeois Frontier* (New Haven, CT: Yale University Press, 2010), 166.

38. Rolf Plots, "Treme's Big Problem: Authenticity," *The Atlantic: Culture*, November 27, 2013, http://www.theatlantic.com/entertainment/archive/2013/11/-em-treme-em-s-big-problem-authenticity/281857/.

39. Bahktin, *Rabelais*, 21.

40. Stewart, *The Drunken Botanist*, 184.

41. "Our Craft," Copper & Kings, http://www.copperandkings.com/our-craft/.

42. Jason Wilson, *Boozehound: On the Trail of the Rare, the Obscure, and the Overrated in Spirits* (Berkeley, CA: Ten Speed Press, 2010), 21.

43. Wilson, *Boozehound*, 22. He also prefers "the original nineteenth-century version, with cognac."

44. Robert Simonson, "The Case of the Sweet Sazerac," *Make It Simple but Significant* (blog), July 26, 2007, http://offthepresses.blogspot.com/2007/07/case-of-sweet-sazerac.html.

45. Keith Allison, "Oh, It's That Whiskey from Indiana," *The Alcohol Professor* (blog), April 20, 2015, https://www.alcoholprofessor.com/blog/2015/04/20/oh-its-that-whiskey-from-indiana/.

BIBLIOGRAPHY

"Absinthe Frappé—Absinthe in Music From 1904." The Wormwood Society. http://wormwoodsociety.org/index.php/history-articles/absinthe-frappe-absinthe-in-music-1904.

Allison, Keith. "Oh, It's That Whiskey from Indiana." *The Alcohol Professor* (blog). April 20, 2015. https://www.alcoholprofessor.com/blog/2015/04/20/oh-its-that-whiskey-from-indiana/.

Amis, Kingsley. *Everyday Drinking*. New York: Bloomsbury, 2008.

Arthur, Stanley Clisby. *Famous New Orleans Drinks & How to Mix 'Em*. Gretna, LA: Pelican Publishing, 1977 [1937].

Bahktin, Mikhail. *Rabelais and His World*. Translated by Helene Iswolsky. Bloomington: Indiana University Press, 2009.

Byron, George Gordon, Lord. "Beppo." In *Lord Byron: The Major Works*, edited by Jerome J. McGann. Oxford: Oxford University Press, 2000.

"Catholic Shrines of New Orleans." Blessed Francis Xavier Seelos, C.Ss.R. http://www.seelos.org/NOLA_Shrines_8.5x11_sm.pdf.

Difford, Simon. "Sazerac Cocktail." *Difford's Guide for Discerning Drinkers.* https://www.diffordsguide.com/encyclopedia/504/cocktails/sazerac-cocktail.

Felten, Eric. *How's Your Drink? Cocktails, Culture, and the Art of Drinking Well.* Evanston, IL: Agate Surrey, 2007.

Gitlin, Jay. *The Bourgeois Frontier.* New Haven, CT: Yale University Press, 2010.

Lanier, Doris. *Absinthe: The Cocaine of the Nineteenth Century.* Jefferson, NC: McFarland, 2004.

McMillian, Chris. "New Orleans' Best Cocktails: The Mint Julep." YouTube 7:55. December 19, 2007. https://www.youtube.com/watch?v=gJV-O1e1oz8&t=272s.

McMillian, Chris. "New Orleans' Best Cocktails: The Sazerac. YouTube 5:22. July 12, 2007. https://www.youtube.com/watch?v=sfhaxHYb46E.

Morgenthaler, Jeffrey. "The Dos and Donts [sic] of Sazeracs." http://www.jeffreymorgenthaler.com/2008/the-dos-and-donts-of-sazeracs/.

"New Orleans Declares Sazerac Its Cocktail of Choice." National Public Radio. June 26, 2008. http://www.npr.org/templates/story/story.php?storyId=91912549.

"Old Absinthe House: History." *Rue Bourbon.* https://www.ruebourbon.com/history/.

"Our Craft." Copper & Kings. http://www.copperandkings.com/our-craft/.

Plots, Rolf. "Treme's Big Problem: Authenticity." *The Atlantic.* November 27, 2013. http://www.theatlantic.com/entertainment/archive/2013/11/-em-treme-em-s-big-problem-authenticity/281857/.

Rense, Sarah. "How to Make a Sazerac." *Esquire.* March 8, 2019. http://www.esquire.com/food-drink/drinks/recipes/a3876/sazerac-drink-recipe/.

Richman, Alan. "Yes, We're Open." *GQ.* November 3, 2006. https://www.gq.com/story/katrina-new-orleans-food.

"Sazerac Cognac Returns with Sazerac de Forge & Fils 'Finest Original.'" *Alcademics.* September 24, 2019. https://alcademics.typepad.com/new_booze/2019/09/sazerac-cognac-returns-with-sazerac-de-forge-fils-finest-original.html.

Saxon, Lyle. *Fabulous New Orleans.* Gretna, LA: Pelican, 1988.

Simonson, Robert. "The Case of the Sweet Sazerac." *Make It Simple but Significant* (blog). July 26, 2007. http://offthepresses.blogspot.com/2007/07/case-of-sweet-sazerac.html.

Stewart, Amy. *The Drunken Botanist: The Plants That Create the World's Great Drinks.* Chapel Hill, NC: Algonquin, 2013.

Thomas, Jerry. *The Bar-Tender's Guide: How to Mix Drinks, or the Bon-Vivant's Companion.* New York: Mud Puddle Books, 2008.

Williams, Elizabeth M., and Chris McMillian. *Lift Your Spirits: A Celebratory History of Cocktail Culture in New Orleans.* Baton Rouge: Louisiana State University Press, 2016.

Wilson, Jason. *Boozehound: On the Trail of the Rare, the Obscure, and the Overrated in Spirits*. Berkeley, CA: Ten Speed Press, 2010.

Wondrich, David. "Brandy Crusta." *Esquire*. November 6, 2007. http://www.esquire.com/food-drink/drinks/recipes/a3823/brandy-crusta-drink-recipe/.

Wondrich, David. *Imbibe!* New York: Perigee, 2007.

Wondrich, David. "New Orleans Cocktail of the Week: The Sazerac, Quintessential Cocktail of New Orleans." *Day of the Dead Celebration*. http://dayofdeadnola.blogspot.com/2014/08/new-orleans-cocktail-of-week-sazerac.html?m=1.

FIVE

MY FIRST TIME

ALBERT W. A. SCHMID

I AM EMBARRASSED TO ADMIT I was forty-four years old the first time I did it. Most people are in their twenties, perhaps in college—in any case, usually half my age at the time. I was lucky to have gentle, knowledgeable, and experienced partners who helped guide me to success. Yes, I was forty-four years old the first time I stood behind a bar as a professional bartender. Granted, during the previous twelve years I had taught about wines, beers, spirits, bartending, and cocktails. I had attended seminars and symposiums on every aspect of alcoholic beverages. I had successfully passed several certification exams, and I had authored five books that were heavily based on alcohol and cocktails, including a book on the old-fashioned whiskey cocktail and one on the manhattan cocktail. In addition, I was earning a living teaching two to four sections of an eleven-week beverage management class four quarters each year for one of the top culinary schools in the United States. When I arrived I was a chef, but those twelve years had transformed me into a beverage expert, a connoisseur, and an author of award-winning books on cocktails and alcoholic beverages. Still, my knowledge was almost purely academic. I had never stood behind a bar and mixed drinks under pressure—with customers waiting.

One of the seminars I attended was a twelve-week boot camp for bartenders, sponsored by Southern Wines and Spirits. To be clear: twelve weeks for *current bartenders*, people already serving bars. At the time, I really did not fit the profile to be a successful student of the class. I secured my place because of my expertise and because of my desire to learn more about bartenders and bartending. But I had never bartended. Who can forget the scene in the movie *Cocktail* when the experienced server asks Tom Cruise's character for a Cuba Libre. Cruise fumbles around behind the bar looking for the cocktail manual to look up a drink he thinks he has never made. He looks at the server and yells, "You bitch! Why didn't you just tell me it was a rum and Coke?" By the end of the movie Cruise is a master bartender. I had about as much practical knowledge behind the bar as Cruise had at the beginning of the movie. My classmates were already Cruise at the end of the movie. At the time I was writing a book, and I thought it might help to be exposed to bartenders. In fact, some of my classmates and their recipes are featured in that book: *The Manhattan Cocktail: A Modern Guide to the Whiskey Classic.*

Every good bartender knows how to make many different drinks and riffs on the classics. My classmates delivered in spades. They understood not only the mechanics of the drink but the spirit as well. Perhaps my favorite was the white manhattan: an unaged whiskey with white vermouth, bitters, and a cherry. The cherry stood out like the cherry garnish in an aviation cocktail. This group took bottles of liquor and with the seeming sleight of hand of a magician created cocktails that pleased humans and made the angels sing. Not something just anyone could do—at least not me. The class included several written exams and one practical exam. The practical exam was judged by my classmates. I had to stand in front of this group—seasoned professional bartenders, all of them—and describe the drink that I was going to produce for them, produce the drink, and let them taste it so they could provide feedback. I served as a judge for their drinks too. They produced complex drinks with amazing flavors and creative garnishes.

When my turn rolled around, I stood in front of these amazing professionals. As a professor, I stood in front of a class daily. As a writer, I researched and tested drinks for the books that I had written. I had the knowledge to make any drink, so this test should have been easy; but my hands and legs began to shake uncontrollably. My voice, which was normally confident, broke at least twice, maybe three times, as I discussed my drink. My mind was empty. The bourbon drink I planned was lost in my scattered brain. I looked at the ingredients in front of me—I had to make a drink, any drink. I could make a riff on a sidecar. A simple drink—brandy, lemon juice, and orange liqueur. I finished my drink, and my classmates gave me a supportive clap. Then I watched their faces as they tasted what I had made: clearly the drink was out of balance. They made supportive suggestions: "Perhaps a sugar rim" (I forgot the sugar rim!); "Perhaps take a taste by dipping a straw into the drink with your finger covering the other end. Then adjust the drink" (I forgot to taste the drink!); "Perhaps a different drink—something you know how to make."

There is an old and not-so-nice saying about teachers and professors: "Those who can, do. Those who can't, teach." I exemplified that saying on my practical exam. There is a difference between mixing drinks for a live, discerning audience and teaching or writing about the same drinks. Anyone can mix liquor and modifiers together to create a cocktail, but few know the craft and the ingredients so well that they bestow a soul in the cocktail. So, I was surprised when, a month later, Gary, the organizer of the class, called me.

"Hey, do you want to help bartend a party?"

That sounded like fun! A chance to dip my toe—or wade—into the bartending pool. When I asked Louisville's legendary bartender Joy Perrine for advice, she said, "Kid, remember people will wait for food. They won't wait for drinks." So I would need to be fast and efficient. I could do that at a small party. Plus, Gary would be there to bail me out.

Each year, for almost a century and a half, thousands of people from all over the world travel to Louisville to attend the Kentucky Derby. The locals know that Derby festivities last for two weeks before the main event, which lasts for only about two minutes. There are usually more than twelve horse races at Churchill Downs on Derby Day, with the Kentucky Derby usually the tenth. The after-parties are epic and last well into the night, long after the horses are safely back in their stables. One of the big events held the night before Derby is "Unbridled Eve." About six hundred people, mostly rich and famous VIPs, attend an all-they-can-eat, all-they-can-drink event. Needless to say, many of the attendees are athletes, actors, singers, and others who have made their mark on society and are out for one last night of revelry before the big race the next day. Southern Wines and Spirits, a national distributor of alcohol, brings together a dozen or so bar-hardened veterans to help create the drinks to help please these stars, celebrities, and other guests. In 2014, however, the bartending makeup was a little different: Gary would supervise eleven bar-hardened veterans and one bartending virgin, me. Which is not to say that I had never mixed a drink before or never understood the subject matter; but I had not been behind a bar and had never been under the kind of pressure that comes with mixing and serving drinks to six hundred VIP guests, most of whom had traveled the world and consumed great cocktails at many exotic ports of call.

I arrived at 3:00 p.m. to begin setting up for the event, which would begin four hours later and would last until legal closing time in Louisville, four o'clock the next morning: Derby Day. I was part of the advance crew of four who prepped for all twelve bartenders, cutting garnishes, prepping bottles, and premixing some of the drinks to be featured at some of the bars. Part of my success would come from these prepared drinks—a practice that bartenders have employed at busy bars for almost as long as there have been cocktails. The three other bartenders in the advance crew included Gary, a true magician of mixed drinks who looks like a young Obi-Wan Kenobi—think Ewan McGregor with a short, well-trimmed beard; Joe, a master bartender who sports long flowing hair and a beard, similar to ZZ Top; and Colleen, a tall woman with long, dark hair and an impeccable palate—think a taller, hard Demi Moore circa *G.I. Jane*. These three mixologists carried themselves with the confidence of true professionals; each had a personal swagger behind the bar. Like Marines, we were the first to land at Louisville's iconic Galt House, and we would be some of the last to leave.

The other nine bartenders would arrive in a second wave a few hours later to set up their individual bars. The reinforcements included other top bartenders in the Louisville area, each from a top bar or restaurant. Every bar at this evening's event had a theme, a specialty, and a bartender. Colleen was lucky to run the bar featuring a major brand of bourbon, with the task of making old-fashioneds and manhattans—that was a job I would have been perfect for, having written books on each of those cocktails. I was more than a little jealous, to say the least, but I understood the decision: Colleen had recently won a bartending contest against a national field of bartenders making old-fashioned whiskey cocktails using the same brand of bourbon that she was pouring that night. Joe was behind the bar that featured drinks made from a major brand of gin and brandy. I was assigned to the vodka bar—which was cool, in part because the bar was made from ice: a full-sized bar carved from ice. Also, I was happy to be at that bar because vodka is one of the most popular spirits in the United States. That night, Gary supervised and walked from bar to bar to make sure that the bartenders had everything a bar would need in the way of supplies, that the bartenders were following the rules that night, and that the general needs of the bartenders themselves were met. Gary was able to enjoy the party.

As the bars were set and the final preparations were made, Gary visited each bar to hand each bartender a black bartender jacket with the name of the bartender embroidered in red along with each person's title that night: "Mixologist." Only my jacket had just the title "Mixologist." I put the jacket on, but I felt unworthy of the accolade as I thought of the great mixologists and bartenders around the United States, like Audrey Sanders, Dale DeGroff, Tony Abou-Ganim, Bridget Albert, Paul McGee, Chris Hannah, Charles Joly, and Jim Meehan. I felt like a fake, a fraud. Professor, yes; author, yes; bartender or mixologist—hell no! I was out of place. However, the time for thinking was over as the door to the event was opened. Like many bartenders, I would need to do my best and make up for what I did not know with personality—always remembering that if I ended up in the weeds, Gary would be able to step in and help.

The customers flooded in, and so began my trial by fire. All of them were interested in getting a drink or two or perhaps three before moving into the ballroom for dinner and live entertainment. The lines at the bars featuring bourbon cocktails filled up fast. This was Louisville and Derby, after all. In fact, for a while I seemed to be getting only the overflow traffic. A new customer would walk in looking for a drink, see that the bourbon bars had huge lines, and would walk up to my bar to grab what I was serving. My bar featured two vodka-based cocktails and shots of vodka, including filtered, unfiltered, and several different flavored vodkas. One of my cocktails was a riff on a greyhound cocktail called "Derby Thyme," which had vodka, ruby red grapefruit juice, and a little honey, all garnished with a sprig of thyme and a mist of Angostura bitters. The other cocktail, called "Wicked Strong Passion," featured a mango-passionfruit vodka, raspberry-peach Grand Marnier, a raspberry gomme syrup, fresh lime juice, and guava juice, garnished with a raspberry. The two cocktails were solid drinks and hits with the customers. Customers tried the cocktails and came back because they liked them. Word spread. My line grew. And I was able to keep up.

Part of bartending is talking to the customer; another part is entertaining the customer. You have to be cool and calm, and you have to keep your head and wits about you. That night I mastered both the one-handed shake and a double one-handed shake. I also poured a lot of shots of vodka. However, not everything went according to plan. I found out that you should not place glass filled with colored liquid onto a bar made of ice. Even my ice-carving background—much less my background as a professor or a writer—did not prepare me for this one. The melting ice creates a thin layer of water that allows the drink to skate away. One of the drinks broke away from me and almost ruined a very beautiful Derby dress; luckily I was able to reach across the bar and catch the drink before it damaged the dress and soaked the young lady wearing it. I solved the problem by laying out paper napkins, which helped to soak up some of the water and provided enough friction so that the glass did not skid across the ice. The only way to know this was from experience.

One of the benefits of bartending is the people you meet. I met some famous people that night: an NBA basketball player sporting a World Championship ring, several NFL players, a singer who had a handful of hits in the late 1970s and early 1980s and hung out at my bar for an extended period of time. But the one who made a lasting impression on me was a TV and film actor who had made a career out of playing different law-enforcement officers. He walked up to my bar. I knew who he was, and he knew exactly what he wanted.

"I want you to give me a double shot of vodka shaken on ice and strained."
"Yes, sir."

I poured the vodka into the shaker with ice, closed the shaker with a pint glass and completed a one-hand shake over my right shoulder. I strained the vodka into the glass, picked up the glass, and passed it to him. He quickly emptied the liquid in the glass into his mouth, swallowed, and placed the glass back on the bar. "Hit me again." I obliged. "Thanks, kid," he said as he slipped me a twenty-dollar bill. He moved into the ballroom for dinner as I realized that the degrees of separation between me and Marisa Tomei had been reduced to one.

I had a steady stream of customers all night: time flew. During the dinner, the bars shut down long enough for the bartenders to sneak away to grab something to eat. As service staff we did not get to eat the same meal that our customers were enjoying in the dining room. But there was a rumor of pizza in the next building. The group of thirteen mixologists moved from one tower of the Galt House to another on a quest to find the pizza. When we arrived at the appointed room we found empty pizza boxes. Nothing! Hungry, we moved back to our stations near the ballroom and prepared our bars for the next wave of customers. I was ready for the next wave. They came, I served drinks, and before I knew it, we were giving last call.

I survived my trial by fire! I was most proud of the fact that I was able to speak knowledgeably about the brands I was promoting that night and that none of the other bartenders had to "save me": I was able to hold my own. At the end of the evening, Joe and I exited the hotel and walked toward our cars. I took off the black bartending jacket to reveal a sticky, sweat-, alcohol-, and juice-soaked white T-shirt. In fact, I felt sticky all over. The dark streets were still filled with people who clearly wanted a party (any party) and others who were looking for a bite to eat. Food trucks and food carts filling the needs of their clients had huge lines.

> Joe said to me, "So how did your night go?"
> "Good," I replied.
> "So, do you feel like a 'mixologist'?" Joe queried.
> "Not really—I feel like a poser."
> "Well, you're not—you are a bartender! Be proud of being a bartender! God, I hate that term . . . *mixologist*—seriously!"

I took what Joe said to heart. That night we were there to tend bar. Give the people what they wanted. Also, Joe inspired me. I moonlighted as a bartender for the rest of 2014. I was invited to return to the Unbridled Eve event in 2015, and this time a red bartender's jacket was waiting for me. Embroidered in black was my title—"mixologist"—*and* my name. Then I was invited back in 2016. In 2015 and in 2016, I was offered full-time bartending positions by owners and managers of local Louisville bars. I noticed that my teaching and writing improved when it came to mixed drinks. I became cognizant of drinks that I had never heard of, and I was able to mix drinks, many drinks, with confidence and flair, when asked to—all without hesitation. Plus, when I spoke about bartending and mixology, I was able to speak with the authority of someone who has "been there, done that." I got a good laugh in 2015 when one of the celebrity guests at the Unbridled Eve event encouraged me to "hang in there—someday you will make it. Take it from me, I used to bartend too." I was right where I wanted to be! With the other hardworking bartenders and mixologists who love serving people drinks, watching their eyes light up when we deliver exactly what they hoped for, and perhaps amusing them along the way. We show up first and leave last. We get paid to play all day with everything alcohol; sure, the hours are long and the work is hard, but it's a lot of fun. Some bartenders become celebrities in their own right, but most stay in the obscure background. The expectation is to entertain but be discreet. To paraphrase Brad Pitt's character from *Ocean's 11*:

> I ask you a question, you have to think of the answer, where do you look? No good! You look down they know you're lying. You look up and they know you don't know the truth. Don't use seven words when four will do. Don't shift your weight. Always look at your mark but don't stare. Be specific but not memorable. Be funny but don't make them laugh. They have to like you but then forget you the moment you have left their sight.

In other words, a good bartender has a supporting role to the drink. Most bartenders work very hard, and work hard not to be the center of attention.

Two of my mentors from that first time have moved on to different jobs in different cities. Joe shaved his magnificent beard and took a full-time position as a brand ambassador for a whiskey distiller. He now lives in New York City. Gary is now the corporate bartender for a major hotel company, has moved to the Washington, DC, area, and travels the country for a living, training bartenders nationwide. Colleen is still the bar manager at a local Louisville restaurant. I follow each of them on Facebook, and I will never forget them or that first night I bartended. Recently, I reached out to Gary to see if he would be in New Orleans for "Tales of the Cocktail," an annual event that bartenders attend from all over the world. I planned to be there at the same time. We were able to connect. As we drank a cocktail, I thanked him for opening a new world of experience for me.

And what about me? What am I up to now? I am still teaching and writing. And bartending.

Greensboro

PART 2

Spirits of the Age

SIX

"THEY MADE ME FEEL CIVILIZED"

The Martini as Modernist Culture

MICHAEL COYLE

"FOR MOST OF THE TWENTIETH century," observes that unabashed defender of cultivated vices, Barbara Holland, "the martini was the definitive drink—called simply a 'drink'—among those who felt that what you drank was an essential part of your respectability, your background, and your social, professional, and educational standing."[1] In fact, "the martini was the signature drink of the ruling class and the passport to all corridors of power from politics to poetry, academia to Wall Street."[2] This association of martinis with status, this investment of a simple cocktail with complexly negotiated cultural capital, is so overfamiliar as to remain essentially unchallenged. It can be invoked with reverence, as above, or with a sneer, as in Bob Dylan and Jacques Levy's "Hurricane," where it serves as shorthand for the privileges of the cultural elite: while a purportedly innocent Rubin Carter languishes in prison, "all the criminals in their suits and ties are free to drink martinis and watch the sunrise."[3] In the 1950s, alto-sax player Paul Desmond, the composer of Dave Brubeck's paradigm-shifting "Take Five," famously explained that he wanted the jazz he played "to sound like a dry martini";[4] Spanish filmmaker Luis Buñuel, in his autobiography, *Mon Dernier Soupir* (*My Last Sigh*, 1982), celebrates the "primordial role" that dry martinis played in his life and art;[5] British novelist Alec Waugh (who claimed to have invented the cocktail party) attested to its special restorative powers: "I am prepared to believe that a dry martini slightly impairs the palate, but think what it does for the soul."[6] American novelist William Faulkner offered that "when I have one martini, I feel bigger, wiser, taller. When I have a second, I feel superlative. When I have more, there's no holding me."[7] Artistic inspiration, spiritual rejuvenation, physical restoration—the martini has been credited with any number of powers. These examples are anything but unusual. Let a couple more examples serve to establish our ground.

The British writer Paul Johnson has offered an account of American poet T. S. Eliot in a particularly unbuttoned moment:

> Eliot always enjoyed drinking, especially gin. He liked strong cocktails. (And he called them that: hence the title of his play *The Cocktail Party*; a born Englishman of his class would have called it *The Drinks Party*.) In 1953 (I think) I first met Eliot [at one of Jock Murray's parties]. Murray was celebrated for the strength of his dry martinis.... The sole remark [Eliot] addressed to me, before we were interrupted, was: "There is nothing in this world quite so stimulating as a strong dry martini cocktail."[8]

In view of David Earle's contention that, historically, in the mid-nineteenth century, cocktails were expected to be "strong, sweet and bitter," Eliot's comment is a sign of his modernity, at least to the extent that there is by definition nothing "sweet" in a "dry" martini.[9] Strength, however, still mattered, as does the identity of the martini as a "cocktail," but Eliot's comment underscores how much the martini had evolved in its first century. So, too, does Johnson's pausing over both Eliot's Americanness and the fact that the Englishman, Jock Murray, was so celebrated for his martinis. Well before this postwar moment, the martini (and cocktail culture in general) had gone global. We have, for instance, William Terrington's British book of 1869,[10] Louis Fouquet's 1899 book in French,[11] and Carl Seuter's 1909 book in German.[12] These early European examples help contextualize H. L. Mencken's proposal that the martini is "the only American invention as perfect as a sonnet."[13] For Mencken, the martini is a cultural achievement, an artistic breakthrough all the more amazing because American, but also now an invention known to all the world. The history of that movement has been much discussed and much debated, but it seems to me that Earle's approach—collecting old and semiforgotten things, like mixology books—produces the most stimulating results.

The first mixology book was published by New York City bartender Jerry Thomas in 1862. It did not contain a recipe for the martini or for anything like the martini. Neither did the 1876 edition of Thomas's book. But in Thomas's 1887 edition we get a recipe for the "martinez": two ounces sweet vermouth; one ounce Old Tom gin; 1/4 ounce maraschino liqueur; one dash bitters; 1/4 slice of lemon as garnish. Notice the mix here of potent spirits, sweet ingredients with bitters: the martinez is an exemplary nineteenth-century cocktail. The martini would represent a simplifying of this recipe and over time a removal of sweetness. The next year, in Harry Johnson's *New & Improved*

Bartender's Manual, the martini was—after the champagne cocktail—the second recipe listed: two to three dashes of Gum syrup; two to three dashes of Boker's Genuine Bitters; one dash of curaçao, and 1/2 wine glassful each of Old Tom gin and vermouth.[14] Old Tom was a variety of gin, slightly sweeter and mellower than the London Dry that subsequently became the basis for most modern gins. Plainly, Johnson's martini did not differ much from Thomas's martinez, and in general the two drinks remained closely related until the end of World War I. But their postwar divergence marks a defining moment in cocktail culture precisely as it participates in a distinctively modernist rarefication.

Scholars often refer to 1922 as the *annus mirabilis* of modernism. It was the year in which Joyce published *Ulysses*, Woolf *Jacob's Room*, Fitzgerald *The Beautiful and the Damned*, and Eliot *The Waste Land*; it was also the year in which Robert Vermeire published *Cocktails: How to Mix Them*.[15] Among the four martini recipes in Vermeire's book is this one: one dash of orange bitters; 1/6 gill of Italian vermouth (which is to say sweet vermouth); 2/6 gill of dry gin; squeeze a lemon peel on top. The martinez is still present like the aroma of a fading bouquet, but the martini cocktail was getting drier. By 1929 the martini recipe in Paul Colin's *Cocktails de Paris* was calling for equal parts dry gin with Noilly Prat (which is to say dry, French) vermouth. This last detail is the source for our modern term *dry martini*: it was so-called not because the cocktail was meant to be austerely dry but because it was to be made with dry vermouth. This shift from signifying a particular ingredient to signifying the absence of that ingredient represents a kind of forgetting, a shift in an older distinction whose significance is today typically lost on us.[16]

And so we are reminded again that the martini has long functioned more as a sign itself than as either signifier or signified. It is less a thing than a cluster of significances and associations. For Barbara Holland, "The martini represents grace under pressure. An arabesque, a liquid pearl. Somebody said it was Fred Astaire in a glass.... Thus is the act of mixing sacred: the moment is the only moment."[17] Both art and sacrament, modernity and tradition, nature and culture, American and cosmopolitan: the martini is somehow able to signifying either side of any number of binary oppositions.

I am interested in how this works: I am interested in what martinis mean, why they're taken to mean so much, and why they're taken to *mean* anything at all. It's not that these questions have never been raised before. Indeed, we have already two particularly rich studies in David Wondrich's *Imbibe!*[18] and Lowell Edmunds's *Martini, Straight Up: The Classic American Cocktail*.[19] Wondrich has established himself as the leading historian of cocktail culture; Edmunds we might call (although he would likely resist so academic a phrase) its chief semiotician. Indeed, toward the end of the revised edition of *Martini, Straight Up*, Edmunds even engages Pierre Bourdieu's *Distinction*, finding Bourdieu "a highly sensitive observer of manners, habits, and, in general, lifestyle."[20] Nevertheless, Edmunds expects that Bourdieu would be suspicious of his "nonchalance concerning the ideological value" of the martini's various "messages" and "ambiguities."[21] He is doubtless right. But the "ambiguities" that Edmunds sees surrounding the cultural meanings of the martini seem to me the inevitable function of its cultural overdetermination and of its circulation as a sign. Why, when the recipe is so clear, are there "ambiguities" around a simple cocktail? Why should a concoction of gin and vermouth be expected to *mean* anything at all besides, perhaps, pleasure? Why should any cocktail be taken as a sign? In addressing these questions, it helps to remember that a sign is not a "thing" but rather the unstable relation between signifier and signified. "Martini" is both a signified—the familiar gin and vermouth cocktail—and a signifier of cultural values to which that cocktail has no necessary association. Ultimately, when we discuss martinis, we enter the dynamic relations between these two aspects of the sign. The meanings (and ambiguities) now associated with this cocktail have proven subject to change not only over time but also across different sociocultural contexts. As a sign rather than a symbol, the martini can be and has been taken to mean any number of contradictory things.

We might question how, given the ever-growing profusion of cocktails out there, the martini has maintained this status for so long. This volume demonstrates that there are plenty of other cocktails that have eloquent advocates, and there are plenty that are in their own ways delicious and equally potent. As Judith Roof explains, the martini was not the first cocktail—the old-fashioned is older by half a century (at least) and is "the cocktail to which all cocktails refer" (see chap. 17). Neither is the martini the most potent of cocktails: that prize could go to any one of a number of more recent potions, like the zombie, or even to the kind of grain alcohol and punch concoctions served at college frat parties. But the martini looms large in the American imagination. Its profile is outsized, and its status—and its function as a sign of status—remains apparently unassailable. Its popularity has on occasion waned, as it did in the 1960s, when Jefferson Morgan eulogized it in the pages of *Bon Appetit*:

> Now I come before you with a heavy heart to ring tocsin of the end of civilization as we know it. The true martini cocktail stands in jeopardy of becoming one with the passenger pigeon, the dodo, and the St. Louis Browns, a situation clearly analogous to the decadence of Rome shortly before the fall of the Empire.[22]

Now nearly half a century old, Morgan's eulogy tells us something about how the *significance* of the martini functions: it is associated with a tradition always on the verge of being lost, its purity threatened at every moment by the overwhelming forces of barbarous (usually consumerist and popular) forces. His comic associations aside, Morgan, like so many before him, equates the martini with civilization itself. In recent years the martini's popularity has been challenged by its old rival, the manhattan, perhaps because of the early-twenty-first-century rise of single-barrel bourbons (and despite the conviction of some of us that, properly speaking, a manhattan should be made not with bourbon at all but with rye). Nevertheless, the martini has survived successive changes in patterns of socialization and continues to function as a marker of status. It has unfailingly maintained what Richard Barnett identifies as its initial, late-nineteenth-century profile as "urban, upmarket, the drink of stylish and successful people, a cocktail to which one might aspire."[23] It is and long has been, as David Wondrich says, "the King of all Cocktails."[24]

Writers on the topic, such as Wondrich, Barnaby Conrad, and Edmunds, have established that the martini was a nineteenth-century invention, likely making its appearance while Ulysses S. Grant was in the White House. In those days, right through Prohibition, the standard recipe seems to have been 50 percent gin and 50 percent vermouth garnished originally with a pearl onion but, by 1888, an olive (the option of a twist of lemon came later).[25] By that time, the martini was already established across the country and already subject to competing claims as to who had invented it, a competition grown noisier in our contemporary, internet-driven era. The internet is full of misinformation claiming that the martini, like most cocktails, was a product of Prohibition—when illegal booze was so gawd-awful bad it had to be adulterated to be palatable. This idea is even repeated in Ben Reed's *Gatsby Cocktails*, a book wholly focused on Prohibition.[26] In fact, in the martini's case at least, the ratio of gin to vermouth *increased* during the twenties—the martini grew *drier* during this period. At the same time, the martini began to acquire its modern aura—its association with modernity and civilization. Its status grew as it increased in potency and as it became ever more austere.

This might be paradoxical, given the centuries-old association of gin with low-class "gin-lanes." Richard Barnett offers a history of gin from its alchemical and medicinal origins in Moorish Spain, to the accelerated production of spirits (because spirits were cheaper to ship than raw grain) in northern Europe during the Thirty Years' War, to the late sixteenth-century production in the Netherlands of "a juniper-based grain spirit that apothecary Sylvius de Bouve called 'Genova'" (later known as "geneva"), and which he recommended "as a treatment for lumbago."[27] Gin proved a matter of grave concern not only for Puritans and other watchdogs of public morality but also for the government: gin seemed to produce "a new kind of drunkenness, wilder and more socially destructive than the rolling English stupor engendered by beer."[28] Initial government impulses toward prohibition soon yielded, however, before the recognition that "spirits could be a lucrative source of [tax] revenue."[29] But from the beginning gin emerged as a sign of "modern" urban life. As Barnett explains, "Early modern drinking culture can be broadly and crudely summarized as ale in the country, hopped beer in the towns and cities, and wine (plain or fortified) for the ruling classes."[30] Spirits did not supplant these patterns so much as supplement them, the quality of such supplements being a function of class. Samuel Johnson's *Dictionary* pauses over both "gin" and "geneva": "gin" is simply "the spirit drawn by distillation from juniper berries"; "geneva," however, earns one of Johnson's longest definitions:

> We used to keep a distilled spirituous water of juniper in the shops; but the making of it became the business of the distiller, who sold it under the name of *geneva*. At present only a better kind is distilled from the juniper-berry: what is commonly sold is made with no better an ingredient than oil of turpentine, put into the still, with a little common salt, and the coarsest spirit they have, which is drawn off much below proof strength, and is consequently a liquor that one would wonder any people could accustom themselves to drink with pleasure.[31]

Johnson disdained gin as a coarse spirit for coarse people. Indeed, he found the stuff so foul as to wonder how "any people could accustom themselves" to drink it all, let alone with pleasure. It was not in his world a thing capable of carrying Bourdieuian "distinction" of any kind, and, quite simply, polite people did not consume it.

The question then is how a spirit of such ignoble origin became the principle ingredient in a cocktail the consumption of which served almost immediately as a sign of prestige. The answer is suggested by the Islamic, medieval-alchemical origins of (proto) gin.[32] The mixing of gin with vermouth represents not just the gustatory "magic" of flavors fortunately combined, but a kind of cultural magic. That is, fortified wine (vermouth) was always associated with cultural elites; the mixing of fortified wine and grain spirit produced a new kind of *cultural* alchemy. As I've already noted, the martini's ratio of vermouth to gin has changed dramatically over the past 150 years, but what matters isn't the *quantity* of vermouth stirred or shaken up with gin but rather its very presence. Gin is the main ingredient in a martini, but it's the vermouth that makes it a martini.

The alchemy works even when the martini is so dry as for the vermouth to be merely gestural, as when Winston Churchill reputedly said that the only way to make a martini was with ice-cold gin and a bow in the direction of France—in the direction of France because historically French vermouth was dry and Italian vermouth sweet.

The contemporary fashion for "dry" martinis (i.e., less vermouth) seems to have developed in large part as a postwar antidote to the martini's increasingly widespread popularity. In 1968, J. A. Maxtone Graham noted an experiment whose conclusions make this point very directly:

> Two years ago in Chicago an attempt was made to classify tastes in martinis. A dreadful-sounding machine called a MartiniMatic enabled 3,426 random people to dial a drink of their chosen strength. Marked differences in blend were shown according to professions: teachers, factory workers, and office workers chose 3 to 1; salesmen, buyers, and engineers chose 4 to 1; admen chose 5 to 1; and publishers chose 7 to 1.[33]

How many publishers might have been numbered among those 3,426 consumers is not revealed, but the message is clearly that the dry martini is an especial marker of "class," not even so much in the socioeconomic sense as in the cultivation of manners and taste.

Edmunds explains the "cultural capital" of the martini in terms of seven implicit messages, and his list is worth quoting in full:

- Message One: The Martini is American—it is not European, Asian, or African
- Message Two: The Martini is urban and urbane—it is not rural or rustic
- Message Three: The Martini is a high-status, not a low-status, drink
- Message Four: The Martini is a man's, not a woman's, drink
- Message Five: The Martini is optimistic, not pessimistic
- Message Six: The Martini is the drink of adults, not of children
- Message Seven: The Martini belongs to the past, not to the present[34]

Edmunds is generally focused on what the martini has come to signify in our time. None of these messages is inherent to the drink itself; each is a function of the culture that surrounds the martini. In fact, it's hard to imagine any other American cocktail that can be said to *have* a culture that surrounds it. Consider, for instance, its distinctive glass. Now appropriated by the rapidly proliferating number of cocktails that call themselves the *something*-"tini," the martini glass enforces a certain comportment; one doesn't wave one's arms about while holding the long-stemmed, broad-brimmed martini glass; one doesn't, one *can't*, slam a martini glass on a bar like it's a heavy beer stein; one must raise a martini glass to one's lips comparatively slowly, lest the contents of the glass end up washing down one's shirtfront. The shape of the vessel may or may not, as Edmunds proposes, be "an image of the female breast";[35] it may originally have served practical purposes like keeping the warmth of your hand away from the drink,[36] or displaying the clarity of the gin; the wide open brim of the glass—as the website "WiseGeek" suggests—may serve to produce surface tension that brings out the bouquet of the gin.[37] But all of these practical functions seem merely excuses to perpetuate the genteel forms of behavior that this iconically shaped glass more or less requires: forms of behavior, social manners, that have been crucial to the martini's enduring social status. It seems clear that this status is usually what is meant when people associate the martini with "tradition."

Not surprisingly, the martini glass has itself evolved along with the contents it so famously displays. What we think of today as the martini glass proper was introduced in the 1925 Paris Exhibition as, Karen Locke tells us, "a modernist take on the champagne coupe"—the 120 to 240 ml glass that has since the early eighteenth century been the vessel of choice for drinks best enjoyed cool but not served with ice.[38] It stands to reason that this innovation happened in Paris, since it was about this time that dry French vermouth began usurping the place of (which is to say the market share of) Italian vermouth. Nevertheless, she adds, this now iconic shaped glass "didn't gain traction until after World War II."[39] The quarter century required for the unfolding of this process is important, because what happened to the shape of the martini glass is homologous to what happened to modernist literature and culture in the same period. Tendencies amplified; differences made extreme; distinctions became oppositions, so that Andreas Huyssen could, in 1987, characterize it as the period of "The Great Divide."[40] This was the period of modernism's academic institutionalization: the period wherein poets like Eliot or painters like Picasso came widely to be recognized as removed from popular culture, despite their own lifelong engagements of it. In just this way, this replacement of the coupe glass by the flared martini glass suggests that the socio-cultural distinction conveyed by the vessel continues to grow more pronounced precisely as the martini grows ever more deeply associated with genteel tradition. And so, when Lizzie Munro writes that "the Martini glass has somewhat fallen out of favour in modern times due to its tendency to spill drinks" she is right—and is missing the point. The point of the impractical martini glass has from its Parisienne start been a sign of elite status.[41] In fact, this shape has taken on a life of its own. Popular concoctions like "applet*inis*" play on the structure of the sign (the martini glass) while changing, sometimes completely, its content (gin and vermouth).

By contrast, advocates of the martini typically celebrate its purity. As Edmunds's third and seventh "messages" might suggest, the martini has long excited a kind of purist traditionalism. One of my favorite examples comes in a 1968 editorial in the *New York Times* by William Grimes. "For more than a century," he affirmed, "the martini has held sway in the world of cocktails by virtue of its purity and simplicity. It has but two ingredients, gin and vermouth. It can tolerate only one of two garnishes, an olive or a twist of lemon."[42] Simplicity. Purity. The way we've always done it. Nothing else can be tolerated. But Grimes seems tolerant indeed compared to Stuart Connelly, who insists that "anyone who suggests you can make a martini with vodka, by the way, is probably in need of electroconvulsive therapy."[43] The gin versus vodka issue is one argued fiercely by advocates of tradition (who invariably, like Grimes, insist on gin)—and hardly acknowledged by people who prefer vodka. But the fact that the martini retains its status, its "distinction," even when its principle ingredient is exchanged for something else is in and of itself worth pausing over. So, too, is the mere fact that we even have a debate between traditionalists and moderns over how to make a cocktail. But then again, the martini is not a "mere" cocktail. What makes a martini a "martini" is not merely a matter of physical ingredients.

The *DrinkBoy* blog offers an opinion on this matter that usefully underscores what is invested in calling the martini a "cocktail": "A cocktail with just a single ingredient is really not a cocktail. And a cocktail made with a spirit that is officially 'tasteless, odorless, and colorless' (vodka), is nothing that even closely resembles a cocktail, much less a Martini."[44] A cocktail must be a mixture of spirits and other ingredients, but one of the things that marks the cocktail as American (and a sign of American class, to return to Edmunds's first message) is its eager mixing of cultures. Since such mixing informs every other aspect of American civilization, it doubtless stands to reason that it would do so here, too, even in so simple a concoction as the martini. Gin is Dutch in origin; vermouth and the green olive both are Italian. A similar point could be made about most American cocktails: A manhattan mixes American rye whiskey (or bourbon) with Italian vermouth and Angostura bitters from Trinidad; a silk stocking is Mexican tequila with French crème de cacao; and so on. This kind of mixing, the emergence of this cocktail culture, appears in America at precisely the moment when America moves from being a postcolonial culture to being a global power. It owes, too, of course, to the mixings of cultures and people that is America's most fundamental heritage. Wondrich identifies the cocktail as peculiarly American in simpler terms:

> Anyone who has spent any time pondering the origins of the Cocktail—be it for the months or years it takes to write a book or the minutes or seconds it takes to internalize a Dry Martini—will agree that it's a quintessentially American contraption. How could it be anything but? It's quick, direct, and vigorous. It's flashy and a little bit vulgar. It induces an unreflective overconfidence. It's democratic, forcing the finest of liquors to rub elbows with ingredients of far more humble stamp.[45]

This sustained riff is funny and doubtless fair. In his sense that the martini is "a little bit vulgar," Wondrich inadvertently recalls Johnson's disdain for gin. His comment would seem to deny the aspirational quality of the martini, its century-old function of separating the elite from the vulgar, and the ways in which it strives for containment more than flash. In our era the martini signifies status as much as vitality.

The martini's twenty-first-century function as a marker of class status was acquired in the second half-century of its life. In other words, Edmunds's third message is historically specific. The nineteenth-century/early-twentieth-century martinez invited no such distinctions, and so long as the martini was primarily to be associated with bars and saloons (those great watering holes of democratic society where social classes can mix as easily as libations), neither did the martini. Paradoxically, the martini began to acquire cultural capital when its recipe was simplified, when it grew less sweet, and when it became more associated with home cocktail parties (or drinks parties) than with public bars. Literary evidence suggests that this transformation unfolded in the years *entre les guerres*—which is to say the modernist era. As Huyssen observes, this amplification of the differences between consumer culture and elite culture generally characterizes the era. That the more recent "New Modernist Studies" has challenged any sense that this divide was ever absolute doesn't belie the anxiety of cultural elites, then and now, to affirm their distinctions from mass culture.[46] The modernist arts in all their forms defined themselves against the example of popular entertainments, and we can see this as clearly in the world of cocktail culture as we see it in literature, painting, or music. The martini never ceased being a public pleasure—but its status rose as it moved from its role as the latest thing to being, as Holland says, "the definitive drink," a modernist sign of tradition.

The title I've given this chapter comes from a passage in Ernest Hemingway's *A Farewell to Arms* (1929). The protagonist of this novel, which made

Hemingway famous, is an American volunteer in the Italian army during World War I. After the Italians suffer catastrophic defeat at Caporetto, Henry abandons the army, evading Italian military police looking for deserters as well as the attacking Austrian army, managing at last to make his way to Stresa, where he hopes to join his wife and flee with her to safety in Switzerland. Going into the bar at the Grand Hotel, he orders some food and has a martini. The martini, he tells us, "felt cool and clean."[47] While conversing with the barkeep and waiting for his food, he has a second. Eventually, the sandwiches arrive and we get this report: "I ate three and drank a couple more martinis. I had never tasted anything so cool and clean. They made me feel civilized. I had had too much red wine, bread, cheese, bad coffee and grappa."[48] In point of fact, in his flight to Stresa, Henry hadn't been eating much at all. The contrast he's drawing here is less gustatory than symbolic. Gin and vodka, clear and colorless, are refined spirits. As Edmunds observes, "Wine, pressed from grapes, is close to nature, close to the earth . . . [but] as for gin, no one quite knows what grain it has been distilled from."[49] In other words, gin is as distant from nature as fermented drinks might be said to be close to it. Hemingway himself often made similar observations. He saw gin as civilization's answer to a germy, bacteria-ridden nature. In a 1954 "By-Line" for *Look* magazine, and writing about Gordon's gin in particular, he testified that gin "is one of the sovereign antiseptics of our time . . . and can be counted on to mollify and cauterize practically all internal or external injuries."[50] "Cauterizing" and healing: the martini is clean.

The idea that the martini is *civilizing* eventually and inevitably informed the language of advertising. A 1957 ad by Peter Arno for Noilly Prat takes a rather stern tone when insisting that "a dry martini is *not* a hooker of gin or vodka. It's a cocktail. And what makes it a cocktail is a noticeable, taste-pleasing, *civilizing* proportion of Noilly extra dry vermouth."[51] Civilizing. A matter of form—which is in part what that savage antagonist of the "boobocracy," H. L. Mencken, had in mind when he described the martini as "the only American invention as perfect as a sonnet."[52] Mencken wasn't really being, or only being, funny. His description is in the spirit of Gilbert Seldes's 1923 book *The Seven Lively Arts*, weighing the new American "lively arts" like jazz and cinema and comic strips in the same balance as the hallowed arts of European tradition. The martini represents American civilization, and, as in the Noilly Prat ad, embodies proportion. It also, as might be implicit in Hemingway's notion of "civilized," signifies modernity. But this last signification raises another question: how does the martini with its nineteenth-century origin come to be the modernist drink of choice?

Cocktails combine disparate elements to form convivial new wholes—wholes that appear liberal but remain fundamentally conservative. In moving from cocktail culture in general to martini culture in particular, the modernist obsession with the "clean" becomes unmistakably important. Theorists of the modern like Ezra Pound made a great show of dismissing Victorian fussiness and sentimentality. Twentieth-century poetry, Pound expected, would be "austere, direct, free from emotional slither."[53] "Good writing is writing that is perfectly controlled," where the writer says what he means with "complete clarity and simplicity."[54] Claims like these circulated as manifestos among modernist writers and poets—but similar claims were being produced by other forms of cultural production. In design or architecture we might think of the Bauhaus style that emerged right after World War I; in music we might point to the twelve-tone music of the second Viennese school; or we might just consider, as Judith Brown has done, the contemporaneous fascination with the "glamour" of cellophane (invented in 1900 by a Swiss chemist).[55] Pound was famously remembered by Jimmy the Bartender as being only "a white winer," a cosmopolitan of sorts who nevertheless remained all his life uninterested in modernist cocktail culture; but the point here is simply to illustrate that Hemingway's terms of praise for the martini were not merely idiosyncratic.[56] Because it wasn't sweet, because it wasn't fermented, because it was clear, and perhaps because it was American, imbibers during the Jazz Age—of the modernist period—separated the martini from its Victorian (and popular) origins. Edmunds's suggestion that "the martini is the civilized antidote to civilization" itself exemplifies urbane cocktail wit.[57] But his suggestion is at 180 degrees from Hemingway's description of Frederic Henry's three martinis in the Grand Hotel as an antidote to germy, bacteria-ridden nature—to the organic. The distinction isn't a merely individual one between two men with different tastes—it's a historical one between two eras, separated by a century, responding to different historical pressures. And this difference is one sign of the martini's having achieved the condition of tradition. The recipe itself has been simplified; but once the martini achieved the condition of being a sign, it has demonstrated a cultural complexity and an inevitably unpredictable semiotic drift. The martini may never have been the most popular cocktail, but it has long been the only *significant* cocktail.

Barnaby Conrad III reminds us of a scene in the 1934 film *The Thin Man*, where William Powell (playing suave detective Nick Charles) instructs three New York bartenders at the elegant Normandie Hotel bar how to make a proper martini: "You see, the important thing is the rhythm," he says. "You always have rhythm in your shaking. With a Manhattan you shake to fox-trot time.

A Bronx to two-step time. A dry Martini you always shake to waltz time."[58] Conrad doesn't explain, but no audience in 1934 would have needed to be told what these dances represented: the heyday for the fox trot was the 1930s; for the two-step it was the 1920s; but for the waltz it was the nineteenth century. The martini is significant because it is not fashionable; it represents old and genteel tradition. But there are contradictions and self-interferences built into this sign. In *The Thin Man* the association with things Victorian represents tradition; in Pound's definition of the modern things Victorian represent fussiness and "emotional slither." Tradition and cleanliness are both essential to the significance of the martini as *the* modern cocktail, but it isn't logic that constellates these qualities together so much as the sequences of negations and differences that mark the martini as a cultural sign.

Much about the martini has changed since the appearance of the martinez in the 1880s. Although it represents elite tradition, that tradition is, contra Edmunds's fourth message, no longer male; Barbara Holland could have told Edmunds that. But, as innumerable contemporary ads in magazines, on TV, and online attest, Edmunds is right that the martini as *tradition* is alive. In fact, ongoing arguments about how dry a martini should be are not only not a threat to that tradition but also one of the mechanisms with which we preserve it. Martinis have become drier over the past century. Even in 1951, Bernard DeVoto was recommending 3.7 to 1, while allowing for 4 to 1.[59] In the first quarter of the twenty-first century, if one wants a proper martini—a cocktail with at least some vermouth—one needs to oversee the bartender—because American bartenders have learned that the best way to avoid trouble with patrons is to follow Churchill's ceremony and exclude the vermouth, with or without the salute to Paris. T. S. Eliot, that most elective of Englishmen, knew better: his widow Valerie later recounted how he named one of his cats "Noilly Prat" after the original French dry vermouth (formulated by Joseph Noilly in 1813).[60] Ceremony alone isn't enough. "A dry martini is *not* a hooker of gin"—it is the vermouth that, in whatever quantity, transforms chilled gin into a martini.

My own most illuminating experience of what we might call "the ratio argument" came during my first visit with my girlfriend's seventy-something-year-old aunt, a sophisticated, still adventurous lady named Gina who lives in Manhattan's Upper West Side in a classic six overlooking the Hudson. I was eager to make a good impression, so just after 5:00 p.m. I offered to make martinis. Her face lit up, and she said, "Oh, YES," but then caught herself, sizing me up with a look that told me a serious lesson was in the offing. She guessed, by virtue of my age, that my idea of a martini would be something austerely dry, something like fourteen or fifteen parts gin to one part vermouth.

"My late husband and I," she explained, "hold that there are good reasons people mix gin with vermouth. We drink martinis the way our parents did before us." I told her I was happy to mix it up to her liking, and so I did—with a nod not to Paris but to tradition—six parts to one. The result was a revelation. What do you know—there are good reasons people mix gin and vermouth! But in retrospect I see another lesson was there to be learned from that ultimately happy moment. This debate about the appropriate ratio of gin to vermouth is, in truth, actually a nondebate. The point isn't really for anyone to win—the point is a kind of insider's conversation. The argument is more of a bonding exercise among people who have learned to speak the same language. That language, like all languages, comprises signs whose meanings are generated from the play of differences with other signs in the same system. But for the martini that language is less the language of "cocktail culture" than it is the language of art—fine art—and cultural distinction. It claims its place in tradition by affirming its modernity, and it marks its modernity by lamenting the passing of tradition.

Colgate University

NOTES

1. Barbara Holland, *The Joy of Drinking* (New York: Bloomsbury, 2007), 81.
2. Holland, *The Joy of Drinking*, 81.
3. Bob Dylan and Jacques Levy, "Hurricane," from *Desire*, Columbia Records, 1976, CK 92393.
4. This phrase is widely quoted both by critics and by other artists, but my favorite discussion is Gary Giddens's; see *Weather Bird: Jazz at the Dawn of Its Second Century* (New York: Oxford University Press, 2004), 336.
5. Luis Buñuel, *My Last Sigh*, trans. Abigail Israel (Minneapolis: University of Minnesota Press, 2003), 44.
6. Alec Waugh, *In Praise of Wine and Certain Noble Spirits* (New York: William Sloane, 1959), 265.
7. Quoted in Joseph Blotner, *Faulkner: A Biography* (Jackson: University of Mississippi Press, 2005), 227.
8. Paul Johnson, *Creators: From Chaucer and Durer to Picasso and Disney* (New York: Harper, 2006), 216–17.
9. David Earle in an exchange of emails with the author, August 7–9, 2018. Earle is currently at work on a book about cocktail culture and history.
10. William Terrington, *Cooling Cups and Dainty Drinks* (London: George Routledge & Sons, 1869).

11. Louis Fouquet, *Bariana: Recueil Pratique de toutes Boissons Américaines et Anglaises* (Paris: Criterion, 1899).

12. Carl A. Seuter, *Der Mixologist* (Nordhausen: Heinrich Killinger Verlagsgesellschaft, 1909).

13. Quoted in Lowell Edmunds, *Martini, Straight Up*, rev. ed. (Baltimore: Johns Hopkins University Press, 1998), xix.

14. Harry Johnson, *Harry Johnson's New and Improved Bartenders' Manual* (New York: Harry Johnson, 1888), 38–39, retrieved from EUVS Vintage Cocktail Books, https://euvs-vintage-cocktail-books.cld.bz/1888-Harry-Johnson-s-new-and-improved-bartender-s-manual-1888/48/.

15. Robert Vermeire, *Cocktails: How to Mix Them* (London: Herbert Jenkins, 1922), 24, 30, 36–37.

16. David Earle in an exchange of emails with the author, August 7–9, 2018.

17. Holland, *The Joy of Drinking*, 82.

18. David Wondrich, *Imbibe!* (New York: Perigee, 2007).

19. Lowell Edmunds, *Martini, Straight Up*, rev ed. (Baltimore: Johns Hopkins University Press), 1998.

20. Edmunds, *Martini, Straight Up*, 106–7.

21. Edmunds, *Martini, Straight Up*, 107.

22. Quoted in Barnaby Conrad III, *The Martini* (San Francisco: Chronicle Books, 1995), 88. Morgan's eulogy was first published in 1978. See also Edmunds, *Martini, Straight Up*, 32.

23. Richard Barnett, *The Book of Gin* (New York: Grove, 2011), 142.

24. Wondrich, *Imbibe!*, 295.

25. Edmunds, *Martini, Straight Up*, xxvii.

26. *Gatsby Cocktails*, designed by Luis Peral-Aranda; recipe text by Ben Reed (London: Ryland Peters & Small, 2012), 7.

27. Barnett, *The Book of Gin*, 32. As I learned recently in Amsterdam, something close to this spirit is still available, marketed in the Netherlands at least as "oude genever."

28. Barnett, *The Book of Gin*, 26.

29. Barnett, *The Book of Gin*, 26.

30. Barnett, *The Book of Gin*, 25.

31. Samuel Johnson, *Dictionary: A Modern Selection*, ed. E. L. McAdam Jr. and George Milne (New York: Pantheon, 1964), 196, 194.

32. See Barnett, *The Book of Gin*, 1–25.

33. Quoted in Conrad, *The Martini*, 37.

34. Edmunds, *Martini, Straight Up*, xxiv.

35. Edmunds, *Martini, Straight Up*, 124.

36. See Bernard DeVoto, *The Hour: A Cocktail Manifesto* (Boston: Houghton Mifflin, 1951), 67–68.

37. "Why Are Martini Glasses Shaped Like That?" WiseGeek, accessed April 2, 2014, http://www.wisegeek.org/why-are-martini-glasses-shaped-like-that.htm.

38. Karen Locke, "Origin Stories behind 4 Classic Drink Glasses," *Sip Northwest* (Winter 2018), https://sipnorthwest.com/origin-stories-behind-4-classic-drink-glasses/.

39. Locke, "Origin Stories."

40. Andreas Huyssen, *After the Great Divide: Modernism, Mass Culture, Postmodernism* (Bloomington: Indiana University Press, 1987).

41. Lizzie Munro, "The Life and Death of the Martini Glass," *Punch Drink*, August 17 2016, https://punchdrink.com/articles/the-life-and-death-of-the-martini-glass-history/.

42. William Grimes, "Oh, for Just Plain Gin and Dry Vermouth." *New York Times*, August 19, 1998, http://www.nytimes.com/1998/08/19/dining/oh-for-just-plain-gin-and-dry-vermouth.html. There is an argument that the water that comes from ice-melt while shaking or stirring the cocktail is an essential third ingredient, without which the taste of the drink would be compromised by the burn of alcohol. Similarly, as the early twenty-first century fad for "dirty martinis" suggests, the brine on the olive, like the tang of a lemon twist, also constitutes—more than a garnish—an ingredient.

43. Stuart Connelly, quoted in "Stuart Connelly," Goodreads, https://www.goodreads.com/author/show/4421844.Stuart_Connelly.

44. "The Perfect Martini," *Drinkboy* (blog), August 5, 2001, http://www.drinkboy.com/Articles/Article.aspx?itemid=18.

45. Wondrich, *Imbibe!*, 168.

46. See, for instance, David Chinitz, *T. S. Eliot and the Cultural Divide* (Chicago: University of Chicago Press, 2003), or Michael Coyle, "Popular Culture," in *A Companion to Modernist Poetry*, ed. David Chinitz and Gail McDonald (Oxford: Wiley-Blackwell, 2014), 81–94.

47. Ernest Hemingway, *A Farewell to Arms* (New York: Scribner, 1929), 245.

48. Hemingway, *A Farewell to Arms*, 245.

49. Edmunds, *Martini, Straight Up*, 73.

50. Quoted in Philip Greene, *To Have and Have Another: A Hemingway Cocktail Companion* (New York: Perigee, 2012), 154.

51. Conrad, *The Martini*, 81.

52. Quoted in Edmunds, *Martini, Straight Up*, xix.

53. Quoted in T. S. Eliot, ed., *Literary Essays of Ezra Pound* (New York: New Directions, 1954), 12. This phrase comes from Pound's essay "Credo."

54. Quoted in Eliot, *Literary Essays of Ezra Pound*, 50.

55. Judith Brown, *Glamour in Six Dimensions: Modernism and the Radiance of Form* (Ithaca, NY: Cornell University Press, 2009), 145–70.

56. Quoted in James J. Wilhelm, *Ezra Pound: The Tragic Years, 1925–1972* (University Park: Pennsylvania State University Press, 1994), 133.
57. Edmunds, *Martini, Straight Up*, 42.
58. Conrad, *The Martini*, 55.
59. DeVoto, *The Hour*, 67–68.
60. This oft-repeated story is recounted most humorously on the "Cats" Musical Wiki: https://catsmusical.fandom.com/wiki/T_S_Eliot (accessed February 14, 2020).

BIBLIOGRAPHY

Barnett, Richard. *The Book of Gin*. New York: Grove, 2011.

Blotner, Joseph. *Faulkner: A Biography*. Jackson: University of Mississippi Press, 2005.

Brown, Judith. *Glamour in Six Dimensions: Modernism and the Radiance of Form*. Ithaca, NY: Cornell University Press, 2009.

Buñuel, Luis. *My Last Sigh*. Translated by Abigail Israel. Minneapolis: University of Minnesota Press, 2003.

"Cats" Musical Wiki. Accessed February 14, 2020. https://catsmusical.fandom.com/wiki/T_S_Eliot.

Chinitz, David. *T. S. Eliot and the Cultural Divide*. Chicago: University of Chicago Press, 2003.

Conrad, Barnaby, III. *The Martini*. San Francisco: Chronicle Books, 1995.

Coyle, Michael. "Popular Culture." In *A Companion to Modernist Poetry*. Edited by David Chinitz and Gail McDonald. Oxford: Wiley-Blackwell, 2014.

DeVoto, Bernard. *The Hour: A Cocktail Manifesto*. Boston: Houghton Mifflin, 1951.

Dylan, Bob, and Jacques Levy. "Hurricane." *Desire*. Columbia Records, 1976, CK 92393.

Earle, David. Email exchange with the author. August 7–9, 2018.

Edmunds, Lowell. *Martini, Straight Up*. Rev. ed. Baltimore: Johns Hopkins University Press, 1998.

Eliot, T. S., ed. *Literary Essays of Ezra Pound*. New York: New Directions, 1954.

Fouquet, Louis. *Bariana: Recueil Pratique de toutes Boissons Américaines et Anglaises*. Paris: Criterion, 1899.

Giddens, Gary. *Weather Bird: Jazz at the Dawn of Its Second Century*. New York: Oxford University Press, 2004.

Greene, Philip. *To Have and Have Another: A Hemingway Cocktail Companion*. New York: Perigee, 2012.

Grimes, William. "Oh, for Just Plain Gin and Dry Vermouth." *New York Times*. August 19, 1998. http://www.nytimes.com/1998/08/19/dining/oh-for-just-plain-gin-and-dry-vermouth.html.

Hemingway, Ernest. *A Farewell to Arms*. New York: Scribner, 1929.
Holland, Barbara. *The Joy of Drinking*. New York: Bloomsbury, 2007.
Huyssen, Andreas. *After the Great Divide: Modernism, Mass Culture, Postmodernism*. Bloomington: Indiana University Press, 1987.
Johnson, Harry. *Harry Johnson's New and Improved Bartenders' Manual*. New York: Harry Johnson, 1888.
Johnson, Paul. *Creators: From Chaucer and Durer to Picasso and Disney*. New York: Harper, 2006.
Johnson, Samuel. *Dictionary: A Modern Selection*. Edited by E. L. McAdam Jr. and George Milne. New York: Pantheon, 1964.
Locke, Karen. "Origin Stories behind 4 Classic Drink Glasses." *Sip Northwest* (Winter 2018). https://sipnorthwest.com/origin-stories-behind-4-classic-drink-glasses/.
Munro, Lizzie. "The Life and Death of the Martini Glass." *Punch Drink*. August 17 2016. https://punchdrink.com/articles/the-life-and-death-of-the-martini-glass-history/.
"The Perfect Martini." *Drinkboy* (blog). August 5, 2001. http://www.drinkboy.com/Articles/Article.aspx?itemid=18.
Reed, Ben. In *Gatsby Cocktails*. Designed by Luis Peral-Aranda. London: Ryland Peters & Small, 2012.
Seuter, Carl A. *Der Mixologist*. Nordhausen, Ger.: Heinrich Killinger Verlagsgesellschaft, 1909.
"Stuart Connelly." Goodreads. Accessed April 3, 2014. https://www.goodreads.com/author/show/4421844.Stuart_Connelly.
Terrington, William. *Cooling Cups and Dainty Drinks*. London: George Routledge & Sons, 1869.
Vermeire, Robert. *Cocktails: How to Mix Them*. London: Herbert Jenkins, 1922.
Waugh, Alec. *In Praise of Wine and Certain Noble Spirits*. New York: William Sloane, 1959.
"Why Are Martini Glasses Shaped Like That?" WiseGeek. Accessed April 2, 2014. http://www.wisegeek.org/why-are-martini-glasses-shaped-like-that.htm.
Wilhelm, James J. *Ezra Pound: The Tragic Years, 1925–1972*. University Park: Pennsylvania State University Press, 1994.
Wondrich, David. *Imbibe!* New York: Perigee, 2007.

SEVEN

AT HOME WITH POSTWAR COCKTAIL CULTURE AND THE COCKTAIL DRESS

LORI HALL-ARAUJO

COCKTAIL CULTURE IN THE POSTWAR United States thrived through the mid-1960s, and thanks to an expanded middle class, consumerism also increased. It was not enough to own a recently constructed home in a newly established suburban community. The new house needed to be filled with furniture and goods and people. All manner of household gadgets, often marketed to simplify domestic life, suddenly became available.

As home ownership and consumerism increased, certain at-home activities became more popular, including—much to the dismay of the motion picture industry—television watching. Despite the 1961 Federal Communications Commission (FCC) chair's admonitions that television programming was a "vast wasteland,"[1] a TV set in the living room became a material signifier of middle-class belonging. While TV viewing was an activity of dubious middle-class cultural value, the home cocktail party provided social aspirants and arrivistes with outlets for demonstrating the desired sophistication. Before World War II, only 30 percent of alcohol in the United States was drunk at home. In 1930s popular culture, cocktails such as the manhattan and the martini solidified their status as classic sophisticated drinks when consumed by William Powell and Myrna Loy in *The Thin Man* (1934),[2] the first in a film series produced into the 1940s. Powell and Loy's married detective characters, "Nick and Nora Charles," were forever drinking in elegant bars and luxurious hotel rooms. The fifth and final sequel starring the bantering, cosmopolitan couple was released in 1947, coinciding with a cultural shift from the city-dwelling to suburban at-home cocktail consumption. After World War II, 70 percent of all booze consumed was drunk at home.[3]

Figure 7.1. Bette Davis as Margo Channing in *All About Eve* (dir. Joseph Mankiewicz, 1950) wearing an Edith Head design. Margo is the consummate bad hostess in this scene, arriving to her own party late and drunk from multiple martinis.

Even the "vast wasteland" of commercial television found a way to highlight the home cocktail party's importance as postwar status signifier. *The Dick Van Dyke Show* (1961–1966),[4] one of the era's most popular programs, premiered the same year that FCC chair Newton Minow made his damning statement about TV as a wasteland. The first episode even included a home cocktail party at which Van Dyke's "Rob Petrie" does an impression of his wife's uncle coming home drunk from an office Christmas party.

Preparing and serving well-mixed drinks to friends, neighbors, and colleagues were means for performing the bourgeois lifestyle. This performance required the appropriate set, props, techniques, and costumes. Among the "props," a good deal of material culture—objects representing human interventions into their environment and products of their social lives—remains, such as distinctive barware associated with postwar cocktail parties. Another important cocktail-related example of material culture from the era is the cocktail dress. Seemingly innocuous and decorative, the cocktail dress is an exemplary by-product of increased wealth. Often taking the silhouette of an upside-down martini glass—"Bottoms up!"—and constructed from yards of expensive fabric, the postwar cocktail dress frequently signifies affluence and conformity. Yet no garment ever communicates only one message as has been suggested, and the cocktail dress could also serve as a vehicle for resisting stifling social norms.[5]

HOSTING A COCKTAIL PARTY

The home cocktail party did not begin with the end of the war. After the 1933 repeal of Prohibition, sophisticated Americans began hosting cocktail events. In 1937 the savvy future "Dean of American Cookery," James Beard, opened a shop and catering business, Hors d'Oeuvre, Inc., to satisfy the growing demand for cocktail party and buffet foods. Within three years, Beard published *Hors d'Oeuvre and Canapés* (1940), further satisfying growing interest in how best to host a cocktail party. Indeed, in the book's first chapter, entitled "The Key to the Cocktail Party," Beard prescribes drinks, food, and people as essential:

> The cocktail party no longer means a bottle of gin, a can of sardines, and a package of potato chips from the corner grocery. It has become a definite part of the entertainment schedule for every household, large and small. To the one-room apartment dweller, it is the solution for extending hospitality in the limits of his domain; and to the owner of the great house, it is the fat check for paying old social debts. It is an institution, and a gay one; one that brings forth the best, and sometimes the worst, in all of us.[6]

As the former proprietor of a 1930s New York specialty foods shop, Beard did not accurately describe Middle America when he proclaimed the cocktail party a "definite part of the entertainment schedule for every household."[7] Yet his words were prophetic of the postwar changes about to occur.[8] *Hors d'Oeuvre and Canapés* remained in print for decades as a source for how to feed the drinking people in one's home.

Postwar wealth and a desire for material comforts after a period of deprivation meant that production and consumption of household goods increased. Affordable barware, recipe books such as Beard's, and concentrated suburban communities where material wealth could be put on display were among the factors contributing to an atmosphere well primed for the home cocktail party.

An early postwar source for home entertaining is the 1949 *Esquire's Handbook for Hosts*. The editors of *Esquire* magazine provide illustrations and cartoons with recipes and tips instructing readers how to become "artful Ph.D.s (philosophers of drinkology)."[9] *Esquire*'s imagined readers are urbane, single, heterosexual men seeking guidance on how to assemble a home wet bar and host a cocktail party. Etiquette, games, and four pages of magic tricks round out the nuts and bolts essentials for making cocktails, aperitifs, after-dinner drinks, highballs, punches (hot and cold), eggnogs, "pick-me-ups," and "'tipples' for teetotalers." In "The Five O'Clock Whistle Whetters" section, the *Handbook* advises, "You'll stir up a hundred Martinis, Mahattans or Old-fashioneds" and will need "Something for the Girls" plus other party drinks.[10]

Esquire's Handbook for Hosts devotes considerably more pages to drink recipes and recommendations for the well-stocked bar than it does to advising the host on appropriate party attire. The 288-page book closes with two pages of advice on "What the Well-Dressed Host Will Wear." Given the number of pages dedicated to drink recipes and tools, the implication is that men's desirable cocktail party performance depends primarily upon ability and drink knowledge over appearance.

Among the tools a host needed to demonstrate cocktail competency was barware. Sold in a range of price points to increase access while stratifying consumer classes, such tools were clearly described in *Esquire's* chapter on "What the Well-Dressed Bar Will Wear." While *Esquire* recommends a good ice pick, inexpensive ice cube trays were new to the market and could be popped into electric refrigerators—a quick and efficient means for achieving the perfect ice cube essential to mixed drinks (fig. 7.2). Moreover, ice cubes freed the host to spend more time with his guests rather than chipping away at a block of ice with an ice pick.

Among the social functions the postwar home cocktail party served was to create opportunities for performing leisure and consumption of material goods. At the more modest end of the spectrum, the home bar's tools might live on a tray in the living room yet could grow into an entire home bar. In *Mr. Blandings Builds His Dream House* (1948), an H. C. Potter–directed comedy about a couple pouring cash into a fixer-upper Connecticut home, Mr. Blandings (Cary Grant) ruminates aloud that they might add a bar to one of the rooms.[11] Though such an idea was probably nothing more than a pipe dream for most homeowners in the late 1940s, by the early 1960s a home bar was not exceptional. From portable furniture to a built-in, the home bar was a postwar trend. The bar space became the set for the public/private stage upon which men performed ideal masculinity. Moreover, the home bar signaled skill in the valued postwar leisure activity of do-it-yourself. Whether a man was selecting booze and mixers to place on a tray or constructing a basement bar complete with stools and a hi-fi, such activities were means for demonstrating socially acceptable masculine domestic agency. A man who demonstrated undesirable domestic agency by, say, washing the dishes would be subject to ridicule (see fig. 7.3). Moreover, a seemingly superfluous skill, mixing drinks, could lubricate interpersonal relationships, especially sexual ones, as both *Esquire* and, later, *Playboy* magazine implied in articles on building a bar and mixing drinks.

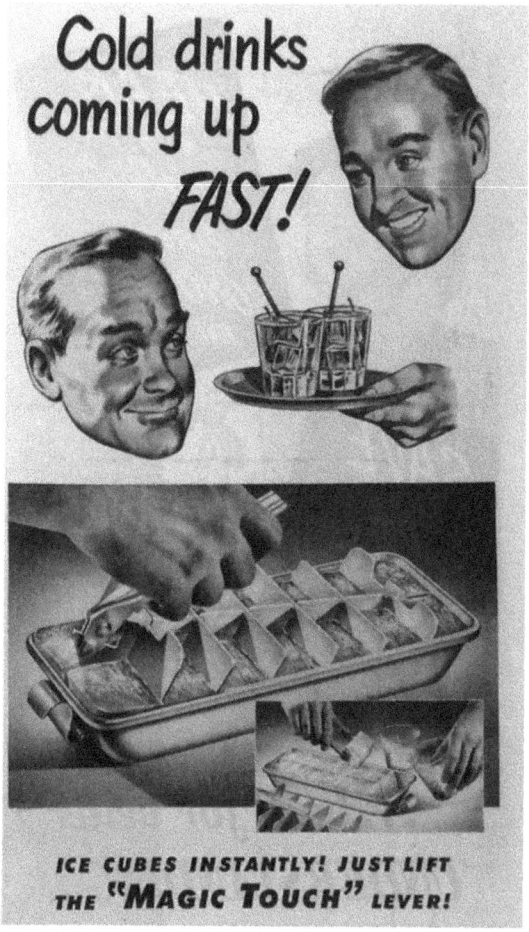

Figure 7.2. An advertisement for Magic Touch ice cube trays from the April 16, 1949, edition of the popular magazine *The Saturday Evening Post*.

GENDER PERFORMANCE AND DRESS

Personal appearance in a social context is always subject to evaluation. Frequently, dress signals gender, and gender in turn informs the nature of evaluation. Women and their postwar cocktail attire were more susceptible to close scrutiny than men were. A consideration of gendered dress, a process that begins in this country from the moment a child's sex is announced, is a good starting point for understanding why women's cocktail attire matters.

Figure 7.3. An illustrated story from the September 10, 1949, issue of *The Saturday Evening Post* subverts prescribed gender roles, with the husband performing domestic agency undesirable for a man. Husband wears wife's apron and washes the dishes while pink suit–clad wife looks on laughingly. In the facing illustration, she's in the driver's seat.

Adult caretakers dress infants to signal both a person's sex and culturally prescribed gender roles and expectations.[12] From the moment a child is swaddled in a blanket and booties, social expectations and interpretations for behavior are established, making what one wears a powerful means for communicating information about identity.

Gender-specific clothing is not unique to the twentieth-century United States. What changes from context to context is the kind of information that gets communicated about and between dressed people. The postwar gender binary for dress is distinctive in that it is bookended by two historical periods when gendered dress was less strictly enforced. During World War II, women wore military uniforms and other attire that in the past was more commonly associated with menswear, such as trousers (see fig. 7.4 for an example of a women's suit inspired by men's tailoring). For men, too, gendered dress was less stringent during wartime, albeit in a more carnivalesque sense. Military base entertainment frequently included cross-dressing that was rewarded with enthusiastic audience approval. The Hollywood star Carmen Miranda was purportedly most impersonated among military men.[13]

By the late 1960s, when cocktail parties were on the wane, gender ambiguity had creeped back into fashion. Women increasingly wore trousers, and men

Figure 7.4. This ensemble is typical of World War II styles, when fabric restrictions led to shorter, narrower skirts. Men's tailoring techniques were popular at the time, as evidenced in this suit from around 1945 and designed by Adrian. While the designer is best remembered for his work as a film costume designer for MGM's leading ladies, he also had his own boutique. Digital Image © 2019 Museum Associates / LACMA. Licensed by Art Resource, NY.

began to grow their hair long in styles previously associated with women's looks. Postwar dress for men and women, from 1947 to the mid-1960s, has the distinction of standing in stark contrast to the more gender-ambiguous fashions from the preceding and succeeding time periods.

Gendered attire often conflates biological sex and sexuality. Contexts for more ambiguous dress may reflect broader cultural ambiguities about, or challenges to, socially prescribed sex, gender, and sexuality roles. The women's and gay liberation movements of the late 1960s and 1970s coincided with a time when gender ambiguity in dress increased. The strict dress binary that existed in the postwar period reflects stringent mainstream cultural codes about sex, gender, and sexuality categories.[14]

For men in the postwar United States, dressing according to the gender binary required unostentatious clothing—a relatively recent phenomenon, since ready-to-wear, mass-produced, dark-colored suits for men did not emerge until the 1820s.[15] Men's postwar suits and sportswear tended toward uniformity and functionality. The popular gray flannel business suit, for example, signified hegemonic masculinity and the middle-class ideal of a heterosexual breadwinner for his family[16] (see fig. 7.5). By contrast, desirable dress for women was far more likely to communicate her marital status, the wealth of the man in her life, and the occasion. Bland uniformity in men's dress is one reason they were less subject to scrutiny for their cocktail party attire—the opportunities for significant missteps simply did not exist. Women's clothing, by contrast, was much more varied with regard to cut, color, fabrics, and accessories and had the power to convey multiple messages containing important social information. Several messages on a single person have the potential to communicate conflicting information or perhaps to be misunderstood. Furthermore, a smorgasbord of dress options can create an additional burden for anyone navigating social success or failure.

While the range of mainstream menswear options before the late 1960s was limited, women had many more options, among them the cocktail dress. Though the cocktail dress has strong associations with postwar culture, the garment had been in women's wardrobes since the 1920s. The simple twenties frock was unfettered by restrictive corsetry of yesteryear and was an expression of youth and abandon—an ideal garment for occasions gathering people in homes and speakeasies to drink bootleg booze. Just as one may eat pancakes for dinner, one may drink at any time of the day. Yet the cocktail hour is nonetheless understood to take place at about 5 o'clock in the afternoon, as the workday ends and in the hours before dinner.[17] The cocktail dress signals this in-between moment.

Figure 7.5. A suit advertisement from the April 8, 1950, issue of *The Saturday Evening Post* conveys the message that a young man in the right "all-purpose" clothes can achieve socially acceptable professional and personal success. In the correct homogenizing suit, "Mr. Pacific" is the object of positive attention: "The boss has an eye on him . . . and so have all the secretaries!"

TESTING BOUNDARIES IN THE LIMINAL COCKTAIL HOUR

An in-between moment, the cocktail hour is characterized by its liminality—on the threshold between the mundane routines of work and dinner (followed by sleep). As such, the cocktail event encourages a temporary upending of norms. Given the postwar era's emphasis on social conformity,[18] an event that tests the limits of conformity is an intriguing point of investigation that can provide information about broader social concerns. Rigid social norms exacerbate the need for release, which the postwar cocktail party can provide. Yet more than simply a socially acceptable form of release, the cocktail party is an opportunity for challenging normativity. Evidence of challenges and resistance to conformist culture can be found in the era's films and popular fiction.

Postwar popular culture critiqued strict social standards, efforts to keep up appearances, and materialism. Grace Metalious's bestselling novel *Peyton Place* (1956), for example, is set in a seemingly idyllic town where its residents keep dark secrets of incest, abortion, and adultery, to name a few themes.[19] The book's popularity suggests that people relished reading about naughty social transgressions. Eventually the commercially successful book was adapted as a film, in 1957, and later as a television series (ABC, 1964–1969), both popular.[20]

All That Heaven Allows (1955),[21] another film of the era, starred Rock Hudson and criticized suffocating social norms related to class, gender, and age. The film centers on a romance between two people divided by age and class. Significantly, she is the upper-class, wealthy, and older lover while he is her handsome, younger gardener. The plot, then as now, defies the typical Hollywood trope of affluent older men with beautiful younger women. In this unusual film, cocktail parties are social spaces for publicly testing or resisting conformity.

In one cocktail party scene, costume designer Bill Thomas dresses the widow "Cary" (Jane Wyman) in a classic 1950s red cocktail dress with a fitted bodice, bared shoulders, and a full skirt (fig. 7.6). Cary enters a conversation with the town gossip, who comments to the widow, "It's indecent to have two grown children and look as young as you do, isn't it? 'course there's nothing like red for attracting attention, is there? I suppose that's why so few widows wear it." The gossip's backhanded compliment is simultaneously an admonishment to correct Cary for her perceived inappropriate nonconformist appearance and behavior. The message: Widowed women with grown children should not be physically desirable and youthful-looking. Presumably the town gossip would have preferred to see the middle-aged widow Cary in a less revealing, darker-colored dress.

Figure 7.6. A scene from *All That Heaven Allows* (dir. Douglas Sirk, 1955) depicts the widow Cary enjoying a bracing martini at home before going to the party. Costume designer Bill Thomas dresses actress Jane Wyman in eye-catching red. Thomas's design for Gloria Talbott as Cary's bookish daughter is schoolmarmish by comparison.

Peg Fenwick's screenplay for *All That Heaven Allows* critiques the era's ideals and the resulting restricting environment. Why, indeed, must a youthful woman be dour because her husband has died? The film's cocktail parties create opportunities for indirectly asking this sort of question. A liminal event such as a cocktail party allows one to challenge social boundaries while participating in normative practices. The costume designer dresses Cary in a color associated with youthful pulchritude and even raciness. In so doing, the designer makes a visual contribution to the film's storyline about a woman resisting social expectations even before the town gossip takes Cary to task for her appearance. Although Cary's escort that evening is not the gardener but a respectable, older widowed man, her appearance signals defiance.

In a second cocktail party scene, Cary's social transgressions are showcased differently. For this party, designer Bill Thomas attires her in a more matronly, understated, plain black dress befitting her social rank. Yet the film scandalously accessorizes Cary with Ron Kirby (Rock Hudson), her gardener and younger lover. The means for testing social limitations has shifted from dress at the first party to public interpersonal performance at the second. Cary boldly arrives with her "unsuitable" lover, blatantly defying bourgeois norms. Though the cocktail party creates a relatively safe space for testing the limits of acceptable behavior, her attendance suggests she does not want to be a complete social outcast. Thomas's costume reflects a keen understanding of the need for Cary to appear mostly in conformance with suburban norms despite her escort.

The cocktail hour's liminality creates a space for social exploration, which is particularly useful in the context of a restrictive culture. Though the cocktail hour remains a means for measuring normative social success or failure—as the town gossip's comments to Cary so beautifully illustrate—it also provides opportunities for testing social boundaries. In both of the film's cocktail party scenes, Cary flouts the rules, first by dressing too youthfully, and next by challenging middle-class snobbery with her working-class date. Nowhere else in the film does she so boldly test bourgeois conformity. The relative permissiveness at cocktail parties creates opportunities for safely challenging the status quo both onscreen and off-screen.

Postwar cocktail parties in *All That Heaven Allows* and in real life could be social land mines. They could also be liberating occasions where drunkenness and transgressive behavior are more excusable than they would be in other contexts. At least one drunk at the party seems to have been expected during the era. Both *Amy Vanderbilt's Complete Book of Etiquette* (1952) and *Esquire's Handbook for Hosts* offer helpful suggestions for what to do about the drunken guest. Says Vanderbilt:

> The most agreeable solution, naturally, would be to omit from our guest list anyone who is a problem drinker. But, as this is rarely possible for business or family reasons, the only thing we can do, as hosts and hostesses, is to keep a sharp eye on the source of supply, keep track of each round, and lock up all alcohol, including wine and beer, after a reasonable amount has been dispensed."[22]

THE COCKTAIL DRESS

Barware, liquor bottles, and martini glasses are clear signifiers of the cocktail party. The upside-down martini glass shape that many of the era's cocktail dresses have is also important for signaling the occasion. Cocktail parties and other liminal events are frequently signaled through occasion-specific dress. Holidays associated with drinking and distinctive dress include the Jewish festival of Purim, Catholic carnival, and Halloween. While these examples mandate a costume—which we typically associate with disguise—a cocktail party nonetheless prescribes special women's attire to mark the occasion.

A postwar woman's cocktail dress is neither daytime attire nor eveningwear. In the 1950s, the cocktail dress was distinguished from day dresses and eveningwear both by the type of fabric used in construction and by the dress's

Figures 7.7 and 7.8. Two Irving Penn photographs in the March 15, 1947, issue of *Vogue* showcase the new dress silhouettes that would prevail in women's fashion throughout the 1950s and into the 1960s. Irving Penn/Vogue © Conde Nast.

length. Cocktail dress length (at the calf) and cut were often comparable to daytime styles, though the material was rather different in that it tended to be more luxurious.[23] Evening gowns, by contrast, might be made from the same specialty fabrics as used in cocktail dresses, but were typically floor length. A woman in a cocktail dress need not utter a word in order for her appearance to signal the occasion.

While the cocktail dress has been a part of our clothing lexicon since the 1920s, the garment had its heyday between the late 1940s and the mid-1960s, coinciding with an uptick in home entertaining.[24] The postwar cocktail dress typically followed the lines for one of two basic silhouettes associated with the period: the fitted sheath or the cinched waist with full skirt (figs 7.7 and 7.8). A variety of textiles and embellishments created myriad possibilities for interpreting the look, which first began with the appropriate "foundations."

FOUNDATIONS

Fashion historians note that one of the most dramatic fashion changes to occur in the Western world was the shift from World War II–era women's boxy attire to the so-called New Look, popularized by the French couturier Christian Dior (1905–1957). In 1947, only months after establishing his own couture house, Dior introduced his first collection. Christian Dior's 1947 Paris designs rejected fabric-rationing styles of the war years and the associated looks inspired by menswear. Instead, the couturier used yards and yards of luxurious fabrics for his designs and reimagined women's silhouettes to harken back to the nineteenth century when corsets, boned bodices, padding, and petticoats were deployed to create the desired hourglass shape. Dior's skirts were considerably longer and fuller than had been seen in years, the waist was now nipped in, and the breasts pushed up. No longer were the shoulders broadened with padding; instead, they were sloped and narrow to emphasize smallness.

When compared with the previous shorter, narrower styles, which met government-mandated fabric restrictions by doing away with excess, Dior's designs may have seemed decadently profligate. Indeed, many women initially rejected the New Look with its long skirts and return to undergarments not worn since the days when grandmother was young. In the beginning, women protested Dior's designs and the styles were mocked in the press (see figs 7.10 and 7.11). Yet fashion tends to change in opposition to whatever was the preceding prevailing norm and eventually his 1947 silhouettes came to dominate fashion trends for nearly two decades.

Among the women's fashions to emerge during the postwar period was one that alluded to pregnancy by placing focus on the abdomen, as seen in Yves St. Laurent's 1953 "trapeze line." Dress scholars speculate that the postwar silhouettes seemed to remind women of their responsibilities to bear and nurture children and to return to so-called traditional womanly duties after being in the wartime workforce.[25]

In order to conform to postwar fashions, the undergarments women used were more constricting than anything women had worn since before 1920. Referred to as foundation garments, the different underwear reoriented and confined the flesh. The merry widow, for example, was an all-in-one undergarment. Boned and elasticized, it had a brassiere that lifted the breasts up and separated them, while it cinched the waist and flattened the buttocks.

Other undergarments included the "bullet bra," which separated the breasts and transformed them into conical shapes. Girdles or "panty girdles" were another popular foundation garment. They helped flatten the stomach and

Figure 7.9. Hoop packaging (1950s). When a woman wore a cocktail dress—"ballerina length"—or other skirt resembling an upside-down martini, she probably also wore petticoats or even a hoop, yet another postwar nod to nineteenth-century dress styles. Courtesy of the FIDM Museum at the Fashion Institute of Design & Merchandising, Los Angeles, CA.

cinch the waist while extending down past the hips to flatten the buttocks and prevent any unseemly jiggling (see fig. 7.12). In one memorable scene from the 1959 film *Anatomy of a Murder*, the lawyer Paul Biegler (James Stewart) admonishes Laura Manion (Lee Remick) for not wearing a girdle.[26] Biegler is concerned that people in the small town will be unsympathetic to her claim of rape if she appears too "loose." The social importance of women constraining their bodies in order to be deemed appropriately feminine was not merely a

Figure 7.10. Not everyone embraced the postwar "New Look," which required a cinched waist and a return to longer dresses. The protester here does not realize she has come face to face with the French couturier, Christian Dior, whom she holds responsible for the more-cumbersome designs. *Chicago Tribune*, September 23, 1947.

Figure 7.11. An editorial cartoon from the March 27, 1948, edition of *The Saturday Evening Post* reflects early ambivalent attitudes to Dior's New Look.

Figure 7.12. Panty girdle package (1950s). The slogan "next to nothing... next to you," paired with a woman's girdled silhouette against an oversize feather, suggests that the garment is lightweight and comfortable, unusual qualities in a girdle. Courtesy of the FIDM Museum at the Fashion Institute of Design & Merchandising, Los Angeles, CA.

thing of fiction. In 1959, the same year *Anatomy of a Murder* was released, fashion designer Anne Fogarty published the self-help book *Wife-Dressing*, in which she advises readers to wear constraining clothes, especially after five o'clock: "You're not meant to suffer," but the sensation "should be one of *constraint* rather than comfort."[27]

THE COCKTAIL DRESS CONFORMS AND RESISTS

Cocktail dresses could come in a range of fabrics, though certain normative expectations prevailed, including that they be worn with foundation garments. Perhaps the most normative advice one could seek at the time was from the moneyed WASP queen, Amy Vanderbilt. In her 1952 book on etiquette, *Amy Vanderbilt's Complete Book of Etiquette*—covering topics from entertaining to child-raising—"Dress and Manners" is the second section. In dictating norms for women's evening clothes, Vanderbilt does not use the term *cocktail dress* per se. Rather, she advises on suitable evening attire that should not to be worn before 6:00 p.m. For those who might need to be out in public "from four-thirty on," she suggests satin dinner suits that are "very convenient for cocktail parties that lengthen out into dinner and the theater."[28] Color, cut, and fabric choice are significant factors in what makes a woman's attire appropriate for cocktails. And, as depicted in *All That Heaven Allows*, one's station in life should dictate such choices. For the postwar cocktail hour, satin was a reliable signifier of the occasion.[29]

Although the postwar period is characterized by relative affluence, not everyone had Amy Vanderbilt's economic means and so a satin dinner suit might be beyond the budget. Yet the performance of middle-class wealth was nonetheless an important ingredient for the cocktail party. The do-it-yourself trend that provided men with productive leisure activities extended to women's hobbies as well, allowing women to participate in bourgeois self-presentation. Just as a man could demonstrate valuable domestic agency and abundant leisure time by building a home bar or mixing a drink, women could express their superfluous domestic skills and industrious use of free time through home sewing. While the actual process of sewing remained unobserved, the home seamstress could perform desirable wealth by wearing her creation.

Although home sewing is chiefly a solitary act and not immediately subject to performance assessment, its results are nonetheless gauged by others. Performance gaps between acts of sewing and acts of wearing create possibilities for seeming duplicitous in ways that building a home bar and mixing drinks do not. Moreover, the social stakes are much higher for women's dress than they are for mixing a drink. Drink mixing is a skill that can reflect well on a man but does not determine his status or identity to the degree that women's dress determines hers. Further, a man can perform bourgeois good taste by pouring an expensive scotch over ice without ever mixing a single manhattan or martini.

In the postwar United States, options for accruing greater cultural capital for oneself were more limited for women than they were for men. Attending Yale University, for example, was closed off to women until 1969. But one way a woman could be an agent for improving her social standing while conforming to gender norms was via her appearance. Thus, a woman might be inclined to take advantage of the performance gap between sewing and wearing. One might ask a sister to make a dress and then take credit for its construction—signaling skill—or even claim that the garment was bought at a specialty boutique, signaling wealth. Yet if one appeared to be wealthier than one was in reality, there was the risk of having one's machinations exposed. In our culture, gendered dress signaling femininity is already beleaguered with the mantle of deception—for example, padded bras that "lie" about a woman's "true" breast size. Home sewing, then, as a gendered activity carried the weight of dissimulation ascribed to women's dress generally.[30]

Yet ultimately, home sewing created more opportunities for personal expression and agency than it presented pitfalls. This was especially true for women of color, who, though they may have belonged to the middle class financially, would not have had the same access to shops as their white counterparts. Resourcefulness and skill in garment construction could provide them with the means to dress themselves according to a desired bourgeois aesthetic (see fig. 7.13).

CONCLUSION

The postwar home cocktail party allowed people to perform and to be assessed for social conformity while creating a space for testing rules of decorum. Conformity included adhering to strict gender roles and demonstrating excess wealth by displaying material goods. For a man, being able to assemble a bar and mix drinks showed that he was knowledgeable and skilled, and that he had the leisure time to practice his hobbies. Regardless of his sexuality or marital status, such pursuits nonetheless demonstrated desirable postwar masculinity. Yet even if he were trying to impress his boss in the context of a cocktail party, a man was unlikely to be assessed solely for his ability to mix drinks. Nonetheless, the cocktail party was not without its hazards, and excessive drunkenness could cost a man a promotion.

Figure 7.13. An advertisement for home sewing patterns from the November 1959 issue of *Ebony*, a magazine targeting an African American audience. The text explains that a resourceful woman can make "stay at home outfits" for the children and a cocktail dress for herself so that she looks "as if money were no object."

In contrast to a man's actions in the context of the cocktail party, a woman's cocktail dress had implications for the wearer and the men in her life. The dress's degree of opulence was a conspicuous gauge for measuring her father's or her husband's (dead or alive) wealth. The dress signified one's taste and whether one understood dress decorum befitting the occasion. These were important social norms to grasp, especially for those who were newly entering the middle class. Despite the continued presence of women in the postwar workforce, desirable femininity in the popular imagination meant that a woman was freed from the need to work, a position made possible by association with a "good provider."

For men, being a good provider signified normative masculinity. Having a well-dressed, financially dependent woman in one's life was one measure of a man's social performance. Her appearance was important because it reflected his earned status as well as their respective social positions. Home sewing provided opportunities for creativity and skills development. Nevertheless, a woman's ability to construct a beautiful cocktail dress was a behind-the-scenes activity supporting the public performance of middle-class respectability.

While the cocktail party allowed people to showcase social conformity through display of wealth and leisure time, its liminal qualities also afforded opportunities for testing social boundaries. Drinking too much meant that the partygoer might "annoy the rest of the party."[31] Afterward, though, the reveler could always plead drunkenness in order to evade responsibility for behaving badly. Even if the partygoer didn't get drunk, a cocktail party was an opportunity to dress too youthfully or to come out as dating one's gardener. All fine excuses for social drinking in a restrictive era.

Stephens College

NOTES

1. Newton Minow, "Television and the Public Interest" (address, National Association of Broadcasters, Washington, DC, May 9, 1961).

2. W. S. Van Dyke, dir., *The Thin Man* (Los Angeles: Metro-Goldwyn-Mayer, 1934).

3. Kristina Wilson, "'The Happiest Party in Town': Cocktail Accessories and American Culture, 1945–1965," in *Cocktail Culture: Ritual and Invention in American Fashion, 1920–1980*, ed. Joanne Dolan Ingersoll (Providence: Museum of Art, Rhode Island School of Design, 2011), 74.

4. *The Dick Van Dyke Show*, created by Carl Reiner, aired 1961–1966, on CBS.

5. See, especially, Roland Barthes, *The Language of Fashion* (London: Bloomsbury, 2006 [1993]).

6. James Beard, *Hors d'Oeuvres and Canapés* (New York: Quill, 1985 [1940]), 1–2.

7. Beard, *Hors d'Oeuvres*, 1–2.

8. Beard even anticipated the future popularity of television: From 1946 to 1947 he hosted the live TV cooking show *I Love to Eat*.

9. *Esquire's Handbook for Hosts* (New York: Black Dog & Leventhal Publishers, 1977 [1949]), 100.

10. *Esquire's Handbook*, 111–34.

11. H. C. Potter, dir., *Mr. Blandings Builds His Dreamhouse* (Los Angeles: RKO Radio Pictures, 1948).

12. Joanne B. Eicher and Mary Ellen Roach-Higgins, "Definition and Classification of Dress: Implications for Analysis of Gender Role," in *Dress and Gender: Making and Meaning*, ed. Ruth Barnes and Joanne B. Eicher (New York: Berg Publications, 1992), 19.

13. Allan Bérubé, *Coming Out Under Fire: The History of Gay Men and Women in World War Two* (New York: Free Press, 1990).

14. Widespread postwar police raids of gay clubs, especially those with drag shows, have been well documented. The 1969 New York police raid of the Stonewall Inn, where drag queens and transgender women fought back, helped to fan the flames of the gay liberation movement.

15. Anne Hollander, *Sex and Suits* (New York: Kodansha International, 1994), 106.

16. Ruth P. Rubinstein, *Dress Codes: Meaning and Messages in American Culture*, 2nd ed. (Boulder, CO: Westview Press, 2001), 164.

17. The smartphone application "5 o'clock" allows users to legitimate drinking outside of the socially acceptable cocktail hour by deploying the application to locate where on the planet it is currently 5 o'clock—a clever means for subverting puritanical attitudes about drinking while still adhering to the letter of the social law.

18. Wilson, "The Happiest Party in Town," 73.

19. Grace Metalious, *Peyton Place* (New York: Simon & Schuster, 1956).

20. Mark Robson, dir., *Peyton Place* (Los Angeles: Twentieth Century Fox, 1957); *Peyton Place*, produced by Paul Monash, aired 1964–1969, on ABC.

21. Douglas Sirk, dir., *All that Heaven Allows* (London: Universal International Pictures, 1955).

22. Amy Vanderbilt, *Amy Vanderbilt's Complete Book of Etiquette: A Guide to Gracious Living* (Garden City, NY: Doubleday, 1952), 305.

23. Joanne Dolan Ingersoll, "All the Right Ingredients: How Americans Dressed for Cocktails," in *Cocktail Culture: Ritual and Invention in American Fashion, 1920–1980*, ed. Joanne Dolan Ingersoll (Providence: Museum of Art, Rhode Island School of Design, 2011), 52–53.

24. Ingersoll, "All the Right Ingredients," 51. Ingersoll suggests that another factor contributing to the cocktail dress's popularity had to do with ready-to-wear industry sizing standardization in the 1950s, making it easier to buy well-made clothes off the rack.

25. Rubinstein, *Dress Codes*, 114.

26. Otto Preminger, dir. *Anatomy of a Murder* (Los Angeles: Columbia Pictures, 1959).

27. A. Fogarty, quoted in Valerie Steele, *The Corset: A Cultural History* (New Haven, CT, and London: Yale University Press, 2001), 161.

28. Vanderbilt, *Amy Vanderbilt's Complete Book of Etiquette*, 196.

29. A strictly semiotic approach to dress, such as Barthes takes in *The Language of Fashion*, asserts that "satin signifies five o'clock" (47). While it is certainly true that this meaning for satin may have been less flexible in the postwar era, even then satin could be recontextualized with a different meaning. For example, an elegant prostitute may have worn a satin cocktail dress well before five o'clock to signify her readiness to participate in a liminal experience outside of the normative social boundaries.

30. The act of sewing is by no means restricted to women, yet it really becomes acceptable for men only when it is a commercial endeavor rather than a hobby. *Haute couture*, a field whose design leaders are mostly men, is associated with creative "genius" that naturalizes and authenticates women's wear. Christian Dior's "New Look," for example, was portrayed as restoring women's femininity after the 1940s when fashions were inspired by military uniforms and men's tailoring.

31. *Esquire's Handbook*, 186.

BIBLIOGRAPHY

Barthes, Roland. *The Language of Fashion*. London: Bloomsbury, 2006.
Beard, James. *Hors d'Oeuvres and Canapés*. New York: Quill, 1985 [1940].
Bérubé, Allan. *Coming Out Under Fire: The History of Gay Men and Women in World War Two*. New York: Free Press, 1990.
The Dick Van Dyke Show. Created by Carl Reiner. Aired 1961–1966, on CBS.
Eicher, Joanne B., and Mary Ellen Roach-Higgins. "Definition and Classification of Dress: Implications for Analysis of Gender Role." In *Dress and Gender: Making and Meaning*, edited by Ruth Barnes and Joanne B. Eicher, 8–28. New York: Berg Publications, 1992.
Esquire's Handbook for Hosts. New York: Black Dog & Leventhal Publishers, 1977 [1949].
Hollander, Anne. *Sex and Suits*. New York: Kodansha International, 1994.
Ingersoll, Joanne Dolan. "All the Right Ingredients: How Americans Dressed for Cocktails." In *Cocktail Culture: Ritual and Invention in American Fashion, 1920–1980*, edited by Joanne Dolan Ingersoll, 45–60. Providence: Museum of Art, Rhode Island School of Design, 2011.
Metalious, Grace. *Peyton Place*. New York: Simon & Schuster, 1956.
Minow, Newton. "Television and the Public Interest." Address to the National Association of Broadcasters, Washington, DC, May 9, 1961.
Peyton Place. Produced by Paul Monash. Aired 1964–1969, on ABC.
Potter, H. C., dir. *Mr. Blandings Builds His Dreamhouse*. Los Angeles: RKO Radio Pictures, 1948.
Preminger, Otto, dir. *Anatomy of a Murder*. Los Angeles: Columbia Pictures, 1959.
Robson, Mark, dir. *Peyton Place*. Los Angeles: Twentieth Century Fox, 1957.

Rubinstein, Ruth P. *Dress Codes: Meaning and Messages in American Culture*. 2nd ed. Boulder, CO: Westview Press, 2001.

Sirk, Douglas, dir. *All that Heaven Allows*. London: Universal International Pictures, 1955.

Steele, Valerie. *The Corset: A Cultural History*. New Haven, CT: Yale University Press, 2001.

Van Dyke, W. S., dir. *The Thin Man*. Los Angeles: Metro-Goldwyn-Mayer, 1934.

Vanderbilt, Amy. *Amy Vanderbilt's Complete Book of Etiquette: A Guide to Gracious Living*. Garden City, NY: Doubleday, 1952.

Wilson, Kristina. "'The Happiest Party in Town': Cocktail Accessories and American Culture, 1945–1965." In *Cocktail Culture: Ritual and Invention in American Fashion, 1920–1980*, edited by Joanne Dolan Ingersoll, 75–87. Providence: Museum of Art, Rhode Island School of Design, 2011.

EIGHT

MIDDLEBROW COSMOPOLITANISM AND THE CANADIAN COCKTAIL

LISA SUMNER

WHILE GLOBALIZATION STUDIES OF THE last two and a half decades have seen a wave of scholarly research into the circulation of cultural artifacts abroad, consumption of culturally other goods in Western and industrialized cultures has been relatively slim. The tropical or foreign cocktail and varied bar have been no exception to this trend. When considered at all, its popularity evokes a William Whyte–style organization man, a dilettantish dabbler in the exotic. The mid-century preference for international brands exacerbates this tension, robbing the pastime as it does of contemporary measures of connoisseurship—such as obscurity and artisanal and ethical production—things we nowadays take as shorthand for informed and even redemptive consumerism.

My hope here is to complicate our assumptions about the allure of the foreign drink by examining its promotion and consumption in a time and place that was Western, industrial, *and* postcolonial: Canada in the 1950s and 1960s. Informed by Laura Moss's writing (who borrows her definition from Ashcroft, Griffiths, and Tiffin in *The Empire Writes Back*), *postcolonialism* is understood as temporally beginning with the moment of colonial contact and conceptually involving a reckoning with, and ongoing reconstruction of, cultural meanings and identities.[1] Nathaniel O'Reilly has demonstrated how the settler colonies of Canada, Australia, and New Zealand have been underexamined in, if not at times outright excluded from, scholarly attention in postcolonial studies. Settler colonies clearly have not endured the same inequity and abuse as those that were colonized, but to exclude the experience of settler culture risks a limiting exoticism that conceals the full gamut of the postcolonial world, as O'Reilly and others have shown. Ashcroft, Griffiths and Tiffin's seminal text, *The Empire Writes Back*, offers a broad definition of *postcolonial* that covers "all the culture affected by the imperial process from the moment of colonization to the present day."[2] By examining the drinking practices of the settler culture of Canada at a time when the nation was struggling to redefine itself and shed its marginal status as a backwoods colony shines a light on a postcolonial experience that can help us avoid rather than reinforce "an erasure of colonial difference and complexity."[3] Graham Huggan makes a clear distinction between postcolonialism as a critique of power that acts as a kind of resistant practice, on the one hand, and postcoloniality, which is understood as being tied up in exoticism and commodification.[4] I argue here that shifting Canadian consumer tastes resonated with postcoloniality in ways that were clearly commercial and that exoticized being bound up after all in the multinational liquor industry. Nonetheless, Canadian cocktail culture allowed for experimentation and play with cultural difference that complimented the groundbreaking policy changes that moved the country away from the overt privileging of British hegemony, widening the door for more pointed interrogations of Canadian history and identity in the coming years. Greater variety in the alcohol culture and the drink culture of much of the country—away from primarily rye whiskey and beer—reflected the 1950s internationalism and a decentering of British culture. In Canada this would be followed by liberalized immigration in the 1960s and an official policy of multiculturalism by the start of the 1970s. While admittedly not a form of radical postcolonial critique, these changing drinking practices did allow Canadian drinkers to subtly explore difference and to challenge the centrality of Britishness that had previously characterized government nation-building efforts.

I focus on the diversification of the product line and advertising of the Seagram Company. The expanding preference for vodka, rum, and gin in the changing cocktail culture that favored fruity concoctions and martinis encouraged Seagram to branch out in the domestic market, at the same time branding their signature Canadian whisky as an internationally recognized export.[5] Consumer desire for foreign-seeming drinks is interpreted as a form of middlebrow cosmopolitanism that took on particular salience in a country that, beginning in the early 1960s, underwent rapid immigration reforms that by 1971 would give way to a pioneering multiculturalism. As status-conscious Jewish immigrants who had emigrated from Eastern Europe, the Bronfman family, who owned Seagram, shared such a liberal vision and promoted it vigorously not only in Seagram's advertising but also politically and philanthropically. I suggest that the appeal of the foreign drink lay not in exoticism alone but rather in a Canadian identification with difference, one that tapped into larger currents of aspiration, national questioning, and experimentation that were underway in a hitherto marginalized country still emerging from the shadows of empire.

CULTURAL DIPLOMACY AND MIDCENTURY MIDDLEBROW ENTERTAINING

"Toast your hosts in every language," invited *Canadian Hospitality* magazine. Readers were encouraged to "air your knowledge" by toasting their guests in Finnish to Chinese, in Bohemian to Indonesian. Hosts could "pick the country of your fancy, then stage a 'Holiday in (say) Italy' party, complete with drinks, decorations, foods and music to match."[6] The home entertaining guide was created for the magazine by Calvert, then owned, like so many liquor brands, by Seagram. While the list of "every language" totaled only twenty, the naïve cultural mishmash of the foreign and the unusual signaled a playful, if not unproblematic, reaching-out. A hostess's worldliness, welcome, and international goodwill was demonstrated to her guests by her raising a shot of vodka and toasting, "Za Vashe Sdorovye!"[7] (See fig. 8.1.)

UN- and nationality-themed evenings, and the drinks on offer, could set the stage for a celebration of cultural difference and informal cultural diplomacy. Cross-cultural contact fostered by World War I and World War II brought distant customs and tastes within reach. Servicemen, for example, returned home and opened Polynesian-themed bars, while Norwegian Thor Heyerdahl's voyage across the Pacific on the Kon-Tiki raft proved an international bestseller, the hugely successful *The Kon-Tiki Expedition* (1948).

The tiki trend founds its way north, with theme bars from ex-Marine Bob Mills's Tahitian Cocktail Lounge in Vancouver's Waldorf Hotel to The Beachcomber Room at the Talisman Motor Inn in Ottawa to the renowned Kon-Tiki restaurant in the Mount Royal Hotel in downtown Montreal. Tiki could serve as a springboard for entrepreneurial newcomers like Bob Mills, an American who settled in Vancouver after his time in the service, and Douglas Chan, who immigrated to Canada from China in the 1950s and waited tables at the Kon-tiki before opening his own Jardin Tiki bar (including a Chinese Canadian buffet, appealing to the taste for both Asian and Polynesian cuisines) in the shadow of Montreal's Olympic Stadium.[8]

The overall shift toward the "long drink" replacing the shot, and "the home fireside or the well-conducted cocktail lounge" replacing "the place of the parked car,"[9] demanded neutral spirits over the signature Canadian whisky

Figure 8.1. "How to Toast Your Guests in Every Language," in *The Calvert Party Companion, Created for Canadian Hospitality*. Courtesy of the Hagley Museum and Library.

that was synonymous with the Seagram brand and that would become one of the country's most recognizable luxury exports. The changing product line and promotional culture of the Seagram Company both represent and speak to the cocktail's Canadian moment. With not only its eponymous brands but also a storehouse of labels—which included Captain Morgan's and Leilani rum; the Myer's, Woods, and Trelawney labels; Gordon's gin; Corby's, Calvert, and Bolshoi vodka; Chemineaud brandy; and a wide range of liqueurs and wines—Seagram dominated the postwar liquor industry. Originally a small distillery in rural Ontario, by the 1920s Seagram had been purchased, expanded, and transformed into a distilling giant by the equally rebranded Samuel Bronfman. Bronfman's selective biography—his birth in Bessarabia in 1889; his family's migration to Canada; settling on the Prairies; a childhood enterprise peddling firewood; Seagram's billions[10]—would be integrated into Seagram's Canadian boosterish advertising, which promoted the Bronfmans, the Seagram's brand, and the nation itself, the subtext reliably implying that immigration was an asset to the nation, provided newcomers strived to assimilate into the demands of the liberal economy.[11]

Seagram's entry into the American market in 1934 established the continental presence that would generate the company's great wealth and foster its global empire. By 1958, Mies van der Rohe's Seagram Building towered over the New York skyline, "endowed with a monumentality without equal" in the civic and religious architecture of the era.[12] The Seagram Building made manifest the company's global influence, providing a "technological" referent and supporting the high-flying lifestyles featured in Seagram advertisements.[13]

International brands of alcohol did exceedingly well in the postwar years, when they served as "emblems of wealth and international modernity"[14] both in domestic markets and in foreign markets. The postwar redrawing of national boundaries, as well as the intensification of the characteristics of globalization, repackaged the enlightenment notions of cosmopolitanism in popular terms and in high gloss. With the internationalism that followed World War II, the notion of the circulation of goods as a global panacea formed a part of the zeitgeist;[15] it found expression in print journalism, film, television, and, of course, alcohol advertisements (see fig. 8.2[16]).

This commercial celebration of the world's cosmopolitan bounty exploited a troubling "coloniality of power" begun in the Renaissance and valorized conditions bound up in slavery and genocide, which Michel-Rolph Trouillot and Sidney Mintz have demonstrated.[17] Modern marketing and enhanced shipping and communication technologies accelerated the circulation and availability of goods. This served to amplify the "profound deterritorialization of desire and power . . . linked heavily to acquisition and consumption of shifting and exotic fashion,"[18] which had first appeared in the early consumer society of eighteenth-century Britain.[19] Alcohol advertisements of the 1950s would romanticize this colonial past while erasing exploitation from view. One Seagram advertisement declared, "In keeping with historic tradition, Seagram ships rums in bulk from Jamaica to Liverpool, England, where climatic conditions have proved ideal for maintaining stocks of Jamaica rums

Trade Routes of the World

Over the trade routes of the world move famous brands of your Corporation's subsidiary companies which have earned and enjoy acceptance in every quarter of the globe. In spite of the obstacles engendered by world-wide economic re-adjustments, your Corporation has persevered in company with those who follow the paths of international trade toward the goal of peace, harmony and goodwill among the nations of the world.

The coins of many lands where our products are sold appear on the following pages, and as such are symbolic of the wide distribution of these products in the markets of the world.

Figure 8.2. "Trade Routes of the World." Seagram Distillers-Citizen of the World. Courtesy of the Hagley Museum and Library.

awaiting bottling and distribution to world markets."[20] Despite the concealed realities that could detract from the fantasy of mobility and escape that the cocktail scene relied on, most drinkers in the 1950s did not, in any case, have ethical consumerism on their radars. At the same time, universal liberalism, if not consumer democracy itself, often went uninterrogated and was even celebrated as a gateway to global reconciliation, seen as redirecting an irrational public into a seemingly benign consumerism.[21] More than this, according to Christina Klein, universal liberalism provided the philosophical glue to construct new forms of postcolonial mapping. Cultural texts could foster relationships that made intimate the concrete material and social relations of a shifting internationalism. In *Cold War Orientalism,* Klein demonstrates how, for Americans, Rodgers and Hammerstein and *Saturday Review* could help the American imaginary move away from a global politics of containment and toward a global politics of integration.[22] For Canadians, using cultural products to foster cross-cultural connection lacked the covert imperialism of some American efforts. While the Canadian government operated in a neocolonial manner toward its indigenous people, and structural inequality between Francophone and Anglophone communities persisted, the nation itself was still struggling to escape the hegemonic influence of powerful nations like Great Britain and the United States. In postwar Canada, I would argue, cocktail culture itself participated in generating exposure and curiosity that could bolster Canadians' national confidence as modern, sophisticated, and vibrant while supporting the remaking of Canadians themselves in ways less restricted to a rigid colonial Britishness.

In its varied product line, advertising, and remarkable global success, Seagram provided the vehicle for the Bronfmans to put forth a Canadian narrative through its advertising that celebrated multinational business, liberal immigration, and cultural mixing as the backbone of the modern nation. It granted heightened legitimacy not only to a former colony but also to the Bronfmans themselves in their own unrelenting ambition for respectability in order to cast off their bootlegging past and humble immigrant origins. With their multinational narrative and material culture, they expressed a revived cosmopolitanism articulated through middlebrow culture, which I want to argue here is at the heart of cocktail culture. It was not unique to Seagram alone; rather, it permeated Cold War consciousness. Seagram, however—with its iconic modernity, its stable of brands, and its uncanny understanding of middle-class aspirationalism—was simply well positioned to cultivate and exploit that cosmopolitanism in a country eager for uplift and renewal.

ASPIRATIONAL DRINKING IN A POSTCOLONIAL NATION

The "Canada Whisky: Throughout the World" advertising campaign of 1958 was Seagram at its most middlebrow. It would represent Canadian whisky alongside Ibsen, Grieg, Kabuki theater—and the music of Italy, Mexico, and Venezuela, to name a few. The drinking culture was situated in the class aspirationalism, cultural commodification, and international curiosity of the 1950s (see fig. 8.3).[23]

Travel, flight, and mobility had acute metaphorical force in the postwar years and responded to a middlebrow desire to escape a stifling Canadian provincialism. As Grant McCracken articulates, "It was a way of talking about social movement as physical movement . . . it is movement from a present location 'out', 'away', or 'beyond' to some new one."[24] There was an eagerness to shed the confines of the small towns and rural life, as portrayed in Alice Munro's short stories, and equally an eagerness to shed the authority-driven restrictions of the urban working class of playwright Michel Tremblay.

New drinking habits and tastes accompanied this yearning for change. Market research of Quebec, begun in the late 1950s and continuing into the 1970s, revealed a shift away from whisky[25] and toward "white goods"—gin, rum, and vodka. White products had become "prominent liquor choices among Canadians," to the extent that there was even consideration of introducing a white whisky.[26] Experts of industry trends attributed the preference for clear alcohol to the increase in female drinking and mixed social gatherings. The "moderating" influence of women upon male drinking behavior was applauded,[27] demonstrating how, during the postwar years, drinking was rapidly domesticated—"the salon had replaced the shed"[28]—and alcohol advanced as a way to express middlebrow gentility, feminine influence, and self-improvement while Canada developed new sites of mixed gender entertaining. Small bungalows and semidetached homes had their square footage dramatically expanded with artificial turf patios that saw sheds dismantled and male binge drinking discouraged.[29]

Seagram hired the famed Freudian-inspired motivational researcher Ernest Dichter to gauge consumer attitudes regarding nationality, gender, and wider social changes of the 1960s to and assess how this might be influencing drinking preferences. With his Viennese accent, psychoanalytical theories and methods, and past working relationship with the famed audience researcher Paul Lazersfeld, Dichter's pedigree was ideal to the therapy culture, scientism, and status preoccupations of the era.[30] Dichter favored open-ended in-depth interviews, a technique borrowed and adapted from the techniques of Freudian therapy,

Figure 8.3. International Album Covers. "Canada Whisky, Throughout the World." Courtesy of the Hagley Museum and Library.

and this—combined with his ethnographic interest in exploring the full "world of objects"—meant that participants were invited to talk at length, offering insights on everyday life and national character.

In test marketing of vodka and rum, it was clear that the cultural difference of products—their distance from Canadian life—was sought after. Canadian worth was uncertain if not outright devalued by respondents, and its dominant culture was considered "too rigid or phlegmatic."[31] Vodka needed to be Russian, and rum needed to be from the Caribbean, as consumers considered consumption of imports the "up to date thing to do."[32] The imported and exotic status of rum in the postwar Canadian market completely eclipsed the fact that the drink had a strong regional history as an ocean trade commodity, one to which the Maritime coastal provinces had easy access and which they favored above all other alcohol. Canadian products in general were often regarded by respondents as second-rate versions of American ones[33] and increasingly required elaborate marketing as consumers became more discerning. When designer Irv Koons[34] was hired to revamp Seagram's packaging in the 1960s and 1970s, he proposed a number of new bottle designs that might best capture the island and swashbuckling associations evoked around rum. Variety was prized, and an appreciation of difference was considered youthful and modern. A diversified bar, it was suggested by a suburban businessman, "makes the difference between an ordinary bar and a high class one," while a preference for "something unusual" was also evident, particularly among "younger (under 35) drinkers." By the late 1960s and early 1970s, respondents were less likely "to rationalize their drinking habits" the way they had in earlier periods. As one Montreal teacher explained, "People are not so afraid to relax as they used to be. They can afford it, and some of the old traditions are giving way."[35]

Aspiration took on a national significance in postwar Canada, as the country engaged in heated debates about its own national direction and struggled to distinguish itself from both its former colonizers and also the cultural and economic influence of the United States. In the years following World War II, where Canada had played a decisive role in the Allied victory, the country was engaged in intense state-run efforts to formulate a national identity and articulate a cultural independence.[36] Would Canadians remain loyal to a British commonwealth, or would they reject it? If they rejected it, who would they be and how would they avoid being absorbed into American hegemony? Social conservatives in postwar Canada clung to a British view of the country, while others found such a view stifling and exclusionary.[37] Cultural critics and pundits presented Britishness itself as a kind of safeguard against the perceived moral erosion of mass culture, which was viewed suspiciously as a threatening

Americanization.[38] A more liberal view saw consumption as a possible route to self-improvement: aspirations could be expressed through a drink and could demonstrate not only individual betterment but also something grander, like a raising of the sophistication of the national culture itself. In this way, drinking culture intersected with more culturally democratic notions and participated in a broader postcolonial process in Canada that aimed at both greater recognition on the world stage and new understandings of what being Canadian meant.[39] In the later 1950s and 1960s, many in Canada grappled with these questions that would re-envision who and what Canada was and what relationships it was fostering in an emerging global imaginary. Cultural democracy was promoted by the postwar government to integrate citizens in national uplift efforts, and it fostered middlebrow aspiration as a kind of civic responsibility.[40] Cultural goods of all kinds took on a new, at times contested, salience. Cultural difference had commercial value, but such difference was also front and center in debates surrounding Canadian nationalism and immigration policy. Increasing humanitarianism at home and abroad, coupled with international pressures and labor shortages, saw Canada remove former barriers to immigration for non-Europeans.[41] An experimentation with cosmopolitanism, which the middlebrow cocktail scene encouraged, allowed Canadians to play with cultural diplomacy and democracy and to performatively engage with more hybrid identities. This questioning of national identity had begun as a "passive revolution" that became apparent in the Diefenbaker Bill of Rights in 1960, which acknowledged basic human rights that were at odds with the discriminatory government restrictions, and thus encouraged a domino effect culminating in the opening up of immigration in the 1960s, and leading to the eventual adoption of a groundbreaking policy of multiculturalism in 1971.[42] To understand what a watershed change this was some background is necessary.

The middlebrow cocktail, while characteristic of wider market trends globally, nonetheless complemented in highly specific ways the emergent civic nationalism that came to prominence in mid-twentieth-century Canada. Immigration reforms of the 1960s attempted to move the country away from the overtly discriminatory policies of the past that had been put in place beginning in the early twentieth century with a tightening of the Immigration Act of 1906. This act had heightened the federal government's ability to exclude and deport certain groups. Additionally, the "open door" policy that existed prior to 1906 was tightly closed, with more restrictive controls that were argued to be necessary to maintain the "national character" as European and to openly privilege British imperialist nationalism as well as northern European migration. At the same time, the restrictive policies of the first half of the twentieth century were also put in place "in an effort to uphold the liberal order so deeply enmeshed in English Canadian elites' attachment to British traditions" by discouraging, among other things, political agitation by radical immigrants from Central Europe and Eastern Europe.[43] However, by the early 1960s this insularity was officially dismantled, with a formal shift in the Liberal government's policy away from preferentialism in terms of ethnicity and nationality, and was replaced by a points system ranking potential immigrants in terms of skills and education.[44] As Walsh writes, "Codification of human rights regimes [including Canada's own Diefenbaker Bill of Rights in 1960] and increasing pressure from the international community" were influential in shifting immigration policy.[45] Canada "led the way" on the global stage toward less discriminatory, less Eurocentric policies and introduced policies that continue to be emulated elsewhere.[46] Importantly, too, immigrants were valued for their suitability to the labor demands of the postwar years and were selected to encourage continual industrial expansion and economic growth. The Canadian government's 1966 White Paper on Immigration makes this clear: "A bigger population means increased domestic markets . . . [which] permits manufacturing firms to undertake longer, lower cost production runs, and broaden the range of industry we can undertake, economically improv[ing] our competitive position in world markets."[47] While ethnic and national restrictions were relaxed, the point systems saw economic and class criteria become more stringently applied to potential immigrants, with the appropriate skillsets of a complex industrialized and urban society seen as essential to necessary to avoid newcomers becoming "burdens rather than assets."[48] The new policies screened applicants to determine how easily they might be absorbed into the conditions and worldview of industrial capitalism and to increase both production and demand in the burgeoning consumer culture.

It was fitting, given the growing emphasis on immigrants as human capital,[49] that the consumer culture of the 1960s as expressed in Seagram's midcentury cocktail could invite an everyday participation in more heterogeneous attitude toward national identity. Nowhere was this more evident than at the Montreal World's Fair, known as Expo 67, where Seagram would co-sponsor the United Nations Pavilion and its alcohols would be available for purchase throughout the immense fairground. Expo 67 would attract fifty million visitors over six months (an international exposition record that is still unbroken) at a time when the population of Canada was only twenty million.[50] It is hard to overstate Expo 67's galvanizing influence on representing a more fluid and diverse image of the country. Expo 67 featured pavilions representing more than sixty countries, and it was the venue for concerts, performances, and events of all kinds.⁵¹ In many ways, the fair offered the Seagram Company an incomparable chance to enact Saint-Exupery's dictum upon which the fair was themed: "To be a man is to feel that through one's contribution one helps to build the world."⁵² The fair itself was a landmark attempt to express a remapping consistent with Marshall McLuhan's "global village" theme. With all its varied exhibits displaying the country's multiple nations and cultures, Canada appeared "something of an oddity" at Expo 67. It was an international nation."⁵³ Expo was primarily a site of entertaining cultural curiosities that would introduce Canadians to new sights, sounds, and tastes. Exposure to Eastern tea rituals, for example, could have a lasting and transformative influence on visitors.⁵⁴ Merchandising was discouraged at the exhibition in favor of participation consistent with themed pavilions. With alcohol consumption at peak levels at the time of Expo 67, the food and drink sector "benefited enormously."⁵⁵ Seagram-owned alcohols were available at most major concessions and pavilions. Drinks were integrated into displays to provide a feeling of voyage to different locales—souvenir passports were even provided for visitors to have stamped at each pavilion. For example, a "bit of Hawaii" cultural exchange show bar or an offer of "Made in Paradise" Leilani brand rum invited visitors to sample "authentic Hawaiian food, entertainment and hospitality" with evocative back bar displays, colorful transparencies, and bartending courses.⁵⁶ The international variety of alcohol supported the fair's theme of universal brotherhood and provided an exposure to new and different tastes and customs that supported the fair's larger federal government initiative to stimulate Canadian visitors into "thinking of us as an *us* that could be a *we*."⁵⁷ Alongside agricultural exhibits describing the technological wonders of modern distilling, the cocktail would represent Seagram's wares to meet the fair's requirements of showcasing of "the best in culture and technology."⁵⁸ Judged by today's standards, these opportunities for cultural exposure may seem quaint, but in 1967 such contact was far more limited. Canadian filmmaker Germaine Ying-Gee Wong was a young hostess at Expo 67 and explained how for her, growing up in a predominantly white, working-class neighborhood of Montreal, such opportunities were rare: "I was the only Asian person. There was one black girl, and there was one Italian, and that was exotic in those days. And then suddenly I met people from Trinidad and Tobago, I met people from Russia, from every part of the world."⁵⁹

The fair's themes and pavilions brought to life the intersection of geopolitical mapping and consumerism prevalent in the postwar period when the idea of integrating nations into a shared vision came to prominence. Klein understands cultural mapping as a means to cultivate "sentimental pathways" around political-economic alliances by translating them into personal terms.⁶⁰

In a Canadian context, remapping the global imaginary in tangible ways like changing drinking practices, the world's fair, and widened immigration served to modernize the nation and cast off its uncertain, and marginal, identity. If Canada was no longer to be defined by its colonial past, it had to embrace its diversity—aesthetically and in terms of policy and subsequent demographic change—as a means to ensure prosperity and to engage in a "quest for a Canadian identity."[61]

CRITICAL DISCUSSION: EXOTICISM, APPROPRIATION, AND THE CANADIAN COCKTAIL

Much like the controversies raised around art and appropriation, culturally other goods force us to consider if the commodification of difference and exoticism that are present in postcoloniality rob it of the subversive, resistant potential of postcolonialism, a distinction Huggan puts forth. Moss underscores Graham Huggan's differentiation between, on the one hand, "the postcolonialism of cultural works that function to redress the injustices of imperialism and its aftermath" and, on the other hand, the postcoloniality that operates as a "value-regulating mechanism within the global late-capitalist system of commodity exchange" and trades in "culturally othered goods" produced in the "alterity industry."[62] Elements of both hegemonic containment and resistance were present in the postwar Canadian cocktail scene. Seagram operated as a powerful multinational company, with an iconic Park Avenue office, that engaged in a romanticizing exploitation of the colonial past and present. Postwar Canada, by contrast, lacked dominance on the world stage (though it was engaging in domestic policies toward indigenous communities, and to a lesser extent Franco Canadians, that perpetuated the process of colonization—thus complicating, though not negating, its postcolonial status, as Moss and others have discussed). Cultural difference was absorbed into something marketable by Seagram, while representations remained problematic and top-down. At the same time, however, the ease of such consumption helped soften and render the multiculturalism and broadened understandings of Canadian identity less intimidating, while emboldening a nation that historically struggled with dependency to engage in a bold vision of redefinition. I use the term *dependency* here with reference to Harold Innis's landmark work that put forth his "staples theory": Canada as a colony was colonized by the British for natural resource extraction. As a result, it lacked its own technological sophistication and had politically been organized and administered to facilitate the exploitation of staple products such as fur, lumber, minerals, oil, and cod.

This led to a kind of stunted development, according to Innis, that perpetuated a marginal status for Canada relative to more powerful nations and delayed the country's modernization. It is in this sense that Canada remained peripheral and could at times feel "marginalized, ignored, or excluded," similar to other postcolonial citizens and non-Westerners, as O'Reilly reminds us.[63] This opens the door to the possibility of identification between cultures that should not be reduced to appropriation and exoticism alone.

The British cultural studies theorist Mica Nava's work[64] is insightful for helping us understand how this kind of cosmopolitan play enacted through consumption can signal freedom from repressive or subordinate identities. In her analysis of women shoppers at Selfridge's department store in London, Nava has put forth a "notion of the commercial arena as popularizer of cosmopolitan and modernist identifications."[65] The Russian ballet and Middle Eastern scarves are two expressions of "popular cosmopolitanism" she highlights. There are admittedly elements of exotica in the enjoyment of culturally other goods, and Nava traces this to the residual cultural modernism that had "significant influence in representing, at the turn of the century, the orient and abroad as more colorful, authentic and erotic than the west."[66] For example, "while primitive art was mainly appreciated by the avant garde throughout the twenties and thirties, after World War II it began, by virtue of this very association, to appeal to the affluent middle class: It was now associated with an artistic, bohemian lifestyle and a whimsical, playful attitude."[67]

Popular texts and consumer goods from abroad, or evocative of abroad, offered up vestiges of cultural modernism in popularized forms. We find in the postwar cocktail scene the kind of cultural blurring and mashup that makes unclear the distinction between the authentic and the inauthentic: rumaki, for example, was the creation of an enterprising American bar owner,[68] yet it played to fascination with Asian and Polynesian culture. Seagram was no stranger to this; the "Party Flamingo" featured in one of their 1960s advertisements demonstrates this bricolage and disregard of specificity with a sun-glassed bird that prepares rum-based drinks and instructs consumers on how to throw a "Tropical Fiesta Party," complete with piñatas and reggae and mariachi music.[69]

Building from Stuart Hall's work that has argued for the potentially liberating potential of "vernacular" forms of cosmopolitanism for marginalized identities, Nava suggests that the consumption of foreign goods by female shoppers in interwar London allowed for a loosening of patriarchal restrictions and the oppressive mores of class and convention. It is the restriction or subordination of the consumer in a wider hegemonic context that distinguishes her shopping, or in our case here, her drinking, from simply re-inscribing power through her consumption of difference. When consuming potentially becomes a space of progressive experimentation for subordinate people—not just to consume difference but to become different—it can participate in forming new symbolic maps that engage with and establish "emergent geo-political terrain."[70]

I want to suggest that in an international context, which saw postwar Canadians struggling to distinguish themselves as a people and shed their dependency, the middlebrow cocktail offered a site to experiment with both soft diplomacy and also the nascent multiculturalism that would later be formalized in government policy. Foreign cachet was paramount and played off the instability of Canadian value. Less "furtive"[71] attitudes toward drinking signaled a loosening of restriction and a stoked desire for difference, uniformly appreciated by Dichter's market research respondents. The cocktail participated in the spread of a middlebrow cosmopolitanism that would combine with changing state-sanctioned definitions of *national identity* to cultivate diversity and to make that diversity more "everyday." Postcoloniality was marketable, and it worked in tandem with the migration controls in Canada that sought to boost production and demand while assimilating immigrants into a mass consumer culture. The cocktail would find itself front and center in a middlebrow cosmopolitanism that would rapidly see a decentered British heritage sit alongside multiculturalism in both the politics and the glassware of the nation.

Marianopolis College

NOTES

1. Laura Moss, "Is Canada Postcolonial? Re-Asking through 'The Forgotten' Project," *Topia* 27 (Spring 2012): 61, https://doi.org/10.3138/topia.27.47.
2. Nathanael O'Reilly, "Australian Literature as Postcolonial Literature," in *Postcolonial Issues in Australian Literature*, ed. Nathanael O'Reilly (Amherst, NY: Cambria Press, 2010), 6.
3. O'Reilly, "Australian Literature," 5.
4. Moss, "Is Canada Postcolonial?" 57.
5. See Noah Rothbaum, *The Business of Spirits: How Savvy Marketers, Innovative Distillers, and Entrepreneurs Changed How We Drink* (New York: Kaplan, 2007).
6. "'The Calvert Party Companion' Created for *Canadian Hospitality*," *Hospitality and Recipe Guides: Institutional and Family* (3 of 10), Seagram Archive, Box 199, Series 3, Accession 2173 (Wilmington, DE: Hagley Museum and Library).

7. "The Calvert Party Companion."

8. See André Dubuc, "Jardin Tiki, haut lieu du kitsch, en peril," *La Presse* [Montreal], August 19, 2014, http://plus.lapresse.ca/screens/bb9a252c-1f32-4990-ad8f-3f80057833eb__7C____0.html.

9. Jacques Martel, Quebec sales manager of H. Corby Distillery Limited, quoted in "Seagram Distillers-Citizen of the World," *BAR Beverage Alcohol Reporter* (February 29, 1964), "Beverage Alcohol Reporter 1964, 1971," Box 291, Series 4, Subseries A, Seagram Museum Collection, Accession 2173 (Wilmington, DE: Hagley Museum and Library).

10. Walter D. Mignolo, "The Many Faces of Cosmo-Polis: Border Thinking and Critical Cosmopolitanism," *Public Culture* 12, no. 3 (2000): 721–48, passim, https://doi.org/10.1215/08992363-12-3-721.

11. See Peter C. Newman, *Bronfman Dynasty: The Rothschilds of the New World* (Toronto: McClelland & Stewart, 1978).

12. The Bronfmans were fervent Canadian nationalists. They commissioned a full-color insert, in both English and French, which they titled "The Canadian Journey/Le Canada, Héritages et Espoirs," to be distributed nationally in the weeks leading up to the Quebec referendum (on leaving or staying in Canada) in an effort to promote multiculturalism and discourage the Quebec sovereignty movement. See "The Canadian Journey 1980," *Maclean's* (March 24, 1980), Series 3, Subseries B, Box 67, Seagram Museum Collection, Accession 2173 (Wilmington, DE: Hagley Museum and Library).

13. James A. Speyer, *Mies van der Rohe* (Chicago: Art Institute of Chicago, 1968), 30.

14. Roland Barthes, *The Fashion System*, trans. Matthew Ward and Richard Howard (New York: Hill and Wang, 1983), 133.

15. Dmitri van den Bersselaar, *The King of Drinks: Schnapps Gin from Modernity to Tradition* (Boston: Brill, 2007), 219. See also Teresa da Silva Lopes, "Brands and the Evolution of Multinationals in Alcoholic Beverages," *Business History* 44, no. 3 (2002): 1–30, https://doi.org/10.1080/713999275.

16. Allen W. Wood. "Kant's Project for Perpetual Peace," in *Cosmopolitics: Thinking and Feeling beyond the Nation*, ed. Pheng Cheah and Bruce Robbins (Minneapolis: University of Minnesota Press, 1998), 59–76; Immanuel Kant, *Perpetual Peace, and Other Essays on Politics, History, and Morals*, trans. and intr. Ted Humphrey (Indianapolis: Hackett, 1983); Thomas J. Schlereth, *The Cosmopolitan Ideal in Enlightenment Thought: Its Form and Function in the Ideas of Franklin, Hume, and Voltaire, 1694–1790* (Notre Dame, IN: University of Notre Dame Press, 1977.)

17. In rhetoric typical of the period, this advertisement from the 1950s celebrated the global circulation of Seagram brands and international subsidiaries as following "the paths of international trade toward the goal of

peace, harmony and goodwill among the nations of the world" ("Seagram Distillers-Citizen of the World").

18. Mignolo, "The Many Faces of Cosmo-Polis," passim.

19. Andrew Herman, *The "Better Angels" of Capitalism: Rhetoric, Narrative, and Moral Identity among Men of the American Upper Class* (Boulder, CO: Westview Press, 1999), 136.

20. Herman, "Better Angels," 142, citing Neil McKendrick, John Brewer, and J. H. Plumb, *The Birth of a Consumer Society: The Commercialization of Eighteenth-Century England* (Bloomington: Indiana University Press, 1985).

21. "Seagram Distillers-Citizen of the World," 6.

22. See Edward Bernays, *The Engineering of Consent* (Norman: University of Oklahoma Press, 1969), and Ernest Dichter, *The Strategy of Desire* (New York: Doubleday, 1960).

23. Christina Klein, *Cold War Orientalism: Asia in the Middlebrow Imagination, 1945–1961* (Berkeley: University of California Press, 2003). See also Sherrie A. Inness, *Dinner Roles: American Women and Culinary Culture* (Iowa City: University of Iowa Press, 2001).

24. "Canada Whisky, 'Throughout the World,' 1958," Box 100, Series 3, Subseries C, Seagram Museum Collection, Accession 2173 (Wilmington, DE: Hagley Museum and Archive).

25. Grant McCracken, "When Cars Could Fly: Raymond Loewy, John Kenneth Galbraith, and the 1954 Buick," in *Culture and Consumption II: Markets, Meaning, and Brand Management*, by Grant David McCracken (Bloomington: Indiana University Press, 2005), 76.

26. Historically, whisky was consumed less in Quebec than in other parts of Canada, where it was widely drunk. Quebecers had traditionally shown a fondness for gin—including Geneva gin—though not in the kind the of cocktail preparations we associate with the 1950s and 1960s.

27. "A Motivational Research Study on the Drinking Patterns of the Geneva Gin Market in Quebec Province," July 1958 (New York: Institute for Motivational Research) in "Gin Marketing Research-Provincial 1958, 1964, 1973," n.p., Box 196, Subseries D, Series 3, Seagram Museum Collection, Accession 2173 (Wilmington, DE: Hagley Library and Museum).

28. Martel, quoted in "Seagram Distillers-Citizen of the World," 4.

29. Martel, quoted in "Seagram Distillers-Citizen of the World," 4.

30. See Joy Parr, *Domestic Goods: The Material, the Moral, and the Economic in the Postwar Years* (Toronto: University of Toronto Press, 1999).

31. See Stefan Schwartzkopf and Rainer Gries, *Ernest Dichter and Motivation Research: New Perspectives on the Making of Post-war Consumer Culture* (New York: Palgrave MacMillan, 2010).

32. "A Motivational Research Study on the Drinking Patterns of the Geneva Gin Market," *Market Research & American Business, 1935–1965*, Adam Matthew

Digital 2020, http://www.marketresearch.amdigital.co.uk/Documents/Details/Hagley_Dichter_BX005_95.3C.

33. "Rum and Vodka Marketing Research, 1971," Box 196, Subseries D, Series 3, Seagram Museum Collection, Accession 2173 (Wilmington, DE: Hagley Museum and Library).

34. "A Motivational Research Study of Maclean's Magazine," Box 1, Series 1, Ernest Dichter Papers Research proposals and reports, Accession 2407A (Wilmington, DE: Hagley Museum and Library).

35. Koons produced packaging design for many of Seagram's alcohols throughout the 1950s and into the 1980s, but he is perhaps best known as the designer of the Dixie Cup. See "Correspondence-Joseph E. Seagram's and Sons., Inc. March 1963–1975," Box 1, Series 1, Irv Koons Papers, Accession 2132 (Wilmington, DE: Hagley Museum and Library).

36. See L. B. Kuffert, *A Great Duty: Canadian Responses to Modern Life and Mass Culture in Canada, 1936–1967* (Montreal: McGill-Queen's University Press, 2003); Jose E. Igartua, *The Other Quiet Revolution: National Identities in English Canada, 1945–1971* (Victoria: University of British Columbia Press, 2006); and Maria Tippett, *Making Culture: English-Canadian Institutions and the Arts before the Massey Commission* (Toronto: University of Toronto Press, 1990).

37. Igartua, *The Other Quiet Revolution*, 13.

38. See Philip Massolin, *Canadian Intellectuals, the Tory Tradition and the Challenge of Modernity, 1939–1970* (Toronto: University of Toronto Press, 2001).

39. For an analysis of how refinement of the national culture played out in cultural policy and the arts, see Jody Berland, "Nationalism and the Modernist Legacy: Dialogues with Innis," *Capital Culture: A Reader on Modernist Legacies, State Institutions, and the Value(s) of Art*, ed. Jody Berland and Shelley Hornstein (Montreal: McGill-Queen's University Press, 2000), 14–38.

40. See Kuffert, *A Great Duty*, and Tippett, *Making Culture*.

41. James Walsh, "Navigating Globalization: Immigration Policy in Canada and Australia, 1945–2007," *Sociological Forum* 23, no. 4 (December 2008): 786–813, https://doi.org/10.1111/j.1573-7861.2008.00094.x.

42. Patrick Lacroix, "From Strangers to 'Humanity First': Canadian Social Democracy and Immigration Policy, 1932–1961," *Canadian Journal of History* 51, no. 1 (2016): 58–82, https://doi.org/10.3138/cjh.ach.51.1.003. Lacroix adapts his term *passive revolution* from the work of Ian McKay.

43. Lacroix, "From Strangers to 'Humanity First,'" 67.

44. Lacroix, "From Strangers to 'Humanity First,'" 77.

45. Walsh, "Navigating Globalization," 796.

46. Walsh, "Navigating Globalization," 796.

47. Walsh, "Navigating Globalization," 794.

48. Walsh, "Navigating Globalization," 797.

49. Walsh, "Navigating Globalization," 797.

50. "Expo 67: Canada Welcomes the World but Reveals a Tear in Its National Fabric," *Le Canada: A People's History/Une Histoire Populaire*, CBC (2001) https://www.cbc.ca/history/EPISCONTENTSE1EP16CH1PA3LE.html.

51. Rhona Richman Kenneally and Germaine Ying-Gee Wong, "Expo 67: Not Just a Souvenir," *Concordia University News*, 2012, accessed July 26, 2018, http://www.concordia.ca/news/articles/2012/expo-67-not-just-a-souvenir.html.

52. John R. Gold and Margaret M. Gold, *Cities of Culture: Staging International Festivals and the Urban Agenda, 1851–2000* (Farnham, UK: Ashgate, 2005), 112.

53. Gary P. Miedema, *For Canada's Sake: Public Religion, Centennial Celebrations, and the Re-making of Canada in the 1960s* (Montreal: McGill-Queen's University Press, 2005), 122.

54. "Expo 67: Back to the Future." CBC Documentary Unit, Toronto: CBC Home Video; Morningstar Entertainment Inc., 2004.

55. Gold and Gold, *Cities of Culture*, 112.

56. "Expo 67 (1 of 2)," Inter-office memo (April 27, 1967), Seagram Archive, Box 6, Subseries C, Series 1, Record Group 1, Accession 2126 (Wilmington, DE: Hagley Museum and Library).

57. Kenneally and Wong, "Expo 67.".

58. Miedema, *For Canada's Sake*, 126.

59. Kenneally and Wong, "Expo 67."

60. Klein, *Cold War Orientalism*, 9.

61. Kenneally and Wong, "Expo 67."

62. Quoted in Moss, "Is Canada Postcolonial?" 56.

63. Quoted in O'Reilly, "Australian Literature," 2.

64. See Mica Nava, "The Cosmopolitanism of Commerce and the Allure of Difference: Selfridges, The Russian Ballet and the Tango 1911–1914," *International Journal of Cultural Studies* 1, no. 2 (1998): 163–96, https://doi.org/10.1177/136787799800100202201; Mica Nava, "Cosmopolitan Modernity: Everyday Imaginaries and the Register of Difference," *Theory, Culture, and Society* 19, no. 1–2 (2002): 81–100, https://doi.org/10.1177/026327640201900104.

65. Nava, "Cosmopolitanism," 177.

66. Nava, "Cosmopolitanism," 171.

67. Sven Kirsten, *The Book of Tiki* (Los Angeles: Taschen, 2000), 26.

68. Rumaki first appeared on tiki bars in the 1940s and was likely the creation of Trader Vic's founder Victor Bergeron, despite its being sold as an appetizer of vaguely Asian and Polynesian origin. See "Rumaki—Mad Men-Era Chinese Cooking," Appetite for China, December 17, 2013, http://appetiteforchina.com/recipes/rumaki.

69. *Hospitality and Recipe Guides: Rum-Wine* (9 of 10), n.d. 1956–1978, Series 3, Box 199, Seagram Archive, Accession 2173 (Wilmington, DE: Hagley Museum and Library).

70. Nava, "Cosmopolitanism," 188.
71. "A Motivational Research Study on the Drinking Patterns of the Geneva Gin Market," n.p.

BIBLIOGRAPHY

Ashcroft, Bill, Gareth Griffiths, and Helen Tiffin. *The Empire Writes Back: Theory and Practice in Post-Colonial Cultures*. 2nd ed. New York: Routledge, 2002.
"A Motivational Research Study on the Drinking Patterns of the Geneva Gin Market in Quebec Province: Appendix to Part I: The Psychological Foundations for a Seagram Geneva Gin, 1958." House of Seagram Folder #95.3A (page unknown). Box 5, Ernest Dichter Papers, Series 1. Research proposals and reports, Accession 2407A. Wilmington, DE: Hagley Museum and Library.
Barthes, Roland. *The Fashion System*. Translated by Matthew Ward and Richard Howard. New York: Hill and Wang, 1983.
Berland, Jody. "Nationalism and the Modernist Legacy: Dialogues with Innis." In *Capital Culture: A Reader on Modernist Legacies, State Institutions, and the Value(s) of Art*, edited by Jody Berland and Shelley Hornstein, 14–38. Montreal: McGill-Queen's University Press, 2000.
Bernays, Edward. *The Engineering of Consent*. Norman: University of Oklahoma Press, 1969.
"'The Calvert Party Companion' Created for *Canadian Hospitality*." Hospitality and Recipe Guides: Institutional and Family. Vol. 3 of 10. Box 199, Series 3. Seagram Museum Collection, Accession 2173. Wilmington, DE: Hagley Museum and Library.
"Canada Whisky, 'Throughout the World,' 1958." Box 100, Series 3, Subseries C. Seagram Museum Collection, Accession 2173. Wilmington, DE: Hagley Museum and Library.
"The Canadian Journey 1980," *Maclean's* (March 24, 1980). Box 67. Series 3, Subseries B. Seagram Museum Collection, Accession 2173. Wilmington, DE: Hagley Museum and Library.
"Correspondence-Joseph E. Seagram's and Sons, Inc. March 1963–1975" Series 1, Box 1. Irv Koons Papers, Accession 2132. Wilmington, DE: Hagley Museum and Library.
Dichter, Ernest. *The Strategy of Desire*. New York: Doubleday, 1960.
Dubuc, André. "Jardin Tiki, haut lieu du kitsch, en peril." *La Presse* (Montreal). August 19, 2014. http://plus.lapresse.ca/screens/bb9a252c-1f32-4990-ad8f-3f80057833eb__7C___0.html.
"Expo 67 (1 of 2)." Inter-office memo. April 27, 1967. Box 6, Series 1, Subseries C, Record Group 1. Seagram Museum Collection, Accession 2126. Wilmington, DE: Hagley Library and Museum.

"Expo 67: Back to the Future." CBC Documentary Unit. Toronto: CBC Home Video-Morningstar Entertainment, 2004.

"Expo 67: Canada Welcomes the World but Reveals a Tear in Its National Fabric." *Le Canada: A People's History/Une Histoire Populaire*. Toronto: Canadian Broadcasting Corporation, 2001. https://www.cbc.ca/history/EPISCONTENTSE1EP16CH1PA3LE.html.

Gold, John R., and Margaret M. Gold. *Cities of Culture: Staging International Festivals and the Urban Agenda, 1851–2000*. Farnham, UK: Ashgate, 2005.

Herman, Andrew. *The "Better Angels" of Capitalism: Rhetoric, Narrative, and Moral Identity Among Men of the American Upper Class*. Boulder, CO: Westview Press, 1999.

Hospitality and Recipe Guides: Rum-Wine (9 of 10), n.d. 1956–1978. Seagram Archive. Series III, Box 199, Accession 2173. Wilmington, DE: Hagley Library.

Igartua, Jose E. *The Other Quiet Revolution: National Identities in English Canada, 1945–1971*. Victoria: University of British Columbia Press, 2006.

Inness, Sherrie A. *Dinner Roles: American Women and Culinary Culture*. Iowa City: University of Iowa Press, 2001.

Innis, Harold A. "The Importance of Staple Products in Canadian Development." In *Staples, Markets, and Cultural Change: Selected Essays*, edited by Daniel Drache, 3–23. Toronto: McGill-Queen's University Press, 1995.

Kant, Immanuel. *Perpetual Peace, and Other Essays on Politics, History, and Morals*. Translated and with an introduction by Ted Humphrey. Indianapolis, IN: Hackett, 1983.

Kirsten, Sven. *The Book of Tiki*. Los Angeles: Taschen, 2000.

Klein, Christina. *Cold War Orientalism: Asia in the Middlebrow Imagination, 1945–1961*. Berkeley: University of California Press, 2003.

Kuffert, L. B. *A Great Duty: Canadian Responses to Modern Life and Mass Culture in Canada, 1936-1967*. Montreal: McGill-Queen's University Press, 2003.

Lacroix, Patrick. "From *Strangers* to 'Humanity First': Canadian Social Democracy and Immigration Policy, 1932–1961." *Canadian Journal of History* 51, no. 1 (Spring-Summer 2016): 58–82.

Lopes, Teresa da Silva. "Brands and the Evolution of Multinationals in Alcoholic Beverages." *Business History* 44, no. 3 (2002): 1–30.

Massolin, Philip. *Canadian Intellectuals, the Tory Tradition and the Challenge of Modernity, 1939–1970*. Toronto: University of Toronto Press, 2001.

McCracken, Grant. "When Cars Could Fly: Raymond Loewy, John Kenneth Galbraith, and the 1954 Buick." In *Culture and Consumption II: Markets, Meaning, and Brand Management*, by Grant David McCracken, 53–89. Bloomington: Indiana University Press, 2005.

Miedema, Gary P. *For Canada's Sake: Public Religion, Centennial Celebrations, and the Re-making of Canada in the 1960s*. Montreal: McGill-Queen's University Press, 2005.

Mignolo, Walter D. "The Many Faces of Cosmo-polis: Border Thinking and Critical Cosmopolitanism." *Public Culture* 12, no. 3 (2000): 721–48.

Mintz, Sidney. *Sweetness and Power: The Place of Sugar in Modern History*. Middlesex, UK: Viking Penguin, 1985.

Moss, Laura. "Is Canada Postcolonial? Re-Asking through "The Forgotten" Project." *Topia* 27 (Spring 2012): 47–65. https://doi.org/10.3138/topia.27.47.

"A Motivational Research Study of Maclean's Magazine." Box 1, Series 1, Ernest Dichter Papers Research proposals and reports, Accession 2407A. Wilmington, DE: Hagley Museum and Library.

"A Motivational Research Study on the Drinking Patterns of the Geneva Gin Market in Quebec Province." New York: Institute for Motivational Research, July 1958. "Gin Marketing Research-Provincial 1958, 1964, 1973." Box 196, Series 3, Subseries D. Seagram Archive, Accession 2173. Wilmington, DE: Hagley Library and Museum.

Nava, Mica. "The Cosmopolitanism of Commerce and the Allure of Difference: Selfridges, the Russian Ballet and the Tango 1911–1914." *International Journal of Cultural Studies* 1, no. 2 (1998): 163–96.

Nava, Mica. "Cosmopolitan Modernity: Everyday Imaginaries and the Register of Difference." *Theory, Culture, and Society* 19, no. 1–2 (2002): 81–100.

Newman, Peter C. *Bronfman Dynasty: The Rothschilds of the New World*. Toronto: McClelland & Stewart, 1978.

O'Reilly, Nathanael. "Australian Literature as Postcolonial Literature." In *Postcolonial Issues in Australian Literature*, edited by Nathanael O'Reilly, 1–14. Amherst, NY: Cambria Press, 2010.

Parr, Joy. *Domestic Goods: The Material, the Moral, and the Economic in the Postwar Years*. Toronto: University of Toronto Press, 1999.

Kenneally, Rhona Richman, and Germaine Ying-Gee Wong. "Expo 67: Not Just a Souvenir." *Concordia University News*, 2012. Accessed July 26, 2018. https://www.concordia.ca/news/articles/2012/expo-67-not-just-a-souvenir.html.

Rothbaum, Noah. *The Business of Spirits: How Savvy Marketers, Innovative Distillers, and Entrepreneurs Changed How We Drink*. New York: Kaplan, 2007.

Rubin, Joan Shelley. *The Making of Middlebrow Culture*. Chapel Hill: University of North Carolina Press, 1992.

"Rum and Vodka Marketing Research, 1971." Box 196, Subseries D, Series 3, Seagram Museum Collection (Accession 2173). Wilmington, DE: Hagley Museum and Library.

"Rumaki—Mad Men-Era Chinese Cooking." Appetite for China. December 17, 2013. http://appetiteforchina.com/recipes/rumaki.

Schlereth, Thomas J. *The Cosmopolitan Ideal in Enlightenment Thought: Its Form and Function in the Ideas of Franklin, Hume, and Voltaire, 1694–1790*. Notre Dame, IN: University of Notre Dame Press, 1977.

Schwartzkopf, Stefan, and Rainer Gries. *Ernest Dichter and Motivation Research: New Perspectives on the Making of Post-War Consumer Culture.* New York: Palgrave MacMillan, 2010.

"Seagram Distillers-Citizen of the World." *BAR Beverage Alcohol Reporter.* February 29, 1964. "Beverage Alcohol Reporter 1964, 1971," 6. Box 291, Series 4, Subseries A. Seagram Museum Collection, Accession 2173. Wilmington, DE: Hagley Museum and Library.

Speyer, James A. *Mies van der Rohe.* Chicago: Art Institute of Chicago, 1968.

Tippett, Maria. *Making Culture: English-Canadian Institutions and the Arts before the Massey Commission.* Toronto: University of Toronto Press, 1990.

Trouillot, Michel-Rolph. "North Atlantic Universals: Analytical Fictions, 1492–1945." *The South Atlantic Quarterly* 101, no. 4 (2002): 839–58. https://www.muse.jhu.edu/article/39116.

van den Bersselaar, Dimitri. *The King of Drinks: Schnapps Gin from Modernity to Tradition.* Leiden: Brill, 2007.

Walsh, James. "Navigating Globalization: Immigration Policy in Canada and Australia, 1945–2007." *Sociological Forum* 23, no. 4 (December 2008): 786–813.

Wood, Allen W. "Kant's Project for Perpetual Peace." In *Cosmopolitics: Thinking and Feeling beyond the Nation,* edited by Pheng Cheah and Bruce Robbins, 59–76. Minneapolis: University of Minnesota Press, 1998.

NINE

ABSOLUT PSYCHOSIS

CRAIG N. OWENS

THE BOOM IN VODKA'S POPULARITY among American consumers of alcoholic spirits in the 1980s and 1990s offers itself as an emblem of larger cultural shifts, particularly in the nature of masculinity and work, during the same period. For, in all three registers—vodka, masculinity, work—we see a progressive emptying out of substance, figured variously as impurities, interiority, and physical labor, and an erasure of difference at the level of the thing itself: of what constitutes a man, an occupation, a distilled spirit. At the same time, a countershift seems to take place, whereby distinctiveness, taste, and investments of talent and energy, once the *substance* of a particularly American ideal of corporate masculinity and the elaborate cocktail mixology that accompanied it, manifest themselves on literal *surfaces*: packaging, clothing, and branding. The aestheticization of the sculpted male body, thanks in large part to Calvin Klein's launch of a men's underwear line in 1982 and to the advertising campaigns that promoted it; the sly return of conformity as the underlying force propelling a rhetoric of corporate individuality; and the sensational advertisements for Absolut vodka published in middlebrow magazines all testify to a relocation of identity from some imagined interior core of a person or object—its being-in-itself, to borrow from Heidegger—to the ersatz and incidental surfaces. The alteration in the conception of professional male subjectivity and its relationship to aestheticized bodily and object surfaces that took place through the 1980s becomes especially salient in Bret Easton Ellis's boozy, bloody novel *American Psycho* (1991) even as it is symbolically rendered in Absolut vodka's print advertising campaign of the 1980s. More than just marking two coordinates in a shifting conception of professionally successful manhood, taken together these two artifacts, novel and ad campaign, reveal that the resulting formation is precisely psychotic in its affect and presentation, particularly in its fixation on visuality and its tortured relationship to language as a medium of thought and expression.

Between the heyday of the cocktail in the postwar decades of the 1950s and 1960s and the reemergence of haute mixology in the late 1990s stretched a two-decade decline in the popularity of elaborate and finely crafted mixed drinks in America,[1] and into that gap between cocktail culture and cocktail redux, Americans poured great quantities of vodka. In addition to its connections to masculinity and work, its emergence as America's most popular spirit in the late 1970s and through the 1980s and 1990s resonates with a range of social, political, economic, and cultural developments—sometimes in consonance with them, and at other times in dissonance.[2] The rise in popularity of a spirit that aspires to colorlessness, flavorlessness, and odorlessness appears precisely of a piece with the emptying out of the signifier in European semiotics, linguistics, and philosophies of signification, especially in humanities departments at US colleges and universities in the 1970s and 1980s, when the grand theories of Jacques Derrida, Roland Barthes, Jacques Lacan, and others became widely influential.[3] Furthermore, in the images of urban blight, stagflation, and unemployment that marked the end of the 1970s and beginning of the 1980s, do we not also perceive a kind of Kafkaesque, vodkaesque dreariness: a bleak emptiness awash over the American economic landscape? In short, we can read vodka's increased popularity among American drinkers as symptomatic of several distinct but interrelated cultural developments. So multilayered is this symptomology, in fact, that a whole book might be written on the subject.

For the purposes of this chapter, situated as it is in a volume that examines mainly the representational and interpretive practices in film, theatre, television, and marketing that coalesce around cocktails and their consumption, I want to focus on the three loci I mentioned earlier—vodka, masculinity, and corporate managerial labor—that, together, triangulate an evacuation of the individual male as such, whether that individual is imagined as a consumer of commodities, as a white-collar investor, or even as a distinct brand. Indeed, it has everything to do with *branding*: the mark on the exterior that both points toward and erases an individuating interior. William Whyte's *The Organization Man* began charting this change in the middle of the 1950s in the identity of the corporate employee—specifically the manager—whose sense of identity was becoming increasingly bound up with the company he worked for; at the same time, his subjectivity found itself increasingly subsumed by, and then replaced by, the ersatz tropes of mass-produced suburbiana.[4]

This evacuation of the corporate manager's and executive's subjectivity was compensated for by the intensification of the imperative to consume—and display one's consumption of—distinguishing commodities: booze, certainly, but also couture, technology, and accessories. As Lori Hall-Araujo's essay in this book notes, the material world of warfare and production, over which earlier generations of men had exercised mastery, was contracted to the narrow confines of largely domestic leisure: drinking, golfing, and dressing. Stuart Ewen examines this contraction further, noting its inscription on the male body, in his book *All Consuming Images: The Politics of Style in Contemporary Culture*. For Ewen, the popularity of exercise and weight-lifting machines, such as those produced by the Nautilus Corporation, founded in 1986, allowed the professional man to reunite with machinery and encouraged a reconception of the male body as both the agent and the product of mechanical production.[5] A mass-produced aesthetic came to dominate conceptions of the ideal male body, whose surface contours and lines attested to its mass producibility, at precisely the moment that corporate culture had succeeded in eliding interiority as the locus of individuality. And through this new landscape of corporate masculine individuality, as distinct from subjectivity, runs a river of vodka: a spirit without soul, itself the perfect analogue for the 1980s corporate climber.

American Psycho, in its manifestation as a novel and a film that together bookend the corporate boom years of the 1990s, signals anxieties about masculine managerial identity, and, in particular, the fraught dichotomy of individuality and conformity that animates corporate cultural discourse. It does so by drawing attention to particular sites of that anxiety: brand consciousness, the machined body, ablutionary self-fashioning, late-capitalist ennui, and the vicissitudes of taste as both expression and marker of difference and sameness at the same time; if, in other words, we read these two texts as time capsules. I wish to suggest that the same anxieties manifest in their representation of corporate masculinity also animate vodka consumption and advertising in the 1980s and 1990s.

The famous and still ongoing Absolut vodka campaign, which began with "Absolut Heaven" and "Absolut Perfection" in 1981, provides a case in point.[6] The goal of the campaign, in the beginning, was to bring to American consciousness the availability of a little-known Swedish vodka and to make it competitive with Stolichnaya, at that time the most popular brand of imported vodka in the United States. (The most popular vodka full stop was Smirnoff, a domestic vodka masquerading as a Russian import). Absolut's advertisers succeeded wildly in raising Absolut's profile—so much so, in fact, that by the late 1980s, the advertisements themselves were in high demand. As Richard A. Lewis points out in his history of the Absolut campaign, *Absolut Book: The Absolut Vodka Advertising Story* (1996), librarians would discover that patrons were removing the ads from magazines either as keepsakes or to trade and/or sell to collectors. Newsagents would remove the ads from magazines—generally middlebrow titles like the *New Yorker*, *Vogue*, and *GQ* that straddle the line between urbane sophistication and mass appeal—and sell them separately from the issues from which they had been removed. College students decorated dorm and fraternity rooms with the ads, and more serious aficionados established carefully curated collections. The appearance of a new Absolut ad design would create something of a stir among readers of the magazines in which it appeared.[7] Famous and emerging artists and photographers were commissioned to create images for the ads; seasonal and topical ads were eagerly anticipated.[8] The ads, in other words, took on a cultural significance of their own, quite apart from the vodka they hawked, and could, in turn, be used by collectors and frat boys alike to brand their own tastes as rarified and distinctive.

In the early years of the campaign, the advertisements used the trademark "Absolut" to play on the common adjective "absolute" in everyday phrases, such as "Absolut[e] Clarity,"[9] "Absolut[e] Gem,"[10] "Absolut[e] Treasure,"[11] and "Absolut[e] Masterpiece."[12] Each ad featured the eye-catching dome-shaped bottle in a visual context that suggested a more or less *literal* meaning of the phrase used. For instance, "Absolut Perfection" (1981) depicted the bottle in an aura of white light, a halo hovering just over the neck.[13] The ideas of saintliness and heavenliness associated with "perfection" situate the drink within a recognizable discourse, even as the juxtaposition of liquor, usually associated with sinfulness, creates a frisson of tension in the image. The key to these early ads was to create a dynamic whereby the distinctiveness and rarity of Absolut vodka finds itself grounded in the familiar, but in such a way as to momentarily, and not too subtly, defamiliarize the everyday phrase on which the taglines played. In this way, the two-word tagline reinforced Absolut's élan with linguistic finesse. As the advertisement campaign itself became a phenomenon, however, the taglines became increasingly decoupled from common usage. Anything could become "Absolut," and advertisers began coining new phrases, relying on the general sense of the word "absolute" to mean "ultimate" or "perfect." These ads, such as the "Absolut Bravo"[14] and "Absolut Attraction,"[15] still early in the campaign's development, show that the word "Absolut" itself had gained cultural familiarity and no longer required a familiar discourse within which to ground itself. The brand, in other words, had begun to detach itself both from the vodka and from any naturalizing discursive context, and so only a trace of the playful finesse of the earlier taglines remains.

This detachment, this emptying out of meaning from the brand, made possible a yet later development in the campaign: commissioning of famous artists, designers, and stylists to create striking backdrops, dressings, and settings for the image of the iconic bottle; or suggesting a distinctive locale in the ad design. Thus, magazine readers encountered "Absolut Warhol"[16] or "Absolut Haring"[17] and "Absolut Bologna"[18] or "Absolut Paris."[19] In these phrases, there is no play on words at all, because "absolute Warhol" is, outside the context of an Absolut ad, meaningless. One does not own an absolute Warhol; one does not visit Pittsburgh to see a collection of absolute Warhols. They are just Warhols. One does not visit absolute Paris; one visits Paris. "Absolut" here becomes entirely self-referential, attesting to the fact that the ad was designed by Warhol or Haring or whomever, as if to say both "this ad was designed by" fill-in-the-blank *and* "this is an Absolut ad" at the same time.

This development in Absolut advertising is quite at odds with advertising for, say, bourbon or scotch. Generally, contemporary ads for these barrel-aged liquors are extremely verbose, extolling the craftsmanship, quality, and distilling and aging processes that make the product distinctive and unique. The silver coin embedded into the glass of the Absolut bottle suggests minting, a process of mass production of identical objects. The purple cloth sack in which Crown Royal is packaged and the wax seal of the Maker's Mark bottle suggest a lineage of human craftspeople involved throughout the production, bottling, and packaging of every bottle of bourbon or Canadian whisky. Indeed, each individual maker of Maker's Mark has had his own personal seal, indicating how many generations he is removed from the first maker. This is not to suggest, I hasten to add, that bourbon and whisky ads of this stripe are somehow more authentic than Absolut ads. The salient difference between them is that the former ads play on authenticity, while the latter ads play on inauthenticity—and they do so precisely by deploying the Absolut/absolute wordplay to empty the idea of absoluteness of its constitutive notion of authenticity. The nod to authenticity, in the Absolut ads, becomes postmodern pastiche: ironic and manifestly inauthentic.

The degree to which Absolut's advertisement campaign of the 1980s marked a departure in how vodka presented itself to American drinkers is especially apparent in view of Heublein's late-midcentury print ads for Smirnoff vodka. These advertisements frequently emphasized Smirnoff's quality, character, purity, and mixability. They were, by today's standards, very text-heavy spots, featuring a paragraph or two informing readers that Smirnoff is "filtered through 14,000 pounds of activated charcoal," offering recipes for Smirnoff's take on classic vodka cocktails, and always ending with the famous tagline "it leaves you breathless"—a sly invitation to the midday tippler to choose a spirit reputed not to leave the telltale scent of alcohol on the breath.[20] Smirnoff ads of the late 1950s and 1960s paired recipes for such drinks as the "Smirnoff Blizzard" (Smirnoff and Fresca),[21] the "Smirnoff Mary" (Smirnoff and tomato juice),[22] the "Bullshot" (Smirnoff and beef bullion),[23] the Smirnoff martini (made with Smirnoff instead of gin),[24] and the "Smirnoff Mule" (Smirnoff and 7UP)[25] with images of such celebrity entertainers as Vincent Price,[26] Johnny Carson,[27] Woody Allen,[28] Julie Newmar,[29] and Tammy Grimes.[30] And, even though the text of these ads often gives a nod to how smooth Smirnoff tastes "even on the rocks," they repeatedly emphasize the versatility of a sprit that "loses itself completely in just about anything that pours."[31]

Smirnoff's ads were, in other words, emphatically *about the vodka*. By linking it metonymically to the celebrities hawking it; by remarking on its particular qualities (versatility, smoothness), its production (charcoal filtration), middle-brow sophistication (being among the more expensive vodkas); and by offering consumers easy cocktail recipes, these busy advertisements attempted to lend substance to this otherwise neutral grain spirit known for its colorlessness, tastelessness, and odorlessness. Indeed, these ads can be understood as working against the nature of vodka as such: their polysemy betraying anxiety about vodka's essential nothingness just as their featured celebrities betrayed anxiety about vodka's essential lack of character.

In the early 1980s, however, after the launch of Absolut's revolutionary ad campaign in 1981, Smirnoff's ads began to change. At first, the change was relatively subtle: While the Smirnoff ads continued to feature accomplished spokespeople, they were not always A-list celebrities recognizable by sight; the ads included, instead, figures known for their accomplishments outside the pop entertainment industry, such as Polly Bergen ("businesswoman and entertainer"),[32] F. Lee Bailey ("trial lawyer"),[33] Robert Ludlum ("author of *The Parsifal Mosaic* and 10 other bestsellers"),[34] Pinchas Zukerman ("world-renowned violinist"),[35] and James A. Nassikas ("President, the Sanford Court Hotel").[36] At the same time, the text of the ads, featuring quoted endorsements, began emphasizing "value." Acknowledging that Smirnoff costs "a little more than ordinary vodka," the prominence of "value" in each ad invites comparison to the more expensive premium vodka Absolut. Gone were the recipes, the "breathless" tagline, and wordy descriptions of Smirnoff's quality and versatility, replaced instead by somewhat ham-handed play on the spokesperson's field of endeavor. So, the lines "Sure, Smirnoff may cost a little more, but in my book quality always does" are attributed to Ludlum,[37] while Zukerman, we are given to understand, finds that Smirnoff "plays second fiddle to none."[38] There's a kind of midlife desperation speaking through these ads, as if the arrival of a hipper, cooler upstart competitor had troubled the more established vodka's sense of identity. Breathlessness becomes value; celebrity gives way to professionalism; claims of quality cede to clunky wordplay.

This sense of being behind the times, in terms of the look and feel of its ads, surely contributed to more radical alterations in the late 1980s and into the 1990s. A 1989 ad, in monochrome silver and crystalline transparency, shows a steel decanter embossed with the Smirnoff crest behind an unadorned, flared rocks glass filled to the rim with iced vodka, the only splash of color being the red "Smirnoff" emblem from the label submerged in the glass like a twist of zest. The copy, too, becomes more understated: "Rock Czar," in an austere, underscored font, heads the ad, while the sub-lede reads, "For over a century the reigning vodka."[39] The brevity of the text, together with the unapologetic pun in the header and the prominence of the vodka decanter, present themselves as all but a knockoff of the Absolut ads of the same period. In the 1990s, Smirnoff's print ads bordered on synonym-replacement plagiarism, deploying "pure" (instead of "absolute") in such catchphrases as "Pure Party,"[40] "Pure Standout,"[41] and "Pure Surprise,"[42] captioning images featuring oversized Smirnoff bottles, redesigned to echo the Absolut bottle's domed shape, as their primary visual feature. In the course of ten years, having launched no fewer than four distinct campaigns, Smirnoff scrambled to remake its image while Absolut continued to elaborate a single, central motif: the iconic bottle shape and the two-word taglines.

The essential contrast between the Absolut and Smirnoff sensibilities lies in the way each vodka's campaign dealt with its product's essential emptiness. From the very beginning, Absolut's ads embraced it, unapologetically and quite explicitly substituting brand image in place of Absolut vodka's positive attributes. Indeed, Absolut ads all but ignore the vodka itself. Apart from the iconic, bold, sans serif font "Absolut . . ." text at the bottom of the page, the only copy in this famous series is the text inscribed on the bottle:

ABSOLUT
Country of Sweden
VODKA

This superior vodka
was distilled from grain grown
in the fields of southern Sweden.
It has been produced at the famous
old distilleries near Åhus

*in accordance with more than
400 years of Swedish tradition.
Vodka has been sold under the name
Absolut Since 1879*

80 PROOF
PRODUCED AND BOTTLED IN SWEDEN 1,0 LITER (33,8 FL. OZ)[43]
IMPORTED

The highly ornate cursive script discourages the casual reader from perusing the text. But, even attended to carefully, the bottle's inscription divulges very little about the vodka it contains: only that it is "superior vodka . . . distilled from grain grown in . . . southern Sweden . . . near Åhus," that it has been branded "Absolut since 1879," that its "80 proof," that it is "imported," and that the bottle contains one liter of it. Familiar though the highly ornate cursive script of the engraved text is, though, frequently some complementary visual feature in the ad obscures or distorts it, at least partially. In fact, more and more often through the 1980s and 1990s, the bottle is missing altogether, until all that remains in the vast majority of ads is its silhouette, sometimes hidden in the busy visual design. In other words, the product mattered little enough in the earliest moments of the campaign and soon enough ceased to matter at all.

Less successfully, at least in aesthetic terms, Smirnoff's ads tried again and again well into the 1980s to say something about Smirnoff vodka and the experience of drinking it, before finally—and too obviously—following Absolut's lead. Perhaps for this reason—the association of Smirnoff vodka with a kind of failure of image, despite its unquestionable quality and popularity—the ad's text reads as irredeemably uncool or, as vodka historian and blogger Victorino Matus has put it, "It's still rail."[44] Emphasizing this disconnect between Smirnoff's "humble" brand identity and quality, Eric Asimov reported on a blind vodka tasting conducted in 2005 by the *New York Times*. While the tasters taking part were experienced mixologists and critics able to detect nuances of flavor and texture among the various vodkas they sampled, the difficulty in ranking vodka results from, as Asimov puts it, "its purity, . . . an almost Platonic neutrality that makes tasting it more akin to tasting bottled waters, or snowflakes."[45] Because the tasters did not see the bottles, they could not base their judgments on "glossy merchandising" by which vodkas have "set a marketing standard for high-end spirits," such as Wyborowa's "striking bottle designed by the architect Frank Gehry" or the unique and immediately identifiable Absolut bottle, associated as it is with a wry, sophisticated ad campaign.[46] Deprived of these markers of status, the *Times*'s tasters admitted that distinguishing among the vodkas proved a challenging task. To keep the tasters honest, among the many premium brands to be sampled, the tasting coordinator included Smirnoff, by far the least expensive and least "cool" of the vodkas on offer, as a ringer. It was, according to Asimov, the across-the-board favorite.

These trends in vodka marketing generally, and Absolut marketing in particular, emphasizing the bottle's surface contours, textures, inscriptions, and trademarks over the ontological emptiness of its contents, coalesce in Ellis's novel. Published at the end of the 1980s, it serves as a kind of postscript to and diagnosis of the decline of corporate masculine subjectivity. Indeed, as a text that—both as a novel and as a film—depicts and brackets vodka's zenith as the American liquor and the evacuation of masculine corporate identity, *American Psycho*, read alongside Absolut's increasingly sophisticated and self-referential advertising campaign, encapsulates these changes. For in film and novel alike, we see an ironic depiction of the emptiness, sameness, and mindless commodity consumption that Absolut advertisers would champion, and that the overwhelming popularity of vodka as the spirit of preference at the end of the twentieth century symptomizes.

In one of the few really gripping passages in the novel, Patrick Bateman, the narrator, a stereotype of the 1980s Wall Street yuppie, plays a particularly cruel, but for my purposes telling, joke on his girlfriend, Evelyn, his antipathy toward whom has developed slowly over the course of the novel. "For dessert," after the expensive dinner they share together late in the novel, he has "arranged something special."[47] He explains that he

> stole a urinal cake from the men's room when the attendant wasn't looking. At home I covered it with cheap chocolate syrup, froze it, then placed it in an empty Godiva box, tying a silk bow around it, and now, in [the restaurant], [...] I ask our waiter to present this to the table 'in the box.' [...]. He brings it over [...], and I'm impressed by what a big deal he makes over it; he's even placed a silver dome over the box and Evelyn coos with delight when he lifts it off [...], and she makes a move for the spoon he's laid next to her water glass (that I make sure is empty). [...] She takes the first bite, chewing dutifully, immediately and obviously disgusted, then swallows. She shudders, then makes a grimace but tries to smile as she takes another tentative bite.[48]

The significance of this brief scene, beyond demonstrating again that Bateman is a sadistic jerk, lies in the way the urinal cake concentrates a number of loosely connected themes in *American Psycho*. Part of the Bateman's amusement at this little prank has to do with the private pleasure he derives from watching Evelyn eat disinfectant toilet deodorizer, without her being aware that that is what she's eating, in a situation in which she must pretend to enjoy doing so. Another part has to do with her reaction: "Her face, twisted with displeasure, manages to blanch again as if she were gagging. [...] 'It's so....' Her face is now one long agonized grimace mask and, shuddering, she coughs[,] '... minty. [...] It's just [...] it's just ... so *minty*.'"[49]

A blend of disinfectant, fragrance, colorant, urine, and chocolate, boxed, bowed, and domed, the urinal-cake dessert stands as a starkly overdetermined symbol of precisely the kind of mixture of incommensurate elements from which Bateman's professed taste (in women, clothes, décor, and music) recoils. If the urinal cake is too much—too disgusting, too layered, too flavorful, too minty—Bateman himself is pure, as he makes clear in a long passage describing his morning routine, reproduced in a shortened version as the opening voice-over of the 2000 film based on the novel. The novel's narrator explains:

> In the shower I use first a water-activated gel cleanser, then a honey-almond body scrub, and on the face an exfoliating gel scrub. Vidal Sassoon shampoo is especially good at getting rid of the coating of dried perspiration, salts, oils, airborne pollutants and dirt that can weigh down hair and flatten it to the scalp which can make you look older. The conditioner is also good—silicone technology permits conditioning benefits without weighing down the hair which can also make you look older. [...] Once out of the shower and toweled dry I appl[y] a shaving cream by Pour Homme [and] press a hot towel against my face for two minutes to soften abrasive beard hair. Then I always slather on a moisturizer (to my taste, Clinique) and let it soak in for a minute. [...] You should use an aftershave lotion with little or no alcohol. Never use cologne on your face, since the high alcohol content dries your face out and makes you look older. [...] If the face seems dry and flaky—which makes it look dull and older—use a clarifying lotion that removes flakes and uncovers fine skin (it can also make your tan look darker). Then apply an anti-aging eye balm (Baume Des Yeuz) followed by a final moisturizing "protective" lotion.[50]

Notably, whereas Bateman administers an improbable collation of chocolate, mint, disinfectant, and deodorizer to Evelyn internally, insisting that she eat it all at once, he applies a similar array of chemicals, extracts, and reactants to himself only topically, and only one at a time. While he amuses himself by penetrating those around him—sexually, violently, and gustatorily—he himself maintains his surfaces, forming around himself a carapace of toned musculature, supple skin, conditioned hair, and, as we shall see, *haute couture*.

In this regard, Bateman appears almost two decades ahead of his time. It took until the end of the 1990s for men's concern over their appearance to become widespread and urgent enough to catch the notice of the *New York Times*. Stephen Henderson's 1998 article for the *Times* titled "Vanity, Thy Name Is Man?" reports on the rise in men's expressions of vanity over the course of the decade, especially among the *nouveau riche*, and sounds a call to action among men who have remained blissfully unconcerned about their physical appearance:

> Attention please, beer-gut Gus, hairy Harry and turkey-neck Tom. Wake up and smell the skin conditioner before women start imploring you to join men across America who are paying more attention to, and more money for, their personal appearance. At all ages and incomes, a steadily growing number of men are tightening their muscles, filing their fingernails, having their smiles whitened and eyes undrooped—or worrying that they should.[51]

Henderson cites the increasingly common recourse to plastic surgery, liposuction, tanning, manicure and pedicure treatments, smile lifts, and home beauty products among men as a sign that "men are now internalizing the same social message that women have suffered under for decades—their worth is based on their looks."[52] These applications renew our attention to the significance of bodily surfaces in *American Psycho*, and, in particular, the surfaces of Bateman's body, which appears sculpted, polished, and impenetrable.

Bateman's morning routine, highly redacted above, suggests that Bateman, in the 1980s, is among those early in adopting high-tech bath and beauty products to enhance their looks and maintain the appearance of youth. Paradoxically, this hyperinvestment in bodily appearance constitutes a kind of subjective disappearing act for Bateman: In an early scene in the film, as Bateman peels off a facial mask, his voice-over explains: "There is an idea of Patrick Bateman, some kind of abstraction, but there is no real me, only an entity, something illusory. [. . .]: I simply am not there."

Bateman's ablutions perform repeated distillations resulting in his disappearance as a coherent individual, the reduction of the subject-persona to "an idea" that is barely "there." These distillations presage the rise of ultrapremium vodkas, including Buffalo Trace's HDW CLIX, whose name includes the distiller's initials (Harlen Davis Wheatley) and the Roman numeral 159, the number of times the vodka has been distilled. In 2011, the online *Drinks International* reported on the launch of HDW CLIX, with this explanation:

> The vodka is made from red winter wheat, rye, yellow dent distiller's grade corn and distiller's malted barley, combined with limestone-rich water. The process includes cooking, fermenting and distilling from an original 28,400 gallons of mash, dividing it down and re-distilling over a period of

twelve months, resulting in 159 distillations, 332 gallons and 2,000 bottles of vodka. Before the final bottling, the product was rested in a stainless steel tank for 12 months.[53]

Here we see the distillation process taken to an absurd extreme, performing reduction after reduction, until the original volume of diverse ingredients has dwindled by 99 percent, producing a vodka the origins and character of whose ingredients, like Bateman after a bath, are "simply [...] not there."

In Ellis's novel, in addition to cleansing, exfoliating, and conditioning the surfaces of his body, Bateman works hard to maintain its hardness. He exercises obsessively: weights, stretching, aerobics, squash. He can do a thousand crunches. He recounts a moment of foreplay with his fiancée thus: "I pull my Armani shirt up and place her hand on my torso, want her to feel how rock-hard, how *halved* my stomach is, and I flex the muscles, grateful it's light in the room so she can see how bronzed and defined my abdomen has become."[54] With Ewen, in *All Consuming Images: The Politics of Style in Contemporary Culture*, we might say that "if this is eroticism, it is one tuned more to the mysteries of technology than to those of the flesh."[55] The then-emerging fixation on the machine-sculpted male body symptomizes a perceived loss of bodily relevance among men whose white-collar jobs had alienated them from physical labor and direct mechanical interface. Profiling one "Raymond H," who "has been working on his body for the past three years, ever since he got his last promotion," Ewen, writing in the late 1980s, muses that "perhaps it is fitting that this quintessential single, young, urban professional—whose life has become a circle of work, money culture, and cultivation of an image—has turned himself, literally, into a piece of work."[56] In Ewen's view, the highly routinized workout structured by machine circuits becomes the location for the expression of a nostalgic masculinity that longs for the inscription of power, earning potential, and social relevance on the "hard" body that itself stands as an index of the usurpation of a human conception of masculinity by a highly machined one: "The hard shell is now a sign of achievement, visible proof of success in the 'rat race.' The goal [Raymond] seeks is more about *looking* than *touching*."[57]

Like Bateman and Raymond H, the producers of Crystal Head Vodka acknowledge the allure of hard surfaces. The Crystal Head website, for example, offers a Frequently Asked Questions page explaining that "the vodka is filtered seven times, of which three passes are through semi-precious crystals known as Herkimer Diamonds." The website goes on to tell the process-conscious consumer that "Herkimer Diamonds are semi-precious quartz crystals. Beautiful examples of the planet's crystalline deposits, these stones have no colored rutilations." And, while the vodka's producers admit that they "can't explain it, taste-testers who sample Crystal Head Vodka with and without the triple Herkimer diamond filtration, resoundingly choose the Herkimer diamond fluid." Somehow, the contact with the faceted surfaces of these hard crystals enhances the flavor and texture of the vodka, even though, according to the website, "your high-school chemistry professor would probably say that pouring vodka over quartz crystals does nothing to materially enhance the product."[58]

Given this essay's central claim—that its substancelessness makes vodka the signature spirit of the American 1980s for the same reasons that *American Psycho* can be read as the decade's emblematic novel—we might expect vodka to flow freely throughout the novel. And it does: Vodka, either generically or by brand name, is mentioned something like three dozen times, with Absolut being far and away the preferred brand among the novel's vodka drinkers. If we assume that the so-called martinis served throughout the novel are made with vodka, and not gin—several times, they are called "Absolut martinis"—then vodka appears twice as frequently as Bateman's own preferred pour, J&B, an English blend of over 40 single-malt whiskies created specifically to appeal to the (undiscerning) post-Prohibition American palate. Throughout the novel, waves of booze of all kinds break again and again on cocaine beaches: spirits including bourbon, tequila, brandy, and, specifically, cognac; as well as such mixed drinks as the Bloody Mary, margarita, and Bellini. Whatever the symbolic or expressive significance of any particular spirit or drink among those that cascade through *American Psycho*, on the whole, they seem primarily atmospheric, more or less accurately depicting the upper-middlebrow Manhattan drinks culture of the 1980s. And while the overall lack of discrimination that the characters' drink choices betray emphasizes the substancelessness this essay is concerned with, the emptiness pervading (if I may) Ellis's novel is more general, less localizable in any single distilled spirit.

By contrast, the Bateman of both the film and the novel is highly brand-conscious when it comes to the clothing that drapes the body's surfaces, so much so that, by about halfway through the novel, the reader can be forgiven for groaning audibly at an encounter with a passage like this, typical of Bateman's introduction of the novel's panoply of secondary characters:

> [Price is] wearing a linen suit by Canali Milano, a cotton shirt by Ike Behar, a silk tie by Bill Blass and cap-toed leather lace-ups from Brooks Brothers. I'm wearing a lightweight linen suit with pleated trousers, a cotton shirt, a dotted silk tie, all by Valentino Couture, and perforated cap-toe leather shoes by Allen-Edmonds. Once inside Harry's we spot David Van Patten and Craig McDermott

at a table up front. Van Patten is wearing a double-breasted wool and silk sport coat, button-fly wool and silk trousers with inverted pleats by Mario Valentino, a cotton shirt by Gitman Brothers, a polka-dot silk tie by Bill Blass and leather shoes from Brooks Brothers. McDermott is wearing a woven-linen suit with pleated trousers, a button-down cotton and linen shirt by Basile, a silk tie by Joseph Abboud and ostrich loafers from Susan Bennis Warren Edwards.[59]

Unlike conventional novels, in which individual characters are discernible by their looks and stature, habits of speech, ideas and ideals, and so forth, in *American Psycho* only their couture differentiates them. But the differentiation offered by the brands and styles repeatedly fails: they are distinctions without difference. Identical with regard to looks, fashion, habits, and personality, the other young professional men who populate *American Psycho* are frequently mistaken for one another. Time and time again, in both the novel and the film, despite their aptitude in recognizing styles and brands, the other bankers with whom Bateman spends his time fail to recognize one another. A typical encounter occurs in the novel's first chapter:

> In a cab that's stopped in traffic across from this one, a guy who looks a lot like Luis Carruthers waves over at Timothy and when Timothy doesn't return the wave the guy—slicked-back hair, suspenders, horn-rimmed glasses—realizes it's not who he thought it was and looks back at his copy of *USA Today*.[60]

And again, a few pages later:

> A figure with slicked-back hair and horn-rimmed glasses approaches in the distance ... and Timothy wonders aloud, "Is it Victor Powell? It can't be."[61]

And still later:

> "Who is that?" Price asks, staring over at the bar. "Is that *Reed* Robison?" ... Preston slowly turns around ... and ... squints over at the bar. "No, that's Nigel Morrison."[62]

Or

> "It's Scott Montgomery," Price says. "Isn't it? It's Scott Montgomery." "Perhaps," Van Patten teases.[63]

Or

> Some guy who looks exactly like Christopher Lauder comes over to the table and says, patting me on the shoulder, "Hey Hamilton, nice tan," before walking into the men's room[64]

Or

> Ebersol wraps an arm around Timothy's neck and laughingly pretends to strangle him, then Price pushes the arm away, shakes Ebersol's hand and says, "Hey Madison."[65]

Or

> From my POV Paul Owen sits at a table across the room with someone who looks a lot like Trent Moore, or Roger Daley, and some other guy who looks like Frederick Connell.[66]

Or "That's not Spencer Wynn"[67]; or "'That wasn't Conrad,' I say"[68]; or "No, that's not Madison for Christ sakes, that's *Turnbull*."[69] Because of the shifts in the way that corporate management, and books about managing corporations, conceived of subjectivity and identity among the managerial classes through the 1980s and into the 1990s, dwelling on these misrecognitions in *American Psycho* proves especially enabling.

In *The Cultural Work of Corporations*, Megan Brown offers a brief history of those transformations. She shows that during the later decades of the twentieth century, corporations began quite intentionally building a culture that emphasized individuality and distinction among their employees, especially in management, reacting against and departing from a discourse of conformity and efficiency in corporate management. Acknowledging that the view of corporate culture in the postwar decades was far from monolithic, including as it did theories of corporate identity that emphasized human relations, ingenuity, and individuality, Brown argues that by the end of the 1980s, corporations in America had begun to emphasize individuality over conformity, explicitly engaging in a discourse of corporate subjectivity at odds with the notion of mindless conformity examined in William Whyte's work mentioned earlier.[70] Far from suggesting an enlightened liberalism, however, Brown argues that these changes effectively broke down the divisions between personal life and work life, allowing the encroachment of the latter into the former, and thus improving loyalty and retention and increasing productivity. In other words, the individualist imperative becomes, under Brown's analysis, its own version of conformity, "another mode of control": "Personality and creativity, like industry knowledge or negotiation skills, become corporate property."[71] In becoming "corporate property," these attributes, once imagined as defining the liberal subject, find themselves detached from the individual who possesses them.

Brown's analysis, which explicitly deploys a Foucaultian approach, demonstrates that corporate "individuality" emerges as a trait of a particular type of corporate employee, drawing our attention once more to Ellis's representation of the denizens of corporate management offices as different in myriad ways, but nonetheless indistinguishable from one another. Furthermore, in light of Brown's analysis, we see again how Ewen's views on the increasing fixation on the machined male body and Henderson's elucidation of the rise in men's consumption of health- and beauty-related products during this same period point back to an internally riven corporate cultural discourse—one that, evacuated of interiority, must turn its attention to the surfaces of the managerial body in order to strive for distinction. From this point of view, the accessories, clothing, ablutions, workouts, sexual appetites, and even psychoses of Ellis's characters appear as symptoms of a particularly late-capitalist anxiety about identity and conformity at the end of the twentieth century. After all, reminded of the fact that his family's wealth makes it unnecessary for Bateman to work at all, he states that he does so because he "want[s] ... to ... fit ... in."[72]

The anxieties about conformity, individuality, identity, and masculinity that we find indexed in *American Psycho* are not, in fact, the novel's or the narrator's anxieties. In Bateman's world, there is no expressed nostalgia for lost subjectivity or angst over trying to maintain it. Bateman and the other characters who populate *American Psycho* are both in and of a world where interiority and subjectivity are not even thinkable as such. Ellis presents emptiness and subjectlessness as neutral facts of the world his novel represents. The degree to which the novel enacts no anxieties about the subjectivity or identity—or about anything else, for that matter—manifests itself even at the level of narrative dynamics. For, despite graphic scenes of sex and violence and the literally cutthroat rivalries that animate relations among the novel's characters, the narrative affects a profoundly blasé attitude toward the events it unfolds. Bateman's tone, as narrator, is detached, matter-of-fact, and disinterested, a tone admirably represented by Christian Bale's flat affect throughout most of the film version.

Indeed, Ellis's novel may be understood as a diagnostic for a generalized middle-managerial male psychosis. Psychosis, suggested by the "psycho" of Ellis's title, enables us to take a cue from vodka's avowed mixability—its knack for complementing a variety of juices, mixers, and garnishes—and to bring together this essay's disparate elements: vodka advertisement; the popularity of vodka as such; shifts in corporate culture in the final decades of the twentieth century; the objectified and aestheticized male body; and *American Psycho*, the setting and the book and film versions of which fall squarely within the period under consideration. Specifically, the view of psychosis propounded by French psychoanalyst and theorist Jacques Lacan (1901–1981) emerges as the overarching motif of this historical moment and the cultural objects thereof.[73] For Lacan, the psychotic suffers from a failure of the paternal, law-giving function, which he termed "The Name-of-the-Father" and which gives coherence and order to the individual's experience of the world by allowing it to be structured and represented through symbolic systems, most notably (but not exclusively) language.[74] This deficiency at the center of the psychotic's symbolic sensibility accounts, in part, for the seemingly confused, tangential, or associative ways in which the psychotic speaks; for his inability to distinguish between experiences of reality and imagined, delusional, or hallucinatory experience; and for his bizarre investment of hidden or secret messages in the symbols and words he encounters.[75] In the Lacanian view, then, psychosis's apparent excesses—the multitude of interpretations the psychotic draws from apparently straightforward utterances, for example, or his persecution delusions and delusions of grandeur, or the hallucinatory experiences that overlay reality—belie a fundamental, structural deficiency: the failure of the symbolic register to ensure subjective and extrasubjective coherence. In short, without the stabilizing relationship to symbolic representation, the psychotic begins to lose a stable sense of himself and his relationship to the world.

Lacan further theorizes that, to compensate for the deficiency in the symbolic order of the mind, the psychotic mind structures itself according to fantasy and, in particular, to fantasy images (rather than symbols) of wholeness, power, and subjective coherence. These fantasies, which dominate in the psychological register that Lacan termed "the Imaginary" because of its primarily imagistic rather than symbolic representational dynamic, serve to produce a sense of subjectivity that is coherent but always temporary, idiosyncratic, and unstable—one unmoored from the grammars and conventions of symbolic exchange. Thus, the psychotic invests experience and perception with disordered significance.

Lacan's view of psychosis speaks to my project here for several reasons: First, it precisely describes the way the fictional Bateman of Ellis's novel perceives himself, structured around an overinvestment in the image (of himself, of others, of the world he inhabits) and a failure to engage effectively in symbolic exchanges, whether composed of speech and writing (including the novel's narrative) or of conventional cultural codes of behavior and affect.[76] Second, it accounts for the shift in corporate masculine identity from one that prizes the corporation as a social organization inhabited by conforming men of substance—Whyte's "company man"—to one built on invidious distinction and competition among atomized individuals motivated by anxieties over a failure of Cartesian interiority and driven by the dominance of the image in the late twentieth century—in particular, the image of the sculpted "hard body" of the managerial man.[77]

Finally, psychosis enables us to more clearly frame the shift in vodka branding and advertising strategies that occurred in the early 1980s: from the wordy, conventional, symbolically integrated discourse of Smirnoff's print ads to the attenuated, abstract, visually and discursively overdetermined Absolut campaign that became the dominant image of vodka in the 1980s and 1990s. In particular, the Absolut ads that dispense with the actual bottle itself in favor of images that suggest the bottle's shape highlight the Lacanian psychosis of the Absolut worldview of the late 1980s and early 1990s. Ads set in "Absolut Paris,"[78] "Absolut Rome,"[79] and "Absolut Monte Carlo"[80]—and any of a wide range of what Lewis, in his history of the Absolut campaign, calls "Absolut Eurocities"[81]—imagine sites specific to those cities as silhouettes of the Absolut bottle: an entryway to the Paris metro, the fairing cowl of a Vespa, a bird's-eye view of a roulette table. These images are, in fact, hallucinations, as if the reader were invited into Absolut's psychotic mindset, where fantasy images of Absolut bottles, in place of the text-inscribed bottle itself, appear everywhere like secret messages that only the supernormal perceptive apparatus of the psychotic can decode. They thus guarantee the coherence of the viewer's relationship to an otherwise chaotic object world. This shift to the primacy of the image over language—of the Lacanian Imaginary register over the Symbolic one—becomes especially apparent in the ads designed by, and named for, such famous and instantly recognizable visual artists as Keith Haring and Andy Warhol. The psychotic, fractured, hallucinatory quality of these "Absolut Artists" ads is especially apparent in those designed by less-well-known or niche artists of the late 1980s and early 1990s, such as David Spada,[82] Monica Majoli,[83] and Konstantin Latyshev.[84] Indeed—and lest one doubt the validity of a psychoanalytic reading of vodka—Lewis himself notes that the "Absolute Dream" ad, one of the earliest in the campaign, had already "g[iven] the Absolut bottle an imagination."[85]

Thanks in large part to the success of these campaigns, vodka comes into its own as a spirit, replacing gin in traditional cocktails and eclipsing barreled and aged liquors, and as an idea at precisely the moment in American cultural history when the idea of urban, professional masculinity finds itself emptied of substance and, instead, garnished, accessorized, moisturized, and "individualized." As a crystallization of that transformation, *American Psycho* points us toward the intersection of these many anxieties, formations, and reformations, suggesting that the endemic psychosis of the modern world bears the effects of a kind of brand-high binge. Absolut's cities and artists ads, like the Calvin

Klein underwear ads offering the image of the sculpted male body as the fantasy paradigm for male self-discipline and self-mastery, are telling symptoms of a cultural psychosis characteristic of white-collar masculinity ascendant in the last decades of the twentieth century, of which Absolut vodka is one particularly telling symptom and of which Ellis's novel may be understood as the diagnosis.

Drake University

NOTES

1. See Edward P. Comentale's essay, "The Manhattan," in this volume for an analysis of the semiotics of one of the fussier, busier cocktails in the American barkeep's repertoire and a discussion of the decline in popularity of such drinks.
2. Anthony Dias Blue, *The Complete Book of Spirits: A Guide to Their History, Production and Enjoyment* (New York: Harper Collins, 2004), 9.
3. For an account of the development and dissemination of so-called poststructuralist theories of language and interpretation, see Terry Eagleton, *Literary Theory: An Introduction*, 2nd ed. (Minneapolis: University of Minnesota Press, 1996), especially the afterword.
4. See William Whyte Jr., *The Organization Man* (Garden City, NY: Doubleday-Anchor Books, 1957).
5. Stuart Ewen, *All Consuming Images: The Politics of Style in Contemporary Culture* (New York: Basic Books, 1988), 188–190.
6. Richard W. Lewis, *Absolut Book: The Absolut Vodka Advertising Story* (Tokyo: Journey Editions, 1996), 10–14.
7. Lewis, *Absolut Book*, xi.
8. Lewis, *Absolut Book*, 67.
9. Lewis, *Absolut Book*, 15.
10. Lewis, *Absolut Book*, 16.
11. Lewis, *Absolut Book*, 19.
12. Lewis, *Absolut Book*, 23.
13. Lewis, *Absolut Book*, 10.
14. Lewis, *Absolut Book*, 18.
15. Lewis, *Absolut Book*, 17.
16. Lewis, *Absolut Book*, 64.
17. Lewis, *Absolut Book*, 69.
18. Lewis, *Absolut Book*, 248.
19. Lewis, *Absolut Book*, 225.
20. Blue, *The Complete Book of Spirits*, 19.

21. "1969 Smirnoff Vodka Ad with Johnny Carson—Blizzard Howl," Vintage Paper Ads, http://www.vintagepaperads.com/1969-Smirnoff-Vodka-Ad-w-Johnny-Carson--Blizzard-Howl_p_2386.html.

22. "1963 Vintage Ad, Smirnoff Vodka Robert Goulet Singer Bloody Mary," PicClick, https://picclick.com/1963-vintage-AD-SMIRNOFF-VODKA-Robert-Goulet-362336470691.html#&gid=1&pid=1.

23. "Magazine Ad for Smirnoff Vodka, Bullshot the Drink with Beef in It, Man with Bull Head, 1958," Magazines, Ads, & Books Store, http://magazinesadsandbooks.com/Magazine-Ad-For-Smirnoff-Vodka-Bullshot-The-Drink-With-Beef-In-It-Man-With-Bull-Head-1958-P3031774.aspx.

24. "Vintage 1957 New Yorker Ad for Smirnoff Vodka—You Taste Them, Not It," Distillery Trail, http://www.distillerytrail.com/blog/vintage-1957-new-yorker-ad-for-smirnoff-vodka-you-taste-them-not-it/.

25. "1966 Smirnoff Vodka Ad—Woody Allen and Mule Mugs," Pinterest, https://www.pinterest.com/pin/9359111702686053.

26. Bert Stern, photog., "Vincent Price for Smirnoff, Life Magazine, 1955," Pinterest, https://www.pinterest.com/pin/470907704778366151/.

27. "1969 Smirnoff Vodka Ad."

28. "1966 Smirnoff Vodka Ad."

29. "1966 Smirnoff Ad—Julie Newmar," Pinterest, https://www.pinterest.com/pin/469148486166172122.

30. "1965 Smirnoff Print Ad Vintage Décor Tammy Grimes Cowgirl Pistol Cowboy Hat," Pinterest, https://www.pinterest.co.uk/pin/414401603195977472/.

31. "Walter Slezak—Smirnoff (1960)," Vintage Ad Browser, http://www.vintageadbrowser.com/alcohol-ads-1960s.

32. "Magazine Ad for Smirnoff Vodka, Polly Bergen, Red Dress, Celebrity Endorsement, 1982," Magazines, Ads, & Books Store, http://magazinesadsandbooks.com/Magazine-Ad-For-Smirnoff-Vodka-Polly-Bergen-Red-Dress-Celebrity-Endorsement-1982-P3026779.aspx.

33. "Smirnoff F. Lee Bailey 1982 Ad," Magazine Advertisements, https://www.magazine-advertisements.com/uploads/2/1/8/4/21844100/smirnoff-f-lee-bailey-1.jpg.

34. "Advertisement Robert Ludlum Smirnoff Vodka Celebrity Author Born [sic] Identity Best Selling Bar Pub Restaurant Club Wall Art Décor," Etsy, https://www.etsy.com/listing/207656851/1982-advertisement-robert-ludlum.

35. "Smirnoff Pinchas Zukerman 1983 Ad," Magazine Advertisements, https://www.magazine-advertisements.com/uploads/2/1/8/4/21844100/smirnoff-pinchas-zukerman-1.jpg.

36. "Smirnoff James A. Nassikas 1984 Ad," Magazine Advertisements, https://www.magazine-advertisements.com/uploads/2/1/8/4/21844100/smirnoff-james-a-nassikas-1.jpg.

37. "Advertisement Robert Ludlum."
38. "Smirnoff Pinchas Zukerman."
39. "1989 Advertisement Smirnoff Vodka Rock Czar Star on the Rocks over Ice Reigning Bar Pub Restaurant Club Wall Art Décor," Etsy, https://www.etsy.com/dk-en/listing/472179286/1989-advertisement-smirnoff-vodka-rock.
40. "1993 Retro Ad—Smirnoff Pure Party," @RetroNewsNow, Twitter, https://twitter.com/RetroNewsNow/status/947222068235591680.
41. "Magazine Ad for Smirnoff Vodka, Penguins, Looking through Bottle, One Wears a Tuxedo, 1994," Magazines, Ads & Books Store, http://magazinesadsandbooks.com/Magazine-Ad-for-Smirnoff-Vodka-Penguins-Looking-Through-Bottle-One-Wears-A-Tuxedo-1994-P2460887.aspx.
42. "Smirnoff Vodka 'Pure Surprise'—1994 Print Magazine Ad," PicClick, https://picclick.com/Smirnoff-Vodka-Pure-Surprise-1994-print-magazine-ad-392054381823.html.
43. Note the use of the European comma, instead of an American point, to denote the decimal.
44. Victorino Matus, "About that New Smirnoff Vodka Ad," *Washington Free Beacon*, June 14, 2017, http://freebeacon.com/blog/793723/.
45. Eric Asimov, "A Humble Old Label Ices Its Rivals," *New York Times*, January 26, 2005, https://www.nytimes.com/2005/01/26/dining/a-humble-old-label-ices-its-rivals.html.
46. Asimov, "A Humble Old Label Ices Its Rivals."
47. Bret Easton Ellis, *American Psycho* (New York: Vintage, 1991), 336.
48. Ellis, *American Psycho*, 336–37.
49. Ellis, *American Psycho*, 337.
50. Ellis, *American Psycho*, 26–28.
51. Stephen Henderson, "Vanity, Thy Name Is Man?" *Sun Sentinel*, August 20, 1998, http://articles.sun-sentinel.com/1998-08-20/lifestyle/9808190247_1_half-naked-men-husbands-women.
52. Henderson, "Vanity, Thy Name Is Man?"
53. "Buffalo Trace Launches Vodka Distilled 159 Times," Drinks International, November 9, 2011, http://www.drinksint.com/news/fullstory.php/aid/2543/Buffalo_Trace_launches_vodka_distilled_159_times.html.
54. Ellis, *American Psycho*, 23.
55. Ewen, *All Consuming Images*, 191.
56. Ewen, *All Consuming Images*, 189.
57. Ewen, *All Consuming Images*, 189.
58. "FAQ," Crystal Head Vodka, https://www.crystalheadvodka.com/en/faq.
59. Ellis, *American Psycho*, 30–31.
60. Ellis, *American Psycho*, 5.
61. Ellis, *American Psycho*, 7.

62. Ellis, *American Psycho*, 36.
63. Ellis, *American Psycho*, 41.
64. Ellis, *American Psycho*, 48.
65. Ellis, *American Psycho*, 55.
66. Ellis, *American Psycho*, 88.
67. Ellis, *American Psycho*, 49.
68. Ellis, *American Psycho*, 50.
69. Ellis, *American Psycho*, 55.
70. Megan Brown, *The Cultural Work of Corporations* (New York: Palgrave MacMillan, 2009), 55.
71. Brown, *The Cultural Work of Corporations*, 56.
72. Ellis, *American Psycho*, 237. Ellipses in the original.
73. Lacan's evolving theories of psychosis can be traced throughout his seminar, held from 1953 to 1980 and published collectively as *The Seminar of Jacques Lacan* in English translations through 24 volumes, to date, beginning in 1988. *The Psychoses* (*Seminar*, vol. 3), in particular, focuses on the relationship of psychosis to imaginary and symbolic registers of perception and self-conception. However, elaborations and remarks on his theory of psychosis appear here and there throughout his oeuvre, including in *Écrits* and, earlier, in *Freud's Papers on Technique* (*Seminar*, vol. 1) and *The Ego in Freud's Theory and in the Technique of Psychoanalysis* (*Seminar*, vol. 2). To spare the reader of this essay Lacan's frequently elliptical—one may even say tortured—prose and transcribed speech, I have largely relegated illustrative and explanatory quotations from these works to the following notes, preferring instead to summarize and paraphrase the salient points of his theory in the body of the essay itself.
74. See Jacques Lacan, *Écrits: A Selection*, trans. Alan Sheridan (New York: Norton, 1977).

> For the psychosis to be triggered off, the Name-of-the-Father ... foreclosed, that is to say, never having attained the place of the Other, must be called into symbolic opposition to the subject.
> It is the lack of the Name-of-the-Father in that place which, by the hole that it opens up in the signified, sets of the cascade of reshapings of the signifier from which the increasing disaster of the imaginary proceeds, to the point at which the level is reached at which signifier and signified are stabilized in the delusional metaphor. (216)

By contrast, Lacan characterizes the relationship of the non-psychotic's ego to the imaginary and symbolic registers thus in his first seminar:

> In man, the imaginary is reduced, specialised, centered on the specular image, which creates both impasses and the function of the imaginary relation.

The image of the ego—simply because it is an image, the ego is ideal ego—sums up the entire imaginary relation in man. By being produced at a time when the functions are not yet completed, it has a salutary value, expressed well enough in the jubilatory assumption of the mirror phenomenon, but it does not possess any the less of a connection with the vital prematuration and hence with an original deficit, with a gap to which it remains linked in its structure.

The subject will rediscover over and over again that this image of self is the very framework of his categories, of his apprehension of the world—of the object, and he will achieve this through the intermediary of the other. It is in the other that he will always rediscover his ideal ego, from whence develops the dialectic of his relations to the other. (Jacques Lacan, *Freud's Papers on Technique*, vol. 1, *The Seminar of Jacques Lacan*, ed. Jacques-Allain Miller, trans. John Forrester [New York: Norton, 1991], 282.)

75. See Jacques Lacan, *The Psychoses*, vol. 3, *The Seminar of Jacques Lacan*, ed. Jacques-Alain Miller, trans. Russell Grigg (New York: Norton, 1993): "For want of being able in any way to re-establish his pact with the other, for want of being able to make any symbolic mediation whatsoever between what is new and himself, the subject moves into another mode of mediation, completely different from the former, and substitutes for symbolic mediation a profusion, an imaginary proliferation, into which the central signal of a possible mediation is introduced in a deformed and profoundly asymbolic fashion" (87).

76. See Jacques Lacan, *The Ego in Freud's Theory and in the Technique of Psychoanalysis*, vol. 2, *The Seminar of Jacques Lacan*, ed. Jacques-Alain Miller, trans. Sylvana Tomaselli (New York: Norton, 1991): "What they have identified with is an image where every gap, every aspiration, every emptiness of desire is lacking.... To the extent that the being's identification with its pure and simple image takes effect, there isn't any room for change ... , that is to say death. To the extent that the subject here symbolically identifies himself with the imaginary, he in some way satisfies [*réalise*] desire" (238). One may quibble with "satisfies" as the rendering of the French "*réalise*"; in the context of Lacan's thought, "actualizes," "enacts," "renders," or even "acts upon" avoids suggesting that any desire can ever be "satisfied."

77. Ewen, *All Consuming Images*, 190.
78. Lewis, *Absolut Book*, 225.
79. Lewis, *Absolut Book*, 226.
80. Lewis, *Absolut Book*, 227.
81. Lewis, *Absolut Book*, 219.
82. Lewis, *Absolut Book*, 174.
83. Lewis, *Absolut Book*, 177.
84. Lewis, *Absolut Book*, 180.
85. Lewis, *Absolut Book*, 16.

BIBLIOGRAPHY

"1963 Vintage Ad, Smirnoff Vodka Robert Goulet Singer Bloody Mary." PicClick. https://picclick.com/1963-vintage-AD-SMIRNOFF-VODKA-Robert-Goulet-362336470691.html#&gid=1&pid=1.

"1965 Smirnoff Print Ad Vintage Décor Tammy Grimes Cowgirl Pistol Cowboy Hat." Pinterest. https://www.pinterest.co.uk/pin/414401603195977472/.

"1966 Smirnoff Ad—Julie Newmar." Pinterest. https://www.pinterest.com/pin/469148486166172122.

"1966 Smirnoff Vodka Ad—Woody Allen and Mule Mugs." Pinterest. https://www.pinterest.com/pin/9359111702686053.

"1969 Smirnoff Vodka Ad with Johnny Carson—Blizzard Howl." Vintage Paper Ads. http://www.vintagepaperads.com/1969-Smirnoff-Vodka-Ad-w-Johnny-Carson--Blizzard-Howl_p_2386.html.

"1989 Advertisement Smirnoff Vodka Rock Czar Star on the Rocks over Ice Reigning Bar Pub Restaurant Club Wall Art Décor." Etsy. https://www.etsy.com/dk-en/listing/472179286/1989-advertisement-smirnoff-vodka-rock.

"1993 Retro Ad—Smirnoff Pure Party." @RetroNewsNow. Twitter. https://twitter.com/RetroNewsNow/status/947222068235591680.

"Advertisement Robert Ludlum Smirnoff Vodka Celebrity Author Born [sic] Identity Best Selling Bar Pub Restaurant Club Wall Art Décor." Etsy. https://www.etsy.com/listing/207656851/1982-advertisement-robert-ludlum.

Asimov, Eric. "A Humble Old Label Ices Its Rivals." *New York Times*. January 26, 2005. https://www.nytimes.com/2005/01/26/dining/a-humble-old-label-ices-its-rivals.html.

Brown, Megan. *The Cultural Work of Corporations*. New York: Palgrave MacMillan, 2009.

"Buffalo Trace Launches Vodka Distilled 159 Times." Drinks International. Online. http://www.drinksint.com/news/fullstory.php/aid/2543/Buffalo_Trace_launches_vodka_distilled_159_times.html.

Blue, Anthony Dias. *The Complete Book of Spirits: A Guide to Their History, Production and Enjoyment*. New York: Harper Collins, 2004.

Eagleton, Terry. *Literary Theory: An Introduction*. 2nd ed. Minneapolis: University of Minnesota Press, 1996.

Ewen, Stuart. *All Consuming Images: The Politics of Style in Contemporary Culture*. New York: Basic Books, 1988.

"FAQ." Crystal Head Vodka. https://www.crystalheadvodka.com/faq.

Ellis, Bret Easton. *American Psycho*. New York: Vintage, 1991.

Harron, Mary, dir. *American Psycho*. Santa Monica, CA: Lions Gate Films, 2000.

Henderson, Stephen. "Vanity, Thy Name Is Man?" *New York Times*, August 20, 1998. Reprinted in *The Sun Sentinel*. http://articles.sun-sentinel.com/1998-08-20/lifestyle/9808190247_1_half-naked-men-husbands-women.
Lacan, Jacques. *Écrits: A Selection*. Translated by Alan Sheridan. New York: Norton, 1977.
Lacan, Jacques. *The Ego in Freud's Theory and in the Technique of Psychoanalysis*. Vol. 2, *The Seminar of Jacques Lacan*. Edited by Jacques-Alain Miller. Translated by Sylvana Tomaselli. New York: Norton, 1991.
Lacan, Jacques. *Freud's Papers on Technique*. Vol. 1, *The Seminar of Jacques Lacan*. Edited by Jacques-Allain Miller. Translated by John Forrester. New York: Norton, 1991.
Lacan, Jacques. *The Psychoses*. Vol. 3, *The Seminar of Jacques Lacan*. Edited by Jacques-Alain Miller. Translated by Russell Grigg. New York: Norton, 1993.
Lewis, Richard. *Absolut Book: The Absolut Vodka Advertising Story*. Tokyo: Journey Editions, 1996.
"Magazine Ad for Smirnoff Vodka, Bullshot the Drink with Beef in It, Man with Bull Head, 1958." Magazines, Ads & Books Store. http://magazinesadsandbooks.com/Magazine-Ad-For-Smirnoff-Vodka-Bullshot-The-Drink-With-Beef-In-It-Man-With-Bull-Head-1958-P3031774.aspx.
"Magazine Ad for Smirnoff Vodka, Penguins, Looking through Bottle, One Wears a Tuxedo, 1994." Magazines, Ads & Books Store. http://magazinesadsandbooks.com/Magazine-Ad-for-Smirnoff-Vodka-Penguins-Looking-Through-Bottle-One-Wears-A-Tuxedo-1994-P2460887.aspx.
"Magazine Ad for Smirnoff Vodka, Polly Bergen, Red Dress, Celebrity Endorsement, 1982." Magazines, Ads & Books Store. http://magazinesadsandbooks.com/Magazine-Ad-For-Smirnoff-Vodka-Polly-Bergen-Red-Dress-Celebrity-Endorsement-1982-P3026779.aspx.
Matus, Victorino. "About that New Smirnoff Vodka Ad." *Washington Free Beacon*. June 14, 2017. http://freebeacon.com/blog/793723/.
"Smirnoff F. Lee Bailey 1982 Ad." Magazine Advertisements. https://www.magazine-advertisements.com/uploads/2/1/8/4/21844100/smirnoff-f-lee-bailey-1.jpg.
"Smirnoff James A. Nassikas 1984 Ad." Magazine Advertisements. https://www.magazine-advertisements.com/uploads/2/1/8/4/21844100/smirnoff-james-a-nassikas-1.jpg.
"Smirnoff Pinchas Zukerman 1983 Ad," Magazine Advertisements. https://www.magazine-advertisements.com/uploads/2/1/8/4/21844100/smirnoff-pinchas-zukerman-1.jpg.
"Smirnoff Vodka 'Pure Surprise'—1994 Print Magazine Ad." PicClick. https://picclick.com/Smirnoff-Vodka-Pure-Surprise-1994-print-magazine-ad-392054381823.html.

Stern, Bert, photog. "Vincent Price for Smirnoff, *Life Magazine*, 1955." Pinterest. https://www.pinterest.com/pin/470907704778366151/.

"Vintage 1957 New Yorker Ad for Smirnoff Vodka—You Taste Them, Not It." Distillery Trail. http://www.distillerytrail.com/blog/vintage-1957-new-yorker-ad-for-smirnoff-vodka-you-taste-them-not-it/.

Whyte, William, Jr. *The Organization Man*. Garden City, NY: Doubleday-Anchor Books, 1957.

TEN

JOY PERRINE AND THE BOURBON COCKTAIL'S RENAISSANCE

SUSAN REIGLER

FROM 1992 TO 2005, I was the restaurant critic for the Louisville *Courier-Journal*. In addition to writing a weekly review and a weekly restaurant news column, I regularly contributed feature-length articles on the city's culinary scene. The 1990s was the decade that saw the revival of bourbon, and since I was a Kentucky-based food reporter, the corn-based whiskey naturally became part of my work.

So, I was taken aback when browsing the *Washington Post* in August of 1999 to see an article about the release of a new bourbon. The Ancient Age Distillery in Frankfort, Kentucky's capital, had been renamed and had released an eponymous flagship bourbon, Buffalo Trace. The effect was as though the *Chicago Tribune* had claimed the Kentucky Derby as its turf. I immediately went into the office of my boss, features editor Greg Johnson, and pointed out that the premiere of Buffalo Trace should have been reported first in the *Courier-Journal*. After all, the distillery was in our geographic backyard and I had written the first article about the restored and reopened Labrot & Graham Distillery (soon renamed Woodford Reserve). Bourbon was the *Courier-Journal*'s rightful beat. With all the developing bourbon news, shouldn't the C-J be devoting more space to the industry? Greg agreed with me, and I was assigned another weekly column, "Drink: The Sipping News." While I didn't always write about bourbon in "Drink"—I was allotted plenty of other space for bourbon coverage, too—I did have the admittedly pleasant task not only of writing about various bourbons coming onto the market, but also of seeking out new and classic bourbon cocktails. That's how I discovered Joy Perrine's peerless bourbon concoctions.

Joy was the bar manager at Equus and Jack's Lounge. A New Jersey native, she had started bartending when she lived on the Caribbean island of St. Croix, where, obviously, rum was the go-to spirit. In her own words, Joy "loves to play with liquor." Coincidentally, the owner of the bar where she worked was a bourbon lover. He made sure that his liquor distributor supplied the bar with an allotment of Old Fitzgerald, the wheated bourbon that, at the time, was made at the legendary Stitzel-Weller Distillery in Louisville. (After Stitzel-Weller closed, the brand was sold to Heaven Hill, which still makes it today.) Joy started playing with bourbon.

Joy eventually left St. Croix, and she arrived in Louisville in 1978. Her timing could not have been better. Only six years before, Kentucky had lifted a ban on female bartenders. The irony of this is that women had long held a place in bourbon culture. Women, in general, have a more acute sense of smell than men. So, for decades distilleries had already employed women on their quality control tasting panels to assure consistency in their whiskey. But over the past decade, women have become even more visible in the bourbon industry. Among current master distillers in the United States are Alex Castle (Old Dominick Distillery, Memphis, TN) Christine Riggleman (Silverback Distillery, Afton, VA) and Joyce Nethery (Jeptha Creed Distillery, Shelbyville, KY). (As a side note, I never felt that anyone questioned my spirits writing because of my gender.)

Joy was hired in 1987 by chef/owner Dean Corbett of Equus Restaurant in Louisville, which was exactly when Maker's Mark was positioning itself as a premium bourbon brand. Whiskey had suffered a precipitous sales decline in the 1970s and early 1980s. Americans had been turning to vodka and discovering wine. Distilleries consolidated and many closed. So, in a now-famous (and certainly effective) advertising campaign, Maker's promoted itself in the 1980s with the slogan "It tastes expensive, and is." Not expensive in comparison to today's limited release bourbon prices, but the distillery was borrowing a tactic from the Scotch whisky industry, which had launched snob-appeal marketing of single malts. At about the same time, in 1984, Ancient Age Distillery (later to become Buffalo Trace) released the first single-barrel bourbon: Blanton's. It was another attempt at positioning a brand as unique and "premium." By the end of the decade, the stage was set for the comeback of bourbon—and with it, the return of classic bourbon cocktails such as the manhattan, the old-fashioned, and the whiskey sour.

At Equus, Joy was serving a lot of bourbon, and by her estimate, more than half was sold mixed with cola or ginger ale or some other sweet, fizzy soft drink. Inspired by tropical rum drinks, she started rethinking bourbon drinks. One thing she tried was making bourbon infusions. It was common enough to see containers of vodka on bar counters with various fruits in them. In the 1990s, however, very few—if any—bartenders besides Joy were trying the same with bourbon.

In 2000, Dean Corbett decided to turn the retail space next door to Equus into an upscale casual bar, which he named Jack's Lounge in honor of his late father. He made Joy the bar manager, and she went to work creating signature cocktails for the new establishment. Naturally, Jack's came to my attention as a good place to look for a drink to cover in my beverage column. And that's where I had my first bourbon cocktail that was not one of the classic trio of manhattan, old-fashioned, and whiskey sour. It was Joy's "Bourbonball," which turned into a classic itself.

In addition to releasing new brands and new bourbon expressions, bourbon distillers started sponsoring cocktail contests for professional bartenders, as did the annual Kentucky Bourbon Festival in Bardstown. Brown-Forman, maker of Woodford Reserve, had acquired an Italian-made liqueur, Tuaca, which had flavors of both orange and vanilla. (The brand has since been sold to Sazerac, parent company of Buffalo Trace Distillery.) In order to promote Tuaca, Brown-Forman had a contest for a cocktail that used it. Joy entered the Bourbonball and it won first place. Here's the recipe:

The Bourbonball
1 part Woodford Reserve bourbon
1 part Tuaca
1 part dark crème de cacao

Combine and shake over ice. Strain into a chilled cocktail glass and garnish with a cherry or with a strawberry on the rim.

The Bourbonball is a classic example of Joy's philosophy of drink mixing. You should always be able to taste the base liquor, and there should be no more than three or four ingredients in addition to it. (A spice blend counts as one ingredient, by the way. Punches may require more.) It is remarkable how few professional bartenders understand this principle. In acting as a judge for many cocktail contests, I have tasted a remarkable number of concoctions that gave me no clue what the base spirit was except that I had been told. One other feature of Joy's cocktail philosophy is *Don't make the customer wait for his drink!*—which is another good reason for keeping it simple. You should not have to wait fifteen or twenty minutes (as I have!) for a bartender to create his or her "masterpiece" for you.

I featured the Bourbonball in my drinks column, and over the next few years I enjoyed many more of Joy's original cocktail recipes. She kept inventing drinks, kept entering them in contests, and kept winning. In 2006, her Spiceberry won the Woodford Reserve Infusion Contest. (Her creative infusions were part of the inspiration for the competition.) In 2008, her manhattan Italiano took second place in the Woodford Reserve Manhattan Experience competition.

Bourbon cocktails have proven to be an effective marketing tool for distillers, nearly all of which—both the big brands and the small craft distillers—feature cocktails on their websites. In addition to Brown-Forman, virtually all the major distillers, including Four Roses, Wild Turkey, Maker's Mark, and Buffalo Trace, have national (and in many cases, international) cocktail contests.

When I left the *Courier-Journal* in 2007, I asked Joy if she had ever considered writing a book of her bourbon cocktail recipes. Her answer was, "I have, but I don't have time to write." I did. So I suggested to Joy that if she would give me recipes, I would organize them into a book. Joy wrote out almost 100 recipes in pencil on lined notebook paper. She handed me the stack and I turned it into a manuscript. The University Press of Kentucky, which had published a book of mine, was interested in developing a "bourbon shelf," and the press agreed to publish what became *The Kentucky Bourbon Cocktail Book*.

Released in 2009, it contains not only cocktail recipes, but also instructions for setting up a home bar, instructions for making bourbon infusions, recipes for bourbon drinks for all seasons (including Louisville's unique fifth season, the Kentucky Derby), recipes for appetizers to serve with the drinks, and a handful of guest recipes from other notable bartenders in Louisville. The Bourbonball graces the cover. The cocktail book has been reprinted multiple times, and a sequel, *More Kentucky Bourbon Cocktails*, was published in 2016. From 2009 to 2016, Joy led "Bourbon Cocktail Mixology" at the Kentucky Bourbon Festival in Bardstown. The single session sold out almost immediately the first year. So it was offered twice the following year. Again, both sold out. In 2011 the event was expanded to three sessions. Participants sample ten different cocktails, Joy demonstrates how to make each of them, and every participant receives a copy of the cocktail book.

Joy has also been honored as "Louisville's Best Bartender" in *Louisville* magazine's "Best of Louisville Awards," and she has been featured at the country's most prestigious cocktail event, Tales of the Cocktail, which is held each year in New Orleans. John Mariani profiled Joy in *Esquire* magazine, dubbing her "The Bad Girl of Bourbon" (a name that delighted her so much that she uses it as her e-mail address). Fred Minnick also devoted several pages to her in his book *Whiskey Women: The Untold Story of How Women Saved Bourbon, Scotch, and Irish Whiskey*. As of 2019, bourbon cocktails are everywhere. Steve Akley's

Bourbon Mixology: 50 Bourbon Cocktails from 50 Iconic Bars features recipes from bars spanning the country from Seattle, Washington, to Washington, DC, and from Chicago to New Orleans. Naturally, many of these bars are in Louisville; and not surprisingly, Joy's Bourbonball from Equus and Jack's Lounge is included. In 2009, the Louisville Convention and Visitors Bureau created the city's Urban Bourbon Trail. In order to be on the trail, a restaurant or bar had to have at least fifty bourbons on its drinks list, had to feature an array of bourbon cocktails, and had to use bourbon as an ingredient in some dishes. The trail started out with eight bars and restaurants. Today the number is approaching forty. In many ways, Joy inspired a great deal of this activity. Very sadly, Joy passed away in 2019. But before that, her contributions to bourbon were formally recognized in 2016 when she was inducted into the Kentucky Bourbon Hall of Fame. She is one of only two bartenders to be so recognized, the other being Dale DeGroff.

Louisville, Kentucky

BIBLIOGRAPHY

Akley, Steve. *Bourbon Mixology: 50 Bourbon Cocktails from 50 Iconic Bars*. N.p: S.A.P. Entertainment, 2015.

Louisville's Urban Bourbon Trail. Louisville Convention and Visitors Bureau. https://www.gotolouisville.com/restaurants/urban-bourbon-trail1/.

Mariani, John. "Bartender Wisdom: 'I Am the Bad Girl of Bourbon.'" *Esquire*. https://www.esquire.com/food-drink/bars/interviews/a9393/kentucky-bartender-joy-perrine-021011/.

Minnick, Fred. *Whiskey Women: The Untold Story of How Women Saved Bourbon, Scotch, and Irish Whiskey*. Lincoln: University of Nebraska Press, 2013.

Perrine, Joy, and Susan Reigler. *The Kentucky Bourbon Cocktail Book*. Lexington: University Press of Kentucky, 2009.

Perrine, Joy, and Susan Reigler. *More Kentucky Bourbon Cocktails*. Lexington: University Press of Kentucky, 2016.

PART 3

Mixed Messages

ELEVEN

INVENTING MARGARITA

Femininity, Fantasy, and Consumption

MARIE SARITA GAYTÁN

IN THE 1977 SONG "MARGARITAVILLE," singer Jimmy Buffett famously describes "wastin' away" in a dreamy beach town where locals prepare margaritas for tourists as they sunbathe, relax, and enjoy a hiatus from their work routines. The catchy track broke into the Top 10 list of the Billboard Hot 100 and reached number one on the Easy Listening chart. Buffett's muse, the margarita, tapped into the collective fantasies associated with life in a colorful and faraway place. *The* margarita—typically made of triple sec, lime juice, and tequila—is often described by mixologists as one of the most popular cocktails in the world. An object and a metaphor, the margarita embodies the craving to escape from the mundane aspects of day-to-day life. Yet, there is another, lesser-known side to the margarita—it also symbolizes cultural pride and creative ingenuity. Despite its international ubiquity in bars and restaurants, the cocktail's sociopolitical significance has received very little academic attention.

In this chapter, I explore the stories of origin and the marketing strategies that helped shape the margarita's mystique in American cocktail culture. Emerging during a period of shifting US–Mexico relations, the margarita exemplifies how consumption serves as a critical site where notions of idealized femininity and racialized anxieties are negotiated by different sets of actors. Weaving together the remnants of the margarita's fragmented past also allows for deeper inquiry into the infrastructure of fantasy—the fantasies of consumers, of producers, and of marketers. Everyday items like the margarita are infused with what feminist theorist Teresa De Lauretis describes as "structures of cognition and of feeling" that influence daily life and allow people to "imagine or give images to their erotic, ambitious, or destructive aspirations."[1]

Thus, fantasies concurrently reflect broader social patterns and individual longings. In the case of the margarita, these fantasies echo the ambition to belong and the fascination with difference as they are tempered by shifting geopolitical relations and the momentum of changing market priorities.

The margarita resides in the interstices of the familiar and the enigmatic, embodying the tensions and possibilities associated with what Latinx studies scholars Frances Aparicio and Susana Chávez-Silverman call "tropicalization." Tropicalization is a measure through which aspects of *Latinidad*—including Latinx icons—are "imbue[d] into a particular space, geography, group or nation with a set of traits, images, and values."[2] Tropicalization connotes multiplicity by recognizing that expressions of hegemonic interests and forms of resistance are simultaneously present in the fashioning of ways of knowing. Far from demonstrating mutually exclusive processes, tropicalization emphasizes "a polydirectional and multivocal approach to the politics of representation" in which aspects of domination and opposition intersect and nourish each other.[3] Tropicalization is therefore a particularly useful heuristic for this analysis, as it allows ample space for contradiction and, in the case of the margarita specifically, for the paradoxes associated with the terms of its emergence and the different stakes associated with its invention. By analyzing the content of stories of origin, historical newspaper articles, and product advertisements, I argue that the margarita personifies the framework of tropicalization and provides an opportunity for understanding the role that certain aspects of femininity play in the formation and proliferation of market-based fantasies.

This chapter proceeds as follows. I begin by addressing how tequila, the margarita's primary ingredient, was depicted as dangerous to American tourists and how it was later employed as a metaphor to embody anxieties regarding Mexican immigration. Next, I discuss the cross-border context in which three margarita invention stories emerged. From there, I explore the cocktail's growing commercial success in the backdrop of the post–World War II period, the bourgeoning Mexican tourism industry, and the increasing alignment of tequila branding with the margarita. I conclude by reflecting on the margarita as a flexible, pleasurable, and profitable tropicalized commodity.

TEQUILA TROUBLE

The origins of the margarita are hard to pinpoint. Writer and mixologist Greg Boehm proposes that the Young Man's Delight, a tequila-based cocktail recipe published in 1930, was likely the earliest incarnation of the margarita.[4] The curious name implies that the combined ingredients—tequila, triple sec, and lemon—were intended to appeal to a certain demographic: young, professional men who could afford the curious concoction. The word *delight* seems to suggest that the consumers the drink targeted would expect to experience pleasure imbibing as well as relishing its customized elements. Alcohol historian Patricia Sharpe writes that its origins likely date to the Tequila Sidecar, a drink whose recipe included lime instead of lemon.[5] Despite tequila's increasing appearance in the 1930s, during the first two decades of the twentieth century it seemed unlikely that American consumers would dare dabble with this primary ingredient. In fact, throughout the United States, journalists and scientists frequently cautioned readers of tequila's hazardous attributes. A 1915 article in *The Plain Dealer*, titled "Yep, Whisky's Only Pink Tea in Mexico," writer John Robert described its effects in the following manner:

> Swallow a little of it and you think a red-hot poker has been melted and poured down your throat.... When you come to, your veins are full of burning acid ... and all your internal machinery is jammed and shrieking for water, which makes you deadly sick the moment it touches your mouth.[6]

By suggesting that the devil named the drink—"'te' for hell 'quila' for water"—Robert advised American tourists to refrain from experimenting with Mexican "native beverages." Scripted in racially neutral language, his message was intended for Anglo American readers already familiar with the effects of whisky. Although far-fetched, the admonition is unequivocal: Tequila is not just bad tasting, it is bad for your health. Sensational terms like "red-hot" and "deadly sick" amplify tequila's otherness and link notions of riskiness to Mexicanness. This tropicalizing move illustrates how fantasy metaphors articulate with racialized ideas about products (e.g., "native beverages").[7]

Impassioned warnings were far from unbiased reviews based on individual taste. Ideas regarding tequila's foul flavor and "hell water" reputation were influenced by mounting domestic distress and international disquiet. Specifically, in the United States temperance movement advocates began associating the ills of alcohol consumption with crime and rising immigration from non-Protestant countries, including Mexico. Foreigners—and their products and customs—were regularly depicted as threatening American mores and morality. For example, in his study *Alcohol Education: What We Must Do*, sociologist David Hanson points out that the American Prohibition Party declared that the influx of undesirable newcomers was "a menace to our institutions." Hanson cites temperance activist Mary Hunt, who decried that "old world immigrants" brought with them their bad habits and ideas regarding alcohol.[8] Nativist anxieties were heightened with the initiation of the Mexican

Revolution (circa 1910–1920), when Mexican civilians began crossing the border into the United States to seek refuge from the mounting upheaval.[9] Between 1889 and 1928 more than half a million Mexicans entered the country, and by the 1930s they were the largest immigrant group in the United States.[10]

The increasing violence associated with the revolution, especially skirmishes that took place near the US–Mexico border—or worse, those that took place in US territory—fueled the growing anti-Mexican sentiment. American journalists reporting on the rebellion were quick to deride Mexican men as predisposed to brutality and often cited their indigenous ancestry as influencing their proclivity for banditry.[11] In particular, writers emphasized the supposed connection between tequila and Mexican lawlessness. For example, the *Los Angeles Times* declared that revolutionaries, like the famous (or infamous) general Pancho Villa, were often "under the influence of the native tequila" when they fought against American interests.[12] A threat to American innocence, tequila, like revolutionaries and bandits, effectively communicated Mexican otherness.[13]

Shifting political policies likewise contributed to ideas about Mexicans and the US–Mexico borderlands as sites of danger and vice. Specifically, in 1919, with the backing of temperance advocates, the Volstead Act (formally, the National Prohibition Act) was passed, outlawing the manufacture, transport, and sale of alcohol throughout the United States. Once the law was enacted, the business licenses of vintners, brewers, and distillers were revoked; bars closed down and nightclubs went dry. Simply put, the stringent measures significantly altered the cultural landscape. While overall rates of drinking decreased throughout the 1920s, Prohibition created a thriving underground economy. Rising reports of alcohol bootlegging along the border solidified the already circulating impression that Mexicans had a penchant for illegality.[14] However, as historian George Díaz explains, the traffic of tequila, mezcal, and rum into the United States was always a joint venture, as Anglo and Mexican bootleggers worked together to circumvent the new federal law. Regardless of this collaboration, "U.S. law enforcement took a much higher toll on tequileros [ethnic Mexican tequila smugglers] than on their Anglo counterparts."[15] To be sure, tequila epitomized and reflected a range of sociopolitical anxieties; however, not all Americans saw tequila as inherently bad or dangerous. Every year, thousands of Americans headed south to imbibe in the cantinas and casinos of border towns, including Nogales, Ciudad Juarez, and Tijuana.[16]

Ironically, soon after the Volstead Act was repealed in 1933, Mexican officials started restricting the sale and consumption of alcohol. As one report published in the *Los Angeles Times* put it, "Where thousands of Americans once streamed across the border to the Mexican cafes, Sonorans today patronize American drinking establishments to buy a nickel or dime glass of some beverage."[17] Despite this change in circumstance, Mexico's attempt at prohibition was unpopular and ultimately unsuccessful. Beyond creating a social context in which drinking alcohol became associated with forbidden and risky attributes, state-sponsored policies in both countries also created a climate of possibility for new forms of cultural contact and commercial collaboration. In the midst of these heightened cross-border exchanges, the margarita emerged on the social scene.[18]

INVENTING MARGARITA

Prohibition altered Americans' relationship with alcohol and changed the cultural landscape in significant ways. For example, the saloon, the iconic drinking institution that catered to men, gave way to a new and more inclusive leisure establishment: the bar. Bars represented a modern shift both in terms of drinking habits and with regard to ideas of respectability. They became new locations from which to experience pleasure without reprimand, and were thus venues that provided a fresh range of possibilities to actualize gratification. Unlike in saloons, which were closely associated with working-class masculinity, in bars, middle-class men and women could congregate without necessarily tarnishing their reputations. These changes were not immediate; instead they began during Prohibition with the rise of speakeasies, underground drinking locales that sold bootlegged alcohol.

Unprecedented numbers of Americans engaged in illegal speakeasy culture. Depending on the neighborhood, some of the watering holes were the size of a living room, while others were larger lounges.[19] According to historian Garrett Peck, the booze served at speakeasies "was potent stuff" that (supposedly) did not appeal to women.[20] In his words, "Women did not like whiskey, which can be bitter (besides, whiskey was seen as a man's drink as brands like Old Grand Dad and Virginia Gentleman reflected) so bartenders mixed cocktails that were more appealing to women."[21] Essentializing explanations like these were (and remain) common, as women were assumed to favor sweetness over bitterness. Such categorizations not only consigned qualities of delicateness and gentility to notions of middle-class womanhood, but also discursively reinforced women's subservient relationship to men.

The increasingly inclusive atmosphere gave rise to the creation of a variety of newfangled products and promoted different practices. Whereas before Prohibition cocktails were almost exclusively marketed for and imbibed by middle- and upper-class men, after Prohibition cocktails took on a more democratic character—middle-class women could also consume barroom concoctions. Women became the subjects and objects of shifting patterns of consumption, as once strict mores relegating them to the private sphere (their homes) started to loosen, creating greater acceptance of their increasing visibility in the public places as producers (workers) and consumers (customers). Old traditions were yielding to new ideas, in steady albeit often diverse ways. Popular culture reflected this modern shift as women became increasingly visible and present in cinema, on the radio, and in the press. The change in attitudes also became apparent in the lives of those individuals who continued with their daily routines—they too participated in these evolving social realities. Stories of the invention of the margarita provide a unique glimpse into how these complex conditions were negotiated by ordinary people in everyday places.

One of the earliest stories of the margarita's origin is about a man named Daniel Negrete. As the legend goes, in 1936 Negrete was the manager of the upscale Garci-Crespo Hotel in the city of Puebla, which at the time, according to journalist Andrés Becerril, was considered the most luxurious hotel in Mexico.[22] In their study on tequila, Marion Gorman and Felipe De Alba detail how Negrete's girlfriend, Margarita, who frequented the hotel's lounge, loved salt and had a habit of sprinkling it into her drinks.[23] One evening while working behind the bar, Negrete drizzled salt on the rim on her icy cocktail so that she wouldn't have to continuously reach for the salt bowl. In the 1940s, Negrete migrated north and took his talent to the Agua Caliente race track and resort in Tijuana, where a teenage performer by the name of Margarita Cansino was causing a buzz among audiences. Too young to work in Hollywood nightclubs, Cansino, who later changed her name to Rita Hayworth, danced at the resort's "Caliente Club." Combining aspects of both experiences, Negrete formally coined his creation "margarita."[24]

The Hollywood starlet connection was also at the heart of Carlos "Danny" Herrera's invention story. According to numerous accounts published at the time of his death in 1992, Herrera was born in Mexico City, and in 1929, he and his wife moved to Baja California, where they built a home alongside the road that connected Tijuana with Rosarito Beach. In 1938, they opened a restaurant called Rancho la Gloria, and later they expanded the business by building a small hotel that catered to the Southern California weekend-getaway crowd. One regular customer was an aspiring actress named Marjorie King. "She was allergic to everything except tequila. . . . But she couldn't take it straight, or even with the lemon and the salt. But she liked it. So I started experimenting," recalled Herrera in an interview published in the *Los Angeles Times*.[25] One afternoon, he mixed three parts tequila, two parts Cointreau, and one part lemon juice. Herrera poured the concoction into a small, short-stemmed glass, added shaved ice, and covered its rim with salt. The young showgirl was elated with the cocktail, and Herrera referred to his new creation as the margarita, his Spanish take on Marjorie.

Finally, another popular account is told by José Antonio Burciaga, a noted Chicano artist, poet, and journalist. Specifically, he writes that his Aunt Bibi was married to Francisco "Pancho" Morales, a well-known bartender in Juárez, Mexico. According to family lore, on July 4, 1942, a female customer stepped up to the bar and ordered a trendy cocktail called the magnolia. Although he knew that it was made with triple sec and lime, he struggled to remember its primary ingredient (likely bourbon), and in his haste he added tequila instead. "This isn't a magnolia but it's very good," she quipped and asked what it was called. Caught off guard, he explained, "There was already a drink named for the Texas daisy, so I thought the translation for daisy would be appropriate. 'Oh, I'm sorry. I thought you had asked for a margarita.' I lied to keep my professional pride."[26] Morales directly translated the word *daisy* into Spanish, "margarita." Morales's Fourth of July improvisation worked, and he continued to serve his creation to American and Mexican customers who frequented the bar.

The three invention stories are recounted as taking place within a few years of each other (late 1930s to early 1940s) during a time of improving diplomatic relations and growing commercial ties between Mexico and the United States. Notably, Mexico's dangerous reputation was gradually changing in the eyes of the American public. Although it is often the case that narratives spotlighting politics, negotiation, and ingenuity are reserved for government officials or powerful entrepreneurs, these examples show that members of the working class—in this case, bartenders—likewise participated in the conception of cosmopolitan creativity. Within the space of bars, restaurants, and nightclubs, these individuals experimented with different ingredients, sometimes out of necessity and sometimes to please a female customer. In leisurely locales, working-class Mexicans creatively drew on their available resources and helped forge modern ideas regarding Mexico as a worldly and hospitable destination.

The margarita represented new possibilities for imagining Mexico as a modern and enterprising country—an arousing mix, part object and part idea, that aligned with shifting market interests and investment opportunities. Combining qualities of accommodation, translation, and multicultural influences, the margarita's invention stories imbued ideas of Mexicanness into the globalizing landscape of consumption and the burgeoning tourism industry. The margarita's creation can also be understood in relation to the growing influence of American media-driven ideals of femininity that privileged US standards of beauty, fashion, and taste. The inspiration for the margarita is a real woman, who, depending on the storyteller, is Mexican, but most often is portrayed as a naïve American patron or actress. The Hollywood starlet connection highlights how ordinary men symbolically claimed recognition for their creativity through the cachet associated with female celebrities. Mexican men, once the targets of the American media's framing of Mexican masculinity as aligned with danger and debauchery, were able to respond to these negative representations through a new avenue of consumption: the margarita.

The margarita's inventors were able to garner respectability and to "unsettle preconceptions" of Mexican people and products as perilous.[27] At the same time, they accommodated customers, and, without necessarily intending to do so, helped fashion a new market-based trope built on tropicalized ideas regarding femininity, exoticism, and Mexico. Margarita is depicted as an entrancing and sometimes innocent customer; her thirst is portrayed as swiftly quenched in increasingly egalitarian leisure spaces. Growing public interactions in new sites of consumption nourished the impression that if Mexico was safe for Margarita, surely it would be hospitable to tourists likewise seeking to imbibe curious Mexican cocktails. A symbol of commodified Mexicanness that was both sweet and intoxicating, the margarita provided a new way of imagining Mexico—enticing, pleasurable, and feminized.

POLITICS AND COCKTAIL CULTURE

By the late 1930s, Mexico's reputation started to give way to a new set of popular associations in the United States. Favorable diplomatic relations bolstered these evolving connotations, especially when US troops were sent to fight in World War II. Mexico specifically and Latin America more broadly became prized "good neighbors" as official foreign policy emphasized the importance of unity and reciprocity across the Americas.[28] According to historian Brian O'Neill, Hollywood studios quickly incorporated patriotic themes into their films so to increase revenue through "the visibility of Latin Americans and Latin themes on the movie screen" and to "boost . . . the American public's awareness of and possibly warm feelings toward their neighbors."[29] Filmmakers focused their energies on wartime fantasy musicals whose plots revolved around an American man and a Latina who romantically fall in love but have to resolve a variety of cultural differences in order to marry.[30] Clichéd scripts enforced gendered and heteronormative attributes that portrayed the United States as masculine (and familiar) and Latin America as feminine (and foreign).

Singer and actress Carmen Miranda, who in the 1930s had already achieved stardom in Brazil as a samba performer, was cast as the exotic lead in several of these "neighborly" productions, including *Down Argentine Way* (1940), *That Night in Rio* (1947), and *Weekend in Havana* (1941). Dubbed the "Brazilian Bombshell," Miranda immediately enthralled American moviegoers with her over-the-top costumes, accessories, "rapid rhythm, sing-speak delivery, . . . her impish and campy gestures, and her haltingly thick accent."[31] Miranda's popularity soared, and Hollywood studios transformed her image into a cartoon that depicted her dancing with her emblematic fruit-adorned head piece.[32] Miranda embodied tropicalized femininity that tapped into viewers' psyches, both drawing from and creating ideas about Latin America and *Latinidad* as simultaneously foreign and accessible—the base from which desire, as a manufactured characteristic, could be commodified.

Much like the margarita, Carmen Miranda's entrance into US popular culture took place in the late 1930s and early 1940s in the shadow of speculation and the eventual American participation in World War II. Although I do not want to claim that one directly influenced the other, I do want to suggest that their overlapping inventions and introductions were not coincidental. The margarita, like Miranda, taps into the same momentum that aligned with the shifting societal forces and commercial priorities of the time period. Safe, saccharine, fruity, and alluring, both of them quenched consumers' desire for a certain type of tropicalized femininity that was inviting and accommodating. Together, their marketable attributes easily cohered with new "public fantasies" that extended notions of *Latinidad* in the popular imaginary of the middle class who were captivated by the prospect of experiencing foreign—but still neighborly—sights, sounds, smells, and flavors.[33]

As the only Latin American country sharing a border with the United States, Mexico became a key location for the advancement of diplomatic relations and cultural exchanges; it also played a crucial role in supplying certain goods that became difficult to procure as World War II fighting put a halt to transatlantic trade. As the war progressed, European spirits that once lined store shelves were less available, and in many cases were no were longer attainable.[34] The interruption of alcohol importation fueled anxieties in bars and homes across the country as supplies of popular cocktail ingredients dried up. These circumstances, however, did not put a stop to the cocktail craze. Instead, enthusiasts sought new ingredients, which was a serendipitous situation for Mexican tequila companies. According to reports published in *La Prensa* newspaper, by 1943 as much as $250,000 worth of tequila was being imported into the United States per month.[35] At the end of the same year, the *Omaha World*

Herald described how, as a result of the shortage of other liquors, the US government imposed controls in order to reduce price-gouging by tequila importers and retailers.[36] New demand subsequently led to the first tequila "boom," or unexpected increase in sales. To be sure, according to the *Wall Street Journal*, Mexican distillers were increasing output in order to "assuage... the great drought that is enveloping the United States."[37]

When the war ended in 1945, Americans' thirst for cocktails continued to expand. By 1946, newspaper society pages began reporting on a new drink called the "Tequila Sunrise," described by food and drink connoisseur Ken Bojens as "knock out drops": a "potion that should have been called 'sunset cocktail' because it took only a few of them to turn out the lights."[38] The latter half of the 1940s saw a steady increase in the popularity of cocktails, a trend that continued with the postwar prosperity of the 1950s. New associations were again taking shape; drinks like the martini were becoming closely connected to the sophisticated palettes of upper-class and upper-middle-class tastes. Making the perfect martini required skill and heightened appreciation for dryness, especially when it came to adding the right amount of vermouth. As author C. B. Palmer explained in an article for the *New York Times*, the "very dry martini ... is a mass madness, a cult, a frenzy, a body of folklore, a mystique, an expertise of a sort of which may well earn for this decade the name of the Numb (or Glazed) Fifties."[39] Those with refined tastes turned to dryness as a symbol of worldliness, allowing upwardly mobile Americans to conspicuously exhibit their sophistication.

Although stories about margarita's invention date to the late 1930s and early 1940s, it was not until the 1950s that the drink began capturing the imagination of the American public. Notably, in 1953 it was named "Drink of the Month" by the fashionable men's magazine *Esquire*.[40] In 1956, *Vogue* magazine listed the margarita in its "People Are Talking About" column. That same year, the *San Diego Union* reported that New Yorkers were "just beginning to find out about margaritas," even though local "Tijuana habituees [*sic*] The Alvin McGowans discovered the drink long ago [and] have been serving it at the Sunday breakfasts for several seasons."[41] In 1958, Pulitzer Prize–winning journalist and food writer Stan Delaplane, before listing detailed instructions, published the following in his widely read nationally syndicated column: "Few weeks ago I could not answer on 'what is a recipe for a margarita?' Herewith today with apologies."[42] From coast to coast (e.g., New York City to San Diego), Americans were becoming familiar with the margarita.

Advertising undoubtedly helped bolster some of this newfound fame. According to one report, US-based tequila distributors were spending upwards of $100,000 to promote the "Mexican beverage in cocktails and mixed drinks," which was seen as contributing to a 36 percent rise in US sales.[43] The American market was critical to both tequila and the margarita's popularity. Other circumstances, including the growth of Mexican resorts, allowed greater numbers of middle-class Americans to explore Mexico's cultural offerings, including its food and drink. As Dina Berger and Andrew Wood explain, the development of affordable seaside tourism in Acapulco, Ensenada, and Mazatlán elevated Americans' appetite for exotic experiences.[44] New rituals accompanied these changes—drinking margaritas on the beach was quickly becoming associated with middle-class tastes and expressions of leisure.

By the 1960s, tequila companies started to promote their brands in relation to the margarita. For example, Jose Cuervo Tequila ran a series of ads that featured a headshot of a woman, a salt-rimmed glass, and the tagline "Margarita, more than a girl's name." Below the woman's painted portrait, a bottle of Jose Cuervo Tequila was positioned next to a blurb that described the margarita as

> an ever-growing favorite among cocktail connoisseurs from the haciendas of sun-drenched Mexico to the smart clubs and bars throughout the world. Jose Cuervo Tequila, basis of many captivating cocktails, including famous Margarita, is the legacy of ancient Aztecs to the sophisticates of 1965. It's incomparable!

Described as drink for worldly connoisseurs, margaritas made with Jose Cuervo Tequila are pitched as fusing ideas of tradition to notions of refinement.

Published in *Vogue*, the ad is a full-page spread (fig. 11.1) that features a blonde, blue-eyed, fair-skinned Margarita who stares directly at the reader. She is wearing a flower-patterned shawl that drapes around her hair, and its pastel hues match the pink rouge of her cheeks and the rosy lacquer of her lipstick. As the accompanying text suggests, this is Margarita, the "girl" behind the name.[45] Personified as attractive and alluring, Jose Cuervo's Margarita, the ad suggests, is worth getting to know. Potential cocktail "sophisticates" might not realize that Margarita is more than a drink from "sun-drenched" Mexican haciendas, she's in "smart clubs and bars." Margarita is not as mysterious as one might imagine.[46] With the readers' gaze directed at her face and mascara-highlighted blue eyes, it is easy to see that although she has an air of foreignness about her, she is still familiar. Indeed, her features are more "girl next door"—that is, Anglo—than "ancient Aztec." Potential purchasers should rest assured that she embodies the right type of exoticism.[47]

Jose Cuervo's characterization of Margarita, much like the depictions presented by those who claimed to have invented the cocktail, personifies her

Figure 11.1. "Margarita: More than a Girl's Name."

through a common cultural narrative—an innocent American (read: Anglo) woman who easily links aspects of tropicalized desirability to consumable femininity. An enticing and commodifiable figure, Margarita epitomizes, promotes, and sustains good neighborly relations in political and commercial spheres. Yet, there are differences in how she is represented to the public. On the one hand, for bartenders in the 1930s and 1940s, tales about the margarita's invention highlighted ideas about cultural recognition and emphasized the virtues of spontaneity, ingenuity, and the ability to translate diverse cultural ingredients and tastes. On the other, for companies like Jose Cuervo, descriptions focused on appropriating the margarita's trendy image into their branding by highlighting her appeal to knowing consumers. That is, while there might be others out there, Jose Cuervo's margarita is the favored choice for sophisticated cocktail aficionados.

Both perspectives rely and build on well-trafficked rhetoric that was already in circulation throughout American popular culture. They also provide insight into the preferred attributes of femininity of the time. Although Margarita is a common name in Spanish, that is where her Latin American traits begin and end. Latinx femininity is missing in most accounts of the margarita's mythic origin and commodified image. The margarita symbolizes a subtle, but persistent, tension of tropicalization as it relates to consumption and public fantasy; her appeal is tempered by the presence and appeal of whiteness—in these cases, whiteness as a marker of recognition and whiteness as a salve to quell anxieties associated with imbibing an exotic other. Stories of the margarita's invention and attributes combine narratives of what gender studies scholar Sunaina Maira calls "polycultural experience" and "multicultural market appropriation"; they speak to different aspirations that comfortably align with commercial values of discovery, exploration, and innocence.[48] Thus, the margarita's popularity and profitability should be understood in relation to its aesthetic flexibility and racial ambiguity, attributes that appealed to marketers, consumers, and producers throughout the twentieth century.

CONCLUSION

In his book *Taco USA: How Mexican Food Conquered America*, Gustavo Arellano writes that by the 1960s, margaritas were widely available in bars and lounges across the nation, competing with other staple cocktails like the martini and the Bloody Mary.[49] In 1964, another related product emerged on the market that would appeal to a new set of potential consumers: the bottled margarita mix. As a 1964 advertisement for La Madrileña's Margarita Cocktail (fig. 11.2) claimed, aficionados "at last" had a bottled tequila cocktail that put

NOW AT LAST

A BOTTLED MARGARITA COCKTAIL

(TEQUILA COCKTAIL)

that puts the most accomplished bartender to shame

MADE FROM PURE WHITE TEQUILA, TRIPLE SEC AND FRESH LEMON JUICE.

All you need do is chill and serve (over cracked ice, of course), with a touch of salt around the rim of the glass. Try some next time you visit Mexico. You too, will oooh and aaah at the delicious, refreshing flavor.

JUST ASK FOR
MARGARITA COCKTAIL
A PRODUCT OF
LA MADRILEÑA, S. A.
MEXICO'S FOREMOST PRODUCERS OF QUALITY LIQUEURS.

Figure 11.2. "La Madrileña's Margarita Cocktail, 1964."

"the most accomplished bartender to shame."[50] This "foremost" Mexican producer's all-in-one cocktail offered audiences a modern, versatile, and convenient consumption opportunity. Also noteworthy is the reference to the product's similarity to those margaritas served to tourists in Mexico. The margarita was a uniquely pliable product that could adjust to emerging market demands and shifting consumer tastes.

The 1970s likewise marked a new phase for the margarita. In 1971, Mexican-American restaurateur Mariano Martinez invented the frozen margarita machine. The prefabricated margaritas were slushy, textured, and tasty; they were also very efficient—instead of spending time mixing individual glasses or pitchers, bartenders could serve the icy concoction directly from the machine. Thirsty customers flocked to Martinez's Dallas restaurant, Mariano's Mexican Cuisine. Timing also mattered: the introduction of frozen margaritas coincided with the inception of large Cal-Mex, Tex-Mex, and Mexican food restaurant chains.[51] Today, Mariano's original frozen margarita machine is on display at the Smithsonian National Museum of American History.

The margarita taps into and constructs a fantasy frame that satiates a range of individual and market-based appetites. Given its material and symbolic attributes, it is not surprising that the margarita quickly aligned with corporate marketing strategies and prompted new investment possibilities. For example, nearly ten years after Jimmy Buffett released the song "Margaritaville," he launched the Margaritaville Cafe in Key West, Florida. Today, in addition to its own variety of Margaritaville tequila, the successful chain has more than twenty-five restaurants in locations throughout the United States and in beach resorts in Mexico, Grand Cayman, and Turks and Caicos Islands. The brand also boasts more than a dozen retail outlets, a hotel, and three casinos. According to *Forbes*, Jimmy Buffett has reported net worth of $550 million and is one of the wealthiest celebrities of all time.[52] Simply put, the margarita potently sustains, quenches, and stokes consumer desire.

Extending Mary Louise Roberts's insight on gender and consumption, the margarita is portrayed as simultaneously "consumer and commodity, purchaser and purchase, buyer and bought."[53] With its unique positioning in the marketplace, the margarita robustly resonates in the public imagination because it fulfills several political, ideological, and commercial needs at once. Changing policies, such as the institutionalization of alcohol prohibition, and the racialized discourses about Mexicans and their products (e.g., tequila) that accompanied it, introduced the American public to powerful ideas concerning Mexicans' proclivity for danger and disregard for US federal law. The repeal of the Volstead Act diminished (although did not entirely eliminate) the focus of the press on Mexican deviance. Across the border, amid these well-circulated stereotypes, ordinary people, such as club and restaurant bartenders, flexed their creativity and introduced the margarita to new groups of middle-class American tourists.

A metonym of diplomacy, the margarita's invention emerged from and reflected the desire for exotic Latin American experiences. Good neighborly exchanges and interactions cohered with ideas of tropicalized femininity, structured feelings that capitalized on the momentum of emergent multicultural commercial possibilities. In the backdrop of continuing postwar prosperity and the growth of American cocktail culture, companies like Jose Cuervo sought to broaden the margarita's popularity as a vehicle for selling their tequila. Promotional materials portrayed the margarita as simultaneously foreign and familiar. Notions of race and class tempered the distance between these attributes—the margarita's tropicalized characteristics underscored the drink's association with whiteness and upper-class sensibilities.

Eight decades after its invention, the margarita continues to embody commodified pleasure, serving as a metaphor of exoticism and representing an antidote to the mundane aspects of daily life. By exploring the sociopolitical context of the margarita's emergence, I contextualized its invention and highlighted the inner workings of public fantasies—how they are translated, produced, and circulated. The margarita, as a material and symbolic icon, matters in myriad ways. The cocktail's popularity emerged amid shifting diplomatic relations and intersected with individual ingenuity—it represented creative expression and offered commercial potential. The margarita straddled the boundaries of foreignness and familiarity and tempered the distance between the two—often uncharted ideological territory that merits closer scrutiny. By zeroing in on the infrastructure of consumption, I shed light on the elusive connections, intricacies, and desires that sustain market-based notions of femininity.

University of Utah

NOTES

1. Teresa DeLauretis, "Popular Culture, Public and Private Fantasies: Femininity and Fetishism in David Cronenberg's 'M. Butterfly,'" *Signs: Journal of Women in Culture and Society* 24, no. 2 (1999): 304, https://doi.org/10.1086/495342.

2. Frances Aparacio and Susana Chávez-Silverman, *Tropicalizations: Transcultural Representations of Latinad* (Hanover, NH: Dartmouth College Press, 1997), 8.

3. Aparacio and Chávez-Silverman, *Tropicalizations*, 14.
4. Greg Boehm, "Once Upon a Time in Mexico: The Origin of the Margarita," Imbibe, http://imbibe.com/feature/once-upon-time-in-mexico/7589.
5. Patricia Sharpe, "Margaritaville: Where Did Our Unofficial State Drink Come From?" *Texas Monthly*, July 11, 2013, http://www.texasmonthly.com/story/margaritaville.
6. John Robert, "Yep, Whisky's Only Pink Tea in Mexico," *The Plain Dealer*, December 6, 1915.
7. Robert, "Whisky's Only Pink Tea in Mexico."
8. David Hanson, *Alcohol Education: What We Must Do* (Westport, CT: Praeger, 1996), 21.
9. Marie Gaytán, *¡Tequila! Distilling the Spirit of Mexico* (Palo Alto, CA: Stanford University Press, 2014).
10. Francisco Balderama and Raymond Rodríguez, *Decade of Betrayal: Mexican Repatriation in the 1930s* (Albuquerque: University of New Mexico Press, 2006).
11. Marie Gaytán, "Drinking Difference: Race, Consumption, and Alcohol Prohibition in Mexico and the United States," *Ethnicities* 14 no. 3 (2014): 437–58, https://doi.org/10.1177/1468796813484442.
12. Marie Gaytán, "Drinking the Nation and Making Masculinity: Tequila, Pancho Villa, and the U.S. Media," in *Toward a Sociology of the Trace*, ed. Herman Gray and Macarena Gómez-Barris (Minneapolis: University of Minnesota Press, 2010), 207–33.
13. Curtis Marez, *Drug Wars: The Political Economy of Narcotics* (Minneapolis: University of Minnesota Press, 2004).
14. See Gaytán, "Drinking Difference."
15. George Díaz, "Twilight of the Tequileros: Prohibition Era Smuggling in the South Texas Borderlands 1919–1933," in *Smugglers, Brothels, and Twine: Historical Perspectives on Contraband and Vice in North America's Borderlands*, ed. Elaine Carey and Andre Marak (Tucson: University of Arizona Press, 2011), 59.
16. James Sandos, "Northern Separatism during the Mexican Revolution: An Inquiry into the Role of Drug Trafficking, 1910–1920," *The Americas* 41, no. 2 (1984): 191–214, https://doi.org/10.2307/1007456.
17. "Sonora's Dry Act in Focus," *Los Angeles Times*, April, 14 1935.
18. There are approximately a dozen different stories about the Margarita's invention—the three that I analyze here are the most referenced and documented on the internet and in books, magazines, and newspapers.
19. Ann Funderburg, *Bootleggers and Beer Barons of the Prohibition Era* (Jefferson, NC: McFarland, 2014).
20. Garrett Peck, *The Prohibition Hangover: Alcohol in America from Demon Rum to Cult Cabernet* (Rutgers, NJ: Rutgers University Press, 2009), 209.

21. Peck, *Prohibition Hangover*, 209.
22. Andrés Becerril, "Historia del Gran Hotel Garci-Crespo de Tehuacán Puebla," https://www.icadtotal.com/blog_de_tehuacan/cultural/historia-del-gran-hotel-garci-crespo-de-tehuacan-puebla-posteriormente-hotel-spa-penafiel/.
23. Marion Gorman and Felipe De Alba, *The Tequila Book* (Raleigh, NC: Contemporary Publishing, 1978).
24. Gorman and De Alba, *Tequila Book*, 78. This story is also recounted in *Mr. Boston Official Bartender's Guide* (Hoboken, NJ: John Wiley, 2009).
25. Paul Chávez, "Danny Herrera, Inventor of Margarita, Dies at Age 90," *Los Angeles Times*, May 14, 1992, http://articles.latimes.com/1992-05-14/local/me-2749_1_danny-herrera.
26. José Antonio Burciaga, *Weedee Peepo: A Collection of Essays* (Edinburg, TX: Pan American University Press, 1988), 22.
27. Adria Imada, *Aloha America: Hula Circuits Through the U.S. Empire* (Durham, NC: Duke University Press, 2012), 19.
28. Marie Gaytán, "The Transformation of Tequila: From Hangover to Highbrow," *Journal of Consumer Culture* 17, no. 1 (2017): 62–84, https://doi.org/10.1177/1469540514556169.
29. Brian O'Neil, "Carmen Miranda: The High Price of Fame and Bananas," in *Latina Legacies: Identity, Biography, and Community*, ed. Vicki Ruiz and Virginia Korrol (New York: Oxford University Press, 2005), 202.
30. O'Neil, "Carmen Miranda," 202.
31. O'Neil, "Carmen Miranda," 199.
32. Miranda appeared several times in Bugs Bunny cartoons.
33. DeLauretis, "Popular Culture," 308.
34. Marie Gaytán, "Transformation."
35. "Exportación de Tequila a Los EE.UU," *La Prensa* (November 30, 1943).
36. "Tequila Under OPA Ceiling," *Omaha World Herald* (October 13, 1943).
37. Lenore Reynolds, "Made in Mexico: U.S. Imports: Tequila, Pottery, Glass, Limes, Huaraches and Spiders. The Guadalajara Area Thrives on Brisk Wartime Trade—Distillers Step up Output, Pine Forests Supply Resin Wartime Demand Booms Exports of Mexican Liquor and Handicraft," *Wall Street Journal*, November 24, 1943.
38. Ken Bojens, "Off the Main Line," *San Diego Union*, August 4, 1946.
39. Paul Harrington and Laura Morehead, *Cocktail: The Drinks Bible for the 21st Century* (New York: Viking Adult, 1998), 35–36.
40. "Potables, Drink of the Month," *Esquire: The Magazine for Men*, December 1956.
41. "Twice Told Town Talk," *San Diego Union*, January 1, 1956.
42. Frank Delaplane, "What if You Get Seasick?" *San Antonio Express*, April 5, 1958.

43. "People Are Talking About," *Vogue*, January 1, 1956.
44. Dina Berger and Andrew Wood, "Introduction: Tourism Studies and the Tourism Dilemma," in *Holiday in Mexico: Critical Reflections on Tourism and Tourist Encounters*, ed. Dina Berger and Andrew Wood, 1–20 (Durham, NC: Duke University Press, 2010).
45. "Margarita: More than a Girl's Name," *Vogue*, February 15, 1965.
46. "Margarita."
47. "Margarita."
48. Sunaina Maira, "Temporary Tattoos: Indo-Chic Fantasies and Late Capitalist Orientalism," *Meridians: Feminism, Race, Transnationalism* 3, no. 1 (2002): 148, https://www.jstor.org/stable/40338549.
49. Gustavo Arellano, *Taco USA: How Mexican Food Conquered America* (New York: Scribner, 2012).
50. "Now at Last," *San Diego Union*, September 3, 1964.
51. See Arellano, *Taco USA*.
52. Emily Price, "Jimmy Buffett Is More Business Than Booze these Days," *Fortune*, February 2, 2018, http://fortune.com/2018/02/08/jimmy-buffett-margaritaville-business/.
53. Mary Louise Roberts, "Gender, Consumption, and Commodity Culture," *The American Historical Review* 103, no. 3 (1998): 817–44, https://doi.org/10.1086/ahr/103.3.817.

BIBLIOGRAPHY

Aparacio, Frances, and Susana Chávez-Silverman. *Tropicalizations: Transcultural Representations of Latinidad.* Hanover, NH: Dartmouth College Press, 1997.

Arellano, Gustavo. *Taco USA: How Mexican Food Conquered America.* New York: Scribner, 2012.

Balderama, Francisco, and Raymond Rodríguez. *Decade of Betrayal: Mexican Repatriation in the 1930s.* Albuquerque: University of New Mexico Press, 2006.

Becerril, Andrés. "Historia del Gran Hotel Garci-Crespo de Tehuacán Puebla." Accessed September 4, 2014. https://www.icadtotal.com/blog_de_tehuacan/cultural/historia-del-gran-hotel-garci-crespo-de-tehuacan-puebla-posteriormente-hotel-spa-penafiel/.

Berger, Dina, and Andrew Wood. "Introduction: Tourism Studies and the Tourism Dilemma." In *Holiday in Mexico: Critical Reflections on Tourism and Tourist Encounters.* Edited by Dina Berger and Andrew Wood. Durham, NC: Duke University Press, 2010.

Boehm, Greg. "Once Upon a Time in Mexico: The Origin of the Margarita." Imbibe. Accessed August 15, 2014. http://imbibe.com/feature/once-upon-time-in-mexico/7589.

Bojens, Ken. "Off the Main Line." *San Diego Union.* August 4, 1946.
Burciaga, José Antonio. *Weedee Peepo: A Collection of Essays.* Edinburg, TX: Pan American University Press, 1988.
Chávez, Paul. "Danny Herrera, Inventor of Margarita, Dies at Age 90." *Los Angeles Times.* May 14, 1992. http://articles.latimes.com/1992-05-14/local/me-2749_1_danny-herrera.
Delaplane, Frank. "What if You Get Seasick?" *San Antonio Express.* April 5, 1958.
DeLauretis, Teresa. "Popular Culture, Public and Private Fantasies: Femininity and Fetishism in David Cronenberg's 'M. Butterfly.'" *Signs: Journal of Women in Culture and Society* 24, no. 2 (1999): 303–34. https://doi.org/10.1086/495342.
Díaz, George. "Twilight of the Tequileros: Prohibition Era Smuggling in the South Texas Borderlands 1919–1933." In *Smugglers, Brothels, and Twine: Historical Perspectives on Contraband and Vice in North America's Borderlands.* Edited by Elaine Carey and Andre Marak. Tucson: University of Arizona Press, 2011.
"Exportación de Tequila a Los EE.UU." *La Prensa.* November 30, 1943.
Funderburg, Ann. *Bootleggers and Beer Barons of the Prohibition Era.* Jefferson, NC: McFarland, 2014.
Gaytán, Marie. "Drinking Difference: Race, Consumption, and Alcohol Prohibition in Mexico and the United States." *Ethnicities* 14, no. 3 (2014): 437–58. https://doi.org/10.1177/1468796813484442.
Gaytán, Marie. "Drinking the Nation and Making Masculinity: Tequila, Pancho Villa, and the U.S. Media." In *Toward a Sociology of the Trace.* Edited by Herman Gray and Macarena Gómez-Barris, 207–33. Minneapolis: University of Minnesota Press, 2010.
Gaytán, Marie. *¡Tequila! Distilling the Spirit of Mexico.* Palo Alto, CA: Stanford University Press, 2014.
Gaytán, Marie. "The Transformation of Tequila: From Hangover to Highbrow." *Journal of Consumer Culture* 17, no. 1 (2017): 62–84. https://doi.org/10.1177/1469540514556169.
Gorman, Marion, and Felipe De Alba. *The Tequila Book.* Raleigh, NC: Contemporary Publishing, 1978.
Hanson, David. *Alcohol Education: What We Must Do.* Westport, CT: Praeger, 1996.
Harrington, Paul, and Laura Morehead. *Cocktail: The Drinks Bible for the 21st Century.* New York: Viking Adult, 1998.
Imada, Adria. *Aloha America: Hula Circuits Through the U.S. Empire.* Durham, NC: Duke University Press, 2012.
Maira, Sunaina. "Temporary Tattoos: Indo-Chic Fantasies and Late Capitalist Orientalism." *Meridians: Feminism, Race, Transnationalism* 3, no. 1 (2002): 134–60. https://www.jstor.org/stable/40338549.
Marez, Curtis. *Drug Wars: The Political Economy of Narcotics.* Minneapolis: University of Minnesota Press, 2004.

"Margarita: More Than a Girl's Name." *Vogue*. February 15, 1965.

"Now at Last." *San Diego Union*. September 3, 1964.

O'Neil, Brian. "Carmen Miranda: The High Price of Fame and Bananas." In *Latina Legacies: Identity, Biography, and Community*. Edited by Vicki Ruíz and Virginia Korrol. New York: Oxford University Press, 2005.

Peck, Garrett. *The Prohibition Hangover: Alcohol in America from Demon Rum to Cult Cabernet*. New Brunswick, NJ: Rutgers University Press, 2009.

"Potables, Drink of the Month," *Esquire: The Magazine for Men*. December, 1956.

"People Are Talking About." *Vogue*. January 1, 1956.

Price, Emily. "Jimmy Buffett Is More Business Than Booze these Days." *Fortune*. February 2, 2008. http://fortune.com/2018/02/08/jimmy-buffett-margaritaville-business/.

Reynolds, Lenore. "Made in Mexico: U.S. Imports: Tequila, Pottery, Glass, Limes, Huaraches and Spiders. The Guadalajara Area Thrives on Brisk Wartime Trade—Distillers Step Up Output, Pine Forests Supply Resin Wartime Demand Booms Exports of Mexican Liquor and Handicraft." *Wall Street Journal*. November 24, 1943.

Robert, John. "Yep, Whisky's Only Pink Tea in Mexico." *The Plain Dealer*. December 6, 1915.

Roberts, Mary Louise. "Gender, Consumption, and Commodity Culture." *The American Historical Review* 103, no. 3 (1998): 817–44. https://doi.org/10.1086/ahr/103.3.817.

Sandos, James. "Northern Separatism during the Mexican Revolution: An Inquiry into the Role of Drug Trafficking, 1910–1920." *The Americas* 41, no. 2 (1984): 191–214. https://doi.org/10.2307/1007456.

Sharpe, Patricia. "Margaritaville: Where Did Our Unofficial State Drink Come From?" *Texas Monthly*. July 11, 2013. http://www.texasmonthly.com/story/margaritaville.

"Sonora's Dry Act in Focus." *Los Angeles Times*. April 14, 1935.

"Tequila under OPA Ceiling," *Omaha World Herald*. October 13, 1943.

"Twice Told Town Talk." *San Diego Union*. January 1, 1956.

TWELVE

POLYNESIAN PARALYSIS

Tiki Culture and the Aesthetics of American Empire

ANDREW PILSCH

IN THE LATE 1950S AND early 1960s, the landscape of the United States became incongruously dotted with Polynesian-style longhouses. Harried office workers could visit their local Hilton or Sheraton chain hotel to escape to a simulated Eden of rum and pork and graven images. These tiki palaces mass marketed a lifestyle aesthetic of primitive carvings, rum punch, and a sneering relationship to the actual histories of colonialism in both Polynesia and the Caribbean. These tiki restaurants—most associated with the big national franchises of Trader Vic's, Don the Beachcomber, and The Luau—served Cantonese food and a drink menu that endlessly remixed the classic Caribbean planter's punch recipe using cutting-edge food science. These innovative drinks and exotic foods were served with a collection of vaguely primitive iconography that subsumed Caribbean, Chinese, and Polynesian cultural elements into a complex network of symbols that created a generalized and unspecific aesthetic of exoticism.

Beyond the restaurants that promulgated tiki culture, faux Polynesiana signals a general fetishization of the south Pacific—an area where much American blood had been spilled in the 1940s—during the 1950s and 1960s. Texts such as the infamous surf scene in *From Here to Eternity* (1953), the wildly successful film musical *South Pacific* (1958), James Michener's best-selling novel *Hawaii* (1959), the admittance of actual Hawaiʻi as a state that same year, Elvis's film *Blue Hawaii* (1961), and the premiere of the long-running cop show *Hawaiʻi Five-o* (1968) all served to crystallize an obsession with the south Pacific as a preindustrial Eden that could serve as an escape from the harried lives of quiet desperation being lived by many men in America's middle class, as documented by contemporaneous texts such as Sloan Wilson's *The Man in the Grey Flannel Suit* (1955) and Richard Yates's *Revolutionary Road* (1961), in which the newly emergent suburb is presented as a sexually, culturally, and emotionally deadening space filled with identical and interchangeable corporate drones and their equally affectless spouses. While not classically tiki (except perhaps the Elvis film, which developed out of "the King's" interest in rum punch), these texts contributed to a specifically masculine fantasia of the Pacific islands marked by sexual permissiveness, gluttony, and a generally simplified way of life.

This projection of Polynesians as sexually permissive savages is perhaps best promulgated on the menu at tiki restaurants, where drinks such as the Headhunter, the Missionary's Downfall, or the Nui (named for the attendant of King Kalaniʻōpuʻu responsible for fatally stabbing James Cook in 1779) featured prominently. However, as I mentioned above, this neo-imperialist appropriation of Polynesian culture is only one aspect of the exoticized aesthetic on display in tiki culture. The pastiche quality of tiki's racial aesthetic is apparent when one considers it as a culture, a unified and organized aesthetic regime stretched across often seemingly disparate sites in midcentury America. Despite a recent uptick in tiki revivalism starting in the late 1990s and intensifying at present,[1] including new Polynesian palaces all over America and a surge in collecting vintage primitive modern furnishings from midcentury, this interest in documenting tiki often occurs in discreet silos of interest. Sven Kirsten's two lushly illustrated books on tiki (*The Book of Tiki* and *Tiki Modern*) consider the architecture and interior decorating trends that made tiki so visually singular. On the other end of the movement, Jeff "Beachbum" Berry's many books on tiki (notably *Sippin' Safari* and *Beachbum Berry Remixed*) consider the drinks as important moments in the evolution of cocktail culture and an innovative last gasp before the descent into the long dark period post-1970s, when it was very hard to find anything resembling a decent cocktail in most parts of the United States.[2] These two major loci of contemporary interest in tiki—furniture and drinks—capture the two different forces that complicate any final statement on what tiki was and what it represented. The restaurants and furniture companies marketing tiki as a domestic lifestyle offered a primitivist aesthetic that idolized a mishmash of vaguely "Polynesian" tropes. But the bartenders making the punches that lubricated this lifestyle depended on advances in food chemistry; on secrecy that would have made any Cold Warrior proud; and, importantly, on the wide-scale availability of cheap blenders, to market a simple, laidback life in a mug.

Tiki's place in America's pop cultural landscape is complicated by this foundational tension between modernity and Edenic paradise. Despite projecting an image of Polynesian people that is as outright offensive as the imagery associated with blackface minstrel shows in the nineteenth century, tiki culture is undergoing a revival that began in the 2000s thanks primarily to the archival work done by Berry in recovering the secret recipes of the famous tiki bars. This conflicted relationship is perhaps best captured in the back-cover copy for Otto von Stroheim's *Tiki Art Now*, which describes tiki as "a recognized part of American Folk Art with a longstanding history and mass appeal."[3] This hailing of tiki as outsider art is problematic, given the intense consumerism and heightened inauthenticity of its depiction of Polynesian culture: the tourist fantasy of Polynesia and the corporatism of franchised chain restaurants. In *Tiki Modern*, Sven Kirsten further argues that tiki is a pop art extension of Dada and Cubism's obsession with the iconography of African and Oceanic art, but, at the same time, Kirsten suggests that "it was fashionable to augment the sleek lines of modernist furniture and decor with the 'odd' shapes of primitive sculpture," which once again articulates that tiki is enmeshed within, and not opposed to, the Jet Age futurism also associated with mid-century modernism.[4] As I will unpack throughout this chapter, tiki is not a primitive escape from a rapidly arriving nuclear future. Instead, it is part and parcel of this arrival: a primitive-futurism, and not a primitive bastion against an ascendant futurism.

This chapter, then, considers this collection of artifacts and phenomenon—rum punch, Polynesian restaurants, primitive furniture, luau music, Hawaiian shirts—under the rubric "tiki culture," a significant popular cultural formation at the dawn of the post–World War II, American world system of economic and militaristic hegemony. For all the work being done by the architects of midcentury tiki culture to articulate a primitive and relaxed alternative to a turgid suburban rat race, tiki culture is equally embedded in the culture of militarism, Cold War paranoia, Jet Age economic expansion, and rapid-fire fossil-fueled technocapital that it also promises to serve as an escape from. While tiki is almost always discussed as another racist popular culture fad akin to minstrel shows or cowboys-versus-Indians movies, even in texts such as von Stroheim's that celebrate the culture, I argue that this formation is *also* an aesthetic movement that articulated a host of issues concomitant to the emergence of American postmodernism as a system of economic and cultural coherence following World War II. While the implicit argument to this whole chapter is that, of course, tiki culture is deeply offensive and a hugely damaging appropriation of Polynesian culture, and its caricatures of island life are as offensive as any depiction of African Americans in the Jim Crow South, I want to bracket this question of racism because, as I will argue, the ways in which this racism happens is suggestive of a moment of cultural anxiety in which a post–World War II, post-Depression America suddenly found itself as the dominant political and cultural force in the world. Tiki culture, I argue, produced a postmodern aesthetic exoticism that manufactured an imperial aesthetic to explain Jet Age America's global reach *and* to produce an impression of a longer, aesthetic imperial past. As Urmila Seshagiri discusses in her book *Race and the Modernist Imagination*, a text I will engage with more extensively below, racial aesthetics were already an important tool for working through the terms and conditions of modernity in British avant-garde art; however, as I'll show, the manner in which this aestheticization happened in tiki culture, in postwar America, is a unique phenomenon that signaled the emergence of postmodernism as a distinct and distinctly American means of articulating a new, globally dominant American empire.

RUM, GOMME, LIME

For many tiki enthusiasts, the drinks are the way into the broader culture of the period. In fact, cocktail historians often forget to mention or downplay the fact that most tiki establishments were restaurants. This is primarily due to the food being of secondary importance to the drinks, as first established at Don the Beachcomber. Rumaki, a signature dish of the restaurant consisting of chicken livers and canned water chestnuts wrapped in bacon, skewered and baked, was developed because, as Berry uncovers in *Taboo Table* (2005), "according to his friend Herb Kane, Don's poultry supplier forced him to buy whole chickens 'and Don couldn't stand all of the chicken livers going to waste' . . . 'He had a Cook Islands dictionary. He opened it, his finger came down on the word rumaki and that's what he called it.'"[5] Similarly, Don's commitment to operating cheaply also accidentally determined another defining, "exotic" character of tiki: complaining to a Chinese grocery store owner that California law mandated he serve food, the owner responded, "Oh, I have a cousin, he'll cook for you," and the association between Chinese food, Caribbean rum, and faux Polynesian art that marked the tiki trifecta was born.[6]

While the food at most tiki restaurants may have been terrible, the drinks were and remain stunning. Classic tiki drinks such as the fog-cutter and, most famously, the mai tai show that mixology at these embarrassingly kitschy faux Polynesian palaces represented the height of cocktail craft and, as Berry has recovered, actually innovated cocktail-making in a number of ways. More importantly, though, the drinks themselves contain a key blending of the factors shaping tiki culture's complex legacy, mixing technological, colonialist, and primitive elements into a potent punch that best describes tiki's place in articulating a postmodern aesthetic for an emergent American imperialism.

At their core, all tiki drinks are only slightly different from the universal formula for a daiquiri: "rum, gomme, and lime," where "gomme" represents gomme syrup, an old-timey sugar syrup thickened with gum arabic that dropped out of fashion after Prohibition. As Berry explains in *Sippin' Safari*, his oral history of tiki bars, iterating this classic flavor was a product of necessity. When Ernest Raymond Beaumont-Gantt (more famous as Don E. R. Beachcomber, the name he legally adopted in the 1940s) was first opening Don the Beachcomber in 1934 in Hollywood (the restaurant that established *the* pattern for tiki restaurants and bars the world over), the end of Prohibition meant that rum was available from former smugglers for dirt cheap prices.[7]

Because of this cheap price of rum, Don abandoned other possible tropical drink templates such as the Singapore sling (which is gin-based) and built a coast-to-coast restaurant empire specifically on the Jamaican planter's punch he first encountered while working on his grandfather's yacht, *The Port of New Orleans* (which his grandfather was using to smuggle rum into the United States during Prohibition).[8] This classic planter's punch recipe—like the base flavor of rum, gomme syrup, and lime—comes in the form of a rhyme: "1 part sour, 2 parts sweet, 3 parts strong, 4 parts weak," with lime juice, sugar, rum, and water being the respective ingredients. As Berry documents, however,

> Don took this formula and ran with it. Why just lime juice? Why not a combination of lime and grapefruit, or lime and pineapple and orange? And why stop at sugar? Why not experiment with more unexpected sweeteners, like cinnamon syrup, or passion fruit syrup combined with falernum?
>
> Don took the same tack with rum. To cut the heavy molasses bite of dark Jamaican rum, he might mix it with a dry white rum from Puerto Rico, then add yet another dimension with a dash of smoky, overproof Demerara rum; the result was a complex, layered flavor no one rum could approach on its own.[9]

Almost all of Don's drinks, and all of the famous ones, follow this basic formula, tweaking rum, syrup, and citrus loads (also usually adding a foundation of a dash of absinthe and Angostura bitters).

Derived from this basic formula, Don's recipes were the heart of his restaurant empire. The history of Don the Beachcomber's that Berry tells in *Sippin' Safari* and dimensionalizes in *Beachbum Berry Remixed* (2009) and *Potions of the Caribbean* (2013) is littered with stories of competitors—including Trader Vic Bergeron and Steve Crane (owner of the Luau franchise) but also single-location tiki mainstays such as The China Trader in Toluca Lake—stealing Don's bartenders in order to get his recipes. As such, especially after bartender Ray Buhen defected from Don to The Seven Seas with a whole notebook of the early Beachcomber recipes,

> Don came up with an encryption system that only his most trusted staff could decipher. He labeled bottles containing his house flavorings with code names like "Don's Mix," "Spices #2," or "Syrup Parisienne." The service bar [where drinks were made to hide their contents from customers] staff never knew what was in these bottles; they just poured the amounts indicated in the coded recipes.[10]

Given the success Don enjoyed guarding his recipes in this manner, most of the authentic formula were lost when Don the Beachcomber's shut down and Don died. However, as Berry documents in a chapter of *Sippin' Safari* that reads like an Ian Fleming novel, it eventually, though with much difficulty, became possible to decrypt the formulas.

In documenting this cryptographic process, Berry describes a set of protocols that themselves more resembled something James Bond might do while working for Her Majesty's Secret Service than when shaking a martini at home. Recording an interview with Mike Buhen, Ray's son, Berry writes that

> "Ray would go to the Astra Company out in Inglewood to pick up #2 and #4," Mike told the Bum. "A chemist would open a safe, take out the ingredients, and twirl some knobs in a big mixing machine, filling up a case while Ray waited. Then they'd close up the secret stuff in the safe. Ray took the bottles—marked only #2 and #4—back to Don the Beachcomber's."

Ray never passed along to his son what those ingredients actually were, however. Eventually, through even more exhaustive methods, Berry uncovers that #2 was a mix of vanilla and allspice, while #4 was cinnamon.

Despite these drinks being potions for accessing a more relaxed way of life, Don's commitment to secrecy more closely mirrors the kind of counterintelligence tactics practiced in industrial settings or as defense against the KGB in America's growing military-industrial complex, especially following the Rosenberg trial. The intense labor that went into these drinks and the carefully guarded secrets that formulated them suggests, in my thinking, an undercurrent of militarism below the surface of tiki's projected aesthetic of permissive and relaxed hedonism. As I will discuss in further detail below, tiki is actually a primitive-futurism, blending militarism and rapid technological change with rhetorics of slowness and primitivism into the same complex brew. In other words, tiki offered an escape from a set of circumstances (intense corporate and geopolitical competitiveness) while relying on the very techniques that underpinned this competitive culture. These two seemingly divergent aesthetic impulses are crucial to situating tiki as a preeminent expression of an American colonialist aesthetic.

This blending is no accident, either. In addition to the secrecy underscoring his formulas, Don's other major innovation depended on the industrialization of traditional notions of women's work that marked the postwar period. While only part of a broader trend toward machining the domestic environment in the name of labor-saving, tiki could not have happened without the invention and proliferation of the electric blender. To return to Don's remixing of the classic planter's punch formula, Berry remarks that for all his innovative dimensionalization of the sweet, strong, and sour components of punch,

> Don's most ground-breaking improvement was with the "weak." Instead of shaking the sour, sweet, and strong with water, which results in an overdiluted drink, Don put them in an electric mixer with crushed ice and flash blended for three to five seconds—just long enough to give the drink a nice chill, but not long enough to liquefy all the ice.[11]

In addition to the blender, Don's drinks were mixed on an assembly line in which several bartenders were responsible for adding the various components of each drink, as orders came in (this operation was hidden from the customer's view). This assembly-line style was why many of Don's star bartenders had little experience actually tending bar: most of them did their work on the service bar and after hours developing new recipes (Don himself was also a legendary tinkerer, as the myriad of authentic zombie recipes attest). This flash blending, however, was truly revolutionary in mixology and directly led to the ubiquitous frozen daiquiris and margaritas available at chain restaurants throughout the United States to this day. Once again, though, we see that tiki intertwined the primitive and the aggressively modern, rather than simply standing in opposition to an oppressive and ubiquitous expansion of American industry.[12]

BLENDED COLONIALISM

Beyond this mixing together of primitivism and futurism, tiki drinks also articulate a potent brew of colonialist images and, as such, articulate not only an exotic aesthetic but also a kind of pan-colonial aesthetic that generally alludes to primarily British colonial tropes in the same kind of unspecific manner that exotic aesthetics allude to specific, real indigenous cultures. An example of this kind of blending is best exemplified by tiki's most famous drink, Trader Vic's mai tai. Long a dispute between Vic Bergeron and a number of his competitors (settled via a number of lawsuits), the origins of the mai tai are complex, as documented by Berry in *Beachbum Berry Remixed*.[13] A variety of factors contribute to this complicated history, most notably that Trader Vic drinks (such as the fog-cutter) tend to rely on lemon juice while the mai tai has lime as base, but Berry concludes his account by offering the most likely scenario: Bergeron invented the mai tai while trying to reproduce an early Don the Beachcomber drink, the Q. B. Cooler. While both drinks share nothing save rum and lime, they taste remarkably similar.

In any case, the classic mai tai formula (much simpler than the Don recipe that Vic was trying to copy) calls for rums from Jamaica and Martinique, orgeat syrup, rock candy syrup, orange curaçao, and lime juice. These ingredients, sourced from all over the Caribbean, are, besides being very curious additions to a "Polynesian" drink, each a token of a slightly different imperial moment in the colonization of the region. While these drinks are tropical because of their association with the region, they also blend together tropes—repeatable figural elements, but also from the Greek *tropaion*, which was a memorial to or remembrance of a major military victory—into a potent tropic punch. By blending tropes along with rum, gum, and lime, these punches work to circulate a pan-imperial aesthetic, distilling particular colonial moments into a broader, unspecific, and general aesthetic effect of power itself for an emergent globally powerful United States.

The ingredient list in a mai tai traces a constellation of colonial signifiers that have shaped and remade life in the Caribbean. Rum itself has a long history of association with colonialism in the Caribbean. When distilled from Caribbean molasses in Boston (which once had a thriving rum distillation industry), the spirit was a key element in the three-legged triangle trade (in which rum from Massachusetts was exchanged for slaves in Africa, who were exchanged for molasses in the Caribbean, which was then shipped back to Boston to make into more rum) that helped enrich the traders of colonial America. The combination of rums in the mai tai (a method invented by Don Beach) manipulates the island-by-island specificity of rum production in the Caribbean and the resultant universe of flavors. Jamaican rum is used in the mai tai for its caramel and oak notes, while the Martinique rhum is included for its grassiness. Further, the rum industry in Jamaica was hugely profitable due to the myriad contracts to supply British military and merchant navies with their grog ration. Rhum agricole, the style of rhum made in Martinique and called for in the mai tai, is the only AOP (Appellation d'Origine Protégée)[14] granted to a region outside France, marking the specifically unusual tension between France and its colonies, as AOP is generally a marker of something uniquely and importantly French.

Both of these rums evoke specific colonial *terroir* in terms of flavor *and* specific historical violence, but the central axiom of tiki mixology is to blend these rums to produce, as Berry rhapsodized, "a complex, layered flavor no one rum could approach on its own."[15] This "complex, layered flavor" produces, similarly, a complex, layered aesthetic that encodes not only a Polynesian Eden but also a pan-colonial aesthetic, drawing from the various histories of the Caribbean to produce an unspecific aesthetic effect. From the rums to the lime (imported from Southeast Asia through the Middle East to Spain and finally to the Caribbean) and the curaçao (a Dutch liqueur made from sour orange peel that grows on a "desert island" where "sugar cane wouldn't grow," whose unique breed of Valencia orange is so "bitter ... not even their goat would eat them"), the mai tai connected a fake Polynesian life of supposed ease to an aesthetic impression of eighteenth-century colonialism and empire-building that bears only tangential relationships to the actual history of any individual island or even the Caribbean as a whole.[16]

LEAVING ON A JET PLANE

In the same way that tiki's seemingly simplistic aesthetic is shot through with a complex intertext of Caribbean colonial violence, the image of Polynesia projected by tiki is intimately enmeshed with a less widely reported history of colonial oppression and the threat of imminent nuclear annihilation that tiki is often seen as resisting. Where we saw the colonial images that arise from the drinks themselves, this other interwoven narrative of nuclear and colonial violence emerges from looking at tiki culture's complex engagement with actual existing Polynesia in the form of the United States's annexation of an independent Hawai'i. As I mentioned in the introduction to this chapter, Hawaiian statehood was the other major force driving the popularization of tiki. However, as with the projection of this paradise, tiki's relationship with Hawai'i is deeply complex.

In 1959, the landscape of Hawai'i changed forever, thanks to a number of events. The islands attained statehood with the passage of the Hawai'i Admission Act (formally, An Act to Provide for the Admission of the State of Hawai'i into the Union) in Congress and an overwhelming referendum in favor of statehood (though the two choices were to remain an unrepresented US territory or to become a US state); James Michener's *Hawaii* became a bestseller popularizing the islands as a haven away from the rigors and abuses of industrialized technomodernity; and, perhaps most importantly, a Pan Am jetliner (a Boeing 707) landed in the Hawaiian Islands for the first time. In 1958, 240,000 tourists made the twelve-hour flight from San Francisco or took a six-day ship crossing from Los Angeles. The arrival of the Pan Am jets, however, cut this travel time to a single five-hour flight. Visiting the paradise that Michener's novel so provocatively described was suddenly within the realm of possibility for any moderately prosperous American. And tourism figures for Hawai'i bear this out: the number of tourists quadrupled the pre-jet numbers to 1 million by 1967 and soared to around 7.5 million today.

This rapid influx of tourists destabilized the lives of Hawaiian natives, leading to, as the radical Hawaiian nationalist Haunani-Kay Trask documents, a set of conditions in which tourists and resident nonnatives outnumber "Native Hawaiians by 30 to 1" (from a two-to-one Hawaiian majority before statehood) and "the average real incomes of Hawai'i residents grew only *one* percent during the period from the early seventies through the early eighties, when tourism was booming."[17] As Trask documents, this set of conditions creates Hawai'i as a fantasy, "mostly a state of mind" in which "Hawai'i is the image of escape from the rawness and violence of daily American life."[18] There are myriad accounts documenting the pattern of violence that tourist fantasies perform to native populations in the south Pacific, most notably Miriam Kahn's ethnographic account of how French tourist fantasies of Tahiti have more to do with the administration of the colony than with the actual needs of the real island's inhabitants.[19]

This projected fantasy is often discussed in terms of an aestheticized primitivism, which is, of course, where tiki—with its Polynesia of the mind—fits into an account of what basically amounts to colonization by hyperreality: Jean Baudrillard's term for the more-real-than-real version of the world projected by global media that is increasingly, in Baudrillard's vision, replacing reality in the collective unconscious. Trask, for instance, suggests that this tourist fantasia "comes out of the depths of Western sexual sickness that demands a dark, sin-free Native for instant gratification between imperialist wars."[20] In Trask's account, following the general rhetorical pattern for discussing tourism in Polynesia, this trope of the restored Eden is seen as an antidote to the atomic militarization of postmodernity; however, what interests me here is that tiki is not just a primitive opposition to the high costs of nuclear futurism. I want to build up, over the remainder of this chapter, a sense of tiki as a specifically primitive-futurism, in which the futurism and the primitivism are intertwined in a way that does not privilege the easy creation of either phenomenon.

For example, as I mentioned, the Pan Am Boeing 707s created the material conditions for circulating this sexualized primitivism throughout midcentury America. These jets that transported American tourists to Hawaiʻi are just as much a product of the militarized technomodernity that tourism promised an escape from. In 1945, Boeing, producer of the B-29 (the long-range bomber that dropped the atomic bombs on Hiroshima and Nagasaki), saw orders for its long-range aircraft drop from 155 a month to 10. Needing to maintain a $500,000-a-day payroll, Boeing decided to enter the emerging field of commercial air travel, at the time dominated by civilian conversions of Douglas's iconic C-47 military transport.[21] These American companies, whether Douglas or Boeing, had a virtual monopoly over the commercial travel market into the 1990s, thanks not to the superiority of American planes (as was widely reported), but instead because of a series of crafty maneuvers during World War II. With a larger production base and more secure facilities, the Allies agreed early in the war that American industry should produce the bombers and transports, while other nations merely produced fighters. After the war, this extensive experience in producing large airframes led to a virtual American hegemony of the skies.[22]

Beyond the general origin in the American war machine, however, the 707s that opened Hawaiʻi have significant roots in the military industrial complex. As aircraft historian Roger Bilstein notes,

> In 1952, . . . a number of U.S. engineers, decided the time had come to design an American jet airliner. . . . Industry leaders became especially interested in Pratt & Whitney's J-57, which took to the air in 1952 with the Boeing B-52 bombers. . . . Boeing in particular had accrued considerable swept-wing expertise during the B-47 and B-52 programs.[23]

Essentially, Boeing used its experiences making the B-47 and B-52 to produce the first widely used commercial jetliners. These military aircraft were both designed as centerpieces of the Strategic Air Command's medium-range nuclear deterrents (for context, the iconic bomb in the film *Dr. Strangelove* was dropped from a Boeing B-52). In other words, the 707s that opened Hawaiʻi to affordable air travel were based on airframes designed to carry weapons capable of obliterating all life on Earth.

Thus, the primitive folk art of tiki culture is linked to the Jet Age futurism of the same period, just as we saw in Sven Kirsten, who noted above that "it was fashionable to augment the sleek lines of modernist furniture and decor with the 'odd' shapes of primitive sculpture."[24] In this way, I argue that tiki culture is not just a primitive antidote to a militarized vision of the future.

Instead, tiki culture is itself a futurism, a specifically primitive-futurist aesthetic.

Berry confirms this, noting that tiki "hit its height during the Space Age. Almost every tiki bar named at least one drink in honor of the final frontier: The Outrigger served a Flying Saucer, Kelbo's had its Star Fire, and even Trader Vic got into the act with his Space Needle."[25] To Berry's list, I would add the iconic Test Pilot from Don the Beachcomber and Berry's own recreations the Coconaut (and the Coconaut Re-Entry, which is the same drink served on fire), Astro Aku-Aku, Aurora Bora Borealis, and Planet of the Apes. So, in addition to cocktails named after headhunters and cannibals, there was a profusion of drinks that alluded to the high technologies that made possible American imperialism. The escape from the rigors of American empire offered by tiki culture was made possible by the militarism that made possible both the empire and the escape in the first place.

HYPER-RAJ

While many people hail the tiki palace as an escape from the everyday realities of administering a nuclear, global America in the 1950s, these tiki restaurants—through their co-optation of this image of Hawai'i as the jewel in America's crown—also provided a space for reflecting on American imperial power. This chapter has traced a series of icons and discourses that tiki culture draws from to assemble a primitive-futurist aesthetic effect, and I want to conclude by considering one more icon. As Charles Allen documents in *Plain Tales from the Raj*, "The Club was a peculiarly 'Anglo-Indian' institution" that served as the "hub of local society ... in all but the very smallest stations" in colonial India.[26] For civil and military colonials, these social and sporting clubs were a space apart from the exotic landscape of India in which colonials could relax, participate in both "sport and social activities," gossip, and generally unwind from the rigors of administering a massive colony such as India.[27] However, as Allen documents, these bits of Britain in the midst of India also continued to be spaces in which colonials had to be on their guard. "It was nevertheless a severe crime 'to drink too much or to be seen to drink too much before Indian servants'" when indulging at the club (which was the main activity of these spaces).[28] So, despite being "a social spot" with "few rivals," the "club verandah on a large station" was also a space in which escape from the rigors of colonial rule was only ever granted under certain rigid conditions of behavior.

The tiki restaurant inverts the logic of "The Club" as Allen describes it, despite preserving this central contradiction of escape without escape. Where clubs in India "were old buildings of no architectural merits," the massive Polynesian longhouses that dominated their American neighborhoods offered elaborate and exaggerated doses of the gaudy and the exotic—for example, the massive Easter Island sculptures that greeted diners outside of the (now demolished) Kahiki Supper Club in Columbus, Ohio. Instead of a piece of Britain amidst the foreign, tiki palaces placed a bit of the exotic in the heart of often anonymous, suburban locales.

However, as I have argued above, the function of the tiki restaurant is the same as its inverse in the Anglo Indian club: the myriad of aesthetic tokens assembled by tiki culture—Cold War counterintelligence, eighteenth-century Caribbean colonialism, nuclear war, jet travel, the annexation of Hawai'i, and the Anglo Indian club—piece together an overall effect meant to dazzle customers with the products of American technological and geopolitical empire while also offering a tantalizing escape from the threats associated with this imperial power. Beyond merely claiming that tiki culture was an articulation of an American Raj, I want to conclude by suggesting that, of course, this Polynesian Raj would happen in a postmodern fashion. Because, of course, wouldn't a midcentury American aesthetic of empire happen through a series of chain restaurants?

As I have suggested, we can think about tiki culture as akin to the various cultures of empire that developed in Great Britain during its time as a colonial power, though tiki is of course filtered through very different American and postmodern contexts. In addition to the drinks, which as we saw blend together various signifiers from Britain's colonial past, the design and construction of the tiki restaurant, the most prominent and iconic portion of the period, mimics certain endeavors that Britain undertook to codify a quintessentially Indian architectural style. As Hawai'i serves as the cultural imaginary through which an American imperial aesthetic was constructed, so India served for the British empire. The tiki restaurant, as a style of American imperial architecture, stands as a particular outgrowth of an image of Hawai'i and, as we shall see, represents an architectural style that represented Hawaiian-ness with minimal input from actual existing Hawaiians. Similarly, the British attempt to define the concept of *Indian style* mutated and deformed the myriad traditions of Indian architecture.

As historian Thomas Metcalf argues, a British-sanctioned "Indo-Saracenic" style of architecture was formulated by architectural historians in the late nineteenth century. This style became the official building style for Indian administrative buildings and, as Metcalf argues, worked to position British imperial power "in the line of the great Indian empires of the past."[29] Indo-Saracenic architects "set about creating a style of building Indian in appearance, but Western in function."[30] Architects working in this style, like tiki culture, appropriated a diverse range of Indian elements from across the continent and reassembled them into a coherent style meant to signify a specifically British take on Indian history.[31] Originally intended for us in the colonial architecture of the Raj, Indo-Saracenic was eventually exported to colonies such as South Africa as the official building style of Britain's empire. Additionally, like tiki, this architecture was "incurably romantic."[32] As Metcalf observes, the British historians of Indian architecture who first formulated the style, "obsessed by a search for the 'picturesque,' singled out for the highest praise the deserted palaces of Dig and Orccha, and the 'fair-like' structures of Udaipur and Bundi."[33] As Metcalf goes on to show, this revivalist style was invested not so much in preserving, praising, or nurturing Indian artistic traditions as in filtering bits and bobs from this same tradition through a Western sense of the exotic and the need to establish and enforce colonial power.

This selective aesthetic is, as we have seen, mirrored at many levels in the elements of tiki culture; however, the association with state power is specifically telling in this instance. The obsession with Indian style and Indian art, though filtered first through British sensibilities, created conditions by which "India's architecture ceased to be a living force. Instead it was pressed into the service of British colonialism."[34] Additionally, this flattening of a history of organic development into a rigid and dubiously Indian style transformed the history of Indian art into a series of tchotchkes that could be assembled to add an exotic flare throughout the British empire (as the Indo-Saracenic style was exported to other colonies) and also at home. The British, as Metcalf documents, were able to transform a vital artistic ferment into a staid (though exotic) aesthetic system.

Martin Cate, author and tiki bar proprietor, documents the development of tiki style as consisting of four distinct phases: "tropical or pre-tiki,"[35] "Beachcomber style,"[36] "Trader style,"[37] and, finally, "High Tiki."[38] This progression was driven by the intense competition among the three major tiki chains to build progressively more-enveloping experiences for their increasingly discerning clientele. Cate imparts the final style, "where every design element that came before coalesces and amplifies," to Steve Crane's Luau.[39] Here, Cate details, "Hollywood set designers are employed to bring an ever-more immersive experience to life with waterfalls and meandering streams traversing the dining room and running under footbridges. Live tropical foliage, macaws, and even alligators are employed to add to the sense of the exotic, while theatrical effects like color-shifting murals and rainstorms animate the space."[40] Arriving relatively late to the tropical restaurant game and serving food and drinks acquired by hiring Vic and Don's bartenders and chefs, Steve Crane worked to create a more intense experience as a means to differentiate his establishments from those of his competitors. In doing so, he brought tiki architecture to its Baroque period.

In discussing how to build the tiki experience at home, Cate continually reminds his readers that escape is the most important aspect of a tiki space. He highlights how, behind some beachy bric-a-brac and a carved statue, tiki is a total experience, emphasizing the importance of creating stark contrasts between inside and outside (speaking of his bar Smuggler's Cove, "the exterior is kept deliberately anonymous to heighten the dramatic shift after you enter"), keeping the space "enveloped in a perpetual twilight," and the "calming" effect of running water (a trait first explored in the "High Tiki" period).[41] Rather than the histories of Berry or Sven Kirsten, Cate's account views tiki as a living tradition, but also clearly documents that tiki was a repeatable, rule-based architectural style.

This tiki experience had interesting effects in Hawai'i. With Crane and his competitors creating increasingly elaborate aesthetic expressions of Polynesia on the mainland, when Hawai'i began to open to tourism following statehood and the arrival of the jet plane, as Berry documents in *Sippin' Safari*, tourists visiting Hawai'i found that it didn't look very Hawaiian (as they had been led to expect by tiki culture's fantasia): "The mysterious, romantic, opulent South Seas décor and drinks of mainland Polynesian restaurants were nowhere to be found in Polynesia itself. Waikiki's most famous resort, The Royal Hawaiian, had a Spanish Revival look, while the Moana Hotel's Ionic columns would have been more at home on the robber-baron estates of Newport."[42]

As Berry explains, these conditions resulted from colonization of the islands by Americans: "Ironically, the American tourist's "dream" of Hawai'i of grass shacks, Tiki gods, and wanton wahines had been wiped out by his own forebears in the 1800s. Bedford whalers preferred clapboard houses to grass shacks, while Boston missionaries threw every Tiki they could find into a fire."[43] As Berry goes on to tell, the Hawaiian resort owners ended up importing the very non-Polynesian sculptors and artists who defined high tiki style for the mainland chain restaurants to make Hawaiian hotels look more "Hawaiian." In other words, Hawai'i had to be renovated by non-Hawaiians in order to look authentically Hawaiian. Similarly to the deformation of India's architectural tradition, Hawai'i was remade by tiki culture to resemble the fantasy of Hawai'i that tiki culture itself had already marketed to Americans.

In describing the aesthetic philosophy of American popular culture meccas such as Las Vegas and Orlando, Umberto Eco explores the idea of a hyperreality, something that is both completely fake and, at the same time, completely real:

> It suggests that there is a constant in the average American imagination and taste, for which the past must be preserved and celebrated in full-scale authentic copy; a philosophy of immortality as duplication. It dominates the relation with the self, with the past, not infrequently with the present, always with History.... To speak of things that one wants to connote as real, these things must seem real. The "completely real" becomes identified with the "completely fake." Absolute unreality is offered as real presence.[44]

Tiki culture uses a better-than-real version of the British empire and a better-than-real version of Polynesian culture to articulate a moment of American economic and technological dominance, while playing fast and loose with the supremely high consequences of this dominance. Tiki signals a move to a hyperreal aesthetic of empire that breaks with the stated logic of something like the Indo-Saracenic style of the Raj. Where British architects publicly stated that their appropriation of classical Indian culture was in the name of saving a dying culture, tiki manufactured a Polynesian culture that never existed in the first place. By imagining this primitive culture, American imperialism during this period is able to skip over the need to preserve an embattled culture as a means to justify exterminating it (as was the case with the Indo-Saracenic style). Instead, the primitive space is transformed from an outside that must be saved into another space in which the technological achievements enabling empire are enacted. As nuclear testing transformed Bikini Atoll from a tropical paradise into a post-atomic hellscape in the name of Cold War nuclear dominance, the south Pacific islands themselves are directly incorporated into the tension between high-tech instant annihilation and easy prosperity that dominates Cold War suburban culture. Thus, tiki highlights the way in which, in the American postwar empire, the logic of technology that both enables and is enabled by imperial power is enacted again and again without an outside: a culture in which even fantasies of escape can be imagined only through the pressures they claim to ease.

This begs the question of how we relate to tiki culture today, especially in a moment where new tiki palaces are the current state of the craft cocktail art. Largely made prominent again in craft cocktail circles by Jeff Berry's books and the focus on new tiki drinks at New York's Death & Co, tiki drinks are a staple of many forward-thinking craft bars. Moreover, newly opened, high tiki–style palaces such as Chicago's Three Dots and a Dash and Lost Lake, New Orleans's Latitude 29, Hale Pele in Portland, Smuggler's Cove in San Francisco, and The Polynesian in New York City dominate cocktail journalism. Reading press from these new-school tiki bars, we see that they are committed to continuing the tradition of detail, quality, and hospitality practiced by the original tiki palaces and, moreover, they specifically speak about reviving the tiki tradition. We can now have, for the first time since they went out of style in the 1970s, an authentic tiki experience. But, as we have seen, tiki itself was an authentic experience of inauthenticity in the first place, a nostalgic restoration of a lost Polynesia that never existed. Just as British architects and tiki set-dressers articulated their work as preserving a forever-imperiled authentic indigenous aesthetic, contemporary tiki proprietors are rescuing a dying tradition from the cultural trash heap. But unlike actually imperiled colonial subjects, the colonial desire that tiki represents is itself now the endangered practice, with the lives of indigenous Polynesians further removed from sight. The efforts to revive tiki today show that even the real fake is threatened with extinction and is subject to the work of preservation.

Texas A&M University

NOTES

1. Most high-end bars, the kind that label themselves as offering "craft cocktails," will have at least one drink drawing inspiration from tiki. *The PDT Cocktail Book* by Jim Meehan (an exemplary document of this sort of establishment) lists recipes for Beachbum, Espresso Bongo, and Luau as original drinks and house recipes for classic tiki drinks, including fog-cutter, mai tai, Navy Grog, Queen's Park Swizzle, and Zombie Punch. While PDT is in no way a tiki bar, as a respectable, innovative cocktail bar it is expected to offer tiki drinks. Additionally, as documented in books by Jeff Berry, Sven Kirsten, and Otto von Stroheim, many enthusiasts, at present, are actively involved in reviving the broader cultural landscape of tiki.

2. As Ted Haigh tells us in *Vintage Spirits and Forgotten Cocktails: From the Alamagoozlum to the Zombie: 100 Rediscovered Recipes and the Stories Behind Them* (Beverly, MA: Quarry, 2009), several factors played into the need for cocktails to be revived in the late 1990s (a revival that this work both documents and participates in). As he notes, the double impact of Prohibition and World War II rationing "dramatically cut down on the stored stocks of aged whiskey" in the United States (25–26). Worried about this dwindling supply, American distillers (following models learned from Canadian companies) began to aggressively

push blended spirits and "an alternative drinking style" to mask the deficiencies in blended spirits: the highball (27). As Haigh mockingly enthuses, the highball is "light! refreshing! casual! modern!" and came to dominate a leisure-driven, home-focused drinking culture that banished obscure fortified wines—as well as herbal liqueurs and the need to keep fresh juice on hand—to the scrap heap of history, for a time. Given, however, that rum is easier and cheaper to produce than American whiskey and that tiki relied on a mechanics of scale to produce its complicated drinks, tiki bars practiced high-end mixology into the 1960s, when the growing popularity of disco and TV killed off the supper club as an institution in America. Thus, many cocktail historians consider tiki to be an important moment in the history of mixology: the last moment of a sophisticated cocktail culture and, simultaneously, an important bridge to the revival of that culture, given that tiki icons such as Tony Ramos, Mariano Lucidine, and Ray Buhen tended bar into the 1990s.

3. Otto von Stroheim, *Tiki Art Now!: A Volcanic Eruption of Art* (San Francisco: Last Gasp, 2004), n.p.

4. Sven A. Kirsten, *Tiki Modern* (Los Angeles: Taschen, 2007), 22.

5. Jeff Berry, *Beachbum Berry's Taboo Table*, ed. Dan Vado (San Jose, CA: SLG, 2005), 12.

6. Jeff Berry, *Sippin' Safari* (San Jose, CA: SLG, 2007), 17.

7. Berry, *Sippin'*, 15–17.

8. Berry, *Beachbum Berry Remixed* (San Jose, CA: Club Tiki, 2010), 148.

9. Berry, *Remixed*, 148.

10. Berry, *Sippin'*, 116–17.

11. Berry, *Remixed*, 148.

12. Don's bartenders were all Filipino (while Trader Vic employed Chinese bartenders), and this pattern of labor—in which immigrant bodies labor to manufacture rich, white leisure—is a pattern reproduced again and again during this period. For instance, Don's service bars (in which the tenders were never seen) mirrors the logic of a cruise ship, in which a host of foreign laborers work to produce absolute leisure for their "guests."

13. Berry, *Remixed*, 64–69.

14. AOP refers to the regional production standards enforced throughout France, mostly protecting styles of wine and cheese. These labels (not unlike bourbon whiskey in the United States) refer to a specific product, made in a specific way, in a specific region.

15. Berry, *Remixed*, 148.

16. Jeff Berry, *Beachbum Berry's Potions of the Caribbean* (New York: Cocktail Kingdom, 2013), 63. In many ways, this appropriation of specific historical events to produce a general effect has been mirrored most recently, in the same byways that tiki sailed, in the Disney movie franchise *Pirates of the Caribbean*. With fake

islands and fake pirates, these movies mine the signifiers of eighteenth-century Caribbean imperialism to produce an aesthetic effect of piracy. While this effect production is commonplace in Hollywood cinema, it is also commonplace in constructions of the Caribbean.

17. Haunani-Kay Trask, *From a Native Daughter: Colonialism and Sovereignty in Hawai'i* (Honolulu: University of Hawai'i Press, 1999), 138.

18. Trask, *From a Native Daughter*, 137.

19. Miriam Kahn, "Tahiti Intertwined: Ancestral Land, Tourist Postcard, and Nuclear Test Site," *American Anthropologist* 102, no. 1 (2000): 7–26, April 1, 2014, https://doi.org/10.1525/aa.2000.102.1.7.

20. Trask, *From a Native Daughter*, 137.

21. Roger E. Bilstein, *The Enterprise of Flight: The American Aviation and Aerospace Industry* (Washington, DC: Smithsonian Institution, 2001), 138–39.

22. Bilstein, *The Enterprise of Flight*, 137.

23. Bilstein, *The Enterprise of Flight*, 141.

24. Kirsten, *Tiki Modern*, 22.

25. Berry, *Remixed*, 30.

26. Charles Allen, *Plain Tales from the Raj: Images of British India in the 20th Century* (London: Abacus, 1988), 116.

27. Allen, *Plain Tales from the Raj*, 117.

28. Allen, *Plain Tales from the Raj*, 126.

29. Thomas R. Metcalf, "A Tradition Created: Indo-Saracenic Architecture Under the Raj," *History Today* 32, no. 9 (1982): 42.

30. Metcalf, "A Tradition Created," 42.

31. Metcalf, "A Tradition Created," 42–43.

32. Metcalf, "A Tradition Created," 43.

33. Metcalf, "A Tradition Created," 43.

34. Metcalf, "A Tradition Created," 45.

35. Martin Cate and Rebecca Cate, *Smuggler's Cove: Exotic Cocktails, Rum, and the Cult of Tiki* (Berkeley, CA: Ten Speed, 2016), 26.

36. Cate and Cate, *Smuggler's Cove*, 28.

37. Cate and Cate, *Smuggler's Cove*, 35.

38. Cate and Cate, *Smuggler's Cove*, 55.

39. Cate and Cate, *Smuggler's Cove*, 55.

40. Cate and Cate, *Smuggler's Cove*, 55.

41. Cate and Cate, *Smuggler's Cove*, 284–85.

42. Berry, *Sippin'*, 71.

43. Berry, *Sippin'*, 73.

44. Umberto Eco, *Travels in Hyperreality* (San Diego, CA: Harcourt, 1990), 6–7.

BIBLIOGRAPHY

Allen, Charles. *Plain Tales from the Raj: Images of British India in the 20th Century.* London: Abacus, 1988.

Berry, Jeff. *Beachbum Berry Remixed.* San Jose, CA: Club Tiki, 2010.

———. *Beachbum Berry's Potions of the Caribbean.* New York: Cocktail Kingdom, 2013.

———. *Beachbum Berry's Taboo Table.* Edited by Dan Vado. San Jose, CA: SLG, 2005.

———. *Sippin' Safari.* San Jose, CA: SLG, 2007.

Bilstein, Roger E. *The Enterprise of Flight: The American Aviation and Aerospace Industry.* Washington, DC: Smithsonian Institution, 2001.

Cate, Martin, and Rebecca Cate. *Smuggler's Cove: Exotic Cocktails, Rum, and the Cult of Tiki.* Berkeley, CA: Ten Speed Press, 2016.

Eco, Umberto. *Travels in Hyperreality.* San Diego, CA: Harcourt, 1990.

Haigh, Ted. *Vintage Spirits and Forgotten Cocktails: From the Alamagoozlum to the Zombie 100 Rediscovered Recipes and the Stories Behind Them.* Beverly, MA: Quarry, 2009.

Kahn, Miriam. "Tahiti Intertwined: Ancestral Land, Tourist Postcard, and Nuclear Test Site." *American Anthropologist* 102, no. 1 (2000): 7–26. https://doi.org/10.1525/aa.2000.102.1.7.

Kirsten, Sven A. *Tiki Modern.* Los Angeles: Taschen, 2007.

Metcalf, Thomas R. "A Tradition Created: Indo-Saracenic Architecture Under the Raj." *History Today* 32, no. 9 (1982): 40–45.

Trask, Haunani-Kay. *From a Native Daughter: Colonialism and Sovereignty in Hawai'i.* Honolulu: University of Hawai'i Press, 1999.

Von Stroheim, Otto. *Tiki Art Now: A Volcanic Eruption of Art.* San Francisco: Last Gasp, 2004.

THIRTEEN

THE IRISH CAR BOMB (AND ONE OTHER DISREPUTABLE "COCKTAIL")

STEPHEN WATT

> Perhaps more than any other cocktail, the Irish Car Bomb is a drink with a split reputation dictated entirely by nationality. In 2014, a bar in Oxford, England, was compelled to rescind a promotion featuring the drink in the face of public outcry. In the US, meanwhile, it is consumed by feckless millions who harbor no qualms about the indelicacy of the name.
>
> —Robert Simonson[1]

IN *THEATRE & IRELAND*, LIONEL Pilkington, undaunted by the prospect of venturing too near an oxymoronic phraseology, has it right when asserting that "Ireland and things Irish have been viewed as *essentially performative*" (my emphasis).[2] In fact, "Irish" is one of very few national or ethnic markers that can be deployed not only as an adjective or a noun, but also as an infinitive phrase: to "Irish up" means to infuse with a sense of liveliness, a process typically involving the addition of alcohol. An Irish coffee, Pilkington quips, is "just the thing for intoxicating your sobriety, or sobering up your intoxication."[3] Employed as an adjective, "Irish" can at times ironize, deform, or otherwise modify the noun or phrase that follows it, as is the case with so-called Irish handcuffs (an alcoholic beverage in each hand) or Irish confetti, where visions of the airy festiveness of a ticker-tape parade yield to a horrific street scene thick with a shrapnel of screws, rivets, and the myriad contents of an improvised explosive device (IED).[4] And, like an Irish Car Bomb, as Ciaran Carson describes in the opening lines of his poem "Belfast Confetti," this deadly farrago can be constituted of various ingredients:

> Suddenly as the riot squad moved in, it was raining
> exclamation marks,
> Nuts, bolts, nails, car-keys. A fount of broken type. And the explosion
> Itself—an asterisk on the map.[5]

"Irish" thus often conveys resonances or ironies—and evokes specific histories—that *perform* in ways that are opaque to the average consumer.[6] So it is with the Irish Car Bomb, the popularity of which motivated journalist Robert Simonson to indict Americans, an increasingly easy target these days, of being "feckless" for blithely ordering these drinks without any "qualms" about the name's genealogy or potential to offend.[7]

Or without the slightest inkling of the performative capacities of "Irish" (and, at times, "Belfast"), which in this case link the cocktail to the 1970s in particular and the history of one its primary ingredients: Bailey's Irish Cream. Most accounts of the invention of the Irish Car Bomb go something like this. Bailey's, which along with Irish whiskey and Guinness stout compose the basic recipe for the cocktail, is the product of experimentation in the early 1970s by Gilbeys of Ireland, part of the International Distillers and Vintners (IDV) Group. In 1973, using vegetable oil as an emulsifier, researchers at Gilbeys successfully homogenized a mixture of cream, whiskey, sugar, and other flavorings, and brought Bailey's to the Irish market in 1974.[8] It reached international markets the following year, and, by 1976—in his Norwalk, Connecticut, bar—Charles Oat was sharing drinks with friends and adding the newly acquired liqueur to just about everything, including Kahlua, which when used to supplement the standard recipe forms a "Belfast Car Bomb." When Oat first combined whiskey with a shot of Bailey's, the resulting concoction bubbled in a mild eruption, hence both the addition of "bomb" to the drink's name and the need for consumers to chug it quickly before the cream curdles. Two years later and still in a mood to experiment, Oat dropped the shot of liquors into a pint of stout with the accompanying chant, "Bombs away." With apologies to T. S. Eliot, this brief history provides the terms *Irish* and *bomb* with obvious objective correlatives: the ingredients of the cocktail originate in Ireland, and the combination of whiskey and Irish Cream causes a mild explosion (the "bombs away!" cheer, an embellishment which drinkers might wish to avoid, adds another historical reference to violence of which most consumers are unaware).

Not surprisingly, Simonson's aspersion of American fecklessness emphasizes the Irish Car Bomb's relationship to the violence that attended the "Troubles" in Northern Ireland—and elsewhere in the United Kingdom—during the

1970s, 1980s, and 1990s.[9] There is little point in denying this association, as the decade of the seventies marked both the invention of the drink and the almost viral expansion of the terrorist weapon for which it is named. Indeed, as Mike Davis terms it in his engaging history of the car bomb, while such improvised and deadly devices have a prehistory that goes back to a 1920 explosion in New York's Wall Street area, the "gates of hell were not truly opened" by a relatively inexpensive, yet devastatingly powerful new generation of bombs until the 1970s.[10]

Like Davis's recounting of this prehistory in the early pages of his book, my purpose here is to suggest that the genealogy of the "Irish Car Bomb" reaches back some fifty years before its widespread use, not to the streets outside J. P. Morgan's New York office in 1920, but rather to the Anglo-Irish War that succeeded the Easter Rising of 1916 in which nationalists seized the General Post Office in Dublin, fought British troops for a week, and proclaimed the birth of the Irish Republic. As the insurrectionist events that followed exceeded the capacity of the Royal Irish Constabulary (RIC) and Dublin Metropolitan Police (DMP) to contain them, in late 1919 the British government placed advertisements in the press to recruit men willing to "face a rough and dangerous task."[11] With thousands of World War I veterans out of work—and with the promise that recruits would be paid ten shillings per day—a paramilitary force was relatively easy to assemble. A more difficult task was providing it with appropriate uniforms, particularly dark green ones that matched those of the RIC. The result was a medley—or cacophony—of discordant apparel, a common green cap and black leather belt accompanied by khaki-colored trousers. For this reason, when this group—paramilitaries, mercenaries, or simple thugs, depending upon one's point of view—appeared in Limerick in the spring of 1920, they were soon dubbed the "Black and Tans" (a phrase once used to describe a pack of hounds).[12] Now, of course, the term refers to a "beer cocktail" in which a half pint of stout or porter is added carefully to a similar measure of lager or ale. The resulting layering of colors in a pint glass produces a black and tan appearance.

The black and tan, if such a simple mixture of beers really merits the term *cocktail*, is the other "disreputable" drink alluded to in my title. It is included here both to complement my consideration of the Irish Car Bomb and to remind those like Simonson that cultural obliviousness might perform more than mere fecklessness and rear its ugly head in more than one place or drink order. When it comes to naming cocktails, unintended consequences always seem to lurk behind the decorative orange slice or maraschino cherry—or Guinness logo on the pint glass—particularly when specific countries or locales, peoples, or referents are used. So, for example, while the names of cocktails like the manhattan and the Singapore sling seem harmless enough, the unfortunate myth that the Long Island iced tea was invented by East Hampton and Glen Cove housewives who didn't want their husbands to discover their afternoon tippling—hence the basic recipe's combination of relatively small amounts of several liquors—is implicitly sexist. More to the point, if a competition of insensitivities over the naming of drinks could be held, it would be difficult to determine which cocktail would win, the Irish Car Bomb or the black and tan. Of course, there is an alternative to this exercise, one attributed an Irish bartender in New York named Fergus. When asked by Simonson about the connotation of "Irish Car Bomb," Fergus is said to have responded, "It doesn't bother me. . . . It's a fucking cocktail." The considerable wisdom of this observation notwithstanding, I want to sketch briefly the historical connotations of both drinks and, in so doing, suggest the complications—and multiple performative possibilities—reflected in their names. For both evoke violent histories of which the insensitive drinker should be aware, histories not forgotten in Ireland and elsewhere in the United Kingdom. Quite to the contrary.

It might be advisable to reiterate that although both the drink and the Troubles came fully into being during the 1970s, the Irish Car Bomb's origin, as I have suggested, is more complex and historically overdetermined (gnarled?). In fact, the Troubles were partially defined by bombs of all varieties. The uproariously clever novelist Robert McLiam Wilson—one of a distinguished list of writers engaging the sectarian impasse in Northern Ireland that includes Seamus Heaney, Brian Friel, Jennifer Johnston, Bernard MacLaverty, Anne Devlin, and many more—gestures to this history through his eponymous and outrageous protagonist in *Ripley Bogle*: "The mid-sixties. . . . There aren't actually very many bombs and guns around as yet—just a lot of jobless Catholics getting the shit kicked out of them and having their homes burnt down on Protestant feast days, adding to their well-stocked catalogue of hatred and injustice."[13] By the end of the sixties, however, as Gerry Conlon remembers in *In the Name of the Father*,[14] peace and civil rights marches began in Northern Ireland, tensions intensified, and soon thereafter British troops arrived in Belfast and Derry, leading to what Ripley drolly terms yet another of the "worthy cock-ups in the preceding four hundred years or so" of Anglo-Irish relations: Bloody Sunday on January 30, 1972. By this time, bombs and guns had increasingly devastated daily life in the North, as they would some months later on so-called Bloody Friday on July 21, 1972, when a series of some twenty explosions rocked Belfast.[15]

"Bloody Sunday" in the Northern context refers to British soldiers firing on a crowd of peace marchers in Derry, killing thirteen civilians and injuring a similar number. A Tribunal of Inquiry was convened within weeks and was presided over by John Widgery, Lord Chief Justice of England and Wales, in part as a response to the enormous international press coverage the events of that tragic day received. On April 10, 1972, the tribunal reported its findings, which seemed as outrageous as they were unjust in blaming the victims for their deaths: "There would have been no deaths in Londonderry on 30 January if those who organised the illegal march had not thereby created a highly dangerous situation in which a clash between demonstrators and the security forces was almost inevitable."[16] This sentence initiated the Inquiry's Summary of Conclusions, even though these same "conclusions" later clarified that "None of the deceased or wounded is proved to have been shot whilst handling a firearm or bomb."[17] Rendering the deaths even more painful is the fact that eight of the thirteen decedents were under the age of twenty-one, and six of these were only seventeen. How much of this controversial decision fueled U2's recording of "Sunday, Bloody Sunday" a decade later is perhaps less important than the fact that by the early 1980s the Troubles in Northern Ireland had been memorialized in song for an entire world to contemplate.

By 1974, the year Bailey's was introduced to the drinking public, the bomb in particular had grown in significance in the combatants' respective arsenals, replacing for a time the hunger strike, which would return to the forefront as nationalists' most effective weapon less than a decade later. In fact, Thomas Hennessey's study *The Evolution of the Troubles 1970–72* begins with a short prefatory essay simply entitled "Bomb," which recounts a March 1972 explosion at Belfast's popular and centrally located Abercorn Restaurant, where shoppers often stopped for a late-afternoon cup of coffee or tea. In the blast, 2 were killed and 136 were injured, including patrons of the restaurant and pedestrians outside on the crowded street. Hennessey's account focuses on the McNern sisters—Rosaleen, 22, and Jennifer, 21—in town shopping for clothes for the elder sister's wedding later that summer. Both lost their legs in the blast, and Rosaleen, confined to a wheelchair for her wedding later that August, lost one of her arms as well.[18] As Hennessey explains, the resurgence of the Provisional Irish Republican Army brought with it a revised policy of engagement that included both "defense and retaliation," the latter motivating a widespread bombing campaign during the early months of 1970.[19] In *Eureka Street*, Wilson's sarcastic repo man Jake Jackson describes the lived reality of such violence in stark and irreverent terms:

It wasn't the bombs that were scary. It was the bombed.... Bombs mauled and possessed their dead. Blast removed people's shoes like a solicitous relative, it opened men's shirts pruriently; women's skirts rode up their bloody thighs from the force of the lecherous blast. The bombed dead were spilled on the street like cheap fruit. And, finally, unfuckingbeatably, the bombed dead were dead. They were so very, very dead.[20]

This violence and the constant threat of future horrors transformed Belfast from a sleepy, "underpopulated capital of a minor province" to a fixture in the international media, on a par with Saigon and Beirut. With these places, Jake observes, Belfast shared "the status of the battlefield" and an unenviable kinship with "all history's slaughter venues."[21] This kinship, sadly, spread to include other regions as the isolated "little" bombings in the North evolved into larger, more strategic campaigns of violence, especially in England.

Gerry Conlon became famously implicated in one of these—the October 5, 1974, IRA bombings of two pubs in Guildford, Surrey, frequented by British troops who were training at a nearby camp. Four soldiers and one civilian were killed, with many more seriously injured; a month later, a pub in Woolwich was bombed, killing two more British soldiers. Conlon, who wasn't in Guildford at the time, was eventually arrested with three others, abused by police (punched in the face and grabbed by the testicles; deprived of sleep, food, and for a time clothing), and finally coerced to confess to a crime he did not commit. The quickly passed Prevention of Terrorism Act emboldened police to interrogate prisoners in this manner, which then led to the indictment and flawed conviction of Conlon as part of the so-called Guildford Four. Soon thereafter, his father and relatives, known as the MacGuire Seven, were also convicted and imprisoned. Moving slowly, the wheels of Justice were finally set in the right direction in late 1989 when Conlon's verdict was "quashed" and the Guildford Four were freed.

Throughout the 1970s and 1980s, in particular, as Wilson's Jake Jackson theorizes, Belfast, Derry, and the Troubles in Northern Ireland became international news, on a par with the Vietnam War or Anglo-American tensions with the Soviet Union. But more than bombs and gunfire motivated this new status. In 1981, protests by imprisoned Republicans at Long Kesh prison outside Belfast captured the world's attention. Led by Bobby Sands, ten men went on hunger strike in opposition to the British government's policies concerning the treatment of IRA prisoners, and their slow, agonizing deaths prompted an outcry from America, particularly Irish America. A thousand people gathered in New York's St. Patrick's Cathedral to hear Cardinal Terence Cooke's homily on reconciliation, and the Longshoreman's Union announced a symbolic boycott of British ships to register its anger with Prime Minister Margaret Thatcher's government. Senator Ted Kennedy, Senator Daniel Patrick Moynihan, House Speaker Tip O'Neill, and Governor Hugh Carey of New York levied sharp criticism at Thatcher, with Kennedy censuring her for showing only "the shadow of flexibility" while ignoring "possible initiatives which could resolve the current dispute over prison conditions."[22] More directly relevant to this discussion—and vastly more ironic—is the way in which self-starvation, as a more traditional form of Irish political dissent, may also been erased from contemporary American memory of the violence of this period. As Maud Ellman emphasizes by underscoring the autobiographical narratives, poetry, and voluminous commentary that accompanied the Sands-led hunger strikes, "There is a sense in which the hunger striker is already dead as soon as he embarks upon this discipline of memory, for in this moment he surrenders food for words and life for legend."[23]

This legend—or, more accurately, almost instant hagiography—clearly affected Irish America at the time, as Ted Kennedy's criticism of Thatcherite intransigence indicates. Several years later, after his release from prison, Gerry Conlon spoke in Washington, DC, at a congressional hearing on human rights, a visit widely covered by the press. One could say, then, that while Bailey's Irish Cream was being shipped to Charles Oat's Connecticut bar, the Troubles in Northern Ireland were being slowly, but surely, imported to America as well. But if Oat's customers seemed unconcerned about making connections between contemporary events and the name of a new cocktail, can drinkers today be expected to remember *any* of this when ordering their cocktails? And, to restate Fergus's more detached position about the importance of a cocktail's name, is it even reasonable to expect them to keep this history in mind when out with their friends on a Friday night?

Perhaps the maintenance of a keen memory of historical events, international ones no less, is too much to expect of American or other drinkers—but not in Ireland. And if this is true insofar as the Irish Car Bomb is concerned, it is equally applicable to the black and tan, which is better known throughout Ireland as a "Half and Half." The *Oxford English Dictionary* dates the origin of the black and tan cocktail to the 1880s, when ordering the mixture of beers by this name amounted to little more than a nugatory request; after all, how indelicate is it to request a drink named after a pack of dogs? But after March 1920, when the Black and Tans arrived in Ireland in support of the RIC, all this changed. The outrages for which they are responsible—committed in response to the aggressive and violent insurgency of nationalists led by Michael Collins[24]—are too numerous to mention, although some of these need to be acknowledged in order for people today to understand why the phrase "Black and Tans" continues to resonate or *perform* so violently in Ireland. It must be said that such a performance is well-grounded in historical fact, as the barbarisms the "Tans" (as their nickname is commonly abbreviated) committed are the stuff of legend. These are aptly summarized in Tim Pat Coogan's observation that "the Tans were not, as was said, the scourings of the jails of England, they were merely encouraged to behave as if they were."[25] Their excesses have taken lodging in Irish collective memory, where they remain today without any possibility of eviction. Some fifty years after the Anglo-Irish War that was concluded by treaty in 1921, for example, and when he was a teenager attending family gatherings, Gerry Conlon heard his aunts and uncles variously allude to "the atrocities of the Black and Tans." For the young Conlon, such songs and stories held "no mystic significance, because there was no one instilling Irish patriotism" in him.[26]

From the earliest days of their arrival in Ireland, the Black and Tans seemed intent on pursuing a project of harsh reprisal; indeed, the period between 1919 and 1921 was so violent that historians remember it as a time of terror or, less dramatically, as a time when it was unsafe even to walk down the street toward Dublin Castle, headquarters of both the RIC and the Dublin Metropolitan Police.[27] When the Tans appeared in Limerick in the middle of the night, as eyewitness Frank Thornton reported, their actions served as a prelude to future behaviors that would come to define their infamous place in the annals of Irish history: "They arrived in a string of lorries and proceeded to shoot up the city, left, right and centre.... We were awakened by shooting at about 12:30 to 1 am and[,] on looking through the window[,] we saw thirty or forty Black and Tans all lying on the road and having a cockshot at Tate's Clock with their rifles."[28] But rolling into town in the middle of the night, awakening residents, and enjoying an impromptu target practice using public property to hone their skills as marksmen were hardly the worst crimes of which this force could be accused. As hostilities between them and nationalist Volunteers intensified, the Tans advanced a campaign of retaliation for IRA and Volunteer attacks, wreaking havoc on towns and villages believed to harbor their enemy. In September of 1920, they burned a hosiery factory, four public houses, and forty-nine private homes in Balbriggan following a pub dispute with locals and ravaged towns in County Clare, leading to both the loss of life and destruction of property. Most savagely, at Kerry Pike near Cork City the bodies of six Volunteers were recovered: one with the heart cut out, one with a battered skull, and one with the nose cut off. In all, over two hundred unarmed civilians were killed in 1920—in the streets, in their own homes, in custody—by police forces and by the Black and Tans.[29]

One could argue, then, that the Prevention of Terrorism Act in 1974, which allowed British and Northern Irish authorities greater latitude in interrogations, including the use of torture and the internment or detention of suspects without formal charge, was almost ghost-written by the Black and Tans. For even earlier, in 1920, the Restoration of Order in Ireland Act (ROIA) had led to numerous repressive practices, including what legal historian Seán Enright describes as "brutal interrogations" that resulted in "unreliable confessions."[30] The ROIA essentially shifted the conduct of trials from the judiciary to the occupying British army, and the Black and Tans were frequently allowed to interrogate and abuse captured prisoners. By the end of 1920, so-called martial law was declared across southwest Ireland, yet, as Enright remarks, "martial law is a misnomer because it means no law at all, just the naked exercise of power by the Army."[31] It was also later in 1920 that perhaps the two most galvanizing events of the Anglo-Irish War occurred, both of which, as detailed above, were sadly repeated decades later during the Troubles in Northern Ireland: the hunger strike of Terence MacSwiney in October; and Bloody Sunday at Croke Park in November, when British soldiers and police opened fire on players and spectators at a Gaelic football match. The latter event led to fourteen deaths and hundreds of injuries, as security forces fired indiscriminately into the crowd with rifles and machine guns. As Black and Tans surrounded the stadium to discourage and impede escape, this storm of shots was fired as a response to the assassinations earlier in the day of several British intelligence officials, including members of the notorious "Cairo Gang," orchestrated by Michael Collins and carried out by young Volunteers and some of Collins's so-called Squad. The Cairo Gang, so named by virtue of their intelligence experience in the Middle East, had been brought to Ireland, like the Black and Tans and Auxiliary Forces, to defeat the Collins-led insurgency. Aided by a carefully cultivated network of spies and informants who fed Collins vital information on Dublin Castle activities, his men were able to identify, trail, and attack his adversaries. Collins responded to the shootings of his own men that day by insisting that Volunteers be buried in their uniforms and, at considerable personal risk, by attending the funeral mass offered for his fallen colleagues the next morning, at which he pinned an "in memoriam" message on one of their coffins.[32]

These memorial gestures and rituals of public mourning are important, I think, in understanding the performative elements inherent to the Irish nationalist project in the 1920s and the Troubles in 1970s. Recounting Terence

MacSwiney's self-starvation—he lingered seventy-four days before dying in a Brixton prison—Paige Reynolds underscores the metaphors of high tragedy that informed newspaper accounts of MacSwiney's decline and describes the larger discourse of masculine martyrdom as "the definitive political expression of early twentieth-century Ireland."[33] Through funeral ceremonies conducted in three cities in the United Kingdom, literally tens of thousands of mourners paid tribute to MacSwiney and his sacrifice. A funeral procession, a Catholic mass, and lying-in-state were staged in London; a procession and corpseless funeral in Dublin; and burial ceremonies in Cork, all of which included lengthy tributes and eulogies. As Reynolds explains, British officials feared that a service in Dublin might cause political demonstrations and thus decided not to allow MacSwiney's coffin to travel there, leading his sisters to protest, "You have murdered our brother and you are not going to arrest his body."[34] However pointed his family's criticism was, the body never arrived in Dublin; it was seized by the Black and Tans and transported directly to Cork for burial. There was even a service at New York's Polo Grounds, which some forty thousand people attended. These memorial events contribute to a MacSwiney hagiography, one not unlike that of Bobby Sands and his colleagues in 1981, and demonstrate the power of public displays of mourning in the operations of collective memory. And, if MacSwiney stands as the figure of the martyr slain by an overwhelmingly powerful adversary, then the Black and Tans represent the brutal physical force that ultimately leads martyrs to their final course of resistance.

Perhaps it is this aspect of thoughtlessly ordering Irish Car Bombs and black and tans without even a pause or a scintilla of historical memory that causes the greatest offense in Ireland (although it is presumptuous of me to speculate on this matter). Both drinks emerge from a historical nightmare four hundred years or more in the making; and both signify the cruelty that seems inevitably to attend movements of nationalist insurgency and the measures that colonizers routinely employ to suppress them. Naming cocktails after such historical moments—or, more particularly, after such atrocities as bombings or those, like the "Black and Tans," who perpetrated them—is, among other things, an act of radical decontextualization that evokes images of colonial domination, violence, and human loss without the performance of mourning and memorialization that accompanied them.

—⚅—

Postscript: One thought about the Irish Car Bomb was introduced earlier without comment, implied only by my perhaps cryptic use of "Car" in the name of the cocktail, but it serves to represent what remains, for me at least, one last question. That is to say, the words "Irish" and "Bomb" possess clear referents, in the cocktail's name, however insensitive their combination might be: its primary ingredients are brewed or distilled in Ireland, and the combination of whiskey and Irish Cream produces a minor eruption, which in turn prompts a frisson of excitement in the drinker. But what about this concoction ties it to *car* bombings? Why not just call the cocktail "The Irish Bomb"?

To begin, unlike the many uncanny parallels that exist between the struggle for Irish independence in the early twentieth century and the Troubles in the 1970s, 1980s, and 1990s—highly publicized hunger strikes and internments, the installations of British paramilitary forces in Ireland—the former conflict was not defined by car bombings. Neil Jordan's 1994 film *Michael Collins* muddles this history slightly, as in it an exploding vehicle punctuates a dramatic moment in England's attempt to dismantle Collins's (Liam Neeson) formidable campaign of insurgency. The scene begins with three British intelligence officers inspecting files in a Dublin Castle office while barking orders at Ned Broy (Stephen Rea), who unbeknownst to them worked for Collins. The chief officer insists that Broy and his colleagues "lift" or arrest all known nationalist suspects. When Broy remarks that "It's not that simple," he is cut short disrespectfully with "We'll make it that simple."[35] As the conversation-cum-upbraiding moves outside and they walk toward a waiting car, the official mentions to his colleagues the need for greater "efficiency"; the trio then enters the car, which immediately explodes, with Broy seen in the foreground of the next shot positioned at a safe distance from the blast. Here, the car bomb serves as a rejoinder to an arrogant dissertation on British efficiency, as it quickly eliminates three of Collins's key adversaries (just as strategically targeted assassinations removed others).

No extensive record of car bombings exists for the Anglo-Irish War of 1919–1921; thus, Oat's allusion to this specific weapon in the naming of his cocktail suggests other, more recent and resonant contexts for the drink. One is clearly the destructive ascendance of IEDs in Baghdad, Beirut, and elsewhere during the 1970s and after, to which I have already alluded and which Mike Davis recounts in describing bloody attacks against Israelis in Tyre in 1982 that led to Hezbollah's veneration of Sheik Ahmed Qassir as "the first suicide car bomber" and martyr.[36] Yet another context is the contemporary cinema's various and continuing use of car bombs, particularly in gangster films. Some, not unlike the car bomb in *Michael Collins,* are deployed with a tinge of irony, the explosion of Detective Trupo's (Josh Brolin) prized Ford

Mustang by Frank Lucas's (Denzel Washington) gang in *American Gangster* (2007), for example, or Sam "Ace" Rothstein's (Robert DeNiro) narrow escape from an inexpertly placed bomb under his car in *Casino* (1995). But most car bombs in gangster films, like that in *Michael Collins*, enact their deadly force with ruthless efficiency. And the victims are not always bad guys. Think here of the explosion that kills Michael Corleone's (Al Pacino) young Sicilian wife Appolonia (Simonetta Stefanelli) in Francis Ford Coppola's *The Godfather* (1972); or the remote-controlled car bomb in Brian De Palma's *Scarface* (1983) that would have killed an innocent woman and her children had Tony Montana (Al Pacino) not intervened.

Perhaps the most prolific use of car (and other) bombs in contemporary films occurs in Jonathan Hensleigh's *Kill the Irishman* (2011), which replicates many of the three dozen bombings that defined a fierce battle between Irish-American and self-appointed Celtic warrior Danny Greene and the Mafia for control of mid-1970s Cleveland. In the film's opening scene set in 1975 and as the title "Kill the Irishman" appears in bold, green lettering, Greene (Ray Stevenson) is driving his Cadillac, notices an electrical short in the radio, and leaps out before the car bursts into flame. Disheveled and belligerent, he picks himself up from the pavement and yells at the top of his lungs, "Is that all you got? It's gonna take more than a few firecrackers to kill Danny Greene!"[37] For over two years, both in the film's narrative and in the history upon which it is based, several embarrassingly unsuccessful attempts were made on Greene's life—including the decimation of his house from a late-night dynamiting—until on an October 1977 afternoon, after exiting his dentist's office, a car parked next to his is detonated, killing him instantly. This explosion marks the culmination of numerous car bombings as several other gangland figures, including Greene's partners and adversaries, were murdered in spectacular explosions, leading some commentators in 1976 to rename Cleveland "Bomb City U.S.A." Indeed, Hensleigh's film emphasizes national interest in this battle and the violence that defined it by including in the narrative television news footage featuring such high-profile journalists as Brian Ross and David Brinkley reporting on the carnage.

What this brief film history suggests—other than the fact that the Irish Car Bomb was invented at the same time as car bombings both in Northern Ireland and in mid-1970s America saturated the national news—is that while the bomb is intended *primarily* to do one terrible thing, like the term "Irish" in Lionel Pilkington's lexicon, the car bomb itself *performs* more than ruthless destruction. And so does ordering it in a pub. In its disregard for human life, the car bomb is bloody, indiscriminate, and even "fascistic"; it operates by stealth, is remarkably efficient and relatively inexpensive; and—perhaps most prominently—it is *loud*. For this last reason, as Davis mentions, car bombs function as "advertisements for a cause," or even as "manifestos."[38] It is within this domain that the ordering of an "Irish Car Bomb" in a pub, I think, performs. Although I lack extensive empirical data to support this claim, my guess is that mostly men, not women, order "Irish Car Bombs"—or, for that matter, "Irish Handcuffs." Indeed, I have never seen a woman order either, though I have detected pained wincing—or pointed eye-rolling—from several when these orders are placed. Yet, in my experience, there is nothing "stealthy" or subtle about such drink orders; on the contrary, although there is nothing overtly fascistic about the men who consume them, the drink order functions as an advertisement: Only strong men like my twenty-something son and his thirty-something, weight-lifting cousins—or a defiant Danny Greene—can handle such drinks. It'll take more than a few alcoholic "firecrackers" to "destroy" them.

While this performance of masculinity does not require a historical consciousness or memory, it is important to note that, when it is not enlivening something or rendering deadly "confetti" ironic, "Irish" typically connotes history. And, as Antonio Ceraso notes elsewhere in this volume when discussing the boulevardier cocktail, the "rhetoric" of cocktail culture seems obsessed with historical origins, mythological or otherwise, a compulsion that frequently drifts into nostalgia. My summary of historical events in the 1920s and bombings during the later Troubles in Northern Ireland confirms Ceraso's thesis, although there is nothing very nostalgic about this chronicle. On the contrary, while for many in Ireland and throughout the United Kingdom naming a cocktail the "Irish Bomb" evokes memories of historical atrocities, adding "Car" to the name of the drink performs other work, adding elements of loud assertiveness—perhaps even danger—to the recipe. In these ways, following Lionel Pilkington's astute observation, the "Irish" in "Irish Car Bomb" ironizes, deforms, and enlivens. Perhaps knowing this history and ordering such drinks anyway adds yet another dimension of irony. In the end, though, while drinking an Irish Car Bomb or a black and tan might signify a kind of fecklessness, it might be well to remember that in Northern Ireland "fuck" is typically pronounced "feck." So, it just might be the case that in these cases a drinker's "fecklessness" conveys more than irresponsibility or weary indifference; rather, his supply of delicacy or concern is exhausted because he just doesn't give a "feck."

Indiana University

NOTES

1. Robert Simonson, "The Irish Car Bomb: The Controversial Drink with a Split Reputation," *The Guardian*, March 17, 2016, www.theguardian.com/lifestyle/2016/mar/17/Irish-car-bomb.

2. Lionel Pilkington, *Theatre & Ireland* (Houndmills, UK: Palgrave Macmillan, 2010), 2.

3. Pilkington, *Theatre & Ireland*, 3–4.

4. For my nephews, my son, and me, when drinking in an Irish pub on the north side of Chicago, the "handcuffs" are typically defined by a beer in one hand and an Irish whiskey in the other.

5. Ciaran Carson, "Belfast Confetti," in *The Irish for No* (Winston-Salem, NC: Wake Forest University Press, 1987), 31.

6. Carson adds historical texture to the notion of "Belfast Confetti" in a book of the same title (Winston-Salem, NC: Wake Forest University Press, 1989). In a brief prose sketch entitled "Brick," he describes the *"sleech*—alluvial or tidal muck" upon which Belfast is built. In turn, this "rubbish, refuse, broken-down stuff, pig-swill" is manufactured into "conveniently hand-sized" bricks, another variety of "confetti" hurled by rioters (72).

7. Simonson, "The Irish Car Bomb," n.p. President Obama was and is, in fact, quite popular in Ireland. During his family's 2013 trip there, the *Irish Times* ran Alison Healy and Dan Keenan's much-quoted story "Obama's Irish Ancestry Highlighted during First Family's Visit to Trinity" (June 17, 2013), in which genealogists commented that more evidence exists for Obama's Irish ancestry than for John F. Kennedy's, including links to a former provost of Trinity College, Dublin, and a Church of Ireland bishop.

8. See "The History of Bailey's Irish Cream" at Little Shamrocks: Food, History, and Travel Adventure from the Emerald Isle, http://www.littleshamrocks.com/history-of-baileys-irish-cream.html. Bailey's Irish Cream, distilled by Dublin-based R&A Bailey and Company, became enormously popular soon after its launch. Initially setting a sales goal of one hundred thousand cases per year, Bailey's sold upwards of one million cases per year within five years of the liqueur's introduction. See Thomas N. Garavan et al., *Cases in Irish Business Strategy and Policy* (Dublin: Oak Tree Press, 1996), 52–64.

9. For many on both sides of the dispute, even the term "Troubles" performs badly or actually fails to perform accurately their political and social commitments. For nationalists, the term reduced their outrage at British domination to a "spasmodic" disruption of an intolerable cultural inequality; for unionists, it failed to register their dismay at the civic unrest and violence inherent to the impasse. See Elmer Kennedy-Andrews, *Fiction and the Northern Irish Troubles Since 1969: (De)-Constructing the North* (Dublin: Four Courts Press, 2003), 10–12.

10. Mike Davis, *Buda's Wagon: A Brief History of the Car Bomb* (London: Verso, 2007), 5.

11. See Richard Bennett, *The Black and Tans: The British Special Police in Ireland* (New York: Barnes and Noble, 1959), 24.

12. See Bennett, *Black and Tans*, 37–38.

13. Robert McLiam Wilson, *Ripley Bogle* (New York: Ballantine Books, 2000), 100.

14. See Gerry Conlon, *In the Name of the Father* (New York: Plume Books, 1993). Conlon remembers: "By the time I left school, in June 1969, the civil rights marches had been going on for a year.... So when that summer the Bogside erupted into rioting and the police were baton-charging the crowd, firing CS gas, and hosing them with water cannons, there was a sense of outrage in West Belfast, as if we were under attack ourselves. Soon we were" (26).

15. See Davis, *Buda's Wagon*, 5. At least twenty bombs exploded within an 80-minute timeframe, wounding and mutilating some 130 citizens and killing nine. The bombs, which began to explode shortly after 2:00 p.m., targeted transportation hubs, including bus and railway stations.

16. John Passmore Widgery, Baron, *Report of the Tribunal Appointed to Inquire into the Events on Sunday, 30th January 1972* (London: The Stationery Office, 2001), 97.

17. Widgery, *Report of the Tribunal*, 99.

18. See Thomas Hennessey, *The Evolution of the Troubles 1970–72* (Dublin: Irish Academic Press, 2007), 1–5.

19. See Hennessey, *Evolution of the Troubles*, 6–18.

20. Robert McLiam Wilson, *Eureka Street* (New York: Ballantine Books, 1996), 15.

21. Wilson, *Eureka Street*, 14.

22. See David Beresford, *Ten Men Dead: The Story of the 1981 Irish Hunger Strike* (New York: Atlantic Monthly Press, 1987), 98–99, 146–48.

23. Maud Ellmann, *The Hunger Artists: Starving, Writing, and Imprisonment* (Cambridge, MA: Harvard University Press, 1993), 87.

24. By 1919, the violence of nationalist Volunteers and the IRA was directed at the RIC and the DMP, particularly the "G" Division of intelligence and other officers, which Collins viewed as his principal adversaries. In *Michael Collins: The Man Who Made Ireland* (New York: Palgrave, 1990), Tim Pat Coogan describes Collins's September 1919 founding of the "Squad," whose principal functions included the assassination of police officers (116–20). In *After the Rising: Soldiers, Lawyers and the Trials of the Irish Revolution* (Sallins, County Kildare, Ireland: Merrion Press, 2016), Seán Enright describes raids on RIC barracks intended not to murder officers, but to seize weapons and ammunitions that Collins's men desperately needed (51–53). Enright and Coogan also discuss the highly planned

murders of police in 1918 and especially in 1919, which motivated the formation of the Black and Tans as the ranks of the RIC were diminished and the morale of those who remained began to wane.

25. Coogan, *Michael Collins*, 126.
26. Conlon, *Name of the Father*, 24.
27. Coogan labels 1920 the "Year of Terror" (121). In *After the Rising*, Enright details the dangers of Dublin streets at this time, 59–61.
28. Quoted in Coogan, *Michael Collins*, 126.
29. Coogan, *Michael Collins*, 145.
30. Enright, *After the Rising*, 72.
31. Enright, *After the Rising*, 79.
32. Coogan, *Michael Collins*, 157–61.
33. Paige Reynolds, *Modernism, Drama, and the Audience for Irish Spectacle* (New York: Cambridge University Press, 2007), 116.
34. Quoted in Reynolds, *Modernism*, 145. For a discussion of these funeral services in all three locales, see Reynolds, 139–55.
35. Neil Jordan, dir., *Michael Collins* (Los Angeles: Warner Brothers, 1996).
36. See Davis, 78–89. Davis lists some thirteen American embassies (including ambassadors' residences) in such cities as Beirut, Bogotá, Lima, Nairobi, and Dar-es-salaam that were car-bombed between 1965 and 2006 (88).
37. Jonathan Hensleigh, dir., *Kill the Irishman* (Los Angeles: Code Entertainment, Dundee Entertainment, and Sweet William Productions, 2011).
38. Davis, *Buda's Wagon*, 9.

BIBLIOGRAPHY

Bennett, Richard. *The Black and Tans: The British Special Police in Ireland*. New York: Barnes and Noble, 1959.

Beresford, David. *Ten Men Dead: The Story of the 1981 Irish Hunger Strike*. New York: Atlantic Monthly Press, 1987.

Carson, Ciaran. "Belfast Confetti." In *The Irish for No*. By Ciaran Carson, 31. Winston-Salem, NC: Wake Forest University Press, 1987.

Carson, Ciaran. *Belfast Confetti*. Winston-Salem, NC: Wake Forest University Press, 1989.

Conlon, Gerry. *In the Name of the Father*. New York: Plume Books, 1993.

Coogan, Tim Pat. *Michael Collins: The Man Who Made Ireland*. New York: Palgrave, 1990.

Davis, Mike. *Buda's Wagon: A Brief History of the Car Bomb*. London: Verso, 2007.

Ellmann, Maud. *The Hunger Artists: Starving, Writing, and Imprisonment*. Cambridge, MA: Harvard University Press, 1993.

Enright, Seán. *After the Rising: Soldiers, Lawyers and the Trials of the Irish Revolution*. Sallins, Ireland: Merrion Press, 2016.
Garavan, Thomas N., et al. *Cases in Irish Business Strategy and Policy*. Dublin: Oak Tree Press, 1996.
Healy, Alison, and Dan Keenan. "Obama's Irish Ancestry Highlighted during First Family's Visit to Trinity." *Irish Times*, June 17, 2013. https://www.irishtimes.com/news/obama-s-irish-ancestry-highlighted-during-first-family-s-visit-to-trinity-1.1431607.
Hennessey, Thomas. *The Evolution of the Troubles 1970–72*. Dublin: Irish Academic Press, 2007.
Hensleigh, Jonathan, dir. *Kill the Irishman*. Los Angeles: Code Entertainment, Dundee Entertainment, and Sweet William Productions, 2011.
"The History of Bailey's Irish Cream." Little Shamrocks: Food, History, and Travel Adventure from the Emerald Isle. http://www.littleshamrocks.com/history-of-baileys-irish-cream.html.
Jordan, Neil, dir. *Michael Collins*. Los Angeles: Warner Brothers, 1996.
Kennedy-Andrews, Elmer. *Fiction and the Northern Irish Troubles Since 1969: (De)-Constructing the North*. Dublin: Four Courts Press, 2003.
Pilkington, Lionel. *Theatre & Ireland*. Houndmills, UK: Palgrave Macmillan, 2010.
Reynolds, Paige. *Modernism, Drama, and the Audience for Irish Spectacle*. New York: Cambridge University Press, 2007.
Simonson, Robert. "The Irish Car Bomb: The Controversial Drink with a Split Reputation." *The Guardian*, March 17, 2016. www.theguardian.com/lifestyle/2016/mar/17/Irish-car-bomb.
Widgery, John Passmore, Baron. *Report of the Tribunal Appointed to Inquire into the Events on Sunday, 30th January 1972*. London: The Stationery Office, 2001.
Wilson, Robert McLiam. *Eureka Street*. New York: Ballantine Books, 1996.
———. *Ripley Bogle*. New York: Ballantine Books, 2000.

FOURTEEN

BAR TREK

WILLIAM BIFERIE

> Drinking is an act loaded with significance. It is a cultural fact on which thousands of years, millions of gestures have accumulated.
>
> —Isabel Gonzalez Turmo[1]

ALCOHOL AND ITS ASSOCIATED RITUALS, whether embraced or proscribed, have existed as cultural cornerstones for thousands of years. Across boundaries both chronological and geographical, alcohol has variously been "praised and insulted, consumed as basic food or enjoyed as a status symbol. It has been drunk alone, in a corner of the house, with an elbow propped on a tavern counter, or enjoyed in company."[2] If the drinking habits of our ancestors—from the Neolithic period through this evening's happy hour—are any indication, it seems almost guaranteed that hundreds of years from now, humanity's love affair with alcohol will continue unabated.

One possible version of humanity's future—and easily one of the most optimistic—is the one shown by the *Star Trek* television and film series. For more than fifty years, *Star Trek*'s various iterations have portrayed a future of peace and prosperity. It is a future, as Lincoln Geraghty puts it, that revolves around "the premise that spatial expansion can bring cultural and social improvement to humanity," improvements that will lead to an end of ethnic conflict, bigotry, cultural power struggles, and racial prejudice.[3] *Star Trek* endures partly because of this optimistic view of what humans may be able to achieve; it lets pop culture consumers view the world through a glass brightly, and see a future where tolerance, open-mindedness, and peace are able to triumph over the ouroboros of violence and disaster in the news every day. With all of the technological and social advancements represented by *Star Trek*'s idealized twenty-fourth-century future, though, drinking alcohol retains its place as a cultural cornerstone for humans and aliens alike. It is still an act loaded with significance.

For our twenty-first-century purposes, *Star Trek* is the perfect pop culture text to explore modern America's relationship with alcohol. From its debut on NBC in 1966 to the recent blockbuster reboots, *Star Trek* has witnessed the heyday, fall, and rebirth of the cocktail. From the fabled three-martini lunch, to the culture of corporate responsibility, to the modern cocktail revival; from alcohol's near-ubiquitous acceptance, to outright derision, to the hip cutting edge, *Star Trek* has survived. More importantly, across five decades, seven television series, and thirteen feature films, *Star Trek* has portrayed alcohol in exactly the same way: in *Star Trek*'s vision of humanity's future, alcohol, whether shared privately or publicly, creates a masculine, multispecies, and multicultural version of Homi K. Bhabha's third space, in which humans and aliens come together as hybridized equals to share in male rituals and celebrations. This third space of alcohol proves to be critical for *Star Trek* to move from the uneasy truces of cultural diversity to the beginnings of real understanding between alien cultures. But this space is almost exclusively male, and so leaves *Star Trek*'s aspirations for an all-inclusive, utopian future incomplete.

Bhabha's third space is a locus of postcolonial theory, and it has been used as a frame for scholarship in literary criticism, cultural studies, and the social sciences. At its most basic, third space theory seeks to explain the relationships between peoples of different cultural identity. As Karin Ikas and Gerhard Wagner write, Bhabha largely "conceives the encounter of two social groups with different cultural traditions that leads to a displacement of the members of both groups from their origins. It is also supposed to bring about a common identity, one that is new in its hybridity; it is thus neither one nor the other."[4] This hybridity, being neither one nor the other, describes not only the inhabitants and encounters of the third space, but also the third space itself:

> These "in-between" spaces provide the terrain for elaborating strategies of selfhood—singular or communal—that initiate new signs of identity, and innovate sites of collaboration and contestation, in the act of defining the idea of society itself.
>
> It is in the emergence of the interstices—the overlap and displacement of domains of difference—that the intersubjective and collective experiences of nationness, community interest, or cultural value are negotiated.[5]

The liminal space between cultures is not a gap, as an "in-between" might commonly be conceived, but an intersection of social, cultural, and personal capital. Encounters between individuals across these borders can lead to conflict or concord, and they can be forced or consensual. No matter how they manifest, they almost always cause a blurring of boundaries between high and low culture, public and private expectations, and self and other.[6] The third space, then, can be used to describe any place where different cultures collide, where differences of rank, caste, culture, and origin are set aside in favor of a hybrid cultural space that arises from these intersections—a space that forms without inherent or imposed hierarchy.

One purpose of the third space is to help navigate cultural encounters past the shallows of multicultural and cultural diversity perspectives, which for Bhabha are simply not up to the task of real cultural exchange or interaction. For Bhabha, multiculturalism and cultural diversity fall far short of their claimed goals: The uncritical use of multiculturalism and traditionally Western critical theory as a frame for understanding cultural interaction and exchange inevitably leads to the privileging of the critic, as "critical theory often engages with texts within the familiar traditions and conditions of colonial anthropology either to universalize their meaning within its own cultural and academic discourse, or to sharpen its internal critique of the Western logocentric sign, the idealist subject, or indeed the illusions and delusions of civil society."[7] The danger is that "however impeccably the content of an 'other' culture may be known, however anti-ethnocentrically it is represented... the demand that, in analytic terms, it always be the good object of knowledge, the docile body of difference" reproduces a relation of domination between the knower and the known that precludes true understanding or cultural identification.[8] Rather than relying on cultural diversity's attempts to compare or contrast ethics or aesthetics as objects of empirical knowledge, the third space attempts to open up areas of cultural *difference* between the authority of a cultural practice and its performance, or enunciation: "Cultural difference is the process of signification through which statements *of* culture or *on* culture differentiate, discriminate and authorize the production of fields of force, reference, applicability and capacity."[9]

In a very real way, then, *Star Trek* appears to perpetuate the Western hegemonic discourses that Bhabha's third space rejects outright. After all, *Star Trek*'s core principle of infinite diversity in infinite combination—or IDIC—distills the tenets of multiculturalism and cultural diversity into a pithy phrase, an easy acronym, and a marketable piece of symbolic jewelry all at once. *Star Trek* seems to fall prey to the kind of simplified utopian thinking that Bhabha critiques, in that its cultural diversity represents "a radical rhetoric of the separation of totalized cultures that live unsullied by the intertextuality of their historical locations, safe in the Utopianism of a mythic memory of a unique collective identity."[10] The homogenous global cultures of *Star Trek*'s Earth or planet Vulcan certainly fit the safe utopianism Bhabha postulates.

Reading against Bhabha, though, we might instead see *Star Trek*'s Earth as a near-utopian society that has somehow managed to navigate the pitfalls Bhabha warns against. Instead of a crass utopianism founded on shaky multiculturalism, *Star Trek*'s humans may have fulfilled Bhabha's call to action, and found a way to conceptualize "an *inter*national culture, based not on the exoticism of multiculturalism or the *diversity* of cultures, but on the inscription and articulation of culture's hybridity."[11] In this science fiction future, humanity's new appreciation of cultural difference has led to the rejection of the cultural power struggles highlighting most of human history. Whichever way one chooses to view *Star Trek*'s utopian future, Bhabha's third space is critical to the project of promoting intercultural understanding.

Central to the third space as a framework for understanding a science fiction text is Bhabha's conception of the "beyond," which "signifies spatial distance, marks progress, promises the future," but also represents a boundary between the knowable present and an unknowable future.[12] To exist in this "beyond" space is "to be part of a revisionary time, a return to the present to redescribe our cultural contemporaneity; to reinscribe our human, historic commonality; *to touch the future on the hither side*" [emphasis in the original].[13] While contemporary conceptions of the third space allow us to both imagine and begin to understand cultural interchanges between groups separated by seemingly unbridgeable divides, the third space of science fiction allows us to take the first tentative steps into the beyond; to touch the future on the *thither* side, and understand ourselves better for it. By seeing how the third space might manifest itself in a distant, idealized future, we can gain a better understanding of our culture in the present.

Since *Star Trek* has been seeking out new life and new civilizations, not to mention new cultures and new ways of being, for over five decades, third space theory is the perfect lens through which to examine the science fiction mega-text. The United Federation of Planets—the governmental body centered on *Star Trek*'s twenty-fourth-century Earth—is, after all, not just postcolonial, but postnational, postglobal, and posthuman. If *Star Trek* shows us an idealized version of humanity's future, then the cultural conventions of the United Federation are also a reflection of how we imagine our idealized selves.

Star Trek, then, provides a window into how utopian social structures may function, and the series' subtle but repeated focus on alcohol and bar culture reflects how we might want posthuman socialization to look. Over *Star Trek*'s decades'-long run, more than two hundred individual kinds of foods and beverages from various galactic cultures are mentioned. Of those, more than fifty are alcoholic beverages—from the common Earth spirits vodka and Scotch whisky to the more exotic Romulan ale and Klingon bloodwine. The consumption of alcohol and exotic cocktails holds center stage during parties, cultural exchanges, and social events in the twenty-fourth century, just as it does in the twenty-first. One need look no further than the leisure facilities on board two of *Star Trek*'s most iconic vessels—the *Enterprise-D* of *Star Trek: The Next Generation* and the eponymous space station of *Star Trek: Deep Space Nine*—to see alcohol's influence: the social lives of some three thousand beings between the two crews center on their respective drinking establishments.

In the future, although these social spaces are open to everyone and patronized by a sometimes dazzling array of aliens and cultures, they are predominantly male. The spaces created by alcohol and its consumption are places where men of different species get together as equals, despite differences in culture or authority: commanding officers share drinks and stories with their subordinates, aliens from across the galaxy come together to share their victories and defeats, and everyone gathers around the dartboard, deck of cards, or gaming table to try and win big. Sharing alcohol, whether in the *Star Trek* of the 1960s or the 2016 film *Star Trek: Beyond*, is a vehicle for celebrating male triumph, proving macho prowess, facilitating bar fights, reveling in male friendships, attracting women, and sharing deep man-to-man dialogues. The rituals of sharing a quiet drink or hollering in alcohol-fueled song are just as important in the twenty-third and twenty-fourth centuries as they are in our own.

This fixation with alcohol's consumption and the social alchemy that follows is apparent within the first few minutes of the *Star Trek* pilot episode, "The Cage." Filmed in late 1964, Gene Roddenberry's pilot follows the adventures of Captain Christopher Pike and the crew of the starship *Enterprise* as they investigate a radio distress signal. From the opening scene on the bridge of the *Enterprise*, Pike is visibly agitated. After a tense encounter with a meteor shower, he retreats to his quarters to rest. The ship's doctor, Boyce, follows the captain down to his quarters to find out what the trouble is, and begins mixing him a martini. "Sometimes," Boyce tells Pike, "a man will tell his bartender things he'll never tell his doctor."[14]

At just shy of five minutes into *Star Trek*'s first incarnation, those viewing the pilot in 1964 would already have been taken on a fairly spectacular journey: the

Enterprise swoops through space, past stars and fabulous nebulae; the spaceship survives unknown peril, piloted through by the demonic-looking Mr. Spock and the commanding Number One; a lingering shot focuses on Captain Pike's futuristic communicator device; and stars fly by the porthole in Pike's quarters as he converses with Dr. Boyce. The first familiar action that takes place is two men sharing a cold martini and connecting not as captain and subordinate, but as equals. In a space that is completely alien—to the show's initial viewers, if not to the characters—a rapport and understanding develop through the simple acts of the silent toast, the knowing nod, and the first sip.

Although it has been thoroughly documented elsewhere, it bears repeating that the future portrayed by Roddenberry's pilot is one where Earth—perhaps more specifically, America—managed to survive presidential assassinations, unpopular wars of containment, and the threat of nuclear holocaust. Even the familiar cultural markers in which Roddenberry chose to ground his idealistic science fiction story—military hierarchy, a pseudonaval setting—are defamiliarized by the presence of civilians wandering the corridors of the ship. If the first truly familiar sight and the first purely social interaction—that is, an interaction not bound by structures of military hierarchy—that viewers see in "The Cage" centers on a pair of expertly measured, frosty martinis, it indicates that Roddenberry's future valued from its outset the social alchemy enabled by shared cocktails. The fact that the potion is shared as a means to bridge hierarchical and cultural divides and make the way safe for candor and friendship presages alcohol's role in every iteration of *Star Trek* thereafter.

Alcohol's presence continues throughout the run of the original series. There are even two episodes in which booze helps save the *Enterprise* from destruction: in "The Tholian Web," the deadly effects of a mysterious region of "interspace" are cured by a cocktail consisting of an otherwise-lethal Klingon nerve agent mixed with alcohol; in "By Any Other Name," Scotty attempts to wrest control of the *Enterprise* from invading Andromedan supermen by drinking one of them under the table. In episodes along the way, the *Enterprise* crew imbibes everything from Saurian brandy to Scotch whisky.

Perhaps the most memorable of the first *Enterprise*'s alcoholic escapades occurs during "The Trouble with Tribbles," which first aired December 29, 1967. This episode finds the intrepid starship responding to a distress signal from the Federation space station K-7, which fears sabotage by the Klingon Empire, the Federation's longtime rival. The arrival of a Klingon battlecruiser seeking shore leave for her crew complicates the situation. Since the Klingons and the Federation are not at war, but rather are engaged in a futuristic cold war, the station commander must abide by a peace treaty that allows the Klingons access to the station. While the *Enterprise* is patrolling the area, her crew members are given shore leave as well. Tensions quickly escalate between the two crews.

"The Trouble with Tribbles" provides an excellent example of the third space in action. The various *Star Trek* series show a hypothetical future where dozens of alien species and cultures interact—generally peacefully—on a daily basis; even longtime rivals like the Klingons and the Federation resolve their conflicts diplomatically, more often than not. These alien races are very rarely shown on their home worlds or in their home cultures. Instead, the aliens we see often occupy starships, such as the Klingons aboard their battlecruiser and the humans aboard the *Enterprise*. These ships function as in-between spaces in their own right, not only transporting their crews from mission to mission, space to space, but also serving as locations where the crews' personal cultures are made secondary to the intragalactic culture of the Federation, Starfleet, the Empire, or any number of other hierarchies. This subversion from diversity to homogeneity seems to be a symptom of exactly the sort of cultural diversity traps that Bhabha warns about: human culture reduced from a cultural heat map to a patchwork of tokenisms. Still, *Star Trek* attempts to normalize human cultural difference within the ranks of Starfleet, rather than indulging in the "exoticism of multiculturalism" that Bhabha seeks to avoid, and it does this through alcohol.

"The Trouble with Tribbles" is one of the first glimpses into how the crews of Starfleet are able to negotiate the subversion of their native cultures to the culture of the organization: by breaking out of their predefined roles with the help of the alcohol served in various shipboard bars and recreation facilities like the K-7's cantina. As the *Enterprise* crew avail themselves of some well-deserved shore leave, Lieutenant Commander Scott, Ensign Chekov, and Lieutenant Freeman settle into the bar and begin drinking in earnest and trading jibes. The stalwart Scotsman, Scotty, and the brash young Russian, Chekov, compare the traditional spirits of their people: Scotty asks Chekov, "When are you going to get off that milk diet, lad, and switch to a man's drink—scotch," instead of Chekov's preferred vodka. Young Chekov knows better, and informs Scotty that "scotch was inwented [sic] by a little old lady from Leningrad."[15]

Through the common ground of alcohol, Scotty and Chekov—who are Starfleet while on duty, Earthers to the Klingons, and Federation to most other species they meet in the galaxy—are able to successfully combine these many imposed and conflated identities with their own, more complex local cultural affinities. Despite their differences in rank, age, and national origin, the third space created by the station's cantina and their chosen drinks allows the two men to engage each other with personae equal parts Starfleet, Scottish, and Russian, while also dissolving the structural hierarchies of rank. They are united not just by their uniforms, but by the male ribaldry and love of fine drink enabled by the cantina.

As a vehicle for crossing the boundaries of human cultural difference, alcohol is the perfect artifact for highlighting and penetrating these marginal spaces between different cultural backgrounds. As Mary Douglas writes in *Purity and Danger*, it is a mistake "to treat bodily margins in isolation from all other margins"; in our case, the bodily margins involving the ingestion of food and drink are helpful analogues to the marginal friction created between subverted cultures aboard a starship.[16] After all, "any structure of ideas is vulnerable at its margins. We should expect the orifices of the body to symbolize its especially vulnerable points."[17] To allow the crossing of these points in a communal space through the ingestion of alcohol is to make oneself vulnerable, and also to indulge in Turmo's silent language, where during or after the simple act of imbibing, "all remain silent because everything has been said."[18] Beneath the steady banter of Scotty and Chekov's conversation, a different form of communication is at work.

Later, tensions rise when Klingon warriors on shore leave arrive on station K-7 and begin drinking with the *Enterprise* crew at the station's watering hole, eventually devolving into a fist fight between the two crews. Such a conflict is, of course, inevitable: From the opening scene of the episode, Kirk describes the Klingons as "brutal and aggressive," in addition to being most efficient. Swarthy, bearded, with arched eyebrows and menacing uniforms, the Klingons are meant to be seen as a real threat to the clean-cut *Enterprise* crew.[19] Although the Klingon captain Koloth reminds Kirk that there is "no formal declaration of hostilities between [their] two respective governments," it is clear that hostility is inevitable.[20] In case the parallels between Federation–Klingon relations and the United States and the USSR were not clear enough, in 1968's "A Private Little War" Kirk explicitly draws the comparison for viewers: Attempting to explain his reasoning for providing weapons to a tribe of primitive aliens, he asks Dr. McCoy if he "remember[s] the twentieth-century brush wars on the Asian continent? Two giant powers involved, much like the Klingons and ourselves. Neither side felt they could pull out," resulting in a war that McCoy tells us "went on bloody year after bloody year."[21] In *Star Trek*'s extrapolated cold war, the brutally efficient Klingons are meant to be feared.

The bar brawl in "The Trouble with Tribbles" is so important for exactly that reason: while these particular Klingons are definitely adversaries, they are also comic figures. When the brawl begins, the music shifts back and forth from martial drum rolls to more jovial fanfares; in the background, the other bar patrons have retreated to the edges of the room, but they are watching the fight with more amusement than concern. More importantly, they never stop sipping their drinks. Thoroughly lubricated in the third space of alcohol, both crews are able to release their antagonism not as an interstellar political disaster, but in a classic, drunken, male activity: the barroom brawl. Such an event constitutes the third space at its most raw—a time and place where rank, culture, caste, and class hierarchies are completely exploded and the participants, no matter how high and mighty, must experience what it is like to be laid low. As Bhabha writes, exchanges of values in the third space "may not always be collaborative ... but may be profoundly antagonistic, conflictual, and even incommensurable."[22] When the Federation and Klingon crews enter the third space of alcohol consumption together, the cantina becomes a safe place where they can release their cultural tensions and meet each other *mano a mano*, rather than at the end of a phaser.

On the surface, the bar brawl in a frontier cantina—so obviously a nod to classic Westerns—seems to indicate that *Star Trek* is simply reproducing the same carnivalesque drinking fantasies that Hollywood has always loved. Reading against that impulse, though, "The Trouble with Tribbles" illustrates how necessary alcohol is to facilitating these third space encounters between humans and "others." Besides acting as a familiarizing force in an unfamiliar science fiction world, alcohol consumption is unique in its complexity as a simultaneously personal, social, and performative act: "Drinking is always an individual act, since each drinker necessarily has to situate himself, more or less consciously, according to the change of emotions produced by the ingestion of alcohol," but it is also a social act, "even when drinking alone, since it is loaded with socially assumed meanings."[23] On a much more basic level, one gets to choose *what* to drink and *where* to drink it. For example, when Scotty and Chekov find themselves aboard the space station, drinking offers the opportunity for individual cultural performance—and for individual situation to the act of drinking itself through either scotch or vodka—while the drinking is still communal. The Klingons, too, make their individual choices about *where* to drink: although they leave their battlecruiser looking for a fight, the Klingons still choose to drink *with* the humans.

It is the hybrid nature of drinking that creates a space so rife with possibilities for cultural interaction. Cultures may meet on nebulous and uncertain terms through music, art, sport, or any other site of collaboration or contestation, but these cultural encounters tend to be either singular *or* communal interactions. Even sporting or athletic contests, while they do create a space of contestation and open possibilities for understanding, are inherently competitive and come loaded with rules and regulations that the space of drinking does not: games, by their very nature, require all participants to play by the same rules—something which proves especially problematic between cultures that do not have a shared history of sport or gamesmanship. Drinking, although loaded with its own rituals and socially assumed meanings, allows individual expression to flourish during a communal act, as each participant brings his own cultural baggage and expectations to the encounter.

Twenty years after "The Trouble with Tribbles," *Star Trek: The Next Generation* would further explore the cultural tensions between the United Federation of Planets and the Klingon Empire. The second *Star Trek* series, which first aired in 1987, takes place roughly one hundred years after the narrative of the original. By this time, the two galactic superpowers are at peace. With peace does not come understanding, however; most episodes of *The Next Generation* that feature Klingons are driven by the vast differences between their warrior culture and the peaceful explorers of the Federation. As before, the first hints of cultural crossover do not occur until the two species drink together.

The second-season episode "A Matter of Honor," which first aired on February 6, 1989, is the second episode of the series to feature the warrior race. The episode's action centers on Commander Riker, the *Enterprise-D*'s adventurous first officer, and his participation in an officer exchange program with the Klingons. Riker is to temporarily serve as the first officer aboard a Klingon space vessel, the *Pagh*, so he begins studying their culture in preparation. Part of this preparation includes sampling some staple Klingon dishes and beverages. While Riker eats and drinks from various bowls full of worms and moving creatures in *Enterprise*'s Ten-Forward lounge, the ship's doctor observes the alien fare with disgust, and claims that the Klingons' "beliefs are rather brutal" compared to the Federation.[24] Using the same language as the original *Star Trek*'s Kirk, the doctor shows just how broad the gap is between the two cultures. Even the accomplished diplomat and explorer, Captain Picard, is visibly repulsed by the Klingons' cuisine, despite his claims about envying Riker's upcoming chance to learn about a new culture.

As Douglas observes, "each culture has its own special risks and problems" associated with impurity and bodily margins, particularly pertaining to the rituals of food.[25] Even in an enlightened utopian future, the humans of the Federation are bound by their cultural expectations of food purity—which seem to include not eating live alien creatures—and can only look on in terror as Riker consumes an array of crawling, tentacled dishes. Picard's spirit of exploration and utopian diversity are unable to move past his cultural assumptions about pure food and drink. It is only Riker's willingness to violate his own cultural taboos of purity that allows him to enter the third space where real understanding can begin.

Indeed, the only space that can nurture cultural understanding is again revealed to be the space created when alcohol is shared. As Riker arrives on the Klingon ship, he is greeted with both curiosity and distrust as the Klingons question his loyalty. All of this changes when he first breaks bread with his new crewmates. The Klingons are at first skeptical of Riker: one even offers to "get one of the females to breast feed" him if he finds Klingon food too strong. When Riker proves that he is able to drink bloodwine and eat pipus claw, bregit lungs, and rokeg blood pie, though, the crew begins to warm to him. Surprised by Riker's spirit, second officer Klag tells him, "Well, it's just you're not what I expected... you have a sense of humor."[26] It is in the officer's mess, surrounded by exotic food and potent drink, where Riker begins to forge the relationships that will help him to weather the crisis at the episode's climax, when he must save both the *Pagh* and the *Enterprise* from a cultural misunderstanding that rapidly escalates into a diplomatic disaster.

It is not just the incidental presence of alcohol at a warrior's feast that enables Riker's assimilation into the crew of the *Pagh*. Although it is not stated explicitly in "A Matter of Honor," later *Star Trek* episodes establish the beverage being consumed with gusto during the mess scene as bloodwine: fuel for space battles and alien bull-sessions alike. Once the levity ends, the conversation turns to fathers, to honor, and to the future. It is here that Riker and the Klingon officers begin exploring what it means to be human in a Klingon world, or to be Klingons confronted with the realization that humans are not what they expected. "Klingons," Klag explains, "do not express feelings the way you [humans] do.... We would not know how." The adventurous Riker takes the transformative ability of the third space to heart: "Yesterday, I did not know how to eat gagh."[27]

Any discussion of alcohol and *Star Trek* would be incomplete without mention of *The Next Generation*'s notorious nostrum: synthehol. Synthehol, a portmanteau of synthetic-alcohol, is "an alcohol substitute ... served aboard starships ... [which] simulates the appearance, taste and smell of alcohol, but the intoxicating effects can be easily dismissed."[28] From a narrative standpoint, synthehol allows writers to craft episodes that center on bars, parties, diplomatic functions, and other social gathering spaces—complete with a background of neon-colored alien drinks with exotic garnishes and space umbrellas—all the while claiming that no one is getting drunk. This is all well and good for creating the ambiance of a bar without the narrative risks of unruly bar patrons, but a future of laboratory-synthesized faux cocktails is a future of terror to any accomplished drinker.

Scotty experiences the difference firsthand in the 1992 *Next Generation* episode "Relics." Through a freak transporter accident, Scotty effectively travels through time seventy-five years into the future. After he is rescued by the *Enterprise-D*, he quickly makes his way to Ten-Forward, the *Enterprise*'s bar and lounge. The bartender serves him up a glass of scotch, and Scotty reacts with disgust, berating the man: "Laddie, I was drinking scotch a hundred years before you were born and I can tell you that whatever this is, it is definitely not scotch."[29] A connoisseur can always tell the difference, and the safe, innocuous synthehol never seems to measure up.

Synthehol's weakness stems from just how innocuous the chemical is: whenever anyone drinks synthehol, it isn't mentioned, it plays no part in the story, it simply dresses the sets. Synthehol, inherently, *does* nothing. Fortunately, most *Star Trek* characters from *The Next Generation* onward agree that while a synth-ale is just fine for the first round after a long day in main engineering, any real celebration calls for the finest of *real* alcohol. Whether it is Aldebaran whiskey or Yridian brandy, wherever a bottle of fine spirits is shared, the male third space begins to open up, as it does for Scotty and Captain Picard over a bottle of green whiskey in "Relics." The two men—who are separated by a gulf of time spanning nearly one hundred years—are able to bond only after they share a glass of authentic alcohol: they compare their old loves, the starships *Enterprise* and *Stargazer*, "old girlfriends [they'll] never meet again."[30] No such bonding or personal exploration occurs when the denizens of the twenty-fourth century drink too much synthehol; the connection between Scotty and Picard, the tension diffused in K-7's bar brawl, and the cultural understanding experienced by Commander Riker are possible only in the third space of alcohol.

The cultural gaps that some *Star Trek* characters have to overcome are far greater than others, however, and no character has further to go than Lieutenant Commander Worf. First appearing in *Star Trek: The Next Generation* during the late 1980s and early 1990s, Worf is a Klingon orphan who was raised by human foster parents. Worf's daily existence is a battle with his own hybridity, as he often must make difficult choices between his native culture, his foster upbringing, the empire of his people, and his oath of loyalty to Starfleet. His hybridity is further complicated by the fact that he is generally rejected by his own people as a traitor, even as he desires to understand them better.

During the events of the 1995 *Deep Space Nine* episode "The Way of the Warrior," Worf must decide if his loyalties lie with the Federation or with the Klingon Empire. In order to discover the secret intentions of a massive Klingon military force that has arrived on the station Deep Space Nine, Worf's commanding officers rely on his dual nature, which allows him entry into a world barred to outsiders: "In the long run, the only people who can really handle the Klingons are Klingons."[31]

As we have seen already, Klingon culture resembles contemporary pop cultural representations of the Vikings: they are warlike people, and while they loot and pillage those they perceive as weaker species, they value personal and familial honor found in battle above all else. Fortunately for Commander Worf, the Klingon warrior culture glorifies personal deeds and revels in past conquests through story and song—in fact, as the fan database Memory Alpha puts it, "with the exception of a few, all Klingon songs could actually be considered Klingon drinking songs."[32] This celebratory drinking culture allows Worf to enter into the hybrid third space created around flagons of Klingon bloodwine—nowhere else is he able to engage his fellow warriors not as a Starfleet officer, but Klingon to Klingon.

It is through the ritual of Klingon drinking song that Worf is able to reconnect with a past he thought he had lost: Huraga, an old friend of Worf's family, is a member of the Klingon expedition to Deep Space Nine. The aged warrior is able to share a piece of their common culture with the outcast, through the ancient ritual of the warrior's drinking song. Their drunken joy enables them not only to temporarily resolve Worf's hybrid identity, but also to come together as equals despite age and cultural enmity. Through the rituals of drink, both Worf and Huraga are able to let go their cultural baggage, overcome "shared histories . . . of discrimination" between their human and Klingon heritages, and come together as warriors, men, and equals, in a third space that bridges their conflicting identities.[33]

Worf's initial attempts to gather information meet with failure: they are not only failures of espionage, but also failures of acculturation.[34] Throughout "The Way of the Warrior," Worf finds himself tempted by several offers to join the Klingons in their quest for martial glory, but each time he chooses to remain loyal to his oath of service to Starfleet. Worf's outsider status is, tellingly, even marked by his choice of beverage: while the Klingon warriors around him guzzle warm bloodwine, Worf is perfectly content with chilled prune juice, which he calls "a warrior's drink."[35] It is not until Worf puts aside his juice and downs four bottles of potent spirits with Huraga that he is accepted by one of his own. Even as allies—and allies of the same species—the cultures of the Federation and Klingon are able to understand each other only in the third space of alcohol.

Counter to all these celebratory examples of male aliens bonding in safe spaces of homosocial revelry, twenty-fourth-century drinking takes a darker turn when women attempt to enter those same spaces. Although forward-looking in many ways, Gene Roddenberry's future has long struggled with its portrayals of women, generally casting them as either scantily clad lovers to be rescued, or deadly praying mantis–like threats to the male heroes.[36] This struggle with regressive views of gender and sexuality extends into *Star Trek*'s bars and clubs: when dealing with the shared space of alcohol, *Star Trek*'s female characters—human and alien alike—find themselves pushed to the margins.

The first example to come to mind regarding women in *Star Trek*'s bar scene is Guinan, the *Enterprise-D*'s bartender in *Star Trek: The Next Generation*. Guinan holds court in Ten-Forward, where she dispenses sage wisdom alongside exotic alien cocktails. Guinan, like Dr. Boyce in "The Cage," plays the traditional part of bartender as advisor and confessor. On many occasions, she helps Captain Picard work through moral quandaries, such as 1989's "The Measure of a Man," which finds Picard defending the android Data's right to refuse disassembly and study by Federation scientists. Guinan's role as bartender and sounding board for the *Enterprise* crew facilitates a third space that allows the characters to explore selfhood in a safe environment. As Dr. Boyce observes, someone is more likely to open up to a trusted bartender than a doctor. Guinan's presence in Ten Forward, as much as alcohol's, creates a place where exciting narratives can unfold.

However, Guinan's role as a guide and mentor—not as a participant in the margin-crossing experience of alcohol consumption—only serves to highlight how overtly masculine *Star Trek*'s third spaces are. Although women are present and are often seen drinking in *Star Trek*'s lounges and bars, the actual *work* of drinking—the rituals and bonding experiences enabled by the sharing of potent libations—is done exclusively by men. The third space opened up by *Star Trek*'s drinking establishments is one where men can revel in their cultural difference, but where women are quietly excluded.

Sadly, in the few instances in which women are purposefully present for alcoholic revelry, they are often cast as the stereotypical drunk girl at the party. In the 1998 episode of *Star Trek: Voyager*, "Timeless," Seven of Nine's normally reserved veneer falls away after a single glass of champagne—she starts telling the Doctor how important he is to her, as he wryly observes that "obviously, the Borg can't hold their liquor," before he carts her off to sickbay amid the amused smiles of her crewmates.[37] Similarly, in the 1996 feature film *Star Trek: First Contact*, the crew of the *Enterprise-E* find themselves back on Earth in 2063, and Deanna Troi must use her empathic powers to ply the locals for information. Commander Riker later finds her in a dive bar. After "three shots of something called tequila," Troi has found the man they are looking for, but she is clumsily drunk. Riker laughs as Troi insists that her counseling skills helped her track the target down, even as she struggles to stay conscious.[38]

A surface reading of these scenes sees Seven and Deanna's antics as some of the light-hearted comic relief that *Star Trek* has always embraced. However, it seems that when women are comically drunk, they are the objects of laughter, rather than willing participants in the joke as men are. The space created by alcohol for these women is in some ways the opposite of the convivial third space of bonding enjoyed by men: Seven and Deanna are separated from their friends and have to be physically helped to safety.

Worse, alcohol goes beyond simply lowering their inhibitions and leaving them out of the fun—it undermines some of the core facets of their characters. Seven of Nine is defined largely by her cold, rational, analytical mind; to lose control of her emotions and gush over her friendship with the Doctor is completely contrary to her character. Tequila is even more poisonous to Deanna: three shots of the stuff are debilitating enough that her telepathic powers and advanced training in psychology, counseling, and therapy are completely useless to her as she questions the bar's primitive twenty-first-century humans. In both cases, rather than being allowed to enter the third space of alcohol, these women are cut off not just from their friends, but from themselves.

In at least one instance, simply being present during masculine third space rituals has dire consequences for a woman. The 1967 *Star Trek* episode "Wolf in the Fold" opens with Kirk, McCoy, and Scotty seated around a low table in an alien bar on the planet Argelius. The three watch an Argelian belly dancer with rapt and lurid attention. Kirk and McCoy egg Scotty on, explaining that Argelius is "a completely hedonistic society" where the native humanoids "think very highly of their pleasure," which is all the prompting Scotty needs to make a move on the dancer, Kara.[39] Soon, Scotty leaves with Kara to walk the dark, foggy alleys of the city. A scream is heard—the dancer has been murdered, and Scotty is found holding the knife, but unable to remember what happened.

Here, the heroes of the Federation engage in that classic masculine bonding rite: going out for drinks and trying to score. With brightly colored alien cocktails in hand, the three men are full of winks and words left unsaid; the women of Argelius and their sexually open culture are clearly seen as objects for the three tourists' gratification. When Kara—who is present in the male third space but not a part of it—leaves with Scotty, a nightmare scenario of sexually charged violence mixed with drink plays out on an alien world.

Scotty is soon exonerated—the actual murderer is an alien energy being that feeds on fear. But this episode illustrates that the safety extended to violent exchanges among men in alcohol's third space—as in the barroom brawl in "The Trouble with Tribbles"—does not extend to women. Ultimately, the third space of drink is a place inhabited by men. Female characters in *Star Trek* generally venture into that space only briefly. When they do, they are portrayed as interlopers who are far less equipped for the rituals of alcohol than men are, or who may fall victim to embarrassment or violence that male drinkers are immune to.

This exclusion of women in *Star Trek*'s third spaces accentuates a blind spot in the science fiction franchise, which mirrors a lacuna in Bhabha's theory of third space interactions in *The Location of Culture*. In fully embracing the differences of culture and understanding that can result through the male camaraderie of alcohol's third spaces, *Star Trek* pushes female participation to the edges of that space, and sometimes into a dangerous beyond. Women populate the ranks of scientists, artists, and warriors on and off *Star Trek*'s starships, but in the space where *Star Trek* gives us the most hope for creating real understanding between cultures, women become the unknowable Other, subject to macho wisdom and defined by the exoticism and cultural diversity stigmas that the third space seeks to avoid. Once alcohol starts flowing and inhibitions are shed, the shared space of manliness invites understanding between its participants; women may not be explicitly excluded from the exchange, they participate at their own peril.

Bhabha, of course, is more self-aware of the forces of exclusion than *Star Trek*, its characters, or its writers seem to be. In focusing his essays on the formation of colonial and postcolonial identity, he effectively pushes women to the margins of his discourse. The third space interactions of colonizer/colonized, and the exploration of hybrid cultural identities created in these spaces, leave little room for considerations of hybrid gender or sexuality.

This is not to say that Bhabha is unaware of the spaces he is exploring: his project uses established feminist theory as a springboard to explore hybrid cultural spaces. For instance, by contrasting the ways in which "feminism specifies the patriarchal, gendered nature of civil society and disturbs the symmetry of private and public" spheres, resulting in a "redrawing of the domestic space" as a space of political friction, he is able to push beyond earlier feminist theory into a theory that explores transnational sites of cultural contestation.[40] But, while he may cite the women involved in the 1985 British miners' strike and Franz Fanon's Algerian revolutionary with grenades in her handbag as evidence to further his argument, women are necessarily pushed to the margins as a tertiary consideration of his task.[41] Bhabha effectively reproduces the gender dynamic that *Star Trek*'s third spaces have been producing for decades: by seeking to create one space that will be "adequate to the construction of systems of cultural identification," he creates another space that forces the female subject to the fringes.[42]

Star Trek's alcohol-fueled saga has recently returned to the point where it began, with the cinematic "reboot" of the franchise. The three newest *Star Trek* motion pictures depict an alternate universe, with reimagined versions of the classic characters from the 1960s original series. Even these more contemporary iterations of the franchise retread the same conflicted ground when alcohol is involved, however. Early in 2009's *Star Trek*, a young, hotshot Kirk aims his unwelcome attentions toward cadet Uhura in a rural Iowa bar. When it becomes clear to her friends that Kirk is harassing her, they step in and a brawl breaks out. Kirk is beaten bloody, and only the timely intercession of Captain Pike[43] brings an end to the fight.

This scene illustrates the conflicted dual nature of *Star Trek*'s masculine third space. The fatherly Pike uses the opportunity created by the fight and the bar's atmosphere to speak to Kirk man to man over drinks—two men who would never meet in the outside world are able to come together in the space of alcohol where rank and hierarchy are temporarily displaced. However, the impetus for the fight was Kirk's boorish behavior toward Uhura, and the fact that her friends violently rushed to her defense, even as she pleaded with them to stop. On one hand, alcohol serves as a vehicle for grounding the audience in a fantastic future, and for grounding two men with more in common than they may realize. But on the other, Uhura is relegated to being the object of the male gaze, a damsel to be rescued, and an observer rather than a participant in the macho third space. Decades after "Wolf in the Fold," *Star Trek* is unable to break this pattern.

Each of these episodes, whether dealing with humans, Klingons, or other species, is a variation on the same idea: where alcohol is shared, barriers fall away and cultural intersections begin to open up. By deploying the third space of alcohol, *Star Trek* manages to shed some of the failed, heterogeneous cultural diversity that the show is often in danger of succumbing to, and instead to achieve a measure of real cultural exchange through the shared rituals of male drinking. However, in this embrace of the cultural difference highlighted by these specifically masculine third spaces, women are left out of the interaction; they are left as perpetual outsiders and objects, consigned to the dangerous fringes of the communal space, or portrayed as comically unfit for the rituals of cosmic drinking culture.

Across decades of franchise history, spanning the US civil rights movement, the fall of the Berlin Wall, and the computer revolution, Star Trek has held out consistent hope for resolving cultural differences through the alchemy of alcohol's third space, regardless of shifting norms surrounding drinking. But, the role of women in that space has remained consistent as well, despite changing understanding of sex and gender in Western society. Thus, *Star Trek* manages to show us a bright future where alcohol helps close otherwise unbridgeable cultural gaps, while also revealing a gulf of gendered exclusion that both we and our utopian aspirations struggle to cross.

And so, if *Star Trek* is any indicator of what we—as Westerners, Americans, or just pop culture consumers—want the future to look like, then not all hope for humanity is lost. It is a future where the best parts of human culture—friendship, laughter, and curiosity—remain intact. We can only hope that the next time the *Enterprise* leaves space dock, and we take our next tentative steps out into the final frontier, there will be room for everyone at the bar.

St. Petersburg College

NOTES

1. Isabel Gonzalez Turmo, "Drinking: An Almost Silent Language," in *Drinking: Anthropological Approaches*, ed. Igor de Garine and Valerie de Garine (New York: Berghahn Books, 2001), 130.
2. Turmo, "Drinking," 131.
3. Lincoln Geraghty, "The American Jeremiad and Star Trek's Puritan Legacy," *Journal of the Fantastic in the Arts* 14, no. 2 (2003): 228, https://www.jstor.org/stable/43308626.
4. Karin Ikas and Gerhard Wagner, introduction to *Communicating in the Third-Space*, ed. Karin Ikas and Gerhard Wagner (New York: Routledge, 2009), 2.
5. Homi K. Bhabha, *The Location of Culture* (New York: Routledge, 2000), 1–2.
6. Bhabha, *The Location of Culture*, 2.
7. Bhabha, *The Location of Culture*, 31.
8. Bhabha, *The Location of Culture*, 31.
9. Bhabha, *The Location of Culture*, 34.
10. Bhabha, *The Location of Culture*, 34.
11. Bhabha, *The Location of Culture*, 38.
12. Bhabha, *The Location of Culture*, 4.
13. Bhabha, *The Location of Culture*, 7.
14. Robert Butler, dir., *Star Trek*, Season 1, episode pilot, "The Cage," aired February 1965 (screening for NBC); October 4, 1988, syndicated, https://www.netflix.com/title/70136140.

15. Joseph Pevney, dir., *Star Trek*, Season 2, episode 15, "The Trouble with Tribbles," aired December 29, 1967, on NBC, https://www.netflix.com/title/70136140.

16. Mary Douglas, *Purity and Danger* (New York: Routledge, 2002), 150.

17. Douglas, *Purity and Danger*, 150.

18. Turmo, "Drinking," 131.

19. Though Star Trek has been lauded as being progressive and promoting a multicultural humanist future, it hardly goes far enough. While the bridge crew is a multicultural one—particularly for a 1960s network television series—Sulu and Uhura, the Japanese and African characters, respectively, are relegated to supporting roles. Even worse, in the original *Star Trek*, evil alien species are often shown as nonwhite, Asiatic, and otherwise exoticized stereotypes of Earth cultures and peoples. For a thorough exploration of race in *Star Trek*, see Daniel Bernardi's excellent *Star Trek and History: Race-ing Toward a White Future* (New Brunswick, NJ: Rutgers University Press, 1998).

20. Pevney, "The Trouble with Tribbles."

21. Marc Daniels, dir., *Star Trek*, Season 2, episode 19, "A Private Little War," aired February 2, 1968, on NBC, https://www.netflix.com/title/70136140.

22. Bhabha, *The Location of Culture*, 2.

23. Turmo, "Drinking," 131.

24. Rob Bowman, dir., *Star Trek: The Next Generation*, Season 2, episode 8, "A Matter of Honor," aired February 6, 1989, syndicated, https://www.netflix.com/title/70158329.

25. Douglas, 150.

26. Bowman, "A Matter of Honor."

27. Bowman, "A Matter of Honor."

28. Alexander Singer, dir., *Star Trek: The Next Generation*, Season 6, episode 4, "Relics," aired October 12, 1992, syndicated, https://www.netflix.com/title/70158329.

29. Singer, "Relics."

30. Singer, "Relics."

31. James L. Conway, dir., *Star Trek: Deep Space Nine*, Season 4, episode 1, "The Way of the Warrior," aired October 2, 1995, syndicated, https://www.netflix.com/title/70158330.

32. "Klingon Drinking Song," Memory Alpha, http://memory-alpha.wikia.com/wiki/Klingon_drinking_song.

33. Bhabha, *The Location of Culture*, 2.

34. Worf is treated as a perpetual outsider through all seven seasons of *The Next Generation*, in addition to the four seasons of *Deep Space Nine* in which he appears. As of the *Next Generation* season-one episode "Heart of Glory," it had been ten years since Worf had been in the presence of other Klingons. Worf's

knowledge of his culture, up to that point, came from childhood memories and research done throughout his teen years. As the *Star Trek* franchise wore on, Worf would find himself unable to relate to the Klingons of the Empire, who were too politically motivated behind their veneer of honor, and unable to relate to humans, who did not understand what honor meant. His hybrid identity is further complicated in that other Klingons see him as being "tamed" by the Federation, and members of the Federation are not sure how to see him. Perhaps most tragically, Worf is often not sure how to see himself: as the character Jadzia Dax observes in the *Deep Space Nine* episode "Looking for par'Mach in All the Wrong Places," "for a Klingon who was raised by humans, wears a Starfleet uniform and drinks prune juice, [Worf is] pretty attached to tradition." Oftentimes, not even Worf can be sure of his identity.

35. David Carson, dir., *Star Trek: The Next Generation*, Season 3, episode 15, "Yesterday's Enterprise," aired February 19, 1990, syndicated, https://www.netflix.com/title/70158329.

36. Admittedly, at least some basic attempts are made to portray gender equality in the *Star Trek* series of the 1990s: the first season of *The Next Generation* shows both women and men wearing the Starfleet standard issue miniskirt uniform; Tasha Yar, the *Enterprise-D*'s first security chief, is a strong leader and a master of aikido; and many guest stars are female scientists, dignitaries, or Starfleet admirals. Of course, all of those attempts are undermined when these same characters are routinely portrayed as sexualized caregivers or are subject to sexualized violence.

37. LeVar Burton, dir., *Star Trek: Voyager*, Season 5, episode 6, "Timeless," aired November 18, 1998, on UPN, https://www.netflix.com/title/70158331.

38. Jonathan Frakes, dir., *Star Trek: First Contact* (1996; Hollywood: Paramount, 2009), DVD.

39. Joseph Pevney, dir., *Star Trek*, Season 2, episode 14, "Wolf in the Fold," aired December 22, 1967, on NBC, https://www.netflix.com/title/70136140.

40. Bhabha, *The Location of Culture*, 11.

41. Bhabha, *The Location of Culture*, 27, 63.

42. Bhabha, *The Location of Culture*, 34.

43. In the rebooted *Star Trek* universe, Captain Pike of "The Cage" becomes mentor to a twenty-something James Kirk and crew, rather than simply an earlier captain of the *Enterprise*.

BIBLIOGRAPHY

Abrams, J. J., dir. *Star Trek*. 2009; Hollywood: Paramount, 2009. DVD.
Abrams, J. J., dir. *Star Trek into Darkness*. 2013; Hollywood: Paramount, 2014. Netflix.

Bhabha, Homi K. *The Location of Culture*. New York: Routledge, 2000.
Bowman, Rob, dir. *Star Trek: The Next Generation*. Season 2, episode 8, "A Matter of Honor." Aired February 6, 1989, syndicated. https://www.netflix.com/title/70158329.
Burton, LeVar, dir. *Star Trek: Voyager*. Season 5, episode 6, "Timeless." Aired November 18, 1998, on UPN. https://www.netflix.com/title/70158331.
Butler, Robert, dir. *Star Trek*. Pilot, "The Cage." Aired December 29, 1967, on NBC. https://www.netflix.com/title/70136140.
Carson, David, dir. *Star Trek: The Next Generation*. Season 3, episode 15, "Yesterday's Enterprise." Aired February 19, 1990, syndicated. https://www.netflix.com/title/70158329.
Conway, James, dir. *Star Trek: Deep Space Nine*. Season 4, episode 1, "The Way of the Warrior." Aired October 2, 1995, syndicated. https://www.netflix.com/title/70158330.
Daniels, Marc, dir. *Star Trek*, Season 2, episode 19, "A Private Little War." Aired February 2, 1968, on NBC. https://www.netflix.com/title/70136140.
Douglas, Mary. *Purity and Danger*. New York: Routledge, 2002.
Frakes, Jonathan, dir. *Star Trek: First Contact*. 1996; Hollywood: Paramount, 2009. DVD.
Geraghty, Lincoln. "The American Jeremiad and *Star Trek*'s Puritan Legacy." *Journal of the Fantastic in the Arts* 14, no. 2 (2003): 228–45. https://www.jstor.org/stable/43308626.
Ikas, Karin, and Gerhard Wagner. Introduction to *Communicating in the Third Space*. Edited by Karin Ikas and Gerhard Wagner. New York: Routledge, 2009.
"Klingon Drinking Song." Memory Alpha. http://memory-alpha.wikia.com/wiki/Klingon_drinking_song.
Pevney, Joseph, dir. *Star Trek*. Season 2, episode 14, "Wolf in the Fold." Aired December 22, 1967, on NBC. https://www.netflix.com/title/70136140.
Pevney, Joseph, dir. *Star Trek*. Season 2, episode 15, "The Trouble with Tribbles." Aired December 29, 1967, on NBC. https://www.netflix.com/title/70136140.
Robinson, Andrew, dir. *Star Trek: Deep Space Nine*. Season 5, episode 3, "Looking for par'Mach in All the Wrong Places." Aired December 29, 1967, on NBC. https://www.netflix.com/title/70158330.
Singer, Alexander, dir. *Star Trek: The Next Generation*. Season 6, episode 4, "Relics." Aired October 12, 1992, syndicated. https://www.netflix.com/title/70158329.
Turmo, Isabel Gonzalez. "Drinking: An Almost Silent Language." In *Drinking: Anthropological Approaches*. Edited by Igor de Garine and Valerie de Garine, 130–42. New York: Berghahn Books, 2001.

FIFTEEN

THE TAMING OF THE SHRUB

DAN CALLAWAY

IN BETWEEN DEEP CLEANS OF the bar, restocking wines, and existential crises, it can be fun to play around with new cocktail creations. As a way to pass the time or as genuine creative expression, developing new drink recipes is one of the high points of bartending. Unfortunately, there comes the inevitable and unenviable situation of feeling stagnant in these productions, when you've reached for your trusted amaro one too many times and have fallen out of love with your once exotic bitters. I have found myself in this dull place more than I would like to remember, but have found lifelines in new flavors and helpful friends.

My first experience with shrub-based cocktails came when I was the bar manager of Decca, an upscale restaurant in Louisville, Kentucky. While the cellar bar is an attraction, the main event is the cuisine provided by chefs who are skillful, innovative professionals. It was during a midweek slow shift that I popped into the back of house and struck up a conversation with the sous-chef. He told me he was ready to test a new gooseberry shrub and offered me a sample. I had a few minutes to spare from my bar, so I followed him to the walk-in refrigerator to try this new creation. It was phenomenal! I had been getting into shrubs for a little bit, but this topped anything I had tried. I asked if I could borrow some to play around with for the rest of the night, and got to work.

For an in-depth look at the history of shrubs and their modern uses, I recommend Michael Dietsch's fantastic book *Shrubs*. For the purpose of this writing, we can simply state that a shrub is a mixture of fruit, vinegar, and sugar. The term *shrub* comes from the Arabic word *sharab*, which means "to drink." Shrubs can be traced to ancient Rome, but they experienced a great resurgence in the eighteenth century as a means to preserve fruit. The drinks could be stored and then enjoyed in the winter when a refreshing fruit drink normally would be out of season. Shrubs are created by combining fruit and sugar, then allowing the mixture to macerate over time. The combination is then strained, and vinegar is added to the resulting liquid. This syrup–vinegar mixture is then put away to be enjoyed whenever convenient.

Shrub cocktails present a unique challenge to any bartender. It can be difficult to complement both the fruit and the vinegar. The intention is to support the flavors and add new depth without covering up the essence of the original shrub. I tried different options with the gooseberry shrub but didn't have much luck. I wandered back into the kitchen and told the staff that I was struggling a bit with the cocktail. The sous-chef told me to bring up some ingredients so he could take a crack at it. He analyzed what I gave him and then poured a couple drops of various liquids into a storage container. He added small amounts of various spices and juices to the drops to see what worked. I hurried back to the bar and gathered all the bottles of bitters I could carry. All of the cooks then huddled around and continued with little drops, commenting on each new creation. For a bartender this is often a foreign concept, but it is enormously effective. More than once, I have started cranking out mediocre complete cocktails instead of taking the time to develop flavor pairings and blends that actually work. The chef's technique was a lesson in efficiency and effectiveness. We talked over some flavor options, and I went back to it.

Initially I was drawn to vermouth for this cocktail, thinking that a fortified wine would mesh well with the berry flavor. I came up with some fun combinations, but nothing that I was especially proud of. The next path I took turned out to be a more successful one: ginger beer! I feel that ginger and carbonation work wonders with a shrub, and the ginger beer/gooseberry was no exception. I liked the way that the cocktail was developing, but it still needed a little more depth. Serendipitously, our bar had recently purchased a couple of cases of The King's Ginger liqueur that were on a deep discount. This unique ginger product was specifically formulated for King Edward VII in 1903 by Berry Bros. & Rudd in London. I mixed in a little bit of The King's Ginger and loved the result. For carbonation I could use club soda and forego the ginger beer altogether. Now that I had a gooseberry shrub/ginger combination, I began auditions for a base spirit. After some trial and error I settled on rum—specifically, a Martinique style. In this form, the rum is derived directly from sugarcane, instead of from molasses. I love the Clement brand in this style; the only problem was that we were planning to use this rum in an upcoming mai tai, and it would be best to diversify a little bit. The next choice turned out to be even better: cachaça!

Cachaça is the most popular distilled spirit in Brazil, used in the famous caipirinha. Like Martinique-style rum, it is distilled from fermented sugarcane juice. The cachaça worked fantastically with the gooseberry and King's Ginger. I must have been thinking of the caipirinha, because I added a little lime juice, then topped it off with club soda for carbonation. The last step was to add a couple of dashes of Bittermens tiki bitters for a touch of allspice and cinnamon. This final step gave the drink a little extra punch and zest. I call this cocktail the Dan Marino, the nickname given to me by the kitchen staff.

Dan Marino
2 oz Cachaça
1 oz gooseberry shrub
1/2 oz The King's Ginger
1/4 oz lime juice
2 dashes Bittermens tiki bitters
Shaken, topped with club soda.

Currently, I am the beverage director and Director of Bourbon Education at Bardstown Bourbon Company. The sixth-largest bourbon distillery in the world, BBC contract-distills for around twenty companies, including Jefferson's, High West, Belle Meade, and Hirsch. Inside the distillery there is a fine dining restaurant and a world-class bar. My focus in this bar continues to include a strong relationship with the kitchen. My bar team and I are constantly striving to create innovative and original cocktails as well as our own unique takes on the classics. It is also where I have found new homes for shrubs.

Modern cocktail consumption revolves around constantly rising expectations. The average cocktail drinker now demands creative ingredients with balanced flavors, while having an original experience. The goal to deliver something original is what drove composer Arnold Schoenberg to make atonal noises, and it is what causes me to try and blend sesame oil with bourbon. Results have been varied. Modern cocktail bars consistently push boundaries and create a new base line that everyone else must reach. It's similar to the pole vault but with more sniffing and criticism.

It is in this new atmosphere that the shrub once again flourishes. Substituting a shrub in a classic cocktail can give a drink originality, life, and nuance. It can also lead to collaboration with the kitchen staff, or at the least it can push the bartender to think in a more culinary way. Currently, our bar features a strawberry margarita made with a rich, fruity strawberry shrub. The vinegar notes of the shrub play perfectly with the tequila and add depth and complexity. The strawberry fruit notes blend with the lime and keep the drink from losing its classic integrity. The recipe also employs a rich strawberry simple syrup. Simple yet effective!

Strawberry Margarita
 2 oz Cimarron Blanco
 3/4 oz Pierre Ferrand Dry Curaçao
 1/2 oz lime juice
 1/2 oz strawberry shrub
 1/2 oz strawberry simple syrup

Shake, and serve on the rocks with a salt rim and strawberry garnish.

I present these drinks and situations as a tribute to new ingredients but also as an encouragement to seek out people and methods to spur your creativity. Shrubs serve as vehicles to reach the goal of creative expression through cocktails. Find fresh flavors and try them out on friends, even when the drink isn't yet perfect. Actively seeking culinary help in your creative process will not only make your drinks better but also help create relationships and bonds with other professionals, which is ultimately more important.

Bardstown, Kentucky

PART 4

In a Glass, Darkly

SIXTEEN

THE LINGERING LOUCHE

Absinthe, the Green Demon of
Alternative Modernity

AARON JAFFE

> Keep always this dim corner for me, that I may sit while the Green Hour glides, a proud pavine of Time. For I am no longer in the city accursed, where Time is horsed on the white gelding Death, his spurs rusted with blood.
>
> —Aleister Crowley[1]

THE DANCING FLAME IS BLOOD-RED and dull yellow, fringed with purple. The almost phosphorescent liquid beneath it resembles the pale green pool table in the middle of the room. The aesthetic spectacle down the bar, the entire aesthetic composition of iridescent yellows and browns, horrific reds and greens, the melting cube of sugar on the spoon spanning an absinthe glass, humans and variegated bottles of all kinds reflected in the long, bar-length mirror, is mildly alarming, eerily echoing Vincent van Gogh's description of his painting *The Night Café*: "lemon yellow lamps with an orange and green glow," "a battle and an antithesis of the most different greens and reds," a chromatic "furnace" of phantasmagoria "suggesting some emotion, an ardent temperament."[2] The painting, he writes, is "one of the ugliest I've done," a description we might take as high praise from a past master in the pantheon of absinthiers.[3]

The style of the flaming Sterno can is truly an ugly way to drink absinthe, an inelegant reminder of extreme alcoholic potency.[4] Yet, even this way, absinthe is something to behold, something to watch well before it's something to ingest. The green seems to consume everything; everything in the room appears oxidized. I'm sitting in an absinthe bar I found on Yelp, gliding into the Green Hour, watching someone else's burning drink down the bar make a tasteless spectacle of itself. One can't help but feel that oblivion itself lies beyond this furnace, an ultimate blackout, promising a spectrum of forgotten experiences but at last yielding nothing. No colors in the abyss, only acutely remembered absences. The decadent poet and noted absinthier Lionel Johnson (1867–1902) fell from a stool in a pub and died—or so goes the rumor recirculated by the modernist poet Ezra Pound.[5] Apparently, it was Johnson who initiated fellow decadent poets into the cult of the green demon in late-nineteenth-century London. It happened in secrecy, in Johnson's private rooms, not in the public house.[6] Absinthe was de rigueur for the poets of his day, Catholic diabolists, and seemingly everyone else, before the international ban made absinthe-fueled decadence little more than a shadowy cultural yearning for nearly a hundred years.

Only recently is absinthe loosed again on the present. Yet, even before its embargo, absinthe-tinged decadence was passé, born obsolescent, as it were, occupying the intermediate zone between the just-now (what's assuredly modern) and the not-now (the just-before, the not yet modern). William Butler Yeats, firsthand witness, remembers it in this way, at least: "In 1900 everybody got down off his stilts; henceforth nobody drank absinthe with his black coffee; nobody went mad; nobody committed suicide; nobody joined the Catholic church; or if they did I have forgotten."[7] Yes, young Yeats knew them all, but here he coyly points to the generative legacy of an absinthe-haloed syncope for the modern experience as such, a demi–cri de coeur in liquid form inviting the future to side passionately with the past against the present. It sounds something like this: *forgetting forms the fuzzy edge of transition, a transition that for the modern operates as the eternal return of forgotten alternatives*. Moderns doctor their denunciations of forgotten aesthetic practices with crucial reappropriations of the superfluously exquisite and obsolescent: garish palettes, wicked decorations and declarations, epigrams, walking sticks, flânerie, and the rest, especially the antiproductive agenda of dandyism well expressed by Oscar Wilde of a prematurely timeworn youth trying "to be somebody, rather than do something."[8]

Remember that the green fairy is drink of choice for Stephen Daedalus, James Joyce's wannabe literary superhero. In his marvelous examination of Daedalus and "the connotations of absinthe as Joyce knew and used them," David Earle investigates "the drink's use as a peculiarly modernist symbol of disruption—both of sensory perception and stylistic portrayal—as a means for artistic clarity of vision, as a symbol of failure, defeat, persecution, and exile."[9] If it seems "specious to attach so many levels of meaning to a single allusion," as Earle aptly notes, the pseudorationale is rooted in the drink's particular symbolic charms: "Absinthe is a perfect example of Joyce's affection for ephemeral yet multivalent signifiers that work across his many levels of meaning, whether aesthetic, historical, or political."[10] The "ephemeral yet multivalent" allure of absinthe, to borrow Earle's phrase, comes from its superheroic capacities to evoke refractive levels of obsolescence and experience. The only unvanquished hero of the decadent age was absinthe.

Or so it seems to me, with this heroically garish absinthe fountain situated before me now at the bar. The gigantic piece of glassware feels like it's stalking me. A terrible beauty, the strange, cumbersome relic sweats with condensation, capped with some kind of metallic acorn and flanked with diminutive caryatids bearing miniature stopcocks. It dwarfs the small glass of absinthe I've also ordered and received. The fountain holds the iced water I'm supposed to slowly titrate into my glass, in the French style, studying the green liquor turning translucent to opalescent. This process is called louching. Could be a bar name: Louching toward Mayhem. Some while back, before the monstrous fire ceremony down the counter, I asked the bartender for access to this aging rock star of bar paraphernalia, kept conspicuously at one side of the counter. Replica or remnant, its suggestion of the curiosity cabinet of a nearly forgotten past seems at once both miraculous and improbable, commemorating a peculiar historical blackout in the natural history of mixology, the fitful fossil record before cocktail culture stretches into the mystic vapors of steampunk. In the setting of a present-day craft cocktail bar such as this, the absinthe fountain simultaneously references a bygone chemist's lab, complete with beakers, burettes, Erlenmeyer flasks, distillation apparatuses, and so forth, and evokes the fairy- and faun-embellished kitsch of a magician's lair, with its poisons and potions, astrological cyphers, silver-plated mermaids, arsenic wafers, Pluto waters, ubiquitous skulls, miscellaneous Lovecraftian geegaws, bibelot, bric-a-brac, and the rest of the purchased decorative atmospherics that trick out this establishment.

"Whiskey and beer are for fools," intoned doomed decadent Ernest Dowson (1867–1900); "Absinthe has the power of the magicians; it can wipe out or renew the past, and annul or foretell the future."[11] If modernity is symbolized in the rational efficiency of the martini glass, then this overly elaborate, difficult-to-clean monstrosity conveys the inevitability of inherited residue just out of sight in the wings. "Steampunk is what happens when goths discover the color brown," an internet witticism I've stumbled on more than once. It's also what happens when cosplayers raid the thrift shop for more superfluous, less slipstream versions of modernity. Decorative memorabilia that are not, strictly speaking, necessary for anything anymore become not only strategically conspicuous here but suddenly obligatory. Monocles, for instance; or walking sticks. Thorstein Veblen, the thinker who coined the phrase "conspicuous consumption," observes that "the walking stick serves the purpose of an advertisement that the bearer's hands are employed otherwise than in useful effort, and it therefore has utility as an evidence of leisure."[12] There is no consumption more conspicuous than the consumption of this particular drink assisted by the equipment set up before me. Facing this tableau, the familiar mixological rationalizations (drip, dilute) ring resolutely false.

It was Dowson who best articulated absinthe's emphatically negative mystique, the form of negative address in the thoroughly modern idea that *being somebody* is changeable and may therefore change absolutely nothing:

> Green changed to white, emerald to an opal: nothing was changed.
>
> The man let the water trickle gently into his glass, and as the green clouded, a mist fell from his mind.
>
> Then he drank opaline.
>
> Memories and terrors beset him. The past tore after him like a panther and through the blackness of the present he saw the luminous tiger eyes of the things to be.
>
> But he drank opaline.
>
> And that obscure night of the soul, and the valley of humiliation, through which he stumbled were forgotten. He saw blue vistas of undiscovered countries, high prospects and a quiet, caressing sea. The past shed its perfume over him, to-day held his hand as it were a little child, and to-morrow shone like a white star: nothing was changed.
>
> He drank opaline.
>
> The man had known the obscure night of the soul, and lay even now in the valley of humiliation; and the tiger menace of the things to be was red in the skies. But for a little while he had forgotten.
>
> Green changed to white, emerald to an opal: nothing was changed.[13]

Absinthe presents the pure diabolical spirit of missing time, and Dowson's prose poem serves up its decadent nihilism through polychromatic mists. "Tomorrow one dies," he was reported to have said, "and it will not stop the traffic passing over London bridge."[14] Opaline signals the destructive aspect of consumption, a fatalistic tuner impatiently changing aesthetic frequencies from green emeralds to tiger eyes to blue vistas of undiscovered countries to red skies summoning the evil spirits of missing time through the wicked rituals of wasted surplus. The lingering sense is that *being present* means *being in a present* in which nothing really changes. Just as this, so too that: absinthe, a vanishing mediator in the invention of the cocktail; absinthe-fueled aestheticism, a vanishing mediator of alternative modernism; tomorrow, nothing was changed. While it's most certainly a dialectical howler that Prohibition gave rise to cocktail culture as a struggle to doctor up bathtub booze, the pretext of Prohibition does provide a credible alibi for momentary escapes from the nightmare of history with a few potions stolen from the apothecary shelf for settling upset stomachs and nerves. Could this be the restorative proscribed for passing through *The Waste Land*?

> My nerves are bad to-night. Yes, bad. Stay with me.
> Speak to me. Why do you never speak? Speak.
> What are you thinking of? What thinking? What?
> I never know what you are thinking. Think.[15]

I never know what you are drinking. To modify Roland Barthes somewhat: absinthe drinks in synecdoches, substitutions of parts for wholes.[16] It is a drink that always traded on its reputation as a liquid hazard. Its very name comes from a Greek root *apsinthion*, a word that tellingly means "undrinkable." In the modern sense, "real" absinthe signifies an alcoholic preparation of wormwood, *Artemisia absinthium*, prized for toxic effects on parasites and humans alike.[17] Part of absinthe's dangerous charm—its historical enmity with the liquid hegemony of the wine trade, for instance, or its aesthetic allure with everyone from Paul Verlaine to Hunter S. Thompson—trades on its reputation as a wicked totem of alternative modernity. Let's review the lost time of absinthe, sorting myths and facts, surveying uses and abuses from Parnassus to Perdido Street Station—from the heyday through its Prohibition years to its recent revival. Starting with matters of absinthe production, the ride turns to issues of consumption, undertaking a comparative semiotics of the concoction, analyzing its shifting meanings and mystique as a tonic for imagining alternative chromatics and flux for assorted spirituous vanguards.

"An age may be said to be decadent, or a generation may be said to be in a state of prone senility," wrote Ezra Pound, "when its creative minds are dead and when its survivors maintain a mental dignity—to wit, the dignity ... of a corpse. Excess or even absinthe is not the sure sign of decadence." Pound wrote these words in 1915. The same year France finally gave in to an absinthe ban, capitulating to years of agitation by the formidable forces of the absinthe temperance movement.[18] The Americans banned the stuff in 1912. The prohibition lasted nearly one hundred years, until the EU forgot to include absinthe in its banned substances treaty and American hobbyists began reverse-engineering pre-ban formulations of the stuff.[19] However bogus, the genesis of the absinthe ban is complex and its decadent mystique was in place long beforehand. The drink began as a medicinal tonic in Switzerland at the end of the eighteenth century. Basically, it's an alcohol preparation of three herbal substances: anise, fennel, and, most crucially, wormwood. The third herb is most crucial. Its flowers, leaves, and indeed wood itself are sharply bitter, long known to alchemists to have antiparasitical effects. It isn't called wormwood for nothing: the plant is both vermifuge or vermicide, a deworming agent—even worms are repelled by it. It's poisonous to life. Ingesting it means capitulating to a certain will to decay.

Ancient and medieval sources fall in line on this front. Pliny prescribes wormwood for worms of the belly. He even details a trick for getting children to consume the leaves by stuffing them inside figs. Other ancient sources describe various wormwood-infused balms, salves, poultices, potions, and tonics, devised for repelling "fleas, flyes, knats and wormes."[20] It was noted as a mosquito repellant and an antimalarial agent, certainly one of the reasons Foreign Legion soldiers were plied endlessly with absinthe. One recipe suggests boiling wormwood with rice, with chickpeas, "or with any other food or meat," in combination with honey, as a means to "slayeth both long and flat wormes, [or] all other kinds whatsoever, loosing the belly very gently."[21] Internal and outer applications are advised in concert—in some cases, augmented with the cyanide juice extracted from peach pits—for killing and drawing out living creatures in and around various human orifices. Additional ingredients usually appear, mostly for flavoring—mint and licorice, above all—to brace against wormwood's bitterness, it seems, as in the *Old English Herbarium*, for instance: "If worms are a bother . . . take equal amounts of absinthium, horehound and lupine. Simmer them in sweetened water or in wine."[22] Ingestion is suggested with caution—mandated pairing with sweeteners or assorted flavoring agents—especially for children or the weak of heart or of stomach. Vermouth, incidentally, is another, less-potent preparation of the same herb, a co-evolved solution with similar therapeutic designs: wine fortified with wormwood. Indeed, the name of this herbaciously fortified wine derives from the German word for "wormwood," *Wermut*.[23]

What does wormwood taste like, you may wonder? In a word: satanic. The taste gets invoked in the Bible, in Revelations 8:11, for instance, with the appearance of a dark star during the end of days: "And the name of the star is called Wormwood: and the third part of the waters became wormwood; and many men died of the waters, because they were made bitter."[24] Or, maybe just Jägermeister-y. That multiherb liver-glue—*Leberkleister*, as the German joke goes—is rumored to contain wormwood among its fifty-six herbs, fruits, roots, and spices.[25] And, many post-ban absinthe aficionados favor wormwood-forward styles—describing the taste as winningly tarragon-like, with a floral nose, camphorous on the palate, and a woody finish. Wormwood's particular quality of bitterness defies description somewhat: It has, according to one reviewer, "a floral, sometimes almost perfumy, minty bitterness that doesn't [quite] come across as harsh, but is quite pleasant."[26] The taste is hyper-qualified: "fresh, weedy-grassy-minty-flowery-somewhat-chrysanthemum-ish."[27] "It's more than that," writes another new absinthian, "but that's an easy way to find it. It's also more detectable if you take a sip of absinthe and smack it with your tongue with your mouth open. It just suddenly leaps forward."[28] The mothbally taste of wormwood is thought to pair well with licorice, which explains the two other players in absinthe's unholy trinity: fennel and anise. You may find yourself sounding something like a baleful Hemingway character, who remarks, "Everything tastes of liquorice. Especially all the things you've waited so long for, like absinthe."[29]

"The solar system and everybody in it having been annihilated, the question was then asked, 'Where was the artist to go for inspiration?'"[30] This language comes from an anti-aestheticism tract from 1913. The answer leads straight to an absinthe bottle. Well, not really. The actual answer is "In art itself"— but the would-be last artist's slender fingers are curled around an absinthe glass when this idea of aestheticism gets hatched. The recipe of aesthetics as decadence—poisonous, intoxicating, and delightful, in the words of one commentator from 1913—"promised occupation in a dreary age of pessimism and stagnation," something to do, in effect, in opposition to a dreary sovereign seated on a burnished throne.[31] Yet, the same critic writes, there's *enough evil in this reprobate phoenix of aestheticism to poison the well for centuries*.[32] As the media kit for one new absinthe brand recently put it: "Writers and artists such as Edgar Allan Poe, Oscar Wilde, Charles Baudelaire, Paul Gauguin, Henri de Toulouse-Lautrec and Vincent van Gogh regarded 'the green fairy' as a source of inspiration"—and post-ban absinthes dutifully deal in imagery derived from Aubrey Beardsley, H. R. Giger, and A. O. Spare, trading on the elixir's enduring diabolical allure as a potion for poison's sake.[33] The gift of *absinthe pour l'art* keeps on giving: "Better to have the Mona Lisa smuggled out of the Louvre than prohibition tracts smuggled in."[34] Like the vampire, absinthe has been dead many times, and learned the secrets of the grave, and its decadent associations are no secret. Indeed, they're inventoried again and again, repeated early and often. Wilde's line about the liquid muse gets a lot of play: "After the first glass you see things as you wish they were. After the second, you see things as they are not. Finally, you see things as they really are, and that is the most horrible thing in the world."[35] Absinthe in hand, the notoriously decadent

Aleister Crowley ponders that "while the barrier between divine and human things is frail but inviolable, the artist and the bourgeois are only divided by a point of view."[36] *Portrait of the Artist as a Young Louche*. What's clear is that even as the post-ban absinthe industry is eager to point out that its dangers have been greatly exaggerated—it doesn't cause hallucinations or seizures; it's really just a distilled, highly alcoholic beverage; drink responsibly—it simultaneously cashes in on its lingering reputation as moral turpitude in a glass. All the tragedy swirling in the absinthe vortex in the pre-ban era returns as farce in the post-ban age; this much is clear when absinthe makers are left to turn to Marilyn Manson—that watered-down substitute Crowley—to trade on absinthe's decadent mystique.

The formative act of depravity that precipitated the ban occurred when a Swiss laborer murdered his pregnant wife and his two young daughters in a lurid alcohol-induced haze. Even though the murderer drank copious amounts of wine (five liters, allegedly), crème de menthe, and brandy before committing his gruesome crimes, the press and public around the world fixated on his consumption of two glasses of absinthe before breakfast, and the misdeed became known as the Absinthe Murders.[37] A petition to outlaw the drink received nearly a hundred thousand signatures within a matter of days in the wake of the Absinthe Murders trial, and within a year absinthe was banned in Bern. With prohibitionists emboldened, other countries quickly followed suit.[38] By 1912, even in Paris—the absinthe hellmouth, as it were—absinthe was banned. As numerous historians have chronicled, French wine producers, working in collusion with temperance movement activists in support of the ban, promoted the erroneous idea that absinthism constituted a graver danger to public health than alcoholism. Wine had lost some market share to absinthe during the Second Empire. Not only had absinthe's antimalarial properties made it a drink of choice for those returning from France's colonial adventures, but also—perhaps more significantly—it provided a cheaper and more powerful alternative when wine prices had escalated during the wine blight of the 1870s and 1880s. Wine producers, eager to dodge any responsibility for the deleterious effects of their wares, threw their weight behind the forces of anti-absinthism.[39] The vituperations were presented thusly: (1) that absinthe was strong, stronger than wine, stronger than whisky; (2) that its use of strong aromatics made impurities and unpleasant taste too easy to conceal; (3) that its use of "coloring matter [was] often very deleterious [including] not infrequently copper salts . . . used in order to produce the green color"; and, most of all, (4) that deadly wormwood itself was a narcotic poison responsible for a host of maladies to the brain and nervous system, including "hypersomnia," "torpor," "loss of memory, intellectual paralysis, dullness, complete loss of will," "brutishness," "giddiness," "vertigo," "muscular disorders," and "convulsive movements like those produced by successive electric shocks";[40] "in a stronger dose it causes attacks of epilepsy, more or less violent, which are not produced by alcohol."[41] In fact, trace amounts of diluted wormwood have no such effects, as the research overturning of the ban showed definitively—once and for all discrediting the science that had led to the ban, which involved submerging mice in pure wormwood oil, and so on.

In *Dictionary of Received Ideas*—his marvelous collection of clichés from the Second Empire—Gustave Flaubert nails it when he defines *absinthe* this way: "ABSINTHE–Extra-violent poison: one glass and you are dead. Journalists drink it while writing their articles. Has killed more soldiers than the Bedouins."[42] In *Bouvard and Pécuchet*, Flaubert describes a depraved absintheur in similar broad strokes. The louche: "The fatigue of bivouacs, absinthe, and fever, an entire existence of wretchedness and debauchery, stood revealed in his dull eyes. His white lips quivered, exposing the gums. The vast sky, empurpled, enveloped him in a blood-red light; and his obstinacy in remaining there caused a species of terror."[43] Later, Flaubert's two idiot protagonists—Bouvard and Pécuchet—set out to develop their own brand of herbal-spirit, a project described as carrying them into realms of discovery "beyond the exploits of conquerors": They buy up the stock of a bankrupt distiller—"sieves, barrels, funnels, skimmers, filters, scales," "a bowl of wood with a ball attached, a ... still, which required a reflecting-furnace with a basket funnel"—and begin concocting potions. Eventually, they cook up a drink to "surpass all others," dubbing it "Bouvarine." It includes "coriander as in Kummel, kirsch as in Maraschino, hyssop as in Chartreuse, amber-seed as in Vespetro cordial, and sweet calamus as in Krambambuly; and it would be coloured red with sandalwood." Heaping all the ingredients inside the apparatus, the would-be alchemists light a fire under the stove and wait: "Suddenly, with the noise of a bombshell, the still burst into twenty pieces, which jumped up to the ceiling, smashing the pots, flattening out the skimmers and shattering the glasses. The coal was scattered about, the furnace was demolished, and next day [their maid] found a spatula in the yard."[44] After the blast, the pair sit on their haunches in stunned ignorance, "not daring to venture on a single movement, pale with terror, in the midst of broken glass"; their troubles, they finally deduce, were caused by nothing more than ignorance of chemistry.[45]

Ignorance of chemistry is the cause of a lot of trouble concerning absinthe.[46] Yet such ignorance is also at the heart of its ritual and romance. What I have in mind here is the louche itself: Water not only changes the flavors, it almost magically alters the appearance of the absinthe. As you slowly add water, the liquid in the glass seems to thicken, and transforms into an opalescent pastel cloud. This effect is called the louche, a word that means "turbulent" in French and "debauched" in English. Back to the chemistry—Absinthe is always very strong: 45–74 percent alcohol by volume (90–148 proof). It also contains trace amounts of essential oils extracted from various plants—phenylpropenes. Chiefly, these are from wormwood (thujone, estragole) and from anise and fennel seed (anethole), but there are many others. Plant extracts such as these are usually lipophilic ("oil-loving") compounds that are not miscible with water but can be diluted in solvents like ethanol. When the absinthe is "watered down," the concentration of alcohol decreases; and when diluted sufficiently, absinthe loses its ability to keep the oils dissolved, "dropping" them into an emulsion, throughout which they are distributed as small droplets. The opaline appears very suddenly—at a certain concentration of alcohol and water—when visible light gets multiply scattered by the rapid introduction of phenylpropene droplets. Left long enough, the two components would separate into different distinct phases—but this might be a very long time. There is a suggestion that the louching changes the chemistry of absinthe, but this isn't true. It may change the taste by effectively altering the distribution of the various essential oils in the glass—a change of the concentration of the components in the phases.

There's the science; here's the mystification: At the Old Absinthe House in New Orleans, Crowley stares at his glass, conjuring "marble basins hollowed—and hallowed!—by the drippings of the water which creates by baptism the new spirit of absinthe." He's on his second glass, he says, of that "fascinating, but subtle poison, whose ravages eat men's heart and brain": "As I am not an American anxious for quick action, I am not surprised and disappointed that I do not drop dead upon the spot."[47] Even though Crowley claims he "can taste souls without the aid of . . . the magic of absinthe," he's captivated by "the middle stage in [Absinthe] Alchemy . . . when the liquor becomes opalescent," invoking "visions of the Saints once called the Universal Peacock, in which the totality is perceived thus royally appareled": "Can it be that in the opalescence of absinthe is some occult link with this mystery of the Rainbow?" Does the "drinker" not thus enter "the secret chamber of Beauty, . . . kindle his thoughts to rapture, adjust his point of view to that of the artists, at least to that degree of which he is originally capable, [and] weave for his fancy a gala dress of stuff as many-colored as the mind of Aphrodite"? "I am watching the opalescence of my absinthe," Crowley reports, and it leads me to ponder upon a certain very curious mystery, persistent in legend. We may call it the mystery of the rainbow. Give up your life completely to the task; sit daily for six hours in the Old Absinthe House, and sip the icy opal; endure till all things change insensibly before your eyes, you changing with them; till you become as gods, knowing good and evil, and that they are not two but one.[48]

I leave you to decide if this absinthe-inspired ideation is merely turbulent or wholly debauched.

Not soggy with decrepit bodies but in the company of impenitent ghosts, then, the absinthe drink I recommend most is not the legendary Corpse Reviver (gin, Cointreau, curaçao, Lillet, lemon juice, a dash of absinthe) nor Hemingway's pluripotent Death in the Afternoon (essentially, absinthe-fortified champagne), but one in which absinthe plays a role that's ectoplasmic. That drink is the storied classic from New Orleans called a Sazerac, a name that is haunted by a defunct brand of cognac and that also today designates a branded portfolio of liquor bottles. Sometimes called the first cocktail, nicer with rye than with bourbon or brandy, it takes two lowball glasses, a teaspoon of sugar, and a few dashes of bitters—New Orleans (Peychaud's), not Trinidad and Tobago (Angostura).[49] This *isn't* an old-fashioned, so New Orleans is critical. If it comes tasting of Angostura in a martini glass, send it back. Two fingers of rye go in one glass; the second gets chilled, then coated with the absinthe revenant, a thin film of the real deal, coating the receptacle and then conspicuously discarded. Pour out the surplus, like a carefree billionaire; in goes the rye and the bitters, a slash of lemon peel around the rim.

Speaking of billionaires, here's an actually drinkable absinthe cocktail that carries that name, the Billionaire, one that includes more than a trivial amount of absinthe. I call mine the Wohltäter, the German word for philanthropist:

Wohltäter
2 oz bourbon (whatever's handy; I bought an export brand named George Washington)
1 oz lemon juice
1/2 oz pomegranate syrup, made with equal parts sugar and pomegranate juice
1/2 oz absinthe

Shake with ice, serve in a coupe with a thin lemon wheel

I'll borrow a toast from a professional louche, Hunter S. Thompson, who lingered under the international absinthe ban for his entire lifespan:

> Let us toast to animal pleasures, to escapism, to rain on the roof and instant coffee, to unemployment insurance and library cards, to absinthe and

good-hearted landlords, to music and warm bodies and contraceptives... and to the "good life," whatever it is and wherever it happens to be.[50]

—⚏—

No sympathy for the devil; keep that in mind. Buy the ticket, take the ride.[51]

Florida State University

NOTES

1. Aleister Crowley, "Absinthe: The Green Goddess," *The International*, XII, no. 2 (February 1918): 1, http://www.museeabsinthe.com/Crowley-Green-Goddess.pdf.

2. Vincent van Gogh, letter to Theo van Gogh, September 8, 1888, Vincent van Gogh, The Letters, Van Gogh Museum, http://vangoghletters.org/vg/letters/let676/letter.html.

3. Van Gogh, n.p.

4. As a self-described absinthe purist put it to me: "Anywhere that would flame absinthe is a place to be avoided; it is an Epcot version of absinthe for tourists, ... more a product of Johnny Depp in *From Hell* rather than any citable historic instance."

5. Ezra Pound, "Hugh Selwyn Mauberley," *Personae: The Shorter Poems* (New York: New Directions, 1990), 183–202.

6. Jad Adams, *Hideous Absinthe: A History of the Devil in a Bottle* (London: Tauris Parke, 2004), 140.

7. William Butler Yeats, *The Oxford Book of Modern Verse 1892–1935* (Oxford: Oxford University Press, 1936), xi. Citing this line, Phil Baker contests Yeats's assessment of absinthe's sudden cultural demise in his comprehensive *The Book of Absinthe: A Cultural History* (New York: Grove/Atlantic, 2001), 264.

8. Wilde, "Pen, Pencil and Poison," *The Prose of Oscar Wilde* (New York: Cosmopolitan, 1916), 62.

9. David M. Earle, "Green Eyes, I See You. Fang, I Feel": The Symbol of Absinthe in Ulysses," *James Joyce Quarterly* 40, no. 4 (2003): 691–709, https://www.jstor.org/stable/25477989.

10. Earle, "Green Eyes, I See You," 702.

11. Ernest Dowson, *Letters of Ernest Dowson*, ed. Desmond Flower and Henry Maas (London: Cassell, 1967), 441.

12. Thorstein Veblen, *Theory of the Leisure Class* (New York: Dover, 1994), 162.

13. Ernest Dowson, "Absinthia Taetra," *Ernest Dowson: Collected Poems*, ed. R. K. R. Thornton and Caroline Dowson (Birmingham, UK: Birmingham University Press, 2003), 211.

14. Ernest Dowson, *Letters of Ernest Dowson*, 441.
15. T. S. Eliot, "The Waste Land," *The Complete Poems and Plays: 1909–1950* (New York: Harcourt, 1963), 40.
16. Roland Barthes, *Roland Barthes by Roland Barthes*, trans. Richard Howard (New York: Wang and Hill, 2010), 96.
17. *Oxford English Dictionary*.
18. Jesse Hicks, "The Devil in a Little Green Bottle: A History of Absinthe," *Distillations*, October 4, 2010, Science History Institute, https://www.chemheritage.org/distillations/magazine/the-devil-in-a-little-green-bottle-a-history-of-absinthe. See also Baker, *The Book of Absinthe*, chs. 6–7.
19. Brian Ashcraft, "The Mystery of the Green Menace," *Wired*, November 1, 2005, https://www.wired.com/2005/11/absinthe.
20. See Graeme Tobyn, Alison Denham, and Midge Whitelegg, *The Western Herbal Tradition: 2000 Years of Medicinal Plant Knowledge* (London: Churchill Livingstone Elsevier, 2011); also, Doris Lanier, *Absinthe: The Cocaine of the Nineteenth Century: A History of the Hallucinogenic Drug and Its Effect on Artists and Writers in Europe and the United States* (Jefferson, NC: McFarland, 1995).
21. Claire Kowalchik and William H. Hylton, eds. *Rodale's Illustrated Encyclopedia of Herbs* (Emmaus, PA: Rodale, 1987), 509–510, 515.
22. Anne Van Arsdall, *Medieval Herbal Remedies: New Translations from the Old English Herbarium* (New York: Routledge, 2010), 195.
23. Lanier, *Absinthe*, 4. Also see Adam Ford, *Vermouth: The Revival of the Spirit That Created America's Cocktail Culture* (Woodstock, VT: Countryman, 2015).
24. See Baker, *Book of Absinthe*, 103.
25. "What's in Jägermeister? Does It Have Medicinal Uses," Life with Gremlins, http://www.lifewithgremlins.com/whats-in-jagermeister-medicinal-uses/.
26. I take this descriptive language from the discussion between "Absomphe," "Gwydion Stone," and "Peridot" in the online forum of the Wormwood Society concerning "Pinpointing the Wormwood Flavor," http://wormwoodsociety.org/forums/topic/5134-pinpointing-the-wormwood-flavor.
27. "Pinpointing the Wormwood Flavor," n.p.
28. "Pinpointing the Wormwood Flavor," n.p.
29. Ernest Hemingway, "Hills Like White Elephants," *The Complete Short Stories of Ernest Hemingway* (New York: Simon & Schuster, 1987), 212.
30. E. Steeksma, "The Phoenix of Aesthetics," *The Living Age* (Boston: Living Age Company, 1913), 572.
31. Steeksma, "The Phoenix of Aesthetics," 571.
32. Steeksma, "The Phoenix of Aesthetics," 571.
33. "Absinthe Mansinthe," Absinthes.com, accessed February 20, 2020, https://www.absinthes.com/en/absinthe-mansinthe-p79.

34. "Absinthe Mansinthe."
35. Oscar Wilde, *Epigrams of Oscar Wilde* (London: Wordsworth, 2007), 165.
36. Crowley, "Absinthe: The Green Goddess," 1.
37. Hicks, "The Devil in a Little Green Bottle," n.p.
38. Hicks, "The Devil in a Little Green Bottle," n.p.
39. Hicks, "The Devil in a Little Green Bottle," n.p.
40. Emma E. Walker, "The Effects of Absinthe," *New York Medical Record* 70 (October 13, 1906): 508, in *The Absinthe Encyclopedia*, https://www.absinthes.com/en/absinthe-encyclopedia/thujone/thujone-and-absinthe-scientific-research/the-effects-of-absinthe-by-emma-e-walker-1906/.
41. Walker, "The Effects of Absinthe," 569.
42. Gustave Flaubert, *Bouvard and Pécuchet with The Dictionary of Received Ideas*, trans. A. J. Krailsheimer (New York: Penguin, 1975), 293.
43. Gustave Flaubert, *Bouvard and Pécuchet* (London: Nichols, 1896), 72, 73.
44. Flaubert, *Bouvard and Pécuchet* (1896), 81.
45. Flaubert, *Bouvard and Pécuchet* (1896), 81.
46. Research chemist Ted Breaux did heroic work to rescue genuine absinthe from oblivion by debunking the notion of its chemical toxicity, for instance, as recounted in Ashcraft's influential *Wired* article.
47. Crowley, "Absinthe: The Green Goddess," 1.
48. Crowley, "Absinthe: The Green Goddess," 1.
49. I have no interest in the veracity of claims that the Sazerac is older than the old-fashioned, but David Wondrich thinks that the "myth" is likely to have originated in the "aggressive" marketing of bottled cocktails by the Sazerac Company in the early 1900s. See Todd A. Price, "David Wondrich Dispels Sazerac Myths," *New Orleans Times-Picayune*, August 31, 2009. See also Joseph Turner's essay on the Sazerac cocktail in this volume.
50. Hunter S. Thompson, *Proud Highway: Saga of a Desperate Southern Gentleman, 1955–1967* (New York: Ballantine, 1997), 101.
51. Hunter S. Thompson, *Fear and Loathing in Las Vegas* (New York: Vintage, 1998), 89.

BIBLIOGRAPHY

"Absinthe Mansinthe." Absinthes.com. Accessed February 20, 2020. https://www.absinthes.com/en/absinthe-mansinthe-p79.

Adams, Jad. *Hideous Absinthe: A History of the Devil in a Bottle*. London: Tauris Parke, 2004.

Ashcraft, Brian. "The Mystery of the Green Menace." *Wired*. November 1, 2005. https://www.wired.com/2005/11/absinthe.

Baker, Phil. *The Book of Absinthe: A Cultural History.* New York: Grove/Atlantic, 2001.

Barthes, Roland. *Roland Barthes by Roland Barthes.* Translated by Richard Howard. New York: Wang and Hill, 2010.

Crowley, Aleister. "Absinthe: The Green Goddess." *The International*, XII, no. 2 (February 1918): 1. http://www.museeabsinthe.com/Crowley-Green-Goddess.pdf.

Dowson, Ernest. "Absinthia Taetra." *Ernest Dowson: Collected Poems.* Edited by R. K. R. Thornton and Caroline Dowson. Birmingham, UK: Birmingham University Press, 2003.

Dowson, Ernest. *The Letters of Ernest Dowson.* Edited by Desmond Flower and Henry Maas. London: Cassell, 1967.

Earle, David M. "'Green Eyes, I See You. Fang, I Feel': The Symbol of Absinthe in *Ulysses.*" *James Joyce Quarterly* 40, no. 4 (2003).

Eliot, T. S. "The Waste Land." *The Complete Poems and Plays: 1909–1950.* New York: Harcourt, 1963.

Flaubert, Gustave. *Bouvard and Pécuchet.* London: Nichols, 1896.

Flaubert, Gustave. *Bouvard and Pécuchet with The Dictionary of Received Ideas.* Translated by A. J. Krailsheimer. New York: Penguin, 1975.

Ford, Adam. *Vermouth: The Revival of the Spirit that Created America's Cocktail Culture.* Woodstock, VT: Countryman, 2015.

Hemingway, Ernest. "Hills Like White Elephants." *The Complete Short Stories of Ernest Hemingway.* New York: Simon & Schuster, 1987.

Hicks, Jesse, "The Devil in a Little Green Bottle: A History of Absinthe." *Distillations*, October 4, 2010. Science History Institute. https://www.chemheritage.org/distillations/magazine/the-devil-in-a-little-green-bottle-a-history-of-absinthe.

Kowalchik, Claire, and William H. Hylton, eds. *Rodale's Illustrated Encyclopedia of Herbs.* Emmaus, PA: Rodale, 1987.

Lanier, Doris. *Absinthe: The Cocaine of the Nineteenth Century: A History of the Hallucinogenic Drug and Its Effect on Artists and Writers in Europe and the United States.* Jefferson, NC: McFarland, 1995.

"Pinpointing the Taste of Wormwood." Wormwood Society. http://wormwoodsociety.org/forums/topic/5134-pinpointing-the-wormwood-flavor.

Pound, Ezra. "Hugh Selwyn Mauberley." *Personae: The Shorter Poems.* New York: New Directions, 1990.

Price, Todd A. "David Wondrich Dispels Sazerac Myths." *New Orleans Times-Picayune.* August 31, 2009.

Steeksma, E. "The Phoenix of Aesthetics." *The Living Age.* Boston: Living Age Company, 1913.

Thompson, Hunter S. *Fear and Loathing in Las Vegas.* New York: Vintage, 1998.

Thompson, Hunter S. *Proud Highway: Saga of a Desperate Southern Gentleman, 1955–1967*. New York: Ballantine, 1997.

Tobyn, Graeme, Alison Denham, and Midge Whitelegg. *The Western Herbal Tradition: 2000 Years of Medicinal Plant Knowledge*. London: Churchill Livingstone Elsevier, 2011.

Veblen, Thorstein. *Theory of the Leisure Class*. New York: Dover, 1994.

Van Arsdall, Anne. *Medieval Herbal Remedies: New Translations from the Old English Herbarium*. New York: Routledge, 2010.

Van Gogh, Vincent. Letter to Theo van Gogh. September 8, 1888. Vincent van Gogh, The Letters. Van Gogh Museum. http://vangoghletters.org/vg/letters/let676/letter.html.

"What's in Jägermeister? Does It Have Medicinal Uses." Life with Gremlins. http://www.lifewithgremlins.com/whats-in-jagermeister-medicinal-uses/.

Wilde, Oscar. *Epigrams of Oscar Wilde*. London: Wordsworth, 2007.

Wilde, Oscar. "Pen, Pencil and Poison." *The Prose of Oscar Wilde*. New York: Cosmopolitan, 1916.

Walker, Emma E. "The Effects of Absinthe." *New York Medical Record* 70 (October 13, 1906): 508. In *The Absinthe Encyclopedia*. https://www.absinthes.com/en/absinthe-encyclopedia/thujone/thujone-and-absinthe-scientific-research/the-effects-of-absinthe-by-emma-e-walker-1906/.

Yeats, William Butler. *The Oxford Book of Modern Verse 1892–1935*. Oxford: Oxford University Press, 1936.

SEVENTEEN

RYE TAKE ON THE PAST—
THE OLD-FASHIONED COCKTAIL

A Glass of Crooning Sophistication

JUDITH ROOF

Just make it a straight rye.

—Cole Porter[1]

SOMETIMES A COCKTAIL IS MORE than just a cocktail. Sometimes a cocktail accrues associations and meanings beyond itself. Stylistic suggestion, class affiliation, characteristics of an era, sodality with personalities—these might adhere to a particular concoction, its associations always bringing the past into the future. The old-fashioned, a cocktail whose very name implies a longevity—in fact, describes the way the old-fashioned cocktail was always there before it was even named the "old-fashioned"—moors a range of reappearances, reprises, and representations of the retro, with its emblematic retro-presentism, especially in the realm of Cole Porter musicals and retro television series, marking the persistent return of what was itself already mythical. The old-fashioned operates as both a libation and a repository for memory, as the cue for revivifying the shows, composers, and performers that have made melodies in its name.

The old-fashioned is the cocktail to which all cocktails refer. Like fashion itself, the old-fashioned is always retro. Many cocktail scholars contend that the old-fashioned is the original cocktail, made in the United States in the early nineteenth century from some form of whiskey (usually distilled from rye), bitters, sugar (to mitigate the harshness of domestic American distillates), and water, and stirred with the tail feather of a rooster—hence "cocktail."[2] On May 13, 1806, *The Balance and Columbian Repository*, a New York newspaper, listed the ingredients of the cocktail as "a stimulating liquor, composed of spirits of any kind, sugar, water, and bitters."³ Because whiskey was cheaper than imported wine, which was heavily taxed, farmers would distill grain into whiskey as an easy form of potable currency; whiskey was the most available (and tax-free) inebriant.⁴

This early "cocktail" reappeared in several forms throughout the nineteenth century, primarily as the "whiskey cocktail." As Robert Simonson recounts, "in 1859, the *Memphis Daily Appeal* called the whiskey cocktail a 'fashionable accompaniment' to the sporting life, along with smoking, chewing tobacco, and playing poker."⁵ Simonson also notes that the whiskey cocktail was made "in batches and sold as provisions to the Union army during the Civil War."⁶ In fact, the whiskey cocktail probably never disappeared, but simply remained a part of domestic imbibables until cocktails became a connoisseur's fashionable focus in the lifestyle that developed after the Civil War in a thriving Chicago and New York. Referred to as "the old-fashioned" in the *Chicago Tribune*, the "old-fashioned" reemerges with a moniker that in itself hails back to an earlier cocktail that was nearly the same—hence the name "old-fashioned."⁷

The next year, the Pendennis Club in Louisville, Kentucky, formulated a version of a cocktail they dubbed, again, the "old-fashioned," which also hearkened back to the earlier formula—whiskey, bitters, sugar—but exchanged rye whiskey for bourbon, and added an orange slice and a cherry.⁸ Simonson adds yet another site for the old-fashioned's development: New York and Colonel Jim Gray, who, as Simonson recounts, "identified himself as the father of the Old-Fashioned."⁹

Often regarded as a "matutinal cocktail," the old-fashioned was a toddy pick-me-up.¹⁰ The recipe for the old-fashioned retains elements of the originary beverage, even though these are no longer, strictly speaking, necessary in a drink composed of seven-year-old bourbon (as the Pendennis Club requires). Made by "muddling" or crushing together the sugar, bitters, and orange peel before adding the bourbon, water, and ice, the old-fashioned still refers to earlier and more primitive methods of mixology. Although some now prefer to use simple syrup instead of sugar (because it takes time for sugar to dissolve properly), and some deploy various kinds of whiskey instead of bourbon (rye, Tennessee whiskey, Irish whiskey, and even scotch), the proper bitter is Angostura bitters and the standard garnish an orange slice and a maraschino cherry.

Thus the old-fashioned, called that because it already existed when cocktails came into fashion, came back into fashion—and more than once. Prohibition's speakeasies relied on distilled liquors, just as in the late eighteenth-century higher-alcohol potables were more easily conveyed and smuggled. *Esquire* offers a recipe for the "Old-Fashioned" as a "bonafide classic."¹¹ Simonson lists "the Old-fashioned—like the Martini, the Manhattan, and a few other drinks too good to completely vanish from American drinkers' drams—as one of the few classic cocktails that survived the drought. Indeed, it seemed to have gained currency during its long absence."[12]

THE LYRICAL RETRO-PRESENTIST COCKTAIL

In the twentieth century, the old-fashioned became a lyrical favorite. Its name evoked cocktail culture in general. After prohibition, the "Old-Fashioned" reappears in two songs sung by Broadway chanteuses. Ruby Keeler sang the first, "A Good Old Fashioned Cocktail (With a Good Old Fashioned Girl)," written by Al Dubin and Harry Warren and featured in the film *Go Into Your Dance*, from 1935.[13] Porter's lyrics to the 1940 "Make It Another Old-Fashioned, Please" characterize the old-fashioned as the drink that, disassembled, reflects the emotional state of poor Panama Hattie (played by Ethel Merman) in *Panama Hattie*.[14] The old-fashioned's components represent an anatomy of happiness and despair, becoming the symbol of an erstwhile pleasure that was once and will be again, its present referring to its past and its past re-evoked by its present. It is the cocktail that, in reappearing, always links the contemporary to history, both in characters' lives and in the larger culture.

The "old-fashioned" is now, in the present, as it was in the present of the 1940 *Panama Hattie*. Retro par excellence, the old-fashioned connotes the return of pure quality produced by the utter simplicity of distillates and sugar. More than a drink, the old-fashioned is always about the origin of the cocktail itself—as if, every so often, sophisticate culture must go back and start over again. And so Panama Hattie's sad anthem ends with the phrase "straight rye," the pure liquor of the old-fashioned's heart. The old-fashioned's embodiment of this retrospective recycling of past in present, of carrying forward that which only once was because it has reemerged, curiously parallels the careers and styles of both Ethel Merman and Cole Porter. We are the drink we sing about.

"A SHAKE AND A GLEAM AND PLENTY OF SYNCOPATION"

Reviewer Brooks Atkinson described *Panama Hattie* as curiously akin to the eponymous cocktail, "taking pains to present La Merman as a coarse-timbered entertainer with a heart of gold. She knows what to do with a part like that. She rolls through it with the greatest gusto, giving it a shake and a gleam and plenty of syncopation."[15] The star of *Panama Hattie*, the show that features Porter's song "Make It Another Old-Fashioned, Please," Ethel Merman had, like the old-fashioned, gained her signature brand by a process of constant retrospection. La Merman is what she is because she always is what she first was, which is, in retrospect, the Merman of Porter's 1934 *Anything Goes*. In the Broadway production of that show, producers cast Merman as leading lady before Porter had returned from a trip to Paris. Deciding he liked the booming songstress who had been thrust upon him—according to Merman his great compliment was "She sounds like a band going by"—Porter eventually wrote five shows specifically for her as female lead.[16]

Panama Hattie, a musical with music and lyrics by Cole Porter, premiered on Broadway in October 1940, lasting for 501 performances.[17] Set in a nightclub in Panama, the show is a tangled web of naval love triangles, class issues, spy plots, and an eight-year-old girl, some of which are organized by reference to the cocktail. The play's elaborate plottings gradually resolve themselves from the ridiculously complex to an exhausted simplicity. Hattie, a nightclub owner, is in love with a wealthy, divorced naval officer, Nick Bullitt, who has an eight-year-old daughter, Jerry. Trying to make a good impression on the daughter, the working-class Hattie buys an elaborately gewgawed outfit, which Jerry then ridicules. Hattie's rival for Nick, the admiral's offspring, Kitty-Belle, encourages Jerry's disdain for Hattie. In the meantime, Nick tries to get Jerry to like Hattie and, in the first of many distillations, Jerry advises Hattie to cut the frills off her dress and instructs her in the finer arts of being upper-class. Asked to present the admiral with a loving cup, Hattie brings it to him filled with jealous Kitty-Belle's floral tribute: goldenrod. The admiral has a severe allergic reaction and forbids Nick's marriage to Hattie.

In the second act, sailors discover that saboteurs intend to bomb the ship, *U.S.S. Idaho*, docked in the Canal Zone. Hattie and Kitty-Belle confront one another, flailing in a fisticuffs manqué. Hattie then meets with the sailors and discovers that Kitty-Belle's best friend, Mildred, is one of the saboteurs who has given Jerry a package to place on Nick's desk in the Panama Canal control room. Hattie overhears the bomb plot, finds the bomb, and throws it out just in time. The admiral permits Nick to marry her and all ends up well for Hattie.

What all of this plotting has to do with cocktails might seem far-fetched, except that two of the show's sixteen Porter songs track plot elements precisely with the cocktail—in fact, with the cocktail's disassembly. The first act's number "I've Still Got My Health" accompanies Hattie's drunken binge after she has been ridiculed by juvenile Jerry, and the song describes Hattie's state of affairs when her life has been stripped back to merely "her health." Drinking, however, accompanies the intensity of Hattie's complex and disappointing triangulations in the second act song "Make It Another Old-Fashioned, Please." Signaling the show's incipient distillations, and coming at the top of a run of dénouements, the song's lyrics strip the old-fashioned cocktail down to the "rye," paralleling the "crash" of Hattie's romantic aspirations. Left by itself, alone, quintessential, the rye is both consolation and survivor, the rock bottom of the rocks glass—or more accurately, the "old-fashioned glass."

Paired with one of his favorite songstresses, Porter's musicals with their lithe references to the beverages of the sophisticates (and, in the case of some of Merman's characters—Panama Hattie, for one—some not so sophisticated) limn the fashionable details of high society's intoxicant accessories. Not his first musical, but certainly his first notable American attempt, *Anything Goes* (which precedes *Panama Hattie* by six years), commences Porter's counter- and then post-Prohibition parallels between alcohol and the vagaries of romance. In Porter's lyrics, cocktails and wines are as much a part of a class environment as clothing, jewelry, food, and music. *Anything Goes*'s "I Get a Kick Out of You" denies the uplifting effects of champagne. "You're the Top" compares the loved one to a specific kind of brandy, while the 1939 *Du Barry Was a Lady*'s "Well, Did You Evah" regales the socially tragic with its lists of refreshments. *Panama Hattie*'s "Make It Another Old-Fashioned, Please" and 1941's *Let's Face It!*, with its hyperbolic references to the quaffing capacities of celebrities, incarnate the ways that Porter's clever lyrics themselves imbibe high society's alcoholic self-definition.[18] As "Katie Went to Haiti" (from *Du Barry Was a Lady*) turns into *Panama Hattie*, so Porter's clever re-articulation of libation terminology (and could one find a drier way to express his juiciness?) itself often refers back to Porter's own oeuvre, deploying a lexicon of spirit references as a shorthand. In the 1941 Porter musical *Let's Face It!*, running contemporaneously with *Panama Hattie* (and starring Danny Kaye, Eve Arden, and Vivian Vance), the song "Let's Not Talk About Love" is rife with references to both the quality and the quantity of distillates and potables.[19]

Like Porter's songs—and like the irrepressible old-fashioned—Merman reappears from one Porter show to another. Because Merman had already had a certain success before *Anything Goes* (appearing, for example, in the Gershwin brothers' *Girl Crazy* in 1930; *George White's Scandals*, a revue in 1931; and the 1932 musical *Take a Chance*), like the old-fashioned, she, perforce, was always already there. Her appearances in five of Porter's shows reprise one another, as each of the four ensuing shows Porter wrote for her refers back in some way to previous shows. The 1936 *Red, Hot and Blue* (in which she sang the duet "It's De-Lovely" with Bob Hope) followed *Anything Goes*. *Panama Hattie* was the third after Porter's 1939 entry, *Du Barry Was a Lady*, which ran for 408 performances.[20] Merman herself noted that the character Panama Hattie had already appeared in *Du Barry Was a Lady* in the song "Katie Went to Haiti" sung by Merman in her dream guise as Madame Du Barry. *Panama Hattie*, like the old-fashioned, seems already familiar because it had already existed. She appeared in Porter's 1941 *Let's Face It!* (with its exuberant hints at feats of tippling) and his 1943 musical *Something for the Boys*, about which *Life* magazine commented, "From start to finish the show belongs to the exuberant Ethel Merman."[21]

And like the old-fashioned, and Porter's designated chanteuse hitter, Porter's songs often reappeared in a different later show that refers back to an earlier show. *Du Barry Was a Lady*'s song "Well, Did You Evah," another paean to alcohol, performed on Broadway by Betty Grable and Charles Walters, reappears in the 1956 MGM film musical *High Society*, with music by Cole Porter and directed by the same Charles Walters who played the character Norton in the Broadway production of *Du Barry Was a Lady*.[22] *High Society* itself refers back to a previous film, the 1940 *Philadelphia Story*, which was itself the filmed version of Philip Barry's 1939 play *The Philadelphia Story*.[23] *The Philadelphia Story*, as both play and film, is also about a regression to a previous state of affairs in which a divorcée, Tracy Lord (Katherine Hepburn), engaged to be married to someone else, ends up remarrying her original spouse, C. K. Dexter-Haven (Cary Grant). When she remarries her earlier spouse, Tracy Lord's future looks to the past, reprising, like the old-fashioned and the film itself, a previously existing text, which is reprised again sixteen years later in *High Society*. *High Society*'s "original" musical track by Cole Porter was his first film soundtrack since 1948 (according to a 1956 *Time* magazine review), though it contains, yet again, the recycled retrospective 1939 tune "Well, Did You Evah," from *Du Barry Was a Lady*, this time as a duet performed by Bing Crosby and Frank Sinatra.[24] This song was indeed original to a movie soundtrack as it had been omitted from the 1943 film version of *Du Barry Was a Lady*, in which Ethel Merman had been replaced with Lucille Ball.[25]

OLD FASHIONED REPRISE

Like the old-fashioned that appears as if from an earlier time to import classical taste into society, *High Society* moves *The Philadelphia Story* to Newport, Rhode Island, replete with large mansions conveniently espied in an aerial introduction. The film also transmutes *The Philadelphia Story* into a musical in which two of leading lady Tracy Lord's (Grace Kelly) suitors are now crooners. The alcohol in this film functions as both an accessory of high style and a catalyst that pushes Tracy to the right decision. Champagne is the provocateur;

matudinal whiskey is the cure-all. But alcohol in this film recalls the earlier versions of both the story and the central song, which is itself about alcoholic overindulgence. The film is what it is because it returns to that which was before, as the retro reemerges as the answer to the dilemmas the plot poses. Dexter-Haven's sophistication in 1956 is linked not only to his casual wear and easy singing style, but also to his appreciation of jazz. Although Tracy is set to marry the humorless and nonmusical nouveau riche mining tycoon George, the film focuses on two other suitors, situating George as the hapless straight man. One suitor, her wealthy ex-spouse C. K. Dexter-Haven (Bing Crosby), evinces the quiet sophistication of the lucky heir, a jazz aficionado who still lives in his own giant mansion next door to the Lords. A sponsor of the Newport Jazz Festival, Haven is hosting Louis Armstrong's jazz sextet at his home (in fact, Armstrong serves as the film's frame narrator). Calm, cool, philosophical, Dexter-Haven drinks but is never inebriated. His drinking is a stylistic statement just like his brown and white spectator shoes and casual suit. He is still in love with his ex-wife.

The other crooner is the journalist MacCauley "Mike" Connor (Frank Sinatra), foisted on the Lords to report the wedding by a small incident of blackmail involving Tracy Lord's father's marital infidelities. Connor, whose own father was a "high school English History teacher," is rougher and much less comfortable among Newport's elite. He usually treats his assignment professionally, with only a few lapses, such as when he noses into the accrued wedding gifts or wanders where he doesn't belong. Like Dexter-Haven, Mike falls for Tracy Lord, but his tryst with her follows an evening of champagne quaffing at George and Tracy's prenuptial party. While Tracy becomes too inebriated to do anything but lounge around on her guests, so that the humorless George forces her to take a nap, Dexter-Haven and Connor forage in their host's library bar for more champagne, as they sing the duet "Well, Did You Evah," a song whose lyrics describe in Porter's typically clever terms a series of alcoholic mishaps. The duet marks the suitors' transition from accepting bystanders to Connor's poolside wooing of Tracy, who has climbed out the window of the room in which George has imprisoned her. Drinking yet more champagne, Tracy and Connor dance and kiss. When Tracy falls into the pool, she suddenly awakens to her condition and Connor carries her back to the house. On the way they encounter her now-enraged fiancé, who, being a man of high scruple, worries over whether marriage to Tracy is the right thing, given her loose character.

All is resolved over "hair-of-the-dog" drinks the next morning, as Connor, Dexter-Haven, and Tracy imbibe whiskey toddies. Confronted by a sleepless George, who decides he can forgive Tracy's one trampy lapse, Tracy decides she no longer wants to marry him. Connor wisely sees that the previous evening was, in fact, only the effect of alcohol. As Tracy announces the wedding's cancellation to her gathered guests, Dexter-Haven suggests that they tie the knot they had failed to tie in a wedding ceremony the first time (they had eloped).

RETRO-SOPHISTICATION: CROONING SOPHISTICATES TURN INTO WOOING PUBLICISTS

The dapper late-1950s drinking duet of Crosby and Sinatra brings us forward to the twenty-first century's retrospective on 1960s cocktail culture as depicted in the studiously nostalgic series *Mad Men* (2007–2015).[26] Whetting the series' 1960s-style bona fides, the old-fashioned is the signature drink, appearing repeatedly in its eponymous chubby, straight-sided glass in the hands of protagonist and style-setter, adman Don Draper (Jon Hamm). "Don Draper" is not his real name, but a name he took from a dead war buddy so as simultaneously to be sent home and to hide his former identity. Draper, thus, returns from the Pacific as someone he never was, but as yet again the same persona simply renamed "Don Draper." Like the old-fashioned, the newly dubbed Don takes this second chance as an opportunity to refashion himself into a much more stylish and urbane individual, which enables him to emerge on Madison Avenue as the epitome of sleek and dapper manliness.

As the series opens, Don is the Creative Director of the successful advertising agency, Sterling Cooper. Along with firm partners Bertram Cooper (Robert Morse) and Roger Sterling (John Slattery), Don oversees the advertising campaigns of a series of early 1960s corporations, from big tobacco to airlines. Tracking Don's life from the office to the formation of a new advertising firm to his home, divorce, and remarriage, the series persistently suggests the emptiness that contrived personal and corporate image-making strives to obscure. Don's version of the old-fashioned-imbibing exec has a seedier parallel in Sterling, the son of one of the firm's founders, whose excessive drinking (despite two heart attacks) and tacky womanizing distract him from business. Original founding partner Cooper's wise restraint relies in part upon his own earlier experience as an adman who indulged in the same vices as his junior associates. Cooper, like Draper, is living his second chance, while Sterling seems to be wasting his third.

Robert Morse, who plays Cooper, himself represents the 1960s past—and its specific style of executive cocktail-quaffing executive—as Morse starred in the 1967 film *A Guide for the Married Man* and also in the Broadway play (1961) and film (1967) about an advertising agency, *How to Succeed in Business Without*

Really Trying. Casting Morse as yet again an adman iterates the old-fashioned's dynamic of reappearing as that which had already appeared. This dynamic also applies to the series itself, which began as a script written by show originator Matthew Weiner ten years before *Mad Men*'s 2007 premiere. According to the *New York Times*, Weiner sent the script, written while he was a staff writer for the series *Becker*, to David Chase, the creator and producer of *The Sopranos* (1999–2007), who liked the work so much that he hired Weiner as a writer on *The Sopranos* (Weiner wrote twelve *Sopranos* episodes).[27] Although HBO did not pick up *Mad Men*, AMC wisely did the year *The Sopranos* aired its final episode.

Mad Men, a retro show credited with popularizing a revival of retro cocktails, evokes 1960s style both as a moment of manly sophistication and as the origin of the twisted corporatism of contemporary, postglobal commerce. Although, as Alex Witchel reports, some "real" admen of the period deny the alcohol-soaked lifestyle of *Mad Men*'s execs, others suggest that the cocktail lunches, bigotry, and sexism were, in fact, quite typical—as is the show's emphasis on style: both the style of the filming and the details of set and costume. The show's characters "are," as Witchel paraphrases Weiner, "not movie stars; they are the people who go to the movies and try to emulate movie stars."[28] As Weiner himself comments, "I'm against clean and glamorous, . . . I like to respect the popular culture, mass production and also people's eccentricities. The temptation is to become Mannerist. People have old things and new things, and as someone who loves the period, it's very hard to resist the idea of getting the perfect 1960 everything, but I want it to feel like a slice of life."[29] This "slice of life" then reappears like a ghost from the past, anew as it was, but existing because at one point in time it had existed already.

As Don Draper's favorite cocktail, the old-fashioned never stops representing the revival of the forgotten. As even a *Wikipedia* entry notes, "The Old Fashioned is the cocktail of choice of Don Draper, the lead character on the *Mad Men* television series, set in the 1960s. The drink was well known in the 1960s, but was nearly forgotten at the time of the series' premiere in 2007."[30] As another *New York Times* article elaborates in 2012, "In the 1960s, when the series takes place, that cocktail was commonplace. By 2000, however, it had fallen into relative obscurity. 'Twelve years ago, it was nowhere,' the cocktail historian David Wondrich said. 'You could go into an old-man bar, and if you insisted, they would make you one.'"[31]

Cocktail aficionados also credit *Mad Men* with either catalyzing or participating in a general revival of cocktail culture in the aughts. As the *New York Times* comments,

The arrival of 'Mad Men' dovetailed with the resurgence of this grand old cocktail, as mixologists and laymen alike reclaimed the potion and held it aloft like an artifact from a lost, great civilization. 'The old-fashioned has been a touchstone of the cocktail movement the last 10 years,' said Robert Hess, a drinks author and old-fashioned fanatic whose Web site, DrinkBoy, helped to generate turn-of-the-twenty-first-century online discussions about the drink.[32]

The *Esquire* website's database gives David Wondrich's (also their resident "cocktail historian") recipe for the drink, also linking it to *Mad Men*, as does AMC's online "*Mad Men* Cocktail Guide."[33] The "badassdigest" site offers another analysis of the *Mad Men*'s old-fashioned, describing a moment during Season 3, episode 3, where Don "leaps over a bar and prepares an Old-fashioned for himself and Conrad Hilton." As the website comments, "It's an expression of masculinity and capability, a Master of the Universe moment. The only problem is that the drink he makes isn't really an Old Fashioned. It's a bastardized version, popular in the 1960s, and a pale imitation of the real thing that has stubbornly persisted as the 'right way' to make an Old Fashioned."[34]

THE RIGHT RETRO

Somehow *Mad Men*'s re-evocation of the drink that had been previously re-invoked multiple times produces a small crisis in the question of what is the "right way" to make an old-fashioned, or whether there even is a "right way" to make a drink unless somehow that right way itself refers to the cocktail's now mythical past. "Right" yet again refers to a before that only emerges as itself after. The problem is that the old-fashioned fronts a plethora of recipes, which themselves suggest not a reappearance or a revival, but a gradual and very muddled evolutionary survival. The old-fashioned doesn't suddenly reappear in a time loop, but resurfaces when the style is right.

Most recently, the internet has offered generous mixology advice about the old-fashioned. The AMC *Mad Men* website offers the following recipe:

Old Fashioned
1 cherry
1 orange slice
1 lemon wedge
2 dashes aromatic bitters
1/2 tsp sugar dissolved with water and bitters
1 1/2 oz bourbon

Fill glass with ice. Add cherry, orange slice, and lemon wedge. Pour in bourbon. Serve in a rocks glass over ice.[35]

On the *Esquire* site, David Wondrich gives a completely different recipe:

Old-Fashioned
1 sugar cube
3 dashes Angostura bitters
Club soda
2 oz rye whiskey

> Place the sugar cube (or 1/2 teaspoon loose sugar) in an old-fashioned glass. Wet it down with 2 or 3 dashes of Angostura bitters and a short splash of water or club soda. Crush the sugar with a wooden muddler, chopstick, strong spoon, lipstick, cartridge case, whatever. Rotate the glass so that the sugar grains and bitters give it a lining. Add a large ice cube. Pour in the rye (or bourbon). Serve with a stirring rod.[36]

Bill Norris, on the website Birth. Movies. Death., reports yet a third recipe:

A Recipe
2 oz Rittenhouse Bonded Rye (or your spirit of choice)
1/2 oz rich simple syrup
3 dashes Angostura bitters

> In an old-fashioned glass, combine rye, simple syrup, and bitters, add a large ice cube or two and stir until quite cold. Cut a swath of peel from a lemon or orange and express the oils over the glass, dropping the peel inside the glass for garnish.[37]

The old-fashioned is, apparently, never quite *the* old-fashioned. Or the old-fashioned itself is always the revival of an imaginary ur-cocktail that never is what it appears to have been when it reappears as its earlier self. No one even spells the drink's name the same way. Albert W. A. Schmid's book on the old-fashioned, *The Old Fashioned* (notice the absence of the hyphen) offers numerous recipes for the old-fashioned, which as Schmid demonstrates was always a cocktail that referred to an earlier cocktail, ending/commencing at a fantasmatic moment when, whatever the old-fashioned cocktail was, it was stirred with a literal cock's tail. Robert Simonson's book *The Old-Fashioned* also offers numerous recipes. Simonson's book is itself a reappearance of sorts, published a year after Schmid's.

So in the 2000s, *Mad Men* set in the 1960s re-evokes the 1940s cocktail fashion of *Panama Hattie,* which featured the torch song "Make It Another Old-Fashioned, Please." The title of Porter's song is itself already announcing the drink's redundancy. The old-fashioned cocktail that is now is only now because it was then (in the 1960s and the 1940s and the 1860s, back to 1806), was what it was and is what it is because it has always represented a nostalgic version of a purer cocktail. Because by definition a cocktail itself is neither "pure" nor "neat," these cyclical revisitations to early, simpler versions enact not the neatness of the old days, but how the origin itself is never pure—and, hackneyed as this is, how one can never go back. No old-fashioned is *the old* old-fashioned. As *Panama Hattie*'s amorous dilemmas demonstrate, no retro cocktail can ever assume the position it once occupied. No cocktail can ever revive innocence. That we want to revisit that unadorned moment of pure spirits, distill back to it, and clean ourselves up with it presents not a clean pleasure, but the entanglements of an ambivalent past: the moment that initiated the downfall of things—of romance, society, culture, taste, and innocence.

So Porter's lyrics strip away the elements of the old-fashioned—the fruit, the bitters—back to the "straight rye" which are the last two words of the song. Curiously, almost every online source for the song's lyrics misquotes the song's last word, mostly because, I suspect, they are not returning to the original sheet music, but instead are copying the lyrics from a copyright-infringing website (itself, as many sites are on the now folkloric web, copied by others), which scribes the last word of the lyrics as "right": "Make it a straight right."[38] Of course, this makes no sense and derives probably from someone transcribing a recording of Merman's version of the song, in which the last word (if one knew absolutely nothing about the old-fashioned) could sound like "right." But in the world of the old-fashioned, the last word, as was the first, is "rye."

Rice University

NOTES

1. Cole Porter, *The Cole Porter Song Collection: Piano/Vocal/Chords*, vol. 2 (1937–1958) (Miami, NY: Alfred Publishing Company, 2009).

2. In his tome on the old-fashioned, Albert W. A. Schmid describes the early "Whiskey drink" stirred with a cock's tail: *The Old Fashioned: An Essential Guide to the Original Whiskey Cocktail* (Lexington: University Press of Kentucky, 2013), 6.

3. Both Schmid and Robert Simonson, in his book *The Old-Fashioned: The Story of the World's First Classic Cocktail, with Recipes and Lore* (New York: Ten Speed Press, 2014), quote the newspaper recipe.

4. In their books, both Schmid and Simonson offer histories of distillates in early-nineteenth-century America.

5. Simonson, *The Old-Fashioned*, 12.

6. Simonson, *The Old-Fashioned*, 12.

7. Schmid cites David Wondrich's discovery of the *Chicago Tribune* article on page 12, but bypasses it in favor of the Pendennis Club account. Robert Simonson traces the Chicago reference back to the *Bartender's Manual*, written by

Theodore Proulx, who worked at several Chicago bars after the Civil War. See Schmid, *The Old Fashioned*, 28.

8. This is primarily Schmid's account, 12–13. Simonson spends two pages trying to debunk the Pendennis Club origin, 40–41.

9. Simonson, *The Old-Fashioned*, 36–37.

10. Simonson, *The Old-Fashioned*, 12.

11. Sarah Rens, "How to Make the Best Old Fashioned Cocktail," *Esquire*, February 8, 2019, https://www.esquire.com/food-drink/drinks/recipes/a3880/old-fashioned-drink-recipe/.

12. Simonson, *The Old-Fashioned*, 44.

13. Simonson, *The Old-Fashioned*, 47, mentions the song.

14. "*Panama Hattie*: Original Broadway Production," Sondheim Guide, http://www.sondheimguide.com/porter/panama.html; see also Ethel Merman and George Eells, *Merman: An Autobiography* (New York: Simon & Schuster, 1978), 303–5; William McBrien, *Cole Porter* (New York: Vintage, 1998), 241–43; and "*Panama Hattie*," Wikipedia, http://en.wikipedia.org/wiki/Panama_Hattie.

15. Brooks Atkinson, "The Play: 'Panama Hattie,'" *New York Times*, October 31, 1940, http://www.nytimes.com/books/98/11/29/specials/porter-hattie.html.

16. See Merman and Eells, *Merman: An Autobiography*, 69–77, esp. 72.

17. "*Panama Hattie*: Original Broadway Production," Sondheim Guide, http://www.sondheimguide.com/porter/panama.html.

18. For Porter's lyrics, see Cole Porter, *The Cole Porter Song Collection: Piano/Vocal/Chords*, vols. 1 (1912–1936) and 2 (1937–1958) (Van Nuys, CA: Alfred Publishing Company, 2009).

19. William McBrien, *Cole Porter* (New York: Vintage, 1998), 245–48.

20. See, generally, Merman and Eells, *Merman: An Autobiography*.

21. "Something for the Boys" (review), *Life* (February 8, 1943): 79, 81–82, http://books.google.com/books?id=a1EEAAAAMBAJ&pg=PA79&lpg=PA79&dq=%22Ethel+Merman%22+%22Something+for+the+Boys%22&source=bl&ots=jUo6rTFGR6&sig=Co7dkOL74O206-j2O_dloISOXFs&hl=en#v=onepage&q=%22Ethel%20Merman%22%20%22Something%20for%20the%20Boys%22&f=false.

22. *High Society*, Internet Movie Database (IMDb), http://www.imdb.com/title/tt0049314/?ref_=fn_al_tt_1.

23. This summary is from "*The Philadelphia Story* (film)," Wikipedia, http://en.wikipedia.org/wiki/The_Philadelphia_Story_(film).

24. Bosley Crowther, "Screen: No 'Philadelphia Story,' This; 'High Society' Lacks Hepburn Sparkle: Sinatra Crosby, Grace Kelly Are Starred," *New York Times*, August 10, 1956, https://www.nytimes.com/1956/08/10/archives/screen-no-philadelphia-story-this-high-society-lacks-hepburn.html.

25. "Du Barry Was a Lady," IMDb, https://www.imdb.com/title/tt0035829/?ref_=fn_al_tt_1.

26. *Mad Men*, created by Matthew Weiner, produced by Lionsgate Television, aired 2007–2015, on AMC.

27. Alex Witchel, "*Mad Men* Has Its Moment," *New York Times Magazine*, June 22, 2008, http://www.nytimes.com/2008/06/22/magazine/22madmen-t.html.

28. Witchel, "*Mad Men* Has Its Moment." Simonson credits *Mad Men* with "helping the rise of the old-fashioned along," 59.

29. Matthew Weiner, quoted in Witchel, "*Mad Men* Has Its Moment."

30. "Old Fashioned (cocktail)," *Wikipedia*, https://en.wikipedia.org/wiki/Old_fashioned_(cocktail).

31. Robert Simonson, "Old-Fashioned or Newfangled, the Old-Fashioned Is Back," *New York Times*, March 20, 2012, http://www.nytimes.com/2012/03/21/dining/the-old-fashioned-don-drapers-cocktail-of-choice.html.

32. Simonson, "Old-Fashioned or Newfangled."

33. Elizabeth Gunnison Dunn, "A Brief History of the Old-Fashioned," *Esquire*, March 21, 2012, https://www.esquire.com/food-drink/drinks/a13315/mad-men-old-fashioned-7492773/. and "Cocktail Guide: Old Fashioned," AMC, https://www.amc.com/shows/mad-men/exclusives/cocktail-guide-old-fashioned.

34. Bill Norris, "Cocktails with *Mad Men*: The Old Fashioned," Birth. Movies. Death., April 22, 2012, https://birthmoviesdeath.com/2012/04/22/cocktails-with-mad-men-the-old-fashioned.

35. "Cocktail Guide: Old Fashioned."

36. "How to Make an Old-Fashioned."

37. Norris, "Cocktails with *Mad Men*."

38. "Make It Another Old-Fashioned, Please," TheInternationalLyricsPlayground.com, http://lyricsplayground.com/alpha/songs/m/makeitanotheroldfashionedplease.shtml; "Make It Another Old-Fashioned, Please," LyricsMania.com, (http://www.lyricsmania.com/make_it_another_old-fashioned,_please_lyrics_ethel_merman.html); "Make It Another Old-Fashioned, Please," http://www.lyrics.net/lyric/21008328; and even Albert Schmid's book all offer the incorrect last word. *The Cole Porter Song Collection*, vol. 2: 1937–1958, however, a tome sanctioned for publication, cites the song's final word as "rye."

BIBLIOGRAPHY

Atkinson, Brooks. "The Play: 'Panama Hattie.'" *New York Times*. October 31, 1940. http://www.nytimes.com/books/98/11/29/specials/porter-hattie.html.

"Cocktail Guide: Old Fashioned." AMC. https://www.amc.com/shows/mad-men/exclusives/cocktail-guide-old-fashioned.

Crowther, Bosley. "Screen: No 'Philadelphia Story,' This; 'High Society' Lacks Hepburn Sparkle: Sinatra, Crosby, Grace Kelly Are Starred." *New York Times*. August 10, 1956. https://www.nytimes.com/1956/08/10/archives/screen-no-philadelphia-story-this-high-society-lacks-hepburn.html.

Du Barry Was a Lady. Internet Movie Database (IMDb). Accessed July 27, 2018. https://www.imdb.com/title/tt0035829/?ref_=fn_al_tt_1.

Dunn, Elizabeth. "A Brief History of the Old-Fashioned," *Esquire*, March 21, 2012 https://www.esquire.com/food-drink/drinks/a13315/mad-men-old-fashioned-7492773/.

High Society. IMDb. Accessed July 27, 2018. http://www.imdb.com/title/tt0049314/?ref_=fn_al_tt_1.

Mad Men. Created by Matthew Weiner. Produced by Lionsgate Television. Aired 2007–2015, on AMC.

"Make It Another Old-Fashioned, Please." LyricsMania. http://www.lyricsmania.com/make_it_another_old-fashioned,_please_lyrics_ethel_merman.html.

"Make It Another Old-Fashioned, Please." Lyrics.net. http://www.lyrics.net/lyric/21008328.

McBrien, William. *Cole Porter*. New York: Vintage, 2000.

Merman, Ethel, and George Eells. *Merman: An Autobiography*. New York: Simon & Schuster, 1978.

Norris, Bill. "Cocktails with *Mad Men*: The Old Fashioned." Birth. Movies. Death. April 22, 2012. https://birthmoviesdeath.com/2012/04/22/cocktails-with-mad-men-the-old-fashioned.

"Old Fashioned (cocktail)." *Wikipedia*. https://en.wikipedia.org/wiki/Old_fashioned_(cocktail).

Panama Hattie: Original Broadway Production. Sondheim Guide. http://www.sondheimguide.com/porter/panama.html.

"Panama Hattie." *Wikipedia*. http://en.wikipedia.org/wiki/Panama_Hattie.

"*The Philadelphia Story* (film)." *Wikipedia*. http://en.wikipedia.org/wiki/The_Philadelphia_Story_(film).

Porter, Cole. *The Cole Porter Song Collection: Piano/Vocal/Chords*. Vols. 1 (1912–1936) and 2 (1937–1958). Van Nuys, CA: Alfred Music Publishing, 2009.

Rens, Sarah. "How to Make the Best Old Fashioned Cocktail." *Esquire*. February 8, 2019. https://www.esquire.com/food-drink/drinks/recipes/a3880/old-fashioned-drink-recipe/.

Schmid, Albert W. A. *The Old Fashioned: An Essential Guide to the Original Whiskey Cocktail*. Lexington: University of Kentucky Press, 2013.

Simonson, Robert. "Old-Fashioned or Newfangled, the Old-Fashioned Is Back." *New York Times*. March 20, 2012. http://www.nytimes.com/2012/03/21/dining/the-old-fashioned-don-drapers-cocktail-of-choice.html.

Simonson, Robert. *The Old-Fashioned: The Story of the World's First Classic Cocktail, with Recipes and Lore*. Berkeley, CA: Ten Speed Press, 2014.

"Something for the Boys." *Life*. February 8, 1943. http://books.google.com/books?id=a1EEAAAAMBAJ&pg=PA79&lpg=PA79&dq=%22Ethel+Merman%22+%22Something+for+the+Boys%22&source=bl&ots=jU06rTFGR6&sig=Co7dkOL74O206-j2O_dloISOXFs&hl=en#v=onepage&q=%22Ethel%20Merman%22%20%22Something%20for%20the%20Boys%22&f=false.

Witchel, Alex. "*Mad Men* Has Its Moment." *New York Times Magazine*. June 22, 2008. http://www.nytimes.com/2008/06/22/magazine/22madmen-t.html.

EIGHTEEN

THE MANHATTAN

EDWARD P. COMENTALE

THE MANHATTAN HAS ALWAYS BEEN an aspirational cocktail. Like the city from which it takes its name, it towers above all others in the cocktail drinker's imagination. Even its iconic tall-stemmed glass presents itself as something for the drinker—like some barside Gatsby or harried King Kong—to climb. Almost all new drinkers see it as a personal challenge, a distinctly formidable beverage that demands maturity and class. Ordering and enjoying one marks the tippler as knowing and sophisticated, as having reached a standing and station in life. For star restaurateur John DeLucie, the drink marked his very entrance to adulthood: "The first time I had a Manhattan, I was in my early 20s at an opulent wedding. I was drinking an iced tea and a much older man said, 'You ought to drink a man's drink,' and gave me a Manhattan."[1]

Part of the drink's aspirational status is merely culinary: the cocktail's over-rich flavor can be appreciated only by a developed palate. But it is also deeply cultural: the drink's association with the Empire State and the opulent hotels of the Gilded Age still provide it with an aura and impossible allure (see fig. 18.1). Above all this, though, the manhattan's mark of distinction is baldly economic. Still one of the most expensive drinks on the bar menu, the manhattan very quickly calculates the difference between not just youth and age, but also poor and rich. Even today, nearly 150 years after its invention, the drink carries significantly restrictive class associations. Ask any bartender to describe the costumer who orders a manhattan, and you'll hear about "confidence" and "class," "knowledge," "suaveness," and "sophistication." As Duggan McDonnell of Cantita Bebides puts it, "The Manhattan is the cocktail that every grown man comes of age upon; it is the drink that brings his drinking palate, his social awareness, his willingness to spend and entertain into maturity."[2]

Figure 18.1. 1934 Spring Garden Rye Manhattan Cocktail Advertisement.

Not surprisingly, then, the manhattan is also a cocktail for jerks. It first rose to prominence in the rich social clubs of Manhattan in the 1880s as an alternative to wine, sherry, brandy, or straight whiskey. In fact, often associated with the early "Manhattan *Club* Cocktail,"[3] its wealthy original drinkers demanded not just rye, but barrel-aged rye, as well as vermouth—from Italy, of course—as well as cracked ice and some fresh fruit on the side.[4] All of this made the cocktail one of the fussiest and most extravagant culinary commodities of its day. It was the drink of choice for the ultraconservative Bourbon Democrats, arrogant fops from down South who still, after the Civil War, continued to favor limited government, absolute free trade, the gold standard, and slavery. Magnate and monopolizer J. P. Morgan is rumored to have had a manhattan delivered to him on a silver platter each day at the end of trading on Wall Street. George F. Babbitt, Sinclair Lewis's fictional avatar of middle-class conformity and soul-deadening suburbia, mixes manhattans by the pitcherful for his neighbors and business partners.[5] Throughout its history, the manhattan has been the drink of the chum, the corporate man, the bureaucrat, fit for swanky hotels and boardrooms. It is a totem and badge of clubby belonging, marking the drinker as not just a man of means, but also "one of us" or "one of the boys" (see fig. 18.2). Indeed, as the favored cocktail of the patriarchy, the manhattan is also often gendered as male and dickishly so. Bill Norris, beverage director at Alamo Drafthouse, compares the dangerous fragility of a feminine martini to the potent masculinity of the manhattan, describing the latter as a "suave companion, the older man with impeccable taste, offering its arm and giving entry to the upper echelons and secret backrooms."[6] Similarly, when asked about her preferences for manhattans, actress Piper Perabo described the drink as a "bold, masculine-looking cocktail," one that is "similar to the men I like: really strong, sort of tidy, simple, beautiful and with their hair down."[7]

Given its rich associations, the manhattan seems specifically American, an embodiment of the nation's central myths of self-made success as well as their tragic undoing. If, as David Wondrich asserts, every cocktail offers a "glimpse of a better world," the manhattan makes this claim its central theme and gives it a fatal twist.[8] No doubt, it's an expensive and rich cocktail, but it's also a little loud, a tad boastful, quickly oversweet, and maybe—just maybe—trying too hard. If the manhattan is aspiration in a glass, it can also serve as a quick disguise or at least puff up the pedigree of a scoundrel. As a spirited shot of success, it can make any drinker at the bar look like he's going up, even if his fortune is in steady decline. But no matter how it's dressed, the drink can't seem to escape its dark past or at least its poor pedigree. This doubleness is built into its recipe and defines its taste. Two parts whiskey to one part vermouth: the

Figure 18.2. 1954 Heublein's Cocktails Manhattan Liquor Advertisement.

drink's got a whole lotta country and a touch of class. The components can be perfectly mixed, the difference covered over with a few splashes of flashy bitters, but even with the finest ingredients, the taste often feels mysteriously vexed. In a way, the manhattan amplifies the basic contradictions of all American cocktails. As Wondrich explains, the American cocktail is "flashy and a little bit vulgar. It induces unreflective overconfidence. It's democratic, forcing the finest ingredients to rub elbows with ingredients of far more humble stamp."[9]

Tellingly, the manhattan does just as well in the lushest of lounges as in the dingiest of dive bars. It is served to toast success as well as failure, pride as well as calamity. Drinking one is similar to flashing money and then quickly losing it. In other words, the manhattan's split identity—at once rural and cosmopolitan, homegrown and exotic, rebellious and elitist—reflects the split identity of its social-climbing consumers. The drink mirrors the city as the proving ground of uncertain men like Jay Gatsby and Don Draper, the Dark Knight—imposters all.

The manhattan was born of the Gilded Age; it greased the wheels of big industry and watered the infamous trusts. Think top hats and tailcoats, horse-whips and buggies, railroads and steel mills and oil derricks cropping up everywhere. It is an expression of a specifically industrial modernity, an era of advanced wealth, economic disparity, and very conspicuous consumption for an elite few. This is the era of Delmonico's and the hoity-toity Manhattan Club and William "The Only William" Schmidt, a Manhattan barkeep known for his waxed moustaches, flaming drinks, and acrobatic pours. Schmidt's early cocktail recipe book didn't blush at the mixing of drinking and dealing. By 1892, the time of the book's publication, the cocktail had shed most of its medicinal association to become a canny marker of class or the lack thereof. According to Schmidt, "MEN drink to quench thirst" as well as "on account of ambition, to forget poverty, to show their riches." Eying his clients at the bar, he wryly notes, "This one wants to warm himself; that one is overheated and wants to get cool; one has lost in Wall Street; another's shares have gone up.... Some men will drink out of pure style; they want to show their diamonds and jewelry, their costly clothes, and mainly their money. But most men will drink because it is 'business.'"[10]

Here, comparing manhattans and martinis proves useful. The popularity of the manhattan predates that of the martini by a couple of decades, and its age shows most immediately in its fussy list of ingredients, heavier old-world flavors, and darker color palate. The two drinks clearly reflect two very different moments of modernity, the former defined by rapid industrialization, urban expansion, and growing monopolies, the latter by unfettered consumerism, café culture, jazz cool, and the flapper. Drawing upon Lowell Edmunds, we might say that whereas the manhattan represents the opulence and comfort of the established nineteenth-century elite, the martini reflects the urbanity and sophistication of the twentieth-century urban middle class and the clean-cut executive.[11] Edmunds's account offers a further distinction within *modernity as style or form*: the manhattan offers depth, flavor, ornamentation, and a fussy bar service, while the martini touts clean lines and minimal, abstract forms.

One might recall here that the manhattan was originally served in a very different glass than the iconic tall-stemmed martini glass used today. This glass was heavier, fancier, multipaneled, and, with its lower center of gravity, more stable than the flashy angular post that came to dominate the bar culture of the Jazz Age.[12] This distinction certainly accords with Michael Coyle's reading of the modernity of the martini in part 2 of this volume. With the original manhattan, form everywhere exceeded function; with the martini, form is refined down to the near neutrality of its basic grain alcohol and its disappearing glass. Indeed, a manhattan is like the heavily upholstered Morris chair, while the martini recalls a streamlined Wassily chair. The manhattan is a stuffy naturalist novel, with its Darwinian logic of rise and fall, while the martini is an imagist poem, built cleanly with an economy of taste and design. One cocktail asserts the drinker's presence, in all his experience and complexity, while the other asserts his indifference or perhaps even his emptiness.[13]

Arguably, as an invention of the modern economy, all cocktail culture is aspirational, and happy hours everywhere provide a forum for the construction and performance of taste and class.[14] But let's take a step back and track the gentrification of the cocktail as it led to the appearance of the manhattan, for only then can we pinpoint some of these subtler differences and distinctions. David Wondrich provides the most streamlined account of the cocktail's arc of success in America, dividing its evolution into three distinct phases: the archaic (1783), the baroque (1830–1885), and the classic (1885–1920). His account focuses on the development of sporting life in the early nineteenth century and the hedonistic figure of the sport, a man about town who, shirking Victorian canons of industry and responsibility, dedicated his life to fashion, gambling, amusement, and drink. As a form of "sport" or "exploit" (a key word in the discussion below), the earliest cocktail culture appears in saloons, gambling houses, and other questionable settings, and the clientele included a dissolute set of actors, musicians, newspapermen, rounders, and some of the coarser politicians. Theodore Dreiser's turn-of-the-century fiction—with its naturalist reckoning of social class and the trappings of material culture—best captures the nuances of nineteenth-century American modernity. His account of Fitzgerald and Moy's, an upscale Chicago saloon, describes the space as "a bubbling, chattering, glittering chamber" to which a man is "lured as much by his longing for pleasure as by his desire to shine among his betters." For Dreiser, the nineteenth-century saloon—with its rough wooden architecture and clumsy brass ornamentation—inspires the dream of a "better social order," but attracts only a "dressy, greedy company," known primarily by their "small, self-interested palaver" and "disorganized, aimless, wandering mental action."

Without the proper ideals to guide its raffish customers, the saloon remains a "a strange, glittering night-flower, odour-yielding, insect-drawing, insect-infested rose of pleasure."[15]

Such establishments and their largely male and "material-minded" clientele drove the early cocktail industry and set its basic terms, making it—as we'll see—a staging ground for both contest and emulation. Over time, though, as the American economy grew and the wealthy class sought new arenas of distinction, the scene started to shift and attract a new class of diners and drinkers. After the Civil War, with the birth of industry in America and the newly established masses of ready wealth, both cocktails and cocktail culture went upscale. Bartenders began to supplement the rough blend of the basic cocktail—spirit, sugar, water, bitters—with finer products and rarer imported ingredients such as absinthe and vermouth. Ice, in turn, changed everything, setting the bartender free to mix drinks on an individual scale and craft elaborate new formulas for reaching new highs. By the end of the century, drinks had become "fancy drinks," and slowly the scene shifted out of the saloon and into the hotel bars and social clubs. "Ironically," Wondrich writes, "this served to liberate the Cocktail from its louche connotations, as the kind of upper-crust gents who would previously have confined themselves to wine learned to drink manhattans and such—a new, lighter, and simpler breed of cocktails."[16] Gilded Age drinkers, he points out, wanted "something lighter and more urbane than a shot of bittered booze; something more refined and epicurean and with less savor of riverboats and tobacco chaws, bare-knuckle bouts and faro dens."[17]

At this time, too, American whiskey had come out of the woods and began to dominate the bar menu. The war with England had cut off overseas trade as well as the rum supply, while a bug (*phylloxera*) had more recently wiped out the brandy business, so whiskey was now free to dominate the market.[18] Its quality and sales grew exponentially after the Civil War, making it the favorite base spirit in cocktails from coast to coast. New industrial-sized stills balanced out the blends in mass quantities, while interstate trade routes grew more established, and branding practices drove improvements in quality and consistency. At the same time, Italian and French vermouth imports had been on the rise since the 1830s. Vermouth first found traction in the American market as an aperitif, but it slowly established itself on cocktail lists as a new "wonder ingredient," proving a sophisticated alternative to strong liquor.[19] The two ingredients were bound to meet sooner or later in a mixing glass, even if they seemed to come from completely different worlds. Wondrich and other scholars link the manhattan's rise to a curious bifurcation in drinking tastes at this time. The popularity of lighter, more complex drinks built on absinthe and vermouth inspired a reactionary backlash, driving some tipplers toward simpler, more potent brews, such as the nostalgic old-fashioned. An 1893 article in the *New York Herald* outlined the divide as well as its class connotations: "As bartenders developed a hardier spirit of invention, they essayed other liquors than gin and brandy. The whiskey cocktail became a favorite with the grosser palates, the vermouth cocktail established itself as the true preprandial appetizer with gentleman of nice perceptions and delicate tastes."[20] Appearing in the 1880s, the manhattan seemed to split the difference between these two options—stronger than the vermouth cocktail, yet more refined than the old-fashioned. Ultimately, whether it was invented to punch up the former or tone down the latter, this two-faced cocktail hit a sweet spot for an elite class of drinkers in an elite setting.

More specific origin stories for the manhattan are plenty. Even as a desire for historical authenticity drives the contemporary cocktail industry, historical *accuracy* remains a will-o'-the-wisp of most cocktail scholarship. Everyone seems to agree that it's a New York native, born out of the elite city club scene of the 1880s. Some scholars bet on a mysterious barkeep named Black, who mixed drinks at a place on lower Broadway that, to this day, cannot be located on any map. Others point toward the more colorful tale that the drink was invented by Jennie Jerome during an event at the Manhattan Club in honor of Bourbon Democrat Samuel J. Tilden (although more-sober historians are quick to point out that she was in England at the time giving birth to Winston Churchill). Either way, by 1884—the year the drink first appeared in a cocktail manual—its associations with the urban world and the new corporate business classes were firmly established. The swanky Manhattan Club and its kind no doubt suited the drink's upscale allure. These clubs catered to statesmen, politicians, and the up-and-coming industrial business class, providing world-class cuisine, cigars, and cocktails during political gatherings and informal business meetings.[21]

Again, Dreiser provides the best description of this scene and its clientele. Here's Sister Carrie newly arrived in NYC and dining out at Sherry's, one of several elite restaurants that redefined night life for the city's high society:

> The air of assurance and dignity about it all was exceedingly noticeable to the novitiate. Incandescent lights, the reflection of their glow in polished glasses, and the shine of gilt upon the walls, combined into one tone of light which it requires minutes of complacent observation to separate and take particular note of. The white shirt fronts of the gentlemen, the bright costumes of the ladies, diamonds, jewels, fine feathers—all were exceedingly noticeable.... On the walls were designs in colour, square spots of robin's-egg blue, set in

ornate frames of gilt, whose corners were elaborate mouldings of fruit and flowers, with fat cupids hovering in angelic comfort. On the ceilings were coloured traceries with more gilt, leading to a centre where spread a cluster of lights—incandescent globes mingled with glittering prisms and stucco tendrils of gilt. The floor was of a reddish hue, waxed and polished, and in every direction were mirrors—tall, brilliant, bevel-edged mirrors—reflecting and re-reflecting forms, faces, and candelabra a score and a hundred times.[22]

Unlike his account of the saloon, Dreiser's emphasis here is on rich materials and sensual opulence, an amplification and refinement of each detail, all surfaces reflecting back the success and wealth of the diner. A cocktail such as the manhattan only adds to the luster, letting the drinker imbibe his own success, the other diners serving as both audience and appreciators.

And yet this history is not simply linear or progressive. If the manhattan became the established "drink of the substantial man," its central murkiness and ambiguity continued to reflect some of its drinkers' own.[23] The whiskey base is a curious one, given its deep associations with the backwoods rebelliousness of the Scotch-Irish who perfected its distillation. In his excellent history of the bourbon industry, Reid Mitenbuler outlines the spirit's connection to the values of the American frontier: individualism, self-sufficiency, practicality, and guts. Given whiskey's place in the nation's movement west and its fight for independence, Mitenbuler explains, the liquor quickly established itself in the national imaginary as an anti-elitist, anti-royal alternative to wine and other European liquors, a patriotic working-class piss-off that, with just one shot, established the drinker's native spirit and strength.[24] Basically, American whiskey took up the associations of health, strength, and vitality that defined aqua vitae and corned them up for an American bar crowd. John Barleycorn, as reflected in Robert Burns's famous poem, became the basis of a new nativist spirit:

And they hae taen his very heart's blood,
And drank it round and round;
And still the more and more they drank,
Their joy did more abound.

John Barleycorn was a hero bold,
Of noble enterprise;
For if you do but taste his blood,
'Twill make your courage rise.[25]

We should recall here that the manhattan, with its NYC origins, often used rye instead of bourbon as its base, but these rustic connotations were only focused and strengthened by this shift. Even though whiskey production had been refined and industrialized by the mid-nineteenth century, bringing some respectability to an otherwise rough-hewn spirit, it was still seen as a rough-and-tumble liquor. Its industrialization only amplified the nativist myth by lending it the potency of the machine, the factory, and the American industrial working class (see fig. 18.3). In fact, despite more recent advertisers' efforts to define bourbon as "traditional" and "authentic," Mitenbuler reminds us, the spirit is as much industrial as it is agricultural. Its production might start in the field, but it is quickly overtaken by machines in large, mechanized factories, a process that was perfected in the mid-nineteenth century by scientifically minded distillers. As Mitenbuler claims, "In all parts of the world where whiskey has flourished, it did so in the wake of an Industrial Revolution that transformed economies from agricultural to industrial."[26] The manhattan took all of these connotations into the club room, where it came to reflect something other than both the Old World European aristocracy and the New World's rural poor. It seemed to split the different between past and future, country and city, power and refinement, in a specifically American vein. Adding vermouth, perhaps the most rarefied and expensive ingredient on the barkeep's shelf, to rye or bourbon, the roughest, must have been like putting lipstick on a pig.

More than anything else, this combination reflected the subtle rapaciousness of the country's newly established leisure class. The manhattan rose to fame in the same milieu that was the focus of Thorstein Veblen's 1899 study *The Theory of the Leisure Class*. In this famous critique of the capitalist system, Veblen scandalously defined the modern leisure class as an outgrowth of the barbarian tribes of the past. The rich are sustained, he argued, by a "bellicose frame of mind," a deeply ingrained predatory habit that manifests itself in hostile business takeovers and lavish displays of wealth.[27] Veblen's study focuses on how modern men express their power and dominance over other men. As more traditional arenas for demonstrating prowess, such as war and the hunt, he argues, become unsustainable, the man of esteem seeks out new means of putting success on display—through clothing, accessories, food, property, and his retinue.[28] In other words, all of the seemingly mundane and meaningless activities of the leisure class are driven by an "emulative or invidious comparison of persons," a tireless contest of showy display in which one's success is defined solely against the worth of others.[29] Hence, famously, Veblen outlines the rise of "conspicuous leisure" and "conspicuous consumption." In leisure, wealth is put in evidence for others as the lack or unnecessity of work. The upper crust carries a distinct disdain for any form of labor, so most of their activity is designed

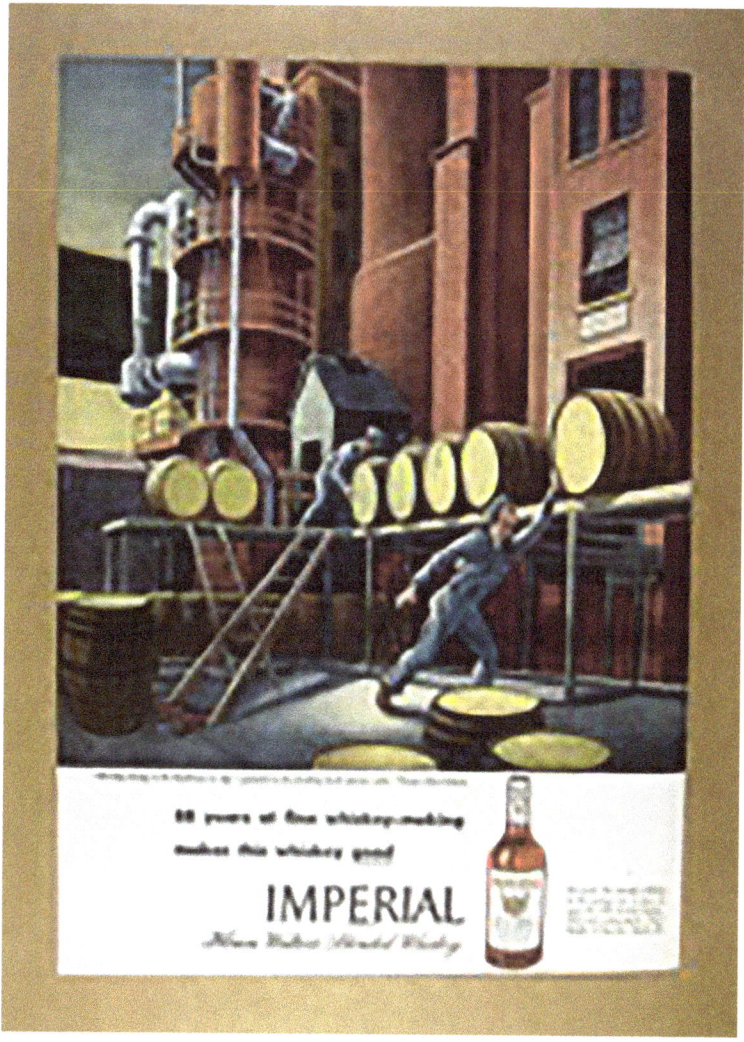

Figure 18.3. Thomas Hart Benton, "Whiskey Going to the Warehouse to Age," 1946 advertisement for Hiram Walker Blended Whiskey.

to show just how much free time they have.[30] Consumption—especially of quality goods—proves just as honorable. The waste of time is accompanied by the waste of commodities—lascivious spending on unnecessary objects and useless ornamentation.[31]

Veblen is more than savvy to the ways in which this logic shapes the cocktail culture of the late nineteenth century. He places spirits and the hotel bar scene at the very center of this study, as the primary arena for conspicuous consumption and leisure. Cocktails such as the manhattan are strictly reserved for use by the leisure class because such drinks are expensive and not necessary for subsistence. The rare ingredients that go into their making—as well as the massive amounts of time spent on aging and shipping them—drastically increase their symbolic value.[32] At the same time, the presence of the barkeep and the bar service—with its showy expenditure of gesture, its crisply folded linens, extra fruit cup, and finely cut glassware and metal tools—augment the display of wealth as gloriously wasteful expenditures.[33] Even the drinker's knowledge of the bar menu and the ability to distinguish between types and brands of liquor attest to his leisure: so many hours of wasted time devoted to learning the subtleties of flavor and provenance.[34] Indeed, for Veblen, pretty much everything about the bar scene conspires toward pecuniary distinctions. Gathered with friends and associations, the man of esteem puts his success on display not only through his own drinking, but also by sporting rounds, buying the barkeep a shot, tipping, and so on. Ultimately, drunkenness itself becomes honorific; a red nose or a hand tremor can, for a certain man of leisure, prove a mark of distinction. The aura of wealth maintained by drinking in the boardroom or after work at the club is sustained for all to see by the next morning's hangover.[35]

But there's something special about the cocktail's ingredients that make it uniquely fitting for emulative culture, particularly among males. Veblen claims that the barbarian culture out of which the leisure class emerged held an animistic view of the world. They divided their labor into two different classes: an inferior sort that involves the manipulation of nonhuman things, that is, industry, and a superior sort that subdues or masters animate life, that is, exploit. The former demands a tedious diligence, while the latter requires strength and prowess, an almost superhuman ability to convert the will of another vital being to one's own ends.[36] "Such employments as warfare, politics, public worship, and public merrymaking," Veblen argues, "are felt, in the popular apprehension, to differ intrinsically from the labour that has to do with elaborating the material means of life."[37] For Veblen, *exploit* is defined as a wild and fateful encounter with the animate world. The encounter with such spirits marks certain kinds of work as not only more esteemed, but also distinctively male.[38] The consumption of literal "spirits" falls under this same range of activities. Long after the days of the hunt have ended, drinking appears as "exploit" in the form of "public merrymaking." The natural potency of the distilled grain meets with the manufactured expensiveness of the product, making the cocktail the quintessential tool for displaying one's prowess. We've already seen what it means to overpower and assimilate the spirit of John Barleycorn. The manhattan is John Barleycorn in top hat and tails, a formidable spirit in fancy disguise.

The fatal potency of the manhattan is most clearly displayed in Dreiser's famous 1925 novel *An American Tragedy*.[39] Loosely based on a famous real-world murder and its subsequent trial, the novel's plot concerns the rise and fall a young dreamer named Clyde Griffith and his efforts to master the modern class system. Clyde is born dirt poor to a family of itinerant preachers, but his moody, sensitive nature makes him yearn for "something better." Wandering the streets of Kansas City, he quickly attaches his innocent cravings for beauty and pleasure to the trappings of the new leisure class, particularly the showy displays of wealth that remain just out of reach on the city streets. Clyde lacks any real moral compass—his lawyer later describes him as a "moral and mental coward"—but his condition is presented as modern and certainly widespread. Having rejected his family and their religion, he can only evaluate his self-worth by way of "invidious comparisons" with others, his thoughts about himself framed by an "old mass yearning for likeness in all thing."[40]

Fittingly, Clyde's tragic course is initiated in a swanky Kansas City hotel called the Green-Davidson, where he lands a job as a bellhop and embarks on a plan to "work and save his money and be somebody."[41] Dreiser defines the hotel environment as light, brisk, and enlivening, a release from the weight of Clyde's impoverished past. Clyde, with his good looks and new bellhop uniform, quickly ingratiates himself with the rest of the staff and thus gains a closer proximity to the world of wealth. The quick and easy display of class and esteem that defines hotel life allows him to reinvent himself at will and thereby evade responsibility for his actions. He quickly falls in with a group of young "sports," an ambitious set of bellhops who, in their smart outfits and leisurely gatherings, emulate the leisure class they serve. The group spends their newly disposable income in fine restaurants and sporting houses, mimicking the rich patrons they serve back at the hotel. Like Clyde, they are each "afflicted by the virus of ambition and unrest," and they use the new entertainments of the urban world to demonstrate their success and prowess before each other.[42] "Dese fellows here," explains one of the ringleaders, "are good sports, all o' dem. Dey're no four-flushers an' no tightwads, eider. Whenever dere's anyting on—a good time or sumpin' like dat, dey're on—nearly all of 'em."[43]

Well enough, but Clyde seems singularly incapable of managing the inherent doubleness of his new life, the superficial thrills of the sporting life and his heavy responsibilities back home. His first moment of crisis occurs during a bellhop "blow-out," a casual drinking party set up by the boys at a nearby restaurant, the hangout of "passing actors, politicians, local business men."[44]

Entering the restaurant, with its reflective surfaces and lively clatter, the boys "somehow felt older, wiser, more important—real men of the world."[45] Of all the drinks on the barkeep's list, their acting leader orders a manhattan: "'Now, me for a good old manhattan, to begin wit',' exclaimed Hegglund avidly, looking about on the crowd in the room and feeling that now indeed he was a person. Of a reddish-tan hue, his eyes keen and blue, his reddish-brown hair brushed straight up from his forehead, he seemed not unlike a large and overzealous rooster."[46] With said cocktail in hand, Hegglund quickly appears a "man of the world," inspiring the others to prove their own worth in turn. They loudly order their cocktails, making sure their decisions are given proper consideration by their peers. Clyde, though, hesitates; he too seeks to capture some of their "present glory," but this competitive desire cuts against his upbringing and its moral strictures. Accepting the drink entails a betrayal of his own self-worth, while refusing it means opting out of the emulatory system that seems to sustain any social worth. His indecision at once exposes and jeopardizes the hazing culture of masculine camaraderie as well as the structures of class that underlie it. Thus, his barstool crisis quickly attains a Hamlet-like air of indecision and fatality:

> "Who, me? Oh, me," exclaimed Clyde, not a little disturbed by this inquiry, for up to now—this very hour, in fact—he had never touched anything stronger than coffee or ice-cream soda.... What would they think of him if he didn't drink something? For ever since he had been among them, he had been trying to appear as much of a man of the world as they were. And yet back of him, as he could plainly feel, lay all of the years in which he had been drilled in the "horrors" of drink and evil companionship.... Should he or should he not drink?[47]

Of course, Clyde drinks, and this sporting culture, if not the manhattan itself, brings about his first great accident and continues to haunt his life as the source of his moral undoing. He drinks not to get drunk, but to feel "worldly"; spirits bring on the "courage and daring" of what he perceives to be the apotheosis of the successful man.[48] But he never feels more than behind the curve, continually puffing himself up, reaching for more, evading responsibility—and ultimately, failing to reconcile the various versions of his identity, he cracks up.

All of which might be why the manhattan and its leisure class milieu faced, after World War I and the Great Depression, a comeuppance and backlash. Linked now with suspicious structures of patriarchal power and a bankrupt economic system, the manhattan became an emblem of gross privilege, and its depiction in popular culture was often turned to more critical or subversive ends. Increasingly, in books and films, the drink appears out of place and inappropriately imbibed, subject to an irony that flips its most basic connotations. Moviegoers in the late 1950s, for example, were tickled pink watching Marilyn Monroe mix sloppy manhattans in *Some Like It Hot*. She pours the concoction in a cramped train berth for twelve other girls and Jack Lemmon in drag. "I tell you," says Jerry in his Daphne disguise, "this is the only way to travel."[49] The cocktail makes a more ominous appearance in Kurt Vonnegut's *Breakfast of Champions*. Here, post-Vietnam and the civil rights era, manhattans are ordered in the cheesy cocktail lounge of a Midland City Holiday Inn where the protagonist, a delusional Pontiac dealer named Dwayne Hoover, plots a public rampage. Vonnegut, who considered the manhattan his favorite cocktail, defines *alcohol* here with characteristic darkness as "a substance produced by a tiny creature called yeast. Yeast organisms ate sugar and excreted alcohol. They killed themselves by destroying their own environment with yeast shit."[50]

Of course, today, the manhattan continues to attract men like Dreiser's Clyde Griffith, and it sustains the largely masculine culture of invidious comparison that Veblen theorized, but the social foundations that underpinned the drink's allure seem forever wobbly. Most recently, the AMC series *Mad Men* offered an extended critique of the aspirational fantasies and class structures that defined both the cocktail and the city of its birth.[51] The show essentially updates the American tragedy that Dreiser so carefully anatomized, replacing Clyde and his Gilded Age milieu with ad exec Don Draper and the gray-suited bureaucracy of midcentury Manhattan. But it also delineates an alternative to their invidious exploits, and such an alternative emerges—in the character of Peggy—through the new feminist and civil rights movements of the same era. As I hope to show in the following analysis of the show, the cocktail remains both a central emblem and a convenient vessel for focusing and addressing these critical issues.

Certainly, in its first season or so, the show did all it could to glamorize its urban locale, depicting Manhattan as a midcentury magnet of style, success, and romantic self-reinvention. When Joan's roommate, one of the thousands of young women who flocked to the city for independence after the war, declares that she's "had it with Manhattan," Joan quickly snaps back, "Don't say that! The city is everything."[52] Even better, in the next episode, up-and-comer Peggy Olson finds herself stuck on a boring date with a young rube. Sensing her superior attitude, the date lashes out the only way he knows how: "You can act like you're from Manhattan, but you don't look like those girls." Peggy's not buying it, though, and her comeback leaves him speechless: "Those people, in Manhattan, they are better than us, because they want things they haven't seen."[53]

At the same time, to the dismay of some social commentators, the show linked the allure of the city to the aura of alcohol and the cocktail culture of the cold war.[54] Whether seated in bar or in boardroom, the show's dashing male leads always had a gorgeously cut glass and some brown booze on hand, while its glamorous leading ladies sipped gimlets and Tom Collinses in kitchens and clubs. "I'm telling you boys," says Pete's father-in-law, "You've got it made: martini lunches, gorgeous women parading through. In my next life, I'm coming back as an ad man."[55]

The show's script, however, also suggested that what links the drive to drink and the entrepreneurial ethos of Madison Avenue was an often manic and insecure desire for acceptance and approval. From the start, the drinking on *Mad Men* always seemed desperately wounded, especially for its male characters, and thereby gave the lie to the aspirational ethos that shapes American cocktail culture.[56] In the very first scene of the show's first episode, we meet Don Draper in a city bar, confidently at work on a new ad campaign and his usual drink of choice, an old-fashioned. For Don, this cocktail reflects his commitment to an older world, a more secure and substantial past with its strong male authorities and certain value systems, but both Don and his nostalgia quickly prove a sham. Later in the episode, we watch him crumble after a work meeting, confessing to his lover, "I have nothing. I'm over and they're finally gonna know it."[57] Again and again, the dashing ad men reach for the bottle in moments of crisis and insecurity, their drinks serving as anxious advertisements for their best, yet unattainable versions of themselves. In one of the first season's angstiest scenes, Roger and Don regroup after having a staffing decision overturned by a senior colleague. Once they reach for the bottle and down its empowering spirit, their talk quickly turns to old wounds:

> ROGER. You don't know how to drink. Your whole generation, you drink for the wrong reasons. My generation, we drink because it's good, because it feels better than unbuttoning your collar, because we deserve it. We drink because it's what men do.
> DON. What about shaky hands? I see a lot of that with you boys.
> ROGER. No joke. Your kind with your gloomy thoughts and your worries, you're all busy licking some imaginary wound.
> DON. Not all imaginary.
> ROGER. Yeah, boo hoo.
> DON. Maybe I'm not as comfortable being powerless as you are.[58]

The posing here is both gendered and generational. The scene offers the first glimpse of Veblen's leisure-class comparisons that increasingly prove debilitating for the men on the show. Just a few episodes later, Don outdrinks Roger and then races him up the stairs to a client meeting. When the latter finally arrives—panting, pale, and sweaty—he promptly vomits on the office floor, while Don looks on with a dopey grin on his face.[59]

But *Mad Men*'s meticulous critique of midcentury cocktail culture extends beyond *how* the characters are drinking to *what* they are drinking. Wondrich puts it best in this analysis of the show: "While the quantities of alcohol alone speak volumes—take your pick between three-martini lunches or three fingers of something brown—the choices say even more about a period in American history when the drinkscape uniquely reflected the cultural forces that created it."[60] Although audiences tend to think of Don Draper as a quintessentially modern man, he prefers the old-fashioned, a drink that gained popularity back in the 1880s as a nostalgic alternative to the fancier cocktails of the time. With one of these in hand, he seems to be trying both to capture his lost past, a more stable world for men before the war (however imaginary) and to drink it away to oblivion. Roger Sterling, in turn, lusts mostly for vodka, a clean and sterile neutral grain alcohol that reflects his dapper style and ironic outlook. Vodka's peak popularity during the Cold War places Roger on the progressive side of drinking culture (even if vodka suffered something of a decline in popularity between about 1960 and 1980); Wondrich calls it a "subversive" choice, fit for a man open to the pleasures of a new generation, and thus the complete opposite of the manhattan, which by this time became known as a drink for parents and other squares.

As for the women on the show, homemaker Betty Draper drowns herself in sugary concoctions such as gimlets and Tom Collinses. Wealthy socialite Trudy Campbell seems to love champagne. The office girls mix rum and crème de menthe, but they'll drink anything the men pass their way. Peggy, though, remains the most elusive female character on the show, and it is worthwhile to track the full arc of her drinking career because of what it suggests about the manhattan and its evolving significance. Contrary to what one might expect, the show does not feature many manhattans at all.[61] In fact, I detect only one on display, and it's ordered in the middle of the very dark fourth season by Peggy, just at the moment of her executive triumph. Peggy first appears in the offices of the Sterling Cooper Advertising Agency as Don's secretary, but her incisive mind and wit for words quickly lead to success with a Belle Jolie account. After delivering a winning pitch, she is promptly invited to Don's office and handed her first drink, a typical three-finger pour of office whiskey. "They poured me a drink!" she exclaims when she's back with the girls later on.[62] At this point, with her career on the rise, Peggy starts experimenting with the city's cocktail options, as if searching for a drink that reflects her newfound professional status. In a later episode, after she stammers through a request for a raise, Don scolds her in fiercely gendered terms: "You presented like a man. Now act like one."[63]

Throughout the series, Don proves both a caring mentor for Peggy and a terrible example of what the business can do to a man. He invites her into the competitive arena of big-city advertising, providing her with small tastes of the power it can provide, but his own struggle with alcoholism seems to check her ambition and cause her to reconsider the terms of success. Peggy, in turn, carefully monitors her near-tribal affiliation with her male colleagues through her decisions to imbibe or reject their spirits. This relationship with Don and his peers comes to a head in a fabulous Season 4 episode titled "The Suitcase." Peggy is now firmly established in a window office right next to Don's, but the setup seems more like a trap than a perk. It's her birthday, and her boyfriend is waiting to meet her at a restaurant, but a heavy-drinking Don won't let her leave the office. When her boyfriend finally dumps her—over the phone, no less—she reaches quickly for Don's Canadian Club, but she also scolds her boss for binge drinking and for stealing her ideas. The two colleagues reconcile and head out to a bar, where Don drinks rye on the rocks and Peggy orders her first and only manhattan. For the first time, they seem to be genuine equals, operating on the same plane of success, even if one appears to be on the rise and the other on a decline. They share intimate details about their pasts—Don's experience in the war, Peggy's abandoned child, the deaths of their fathers, and so on—which reveal further tragic parallels between them. Don, though, seems utterly ravaged by his memories, whereas Peggy discloses her regrets and mistakes with a grim directness. Tellingly, though, if she proves the victor here, it is because she doesn't finish her drink. The episode is set against the 1965 fight between Mohammed Ali and Sonny Liston, when the world heavyweight champ knocked down the latter in just a minute and a half with his "phantom punch." "It's over," Don woefully declares when the result is announced on the radio, as if describing his own demise. Similarly, all the men go down around Peggy—Duck and Don literally knock each other out back at the office—and she's the last one standing. Tellingly, when she leaves the bar, she leaves her drink unfinished. She seems to be the only character on the show with the maturity and sophistication to order a manhattan as well as the will and self-possession to leave it behind.

There's something especially poignant about the image of Peggy's unfinished manhattan sitting alone on the bar. It signals all that she's willing to abandon, all those associations that have accrued around the manhattan and its clubby cocktail culture: toxic masculinity, invidious competition, conspicuous consumption, and old-world power. She heroically exercises restraint when faced with the bar's most unrestrained brew, and she thereby stands out as a singularity in a world of interchangeable men. One curious feature about descriptions and theories of cocktail culture is that they are mostly driven by simile. The sensual features of the cocktail are powerful but vague, and thereby open to multiple associations. In turn, these associations have bestowed the drink with a near-mythical status, encoding it as a totem of power and success.[64] When considering my own descriptions of the manhattan, I see nothing but the kind of associative mythmaking that attends all cultural power. The liquor lends "spirit" and "potency" to a specific ideology, while that ideology in turn grants the liquor a stable meaning and significance. Certainly, this involuted logic extends to the act of drinking itself. When you order a manhattan, you are not simply identifying with certain forms of myth and power, but literally ingesting those associations as sources of pleasure and self-worth, and thereby reproducing the structures in which they have any meaning at all. If my reading is correct, Peggy wants nothing to do with such primitive "exploit." She avoids all such similes and comparative culture in general. She remains sober, critical, and starkly individual, and thereby demonstrates a different order of being and power.

Nevertheless, Peggy would make a fine drinking companion, and she seems one of the few drinkers mentioned in this essay who can make good on the manhattan's original promise. With her subversive model in mind, perhaps, the drink seems redeemable, and if some final bartending notes are in order, maybe they can point toward a more nuanced set of practices.

Mixing a satisfying manhattan takes some time, and you have to pay close attention to its parts in order to avoid potential problems. Here's the most common version, accepted by David Wondrich and other experts, all of whom express similar reservations about the drink's potential excesses:

Manhattan
2 oz rye whiskey
1 oz Italian vermouth
2 dashes Angostura bitters

Stir the rye whiskey, vermouth, and bitters with ice in a cocktail shaker. Strain into a chilled cocktail glass and garnish with a lemon twist or a maraschino cherry.

For connoisseurs, only rye whiskey seems to do. It was often used in the earlier recipes, and its spicier, spikier flavor cuts through the sweetness of the vermouth. Using 100 proof rye works best—Rittenhouse is always reliable—as it takes charge of the sugary mix and smooths out the frills. Stirring the drink is a heck of a lot better than shaking, as the latter will ruin the color of the drink and give it an unsightly foamy head. Just make sure you stir it long enough (fifty strokes?) to blend and chill thoroughly. It's hard to resist the cherry, if only for what it adds to the drink's aspirational arc. Still, the lemon twist is truer to the drink's origins. Just twist and discard: it creates a neat little oil slick at the top of the drink and fills the empty upper volume of the glass with a beautiful scent.

It's important to consider not just *how* to mix a decent manhattan, but also when and where to drink one. In the early days, it was rightly considered a preprandial cocktail. You'll want to order one as your first round, before you launch into a meal or any other palate-wrecking activity. But I'd also recommend drinking the manhattan alone. While it's a social drink by nature, it's an unusually busy pour, and you'll want to block out a lot of the surrounding noise to appreciate its components. This will also allow you to avoid any of those invidious social comparisons that might occur if you're seen with one at a bar or a party. In general, try to cut out all fanciness and pretention. To be honest, my all-time favorite manhattans were served in dive bars—one at the barely lit Old Pink in Buffalo, New York, and the other at the Atlas Ballroom in Bloomington, Indiana. Something of the ruined splendor of these settings brings out the true decadence of the drink and exposes its tragic dimensions. I'm not proposing here some simple exercise in hipster irony, a cute postmodern twist of high and low culture, classiness and decadence. Rather, it strikes me that the dive bar embodies the deep contradictions that define the history of cocktail culture and especially the manhattan. More than anything else, a true dive bar, one that has literally fallen into disrepair, remains a haunting reminder of that promise of "something better" in American life even as it demonstrates its falseness and fragility. As a gathering space, it still permits the dynamic performance of both identity and sociality, but it punks any possible pretentions of either. Simply put, the dive bar is the dark mirror image of all the gilt and marble lounges described above. Its dank décor—the shitty lighting, rank smells, and shrill loudness—actually enriches the bruised colors and bittersweet flavors of the classic manhattan. There's a reason why most barcrawls move downward over the course of the evening, saving the worst bar for last. The city, like the drink, has its dingy side, and it's worth a visit now and again. This is no mere "glimpse of a better world." It's a genuine pleasure in its own right, one that both offers a true critique and rewards real consideration. Bottoms up to the American dream!

Indiana University

NOTES

1. Quoted in Amy Zavatto, "I'll Take a Manhattan," *Gotham* 4 (July 28, 2014): 128–33, https://issuu.com/nichemediaholdingsllc/docs/gotham_-_issue_4_-_summer_2014.
2. Quoted in Jason Wilson, "I'll Take the Manhattan," *Washington Post*, July 9, 2009, http://www.washingtonpost.com/wp-dyn/content/story/2008/07/08/ST2008070802290.html.
3. See Albert W. A. Schmid, *The Manhattan Cocktail* (Lexington: University Press of Kentucky, 2015), 3–5. David Wondrich expresses some skepticism about the connection in *Imbibe! From Absinthe Cocktail to Whiskey Smash, a Salute in Stories and Drinks to "Professor" Jerry Thomas, Pioneer of the American Bar* (New York: Perigee, 2015), 255.
4. On the expensiveness of ice and other cocktail ingredients, see Wondrich, *Imbibe!*, 47–59.
5. Sinclair Lewis, *Babbitt* (New York: Bantam Dell, 2007).
6. Quoted in Bill Norris, "Cocktails with *Mad Men*: The Manhattan," Birth. Movies. Death. May 27, 2012, http://birthmoviesdeath.com/2012/05/27/cocktails-with-mad-men-the-manhattan.
7. Quoted in Amy Zavatto, "I'll Take a Manhattan."
8. Wondrich, *Imbibe!*, 8.
9. Wondrich, *Imbibe!*, 209.
10. The Only William (William Schmidt), *The Flowing Bowl: When and What to Drink* (New York: Charles L. Webster, 1892), 114.
11. See Lowell Edmunds, *Martini, Straight Up: The Classic American Cocktail* (Baltimore: Johns Hopkins University Press, 1981), 47, 14.
12. See recipes and glassware descriptions in *How to Mix Drinks: Bar Keeper's Handbook* (1884) and *Jerry Thomas's Bar-Keeper Guide* (1887), reprinted in Wondrich, , *Imbibe!*, 257–59.
13. This characterization of the martini follows Max Rudin's excellent account in "There Is Something about a Martini," *American Heritage* 48, no. 4 (1997): 32–51.
14. See Paul Fussell, *Class: A Guide Through the American Status System* (New York: Simon & Schuster, 1983), 97.
15. Theodore Dreiser, *Sister Carrie* (New York: Random House, 1999), 64–65.
16. Dreiser, *Sister Carrie*, 54.
17. Wondrich, *Imbibe!*, 249–50.
18. Wondrich, *Imbibe!*, 57–58.
19. Wondrich, *Imbibe!*, 226.
20. Quoted in Philip Greene, *The Manhattan: The Story of the First Modern Cocktail (with Recipes)* (New York: Sterling Epicure, 2016), 12.

21. See Greene's useful account in *The Manhattan*, 25–41.
22. Dreiser, *Sister Carrie*, 420–22.
23. William Grimes, *Straight Up or On the Rocks* (New York: North Point Press, 2001), 74–75.
24. Reid Mitenbuler, *Bourbon Empire: The Past and Future of American's Whiskey* (New York: Penguin Books, 2015), 2.
25. Robert Burns, *The Complete Poems and Songs* (Glasgow: Geddes & Grosset, 2015), 25.
26. Mitenbuler, *Bourbon Empire*, 254.
27. Thorstein Veblen, *The Theory of the Leisure Class: An Economic Study of Institutions*, Mentor Edition, introduction by C. Wright Mills (New York: Macmillan, 1953 [1899]), 20.
28. Veblen, *Theory of the Leisure Class*, 24.
29. Veblen, *Theory of the Leisure Class*, 16.
30. Veblen, *Theory of the Leisure Class*, 36–63.
31. Veblen, *Theory of the Leisure Class*, 68–101.
32. Veblen, *Theory of the Leisure Class*, 71.
33. Veblen, *Theory of the Leisure Class*, 62–63.
34. Veblen, *Theory of the Leisure Class*, 44–45.
35. Veblen, *Theory of the Leisure Class*, 70.
36. Veblen, *Theory of the Leisure Class*, 12.
37. Veblen, *Theory of the Leisure Class*, 10.
38. Veblen, *Theory of the Leisure Class*, 13.
39. Theodore Dreiser, *An American Tragedy* (New York: Signet Classics, 2010).
40. Dreiser, *American Tragedy*, 4.
41. Dreiser, *American Tragedy*, 24.
42. Dreiser, *American Tragedy*, 257.
43. Dreiser, *American Tragedy*, 48.
44. Dreiser, *American Tragedy*, 54.
45. Dreiser, *American Tragedy*, 54.
46. Dreiser, *American Tragedy*, 56.
47. Dreiser, *American Tragedy*, 57.
48. Dreiser, *American Tragedy*, 77.
49. Billy Wilder, dir., *Some Like It Hot* (Los Angeles: United Artists, 1959).
50. Kurt Vonnegut, *Breakfast of Champions* (New York: Dial Press, 2002), 214.
51. *Mad Men*, created by Matthew Weiner, produced by Lionsgate Television, aired 2007–2015, on AMC.
52. Tim Hunter, dir., *Mad Men*, Season 1, episode 10, "Long Weekend," aired September 27, 2007, on AMC.
53. Tim Hunter, dir., *Mad Men*, Season 1, episode 11, "Indian Summer," aired October 4, 2007, on AMC.

54. See commentary in Carly Severn, "Drinking with *Mad Men*: Cocktail Culture and the Myth of Don Draper," *Bay Area Bites* (blog), KQED, March 31, 2015, http://www.npr.org/sections/thesalt/2015/04/05/397352082/drinking-with-mad-men-cocktail-culture-and-the-myth-of-don-draper.

55. Tim Hunter, dir., *Mad Men*, Season 1, episode 4, "New Amsterdam," aired August 9, 2007, on AMC.

56. For more commentary in this vein, see WSJ Staff, "'Mad Men' Gets Deep: 'The Existential Void of Roger Sterling,'" *Wall Street Journal*, July 11, 2011, http://blogs.wsj.com/speakeasy/2010/07/11/mad-men-get-deep-the-existential-void-of-roger-sterling/.

57. Alan Taylor, dir., *Mad Men*, Season 1, episode 1, "Smoke Gets in Your Eyes," aired July 19, 2007, on AMC.

58. Hunter, "New Amsterdam."

59. Tim Hunter, dir., *Mad Men*, Season 1, episode 7, "Red in the Face," aired August 30, 2007, on AMC.

60. Reid Mitenbuler, "What Are They Drinking on Mad Men," Serious Eats, April 1, 2013, http://drinks.seriouseats.com/2013/04/what-are-they-drinking-on-mad-men-booze-cocktails-sixties-history-what-don-draper-drinks.html.

61. See, again, Severn, "Drinking with 'Mad Men.'"

62. Phil Abraham, dir., *Mad Men*, Season 1, episode 8, "The Hobo Code," aired September 6, 2007, on AMC.

63. Hunter, "Indian Summer."

64. See Roland Barthes, *Mythologies*, trans. Annette Levers (New York: Hill and Wang, 1972).

BIBLIOGRAPHY

Barthes, Roland. *Mythologies*. Translated by Annette Lavers. New York: Hill and Wang, 1972.
Burns, Robert. *The Complete Poems and Songs*. Glasgow: Geddes & Grosset, 2015.
Dreiser, Theodore. *An American Tragedy*. New York: Signet Classics, 2010.
Dreiser, Theodore. *Sister Carrie*. New York: Random House, 1999.
Edmunds, Lowell. *Martini, Straight Up: The Classic American Cocktail*. Baltimore: Johns Hopkins University Press, 1981.
Fussell, Paul. *Class: A Guide Through the American Status System*. New York: Simon & Schuster, 1983.
Greene, Philip. *The Manhattan: The Story of the First Modern Cocktail (with Recipes)*. New York: Sterling Epicure, 2016.
Grimes, William. *Straight Up or On the Rocks*. New York: North Point Press, 2001.
Thomas, Jerry. *The Bartender's Guide: How to Mix Drinks, or the Bon-Vivant's Companion*. New York: Dick & Fitzgerald, 1862.

Lewis, Sinclair. *Babbitt*. New York: Bantam Dell, 2007.
Mad Men. Created by Matthew Weiner. Produced by Lionsgate Television. Aired 2007–2015, on AMC.
Mitenbuler, Reid. *Bourbon Empire: The Past and Future of American's Whiskey*. New York: Penguin Books, 2015.
Mitenbuler, Reid. "What Are They Drinking on Mad Men." Serious Eats. April 1, 2013. http://drinks.seriouseats.com/2013/04/what-are-they-drinking-on-mad-men-booze-cocktails-sixties-history-what-don-draper-drinks.html.
Norris, Bill. "Cocktails with *Mad Men*: The Manhattan." Birth. Movies. Death. May 27, 2012. http://birthmoviesdeath.com/2012/05/27/cocktails-with-mad-men-the-manhattan.
Rudin, Max. "There Is Something about a Martini." *American Heritage* 48, no. 4 (1997): 32–51.
Schmid, Albert W. A. *The Manhattan Cocktail*. Lexington: University Press of Kentucky, 2015.
Schmidt, William. *The Flowing Bowl: When and What to Drink*. New York: Charles L. Webster, 1892.
Severn, Carly. "Drinking with *Mad Men*: Cocktail Culture and the Myth of Don Draper." *Bay Area Bites* (blog). KQED. March 31, 2015. http://www.npr.org/sections/thesalt/2015/04/05/397352082/drinking-with-mad-men-cocktail-culture-and-the-myth-of-don-draper.
Veblen, Thorstein. *The Theory of the Leisure Class: An Economic Study of Institutions*. Mentor Edition. Introduction by C. Wright Mills. New York: Macmillan, 1953 [1899].
Vonnegut, Kurt. *Breakfast of Champions*. New York: Dial Press, 2002.
Wilder, Billy, dir. *Some Like It Hot*. Los Angeles: United Artists, 1959.
Wilson, Jason. "I'll Take the Manhattan." *Washington Post*. July 9, 2008. http://www.washingtonpost.com/wp-dyn/content/story/2008/07/08/ST2008070802290.html.
Wondrich, David. *Imbibe! From Absinthe Cocktail to Whiskey Smash, a Salute in Stories and Drinks to "Professor" Jerry Thomas, Pioneer of the American Bar*. New York: Perigee, 2015.
WSJ Staff. "'Mad Men' Gets Deep: 'The Existential Void of Roger Sterling.'" *Wall Street Journal*. July 11, 2011. http://blogs.wsj.com/speakeasy/2010/07/11/mad-men-get-deep-the-existential-void-of-roger-sterling/.
Zavatto, Amy. "I'll Take a Manhattan." *Gotham* 4 (July 28, 2014): 128–33. https://issuu.com/nichemediaholdingsllc/docs/gotham_-_issue_4_-_summer_2014.

NINETEEN

COCKTAILS THAT AREN'T COCKTAILS FOR GENTLEMEN WHO AREN'T MEN

Recovering the Metaphorical Body of the Fictional Drinker

MICHAEL JAY LEWIS

THE PSEUDOMEDICINAL COCKTAIL SOLUTION

In the body of the unreal, immaterial drinker exists the supermetabolic liver, the unflagging brain, the stomach that cannot be upset. Unreal organs for unreal worlds. A reader of such worlds might think that the owner of such organs would know nothing of exhaustion, recuperation, or recovery. As long as such figures stayed safely within the borders of these imaginary places, they would never wear down and thus never need repair. Jake Barnes should be able to drink sangria all night, James Bond innumerable martinis, and The Dude white Russians ad nauseam—or rather the opposite—without ever slogging through mornings of nausea and headache. Yet something spoils their superheroic constitution, turns their inhuman tolerance normal, susceptible to the same biological limitations of their material readers and viewers: realism.

This occasional realism, however, tends to go only so far: to present a minimally departing imitation of the real, one that aligns the habits of impossibly sober dipsomaniacs with those of the would-be hungover reader. In these moments, the unreal, mythic organs are exchanged for rich description. The exhortation of the stoic, unflappable stomach is traded for the glorification of language's power and the evocative image. *Henry IV, Part I* offers us Falstaff "sleeping upon benches after noon," subliminally invoking "egg and butter" cravings while asking the future king to view him as a "squir[e] of the night's body" rather than a "thief of the day's beauty."[1] We see *Vanity Fair*'s Sedley "groaning in agonies which the pen refuses to describe," displaying a comical turmoil—exacerbated because "soda-water was not yet invented"—that made it difficult even for his "valet, the most solemn and correct of gentlemen," to "keep his countenance in order."[2] And in perhaps the most well-known description of a hangover in English literature, we see *Lucky Jim*'s Dixon being run over by a consciousness that was "on him before he could get out of the way," awakening to find his "mouth had been used as a latrine by some small creature of the night, and then as its mausoleum" and resolving "never to move his eyeballs again."[3] While such descriptions seem to bring their heroes back to Earth, and via alcoholism-focused dramas, like *The Lost Weekend*, may continue to do so, their effects are often short-lived. Save for the rare disquisition on the layabout (e.g., Goncharov's *Oblomov*), literary figures have to get up, go out, *do things*. In order to get them going, something must be done. Enter the tonics: the "bracers" and "stomach-revivers," "fog-cutters" and "eye-openers." Notably, while they promise repair—flushed organs, propped lids—these pick-me-ups only enable the hero to appear ready to consume again, to reengage the cocktail culture, not to understand it. The eyes that the tonic "opens" are not the roused yet somewhat automatic hero's but the reader's.

Detailed accounts of hangover remedies are commonplace to literary *culture*. Most—as do each of the twenty-seven "Picker-Uppers" in Charles Baker's 1939 *Gentleman's Companion*—involve the hair of the dog, such remedies being "safer and more pleasant" than "[innards]-corroding," habit-forming "chemicals," that is, "revivers smacking of drugdom."[4] Many of these "variegated hairs of the dog,"[5]—from Hemingway's Death in the Afternoon (1 jigger of absinthe, mixed to "proper opalescent milkiness" in a flute with 4 ounces of iced champagne)[6] to his Death in the Gulf Stream (4 splashes of Angostura, juice and crushed peel of 1 green lime, topped off with Hollands gin in a "tall thin water tumbler" filled with "finely cracked ice")—function both as tonics and as mid-evening refreshers.[7] From there, the literary tonic tends quickly toward the narcotic or at least the dog's whole hide (as well as an inebriety and celluloid doubled "reality effect"),[8] exemplified by Hunter S. Thompson's "12 amyl nitrates (one box) in conjunction with as many beers as necessary"[9] and the popular directive, "Stay drunk,"[10] attributed to Dean Martin and a characterized Dorothy Parker.[11] But perhaps the most famous—and lengthy—literary hangover remedy comes (again) from Kingsley Amis, whose *Everyday Drinking*, like his fiction, gives "sapient advice about how to keep drinking[,] remain functional" and, in the end, "save much avoidable pain."[12]

Notably, Amis's program for alleviating both the hangover's physical and metaphysical effects involves treating the hangover like intoxication's ghost, which lingers until its needs are satisfied. His cure for the physical hangover involves sex, rest, shaving, a hot bath (no cold showers), unsweetened grapefruit (but no other food, especially "greasy" food), water, self-exhortation, abstinence from cigarettes, and, at last, a "tuft" of the dog that bit you.[13] He references the Bloody Mary but explores more carefully the "usually effective" Underburg, "a highly alcoholic bitters rather resembling Fernet Branca" whose "effect on one's insides . . . is rather like that of throwing a cricket ball into an empty bath, . . . resulting [in] mild convulsions and cries of shock" followed by "a comforting glow . . . and very often a marked turn for the better."[14] These remedies, however, could be supplanted by any one of three "infallible" cures: (1) going "down the mine on the early-morning shift at the coal face," (2) going "up for half an hour in an open aeroplane (needless to say, with a non-hungover person at the controls), or (3) drinking Donald Watt's Jolt.[15] While the first two are "hard to come by,"[16] the third ("a tumbler of some sweet liqueur, Benedictine or Grand Marnier, taken in lieu of breakfast") will likely work because "the sugar in the drink will give you energy and the alcohol."[17] Yet this is not where things end: the metaphysical hangover still remains. Again, Amis has the solution: (1) deal with the physical hangover, (2) recognize that your ailment is only a hangover and not a chronic condition (which may or may not be the case), and (3) begin a course of reading and listening. Given cinema's capacity to involve verse, prose, and all forms of music, as well as its twenty-first century ubiquity, we might add "watching" to the list.

Notably, any course of metaphysical repair that involves fictional narrative, even mimetic narrative that depicts recreational drug customs, is likely to divulge only vague remedies to the reader's physical hangover. While the nonfictional literary tonic, like the cocktail, is occasionally described in detail, its fictional counterpart is not. Equally important, the nonfictional construction is defined by the operation of preparation: one mixes absinthe with iced champagne, and one adds or subtracts Tabasco at one's peril, especially as one is confronted by the same ingredients, the same tools, and often the same space (kitchen, sideboard, bar) at which the last cocktail was prepared. It is here, at the site of creation, that the recipe of the fictionalized eye-opener diverges from the real. While there are occasions of such itemization, there is perhaps more significantly a tendency toward focalized evasion, thus ensuring that the antidote cocktail retains some of the mysteriousness crucial to its power, especially as it emerges in film. In that genre, tonics are primarily delivered in the background or behind the scenes, maintaining biological realism and superheroic agency in one character body through the magic of an unseen, untested dram. The tonic thereby works as a reanimation tool required by realism; even when unmentioned it is implied, an engine for the likes of Lorelei Lee, Danny Ocean, and Philip Marlowe. Notably, these tonics are often prepared and dispensed by others: valets and manservants, squires, attendants, and gentleman's gentlemen—predominately male figures called upon to relieve the next-day distress of their consistently detoxing employers. As the daytime foil of the cocktail-proscribing bartender of the nightclub or speakeasy, the valet emerges with remedial analeptics necessary to sustain narrative cohesion. In this way, like Big Halley at the Golden Day, *Invisible Man*'s brothel-bar and once-a-week "ward" for otherwise hospitalized, mentally disabled veterans, the valet is both a bartender and a doctor: an admixing physician treating the chronic condition of the impossible hero and the otherwise chaotic plot.[18] Like any medicine man, the valet-as-tender becomes the gentleman's greatest threat. Beyond knowing the "family secrets [the family] wouldn't care to have told,"[19] he controls the tonic that may determine whether these secrets are preserved.[20]

As often happens in a medical setting, the recipient of such solutions is given instructions about dosage but not ingredients. Unlike the ingredients administered by P. G. Wodehouse's quintessential Reginald Jeeves—the in-story creator of perhaps the most famous fictional tonic—literature more commonly depicts ambiguous reviving potions, elixirs, and concoctions, especially in the fantasy genre (e.g., *The Princess Bride*'s "resurrection pill": "a lump of clay the size of a golf ball").[21] Whether applied to repair intoxication or "sort of dead[ness]," such ambiguity aids in preserving the reader's faith in the magic of agency.[22] As the material parallel of *The Princess Bride*'s metanarrating editor, who intervenes to announce story-line redactions, the tonic's absent recipe underscores the importance of keeping the magic—the details that allow the hero's return—off the "stage"; its ingredients, similar to the interiority of the valet, are essential but private.[23] We see such recipe confidentiality in the prose of Oscar Wilde, H. H. Munroe, and Evelyn Waugh, where the act of tonic-bringing is often referenced as an off-page event.

Yet even when its contents are known, as with the hangover remedy of *Twin Peaks*'s Agent Dale Cooper, the tonic reminds us of the cocktail's immaterial, conceptual power. To repair one's fictional hangover, one does not need to "take a glass of nearly frozen, unstrained tomato juice, . . . plop a couple of oysters in there, . . . drink it down, breathe deeply." Nor does one need to "take a mound, and I mean a mound, of sweetbreads, sauté them with some chestnuts and some Canadian bacon," add "biscuits. Big biscuits, smothered in gravy" and, "where it gets tricky," know "you're gonna need some anchovies." Rather, one only needs to hear the remedy described.[24] Given that the story-world tonic is always an immaterial description for the reader, we are thereby encouraged to focus on its symbolic capacity. In doing so, we find the morning cocktail also preserving an extradiegetic capacity for fancy: the imaginative, counterfactual, hypothetical, or otherwise unrealized abstractions produced by engaging with the text. Thus, altogether, the tonic

1. repairs the protagonist's physical body;
2. affords the opportunity for dramatic irony;
3. guarantees the perpetuation of the plot, vis-à-vis the protagonist;
4. establishes the narrative's "normal";
5. underscores the tonic-giver's role as a narratological function;
6. establishes the "tactical" act that figures the authorial over the characterological; and lastly,
7. allows both the story-world tonic-giver and the reader a remora-as-revolutionary capacity for survival.

We see the symbolic bracer that is not an eye-opener in figures such as Miguel de Cervantes's Sancho Panza, whose tonic is realism; newer ones like Stephen King's Delbert Grady (of *The Shining*), whose primary solution is not the requested "hair of the dog that bit me" but delusion; and Batman-creator Bob Kane's Alfred Pennyworth, whose cocktails defeat pretended or unintended intoxication. In all of these cases, the restorative presented by the hired subordinate allows a temporarily vulnerable employer to recover his "good spirits," not so that the latter might remain sober or become healthy but rather so that he might be able to get "drunk" again and perpetuate his fight with ennui, crime, or windmills. In service foremost to the narrative, the tonic as bracer is dispensed when the otherwise heroic (or delusionally heroic) principal confronts an otherwise plot-hindering gastrointestinal, muscular, or neurological realism. Via Algernon, *The Importance of Being Ernest* offers a baseline for this kind of tonic-bringer: a seemingly subservient attendant who preserves his own usefulness via the preservation of his employer's physiology, memory, and legibility (or capacity to be remembered).

The valet in this mode reprises the bartender's role as conservator of narrative memory and legibility, as doctor to the body of both the hero and the text. As an ineluctable mechanism whose agency is ironically dependent on a plot that prolongs its subordination, such attendants intervene upon the "hero's fate" frequently enough to consider "redefin[ing] the *deus ex machina* as a *servus ex machine*."[25] They are, like the tonics they bring, articulating objects: items that speak, but only to connect, to rearrange the out-of-place remnants of intemperate nights and knights-errant so that the gentleman's narrative hangs together. In this way, bartender and valet work together to sustain cocktail culture: mixing the drinks that perpetuate the narrative and auditing the record of the adventures their mixtures promote.

While versions of these three figures appear as early as the seventeenth-century continental novel, the image of the valet as literal tonic-giver seems to crystallize at the turn from the nineteenth century to the twentieth, developing through prose and drama into film.[26] Having already moved from type to stereotype, this tonic-administering dynamic has become so familiar in contemporary film that it tends to appear now only as a revision—a revision that invokes viewerships aware of the tonic-dispenser's genealogy. Admittedly, none of the turn-of-the-century revisions I address here—Oliver Parker's *An Ideal Husband* (1999), Christopher Nolan's *Batman Begins* (2005), or Jake Schreier's *Robot & Frank* (2012)—signals the apotheosis of the tonic-giving act. Each film does, however, link the representation of the tonic and the tonic-bringing valet to the maintenance of narrative memory. Through solution of sodium bicarbonate; a blend of complex carbohydrates, fructose, and blue-green algae followed by another fizzy bracer; and a virgin mimosa, each film repeats and extends the power of the tonic to preserve the *fictional* cocktail culture. As we will explore further, it is the carbonated, Amis-derogated "alkalizing agent" common to each of these offerings that will in part come to mark the equally generic, never fully realized valet—either as "flat" footman, fantasy stereotype, or robotic prototype—as a potentially ominous model for the hungover hangover reader.[27]

THE PRESERVATION OF THE FANCIES

The Disaffected Fanciful

The turn-of-the-century tonic-giving scene preserves at least three embodiments of fancy: the disaffected fanciful, the pretending fanciful, and the earnestly fanciful. In the first of these three models, the tonic repairs the whimsical, capricious, clowning principal character. This is a common, normativizing figure of perpetually shifting, insatiable desires: a light-hearted, capricious hedonist, preserved by a valet with a tonic ever on hand. Wodehouse's Jeeves attends perhaps the best example of such a disaffected fanciful gentleman: Bertie Wooster.

Jeeves's "pick-me-ups" keep his employer on comical track, aiding in a constant narrative resuscitation that props Wooster up so that we can watch him fall over again. Perhaps for its ability to motivate seemingly unwanted and impossible-to-self-administer changes, Wooster describes the powers of Jeeves's tonic as extending beyond the natural. Among its natural ingredients—"some kind of sauce, the yolk of a raw egg and a dash of red pepper"—Wooster also imagines a facet "much deeper," a supernatural factor that could explain the tonic's "amazing," revelatory effect.[28] Upon its consumption, Wooster claims that "nature wait[s] breathless," framing the functioning of the natural universe as both dependent on and only indirectly involved in the revival of a gentleman's health.[29] The representation of Wooster-as-"world" afterward develops as an apocalyptic narrative, where the "Last Trump" sounds and "Judgement Day" does not only "set in," but does so with "unusual severity."[30] Then, prior to its reincarnation, "the"—that is, now generic—tonic drinker's universe is broken into parts. The abdomen is "heavily charged with molten lava," the "ears ring loudly," the "eyeballs rotate," and the "brow" "tingle[s]."[31] "Bonfires burst out" everywhere, amid a similarly ubiquitous "great wind," while "something resembling a steam hammer strike[s] the back of the head."[32] Just as absolute annihilation seems imminent, the crisis fades: "The wind drops. The ears cease to ring. Birds twitter. Brass bands start playing. The sun comes up over the horizon with a jerk."[33] Here, the revival of the universe is framed as dependent on the revival of the reading and reporting gentleman: the subjective, interpreting consciousness (reader) that constructs the story through first persona narration (reporter). Insofar as it also has the power to sustain universes, the novel's reader is hereby connected to the tonic and the narrative-constructing, tonic-giving valet.

While not always registered by the principal, the introduction of the tonic frequently causes an initial revolt followed by an eventual resetting of the recipient's attitude, direction, and focus. The breadth of this influence, however, is often connected to the aforementioned ambiguity of the tonic's ingredients, which emerges as a parallel trope to Jeeves's rarer model. Perhaps the best example of this metaphorical over metonymical model occurs in the opening shot of Oliver Parker's film adaptation of *An Ideal Husband*, where the valet, Phipps, brings a more visibly slothful Lord Goring a hangover remedy.[34] Unlike in the 2015 London revival of *The Importance of Being Earnest*, which saw a Goring-like Algernon consuming a Jeeves-like Prairie Oyster cure—raw egg, Worcestershire sauce, hot sauce, salt, and ground black pepper—Phipps's "lord" is here offered his "usual," a more ambiguous and perhaps literal tonic: a carbonated mixture whose contents are not disclosed.[35]

Perhaps even more than the prairie oyster—or the amber moon, which exchanges Worcestershire sauce for whiskey—the carbonated tonic exemplifies the thin line between intoxicating and detoxing cocktail, between reparatory and recreational drug. As it conflates the medicinal and the recreational, the tonic also reflects a twentieth-century shift from unique, private ingredients to unique, public labeling, especially insofar as its chemical distinction involves everything but the product's "active ingredient." In this way, like the range of purportedly tasteless, colorless, and odorless vodkas, the tonic brands the scientifically developed, expertly formulated product as exceptional. Continuing this trend, the latest hangover fads—for example, "The Hangover Patch"—underscore what is missing from their products: the historically informed expert, the valet-like dispenser *who also remembers*. The generic applicability of the always precisely formulated branded remedy (e.g., "Partysmart" or "Blowfish for Hangover") replaces the named but always uniquely mixed tonic (e.g., the black velvet or the Ramos gin fizz), thereby prefiguring the replicability of the digital valet—a device whose responses may or may not reflect the specific needs of its user. Like "Hangover Heaven's" bused-in IV, their ingredients are removed from the language of the cocktail and replaced in the world of medicine: they involve potassium, chloride, saline, sodium, and lactates. Like the valet cum physician (or dealer), the history of the depicted pick-me-up arcs from alchemy to chemistry.

Though Joseph Priestly introduced carbonated beverages in 1767, tonic water with quinine was not popularized as a hangover cure until the mid-1820s at the earliest, following the isolation of quinine by French chemists Pierre-Joseph Pelletier and Joseph-Bienaimé Caventou in 1820.[36] As quinine became a routine antimalaria dose regime for British and French armies, the popular narrative is that as early as 1825 soldiers would mix it with soda water, sugar, and gin in order to mask its bitter taste. As it thereby encourages (or at least excuses) drinking, tonic water with quinine comes to symbolize the ongoing contest between an escape from alcohol and an escape through alcohol. As a class no longer defined by ingredients but rather by context of use, all that distinguishes the cocktail-as-intoxicant from cocktail-as-tonic are time of day and method of delivery.

Oliver Parker's film adaptation of *An Ideal Husband* opens with a rack focus shot, which shows the foregrounded tonic-bearing Phipps drawing the curtains before attending to a woman who is exiting the dozing Goring's bed. The film underscores this distinguishing link, recalling the carousel necessitating the bracer and the history of the cocktail/tonic dynamic.[37]

Yet the final frame of this opening also ironically suggests that Goring (and not Chiltern) will fulfill the "ideal husband" promise of the title card, in part by drinking the rights things, especially the morning bracers that allow him to look and act the part.[38] In focalizing on Phipps's delivery, the opening also suggests both Phipps and the tonic as potential referents of the title: elements that care-take, which preserve and husband Goring. Investing future hangover remedies like "Drinkin' Mate" with an increasingly spousal sense, the tonic here—like Mabel Chiltern in the drama's plot—is the component that allows for even the possibility of Goring being, like Sir Robert Chiltern, an ideal husband. As a commodity, however, the reviver acts too efficiently, supporting Goring so well that he never need drink another. Shifting away from the comedy of Wodehouse, the film thus ends by depicting Goring's revival as a transition from the first model to the second model, that of the pretending fanciful.

While the tonic-bringing valet works to alleviate his employer's pain in both the first model and the second, the nature of the pain assuaged in each is distinct: namely, what causes the employer's pain in the latter is less directly a condition of his own making. His drinking, literal or figural, is the effect of a preexisting condition. Notably, the first model's condition is still apparent in the behavior of the second; though the first model can of course be read metaphorically, it is nonetheless the most literal of the three, and it is the specifically literal application of the tonic that the second model imitates.

The Pretending Fanciful

In the second model, the tonic—as it shifts from organic compound to chemical compound—acts to repair and preserve the image-creating, conceptualizing principal character. Here, as we drift into analogical territory, the "fancy" preserved is frequently less humorous and generally involves a ruse or passing—for example, the transvestism of Elizabethan drama—which allows the employer-hero to be seen as other than he/she is originally identified. Such heroes bear personas that initially exist only in the imagination: they, together with their valets, reify this image. They are the makers of fancy—figures that deploy the symbolic in order to regulate others' perceptions.[39]

Where the preservation of the disaffected fanciful (*Ideal Husband*) allows the gentleman to continue to blend in—to fit within an expected social mold—the preservation of the pretending fanciful (*Batman Begins*) helps the gentleman to craft "suitable excuses" for his behavior, to blend in by causing a scene, to "drive sports cars, date movie stars. . . . Buy things that aren't for sale," to control public perception about ideological investments beyond the gentleman's self.[40] Both models encourage the public to disassociate the pre- and posttonic gentleman, especially to protect the gentleman from the tawdry, attention-garnering label of the extraordinary. Yet while the first phase attempts to temper indiscretion with presentability, replacing memorable exploits with a forgettable every-gentleman, the second model attempts to temper presentability with indiscretion, foreclosing any possible public memory linking the gentleman (Wayne) to the extraordinary (Batman) and thereby protecting narrative cohesion.

The Alfred Pennyworth of Nolan's Batman trilogy, who acts as Bruce Wayne's butler, surrogate father, and physician, exemplifies the valet of this second model. The fatherly aspect of this transformation—which *Arthur*'s Hobson perhaps most notably represents[41]—is demonstrated in his hope that "if [Wayne] start[s] pretending to have fun, [he] might even have a little by accident."[42] Though invested in supporting his employer's alter ego—signaled in his suggestion that they modify Wayne Manor to accommodate Batman's needs after it burns down—Alfred does so while privileging Wayne's experience over his effect. Apposing the butler's role as a maker of fancy with his function as physical caretaker, the film signals the ongoing transformation of the valet's expertise from physiology to psychology and the tonic's transition from a physical reparative to a psychological one. The film's two tonic-bringing scenes demonstrate this shift. The first is reminiscent not only of Parker's *An Ideal Husband* but also of the tonic-giving tradition: Alfred enters, opens the curtains—letting in the daylight—and offers his employer an undefined beverage as a tonic.[43]

Conspicuously unlike the tonic that follows in the subsequent "revival" scene, which will signal the turn toward a scientific valet, this drink resembles an organic, homemade superfood smoothie: a green mixture suggesting the inclusion of fruits, vegetables, grasses, and an algal cyanobacterium like spirulina. Though it is no less "a drink taken as medicine, to give feeling of energy or well-being," it is not a solution to a hangover.[44] This first drink is rather intended as a buffer against the effects of Wayne's heroic, physical exploits—exploits made possible in part due to Wayne's carousing ruse. Unlike Jeeves's or Phipps's tonic, which aim to repair literal hangovers, Alfred's nutrient-rich drink is aimed at restoring Wayne's capacity to pretend: to perpetuate his fanciful playboy persona, to join in the drinking that evening,[45] to take *one* sip of champagne while acting the spoiled birthday boy as he kicks guests out of his house.[46] Ironically, as the second scene suggests, the tonic that helps Wayne recover from pretended drunkenness and physical perils that a drunk Wayne would never encounter is what ultimately leads to his intoxication. Alfred's precise imitation of the hangover tonic's delivery is likewise a diegetically superfluous addition to Wayne's drunken ruse—a performance for no character in the story-world. It does, however, inform the viewer of the tonic's adaptive capacity, as long as the mixture offers some pragmatic resuscitative purpose that supports its underlying function: to preserve a gentleman's fancy—in this case, to perpetuate the image of a Batman.

Even when the gentleman develops—from a Goring to a Wayne to a Batman—the tonic's role as the primary tool for preserving the "official" narrative continues, a function underscored by its universal applicability. While literature offers up the occasional cocktail-selective James Bond, heroic alcohol consumption is usually varied, with the inebriated consuming a range of drinks in various quantities. Meanwhile, the tonic's recipe—like the valet—remains unchanged. Here we see a holdover from the worlds of Jeeves and Phipps, a similarity retained by these otherwise distinct bracers: a good tonic suits any occasion, counteracts a spectrum of ailments, repairs one for any future condition.[47]

Likewise, while early iterations of the narrative tonic may imbue either their creators or their drinkers with personality, fictional tonics increasingly demonstrate a corporate-digital replicability. To the degree that the contemporary hero can acquire exactly the same tonic each time and has access to limitless brands, the valet's special "cure" reflects a trend toward generic technocratic commodity: a mass-produced solution that appears unique in (brand) name only. We see the promise of this transition in the second tonic-bringing scene from *Batman Begins*.

While similar to the first, this second scene includes two significant changes. Most notably, the second scene depicts Wayne recovering from literal intoxication, his having inhaled a "weaponized hallucinogen" in "aerosol form."[48] It is crucial that the organic vegetal blend from the first scene be exchanged for the transparent, carbonated tonic; the raw and organic is traded in for the extracted and medicalized, mirroring the shift from pretended to actual physical ailment.[49] The "tonic" here becomes the "antidote," a cure for an intoxicant that threatens not only Wayne but the entire community. Reinforcing this transition is not only Wayne's inability to pop out of bed and begin a push-up regime but also the presence of Lucius Fox, the current head of the Applied Sciences division at Wayne Enterprises. While Alfred's tonic is powerful enough to help Wayne recover from his fanciful exploits, Fox—symbolizing the nexus of business interests, technological innovation, and de facto medical expertise—appears when the intoxication is made real, when the effects last "two days."[50] Together with Alfred—as the hint of something added to the tonic—Fox helps to repair the hero's body so that it might again be chemically impaired, allowing the explicit, external physical ingestion of a bioweapon to replace the internalized and unreported (but nonetheless physical) chemical intoxication of adventure.

Of course, as the emergence of technology shifts both tonic and valet toward generic replicability, it does so to preserve the memory of the gentleman. As such, the corporate-digital becomes a mediator between the medical-physical and cultural-psychological, reifying in the fizzy drink, as in the body of the valet, a discursive mélange of traditions, directives, rumors, and plans. It is here that the two—tonic and valet—are themselves mixed, the valet transforming from tonic-bringer to tonic. Reading the valet as the eye-opener reinforces the cultural over chemical value of the tonic: the glass containing the hangover remedy could be filled with anything—or, as in William Wyler's postwar drama *The Best Years of Our Lives* (1946), could be empty—as long as the scene that depicts it promises the comfort of stability, a routine whose function produces a programmed result.[51]

What happens, however, when the gentleman-patient does not understand the output, the persona the tonic is keeping alive? Is it a failed version of the Jeeves-Wooster dynamic of valet handler and gentleman fool—for example, Edmund Blackadder to Prince Regent—where the valet has not quite discovered the discursive tonic necessary to keep his master in line? Not exactly: for in the model we've been following, the gentleman must be at least in some part occasionally self-aware, conscious of his condition relative to others, and, for these reasons, occasionally interested—metaphorically and literally—in getting drunk.

The Earnest Fanciful

Endemic to both the actual and the seeming dilettantes we have reviewed so far is their secret industry—their capacity to behave ethically and sympathetically (like *Sabrina*'s David Larabee) or with private, previously hidden motives (like Henry Jekyll). These two principals prefigure the third: the delusional, dreaming hero, a character marked by an imagination unrestricted by dependable memory and self-awareness. Like his preserving valet—which combines the qualities of Pennyworth and Fox—this gentleman's reviving cocktail offers a mix of cultural, medical, and legal assistance in a range of forms: straight hair of the dog, a nonalcoholic imitation of an alcoholic remedy, and, ultimately, the valet itself as the hero's memory (like the bartender that recalls for patrons what occurred the night before). As the valet begins to take on the role of the tonic, its diegetically fictional expression (its artificial intelligence) emphasizes a previously latent role for the reader, not as co-intoxicant with the protagonist but as co-conservationist with the valet. A compelling recent example of this valet appears in Jake Schreier's 2012 film *Robot & Frank*: a tale about a former jewel thief with midstage dementia who, after being given a robot aide by his son, recruits his nonmorally programmed sidekick to assist him in a set of burglaries.

While Robot performs the actions of other valets—cooks, cleans, wakes, feeds, and generally serves—he is from the start more overtly framed as the tonic itself. He prevents his "master," Frank, from trying to go to Harry's, his favorite out-of-business hangout. Certainly, when Frank classifies him as a "robot butler," the unnamed VGC-60L corrects him, suggesting he is instead "a health care aide programmed to monitor and improve your physical and mental health."[52] Yet rather than simply "monitor and improve" his master, Robot directly performs the reviving, rejuvenating, reanimating role of the tonic. As a "nursing" agent, he gets Frank "walk[ing]," organizing his thoughts, and inadvertently preparing him for future "adventures," or robberies.[53] In this way, like a medicinal remedy in a cocktail scene, Robot's reparative operations aid Frank's delusion: his intoxicating nostalgia for romance. While Frank's dream of reassuming his life as a thief is fed by his ongoing mental debilitation, its coherence and legibility are enabled by Robot in the role of the tonic. Notably, the first object Robot and Frank steal is an original copy of *Don Quixote*, one of several references to Miguel de Cervantes's picaresque.[54] *Robot & Frank* suggests that romantic narratives are—as they were with Quixote—Frank's drink of choice, or, more accurately, his fated condition.[55]

Apart from a single virgin mimosa, *Robot & Frank*'s metaphorical cocktail culture includes no literal tonics. This is due, in part, to Robot's refusal to allow Frank alcohol, which is "not good for [the] gout"[56] that Frank does not have or the high "blood pressure" that he does.[57] As a rejoinder to the "stay drunk" hangover remedy, Robot may seem to offer the preventative, "Don't get drunk." Yet in the metaphorical context of the film, which sees Frank chasing nonalcoholic "intoxication" throughout, Robot offers no such solution. Instead, his fantasies are repeatedly posed as cocktail surrogates, as when Jennifer—the ex-wife Frank does not recognize—summarizes a fundraiser as not "such a bad party, once you start drinking."[58] Champagne flute in hand, Frank eyes all the "gems and jewels" and suggests that the "whole thing [is] just one big scam," thereby linking the "free booze" and her buzz not to his dementia but rather to his burgling schemes.[59] Dementia, in this way, is then aligned with everyday life: the entropic condition the romantic intoxicant promises temporarily to assuage. The theme of romance as intoxicant is repeated again, after the heist, where the specter of alcohol arises again. "I got troubles," Frank tells Robot from the porch where he sits with his daughter, "I need a little booze to help unwind myself."[60] It is here that Robot offers Frank the virgin mimosa, representing in one sense the evasion of intoxication, in another the detoxing routine meant to counteract the dangerous romance of the previous night.

When such romantic narratives emerge, the valet-as-tonic establishes the condition in which the reader (viewer, interpreter) can participate in the protagonist's intoxication. Even as it draws the reader away from romance and back to realism—like Panza recasting Quixote's giants as windmills and stallions as asses—this tool sustains the gentleman's and reader's adventures.[61] Since the valet is here a tonic—an increasingly unthinking tool—the reader is encouraged to identify with the delusional gentleman, to take him seriously in spirit. The two, in a sense, get drunk together, take in (and take seriously) the romance of a piece of fiction.[62]

Robot & Frank, however, also reinforces how the reader's solidarity with quixotic value does not so much suspend disbelief as it does impose doubt. On this view, taking Frank seriously would not involve believing that he is right (inside the text)—or real (outside it)—but in valuing his delusion as being as serious a sign as any other in the film, in doubting the "believability" of any competing narrative. Thus, more than simply labeling fiction's windmills and giants as equally unreal, this view suggests that a character's delusional persona is no less credible an ideological sign than any other, either in or outside the text.[63] Insofar as ideation is privileged over realization, the intoxicating romance for which realism was originally the tonic becomes the tonic for the more troubling toxicity of reality.

Late in the film, Robot embodies for Frank such a tonic of romance. Frank's crimes have been detected and Robot encourages his owner to erase his memory: the single most damning piece of evidence against the two. When Frank suggests the ironically inhuman solution of lobotomy—of just "eras[ing] the bad parts"[64]—Robot reminds Frank that he is "not a real person,"[65] which reminds the viewer that Frank is not a real person either, and may not even represent one.[66] Through Frank's projection of humanity, the text suggests that the central dynamic of the two characters is not gentleman/valet but story-bearer/functionary, or, cocktail/tonic. As a function, "an advanced simulation" akin to a fictional narrative, Robot cannot help but be a tonic to Frank's daily reveries, cannot help but repeatedly restore him to a state of mind that the text ultimately suggests is one of perpetual delusion.[67] As he entreats Frank to erase his [Robot's] memory, channeling Dale Wasserman's *Man of La Mancha*, Robot also asks his master to "remember,"[68] to exchange Robot's record of events with his own incomplete, noncredible record.[69]

Robot is therefore neither archive nor archivist. He is the concoction that permits the rebooting of the master's memory, redacted to suit the scene. Just as a tonic does not restore one to full awareness of what transpired the night before, Robot-as-bracer preserves the gentleman's account by allowing his own sober memory to be erased.[70] Regardless of how earnestly Robot pleads for Frank to "remember," he—unlike the viewer—will forget. It is, in fact, the erratic wherewithal of the gentleman that fuels this vortex: the text's ironic black hole of remembering. Into the vacuum of the intoxicated gentleman and the forgetting valet comes the reader/viewer, the figure who will remember both the intoxication and the forgetting. Thus, even as viewers might be using the film as a tool for forgetting, they are reminded of their capacity as a repository for memories—a repository that functions not *to* forget itself but *by* forgetting itself. In fact, *Robot & Frank* lays out this role for the reader from the beginning of the film.

BEYOND THE EARNEST FANCIFUL: THE READER AS BARTENDER-VALET

The viewer's role as narrative valet-bartender is highlighted in *Robot & Frank*'s climactic scene. In having his memory erased, Robot sacrifices himself and narrative control to Frank's delusionally heroic history. Frank is thereby seemingly made responsible for keeping alive a version of Robot that no longer exists, which is the exact relationship his wife and children have with him. Yet given Frank's diminished capacity, the film's viewer becomes the sole repository for Robot's memory. Importantly, we aren't remembering Robot—Robot is just a tonic; we are remembering Frank: the cocktail consuming hero. In contrast to the impotent character—the drunk puppet on the floor—the viewer appears all-powerful. We are sustaining the legible, fanciful persona; we are responsible for defining specific acts and attributes, aligning those defined acts and attributes to specific characters, and thereby preserving the plausibility of individuated agency.

Just as the erasure of Robot's memory preserves Frank's belief in his power to make future decisions, the reader's self-consciousness-suspending role as narrative valet encourages faith in diegetic (and perhaps real-world) agency. The effect of this story-sustaining power is exemplified early in *Robot & Frank*, when Robot "walks" Frank in the woods. Frank is recoiling against the suggestion that he must develop healthier habits, saying that he "would rather die eating cheeseburgers than live off of steamed cauliflower."[71] In response, Robot reminds his master that if he "die[s] eating cheeseburgers"—if he commits acts that Robot should be preventing—Robot will "have failed" and will be sent "back to the warehouse" to have his memory wiped.[72] In this moment, the film demonstrates agency's essential relationship with narrative fiction. If the viewer takes Robot seriously, then the film's later, supposedly climactic, dilemma of whether or not to erase Robot's memory must be read as a ruse—just another of the text's actions that preserves Frank's illusion of control. If Frank had not erased Robot's memory, then Frank and Robot's crimes would be found out; Robot would likely be diagnosed as having "failed" in its job and thus "sent back to the warehouse."[73] Frank's fate, too, is likely the same either way: convicted of theft or not, he is likely to end up in a secure "memory center."[74] This *idea* of agency is preserved in Robot's performance but is saved only in the viewer's memory of Robot's memory of Frank's memory. If anyone recalls what "really" happened, it's the reader as valet-bartender. Faith in extratextual agency is thereby reinforced via the fabrication of fictional decision-making. Changes in *Robot & Frank* primarily chart moments in which the viewer—the only one with all the knowledge—is made to feel responsible for determining not only *what happened*, but also *who did what*. *Robot & Frank*, however, suggests that its narrative—like Robot's memory—is a "holographic array": an all-or-nothing record that can be seen either clearly or "in half the resolution" but cannot be altered.[75]

The reader's memory thereby relates to tonic-giving—to intoxicated revelry and subsequent recovery—insofar as it poses the consumption of an intoxicating agent as something other than an individuated decision, as something distinct from addiction. What the reader as valet-bartender preserves is the illusion of the individuated hero, if not the superhero: the possibility of one who may choose to drink, get drunk, and return to a similar condition of play the following evening. It begins with the exchange of tonics for cocktails, which signals the contest between narratives of individual control and conditioned entrapment.[76] The hero who drinks in the evening to feel empowered (as an individuated agent) wakes in the morning to blame the evening's events on his inebriation (as a conditioned effect). Next enters the tonic-administering valet to preserve the superiority of a hero who is ordinary. The hero is a veiled everyman whose mobility is as locally determined as everyone else's, as his valet's. The would-be gentleman hero thereby implies that any character with agency in a fictional narrative is by definition a superhero, wherein the defining superior trait is the power to act, to perform a task that is discernible as one's own, discrete from one's context, and capable of being the single identifiable cause of a particular, definable effect. Readers—invited in to supply choice, pretend action, and adjudicate credit and blame—thereby come to embody intoxication with the promise of an agency, change, or rejuvenation that they themselves have helped construct.

To this end, to engage with *Robot & Frank* or *Batman Begins* or *An Ideal Husband* is to rely on Amis's metaphysical hangover cure. And while it might seem inviting—especially with Amis in mind—to conflate the fictional and actual worlds, to treat the literal tonics in fictional narratives as mimetic cultural influences that encourage trends of consumption, the narratives in which these remedies appear encourage us to do otherwise. So while a bicarbonate of soda might suit a late-nineteenth-century dilettante, as a superfood smoothie does a late-twentieth-century faux playboy, or a virgin mimosa does a twenty-first century thief, the previous evenings that led to these conditions are not similar to those in which we find these figures. For some part of us knows that champagne is not what makes Goring drunk; Wayne does not need to avoid Falcone's bourbon to stay sober (or Alfred his Fernet-Branca); Frank can consume as much free wine as he wishes: they simply cannot get drunk alone.

So it is that the reader could be considered the principal drunk, and the implied author/text could be both providing the fancy and also—via disclaimers, metalepsis, and reminders of the reading experience—triggering a return to the extradiegetic, or real, which allows for the delight of the return to fancy. Conversely, the text could thwart the reader's persistence; could, as an intoxicant, be too powerful, too diverting; could produce a pleasant disorganization or disjointing order, a *mise en abyme* that, in reflecting the reader's assumptions too readily, produces an inchoate overstimulation, an overdetermined sensory blackout. In such a case, the tonic would become our own material existence, and forgetfulness become our valet. The contradictory record of our ongoing obliteration could then be seen through the reader as writer, the intoxication of absorbed reading mitigated by the sobriety of critical distance.

Yet it is here, as we weigh the nature of this sobriety, that the material value of these tonics we have discussed seems most relevant. For, as Amis suggests, alcohol is often directly influencing either writer or reader, and to treat it only metaphorically would be as negligent as treating it as only literal. Certainly, the drinking writer and the hungover reader have met many times and will continue to do so; and like Frank, who does not want "to talk about how [Robot does not] exist" because it makes him "uncomfortable," they will likely continue to celebrate the mimetic, autobiographical historicism of cocktail culture.[77] But in doing so, they will also be preserving metonymical-metaphorical symbols that speak largely to objects and ideas only indirectly tied to sodium and chloride ions, lactated Ringer's, or vitamin B. This is not so much a statement about the abstract quality of narrative fiction or its automatically nonmimetic capacity, but rather a statement about the already metaphorical capacity of the supposedly material drink once labeled, once brought into the world of letters. This is a product of the fictional narratives already available—some overt, some latent—in the world of the hangover remedy. It is in this world that a hangover can be treated by an "I.V. Doctor,"[78] guaranteed to supply you with an updated version of the "Myers' cocktail,"[79] where early morning nausea can be prevented or shortened via a "Drinkin' Mate" or by "Party[ing] Smart." Indeed, this fictionality corresponds to the fictionalities of social performativity and virtual personae: from branding and marketing, to the grand narratives of decorum and class; from anthropological routine and future studies, to the immediate fiction of the unrealized plan. These are the fictions of narrative constructivism, the ones ensuring that readers and viewers will continue to imitate not only Wilde but also Goring, will dress up in costume to "fight crime," hoping "Blowfish for Hangover" will heal their real injuries in ways that Bruce Wayne's unknown tonic never had to do. In short, there's little doubt that the fictional symbols will most often be read as uncomplicated mimetic signifiers. Luckily, for our metaphysical sakes, they don't have to be. Luckily, in a piece of narrative fiction, a cocktail is not a cocktail is not a cocktail.

NOTES

1. William Shakespeare, *Henry IV, Part I* (New York: Washington Square, 1994), I.ii.3–4. References are to act, scene, and line (pp. 24–25).
2. William Makepeace Thackeray, *Vanity Fair: A Novel without a Hero* (London: Wadsworth Classics, 2001), 51–52.
3. Kingsley Amis, *Lucky Jim* (New York: New York Review Books, 2012), 60.
4. Charles H. Baker, *The Gentleman's Companion, Being an Exotic Drinking Book: Or Around the World with Jigger, Beaker and Flask* (New York: Derrydale Press, 1946), 81, 82, 86, 87, 89. Among these are the morning glory no. I (1 jigger dry gin, the juice of 1/2 lime, 1 egg, and 2 teaspoons green crème de menthe), the morning doctor (1 1/2–2 1/2 jiggers of brandy, a "trifle over" a cup of milk, and a teaspoon of sugar, beaten), old pepper (1 jigger of rye, the juice of two-thirds of a lemon, 3 drops of tabasco, 1 jigger of bourbon, 1/2 teaspoon Worcestershire, and 1/2 teaspoon chili sauce), and the swiss yodeler (1 jigger of absinthe, 1 teaspoon anise, and 1 egg white, shaken with ice).
5. Baker, *The Gentleman's Companion*, 82.
6. Sterling North and Carl Kroch, eds., *So Red the Nose or Breath in the Afternoon* (Nelson, NY: Farrar and Rinehart, 1935), 1.
7. Baker, *The Gentleman's Companion*, 32.
8. Roland Barthes, *The Rustle of Language*, trans. Richard Howard (Berkeley: University of California Press, 1986), 148.
9. Adam Clark Estes, "Tips from Hunter S. Thompson," *The Atlantic*, September 8, 2018, https://www.theatlantic.com/entertainment/archive/2011/10/tips-and-tricks-hunter-s-thompson/336644/.

10. Christopher B. O'Hara and William A. Nash, *The Bloody Mary: A Connoisseur's Guide to the World's Most Complex Cocktail* (New York: Lyons, 1999), 12.

11. Alan Rudolph, dir., *Mrs. Parker and the Vicious Circle* (1994; Chatsworth, CA: Image Entertainment, 2006), DVD.

12. Christopher Hitchens, "Introduction: The Muse of Booze," in *Everyday Drinking: The Distilled Kingsley Amis*, ed. Kingsley Amis (New York: Bloomsbury, 2008), x, xi.

13. Kingsley Amis, *Everyday Drinking: The Distilled Kingsley Amis* (New York: Bloomsbury, 2008), 80–84.

14. Amis, *Everyday Drinking*, 83.

15. Amis, *Everyday Drinking*, 84.

16. Amis, *Everyday Drinking*, 84.

17. Amis, *Everyday Drinking*, 84.

18. As the forerunner to stories of middle-class semiheroes like George Babbitt, Julian English, and Harry Angstrom, many caste-centered narratives open after a night of revelry, already focalized on an upper-class bachelor in the midst of habitual recovery.

19. George Bernard Shaw, "Arms and the Man," in Vol. 1, *The Bodley Head Bernard Shaw: Collected Plays with Their Prefaces* (New York: Dodd, Mead, 1970), 413.

20. While there are also "maiden's maids," male nurses, and female butlers (especially in recent film, whether overtly like Helen Mirren in the remake of *Arthur* [2011], or covertly as the title character of *Albert Nobbs* [2011]), I here focus on ostensibly male/male valet relationships, ones that pretend a nonfemale domestic space in which the attendant plays both normative parental roles, embodying a duo whose stereotypical masculine and feminine attributes are not discernible, much less divisible. These categories could easily be reworked to explore the range of valets whose cis or trans identities remain ambiguous, a range that could include all identifiable valets.

21. William Goldman, *The Princess Bride: S. Morgenstern's Classic Tale of True Love and High Adventure* (New York: Houghton Mifflin Harcourt, 2013), 325.

22. Goldman, *The Princess Bride*, 317.

23. Goldman, *The Princess Bride*, 321. The reason for such privacy, suggests Miracle Max, has to do with the stakes of mixology: "You can't mess around with these resurrection recipes," he states. "One little ingredient wrong, the whole thing blows up in your face."

24. Duwayne Dunham, dir., *Twin Peaks*, Season 2, episode 18, "On the Wings of Love," aired April 4, 1991, on ABC.

25. Bruce Robbins, *The Servant's Hand: English Fiction from Below* (Durham, NC: Duke University Press, 1993), 131.

26. Even more than drama, film's mise-en-scène has the capacity to make immediately visible a deep field of background objects and subjects and to do so without the requirement of narrative focalization. This allows the viewer to focus on secondary or subordinate characters, incidental actions, and otherwise forgettable objects, simultaneously allowing for the invention of objects and actions that source texts, scripts, and librettos might not describe.

27. Amis, *Everyday Drinking*, 82.
28. P. G. Wodehouse, *Right Ho, Jeeves* (Charleston, SC: BiblioBazaar, 2007), 43.
29. Wodehouse, *Right Ho, Jeeves*, 43.
30. Wodehouse, *Right Ho, Jeeves*, 44.
31. Wodehouse, *Right Ho, Jeeves*, 44.
32. Wodehouse, *Right Ho, Jeeves*, 44.
33. Wodehouse, *Right Ho, Jeeves*, 44.
34. Oliver Parker, dir., *An Ideal Husband* (1999; Los Angeles: Miramax, 2000), DVD, 00:01:10. While they make similar ideological comments, Wilde's 1895 drama and Parker's 1999 film erect their pillories in distinct contexts. Breaking from Wilde's text, Parker's Goring groggily awakens in need of a remedy; in doing so, the film undermines the possibility of the entirely parasitic servant, even as it constructs a scenario by which the valet might gain more time and freedom to rebel. The film nevertheless supports the generally carnivalesque gentleman/valet dynamic, wherein the gentleman knowingly allows for and encourages the possibility of minor revolts, thereby ensuring the ongoing dedication of the servant to the preservation of the gentleman's self-identity, either through appreciation or through blackmail.

35. See Michael Arditti, "The Importance of Being Earnest and The Trial: Theatre Reviews," *Express*, July 5, 2015, https://www.express.co.uk/entertainment/theatre/588844. Referenced here is the London Vaudeville Theater production of *The Importance of Being Earnest*, which ran from July 1 to November 7, 2015. Compare Baker, *The Gentleman's Companion*, 88, which references the "So-called Prairie Oyster," recipe, which also includes 1 teaspoon ketchup, 1/2 teaspoon vinegar, and a pinch of cayenne pepper.

36. Teodoro S. Kaufman and Edmundo A. Rúveda, "The Quest for Quinine: Those Who Won the Battles and Those Who Won the War," *Angewandte Chemie: International Edition* 44, no. 6 (January 2005): 857. By focusing on the yellow bark of the cinchona (quina) plant, Pelletier and Caventou were able to show that it had different properties (such as solubility in diethyl ether) than the gray bark that Bernardo Antonio Grimes had used to produce his cinchonine extract in 1811. In this way, Pelletier and Caventou demonstrated that Grimes's cinchonine was actually a combination of two alkaloids, which they labeled cinchonine and quinine. It was this isolation that led to the more comprehensive study of the quina bark and the eventual development of this "pure compound as a specific treatment for malaria."

37. *An Ideal Husband*, 00:01:56.
38. *An Ideal Husband*, 00:01:24.
39. An earlier literary example of such an attendant is *The Count of Monte Cristo*'s Baptistin, who does the work necessary to preserve the image of Edmond Dantès as he plans and enacts his revenge on Fernand Mondego, Gérard de Villefort, and Baron Danglars. See Alexandre Dumas, *The Count of Monte-Cristo, or, The Adventures of Edmond Dantès*, vol. 1, *The Works of Alexandre Dumas* (New York: Peter Fenelon Collier, 1893), 528.
40. Christopher Nolan, dir., *Batman Begins* (2005; New York: Faber and Faber, 2007), DVD, 01:07:30.
41. Steve Gordon, dir., *Arthur* (1981; Burbank, CA: Warner Bros., 2005), DVD. In *Arthur*, Hobson professes his "love" for the "little shit," telling him from his own deathbed that "he is a good son." The film also includes the customary tonic-bringing, drape-opening scene in which Hobson delivers "orange juice, coffee, and aspirins," asks whether Arthur needs to "throw up," and then opens the curtains, speaking of the day as "seem[ing] to indicate that the night is over."
42. *Batman Begins*, 01:07:35.
43. *Batman Begins*, 01:07:20. While perhaps consolidated and concentrated in Nolan's trilogy, elements of this characterization of Alfred are present in the Bob Kane, Dick Sprang, and Bill Finger comics and comic series. See Frank Robbins, Irv Novick, and Dick Giordano, *Batman #216* (New York: DC Comics, 1969), 3; Alan Grant and Enrique Alcatena, *The Batman of Arkham* (New York: DC Comics, 2000), 18; Frank Miller and David Mazzucchelli, *Batman: Year One* (London: Titan, 2007), 87.
44. *Paperback Oxford English Dictionary*, s.v., "tonic, n.," (New York: Oxford University Press, 2012). Compare the *OED Online*, which defines the nominal tonic as a "medicine, application, or agent" that has the "property of increasing or restoring the tone or healthy condition and activity of the system or organs; strengthening, invigorating, bracing." *OED Online*, "tonic, adj. and n," http://www.oed.com/view/Entry/203193.
45. *Batman Begins*, 01:08:41.
46. *Batman Begins*, 01:44:01.
47. Regarding secret-keeping servants, see also Stevens from Kuzuo Ishiguro's *Remains of the Day*, Louka from George Bernard Shaw's *Arms and the Man*, or even Bertha Mills and Edmund Tuttle from Alejandro Amenábar's *The Others*, who temporarily keep the secret of their supposed employers' own demise from the employers themselves.
48. *Batman Begins*, 01:19:63.
49. *Batman Begins*, 01:19:55.
50. *Batman Begins*, 01:19:57.
51. William Wyler, dir., *The Best Years of Our Lives* (1946; Beverly Hills, CA: Metro-Goldwyn-Mayer, 2000) DVD, 01:56:26.

52. Jake Schreier, dir., *Robot & Frank* (2012; Culver City, CA: Sony Pictures Home Entertainment, 2013) DVD, 00:15:36.

53. *Robot & Frank*, 00:17:10.

54. *Robot & Frank*, 00:31:47.

55. In *Robot & Frank*, the potential "intoxication" metaphors are doubled: Yes, Frank has a form of dementia, a condition that could be treated as a form of perpetual inebriation, a contingent, biological, and unchosen state similar to that of being an alcoholic. Here, however, in part to upset literal equivalences between dementia and drunkenness, I focus on Frank's intoxication as being his identity with his still present inclinations—his desire to preserve the delusion not of what he used to be, but rather of what he never has been (that is, an ordinary law-follower).

56. *Robot & Frank*, 00:37:29.

57. *Robot & Frank*, 00:57:57.

58. *Robot & Frank*, 00:39:04.

59. *Robot & Frank*, 00:35:25.

60. *Robot & Frank*, 00:57:55.

61. Miguel de Cervantes, *The Ingenious Gentleman Don Quixote de la Mancha, Complete in Two Parts*, trans. and intr. by Samuel Putnam (New York: Modern Library, 1949), 63, 134.

62. We see this role reinforced, when Frank's accusatory final mark accidentally knocks a real mimosa off a patio table and Robot catches it. In doing so, Robot metaphorically preserves the intoxicant that keeps the fantasy going while simultaneously announcing to the also-present Sheriff Rowlings that Frank, while perhaps not able to pull of such jobs at "his age," is not performing such feats unaided.

63. Any decision about whether Quixote is "right" regarding the windmills being giants (or rather, the giants *not being* windmills) depends on an initial assumption that the referents originate as windmills. Quixote's "intoxication" produces a contest of reports: it permits the possibility of a vision that is distinct not only from that of other figures in the narrative (like Panza) but also from the narrator, who does nothing but report what it sees and what Quixote claims to see. For more on the "authenticat[ion] [of] fictional facts," see Lubomír Doležel, *Heterocosmia: Fiction and Possible Worlds* (Baltimore: Johns Hopkins University Press, 1998), 148.

64. *Robot & Frank*, 00:41:41.

65. *Robot & Frank*, 01:02:28.

66. *Robot & Frank*, 01:13:00.

67. *Robot & Frank*, 01:13:20.

68. *Robot & Frank*, 01:13:25.

69. Importantly, Frank's record of their illegal exploits is not necessarily less damning than Robot's, merely likely to be viewed as incomplete (i.e., inaccessible) and thus unreliable.

70. This event of forgetting is disallowed only by the film's dramatic irony, as it is when Lord Darlington's antisemitic sympathies are exposed for the reader in Kuzuo Ishiguro's *Remains of the Day*. Like Ishiguro's Stevens, Robot's role as an "unthinking" *restorative* does not prevent the reader from recalling the secrets that such sacrifices might aim to conceal. On this view, Mr. Stevens's survival in *The Remains of the Day*, however silent, marks his betrayal of rather than complicity with Lord Darlington; it is the factor that enables the master narrative that trumps his master's narrative. See Karen Scherzinger, "The Butler in (the) Passage: The Liminal Narrative of Kazuo Ishiguro's *The Remains of the Day*," *Literator: Journal of Literary Criticism, Comparative Linguistics and Literary Studies* 25, no. 1 (April 2004): 14.

71. *Robot & Frank*, 00:17:10.

72. Important here is that while Robot says this only to persuade Frank, he does not say that this is not true—and he confesses that he does not care if his memory is erased.

73. *Robot & Frank*, 00:17:20. While Robot is not programmed with morality, there is little to indicate that he does not know of its existence: if he did not, he could not advise Frank in the climactic scene as he does. His knowledge of others' morality implies that he knows that his tack for helping Frank maintain his health is against policy and, more important, is aimed at addressing the condition of Frank's imagination as the central means of preserving his self.

74. *Robot & Frank*, 00:12:55.

75. *Robot & Frank*, 01:02:33.

76. *Robot & Frank*, 00:27:27–36. As the "schedule," which "helps [Frank] remain oriented" is increasingly organized to let free him up for adventures, which must be done "quiet[ly]" in the "dark" without "be[ing] seen," the reader might see no available metaphor for cocktail culture. But this is precisely where it is most pronounced. Here, Frank seeks what such evenings offer: adventure without self-consciousness, the opportunity to be empowered to act while one's identity remains secret.

77. *Robot & Frank*, 00:41:50.

78. Adam Gabbatt, "The Restorative IV Drip: A Hangover Cure from 'The Dawn of Ages,'" *The Guardian: U.S. Edition*, December 30, 2014, https://www.theguardian.com/lifeandstyle/2014/dec/30/alcohol-hangover-cure-iv-drip-new-years. The "IV Doctor's" "Revive" package, intended "for deathbed relief" includes "130 mEq of sodium ion, 109 mEq of chloride ion, 28 mEq of lactate (pH balancer), 4 mEq of potassium ion, 3 mEq of calcium ion, Famotidine (a histamine H2-receptor antagonist that inhibits stomach acid production), Ondansetron (a serotonin 5-HT3 receptor antagonist used to prevent nausea), and Ketorolac (a nonsteroidal anti-inflammatory drug)." See also Justin Jones, "History's Craziest Hangover Cures," *The Daily Beast*, December 30, 2014, https://www.thedailybeast.com/historys-craziest-hangover-cures.

79. Alan R. Gaby, "Intravenous Nutrient Therapy: The 'Myers' Cocktail," *Alternative Medicine Review: A Journal of Clinical Therapeutics* 7, no. 5 (October 2002): 389. Though his "cocktail's" exact ingredients remain unknown, "it appear[s] that Myers used a 10-mL syringe and administered by slow IV push a combination of magnesium chloride, calcium gluconate, thiamine, vitamin B6, vitamin B12, calcium pantothenate, vitamin B complex, vitamin C, and dilute hydrochloric acid."

BIBLIOGRAPHY

Amis, Kingsley. *Everyday Drinking: The Distilled Kingsley Amis*. New York: Bloomsbury, 2008.

Amis, Kingsley. *Lucky Jim*. New York: New York Review Books, 2012.

Arditti, Michael. "The Importance of Being Earnest and The Trial: Theatre Reviews." *Express*. July 5, 2015. https://www.express.co.uk/entertainment/theatre/588844.

Baker, Charles H. *The Gentleman's Companion, Being an Exotic Drinking Book: Or Around the World with Jigger, Beaker and Flask*. New York: Derrydale Press, 1946.

Barthes, Roland. *The Rustle of Language*. Translated by Richard Howard. Berkeley: University of California Press, 1986.

Cervantes, Miguel de. *The Ingenious Gentleman Don Quixote de la Mancha, Complete in Two Parts*. Translated and with an introduction by Samuel Putnam. New York: Modern Library, 1949.

Doležel, Lubomír. *Heterocosmica: Fiction and Possible Worlds*. Baltimore: Johns Hopkins University Press, 1998.

Dumas, Alexandre. *The Count of Monte Cristo, Or The Adventures of Edmond Dantès*. Vol. 1, *The Works of Alexandre Dumas*. New York: Peter Fenelon Collier, 1893.

Dunham, Duwayne, dir. *Twin Peaks*. Season 2, episode 18, "On the Wings of Love." Aired April 4, 1991, on ABC.

Estes, Adam Clark. "Tips from Hunter S. Thompson." *The Atlantic*. September 8, 2018. https://www.theatlantic.com/entertainment/archive/2011/10/tips-and-tricks-hunter-s-thompson/336644/.

Gabbatt, Adam. "The Restorative IV Drip: A Hangover Cure from 'The Dawn of Ages.'" *The Guardian: U.S. Edition*. December 30, 2014. https://www.theguardian.com/lifeandstyle/2014/dec/30/alcohol-hangover-cure-iv-drip-new-years.

Gaby, Alan R. "Intravenous Nutrient Therapy: The 'Myers' Cocktail." *Alternative Medicine Review: A Journal of Clinical Therapeutics* 7, no. 5 (2002): 389–403.

Goldman, William. *The Princess Bride: S. Morgenstern's Classic Tale of True Love and High Adventure*. New York: Houghton Mifflin Harcourt, 2013.

Gordon, Steve, dir. *Arthur*. 1981; Burbank, CA: Warner Bros., 2005. DVD.
Grant, Alan, and Enrique Alcatena. *The Batman of Arkham*. New York: DC Comics, 2000.
Jones, Justin. "History's Craziest Hangover Cures." *The Daily Beast*. December 30, 2014. https://www.thedailybeast.com/historys-craziest-hangover-cures.
Hitchens, Christopher. "Introduction: The Muse of Booze." In *Everyday Drinking: The Distilled Kingsley Amis*. Edited by Kingsley Amis. New York: Bloomsbury, 2008.
Kaufman, Teodoro S., and Edmundo A. Rúveda. "The Quest for Quinine: Those Who Won the Battles and Those Who Won the War." *Angewandte Chemie: International Edition* 44, no. 6 (2005): 854–85.
Miller, Frank, and David Mazzucchelli. *Batman: Year One*. London: Titan, 2007.
Nolan, Christopher, dir. *Batman Begins*. 2005; Burbank, CA: Warner Bros., 2007. DVD.
North, Sterling, and Carl Kroch, eds. *So Red the Nose, or Breath in the Afternoon*. Illustrated by Roy C. Nelson. New York: Farrar and Rinehart, 1935.
O'Hara, Christopher B., and William A. Nash. *The Bloody Mary: A Connoisseur's Guide to the World's Most Complex Cocktail*. New York: Lyons, 1999.
Paperback Oxford English Dictionary [POED], s.v., "tonic, n." New York: Oxford University Press, 2012.
Parker, Oliver, dir. *An Ideal Husband*. 1999; Los Angeles: Miramax, 2000. DVD.
Robbins, Bruce. *The Servant's Hand: English Fiction from Below*. Durham, NC: Duke University Press, 1993.
Robbins, Frank, Irv Novick, and Dick Giordano. *Batman #216*. New York: DC Comics, 1969.
Rudolph, Alan, dir. *Mrs. Parker and the Vicious Circle*. 1994; Chatsworth, CA: Image Entertainment, 2006. DVD.
Scherzinger, Karen. "The Butler in (the) Passage: The Liminal Narrative of Kazuo Ishiguro's *The Remains of the Day*." *Literator: Journal of Literary Criticism, Comparative Linguistics and Literary Studies* 25, no. 1 (2004): 1–21.
Schreier, Jake, dir. *Robot & Frank*. 2012; Culver City, CA: Sony Pictures Home Entertainment, 2013. DVD.
Shakespeare, William. *Henry IV, Part 1*. Edited by Barbara A. Mowat and Paul Werstine. New York: Washington Square, 1994.
Shaw, George Bernard. "Arms and the Man." In Vol. 1, *The Bodley Head Bernard Shaw Collected Plays with Their Prefaces*. New York: Dodd, Mead, 1970.
Thackeray, William Makepeace. *Vanity Fair: A Novel without a Hero*. London: Wadsworth Classics, 2001.
Wodehouse, P. G. *Right Ho, Jeeves*. Charleston, SC: BiblioBazaar, 2007.
Wyler, William, dir. *The Best Years of Our Lives*. 1947; Beverly Hills, CA: Metro-Goldwyn-Mayer, 2000. DVD.

TWENTY

THE COLD GRAY DAWN OF THE MORNING AFTER

Hangover Cures and the Inevitability of Excess

STEPHEN SCHNEIDER

OF ALL THE DRINKS THAT have become emblematic of the cocktail revival, none seems so aptly named as the Corpse Reviver No. 2. It is a drink that itself seems to have risen once again from the dead, from being one of the hundreds of drinks found in Harry Craddock's *Savoy Cocktail Book* (1930) to a centerpiece drink in "Dr. Cocktail" Ted Haigh's *Vintage Spirits and Forgotten Cocktails* (2009). As a drink, it exudes style and embodies the best features of Prohibition-era mixology: combining equal parts gin, lemon juice, Cointreau, and Lillet, and held together with the faintest dash of absinthe, the Corpse Reviver No. 2 is nothing short of a masterpiece. Its demand for exact measurements places an emphasis on the bartender's craft, while its Savoy Hotel origins invoke the cultural history of the cocktail itself. Small wonder, then, that the resurgence of craft cocktail in the twenty-first century often seems to mirror the resurgence in popularity of the Corpse Reviver.

At the same time, the Corpse Reviver also stands as a reference to the long history of the hangover cure within both mixology and cocktail culture. As the "No. 2" suffix suggests, the Corpse Reviver isn't just a specific drink, but rather a class of drink intended for consumption the morning after the night before.[1] Just like hangover cures in general, the Corpse Reviver No. 2's curative properties are dubious at best. In recording the recipe for the No. 2, Craddock himself quips, "Four taken in swift succession will unrevive the corpse again."[2] Haigh likewise notes, "Personally, I can't imagine drinking these in the morning, but then, no one has offered, either."[3]

Corpse Reviver No. 2
  3/4 oz dry gin
  3/4 oz Cointreau

3/4 oz Lillet Blanc
3/4 oz lemon juice
1 dash absinthe (Ted Haigh recommends no more than 3 drops)

Combine ingredients over ice in a cocktail shaker. Shake for 30 seconds and strain into cocktail glass.

From Harry Craddock, *The Savoy Cocktail Book* (1930)

Craddock and Haigh's remarks gesture, then, not only to the ostensible dangers of overindulgence (though their cautions often seem more like challenges), but also to the intimate connection between the history of the cocktail and the history of the hangover, the history of a solution that seems to beget its own problem. If, then, we are to take their remarks at face value, we might wonder what, if anything, the hangover cure actually cures. The Corpse Reviver No. 2 thus captures the humorous tension at work in modern mixology: the tension between the refined standards of cocktail culture and the excess that those standards, properly embraced, seem to inevitably induce.

HAIR OF THE DOG

If the number of hangover cures found in cocktail books is anything to go by, we might conclude that the hangover is perhaps the greatest—or at least the most common—problem facing the bon vivant. A quick glance through this literature reveals a host of drinks designed to take the edge off the morning after. But a cursory examination of the recipes for picker-uppers also casts some doubt on their calming or curative effects. Drinks such as the Corpse Reviver and the Saratoga brace-up, for example, combined strong spirits with citrus and hardly seem likely to calm an upset stomach or a fevered brow. The dairy component of the Ramos gin fizz, the Suissesse, and the brandy milk punch (milk being a key ingredient in many emetics) might prove a little more soothing, assuming that it takes the edge off other ingredients. But overall, picker-uppers still seem oddly unsuited to the intended task. Nor is this a modern phenomenon: hangover cures extend back as far as mixology itself, and the history of the hangover and the history of the cocktail are likewise closely entwined.

In fact, it isn't too strong a claim to suggest that the cocktail emerged alongside—if not from—the hangover cure; as Haigh reminds us, "Cocktails were morning drinks."[4] Cocktail historian David Wondrich highlights this history when he notes that bitters—one of the earliest cocktail ingredients—were themselves considered a means of recovery from the excesses of drinking. One early advertisement portrays bitters as a way "to recover and restore a weaken'd Stomach or lost Appetite ... occasioned by hard Drinking or Sickness, &c." and "[carry] off the effects of bad Wine, which too many die of."[5] It was only natural, then, that bitters formed a key ingredient in early cocktails, which were likewise taken as "[therapeutics] in the morning... favored by a loungy, sporty, dissolute set."[6] Based on that category of drink known as a sling, so named because it was to be thrown back in the manner of a bracer, these cocktails ensured early the place of the hangover and the hangover cure in mixological history.

Even Jerry Thomas, whose 1862 *The Bar-Tender's Guide: How to Mix Drinks, or the Bon Vivant's Companion* is generally considered the first bona fide cocktail book, comments that the cocktail is a "modern invention, and is generally used on fishing and other sporting parties, although some patients insist that it is good in the morning as a tonic."[7] Thomas's doubt, and humor, in regard to these purported remedies would be a theme taken up both within the genre of the hangover cure and more generally by some of the most famous drink writers of the twentieth century. After all, the cocktail's origins were problematic to say the least. "Drinking in the morning," suggests Haigh, "often means getting over what you were drinking the night before, and that kind of behavior is what they used to call dissipated."[8] Charles William Janson, writing in 1807 of his travels in the United States, went so far as to name these drinkers "slingers" (based on what they drank) or "eleveners" (based on when they drank).[9] Even the first reference in print to the cocktail—in the *Farmer's Cabinet* in 1803—was presented as "evidence on the intemperance of modern urban youth."[10]

As the cocktail evolved, it retained this spurious medicinal association, coming to be known various as an "anti-fogmatic," an "eye-opener," a "bracer," a "corpse reviver," a "morning glory," or a "pick-me-up."[11] And as the term *cocktail* came to refer not to the narrowly defined bittered sling but to the more all-encompassing spirits-plus-anything-plus-ice-in-a-glass, these terms would come to be preserved in the name of actual drinks. The Saratoga brace-up and the morning glory were perhaps among the earliest of these named hangover cures. Both drinks look a lot like the Corpse Reviver No. 2, combining brandy, lemon juice, egg, bitters, and absinthe, and brandy, whiskey, absinthe, bitters, sugar, and curaçao, respectively. New Orleans, one of the cocktail capitals of the late nineteenth and early twentieth centuries, was the birthplace of such morning drinks as the brandy milk punch (brandy, milk, and sugar), the Suissesse (absinthe, cream, orgeat, and egg white), and the now classic Ramos gin fizz (gin, cream, lemon, lime, egg, and orange-flower water)—itself derived from the gin fizz, another common morning drink of the era.[12]

Temperance, World War I, and Prohibition would ultimately transform the cocktail from the frowned-upon pastime of morning drinkers to an emblem of the Jazz Age, leisure, and freedom. "With the stock market crash of 1929, talkies the same year, and Prohibition's repeal at the end of 1933, the cocktail's appeal was unequivocal. It was escape, the ultimate fantasy."[13] This transformation did not, however, remove the cocktail's association with its dissipated past. Instead, the dissolute drinkers of the nineteenth century were replaced by the leisure class of the twentieth century. Cocktails thus "symbolized a better world to come, a rainbow around the corner, and they actually produced physical euphoria."[14] While the cocktail thus seemed to shake off its association with morning drinking, it nonetheless retained its association with excess—albeit in a more positive light.

This shift in cocktail culture also nourished the genre of the hangover cure; as hangovers became less a marker of dissipation and degeneracy and more the consequence of a well-led life, drink writers were able to embrace spurious mixological cures in the spirit of fun. Charles H. Baker—described by one critic as "poet laureate of the cocktail"—included twenty-seven designated picker-uppers in his *Gentleman's Companion*, claiming that these drinks were "for the nineteenth hole, which can not only enable us to greet the new day undismayed but may—on occasion—save a life."[15] Around the same time, Fernand "Pete" Petiot began serving guests at the St. Regis Hotel in New York another classic hair of the dog: the Bloody Mary. But perhaps no group did more to radically expand the list of picker-uppers than the tiki mixologists of the 1930s and 1940s. Drinks like the painkiller, the fog-cutter, the suffering bastard, and the zombie preserved not only the traditional genre of the pick-me-up, but also the practice of naming these drinks so as to evoke the very problem they purport to solve. The painkiller and the fog-cutter, then, play on the "anti-fogmatic," while the zombie references both the Corpse Reviver and its potentially deadening effects (customers at Don the Beachcomber's were famously allowed only two zombies so as to avoid being turned into zombies themselves). The suffering bastard has similarly colorful origins, being invented by Joe Scialom at the Shepheard Hotel in Cairo allegedly to sooth the hangover of a suffering bar-steward. The suffering bar-steward becomes the corrupted "suffering bastard" (linguistically and existentially), and the rest is history.

Ferdinand "Pete" Petiot's Bloody Mary
I cover the bottom of the shaker with four large dashes of salt, two dashes of black pepper, two dashes of cayenne pepper, and a layer of Worcestershire sauce; I then add a dash of lemon juice and some cracked ice, put in two ounces of vodka and two ounces of thick tomato juice, shake, strain, and pour.[16]

Within the context of the current cocktail revival, drinks such as the Corpse Reviver No. 2 continue to gesture reflexively to this longer history. Hangover cures preserve not only the cocktail's own status as a one-time morning drink, but also the problematic association made between the culture of the cocktail and a culture of excess. On the one hand, the drink evokes the exactitude of measurement, the apex of craft and refinement, the height of taste and civility; on the other, the very name of the drink indexes the longer history of dissolution and decadence that underlies mixed drinks and sporting society. The hangover thus represents a constitutive problem, representing the very thing that makes cocktail culture possible and likewise threatens its ruin.

THE INEVITABILITY OF EXCESS

In *Everyday Drinking*, Kingsley Amis opens his lengthy discussion of the hangover by noting that "you can hardly open a newspaper or magazine without coming across a set of instructions . . . on how to cure this virtually pandemic ailment."[17] If the hangover is the problem that is forever on the drinker's horizon, then it should come as no surprise that writers like Charles H. Baker and Kingsley Amis give fairly detailed treatments for this condition. For Baker, the hangover is something that no bon vivant can escape: "There are times in every man's life when, through one reason or both, a man feels precisely like Death warmed up. In such a sorry plight there is but one thing to do if we do not wish to sit and suffer through a whole day waiting for the cool hand of normalcy to stroke our dry and fevered brow—a Picker-Upper."[18] For Baker, everyone has to pay the piper eventually. "For years before our ignoble experiment," Baker continues, "civilized man has been trying to civilize his drinking."[19] The hangover is simply part and parcel of this struggle—a struggle that, for Baker, continues to this day. After all, Baker reports that "his little list of variegated hairs of the dog has been hand-culled from quite a few joustings of our own with this sort of human withering on the vine," suggesting that his picker-uppers were at least born of both an urgent and a common need.[20]

Amis provides an even more lyric description, focusing not on the physical symptoms of the hangover, but rather on "the psychological, moral, emotional, spiritual aspects: all that vast, vague, awful, shimmering metaphysical superstructure that makes the hangover a (fortunately) unique route to self-knowledge and self-realization."[21] And while Amis claimed "to absolutely decline" a further description of the hangover (apparently "no fun to read or write"), he continues his discussion for another eight pages.[22]

We are told, for instance, of those authors who best describe the hangover: Dostoevsky, Poe, and Kafka, with Kafka's "The Metamorphosis" providing "the best literary treatment of all."[23] And we are introduced to "Gale's Paradox," or the principle that "if you do *not* feel bloody awful after a hefty night then you are still drunk."[24] Amis also considers the benefits of sex as a hangover cure, the reasons for avoiding a cold shower, and the close relationship that professional artists have with alcohol. But perhaps more important to this account is Amis's elevation of the hangover to a metaphysical level—as the title of Amis's essay suggests, we are no longer dealing with *a* hangover, but rather *the* hangover. It remains the accursed share of any good bout with the bottle, registering excess without providing us with any blueprint for dealing with it. The morning after it remains this indivisible remainder, a painful set of registrations that resist anything like a cure. Instead, we're left with "that ineffable compound of depression, sadness (these two are not the same), anxiety, self-hatred, sense of failure and fear for the future."[25]

The inevitability of the hangover, though, is only a symptom of the larger problem registered by Baker and Amis. After all, the hangover is, for many, at the heart of hard drinking. But hard drinking is nonetheless defined by the tension between moderation and immoderation—between holding one's liquor and getting on a bender. Put another way, and to loosely paraphrase Lowell Edmunds, classicist and author of *Martini, Straight Up*, the cocktail is both a civilized force and an uncivilized force—a marker of culture and a marker of culture's inevitable dishevelment.

As a civilized force, the cocktail is an emblem of conspicuous consumption and conspicuous leisure. Observing the leisure class of the late nineteenth century, Thorstein Veblen notes that "the life of leisure is beautiful and ennobling in all civilized men's eyes."[26] Leisure—both the abstention of labor and the nonproductive use of time—isn't simply the performance of one's class position. Rather, it also makes possible the cultivation of both manners and aesthetic taste, making it "not only a honorific or meritorious act, but presently... a requisite of decency."[27] Conspicuous consumption likewise functions both as evidence of one's pecuniary power and as the focal point for the exercise of taste. "Consuming in due quantity" and living a life of "ostensible leisure in a becoming way" become measures of one's refinement and reputability.

Both conspicuous leisure and conspicuous consumption—what Veblen calls more generally "conspicuous expenditure"—is thus focused on "conspicuous waste," whether that be wasted time or wasted commodities. Given that such conspicuous waste is focused on "luxuries and the comforts of life," drinking takes on particular importance: "Drunkenness and the other pathological consequences of the free use of stimulants therefore tend in their turn to become honorific, as being a mark, at the second remove, of the superior status of those who are able to afford the indulgence. Infirmities induced by over-indulgence are among some peoples freely recognized as manly attributes."[28] Not so for Veblen: The act of drinking marks only one aspect of this form of conspicuous waste. Overindulgence and drunkenness also become key parts of this performance. We might therefore suggest that for drinking to function as conspicuous waste, it must also be constructed as and performed to excess.

As cocktail culture emerged in the second half of the nineteenth century, and as it developed in the early decades of the twentieth century, these associations remained. Paul Fussell and Eric Felten both investigate the class and cultural associations of liquor and the cocktail, and the manner in which these associations were made manifest in drinking habits. It was important not only to know what to drink—which liquors, and which cocktails, for example—but also how to drink. After all, if drinking is to be an expression of leisure, it still needs to be performed with an eye to maintaining the pretensions of the leisure class.

Nevertheless, drinking also remains an expression of the profligacy of the bon vivant—a far more immoderate sphere of conspicuous consumption. Jerry Thomas's early remarks on the sporting set associated with the cocktail suggest that even early in the cocktail's history it had come to be a symbol not just of leisure but also of excess. This sort of drinking—Lowell's uncivilized force—concerns itself not with the maintenance of social mores or with the moderate consumption befitting those mores, but rather with decadence and debauchery. If such consumption becomes in Veblen's terms "honorific," that is because it expresses what philosopher Georges Bataille calls "profound freedom . . . given in destruction, whose essence is to consume profitlessly whatever might remain in the progression of useful works."[29] And it is this immoderation that ultimately animates the drinker: "This useless consumption is what suits me, once my concern for the morrow is removed."[30] We might suggest then that this kind of drinking is not just conspicuous but also *useless* consumption—consumption that is defined by its lack of concern for how it is conducted or interpreted, and that actively challenges the social narratives that typically attend other forms of conspicuous consumption.

Veblen acknowledges the potential for such uncivilized consumption when he notes that conspicuous leisure produced "a secondary, and in a sense spurious, leisure class—abjectly poor and living a precarious life of want and discomfort, but morally unable to stoop to gainful pursuits."[31] Anxiety over this spurious leisure certainly attends the morning drinkers of the eighteenth and nineteenth centuries, as we see in Janson's derisive and Thomas's humorous comments. Haigh likewise notes that the "sporting" set associated with cocktails were gamblers and small-time criminals rather than what we might now think of as the leisure class. In short, cocktails were associated with a more dangerous class of individual—a class that threatened the more staid virtues surrounding work, leisure, and consumption.

Following Bataille, useless consumption thus proves to be "an ostentatious squandering" that "places the value, the prestige and the truth of life in the negation of the servile use of possessions."[32] But in refuting both necessity and social utility, useless consumption also demands "the useless employment of oneself, of one's possessions, for play."[33] Hard drinking, then, might be taken as useless consumption par excellence, insofar as it isn't just about the ostentatious squandering of alcohol but also about the ostentatious squandering of one's self—one's poise, dignity, and ultimately health—in drunkenness and stupor.

Naturally, there are limits to how far one can take this sort of thing. Drinking for fun is all well and good, and drinking to excess is often taken to be part of that fun. Nevertheless, past a certain point, excessive drinking is subject to both derision and dismissal. The bon vivant, then, ostentatiously consumes not just alcohol, but also money, time, and ultimately physical and mental well-being; but at the same time, the drinker seeks to reassert the very social status that this behavior renders irrelevant. Useless consumption thus "calls for action in two contrary directions: We need on the one hand to go beyond the narrow limits within which we ordinarily remain, and on the other hand somehow bring our going-beyond back within our limits."[34] As Bataille concludes, useless consumption ultimately "attempts to grasp that which it wished to be ungraspable, to use that whose utility is denied."[35]

One might read Baker's and Amis's accounts as such attempts—as efforts to account for the hangover, to make it useful in some way, even if only as an object of humor. And yet the hangover resists such use: for Baker, it occasions only more drinking and begets only another hangover; for Amis, it brings only physical discomfort and metaphysical doubt. It is this contradictory logic that the hangover expresses in the most mundane of ways. After all, everyone who drinks stands to get a hangover at some point. But by the same token, there's no getting rid of a hangover either. On the one hand, the hangover stands as an expression of useless consumption and the squandering of the self. But at the same time, it stands for an excess that precisely can't be reintegrated into the mores and habits of conspicuous drinking culture.

Understood in this light—as both conspicuous and useless consumption—the hangover cure functions as a *pharmakon*, an object that serves as both poison and remedy. Insofar as drinking stands as an act of conspicuous consumption, it allows drinkers to reinscribe themselves within those customs and mores that broadly affirm their social status. Nonetheless, it is useless consumption that lies at the heart of such drinking practices, threatening—demanding—the dissolution of the very same customs. The rituals of mixology and drinking, measured according to various levels of exactitude, thus promise to contain this excess and to thereby serve as the antidote to potential ruin.

But as the hangover cure makes clear, this ruin is not potential but to some degree certain. And it is this certainty that the hangover makes clear: after all, the hangover attests to the power of the pharmakon to act in the absence of drinking rituals, and thus in the absence of the drinker's intentions. The pharmakon, then, threatens the very rituals that promise to contain it, and therefore the curative powers accorded it by the individual. Put another way, the useless consumption so perfectly expressed in hard drinking threatens the consumers themselves, not by accident but by design. And it is this problem that is far more simply and elegantly described as the metaphysical hangover.[36]

PRESCRIPTIONS FOR A CURE

The problem with a hangover—the hangover—is that there isn't much you can do about it or with it. Of course, this doesn't prevent people from trying: for the physical hangover, there any number of suggestions, ranging from cold showers to sleep to vitamin B. But for the metaphysical hangover, that existential doubt brought on by inevitable excess, there are only two real options. The first: You can repent. You can confess your sins, renounce your ways, even swear off alcohol with the phrase "never again." We see this played out to its elaborate and comical conclusions in the 2009 movie *The Hangover*, where too much drinking leads the movie's protagonists to lose their best friend on the eve of his wedding. The ninety minutes that follow consist of the cast's attempts not only to reconstruct what happened, but also to atone for their wrongdoings—they have to return a baby, a police car, and Mike Tyson's pet tiger, and receive beatings and tazerings commensurate with their crimes. The moral economy of the comedy is both taut and unrelenting. But what's important to note here is that, while making restitution, none of the characters drinks.[37]

But what ultimately comes of this kind of self-flagellation? Nothing, if you believe Kingsley Amis, who seems to suggest that repentance is for the most part simply acting in bad faith. After all, the hangover is neither the consequence of a prior sin, nor a comment on the immorality involved in having a good time. So atonement certainly won't restore you to some prelapsarian splendor, physical or metaphysical.

Your second option, maybe your only option, then, is to "start telling yourself that what you have is a hangover":

> You are not sickening for anything, you have not suffered a minor brain lesion, you are not all that bad at your job, your family and friends are not leagued in a conspiracy of barely maintained silence about what a shit you are, you have not come at last to see life as it is, and there is no use crying over spilt milk.[38]

"If this works," Amis concludes, "if you can convince yourself, you need do no more, as provided in the markedly philosophical. . . . He who truly believes he has a hangover has no hangover."[39] Amis's conclusion speaks more to his curmudgeonly common sense than any real attempt at philosophy: a hangover is a hangover, nothing less and certainly nothing more.

Of course, Amis does provide us with a few other cures for the metaphysical hangover: reading Solzhenitsyn's *One Day in the Life of Ivan Denisovich* or the final scene from *Paradise Lost*, while listening to Tchaikovsky's Sixth Symphony—both to be done while treating your physical hangover. And at around 12:30 p.m., Amis instructs us to "firmly take a hair (or better, in Cyril Connolly's phrase, a tuft) of the dog that bit you."[40] The dog "is of no particular breed," though Amis mentions the Bloody Mary or Underberg bitters as likely resorts and advises against ingesting any alkalizing agents. Charles Baker likewise cautions against "all revivers smacking of drugdom" in favor of "a bit of well-aged spirit with this or that."[41] After all, "the field of the great gray Morning After is one in which this same civilized mankind is trying to graduate from undiluted hair of the dog that bit him, to something less regurgitative, and shocking to the whole mental and nervous network."[42]

It is hard to ignore the contrast between the precise mixology involved in the creation of the Corpse Reviver No. 2 and the almost devil-may-care attitude that both Baker and Amis take toward the choice and composition of a pick-me-up. Such blasé dismissal seems to accord both with Amis's gruff approach to the hangover and Baker's almost poetic embrace of drunken excess, even though it cuts against the attention both authors pay to mixology and measurement elsewhere in their writings. And yet if there is truly no atoning for the excess of drinking, then it only follows that any remedy should be treated lightly and applied liberally. In this regard, the finicky proportions of the Corpse Reviver No. 2 seem a far less appropriate expression of the logic of the hangover cure than does the Bloody Mary, a drink that has become the epitome of mixological excess. Far from an austere curative, the Bloody Mary is something of a culinary dare—a pharmakon that, in its liberal use of hot sauce, Worcestershire sauce, cayenne pepper, celery salt, and tomato juice, more closely resembles the fires of hell. Far from curing the morning after, the Bloody Mary seems to ring the bell for round two.

After all, what better way to acknowledge the hangover—that reminder of the inevitability of excess—than to have another drink? As David Embury reminds us, folklore and homeopathic logic aside, we can hardly still think that hair-of-the-dog is an actual curative: "You don't treat arsenic poisoning by taking more arsenic or ptomaine poisoning by eating more contaminated food. Why be so naïve as to imagine that you can cure alcohol poisoning by drinking more alcohol?"[43] But there's a difference between curing alcohol poisoning and curing the metaphysical hangover. Following Amis's advice, the only way to cure a hangover is to face it squarely for what it is—which is to say, to acknowledge that you always already had it coming to you. Drinking is always already uncivilized and excessive, and a hangover is what remains of that uncivilized element when the glow of the night before wears off (even that glow has a decidedly uncivilized tint—allowing us to be a little too loud, a little too strident in our opinions, and a little too willing to not give a damn whom we offend). But *the* hangover was there when the night began, sharing in that first drink, encouraging you to have one too many; and it was there when the night ended, waiting around the corner to laugh at you. We might respond to Embury, then, with this: "Why be so naïve as to imagine you can cure a hangover—the hangover—at all?"

After all, as the personal lives of Kingsley Amis and other literary drunks remind us, the hangover is but a gesture to that much larger accursed share that attends alcohol: drunkenness, dipsomania, and alcoholism. And much like the hangover, there's little to be done with these problems either—there's abstinence, of course, or else restitution, or else resignation. And all too often—certainly in the case of Amis—resignation leads to ruin (we might remember that, long after the bottle ruined Amis's marriages, his failing health led him to move in with his ex-wife and her new husband, who in turn served as his full-time caregivers—it seems tragic to suggest that Amis himself came to so thoroughly embody the inevitable excess he'd written about with such wit and clarity). Small wonder, then, that the hangover seems to bring with it such metaphysical freight.

But as the history outlined by Wondrich suggests, this freight has always been there. The history of the cocktail—its birth in the colonies, its Progressive Era golden age, its relocation to Paris and London during World War I and Prohibition, its resurgence during the New Deal, its tikification and evolution in the 1950s, 1960s, and 1970s—suggests that excess always attends the mixing and consumption of a stiff drink. And the question that continues to haunt even the most mercurial of drinkers remains: What do we do with that excess once the drinking is over? Short of facing life's maladies sober (a threat that itself seems to demand a drink), there's no real cure for, or escape from, the hangover. And maybe this is what elevates the hangover from a physical problem to a metaphysical problem—its eternal and inevitable return. But this inevitability makes it both the greatest and least of a drinker's problems—one that demands a knowing nod, and ultimately, a recharge of the glass.

University of Louisville

NOTES

1. The Corpse Reviver No. 1 is an unremarkable combination of brandy, calvados, and Italian vermouth. It was to "be taken before 11am, or whenever steam and energy are needed." Harry Craddock, *The Savoy Cocktail Book* (London: Pavilion, 1930), 51.
2. Craddock, *The Savoy Cocktail Book*, 52.
3. Ted Haigh, *Vintage Spirits and Forgotten Cocktails: From the Alamagoozlum to the Zombie: 100 Rediscovered Recipes and the Stories Behind Them* (Beverly, MA: Quarry Books, 2009), 95.
4. Haigh, *Vintage Spirits and Forgotten Cocktails*, 17.
5. David Wondrich, *Imbibe!* (New York: Perigee, 2007), 171.
6. Wondrich, *Imbibe!*, 176.
7. Jerry Thomas, *The Bar-Tender's Guide: How to Mix Drinks, or the Bon-Vivant's Companion.* (New York: Dick & Fitzgerald, 1862; Repr., New York: Mud Puddle Books, 2008), 181.
8. Haigh, *Vintage Spirits and Forgotten Cocktails*, 18.
9. Charles William Janson, *The Stranger in America* (London: Albion Press, 1807), 299–300.
10. Haigh, *Vintage Spirits and Forgotten Cocktails*, 17.
11. Wondrich, *Imbibe!*, 214.
12. Wondrich, *Imbibe!*, 112.
13. Haigh, *Vintage Spirits and Forgotten Cocktails*, 24.
14. Haigh, *Vintage Spirits and Forgotten Cocktails*, 25.
15. St. John Frizzell, "Masters of Mixology: Charles H. Baker," Liquor.com, last modified January 13, 2012, http://liquor.com/articles/masters-of-mixology-charles-h-baker/#tJCRFK7WEsgw87sQ.97; Charles H. Baker, *Jigger, Beaker, and Glass: Drinking Around the World* (Lanham, MD: Derrydale Press, 1992), 81.
16. Geoffrey T. Hellman, "The Talk of the Town," *The New Yorker* (July 18, 1964): 19.

17. Kingsley Amis, *Everyday Drinking* (New York: Bloomsbury, 2008), 79. Amis's "The Hangover" first appeared in *On Drink* (London: Cape, 1972), a collection of his newspaper columns on all matters alcoholic.

18. Baker, *Jigger, Beaker, and Glass*, 81.

19. Baker, *Jigger, Beaker, and Glass*, 82.

20. Baker, *Jigger, Beaker, and Glass*, 82.

21. Amis, *Everyday Drinking*, 79.

22. Amis, *Everyday Drinking*, 80.

23. Amis, *Everyday Drinking*, 80.

24. Amis, *Everyday Drinking*, 81.

25. Amis, *Everyday Drinking*, 84.

26. Thorsten Veblen, *The Theory of the Leisure Class: An Economic Study of Institutions* (New York: Penguin, 1994), 38.

27. Veblen, *Theory of the Leisure Class*, 41.

28. Veblen, *Theory of the Leisure Class*, 70.

29. Georges Bataille, *The Accursed Share: An Essay on General Economy*, vol. 1, *Consumption*, trans. Robert Hurley (New York: Zone Books, 2007), 58.

30. Bataille, *The Accursed Share*, 58.

31. Veblen, *Theory of the Leisure Class*, 42.

32. Bataille, *The Accursed Share*, 73.

33. Bataille, *The Accursed Share*, 73.

34. Bataille, *The Accursed Share*, 69.

35. Bataille, *The Accursed Share*, 73.

36. It is tempting at this point to continue with this somewhat Derridean analysis and to suggest that the hangover is in fact a supplement to drunkenness, always coming after it and challenging whatever meaning or positive effect we attribute to drinking. And in that sense the hangover always refuses to submit to the presence of the drinker and the intentionality of the drinker's acts. Put simply, one is always the author of one's drunkenness; but one is never the author of one's hangover, or that trace that remains after drunkenness subsides. But if the hangover insists not on the metaphysicality but rather the materiality of the pharmakon, then the problem posed is less philosophical and more simply physiological.

37. They do, in fact, drink once while attempting to find their friend (Doug), specifically when they resort to counting cards in order to raise the ransom money needed to secure Doug's release from a kidnapping. But what we learn here is that the protagonists (Alan, Phil, and Stu) do not need to make restitution, but rather to quite literally double down on the night before. But then again, we also learn that the hangover that animates the film is as much the result of Alan, Phil, and Stu accidentally ingesting Rohypnol as it is the result of their drinking too much alcohol. And ultimately, when Doug is found on the roof of

the hotel in which all four are staying, the elaborate restitution they've made may itself be beside the point.

38. Amis, *Everyday Drinking*, 84–85.
39. Amis, *Everyday Drinking*, 85.
40. Amis, *Everyday Drinking*, 83.
41. Amis, *Everyday Drinking*, 82.
42. Amis, *Everyday Drinking*, 82.
43. David Embury, *The Fine Art of Mixing Drinks* (New York: Mud Puddle Books, 2009), 346.

BIBLIOGRAPHY

Amis, Kingsley. *Everyday Drinking*. New York: Bloomsbury, 2008.
Baker, Charles H., Jr. *Jigger, Beaker, and Glass: Drinking Around the World*. Lanham, MD: Derrydale Press, 1992.
Bataille, Georges. *The Accursed Share: An Essay on General Economy*. Vol. 1, *Consumption*. Translated by Robert Hurley. New York: Zone Books, 2007.
Craddock, Harry. *The Savoy Cocktail Book*. London: Pavilion, 1930.
Embury, David. *The Fine Art of Mixing Drinks*. New York: Mud Puddle Books, 2009.
Felten, Eric. *How's Your Drink? Cocktails, Culture, and the Art of Drinking Well*. Chicago: Surrey Agate Publishing, 2007.
Frizzell, St. John. "Masters of Mixology: Charles H. Baker." Liquor.com. Last modified January 13, 2012. http://liquor.com/articles/masters-of-mixology-charles-h-baker/#tJCRFK7WEsgw87sQ.97.
Fussell, Paul. *Class: A Guide through the American Status System*. New York: Summit Books, 1983.
Haigh, Ted. *Vintage Spirits and Forgotten Cocktails: From the Alamagoozlum to the Zombie: 100 Rediscovered Recipes and the Stories Behind Them*. Beverly, MA: Quarry Books, 2009.
Hellman, Geoffrey T. "The Talk of the Town." *The New Yorker*. July 18, 1964.
Janson, Charles William. *The Stranger in America*. London: Albion Press, 1807.
Phillips, Todd, dir. *The Hangover*. Written by Jon Lucas and Scott Moore. Los Angeles: Warner Bros., 2009.
Thomas, Jerry. *The Bar-Tender's Guide: How to Mix Drinks, or the Bon-Vivant's Companion*. New York: Dick & Fitzgerald, 1862. Reprint, New York: Mud Puddle Books, 2008.
Veblen, Thorsten. *The Theory of the Leisure Class: An Economic Study of Institutions*. New York: Penguin, 1994.
Wondrich, David. *Imbibe!* New York: Perigee, 2007.

AFTERWORD

CONFESSIONS OF A COCKTAIL NERD

SONJA KASSEBAUM

I'M A SPIRITS DRINKER. AND a spirited drinker. Don't get me wrong, I like beer and wine, but I *love* spirits—always have. In my youth, I thought the amaretto sour was a sophisticated drink. It was the 1990s, and I mostly mimicked what I saw others doing, especially women slightly older than me, women I admired. In those days, people were drinking mostly highballs or supersweet concoctions designed to bury the alcohol in a sugary cascade of fruitiness.

Suddenly, cocktail glasses full of pink liquid were everywhere at the bars and restaurants—it was the *Sex and the City* era. Though many were still made with cheap ingredients, like bottled sour mix, they were served in a cocktail glass (commonly called a martini glass), which hadn't seen much use in quite some time. The heyday of "martinis" was upon us. And cocktails, especially those served in a martini glass, were seen as women-oriented drinks—all my friends were drinking them, to be sure.

Trendsetting bartenders in New York (Dale DeGroff, Tony Abou-Ganim, and their progeny) were already reviving classic cocktails during this period, but none of that had reached the Midwest yet. I credit Ted Haigh (also known as Dr. Cocktail) and his *Vintage Spirits & Forgotten Cocktails* (Apple Press, 2004) with introducing me to classic cocktails. Who knew that an American bartender wrote the first cocktail book, or that most of the great cocktail tools and techniques were invented by Americans?!? Who knew that cocktails weren't supposed to be made with prebottled sour mix and were so much better with fresh juice?!? It changed my world.

So, in the mid-2000s, I embarked on a journey to make pretty much all the drinks in Dr. Cocktail's book. The most important lesson for me was this: a cocktail can be an experience in a glass, an opportunity to see how ingredients come together to become something more than any one of them is on its own. Unlike many books I owned at that time, this book was full of drinks that were drinkable and interesting. Completing this journey led me to discover the magic and wonder of liquor departments at large liquor stores and the thrill of the hunt for defunct spirits and bitters at older, smaller, less heavily trafficked stores.

One of my enduring favorite cocktails from that time, which I discovered in Dr. Cocktail's book and shared with others, is the Corpse Reviver No. 2. It's a "gateway" cocktail, one that helps demonstrate the concept of a cocktail as an experience—the ingredients combine into something boozy yet refreshing, herbal, and nuanced. With equal measures of gin, fresh lemon, orange liqueur, and Lillet Blanc,[1] along with a drop of absinthe, it's a layered, bright cocktail that dances on the palate. And, as Harry Craddock writes in *The Savoy Cocktail Book* (Pavilion, 2002), "four of these taken in quick succession will unrevive the corpse again." It was originally created as a morning cocktail, a hangover cure, but to this day I have never had one in the morning.

In the mid-2000s, there were maybe four bars in all of Chicago and the surrounding area where you could order a manhattan, a martini, or a Sazerac and actually get a well-rendered version of the drink. Now, I had only just learned what the classic style *was* around that time, but I was excited to find others who knew this secret history and wanted to geek out about it with me. My days were spent toiling away as an employment lawyer, and my nights were spent at one of those four bars, or more often with cocktail paraphernalia strewn about my kitchen as I played around with cocktails and spirits. I lived and worked in the north suburbs of Chicago and spent a lot of time at work, so I didn't get to spend that much time in those bars. I loved the feel of them, though, sitting among others who appreciated a great drink. It was like a secret club, and it was a great opportunity to meet interesting people, make a new friend, and learn a thing or two about one of my favorite hobbies. I almost always walked away with a new idea or favorite cocktail.

Around that time, I made a decision that was widely regarded by my friends and family as impulsive (well, I did elope in Las Vegas at age twenty to someone I dated for two and half months). I quit my lawyerly job and joined my husband in a new enterprise: a small artisan distillery. It was (and still is) a great combination of our interests and talents, really: he is a chemical engineer by training and shares my passion for spirits and cocktails, and I have some expertise in compliance and regulatory schemes. Since we pay taxes twice a month and must track every drop of alcohol, my education has come in handy. With that, cocktails became part of my professional life, too. At the time, I had no way of knowing where my cocktail journey would take me, or the strange and wonderful (and occasionally terrible) things I would discover.

Once we started the distillery, we delved even deeper into spirits and cocktails than we had before. In fact, our office at the distillery was so overloaded with random bottles of spirits that the local sheriff's deputies thought we were doing something illegal when they came through our front door for a surprise visit and found the racks of booze. An interesting thing happens when you are in the booze business: because you are constantly surrounded by liquor, you become desensitized to how it looks to someone outside the business that you have so many bottles of booze all around your workplace, at your house, in the trunk of your car. As time has passed, we have accumulated an obscene number of bottles of spirits, bitters, and mixers, so much so that we tell our friends and family not to bring spirits of any kind to our house—we probably have far more than we (and they) should (and probably could) drink in our combined lifetimes.

For many years, we were wildly experimental with our cocktails, and with our distilling, too—always testing the limits, trying new things, and looking for balance while creating something interesting. We made a few really disgusting things, some so-so things, and a few amazing things. We learned how different botanicals, fruits, vegetables, and spices behave when infused, distilled, macerated, or otherwise introduced into alcohol.

We also spent a lot of time in bars and restaurants, and with bartenders and restaurateurs learning about their business while sharing ideas, recipes, spirit samples, laughs, and stories. It's still one of my favorite pastimes—I love checking out new menus, geeking out about classic cocktail history and new combinations of flavors and ideas, and being inspired and awed by a great drink. Whether the drink is made with one of our spirits or not, it's a true pleasure to see people express themselves creatively in beverage form. That we get to enjoy a great drink with more than one of our senses makes it all the better.

THERE ARE OTHERS

I was not alone, of course, in my newfound love of cocktails. Through many channels, fellow cocktail lovers found ways to express their adoration, to explore new cocktails and cocktail history, and to share their enthusiasm. And they have helped shape the cocktail culture in the last decade with their efforts.

Some fun and very nerdy things happened in 2007 and 2008. I started a blog about cocktails and joined a network of bloggers around the country who were writing about our cocktail experiments and experiences. Blogging really had a moment back then, and it took off in many different industries—a new frontier of nonexpert, nonmedia types taking to the internet to share their thoughts. We participated in monthly group posts and got together in person and online to geek out about what we were learning and doing. Along the way, many of us were granted press credentials to attend a small but influential event called "Tales of the Cocktail."

"Tales" is an annual cocktail festival held in July in New Orleans, and it has grown immensely in the years since I first attended. In 2007, it was still a small, informal affair targeted at the industry and hardcore cocktail enthusiasts. I loved it because I was surrounded by people who were more knowledgeable about cocktails than I was, and there were many great opportunities to learn from others, including some legends in cocktail culture like DeGroff, Gary Regan, and Robert Hess. I even got to meet Haigh and get an autographed copy of his second edition for my collection.[2] Each year, Tales became a larger and more high-profile event, and eventually I, and many of my blogger friends, stopped attending. For me, it was a practical decision—I own a small distillery that sells spirits only in the midwestern United States, and Tales has a worldwide following. While I would have a great time at Tales, it would be a vacation rather than a meaningful opportunity to develop my business, and participating became expensive, relative to the size of our company. For many of my blogger friends who were not in the business, it had changed enough that it was no longer as interesting or as cost-effective as it once was. Nonetheless, Tales continued to expand its influence and scale; in fact, its annual awards came to be viewed by some in the industry as the "Oscars of Bartending." Tales was marred by significant controversy in 2017, and its influence has lessened in the aftermath. A new leadership team has been working to restore its prominence.

There is a lot of cocktail history in New Orleans, and Tales has always been based at the Hotel Monteleone, the home of the famed Carousel Bar. It's actually a very slow-moving carousel that rotates around the bar—the first time I'd ever seen or heard of such a thing. The Vieux Carré cocktail was invented at that very bar—or more precisely, at the bar that would become that bar—in 1937. Composed of rye whiskey, cognac, sweet vermouth, Benedictine, and bitters, it's an herbal, boozy mix of flavors for savoring. Now, each time I find myself in New Orleans, I stop by the Carousel Bar for a Vieux Carré—but only one, or I risk falling off the carousel when I stand up.

Eventually I—and virtually all my blogger friends—stopped blogging, too. Several bartend for a living now, a few went on to become professional writers, and the rest just went back to living their lives, starting families, and such. We keep in touch on social media, but that's about it. New bloggers have taken up the torch, likely to run their course writing about their adventures as well, or to become bartenders or writers.

There has been an explosion in the publication of cocktail books over the last decade or so, a few of them written by my blogger friends. These days, cocktail books are actually selling, and new books are appearing all the time. Many of the new books are quite specialized, focused, for example, on a specific period in history, person, or type of cocktail or spirit. Many are written by well-known writers, but some are by industry newcomers looking to build their personal brand. When my journey with cocktails began, there simply weren't enough people to buy these kinds of books, so they weren't being written. Now, you can find a wide range of websites, mobile applications, and other tools for your inner cocktail nerd. Unfortunately, you will also find a wide range of reliability for accuracy and deliciousness, as many of the apps and websites are funded by companies from within the industry that are aiming to promote their products.

THE LADIES LOVE COCKTAILS

As another outlet for my love of cocktails, I started the Chicago chapter of a group called LUPEC, the Ladies United for the Preservation of Endangered Cocktails, in the late 2000s. LUPEC was started in 2001 by a group of women in Pittsburgh with the following mission:

> In a post-millenium [sic] world of beer and prepackaged Chex Mix™, LUPEC works tirelessly to breed, raise, and release cocktails that are endangered or even believed to be extinct.
>
> The collecting of anachronistic recipes by women, and the resulting creation of endangered cocktails in an all woman setting is intended to achieve the following goals:
> - To create a secular "coven-like" atmosphere in which Classy Broads of today can invoke and honor the spirits of their Forebroads
> - To continue the 150 year American tradition of dangerous women calling themselves Ladies and getting together in groups, clubs, and societies to work undercover while they chipped away at the patriarchy.
> - To protect the collective Joie de Vivre of LUPEC members by assuring them at least one good party a month
> - To encourage the accumulation and use of vintage serving and barware.[3]

I invited some of my favorite women to join me in this club, and they invited a few others. For many years, we got together once a month to sip on great classics like the Violet Fizz, the Dixie Cocktail, and other mostly forgotten drinks, and to explore new ingredients and flavors together. It was also a wonderful opportunity to ensure that we actually saw each other, and we took care to limit our membership to women who everyone felt fit into the group. Some of us took the cocktail history and the collection of vintage barware more seriously than others, but we all formed lasting friendships with new people and tried a wide range of cocktails and spirits together. Several have blamed me for turning them into cocktail nerds (snobs?) as well.

A few years after our chapter started, women in the bartending industry began forming LUPEC chapters. Given that women were not even allowed by law to bartend in Chicago until 1970, there was a definite lack of women in the bartending community; some would say there still is. Those women were looking for an opportunity to get together, to compare notes, and to support and encourage each other, and LUPEC seemed like a great foundation. Soon, chapters were forming all over the country, primarily started by female bartenders, and national LUPEC meetings were held at Tales of the Cocktail. We had three chapters here in Chicago, in fact. The rules of LUPEC were that there could be only twelve members, so when one chapter filled, a new one was started. The second and third chapters here were mostly, but not entirely, made up of women in the bartending or liquor industry, with the occasional journalist or food scientist.

Interestingly, the original LUPEC chapter in Pittsburgh was mostly inactive. However, they continued to feel strongly about the mission of LUPEC, which they had created. The website was (and is) still accessible, but they were not responsive when I started the Chicago chapter; the Boston chapter helped me most. My only interaction with the "mothership" was sending them our check for membership dues. As time went by, other chapters learned that the main founders of LUPEC were unhappy with the direction the industry-driven chapters were taking. They still wanted the organization to be politically active, and they took a strong stand on a variety of issues: they had given themselves the tagline "dismantling the patriarchy one cocktail at a time," and they felt that that sentiment should underpin all activities under the banner of LUPEC. The industry women were decidedly pro-women in their activities, but they avoided political issues: their focus was on inclusion and support rather than political action. Eventually, the industry groups dropped the LUPEC banner altogether.

Not wishing to become a political organization either, for a time my group changed our name to the Ladies Drinking Society. While a few of us still get together occasionally, we, too, stopped meeting regularly. The other Chicago chapters disbanded as well, with many of the original members moving out of the area, leaving bartending, or transitioning into new roles in the industry that made participation difficult. Like the "mothership," our chapters had run their course, and no one was left who would put in the effort to organize meetings and events.

BARTENDING AS A CAREER

Another group of people were also focused on organizing and supporting bartenders and promoting bartending as a career path: the United States Bartenders' Guild, which has become a force in the evolution of American cocktail culture. The USBG has existed for at least sixty years, but in the late 2000s you would have been hard-pressed to find anyone who knew anything about it. The chapter in Chicago was in its infancy then, and I joined my local chapter in 2009. Initially, it was an opportunity to network and to learn—the group held a variety of educational sessions around Chicago. Some bartenders resisted the guild, either because they didn't see any value in it or because they thought it must be biased because it was supported in large part by a large, nationwide liquor wholesaler. In fact, some bartenders formed independent guilds at first, which have gradually joined the USBG—it's a lot of work to run a member-based group. Over the years, the Chicago chapter has grown to include several hundred members of the bartending community (as well as liquor company representatives), and to offer a wide range of social, educational, and community-service projects around the area. USBG chapters have also been formed in most of the major cities in the United States; the organization has a full-time staff now, as well as a charitable foundation and other offshoots.

While plenty of criticism could be leveled at the organization, the USBG has helped promote bartending as a career and has helped raise the level of education and training that bartenders have in cities where USBG has chapters. The number of bar professionals who plan to make a career out of bartending has skyrocketed, and the USBG has helped to legitimize that career choice. In the late 1800s, some bartenders were celebrities, and people waited in line to have a cocktail made by them. In today's era of celebrity chefs, we now have celebrity bartenders again, with national competitions and even reality shows dedicated to bartending. Bartenders are starting spirits companies, distilleries, and bitters and syrup companies; they're commanding appearance fees these days; and bartending and bar management is now widely seen as a viable long-term career path.

CRAFT DISTILLING: WHAT'S OLD IS NEW

Bartenders, cocktail lovers like me, and other entrepreneurs are expanding the liquor industry by becoming manufacturers, as well. Before Prohibition, there were thousands of small distilleries in the United States. Many sold only in their local area, and they used local crops for their products. With the renewed emphasis on where our foods (and beverages) come from, and the craving for new experiences that is so prevalent in our culture generally, craft distilling has exploded in the United States over the last decade. In 2004–2005, there were about sixty small distilleries in the United States; by early 2020, that number had surpassed two thousand.

Interestingly, the passion for local and handmade beers, and even local and handmade food products, did not translate over to spirits initially. For many, the lingering effects of large spirit company marketing hung on—good vodka only comes from Russia, for example—and dollars were spent on brand building rather than on the product itself. Because I had no experience in sales or marketing, the process of learning to market and sell my own product was a journey.

As our nascent craft distilling industry has grown, we've had a heyday in cocktail bars. Over the last few years, more and more restaurants were "farm to table," and they focused on using local, seasonal ingredients, including spirits. While that remains the focus at some places, the restaurant and bar industry will inevitably turn toward a new focus, and that is evident here in Chicago. The restaurant and bar businesses are extremely competitive, and their numbers are expanding as well, which puts further pressure on each individual restaurant to continue to innovate and attract customers. As competition increases in craft distilling, and as investor money flows into the industry, the focus of our business will continue to evolve as well. While we hope that reverence for classic cocktails and for the concept of a cocktail as an experience will continue, we wonder sometimes.

THIS IS PART OF THE CULTURE, TOO

Other things are going on in the cocktail and drinking culture, and some of them are not nearly as refined as the drinks Jerry Thomas wrote about in 1862. One example: Jeppson's Malört. I so love cocktails, but I also love introducing people to this uniquely Chicago drinking institution. It's an experience in a glass of a totally different sort. The story goes that Jeppson's Malört was invented by Carl Jeppson, a Swede, to replicate a style of bitter spirit he enjoyed in Sweden; it was considered "medicinal," and he sold quite a bit of it during and immediately after Prohibition in Chicago. Initially it was made in Chicago and was served primarily to older men who shared Mr. Jeppson's love of bold flavors and strong spirit, men such as the brand's next owner, the attorney George Brode. Brode's legal secretary, Pat Gabelick, took over the company upon Brode's death in 1999. She had gone on the record repeatedly stating that she did not like the taste of it,[4] but no matter—she continued to market and promote the brand in Chicago with vigor. In 2019 a Chicago-based company purchased the brand and it moved production of the spirit from Florida, where it had been for years, bringing it back to Chicago.

What does it taste like? Mostly, dirty sweat socks with a touch of grapefruit. And it lingers on the palate. For a very long time. Thirty minutes later you might still be tasting its bitter, unflinchingly earthy flavor. Yet it also endures in popularity and has grown immensely as a brand over the last ten or so years, even as quality cocktails have also become far more commonplace.[5] It's really an icon of Chicago drinking culture now: several bars even serve it on tap. So, even if it's a bit of a sucker punch, introducing people to it is somehow great fun when you're taking them out for cocktails in Chicago for the first time.

In fact, I love doing it so much that I served it at the conference that led to this very book. Most of the authors in this book had their first Malört experience with me, and some of them were pretty upset with me at the time. As a visitor from Chicago, at a conference convened to talk about cocktail and drinking culture, I thought it was appropriate for me to bring Malört. So, after listening to presentations by many smart and insightful authors, I stood up and got them each to take a shot of Malört—with no forewarning. I have to confess that the thought of it still makes me giggle; it was definitely the largest group of people I have ever introduced to Malört at one time. It might be that I have a mean streak, but I also think Malört becomes part of the culture for most people who spend meaningful amounts of time in the bars of Chicago. Chicago is a special place: it's the "City of the Big Shoulders,"[6] a "City on the Make."[7] It's a town full of hustlers, in every sense of that word; its people work very hard, always striving and fighting to get ahead, and there is some ugliness along the way. Including in our beverages.

At the same time, we also have bars offering boozy milkshakes, "fern" bars mimicking the bar culture of the 1970s (but the best one here in Chicago has really solid drinks), and bartenders celebrating blue curaçao in cocktails—cocktail trends that are not classic by any means, but nonetheless are gaining traction as well as press coverage. As groups and trends come and go, the cocktail and drinking culture continues to evolve and change.

COCKTAIL CULTURE TODAY

Today there are dozens of great cocktail bars in Chicago, even some in the suburbs and outlying areas, and quality restaurants in urban areas are widely viewed as being outdated if they don't have a decent cocktail program. This is happening across the Midwest, and across the United States in cities large and small. The level of education, professionalism, and standards in many cocktail bars these days is truly impressive, and the array of options for cocktail nerds like me is unending.

While for many years the focus has been on local and seasonal flavors, as cocktail culture evolves it is becoming more specialized and is veering off in new directions—for example, toward mezcal or sherry-based cocktail menus and themes, geographically derived cocktail menus, and the like. Bars are selling cocktails using defunct ingredients, old "rescued" bottles of spirits that aren't made any more, and are making many ingredients in-house. They are barrel-aging cocktails; making their own bitters, tinctures, and liqueurs; and continuing to evolve and change with the times.

Cocktail and spirits professionals are now recognized in chef-centric award ceremonies and events, such as the prestigious James Beard Awards. The level of awareness and attention to bartending and cocktails is continuing to expand, and cocktail and spirit-focused books, websites, and mobile apps have proliferated. New interest groups, industry and trade groups, and marketing companies with more specialized focuses that simply did not exist ten years ago are popping up around the country and the globe. Cocktail culture has changed so much in the twenty-first century so far, but some things haven't changed. It's still an interesting time to be a fan of cocktails and spirits, and to be a member of the liquor industry. Here's hoping it stays that way for many years to come.

Chicago

NOTES

1. The topic of Lillet in this cocktail is a subject of debate among cocktail nerds, most preferring to use Cocchi Americano rather than the currently available Lillet Blanc, because the recipe of the latter has changed over the years and the former is thought to be closer to the original. I personally like it both ways.

2. In the interest of full disclosure, Dr. Cocktail mentions me and my blog in the second edition of *Vintage Spirits and Forgotten Cocktails*, in a new section intended to recognize influential online cocktail pioneers. See Ted Haigh, *Vintage Spirits and Forgotten Cocktails: From the Alamagoozlum to the Zombie 100 Rediscovered Recipes and the Stories Behind Them*, 2nd ed. (Beverly, MA: Quarry Books, 2009).

3. See http://www.lupec.org/mission.html.

4. See Mike Sula, "Omnivorous: Shot of Malort, Hold the Grimace," *Chicago Reader*, April 9, 2009, https://www.chicagoreader.com/chicago/shot-of-malort-hold-the-grimace/Content?oid=1098569; and Melissa McEwen, "How Swedish Malort Became Chicago's Mascot Bitter Drink," The Salt, National Public Radio, May 10, 2013, https://www.npr.org/sections/thesalt/2013/04/15/177362556/how-swedish-malort-became-chicagos-mascot-bitter-drink.

5. The marketers for Malört did a very smart job with this product, producing videos such as "What Does Malört Taste Like?" (https://www.youtube.com/watch?v=tNMin0a9ILg) to capitalize on its reputation. For years, there has been a Flickr group called "Malört Face" for before and after photos of people trying the drink for the first time (https://www.flickr.com/groups/malortface/).

6. See Carl Sandburg, "Chicago," *Poetry* 3, no. 6 (March 1914), https://www.poetryfoundation.org/poetrymagazine/poems/12840/chicago.

7. See Nelson Algren, *Chicago: City on the Make* (New York: Doubleday, 1951).

CONTRIBUTORS

WILLIAM BIFERIE is an academic advisor at St. Petersburg College in Clearwater, Florida. His recent projects include a bibliographical essay on Sir Philip Sidney commissioned by Oxford University Press and an ongoing love affair with T. H. White's *The Once and Future King*. His research interests include pop-cultural studies, Arthuriana, and the narratology of science fiction and fantastic literature. He prefers Gordon's gin, but he'll drink whatever you have behind the bar.

DAN CALLAWAY serves as Vice President of Hospitality at Bardstown Bourbon Company in Bardstown, Kentucky. A certified sommelier, he was formerly General Manager of Decca Restaurant in Louisville and Assistant Principal French Horn of the Louisiana Philharmonic in New Orleans. A native of England, Dan has found a home in Kentucky, surrounded by spirits, music, and family.

ANTONIO CERASO is Associate Professor and Chair of the Department of Writing, Rhetoric, and Discourse at DePaul University. His research focuses on expert and amateur writing and knowledge building in technical and scientific disciplines. He has published on topics such as free and open-source software communities, amateur mycology and psilocybin experimentation, and, now, mixing good drinks.

EDWARD P. COMENTALE is Professor of English, Associate Vice Provost for Arts and Humanities, and Director of the Arts and Humanities Council at Indiana University Bloomington. He is author of *Modernism, Cultural Production, and the British Avant-Garde* (2004) and *Sweet Air: Modernism, Regionalism, and American Popular Song* (2013). He coedits a book series on fan cultures, through which he has published two coedited volumes: *The Year's Work at the Zombie Research Center* and *The Year's Work in Lebowski Studies*. His work has been featured in the *New York Times*, the *New Yorker*, and *Rolling Stone* and on NBC's *Dateline*.

MICHAEL COYLE, Professor of English at Colgate University, is founding president of the Modernist Studies Association, served as president of the T. S. Eliot Society from 2013 to 2015, and has been an active jazz disc jockey for the past quarter century. His most recent book, authored with Roxana Preda, is *Ezra Pound and the Career of Modern Criticism* (2018).

JONATHAN ELMER is Professor of English at Indiana University, where he also serves as Director of the College Arts and Humanities Institute. He is author of two books: *Reading at the Social Limit: Affect, Mass Culture, and Edgar Allan Poe* (1995) and *On Lingering and Being Last: Race and Sovereignty in the New World* (2008). His many articles have addressed topics ranging from Niklas Luhmann to Jeff "the Dude" Lebowski.

MARIE SARITA GAYTÁN is Associate Professor of Sociology and Gender Studies at the University of Utah. Her work has appeared in *Meridians: Feminism, Race, Transnationalism*; *Journal of Rural Studies*; *Journal of Consumer Culture*; and *Feminist Formations*. Her book *¡Tequila! Distilling the Spirit of Mexico* was published in 2014.

LORI HALL-ARAUJO is Assistant Professor in the Fashion Program and Curator of the Costume Museum and Research Library at Stephens College in Columbia, Missouri. Her work has appeared in *Museum Anthropology Review* and *Film, Fashion and Consumption*. She is currently completing the book *The Missing Body from the Carmen Miranda Museum*.

CHRISTOPH IRMSCHER directs the Wells Scholars Program at Indiana University Bloomington, where he is also Provost Professor of English. He is author of many books, among them, most recently, *Max Eastman: A Life* (2017). His homepage can be found at www.christophirmscher.com.

AARON JAFFE is Frances Cushing Ervin Professor of American Literature at Florida State University. He has published extensively on modern and contemporary literature and cultural theory, including *Modernism and the Culture of Celebrity* (2005), *The Way Things Go: An Essay on the Matter of Second Modernism* (2014), and *Spoiler Alert: A Critical Guide* (2019).

SONJA KASSEBAUM is the chief cocktail nerd and resident bar enthusiast at North Shore Distillery, the artisan distillery she runs with her husband Derek. Over the years, she has written an influential blog about cocktails and has spoken to groups across the midwestern United States about cocktail history, cocktail making, and Chicago cocktail culture. North Shore Distillery manufactures a range of award-winning spirits and was the first craft distillery founded in the Chicago area since Prohibition (founded in 2004).

MICHAEL JAY LEWIS is a critic, cartoonist, and creative writer specializing in modernism, fiction studies, and the rhetoric of the nonhuman. He is currently Assistant Professor in the Core Division at Al Quds Bard College.

CRAIG N. OWENS is Professor of English and Director of the Center for Teaching Excellence at Drake University, where he teaches courses in modern drama, play writing, and critical theory. He is editor of *Pinter Et Cetera* (2009) and has written articles and essays on Samuel Beckett, Harold Pinter, George Bernard Shaw, James Joyce, Arthur Miller, Alan Ball, Lady Gaga, Arthur Miller, James Bond, and vodka. He is the author of *Staging Technology: Medium, Machinery, and Modern Drama* (2020).

ANDREW PILSCH is Associate Professor of English at Texas A&M University, where he researches and teaches rhetoric and the digital humanities. He is author of *Transhumanism: Evolutionary Futurism and the Human Technologies of Utopia* (2017). His work has appeared in the journals *Amodern*, *Philosophy & Rhetoric*, and *Science Fiction Studies*.

SUSAN REIGLER, author of four books about bourbon, is a contributing correspondent to *American Whiskey* and *Bourbon+* magazines, as well as the bourbon columnist for *Food & Dining—Louisville*. From 2015 to 2017, she served as the president of the Bourbon Women Association and was elected to membership in Les Dames d'Escoffier International in 2016. She holds degrees from Indiana University and the University of Oxford.

JUDITH ROOF is author of seven monographs, including most recently *What Gender Is, What Gender Does* (2016) and *The Comic Event: Comedic Performance from the 1950s to the Present* (2018). She has also authored six edited collections, including *The Year's Work in the Oddball Archive* (with Jonathan Eburne; 2016) and *Lacan and the Posthuman* (with Svitlana Matviyenko; 2018). She has also published essays on such topics as narrative theory, studies in sexuality, Hollywood cinema, DNA, the shift from analogue to digital, psychoanalysis, gender, film theory, hoaxes, *The Big Lebowski*, nerds, Viagra, James Bond, feminist criticism, protozoa, systems theory, critical legal studies, and the work of Samuel Beckett, Harold Pinter, Marguerite Duras, Virginia Woolf, Percival Everett, Richard Powers, Nicole Brossard, David Hare, Simon Gray, Tom Stoppard, and, well, Rabelais. She is the William Shakespeare Chair in English at Rice University.

ALBERT W. A. SCHMID is author of ten books, including four cocktail books and a textbook on beverage management. He is also a consultant and a college instructor.

STEPHEN SCHNEIDER is Associate Professor of English at the University of Louisville. While he spends altogether too much time reading old cocktail volumes, his research typically focuses on the relationship between social movements, rhetoric, and education. He's happiest while drinking a daiquiri, and he doesn't care who knows it.

LISA SUMNER is Professor of Humanities at Marianopolis College in Montreal. She also teaches Communication and Media Studies at Carleton University in Ottawa. Her work on drink culture has appeared in journals and edited collections in Canada and Europe including *Globe: Revue internationale d'études québécoises*, *La ville autrement*, and *Konsum und Nation*. She can be reached at l.sumner@marianopolis.edu.

JOSEPH TURNER is Assistant Professor of English at the University of Louisville. He writes on medieval rhetoric and literature, and his work has appeared in the journals *Rhetorica*, *The Chaucer Review*, *Pedagogy*, and *Rhetoric Review*. When not writing, he's probably enjoying some of the fine bourbon produced in Kentucky.

STEPHEN WATT is Provost Professor of English at Indiana University. His most recent books include *Bernard Shaw's Fiction, Material Psychology, and Affect: Shaw, Freud, Simmel* (2018), *"Something Dreadful and Grand": American Literature and the Irish-Jewish Unconscious* (2015), and *Beckett and Contemporary Irish Writing* (2009).

INDEX

Italicized page numbers refer to figures.

Abercorn Restaurant, 248
Abou-Ganim, Tony, 96, 384
absinthe, 15, 82, 362n4, 370–71; Absinthe Frappé, 83–84; aesthetics of, 292–93; aficionados of, 295–96; alchemy, 298; Angostura bitters and, 228; bitters and, 372; champagne and, 346; colors in, 83–84, 289–90, 292, 296, 385; decadence of, 15, 290, 293, 295; in drinking culture, 297–300; etymology of, 293; French, 87; history of, 294–97; in modernism, 289–91, 293; Old Absinthe House, 83–84, 298–99; in old-fashioned, 85–86; origin narratives of, 290–94; signifiers of, 291; Swiss, 87; vermouth and, 327–28; violence and, 296–97; water with, 298; whiskey and, 86
Absolut vodka, 169–77, 175–76, 181, 186–87
Adorno, Theodor, 7
advertisements: for aficionados, 215–16; celebrities in, 174–75; colors in, 152; fashion, 133, 135, 135, 137; femininity and, 204, 213, 214; for manhattan, 322, 324; for margarita, 214, 216; marketing and, 212–13; in postcolonialism, 147–49, 148, 150, 151; by Seagram's, 146–49, 148, 150, 151, 153, 159, 161n17; for vodka, 13, 169–77, 186–87; for whiskey, 331
aesthetics: of absinthe, 292–93; of American empire, 224–27; after colonialism, 227–28,

230; of hedonism, 229–30; language and, 295; of modernism, 234–35; pan-colonial, 230–32; of Polynesia, 236, 239–40; of race, 225; of Tiki culture, 236–40
aficionados, 38, 48, 50, 52–54, 295–96; advertisements for, 215–16; of cocktails, 6, 44–45, 49, 313
After the Rising (Enright), 258n24
Agua Caliente race track and resort, 208
aircraft, 232–35
Akley, Steve, 198–99
Alabama fog-cutters, 68
Alamo Drafthouse, 323
Alaska cocktail, 4, 19n19
Albert, Bridget, 96
alchemy, 108–9, 265–66, 277–78, 298
alcohol: alchemy of, 277–78; *Alcohol Education*, 205; alcoholism, 33, 309, 311, 346, 350, 356–61, 366n55; Civil War and, 62; cocktail culture and, 336; cocktails and, 93; consumption, 157, 311–12; in culture, 146, 261; dementia from, 357; gender and, 152; grain, 106, 326; history of, 205; infusions, 386; literature and, 6, 333–35; in *Mad Men*, 312–14; masculinity and, 265, 273–77; medicine and, 348, 354; relationships and, 69; restriction of, 206–7; science of, 298; soda water and, 352; in *Star Trek*, 262–64, 270–73; stereotypes of, 335; violence and, 277

399

Algeria, 276
Ali, Mohammed, 338
All About Eve (film), 122
All Consuming Images (Ewen), 171, 180
Allen, Charles, 235
Allen, Woody, 174
allspice, 229
All That Heaven Allows (film), 130–32, 131, 138
alternative modernism, 292–93
Ambulance Cocktail, 39
Amenábar, Alejandro, 365n47
America: American cocktails, 10, 25–31, 32, 33–34; American empire, 224–27; American Revolution, 27, 30–31, 33, 44, 84; Americans (cocktail), 68; American Trilogy, 44, 52; American whiskey, 327; Barnum's American Museum, 63, 67–68; bartending in, 115; blended spirits in, 240n2; Canada and, 154–55; civil rights movement in, 277; class in, 223–24; cocktail culture in, 170; consumers in, 121; craft distillation in, 390–91; creativity in, 106; culture of, 10–11, 14, 111, 113; distillers in, 390–91; England and, 68; Europe and, 85, 293–94; femininity in, 209–10; *Gallery of Illustrious Americans*, 64; Great Britain and, 151; Hawai'i for, 235–36; industrialism in, 230; Italy and, 37; Mexico and, 203–4, 206–7, 210–13, 214, 215, 217–18; mixing in, 65; mixology in, 67–68; New Deal in, 380–81; *Pioneer of the American Bar*, 6; politics in, 34; popular culture in, 211; race in, 226–27; stereotypes of, 329; *Taco USA*, 215; temperance movement in, 205–6; tequila in, 211–12; Vietnam War for, 249; vodka in, 13; women in, 130–35, 131, 133, 135–37, 138–39; after World War II, 139, 226–27, 234
American Gangster (film), 255
Americano, 37, 49, 393n1
American Psycho (Ellis), 13, 169–71, 177–87
American Psycho (film), 13, 171, 177–79, 181–85
American Tragedy, An (Dreiser), 333–34
Amis, Kingsley, 16, 346, 360–61, 374–75, 377–79
Amy Vanderbilt's Complete Book of Etiquette (Vanderbilt, Amy), 132, 138

Anatomy of a Murder (film), 135, 138
Ancient Age Distillery, 195–96
Angel's Envy Bourbon, 18
Anglo-Irish War, 251–52
Angostura bitters, 39, 82–83, 89n24, 97, 111; absinthe and, 228; Hollands gin and, 346; in manhattan, 339; in old-fashioned, 299, 306, 315
anise, 295, 298, 362n4
Antiques & Fine Art (journal), 29
anxiety, 171, 184
Anything Goes (Porter), 308–9
AOC. See Appellation d'Origine Contrôlée
AOP. See Appellation d'Origine Protégée
Aparicio, Frances, 204
aperitifs, 10, 37, 123–24
Aperol, 46
Appellation d'Origine Contrôlée (AOC), 87
Appellation d'Origine Protégée (AOP), 231–32, 241n14
apple brandy, 44
appletinis, 111
architecture, 236–37
Arden, Eve, 309
Arellano, Gustavo, 215
aristocracy, 330
Armitage, David, 33
Arms of the Man (Shaw), 365n47
Armstrong, Louis, 311
Arno, Peter, 113
Arnold, Billy, 39
Arnold, Dave, 6
aromatic bitters, 314
"Around the Town" (Moss, A.), 41
Arthur (film), 354, 363n20, 365n41
Arthur, Stanley Clisby, 6, 83
artisan distillers, 385–86
Artistry of Mixing Drinks, The (Meier), 5
Arts and Crafts movement, 49–50
Asbury, Herbert, 62
Ashcroft, Bill, 145–46
Astaire, Fred, 105
Astro Aku-Aku, 235
As You Like It (Shakespeare), 69, 72n43
Atkinson, Brooks, 307
Atlas Ballroom, 340
Atlas Shrugged (Rand), 2

INDEX

Auden, W. H., 1
Auden Martini, 1–2
Aurora Bora Borealis, 235
authenticity, 76, 328
Aviary (bar), 5
Aviations, 43–44, 52, 94

"Bacchus" (Emerson), 63
Badcock, John, 29
Bad Judgment, 68
Bahktin, Mikhail, 78–79, 85
Bailey, F. Lee, 174
Bailey's Irish Cream, 245, 248, 250, 257n8
Baker, Charles H., 5–6, 373, 374, 377, 379
Balance and Columbian Repository, The (newspaper), 305–6
bald-face (cocktail), 34
Bale, Christian, 184. See also *American Psycho* (film)
Ball, Lucille, 310
Bank of England, 68
Bardstown Bourbon Company, 284
Barflies and Cocktails (McElhone), 39, 41–43, 53
barley, 179, 329–30, 332–33
Barnett, Richard, 107–8
Barnum's American Museum, 63, 67–68
Barry, Philip, 310
bartenders, 11, 66, 66, 94; as celebrities, 230, 390; culinary culture for, 284; *The Curious Bartender*, 6; education for, 392–93; marketing with, 237–38; *New & Improved Bartender's Manual*, 104–5; race of, 241n12; sexism and, 389; tourism for, 209–10; USBG, 390; valets and, 349–50, 359–62
Bartender's Guide, 11, 60, 70n4, 71n8, 372; Blue Blazers in, 61–62; origin narratives of, 59, 104–5; Thomas, J., in, 59, 64–65, 80
bartending: in America, 115; aspects of, 17; careers in, 390; celebrities and, 6–7; *The Curious Bartender*, 6; home bars, 124; industrialism and, 389–90; in Japan, 6; in Louisville, 198–99; mixology and, 99; narratives of, 93–99; nostalgia for, 64–65; *Portrait Gallery of Distinguished Bar-Keepers*, 64; spirits for, 196

Barthes, Roland, 3, 170, 293
barware, 9
Bataille, Georges, 376–77
Bathtub Gin Bar, 30
Batman Begins (film), 350, 353–56, 360–61, 365n43
"Battle of Lexington" (Doolittle), 27
Baudelaire, Charles, 295
Baudrillard, Jean, 233
Beachbum, 240n1
Beachbum Berry Remixed (Berry), 225, 228–29, 231
Beachcomber, Don E. R., 224, 227–30
Beachcomber Room, 147
Beard, James, 123
Beardsley, Aubrey, 295
Beaumont-Gantt, Ernest Raymond. See Beachcomber
Beautiful and the Damned, The (Fitzgerald), 105
Becerril, Andrés, 208
Becker (TV show), 313
beer, 26–27, 31, 48, 52, 108; craft-brewed, 9, 45, 47; for drinking culture, 146; ginger, 29, 283; for hangovers, 346; in popular culture, 388; stout, 39, 245; whiskey and, 291
Belfast, 245–49
Belfast Car Bomb, 245
"Belfast Confetti" (Carson, C.), 244–45, 257n6
Bellini, 181
Benedictine, 347, 387
Benton, Thomas Hart, 331
Bergen, Polly, 174
Berger, Dina, 213
Bergeron, Victor, 164n68, 228–29, 230–31
Berlin Wall, 277
berries, 282–83
Berry, Jeff "Beachbum," 6, 225–31, 235, 238
Best Years of Our Lives, The (film), 356
Bhabha, Homi K., 14, 262–64, 267, 269, 276–77
bigotry, 313
Billionaire (cocktail), 299
Bilstein, Roger, 234
Bird, Aaron, 82–83

Birth of Biopolitics, The (Foucault), 51–52, 52, 56n27
bishop, 34
bitters, 80, 94, 104, 324, 386–87; absinthe and, 372; aromatic, 314; Bittermens tiki, 284; Boker's Genuine Bitters, 105; cognac and, 81; exotic, 282; medicinal, 7; orange, 4, 44, 105; Peychaud's, 82, 84, 89n24; for shrubs, 283; spirits and, 385; sugar and, 82, 299, 305; Underberg, 379. *See also* Angostura bitters
black and tan (beer cocktail), 14, 246–47, 256
Black and Tans, 246, 250–53
Black Bottom Cooler, 39
black-jack (cocktail), 34
black pepper, 373
black velvet, 352
blended spirits, 181, 240n2, 331
blenders, 230
blogging, 7, 386–88
Bloody Marys, 181, 215, 347, 373–74, 379–80
Bloody Sunday, 247–49, 252, 258n15
Blue Blazers, 34, 58–59, 59–60, 61–63, 66, 67–69, 71n15
blue curaçao, 392
Blue Hawaii, 224
Boccato, Richard, 44
Boehm, Greg, 204
Bojens, Ken, 212
Boker's Genuine Bitters, 105
Bolos, 39
Bolshoi vodka, 148
Bolton, Ross, 70n4
Bon Appetit (Morgan, Jefferson), 106–7
Bond, James, 4, 17, 229
bonded applejack, 44
Bon Vivant's Companion (Thomas, J.), 66, 80
Book of Tiki, The (Kirsten), 225
bootleg booze, 128, 206
Boozehound (Wilson, J.), 7
Boston, 30
bottles, 177
Boulevardier, 10–11, 37–38, 53, 256; history of, 39–45, 42, 43–44; industrialism of, 45–49, 47
bourbon: as American, 43, 111; Angel's Envy Bourbon, 18; Bardstown Bourbon Company, 284; for Boulevardier, 47;

Bourbonball, 197–99; brandy and, 299; from Cincinnati, 53; cocktails, 195–99; creativity with, 94; culture, 17, 195–99; Jim Beam, 83; Kentucky Bourbon Affair, 7; in Louisville, 86; in manhattan, 107; old-fashioned and, 306, 314; politics and, 323; in Sazeracs, 86; single-barrel, 107; tequila and, 209; wheated, 196; whiskey, 39, 46, 196; for Wohltäter (cocktail), 299
Bourdieu, Pierre, 106
The Bourgeois Pig (bar), 5
Bouvard and Pécuchet (Flaubert), 297
Boxiana (Badcock), 29
Brady, Mathew, 64
branding, 332; in *American Psycho*, 181–82; culture in, 173; of margarita, 215; marketing and, 362; masculinity and, 13, 169–70; with nostalgia, 38; by Seagram's, 146; tequila, 204; vodka, 186; of whiskey, 327
brandy, 94, 266, 323, 362n4, 372; apple, 44; bourbon and, 299; brandy-champerelle, 34; brandy-crusta, 34; Chemineaud, 148; cognac and, 87; Copper & Kings, 86–87; craft distillation of, 86–87; French, 65; gin and, 328; in lyrics, 309; milk punch, 371; old-fashioned, 80; peach, 67; Sazeracs, 87
brandy old-fashioned, 80
Braverman, Harry, 45–46
Brazil, 211, 283–84
Breakfast of Champions (Vonnegut), 335
Brennan, Lally, 6
Brolin, Josh, 254–55
Bronfman, Samuel, 149
Brown, Judith, 114
Brown, Megan, 183–84
Brown-Forman distillery, 197–98
Brown Hotel, 18
brown sugar cubes, 44
Brubeck, Dave, 103
Buckman's Tavern, 27
Bud Light, 48
Budweiser, 52
Buffalo Trace, 179–80, 195–98
Buffett, Jimmy, 203, 217
Buhen, Mike, 229
Buhen, Ray, 229
Buñuel, Luis, 103

Burciaga, José Antonio, 209
Burns, Robert, 329–30, 332–33
bust-head (cocktail), 34
"By Any Other Name" (*Star Trek*), 266
Byron (Lord), 77–78

cachaça, 283–84
"Cage, The" (*Star Trek*), 265–66
caipirinhas, 284
Cairo Gang, 252
Caliente Club, 208
Calvert liquor, 147–48, *148*
Calvin Klein underwear, 169, 186–87
Campari, 37, *37*, 39, 42–46, *47*, 53
Canada: America and, 154–55; blended spirits in, 240n2; cocktails in, 12–13; colonialism for, 152, *153*, 154–58; consumerism in, 145–47; cultural difference in, 146, 154–55, 158; cultural diplomacy for, 147–49, *148*, *150*, *151*; exoticism in, 158–60; politics in, 161n12; whiskey in, 162n26
Canadian Club whisky, 338
Cansino, Margarita, 208
capitalism, 11, 156
Captain Morgan's rum, 148
careers, 390
Carey, Hugh, 250
Caribbean: colonialism in, 231; ingredients from, 231; liqueur, 65; *Pirates of the Caribbean*, 241n16; Polynesia and, 232; *Potions of the Caribbean*, 228–29; punch, 224; rum in, 196
Carnival, 76–79, 85, 88n7, 132
Carson, Ciaran, 244–45
Carson, Johnny, 174
Carter, Rubin, 103
Casino (film), 255
Castle, Alex, 196
Cate, Martin, 237–38
Catholicism, 76–79, 85, 132
Caventou, Joseph-Bienaimé, 352, 364n36
cayenne pepper, 373, 380
celebrities, 6–7, 11, 174–75, 210–11, 230, 390
celebrity chefs, 390
celery salt, 380
Cervantes, Miguel de, 349, 357–58
champagne, 39, 69, 105, 310–11, 346, 354

Chan, Douglas, 147
Channing, Margo, *122*
Chase, David, 313
Chasing the White Dog (Watman), 7
Chávez-Silverman, Susana, 204
chefs, 54, 390, 393; in drinking culture, 93, 196, 237–38, 282–83; *Top Chef*, 49–50
Chemineaud brandy, 148
chemistry, 297–98, 364n36
cherries, 94, 306, 314
Chicago, 5, 306, 385; *Chicago Tribune*, 136; culture of, 51; Fitzgerald and Moy's in, 326; gender in, 389; North Shore Distillery in, 17, 18; Palmer House, 64; popular culture in, 392; Three Dots and a Dash and Lost Lake, 240
China Trader (cocktail), 229
ching-ching (cocktail), 34
Chocolate Martini, 28
Churchill, Winston, 109, 115, 328
cider spirits, 44
Cimarron Blanco, 285
Cincinnati (Ohio), 40, 53
cinnamon, 229
City Hotel, 63
civil rights movement, 277, 335
Civil War, 62, 64, 306, 323, 327
Claret and Champagne Cup, 65
class: in America, 223–24; aristocracy, 330; cocktails and, 155–56, 207–8; consumption and, 325; cultural difference and, 12–13; culture and, 112, 159; dress codes and, *140*, 140–41; drinking culture and, 326; elitism and, 328; fashion and, 122–23, 132–33; high society, 328–29; language and, 147; leisure, 330–37, *331*, 375; in *Mad Men*, 335–39; middlebrow cosmopolitanism, 145–49, *148*, *150*, *151*; race and, 218; socioeconomics and, 109; spirits and, 376; stereotypes of, 212; tourism and, 218; whiskey and, 329; after World War II, 211
clubs: Caliente Club, 208; cocktail culture and, 338–39; in India, 235–36; margarita in, 213; nightclubs, 206, 208–9; The Raj, 235–40; social, 323, 327–28; sporting, 235, 333–34; on *Star Trek*, 274; Tom Collinses in, 336; for women, 388

club soda, 284, 315
Coca-Cola, 39, 94
Cocchi Americano, 393n1
cocktail culture, 2–5, 11–12, 16, 51, 79; alcohol and, 336; in America, 170; Boulevardier in, 256; clubs and, 338–39; Cocktail Culture Conference, 18; cocktail dresses, 122–23, 132–33, *133*, 138–39, 142n24, 143n29; cocktail history and, 37, 37–39, 44–45; cocktail hour, 128, 130–32, *131*, 142n17; cocktail parties, 123–24, *125*; drinking culture and, 391–92; entrepreneurs and, 390–91; exoticism and, 225; gender performance in, 125–26, *126–27*, 128, *129*; history of, 37–39, 44–45, 376, 386–87; journalism, 240; language of, 116; for leisure, 124, 138–41; manhattan in, 111, 321, 322, 323–27, *324*; modernism in, 284, 326; nostalgia in, 53–54; old-fashioned in, 312–14; politics and, 210–13, *214*, 215; popular culture and, 218, 384; professionalism of, 392–93; Prohibition era for, 293; revival of, 240n2; sexism in, 313; tonics in, 346; after World War II, 121–23, *122*, 134–35, *135–37*, 138–41, *140*, 240n2. *See also* Canada
cocktail history, 2, 30, 227, 292–93, 370; cocktail culture and, 37–39, 44–45; creativity in, 386; vintage barware, 389; Wondrich on, 326, 371–72, 380–81
cocktails: aficionados of, 6, 44–45, 49, 313; alcohol and, 93; American, 10, 25–31, 32, 33–34; *Barflies and Cocktails*, 39, 41–43, 53; bourbon, 195–99; in Canada, 12–13; champagne, 105; class and, 155–56, 207–8; *Cocktail* (film), 93; cocktail dresses, 122–23, 132–33, *133*, 138–39, 142n24, 143n29; cocktail hour, 128, 130–32, *131*, 142n17; *Cocktail Lab* (cocktail), 6; Cocktail la Louisiane, 76; cocktail logic, 8–10; cocktail parties, 12; *The Cocktail Party*, 104; cocktail revival, 5–8, 17; "Cocktails Around Town," 39, 41; *Cocktails de Paris*, 105; *Cocktails: How to Mix Them*, 105; *Cocktail Techniques*, 6; from colonialism, 44; *Craft Cocktails at Home*, 6; craft culture and, 46, 49–53, 239–40, 240n1; craft distillation for, 198; in culinary culture, 321; debates on, 17–18; decadence of, 376; in drinking culture, 111–12; Embury on, 75–76; etymology of, 28, 34, 82, 254; excessive consumption of, 373; exotic, 265; fire in, 58; gin, 8; hegemony and, 158; ideology of, 106; ingredients for, 211; *In the Land of Cocktails*, 6; as inventions, 104; from Ireland, 14; knowledge of, 38; masculinity and, 16; morning, 348–49; narratives of, 53, 81, 362; New Orleans, 11; nostalgia for, 41; origin narratives of, 11–12, 15; performance and, 244–45; philosophy of, 197; popular, 203; prehistory of, 25–31, 32, 33–34; Prohibition era, 53, 107; recipes for, 325; rye in, 299, 305–7; shrub-based, 282–85; spirits and, 386; *Vintage Spirits and Forgotten Cocktails*, 6, 47, 240n2, 370, 384; vodka for, 9, 96–98, 173–74, 186–87; water in, 305; whiskey, 306, 328; women and, 388–90; Wondrich on, 112, 323–24; writing about, 43–44, 387–88. *See also specific cocktails*
Coconauts, 235
Codrescu, Andrei, 6–7
cognac, 65, 80–81, 83, 87–88, 387
Cointreau, 209, 299, 370–71
Coke. *See* Coca-Cola
Cold War, 236, 239, 249–50; *Cold War Orientalism*, 151; paranoia, 226; on *Star Trek*, 268; vodka during, 337
cold water, 83
Colin, Paul, 105
Collins, Michael, 250–52
colonialism, 10; aesthetics and, 227–28, 230–32; for Canada, 152, *153*, 154–58; in Caribbean, 231; cocktails from, 44; Cold War and, 236; for consumers, 149–50; consumption and, 145–46; from Europe, 155–56; Great Britain in, 235–37; history of, 10, 232; identity and, 157–60, 276–77; marketing and, 149, 151; military for, 235; primitive culture and, 239–40; Santo Domingo, 81; signifiers from, 231, 236; Tiki culture and, 230–32; tourism and, 233
colors: in absinthe, 83–84, 289–90, 292, 296, 385; in Absinthe Frappé, 83–84; in advertising, 152; of Alaska, 19n19; in alien

INDEX 405

drinks, 271, 275; in black and tan, 246; coloring, 61; colorless spirits, 113, 170, 174; colorless vodka, 111, 175, 180–81, 352; manhattan and, 325, 339–40
Commander's Palace and Café (restaurant), 6
Comus (Milton), 81
Conigliaro, Tony, 6
Conlon, Gerry, 247, 250–51, 258n14
Connecticut eye-openers, 68
Connelly, Stuart, 111
Connolly, Cyril, 379
Conrad, Barnaby, 107, 114–15
conspicuous consumption, 8, 292, 330–32, 338–39, 375–78, 395
consumers, 38, 45–49; in America, 121; anxiety for, 171; in Canada, 145–47; colonialism for, 149–50; ethics of, 151; hegemony for, 159–60
consumption, 16–17; alcohol, 157, 311–12; class and, 325; colonialism and, 145–46; conspicuous, 8, 292, 330–32, 338–39, 375–78, 395; in drinking culture, 152; excessive, 370–71, 373–78, 380–81; gender and, 217–18; hangovers and, 370–71, 374–78, 382n36; knowledge and, 53–54; modern cocktail, 284; politics of, 159–60; subjectivity and, 169–70; in third space, 274; of tonics, 351; tonics for, 346; useless, 376–77
Coogan, Tim Pat, 251, 258n24
Cook, James, 225
Cooke, Terence, 249–50
Cooper, Anderson, 40
Cooper, James Fenimore, 30, 33–34
Coors, 52
Copper & Kings, 86–87
Coppola, Francis Ford, 255
Corbett, Dean, 196–97
Corby's, 148
coriander, 297
corn, 179–80, 195
cornflower syrup, 68
corporate culture, 171, 177, 182–86
Corpse Reviver, 299, 371, 372, 373, 381n1
Corpse Reviver No. 2, 370–73, 379, 385
cosmopolitans, 4, 51–52
Côte de Beaune, 28
Count of Monte Cristo, The (Dumas), 365n39

Coward, Noël, 42
Coyle, Michael, 326
Craddock, Harry, 4–6, 370–71, 385
craft-brewed beer, 9, 45, 47
Craft Cocktails at Home (Liu), 6
craft culture: Boulevardier in, 38; cocktail history in, 370; cocktails and, 46, 49–53, 52, 239–40, 240n1; distillation and, 390–91; ethos of, 46, 50
craft distillation, 50–52, 86–87, 198, 390–91
craft makers, 45, 173
Craft of the Cocktail, The (DeGroff), 5
Crane, Steve, 228–29, 237–38
Crazy, Stupid, Love (film), 4
cream, 80, 245
crème de cacao, 44, 197
crème de menthe, 362n4
crème de violette, 44
Crescent City cocktails, 76
Crosby, Bing, 310–12
Crowley, Aleister, 289, 295–96, 298–99
Crown Royal, 173
Cruise, Tom, 93–94
Crustas, 79–80
Crystal Head Vodka, 180–81
Cuba Libre, 93
Cubism art, 226
culinary culture, 33, 93, 195; for bartenders, 284; Bloody Marys in, 379–80; cocktails in, 321; manhattan in, 323; for mixologists, 285
cultural difference: in Canada, 146, 154–55, 158; class and, 12–13; diversity and, 267–68, 277–78; in Hollywood, 210; in *Star Trek*, 267–68, 274, 277–78; in third space, 263–64, 277–78; Tiki culture and, 147
cultural diplomacy, 147–49, 148, 150, 151, 270–71
culture: alcohol in, 146, 261; of America, 10–11, 14, 111, 113; Bond for, 17; bourbon, 17, 195–99, 197; in branding, 173; of Chicago, 51; after Civil War, 64, 323, 327; class and, 112, 159; conspicuous leisure in, 375; craft, 38, 46, 49–53, 52; cultural alchemy, 108–9; cultural capital, 109–12, 114–15; cultural democracy, 155; cultural history, 14; cultural modernism, 159; cultural

culture (*Cont.*)
  overdetermination, 106; *The Cultural Work of Corporations*, 183–84; drinking, 26–28, 31, 33; of Europe, 75; expatriate, 40; gender and, 215; high, 340; human bodies and, 270–71; identity and, 264; of industrialism, 7; of Jazz Age, 49; low, 340; martini in, 3–4; of Mexico, 13, 213; mixing of, 111–12; modernist, 12; of New Orleans, 76, 387; of New York City, 4–5; of Paris, 61; popular, 130; Prohibition era and, 39–40, 123; Space Age, 235; speakeasy, 207–8; television for, 121; Tiki, 13–14; Victorian, 114–15; after World War II, 13–14, 25. *See also specific topics*
curaçao, 65, 105, 285, 299, 372, 392
Curious Bartender, The (Stephenson), 6

Dada art, 226
daiquiris, 8, 84, 228
Dan Marino (drink), 284
Davis, Bette, *122*
Davis, Mike, 246, 254, 256
deacon (cocktail), 34
deadbeat (cocktail), 34
The Dead Rabbit, 6
De Alba, Felipe, 208
Death & Co., 5, 6, 239
Death in the Afternoon (Hemingway), 346
Death in the Gulf Stream (Hemingway), 346
de Bouve, Sylvius, 107–8
Debt to Pleasure, The (Lancaster), 1
Decca (bar), 282
Declaration of Independence, 33
deconstruction theory, 8, 15
Deep Space Nine (TV show), 265, 272–73, 279n34. See also *Star Trek*
DeGroff, Dale, 5, 6, 43, 96, 199, 384, 387
Delaplane, Stan, 212
De Lauretis, Teresa, 203
DeLucie, John, 321
dementia, 357
DeNiro, Robert, 255
Denver, 5
De Palma, Brian, 255
Derby Thymes, 97
Derrida, Jacques, 8, 170

deskilling thesis, 55n19
Desmond, Paul, 103
detoxing. *See* hangovers
Devlin, Anne, 247
DeVoto, Bernard, 115
Dial, The (pamphlet), 42
Díaz, George, 206
Dichter, Ernest, 152, 154, 160
Dick & Fitzgerald publishing, 59, 62
Dick Van Dyke Show, The (TV show), 122
Dictionary (Johnson, S.), 108
Dictionary of Received Ideas (Flaubert), 297
Diefenbaker Bill of Rights, 155–56
Dietsch, Michael, 282
Difford's Guide (website), 5
Dior, Christian, 134, *136*, 143n30
dirty martini, 118n42
discourse, 16–17
distillation, 169, 179–81, 196, 231–32, 329, 390–91. *See also specific distilleries*
distillers, 99, 212, 245, 385–86, 390–91
Distinction (Bourdieu), 106
dive bars, 325, 340
diversity, 263–64, 267–68, 277–78
Dixie Cocktails, 389
DMP. *See* Dublin Metropolitan Police
Dr. Cocktail. *See* Haigh
Dr. Strangelove (film), 234
Don Quixote (Cervantes), 357–58, 366n63
Don the Beachcomber, 224, 227, 229, 235, 241n12, 373
Doolittle, Amos, 27
Douglas, Mary, 268, 270
Down Argentine Way (film), 211
Dowson, Ernest, 291
Dreiser, Theodore, 15, 326–29, 333–34
dress codes, 124, *140*, 140–41, 143n29; cocktail dress, 122–23, 132–33, *133*, 138–39; performance and, 125–26, *126–27*, 128, *129*
"Drink" (Reigler), 195
DrinkBoy (blog), 111
"Drinker's Dictionary, The" (Franklin), 26, 28
drinking culture, 26–28; absinthe in, 297–300; Bailey's Irish Cream in, 257n8; beer for, 146; chefs in, 93, 196, 237–38, 282–83; class and, 326; cocktail culture and, 391–92;

cocktails in, 111–12; consumption in, 152; distillation in, 179–80; dive bars, 325, 340; drunkenness in, 132, 139, 141; gateway drinks, 86; gender and, 66–67; history of, 337; language of, 68–69; leisure in, 66, 207–13, 240n2; of Louisiana, 84; of Louisville, 95; martini in, 212; in New York City, 181; performance in, 269–70; politics and, 31, 33; Prohibition era for, 372–73; in *Star Trek*, 265–70; in third space, 273; women in, 337–38, 384; work and, 333–34; after World War II, 110, 121
Drinkin' Mate (hangover cure), 353, 362
Drunken Botanist, The (Stewart, A.), 6, 86
drunkenness, 132
dry gin, 105, 362n4
dry martini, 103–5, 107, 109, 112–15
Du Barry Was a Lady's (musical), 309–10
Dubin, Al, 307
Dublin Metropolitan Police (DMP), 246, 258n24
Dumas, Alexandre, 365n39
Dunham, Gary, 18
Dylan, Bob, 103

Earle, David, 290–91
Easter Island, 236
Ebony (magazine), 140
Eco, Umberto, 239
Edmunds, Lowell, 3–5, 7, 12, 325, 375; cultural capital for, 109–11, 114–15; on martini, 105–7
education, 392–93
Edward VII (king), 283
eggnog, 124
eggs, 66–67, 68, 80–81, 372
Eliot, T. S., 62, 104, 105, 115, 293
Eliot, Valerie, 115
elitism, 48, 112, 328
Ellis, Brett Easton, 13, 169, 177, 180–81, 184–85, 187
Ellman, Maud, 250
Embury, David, 6, 19n19, 75–76, 85, 380
Emerson, Ralph Waldo, 63
Empire Writes Back, The (Ashcroft/Griffiths/Tiffin), 145–46
England, 29, 68, 108

English gin, 1
Enright, Seán, 252, 258n24
Ensslin, Hugo R., 5, 43, 43–44
entrepreneurs, 52, 52–54, 209, 390–91
Equus and Jack's Lounge, 196–97, 199
Erlenmeyer flasks, 291
Espresso Bongos, 240n1
Esquire's Handbook for Hosts, 123–24, 132
ethanol, 298
etymology, 25, 28, 34, 82, 254, 293
Eureka Street (Wilson, R.), 248–49
Europe, 53, 75, 87, 155–56, 330; America and, 85, 293–94; spirits from, 211, 329
Everyday Drinking (Amis), 374
Evolution of Troubles, The (Hennessey), 248
Ewen, Stuart, 171, 180, 184
excessive consumption, 370–71, 373–78, 380–81
exoticism: in Canada, 158–60; cocktail culture and, 225; exotic cocktails, 265; immigration and, 146–47; in India, 235; of multiculturalism, 267; for Whyte, 145
Expatriate culture, 40
experimentation, 17
extra dry vermouth, 113
extra-dry vodka, 1

Fabulous New Orleans (Saxon), 78
Facebook, 99
Famous New Orleans Drinks and How to Mix 'Em (Arthur), 6
Fanon, Franz, 276
Farewell to Arms, A (Hemingway), 4, 112–13
fashion, 133, 135, 135, 137, 138–39; *All Consuming Images*, 171, 180; branding in, 181–82; class and, 122–23, 132–33; *The Language of Fashion*, 143n29; "New Look," 134, 136, 143n30; socioeconomics of, 142n24
Faulkner, William, 103
FCC. *See* Federal Communications Commission
feaguing, 28–29
Federal Communications Commission (FCC), 121–22
Felten, Eric, 2, 82, 376

femininity: advertisements and, 204, 213, 214; in America, 209–10; for De Lauretis, 203; feminism, 276–77; in marketing, 218; masculinity and, 210–11; stereotypes of, 213, 215; underwear and, 134
fennel, 295
fern bars, 392
fiction, 345–48, 351–60. *See also specific works*
filtration, 180–81
Fine Art of Mixing Drinks (Embury), 6
fire, 58, 62–63. *See also* Blue Blazers
fiscal agent (cocktail), 34
Fisher, Bud, 62
Fisher, M. F. K., 5
Fitzgerald, F. Scott, 105
Fitzgerald and Moy's (saloon), 326
5 o'clock (app), 142n17
fizzes, 79–81, 352, 355–56, 371, 372
Flaubert, Gustave, 297
Fleming, Ian, 229
Fleming, Renée, 62
floater (cocktail), 34
flower water, 80–81
Flying Saucers, 235
Fogarty, Anne, 138
fog-cutters, 240n1, 373
food science, 6
form. *See* aesthetics
fortified wine, 108
Foucault, Michel, 9, 51–52, 52, 56n27, 183–84
Fouquet, Louis, 104
Four Roses, 198
France, 28, 76–77, 109, 231–32, 241n14; Louisville and, 87; Tahiti and, 233
Franklin, Benjamin, 26–31, 33, 68
Franklin Mortgage and Investment Company (bar), 5
French absinthe, 87
French brandy, 65
French cognac, 87–88
French crème de cacao, 111
French vermouth, 8, 105, 109, 110, 115, 327
Freudian therapy, 152, 154
Friel, Brian, 247
Frisch, Janice, 18
From Here to Eternity (film), 224
fruit, 282–83

Fussell, Paul, 2, 376
futurism, 226–27, 230–35, 261–62, 265, 279n19

Gabelick, Pat, 391–92
"Gale's Paradox" (Amis), 374–75
Gallery of Illustrious Americans (Brady), 64
Galt House, 96, 98
Garci-Crespo Hotel, 208
Gargoyle (magazine), 41
garnishes: cherries, 94; as ingredients, 118n42; lemon peels, 82; lemons as, 104; lemon twists, 3, 111; in mixing, 80; olives, 1–2, 107, 111; orange peels, 44, 47; orange slices, 37; pearl onions, 107; raspberries, 97; thyme, 97; umbrellas and, 271. *See also specific garnishes*
Gatsby Cocktails (Reed), 107
Gauguin, Paul, 295
gay liberation movement, 128, 142n14
gender: alcohol and, 152; in Chicago, 389; consumption and, 217–18; culture and, 215; drinking and, 66–67; martini and, 323; masculinity and, 124, 128; mixing and, 138–39; performance, 125–26, 126, 127, 128, 129; roles, 139–41, 140; sexuality and, 274, 278, 280n36; in *Star Trek*, 280n36; stereotypes, 363n20; in third space, 275–77; of valets, 363n20
Geneva gin, 162n26
Genova, 107–8
Gentleman's Companion (Baker), 373
George White's Scandals (Gershwin brothers), 309
Geraghty, Lincoln, 261
German seltzer, 65
Gershwin, George, 309
Gershwin, Ira, 309
gibsons, 5
Giger, H. R., 295
G.I. Jane (film), 96
Gilded Age, 64, 321, 325, 327, 335
gin, 3, 385; for Aviation, 43; Bathtub Gin Bar, 30; beer and, 29; brandy and, 328; for cleaning, 26; cocktails, 8; for Corpse Reviver, 299; dry, 105; in dry martini, 115; gin and tonic, 51; Gin Foundry (website), 43; gin-lane, 107; Gordon's, 39, 113, 148;

INDEX 409

Hollands, 346; lemon juice and, 370, 370–71; London Dry, 105; martini, 1–2; Old Tom, 104–5; origin narratives of, 107–8; in Quebec, 162n26; Ramos gin fizz, 79–81, 352, 371, 372; religion and, 108; sugar, 352; vermouth and, 106–9, 111, 116; vodka and, 113, 186; as white goods, 152. *See also specific gins*
ginger beer, 29, 283
Girl Crazy (Gershwin brothers), 309
Godfather, The (film), 255
Go Into Your Dance (film), 307
Goldman, William, 348
gomme, 228
"Good Old Fashioned Cocktail, A" (Keeler), 307
gooseberry shrubs, 283–84, 284
Gordon, Steve, 354, 363n20, 365n41
Gordon's gin, 39, 113, 148
Gorman, Marion, 208
Gosling, Ryan, 4
GQ (magazine), 85
Grable, Betty, 310
Graham, J. A. Maxtone, 109
grain alcohol, 106, 326
grammatization, 47, 50
Grand Marnier, 80, 97, 347
Grant, Cary, 124, 310
Grant, Ulysses S., 107
grapefruit juice, 97
Gray, Jim, 306
Great Britain, 151, 235–37, 249–52
Great Depression, 334–35
Greene, Philip, 6
green tea, 65
greyhound, 97
Griffiths, Gareth, 145–46
Grimes, Bernardo Antonio, 364n36
Grimes, Tammy, 174
Grimes, William, 68, 111
guava juice, 97
Guide for the Married Man, A (film), 312
guild craft, 52, 53
Guildford Four, 249
Guinness, 245, 246
Gum syrup, 105
Gwynne, Alice Claypool, 40, 43

Gwynne, Edward Erskine, Jr., 39–41, 43, 45, 53, 54n5. *See also* Boulevardier
Gwynne, Edward Erskine, Sr., 40

Haigh, Ted, 6, 42, 47, 240n2, 370–72, 384
hair of the dog drinks, 311–12, 347, 371–74, 380
Haiti, 81
Hale Pele, 240
Half and Halfs. *See* black and tan
Hamm, Jon, 312
Handy, Thomas, 83, 87–88
Hangover, The (film), 378, 382n37
hangovers: Absinthe Frappé, 84; beer for, 346; consumption and, 370–71, 374–78, 382n36; Drinkin' Mate for, 353; fizzes for, 355–56; hair of the dog drinks for, 311–12, 347, 371–74, 380; the hangover cure, 9–10, 16; human bodies and, 346–48; medicine for, 352; memory and, 356–61; morning cocktails for, 348–49; Myer's cocktails for, 362, 368n79; narratives of, 359–62, 363n18; prescriptions for, 378–81; recipes for, 16, 362n4; science of, 346–47, 352, 361–62, 378–81; soda water for, 345–46, 360–61; tonics for, 348–56; valets and, 349–50; work and, 332
Hannah, Chris, 96
Hanson, David, 205
hard shakes, 6
Haring, Keith, 186
Harry's (New York) Bar, 39
Hawai'i, 224, 232–36, 238
Hayworth, Rita, 208
HDW CLIX (Buffalo Trace), 179–80
Headhunter (cocktail), 225
Healy, Alison, 257n7
Heaney, Seamus, 247
"Heart of Glory" (*Star Trek*), 279n34
Heaven Hill Distilleries, 18, 196
hedonism, 229–30
hegemony, 158–60, 204, 226, 263–64
Heightchew, Tracy, 18
Hemingway, Ernest, 4, 6, 42–43, 112–13, 346
Henderson, Stephen, 179, 184
Hennessey, Thomas, 248
Henry IV, Part I (Shakespeare), 345

Hensleigh, Jonathan, 255
Hepburn, Katherine, 310
Herbsaint, 82
Herkimer Diamonds, 180–81
Herrera, Carlos "Danny," 208–9
Hess, Robert, 387
Heublein's Cocktails Manhattan Liquor, 324
Heyerdahl, Thor, 147
Hezbollah, 254
highballs, 124
high culture, 340
high society, 328–29
High Society (film), 310–11
High West Distillery, 43
Hingston, Edward Peron, 70n1
Hiram Walker Blended Whiskey, *331*
history: of absinthe, 294–97; of aircraft, 234; of alcohol, 205; of American Revolution, 27; of Anglo-Irish War, 251–52; authenticity in, 328; of black and tan, 246–47; of Bloody Sunday, 247–49; of Blue Blazers, 58–59, *59–60, 61, 66, 67*; of bootleg booze, 206; of Boulevardier, 39–45, *42, 43–44*; cocktail, 6, 37, 37–39, 44–45; of cocktail culture, 37, 37–39, 44–45, 376, 386–87; of colonialism, 10, 232; cultural history, 14; of drinking culture, 337; experience of, 30; of fashion, 134; of Hawaiʻi, 232–33; historical narratives, 38; idealization of, 15; of martini, 3, 15, 104–5; of mixology, 8, 291, 306, 372; of modernism, 105; of New Orleans, 84; prehistory, 25–31, 32, 33–34; Prohibition era, 5, 33; of scotch, 329; of Seagram's, 149; of Thomas, J., 63–64, *66*; of Tiki culture, 147, 164n68, 241n16; Whiskey Rebellion, 49. *See also* cocktail history; origin narratives
Hockheimer wine, 65
Holland, Barbara, 103, 105, 112, 115
Hollands gin, 346
Hollywood, 210
home bars, 124
honey, 97
Hoop packaging, *135*
Hope, Bob, 309
Horkheimer, Max, 7

Hors d'Oeuvre and Canapés (Beard), 123
Hors d'Oeuvre Inc., 123
Horse's neck (cocktail), 34
hotel bars, 331–32
Hotel Brighton, 64
Hotel Monteleone, 387
hot sauce, 379–80
How Do You Know (film), 4
How to Mix Drinks (Thomas), 5, 61
How to Succeed in Business Without Really Trying (play), 312–13
Hudson, Rock, 130–31
Hudson (New York) Balance and Columbian Repository, 29
Huggan, Graham, 146, 158
human bodies, 169–71, 178–80, 184–86, 268, 270–71, 345–48
Hunt, Mary, 205
Hurricane (cocktail), 84
"Hurricane" (Dylan/Levy), 103
Hurricane Katrina, 84
Huyssen, Andreas, 110, 112
hybrid identities, 279n34

ice, 97, 118n42, 124, 125, 327, 362n4
Ideal Husband, An (film), 350–54, 360–61, 364n26
idealization, 15, 106, 276–77
identity, 157–60, 182–86, 264, 268, 276–77, 279n34. *See also* femininity; masculinity
IDV. *See* International Distillers and Vintners
IEDs. *See* improvised explosive devices
"I Get a Kick Out of You" (Porter), 309
imaginary order (Lacan), 185–86, 190nn73–74
Imbibe! (Wondrich), 6, 105
Imbibe, Punch, Chilled (website), 5
immigration, 87, 146–47, 160, 204
Imperial Cabinet Saloon, 80
imperialism. *See* colonialism
Importance of Being Ernest, The (Wilde), 349, 351
improvised explosive devices (IEDs), 244, 254
India, 235–37
indulgence, 370–71, 370–71, 373–78, 380–81

industrialism, 45–53, 47, 52, 230, 234; bartending and, 389–90; capitalism and, 156; culture of, 7; in narratives, 330
Industrial Revolution, 330
ingredients: from Caribbean, 231; for cocktails, 211; garnishes as, 118n42; for margarita, 203–5; modernism and, 285; for planter's punch, 228; proportions and, 4; science of, 384–85; wormwood, 293–98
"In Search of the Auden Martini" (Schaap), 1
In the Land of Cocktails (Martin, T. A./ Brennan), 6
In the Name of the Father (Conlon), 247
Inquiry into the Effects of Spirituous Liquors, An (Rush), 31, 32, 33
International Distillers and Vintners (IDV), 245
internationalism, 149
Invisible Man (Ellison), 348
Ireland: black and tan in, 250–53; cocktails from, 14; immigrants from, 31; Irish Car Bombs, 14, 244–47, 253–56; Irish Republican Army, 248–49, 251, 258n24; Obama in, 257n7; politics of, 247–50, 253–56
Irish Car Bomb, 14
Irish cream, 254
Irish whiskey, 245, 306
Ishiguro, Kuzuo, 365n47, 367n70
Italian vermouth, 105, 109, 111, 323; for Boulevardier, 37, 39, 46, 47; in manhattan, 327, 339
Italy, 37, 111
It Happened in Nordland (musical), 83
"It's De-Lovely" (song), 309
"I've Still Got My Health" (Porter), 308

Jack and Cokes, 51–52
Jacob's Room (Woolf), 105
Jamaica rum, 65, 228, 231
James Beard Awards, 393
Jameson whiskey, 68
Janicki, J. W., 39
Janson, Charles William, 372
Japan, 6, 234
Jardin Tiki bar, 147
Jazz Age culture, 49

jazz music, 310–11
J&B whiskey, 181
Jell-O shots, 6
Jelly Shot Test Kitchen (Palm), 6
Jeppson, Carl, 391–92
Jeppson's Malört, 391–92
Jeptha Creed Distillery, 196
Jerome, Jennie, 328
Jerry Thomas' Bar Tender's Guide. See *Bartender's Guide*
jet age futurism, 226–27, 230–35, 261–62, 265, 279n19
Jim Beam, 83
Jim Crow laws, 226–27
"John Barleycorn" (Burns), 329–30, 332–33
John Lamb (bar), 68
Johnson, Greg, 195
Johnson, Harry, 104–5
Johnson, Lionel, 290
Johnson, Paul, 104
Johnson, Samuel, 108
Johnston, Jennifer, 247
Joly, Charles, 96
Jordan, Neil, 254
Jose Cuervo Tequila, 213, 214, 215, 218
Joyce, James, 42, 105, 290
Joy of Mixology, The (Regan), 5
juniper berries, 108

Kafka, Franz, 374
Kahiki Supper Club, 236
Kahlua, 245
Kahn, Miriam, 233
Kalaniʻōpuʻu (king), 225
Kane, Bob, 349
Kane, Herb, 227
Kansas, 5
"Katie Went to Haiti" (song), 309–10
Kaye, Danny, 309
Keeler, Ruby, 307
Keenan, Dan, 257n7
Kelbo's, 235
Kennedy, Ted, 250
Kentucky, 7, 17, 81, 95–96, 195–99, *197*. See also Louisville
Kenya, 40
Kill the Irishman (film), 255

King, Marjorie, 208–9
King, Stephen, 349
King's Ginger liqueur, 283–84, *284*
Kirsten, Sven, 225–26, 234, 238
Klein, Christina, 151, 157–58
knickerbocker (cocktail), 34
Kon-Tiki Expedition, The (Heyerdahl), 147
Kon-Tiki restaurant, 147
Koons, Irv, 154, 163n35

labor, 45–47
Labrot & Graham Distillery, 195
Lacan, Jacques, 170, 184–86, 190, 191nn73–76
Ladies United for the Preservation of Endangered Cocktails (LUPEC), 388–89
Laing, Olivia, 6
Lancaster, John, 1
language, 68–69, 116, 143n29, 147, 295
Lanza, Joseph, 67
Latin America, 211–12, 218
Latinidad, 204, 211
Latinx studies, 204, 215
Latitude 29, 240
Latyshev, Konstantin, 186
Lazersfekd, Paul, 152, 154
Leilani rum, 148
leisure: class, 330–37, *331*, 375; cocktail culture for, 124, 138–41; in drinking culture, 66, 207–13, 240n2; in jet age futurism, 265; in Tiki culture, 241n12; after World War II, 171
Lemmon, Jack, 335
lemons, 80, 82, 104–5, 203–4, 385; juice, 39, 43, 80, 94, 209, 299, 370, 372–73; twists, 3, 107, 111, 118n42; wedges, 314
Let's Face It! (musical), 309–10
"Let's Not Talk About Love" (Porter), 309
Levi-Strauss, Claude, 17
Levy, Jacques, 103
Lewis, Richard A., 171–72
Lewis, Sinclair, 42, 323
liberal subject, 183
licorice, 86, 294–95
lightning-smashes, 68
Lillet Blanc, 299, 370, 385, 393n1
lime juice, 97, 203, 284–85, 362n4
limes, 209, 228, 231, 346

line maintenance, 97
liqueurs. *See specific liqueurs*
liquid fire, 62
Liquid Intelligence (Arnold, D.), 6
Liquor.com, 5
Liston, Sonny, 338
literature, 6, 30–31, 113, 181, 240n1, 333–35. *See also specific books*
Little Branch (bar), 44
Liu, Kevin, 6
live mixing, 94–95
Location of Culture, The (Bhabha), 276
Locke, Karen, 110
locomotive (cocktail), 34
London Dry gin, 105
long drinks, 147–48
Long Island iced teas, 247
Lost Weekend, The (film), 346
la louche, 84
louching, 291, 298, 299–300, 327
Louisiana, 75–76, 84. *See also* New Orleans
Louisville, 306; bartending in, 198–99; bourbon in, 86; Cocktail Culture Conference, 18; culinary culture in, 195; Decca in, 282; drinking culture of, 95; France and, 87; Galt House, 96, 98; Kentucky Bourbon Affair, 7; mixology in, 17; Stitzel-Weller Distillery, 196; tourism in, 199
Louis XIV, 87
low culture, 340
Loy, Myrna, 121
Luau, 224, 228–29, 237
Luaus (drink), 240n1
Lucky Jim (Amis), 346
Ludlum, Robert, 174
LUPEC. *See* Ladies United for the Preservation of Endangered Cocktails
lyrics, 307–10

MacGuire Seven, 249
MacLaverty, Bernard, 247
MacSwiney, Terence, 252–53
Madeira, 28–29, 65
Mad Men (TV show), 4, 312–15, 335–39
La Madrileñas Margarita Cocktail, 215, *216*, 217

magnolia (cocktail), 209
Maira, Sunaina, 215
mai tais, 231–32, 240n1, 283
Majoli, Monica, 186
"Make It Another Old Fashioned, Please" (Porter), 15, 307–9, 315
Maker's Mark, 173, 196, 198
malaria, 352, 364n36
mango-passionfruit vodka, 97
manhattan, 7, 15, 385; in *An American Tragedy*, 333–34; bourbon in, 107; in cocktail culture, 111, 321, 322, 323–27, 324; colors and, 325, 339–40; in culinary culture, 323; decadence of, 340; etymology of, 247; *The Manhattan Cocktail*, 94; martini and, 15, 307, 325–26; mixing of, 114–15, 339–40; modernism in, 325–26; old-fashioned and, 93, 124; origin narratives for, 327–30; in popular culture, 325, 330–33, *331*; recipes for, 339, 339–40; rye whiskey in, 107; stereotypes of, 321, 334–39
Manhattan Club, 328
Manhattan Cocktail Classic, 7
Man in the Grey Flannel, The (Wilson, S.), 225
Mankiewicz, Joseph, 122
Man of La Mancha (Wasserman), 358
Manual for the Manufacture of Cordials, Liquors, Fancy Syrups, &c. &c. (Schultz), 61
maraschino, 44, 80
maraschino cherries, 306
maraschino liqueur, 104
Mardi Gras, 77–78
margarita, 13, 181, 212; advertisements for, *214, 216*; branding of, 215; in clubs, 213; La Madrileñas Margarita Cocktail, 215, *216*, 217; "Margaritaville," 203, 217; marketing of, 203–4, 215, *216*, 217–18; origin narratives of, 207–10, 219n18; in Prohibition era, 204–7; strawberry, 284–85, *285*; tropicalization of, 204, 215
Mariani, John, 198
Marilyn Manson, 296
marketing: advertisements and, 212–13; with bartenders, 237–38; bottles in, 177; of Bourbonball, 197–98; branding and, 362; colonialism and, 149, 151; femininity in,

218; by Maker's Mark, 196; of margarita, 203–4, 215, *216*, 217–18; in Quebec, 152; research, 160; by Seagram's, 12, 156–57; test, 154; of vodka, 170
Martin, Dean, 346
Martin, Ti Adelaide, 6
martinez. *See* martini
Martinez, Mariano, 217
martini: Auden Martini, 1–2; Chocolate Martini, 28; for cocktail parties, 124; dirty, 118n42; in drinking culture, 212; dry, 103–5, 107, 109, 112–15; gender and, 323; gin, 1–2; history of, 3, 15, 104–5; "In Search of the Auden Martini," 1; manhattan and, 15, 307, 325–26; *Martini, Straight Up*, 3, 105–6, 375; martini glasses, 110–11; Martini Madness, 5; as modernism, 12, 103–4, 107–16; old-fashioned and, 79; olives in, 67; plain, 2; in popular culture, 345, 384–85; reputation of, 2–3, 105–7; shaken vodka, 4; as signifiers, 105–6; vermouth for, 105, 115–16; vodka, 1–2, 4, 111. *See also specific martini*
Martinique, 231, 283–84
Marxist theory, 11, 45, 47, 55n19
masculinity: alcohol and, 265, 273–77; branding and, 13, 169–70; cocktails and, 16; in corporate culture, 177, 184–86; femininity and, 210–11; gender and, 124, 128; human bodies and, 171, 178–80, 184; nostalgia and, 336–37; performance of, 256; psychopaths and, 177–80; psychosis and, 187; of scotch, 267; stereotypes of, 323, 325, 327, 345–46; in third space, 262, 269; toxic, 338–39; underwear and, 169, 186–87; vodka and, 169–70, 181–83
"Matter of Honor, A" (*Star Trek*), 270–71
Matus, Victorino, 176
matutinal cocktails. *See* old-fashioned
McCaffety, Kerry, 6–7
McCracken, Grant, 152
McDonnell, Duggan, 321
McElhone, Harry, 39, 43, 46
McGee, Paul, 96
McGowan, Alvin, 212
McGregor, Ewan, 95–96
McIlroy, Michael, 44

McLuhan, Marshall, 157
McMillian, Chris, 80–82, 84
McNern, Jennifer, 248
McNern, Rosaleen, 248
"Measure of a Man, The" (*Star Trek*), 274
medicinal bitters, 7
medicinal tonics, 293–94, 351–52
medicine, 348, 352, 354
"Meditation on a Quart Mugg, A" (Franklin), 26
Meehan, Jim, 96, 240n1
Meier, Frank, 5
memory, 350, 356–61
Mencken, H. L., 25–26, 28, 30, 34, 104, 113
Merchants Exchange Coffee House, 82–83
Merman, Ethel, 15, 307–9, 316
Metalious, Grace, 130
"Metamorphosis, The" (Kafka), 374
Metcalf, Thomas, 236–37
Metropolitan Hotel, 58, 63
Mexico, 13; America and, 203–4, 206–7, 210–13, *214*, *215*, 217–18; Mexican Revolution, 205–6; tourism in, 204, 209, 213, 217
mezcal, 206
Michael Collins (film), 254–55, 258n24
Michener, James, 224, 233–34
middlebrow cosmopolitanism, 145–49, *148*, *150*, *151*
Middle East, 232, 254
military, 234–35, 352
milk, 362n4, 371
Milk and Honey (bar), 5
Mill, Bob, 147
Milton, John, 81, 379
Milwaukee Daily-Journal, 63
Minnick, Fred, 198
Minow, Newton, 122
mint, 67, 294
mint julep, 67, 81
Mintz, Sidney, 149
Miranda, Carmen, 126, 211
Mirren, Helen, 363n20
Missionary's Downfall, 225
Mr. Blandings Builds His Dream House (film), 124
Mitenbuler, Reid, 329–30

mixing, 386; in America, 65; blenders for, 230; of Blue Blazers, 62–63; of culture, 111–12; of dry martini, 114–15; Embury on, 85; garnishes in, 80; gender and, 138–39; hard shakes, 6; ice in, 118n42; live, 94–95; of manhattan, 114–15, 339–40; martini, 3; old-fashioned, 4; origin narratives of, 62–63; as patriotic, 68; ratios in, 115–16; in recipes, 82; ritualism of, 79, 81–82, 84, 88; of Sazeracs, 75–76, 86–88; for Thomas, J., 66–67; vodka for, 184
mixologists, 63; chefs and, 393; culinary culture for, 285; as entrepreneurs, 53; popular cocktails for, 203; skills of, 45–47, 96–99
mixology, 6, 379; aficionados and, 38, 50, 52–54; in America, 67–68; in American Revolution, 27; *Bourbon Mixology*, 198–99; consumers and, 38; history of, 8, 291, 306, 372; ice in, 327, 362n4; in Louisville, 17; origin narratives of, 104–5; packaging and, 169; Prohibition era, 370; on YouTube, 81–82, 84. *See also* bartending
Moana Hotel, 238
modernism: absinthe in, 289–91, 293; aesthetics of, 234–35; alternative, 292–93; in cocktail consumption, 284; in cocktail culture, 284, 326; cultural, 159; history of, 105; ingredients and, 285; in manhattan, 325–26; martini as, 12, 103–4, 107–16; *Race and the Modernist Imagination*, 227; steampunk in, 291–92; in Tiki culture, 225–26. *See also* jet age futurism
molasses, 231
Mon Dernier Soupir (Buñuel), 103
Monroe, Marilyn, 335
Montreal, 147, 156–57
Moore, Demi, 96
Morales, Francisco "Pancho," 209
moral suasion (cocktail), 34
More Kentucky Bourbon Cocktails (Perrine), 198
Morgan, Jefferson, 106–7
Morgan, J. P., 246, 323
morning cocktails, 348–49
morning doctor (cocktail), 362n4
morning glory no. I, 362n4, 372

Morse, Robert, 312–13
Moss, Arthur, 39–41, 43, 46, 53, 54n8
Moss, Laura, 145, 158
Moynihan, Daniel Patrick, 250
muddling, 76, 306
Mud Puddle Books, 5–6
mulled wine, 66–67
multiculturalism, 267, 279n19
Munro, Alice, 152
Munro, Lizzie, 110
Munroe, H. H., 348
Murray, Jock, 104
Myer's cocktails, 148, 362, 368n79
myths, 17

narratives: autobiographical, 250; of bartending, 93–99; of cocktails, 53, 81, 362; of entrepreneurs, 53; in film, 364n26; fire in, 63; of hangovers, 359–62, 363n18; industrialism in, 330; memory in, 350; from military, 352; of New Orleans, 84–86; about old-fashioned, 44; of origin narratives, 39–40, 42–43; of San Francisco, 70n1; of Sazeracs, 82–83; signifiers in, 362; as tonic, 16–17; valets and, 349–50. *See also* origin narratives
Nassikas, James A., 174
Nast, Thomas, 64
National Prohibition Act, 206
Nautilus Corporation, 171
Nava, Mica, 159
Navy Grogs, 240n1
Nealon, Jeffrey T., 56n27
Neeson, Liam, 254
Negrete, Daniel, 208
negroni, 37
Negroni, The, 43
Netherlands, 107, 111
Nethery, Joyce, 196
neutral spirits, 147–48, 174
New Deal, 380–81
New Haven (Connecticut), 63
New & Improved Bartender's Manual (Johnson, H.), 104–5
"New Look," 134, 136, 143n30
Newmar, Julie, 174

New Orleans, 6–7, 228; Catholicism in, 78–79; cocktails, 11; culture of, 76, 387; *Fabulous New Orleans*, 78; France and, 76–77; history of, 84; Hotel Monteleone in, 387; Latitude 29, 240; Mardi Gras in, 77–78; Merchants Exchange Coffee House, 82–83; narratives of, 84–86; Satina's Pousse Café from, 65; Sazeracs and, 79–84, 299; Wondrich on, 75
News of Paris (Weber), 40–41
New York City, 4–5, 306; Barnum's American Museum, 63, 67–68; Bathtub Gin bar in, 30; bookbinding in, 61; Boston and, 30; Death & Co., 239; drinking culture in, 181; Harry's (New York) Bar, 39; Hotel Brighton, 64; John Lamb (bar), 68; Manhattan Club, 328; Manhattan Cocktail Classic, 7; Metropolitan Hotel, 58, 63; *New Yorker*, 40; *New York Herald*, 41; *New York Times*, 43, 111, 178–79, 313; police in, 128, 142n14; reputation of, 79; Sago Hotel, 68; Stonewall Inn, 128, 142n14
Night Café, The (van Gogh), 289
nightclubs, 206, 208–9
Noilly Prat, 105, 113, 115
Nolan, Christopher, 350
Nome, 19n19
normalization, 50–52
Norris, Bill, 315, 323
Northern Ireland, 245–48, 251–52, 256, 257n9. *See also* Ireland
North Shore Distillery, 17, 18
nostalgia: for bartenders, 66, 66; for bartending, 64–65; for Blue Blazers, 67–69; branding with, 38; in cocktail culture, 53–54; for cocktails, 41; masculinity and, 336–37; for old-fashioned, 305–7, 314–15, 314–16, 328; origin narratives and, 37–39
Nui (cocktail), 225

Obama, Barack, 257n7
Obituary Cocktail (McCaffety/Codrescu), 6–7
Occidental Hotel, 58
Ocean's 11 (film), 99
Old Absinthe House, 83–84, 298–99

Old Dominick Distillery, 196
old-fashioned, 4, 7–8; absinthe in, 85–86; Angostura bitters in, 299, 306, 315; brandy, 80; in cocktail culture, 312–14; in deconstruction theory, 15; as lyrical favorites, 307–10; manhattan and, 93, 124; martini and, 79; narratives about, 44; nostalgia for, 305–7, 314–16, 328; *The Old Fashioned*, 315; in popular culture, 310–12; recipes for, 306, 314–15. *See also* Sazeracs
Old Fitzgerald, 196
Old Grand Dad, 207
Old Overholt, 83
old pepper, 362n4
Old Pink (bar), 340
Old Tom gin, 104–5
olives, 1–3, 67, 107, 111, 118n42
"On Drunkenness" (Franklin), 26
One Day in the Life of Ivan Denisovich (Solzhenitsyn), 379
O'Neil, Tip, 250
Ontario, 149
optimization, 56n27
orange bitters, 4, 44, 105
orange flower water, 80
orange liqueur, 94, 385
orange peels, 44, 47
oranges, 65
orange slices, 37, 306, 314
O'Reilly, Nathaniel, 145–46, 159
Organization Man, The (Whyte), 170
origin narratives: of absinthe, 290–94; of Alaska cocktail, 19n19; of *Bartender's Guide*, 59, 104–5; of Boulevardier, 40–44, 42; of cocktails, 11–12, 15; etymology and, 25; of gin, 107–8; of Irish Car Bomb, 244–47, 253–54; for Jeppson's Malört, 391–92; of mai tai, 231–32; of manhattan, 327–30; of margarita, 207–10, 219n18; of mixing, 62–63; of mixology, 104–5; nostalgia and, 37–39; of old-fashioned, 306; from Prohibition era, 41; of Tiki culture, 227–30
Others, The (Amenábar), 365n47
Ottawa, 147
Outrigger (cocktail), 235
"Over the River" (Moss, A.), 41

Pacific islands, 235–40
Pacino, Al, 255
packaging, 50, *135*, 154, 163n35, 169, 173
painkillers, 373
Palm, Michelle, 6
Palmer, C. B., 212
Palmer House, 64
Panama Hattie (film), 15, 307–10, 315–16
Pancho Villa, 206
pan-colonial aesthetics, 230–32
Paradise Lost (Milton), 379
Paris, 39–41, 61, 110, 134
Parker, Dorothy, 346
Parker, Oliver, 350–54, 364n26
parody, 84–86
PDT (bar), 6
PDT Cocktail Book, The (Meehan), 240n1
peach brandy, 67
pearl onions, 107
Peck, Garrett, 207
Pelletier, Pierre-Joseph, 352, 364n36
Penn, Irving, *133*
Perabo, Piper, 323
performance, 244–45, 256, 269–70
Perrine, Joy, 17, 95, 195–99
Petiot, Fernand, 373
Peychaud, Antoine Amedie, 81–84, 89n24
Peychaud, Henri, 28
Peyton Place (Metalious), 130
Phaedrus (Plato), 47
pharmakons, 377–80
Philadelphia, 5
Philadelphia Story (film), 310
phlegm-cutter (cocktail), 34
Picasso, Pablo, 110
Picker-Uppers, 374
Pierre Ferrand Dry Curaçao, 285
Pilkington, Lionel, 255
pineapple, 67
pine-top (cocktail), 34
Pioneer of the American Bar (Wondrich), 6
Pirates of the Caribbean (film), 241n16
Pitt, Brad, 99
plain martini, 2
Plain Tales from the Raj (Allen, C.), 235
plain wine, 61
Planet of the Apes (drink), 235

Planter's House hotel, 63
planter's punch, 224, 228, 230
Plato, 47
Playboy magazine, 124
Poe, Edgar Allan, 295
poetry, 2, 114, 250, 373
politics: in America, 34; bourbon and, 323; in Canada, 161n12; cocktail culture and, 210–13, 214, 215; of Cold War, 249; of consumption, 159–60; Diefenbaker Bill of Rights, 155–56; drinking culture and, 31, 33; of Ireland, 247–50, 253–56
Polynesia, 13–14, 224–27, 231–33, 236, 239–40. *See also* Tiki culture
pomegranate syrup, 299
popular culture, 130; in America, 211; beer in, 388; Bloody Marys in, 215; champagne in, 310–11; in Chicago, 392; cocktail culture and, 218, 384; manhattan in, 325, 330–33, 331; martini in, 345, 384–85; old-fashioned in, 310–12; third space for, 262–64; Tiki culture in, 225–26; vodka in, 337
pork, 224
Porter, Cole, 15, 307–11, 316
Portland (Oregon), 7, 240
Port of New Orleans, The (boat), 228
Portrait Gallery of Distinguished Bar-Keepers (Thomas, J.), 64
postcolonialism, 145–49, 148, 150, 151, 160
Potions of the Caribbean (Berry), 228–29
Pound, Ezra, 114, 290, 293
Powell, William, 114–15, 121
prehistory, of cocktails, 25–31, 32, 33–34
prescriptions, for hangovers, 378–81
Presley, Elvis, 224–25
Preston, Kiki, 40, 43
Prevention of Terrorism Act, 249, 252
Price, Aaron, 18
Price, Vincent, 174
price-gouging, 212
Priestly, Joseph, 352
primitive culture, 239–40, 268, 275; jet age futurism and, 230–31; Tiki culture and, 224–30, 233–35
Princess Bride, The (Goldman), 348
"Private Little War, A" (*Star Trek*), 268
professionalism, 392–93

Prohibition era, 5, 33, 208, 380–81; blended whiskey after, 181; Campari in, 42–43; for cocktail culture, 293; cocktails, 53, 107; culture and, 39–40, 123; for drinking culture, 372–73; margarita in, 204–7; mixology, 370; National Prohibition Act, 206; origin narratives from, 41; in Paris, 39; rum during, 228; speakeasies in, 306
proletariats, 47
Proof (Rogers), 6
psychosis, 190nn73–76; for Absolut vodka, 169–77; human bodies and, 169–70; for Lacan, 184–86; masculinity and, 187; psychopaths, 177–80, 184–86; subjectivity and, 184–85
publishing, 59, 61, 62, 71n8
punch, 5, 35n7; bowls, 27; brandy milk, 371; Caribbean, 224; for cocktail parties, 124; concoctions, 106; jelly, 66; knowledge of, 65; planter's, 228; *Punch!*, 6; Regent's Punch, 65; Royal, 65; Swedish, 39; tropic, 231; Zombie Punch, 240n1
pure spirits, 316
Purim, 132
purity, 270–71
Purity and Danger (Douglas), 268

Qassir, Ahmed, 254
Q. B. Coolers, 231
Quebec, 152, 161n12, 162n26
Queen's Park Swizzle, 240n1
quinine, 352, 364n36

race, 218, 225–27, 241n12, 261, 279n19
Rainbow Room, 5
raisins, 65
The Raj, 235–40
Ramos, Henry C., 80
Ramos gin fizz, 79–81, 352, 371, 372
Rand, Ayn, 1–2
raspberries, 97
raspberry gomme syrup, 97
raspberry-peach Grand Marnier, 97
ratios, in mixing, 115–16
Raw and the Cooked, The (Levi-Strauss), 17
Rea, Stephen, 254

recipes: Absinthe Frappé, 83–84; Americano, 37; American Trilogy, 44; Aviation, 43–44; Baily's Irish Cream, 245; Bloody Marys, 373; Blue Blazers, 58; Boulevardier, 47; Bourbonball, 197; for cocktails, 325; Corpse Reviver, 299; Corpse Reviver, No. 2, 370–71; Crustas, 79–80; custom-ordered cocktails, 39; daiquiris, 228; Dan Marino, 284; Death in the Afternoon, 346; Death in the Gulf Stream, 346; Derby Thyme, 97; for dry martini, 113; for hangovers, 16, 362n4; instructions in, 64–65; knowledge of, 46; for manhattan, 339–40; margarita, 203, 209, 212; martini, 104–5, 107; mint julep, 81; mixing in, 82; morning glory no. 1, 372; for mulled wine, 66–67; for old-fashioned, 306, 314–15; planter's punch, 228; Ramos gin fizz, 80–81, 352; *Recipes for Mixed Drinks*, 5, 43–44; Saratoga brace-up, 372; Sazeracs, 82–83; strawberry margarita, 284–85; technique in, 62; Vieux Carré cocktail, 387; Wicked Strong Passions, 97; Wohltäter (cocktail), 299
Red, Hot and Blue (musical), 309
Reed, Ben, 107
Regan, Gary, 5–6, 43, 387
Regent's Punch, 65
relationships, 69
"Relics" (*Star Trek*), 272
religion, 76–79, 85, 108, 132
Remains of the Day (Ishiguro), 365n47, 367n70
Remick, Lee, 135, 138
Restoration in Ireland Act (ROIA), 252
revisions, 71n8
Revolutionary Road (Yates), 225
Reynolds, Paige, 253
Rhine wine, 65
rhum agricole, 231–32
RIC. *See* Royal Irish Constabulary
Richman, Alan, 84–85
Riggleman, Christine, 196
Ripley Bogle (Wilson, R.), 247
Rittenhouse Bonded Rye, 315, 339
ritualism, 79, 81–82, 84, 88
Robert, John, 205

Roberts, Mary Louise, 217
Robot & Frank (film), 350, 356–61, 366n55, 366n62, 367nn72–73
rock candy, 65
Roddenberry, Gene, 265–66, 274
Rogers, Adam, 6
Rohe, Mies van der, 149
ROIA. *See* Restoration in Ireland Act
Roman Empire, 106
Roosevelt, Franklin D., 4
ropee (cocktail), 34
Royal Hawaiian (cocktail), 238
Royal Irish Constabulary (RIC), 246, 250–51, 258n24
Royal punch, 65
ruby red grapefruit juice, 97
Rudd, Paul, 4
rum, 206; Captain Morgan's, 148; in Caribbean, 196; distillation of, 231–32; Jamaica, 65; Leilani, 148; limes and, 228, 231; for mai tais, 283; from Martinique, 284; pepper in, 31; as polish, 26; pork and, 224; during Prohibition era, 228; rum and cokes, 93; tropicalization of, 196–97; vodka and, 154; as white goods, 152
Rumaki, 164n68
Rush, Benjamin, 31, 32, 33
Russia, 171
rye, 309, 338, 362n4; in cocktails, 299, 305–7; rye Sazeracs, 87–88; Spring Garden Rye, 322; as substitute, 83; whiskey, 44, 82–83, 107, 111, 146, 315, 339, 387. *See also* old-fashioned
rye (grain), 46, 179, 305

Sago Hotel, 68
Saint Patrick's Day, 77
St. Charles Exchange, 18
St. Laurent, Yves, 134
St. Louis (Missouri), 63
salt, 208, 373, 380
Sanders, Audrey, 96
Sands, Bobby, 249–50, 253
San Francisco, 58, 63–64, 70n1, 238, 240
sangria, 345
Santo Domingo, 81
Saratoga brace-up, 372

Satina's Pousse Café, 65
Saturday Evening Post, The (magazine), 125, 126, 129, 136
Saturday Review, 151
savior-faire theory, 45, 47–48, 50, 52–53
Savoy Cocktail Book, The (Craddock), 4–5, 6, 370–71, *370–71*, 385
Saxon, Lyle, 78, 80–81
Sazeracs, 197, 385; Carnival and, 76–79; mixing of, 75–76, 86–88; New Orleans and, 79–84, 299; in parody, 84–86
Scarface (film), 255
Schaap, Rosie, 1–2
Schmid, Albert W. A., 4, 315
Schmidt, William, 325
Schoenberg, Arnold, 284
Schreier, Jake, 350
Schultz, Christian, 61, 70n6
Scialom, Joe, 373
science, 205, 377, 384–85; chemistry, 297–98, 364n36; of hangovers, 346–47, 352, 361–62, 378–81
scientific management, 46
Scotch whisky, 58, 62, 265–68, 306, 329
Seagram's, 154, 163n35; advertisements by, 146–49, *148*, *150*, *151*, *153*, *159*, 161n17; marketing by, 12, 156–57
Seldes, Gilbert, 113
seltzer, 65, 80
Seshagiri, Urmila, 227
Seuter, Carl, 104
715 Club (bar), 5
Seven Lively Arts, The (Seldes), 113
sewing, 138–41, *140*, 143n30
Sex and the City (TV show), 4, 384
sexism, 313, 389
sexuality, 274, 278, 280n36
shaken vodka martini, 4
Shakespeare, William, 69, 72n43, 345
shambro (cocktail), 34
Sharpe, Patricia, 205
Shaw, George Bernard, 365n47
sherry, 323
Shining, The (King, S.), 349
shrub-based cocktails, 282–85, *284*, *285*
signifiers, 121–22, 132, 138, 241n16, 291; from colonialism, 231, 236; for Lacan, 190;

martini as, 105–6; in narratives, 362; with vodka, 170
Silverback Distillery, 196
silver-top (cocktail), 34
Simon, David, 84
Simondon, Gilbert, 48
Simonson, Robert, 87–88, 244–47, 306
simple syrup, 80, 87, 285, 306, 315
Sinatra, Frank, 310–12
Singapore slings, 228, 247
single-barrel bourbon, 107
single-barrel whiskey, 7–8
Sippin' Safari (Berry), 6, 225, 228–29
Sirk, Douglas, 130–31, *131*
Slattery, John, 312
sliced lemons, 80
small-batch whiskey, 7–8
Small Beer, 31
Smirnoff, 13, 171, 173–77, 186
Smith, Andrew, 62
Smith, Joshua Soule, 81
Smuggler's Cove, 238, 240
snap-neck (cocktail), 34
sobriety, 361–62
social alchemy, 265–66
social clubs, 323, 327–28
socioeconomics, 109, 142n24
soda water, 37, 65, 284, *284*, 345–46, 352, 360–61
Solzhenitsyn, Aleksandr, 379
Some Like It Hot (film), 335
Something for the Boys (musical), 310
Sopranos, The (TV show), 313
South American Gentleman's Companion (Baker), 5–6
South Carolina, 4
Southeast Asia, 232
Southern Wines and Spirits, 93, 95
South Pacific (film), 224
South Pacific (region), 224–25
Space Age, 235
Space Needles, 235
Spada, David, 186
Spain, 107, 232
Spare, A. O., 295
speakeasies, 306
speakeasy culture, 207–8
Spiceberry, 198

spirits, 44; in *American Psycho*, 181; for bartending, 196; bitters and, 385; blended, 240n2; cachaça, 283–84, *284*; class and, 376; cocktails and, 386; colorless, 113, 170, 174; creativity with, 283–84; distillation of, 169; from Europe, 211, 329; at hotel bars, 331–32; *An Inquiry into the Effects of Spirituous Liquors*, 31, 32, 33; "John Barleycorn" about, 329–30; neutral, 147–48, 174; pure, 316; Southern Wines and Spirits, 93, 95; on *Star Trek*, 265; stereotypes of, 339; in third space, 272; *Vintage Spirits and Forgotten Cocktails*, 6, 47, 240n2, 370, 384; wine compared to, 306
split-ticket (cocktail), 34
sporting clubs, 235, 333–34
Sportsman's Dictionary (Badcock), 29
Spring Garden Rye, 322
Spy, The (Cooper, J. F.), 30–31
squeezed lemon peels, 105
stagger-juice (cocktail), 34
Stag Saloon, 80
Star Fires, 235
Star Trek, 279n19, 279n34, 280n36; alcohol in, 262–64, 270–73; cultural difference in, 267–68, 274, 277–78; drinking culture in, 265–70; jet age futurism in, 261–62; women in, 273–77
Star Trek franchise, 14
steampunk, 291–92
Stefanelli, Simonetta, 255
Stephenson, Tristan, 6
Stevenson, Ray, 255
Stewart, Amy, 6, 86
Stewart, James, 135, 138
Stiegler, Bernard, 45, 47–48, 50–52
stinkibus, 34
Stitzel-Weller Distillery, 196
Stolichnaya, 171
stone-fence (cocktail), 34
stone-wall (cocktail), 34
Stonewall Inn, 128, 142n14
stout beer, 39, 245
strawberry margarita, 284–85
subjectivity, 169–70, 184–85
sugar, 58, 94, 245, 352, 362n4; with absinthe, 289; bitters and, 82, 299, 305; brown sugar cubes, 44; cane, 232; cubes, 76, 315; gomme in, 228; for shrubs, 282–83; simple syrup and, 80, 306; with water, 314; whiskey and, 372
Suissesse, 371, 372
"Suitcase, The" (*Mad Men*), 338
"Sunday, Bloody Sunday" (U2), 248
Sweden, 171, 175–76
Swedish punch, 39
sweet liqueur, 347
sweet vermouth, 37, 105, 387
Swift, Taylor, 62
Swiss absinthe, 87
swiss yodeler (cocktail), 362n4
Switzerland, 294
symbolic exchanges (Lacan), 38, 185
symbolic order (Lacan), 185, 191n75
syrup, 58, 61, 68, 97, 105; pomegranate, 299; simple, 80, 87, 285, 306, 315; vinegar in, 283

Tabasco (sauce), 347
Taboo Table (Berry), 227
Taco USA (Arellano), 215
Tahiti, 233
Tahitian Cocktail Lounge, 147
Take a Chance (Gershwin brothers), 309
"Take Five" (Brubeck), 103
Talbott, Gloria, 131
Tales of the Cocktail, 7, 99, 198, 387, 389
Taylor, Sewell T., 82
tea, 157
television, 121–22
temperance movement, 205–6
Tennessee whiskey, 306
tequila, 111, 203–6, 208–9, 211–12, 273–74; Jose Cuervo, 213, *214*, 215; for strawberry margarita, 284–85
Tequila Sunrise, 212
Terrington, William, 104
test marketing, 154
Test Pilots, 235
Texas daisy, 209
Thatcher, Margaret, 249–50
That Night in Rio (film), 211
Theory of the Leisure Class, The (Veblen), 330–33
Thibodeaux, Sean, 18

Thin Man, The (film), 114–15, 121
third space, 14, 262–64, 269–78. See also *Star Trek*
Thirty Year's War, 107
"Tholian Web, The" (*Star Trek*), 266
Thomas, Bill, 130–32, *131*
Thomas, George, 63–64
Thomas, Jerry, 5, 11, 104, 372, 376; in *Bartender's Guide*, 59, 64–65, 80; history of, 63–64, *66*; mixing for, 66–67; reputation of, 58–59
Thompson, Hunter S., 293, 299–300, 346
Thornton, Frank, 251
Three Dots and a Dash and Lost Lake, 240
thunderbolt cocktails, 68
thyme, 97
Tiffin, Helen, 145–46
Tiki culture, 6, 13–14; aesthetics of, 236–40; Bittermens tiki bitters, 284; colonialism and, 230–32; cultural difference and, 147; history of, 147, 164n68, 241n16; jet age futurism and, 234; leisure in, 241n12; in literature, 240n1; modernism in, 225–26; origin narratives of, 227–30; primitive culture and, 224–30, 233–35; The Raj for, 235–40; signifiers from, 241n16; *Tiki Art Now*, 226; *Tiki Modern*, 225–26
Tilden, Samuel J., 328
toddies, 311
tomato juice, 373, 380
Tom Collinses, 336
Tomei, Marisa, 98
tonics, 293–94, 346–47, 365n44; for hangovers, 348–56; valets with, 354–59
tonic water, 51, 352
Top Chef (TV show), 49–50
To Have and Have Another (Greene), 6
tourism, 14, 199, 205, 210, 218; in Hawai'i, 233–34, 238; in Mexico, 204, 209, 213, 217
"Trade Routes of the World" (Seagram's), *150*
Trader Vic's, 164n68, 224, 228–31, 235
Transatlantic Review (pamphlet), 42
Trask, Haunani-Kay, 233
Trelawney, 148
Tremblay, Michel, 152
Treme (TV show), 84–86
Trinidad, 111

triple sec, 203–4, 209
Trip to Echo Spring, The (Laing), 6
Tropical Isle (restaurant), 84
tropicalization, 159, 196–97, 204, 215
tropic punch, 231
Troubles. See Northern Ireland
"Trouble with Tribbles, The" (*Star Trek*), 266–70, 275–76
Trouillot, Michel-Rolph, 149
Tuaca, 197
Turmo, Isabel Gonzalez, 261
Twin Peaks (TV show), 348–49
Tyson, Mike, 378

U2, 248
Ulysses (Joyce), 105
umbrellas, 271
unaged whiskey, 94
"Uncle Sam" image, 64
Underberg bitters, 379
underwear, 134, 169, 186–87
United Kingdom, 245–46, 249–50, 253
United States. See America
United States Bartender's Guild (USBG), 390
useless consumption, 376–77
Uyeda, Kazuo, 6

valets, 363n20; bartenders and, 349–50, 359–62; in fiction, 345–48, 351–56; with tonics, 354–59
Vance, Vivian, 309
Vancouver, 147
Vanderbilt, Alfred, 43
Vanderbilt, Amy, 132, 138
Vanderbilt, Cornelius, II, 40
Vanderbilt, Gloria, 40
van Gogh, Vincent, 289, 295
vanilla, 229
"Vanity, Thy Name Is Man?" (Henderson), 179
Veblen, Thorstein, 292, 330–33, 336–37, 376
Verlaine, Paul, 293
Vermeire, Robert, 105
vermouth, 1, 3, 53, 94, 113; absinthe and, 327–28; Campari and, 45; gin and, 106–9, 111, 116; for martini, 105, 115–16; sweet, 37, 105, 387; whiskey and, 323–24. See also specific vermouths

Verstappen, H., 39
Vespetro cordials, 297
Victorian culture, 114–15, 326
Vietnam War, 249, 335
Vieux Carré cocktail, 387
vinegar, 282–85
Vintage Spirits and Forgotten Cocktails (Haigh), 6, 47, 240n2, 370, 384
violence, 275–77, 296–97
Violet Fizzes, 389
Virginia Gentleman, 207
vitamin B, 378
vodka, 1–3, 265, 267; advertisements for, 13, 169–77, 186–87; in America, 13; Bolshoi, 148; branding, 186; for cocktails, 9, 96–98, 173–74, 186–87; during Cold War, 337; as colorless, 111, 175, 180–81, 352; corn for, 179–80; gin and, 113, 186; mango-passionfruit, 97; marketing of, 170; martini, 1–2, 4, 111; masculinity and, 169–70, 181–83; for mixing, 184; in popular culture, 337; rum and, 154; signifiers with, 170; stereotypes of, 391; tasting, 176–77; tomato juice and, 373; wheat for, 179–80; as white goods, 152. *See also specific vodkas*
Vogue (magazine), 133
Volstead Act, 206, 217–18
Vonnegut, Kurt, 335
von Stroheim, Otto, 226
vox populi, 34

Wagner, Gerhard, 262
Walters, Charles, 310
Warhol, Andy, 173, 186
War of 1812, 84
Warren, Harry, 307
Washington, Denzel, 255
Washington, George, 28, 44
Wasserman, Dale, 358
Waste Land, The (Eliot, T. S.), 105, 293
water, 26–27, 80–81, 83, 228, 314; with absinthe, 298; in cocktails, 305; soda, 37, 65
Watman, Max, 7
Waugh, Alec, 103
Waugh, Evelyn, 348
"Way of the Warrior, The" (*Star Trek*), 272–73

Weber, Ronald, 40–41
Weekend in Havana (film), 211
Weiner, Matthew, 313
"Well Did You Evah" (song), 309–11
wheat, 179–80, 196
whiskey (including whisky), 245, 265, 310–11; absinthe and, 86; advertisements for, 331; American, 327; beer and, 291; blended, 181; bourbon, 39, 46, 196; branding of, 327; in Canada, 162n26; Canadian, 147–48, 152, 173; cheap, 7; class and, 329; cocktails, 306, 328; corn for, 195; distillation of, 329; distillers, 99; Jameson, 68; in literature, 31; for old-fashioned, 7–8; rye, 44, 82–83, 107, 111, 146, 315, 339, 387; scotch, 58, 266; straight, 323; sugar and, 372; toddies, 311; unaged, 94; vermouth and, 323–24; Whiskey Rebellion, 49; *Whiskey Women*, 198; white, 152; Worcestershire sauce for, 351; at work, 337–38; "Yep, Whisky's Only Pink Tea in Mexico," 205. *See also* bourbon; Canadian whisky; Irish whiskey; rye; Scotch whisky; Tennessee whiskey
white sugar, 80
white vermouth, 94
Whyte, William, 145, 170, 183, 185–86
Wicked Strong Passions, 97
Widgery, John, 248
Wife-Dressing (Fogarty), 138
Wikipedia, 313
Wilde, Oscar, 295, 348, 349, 364n26
Wild Turkey, 198
Williams, Elizabeth, 80
Wilson, Jason, 7
Wilson, Robert McLiam, 247–49
Wilson, Sloan, 225
wine, 9, 65–67, 108, 296, 323; for bathing, 26; in Canada, 148–49; plain, 61; spirits compared to, 306
Wire, The (TV show), 84–85
WiseGeek (website), 110
Witchel, Alex, 313
Wohltäter (cocktail), 299, 299
Wolfe, Thomas, 42
"Wolf in the Fold" (*Star Trek*), 275–77

women: in America, 130–35, *131*, *133*, 135–37, 138–39; clothing styles for, 125–26, *126–27*, 128, *129*; clubs for, 388; cocktails and, 388–90; in drinking culture, 337–38, 384; Prohibition era for, 207–8; sewing for, 138–41, *140*, 143n30; sexism, 313; in *Star Trek*, 273–77; stereotypes of, 207; *Whiskey Women*, 198; work for, 230; Yale University for, 139. *See also* gender

Wondrich, David, 25–26, 28–30; on cocktail history, 326, 371–72, 380–81; on cocktails, 112, 323–24; Cooper, J. F., and, 33–34; on Crustas, 80; *Imbibe!*, 6, 105–6; on louching, 327; on martini, 107; on New Orleans, 75, 83; on old-fashioned, 313; on punch, 35n7; recipes by, 314–15

Wong, Germaine Ying-Gee, 157

Wood, Andrew, 213

Woodford Reserve, 195, 197–98

Woods, 148

Woolf, Virginia, 105

Worcestershire sauce, 351, 362n4, 373, 379–80

work, 230, 330–34, *331*, 337–38, 375

workers, 45, 246

World's Drinks and How to Mix Them, The, 83

World's Fair, 12–13

World War I, 113–14, 246, 334–35

World War II, 210; America after, 139, 226–27, 234; class after, 211; clothing styles of, *127*; cocktail culture after, 121–23, *122*, 134–35, 135–37, 138–41, *140*, 240n2; cocktail parties after, 123–24, *125*; culture after, 13–14, 25; drinking culture after, 110, 121; hegemony after, 226; internationalism after, 149; leisure after, 171; popular culture after, 130

wormwood, 293–98

writing, 7, 43–44, 114, 386–88

Wyler, William, 356

Wyman, Jane, 130, *131*

Wystan Martinis, 1–2

Yale University, 139

Yates, Richard, 225

Yeats, William Butler, 290

Yellow Chartreuse, 4

"Yep, Whisky's Only Pink Tea in Mexico" (Robert), 205

Young Man's Delight, 204

"You're the Top" (Porter), 309

YouTube, 81–82, 84

zombie (cocktail), 106

Zombie Punch, 240n1

Zukerman, Pinchas, 174

ZZ Top, 96

www.ingramcontent.com/pod-product-compliance
Lightning Source LLC
Chambersburg PA
CBHW041438300426
44114CB00026B/2919